THE CONTEXT OF SCRIPTURE

Canonical Compositions, Monumental Inscriptions, and Archival Documents from the Biblical World

General Editor William W. Hallo
Associate Editor K. Lawson Younger, Jr.
Project Editor David E. Orton

TUTA SUB AEGIDE PALLAS 1683

BRILL

The Context of Scripture

VOLUME 4

Supplements

Edited by

K. LAWSON YOUNGER JR.

BRILL

LEIDEN | BOSTON

Cover image courtesy of the Neubauer Expedition to Zincirli of the University of Chicago.

The Library of Congress Cataloging-in-Publication Data is available online at http://catalog.loc.gov
LC record available at http://lccn.loc.gov/2016041628

ISBN 9789004166745 (hardback)

This book is printed on acid-free paper and produced in a sustainable manner.

FSC www.fsc.org MIX Paper from responsible sources FSC® C004472

CONTENTS

AKKADIAN INSCRIPTIONS

SUMERIAN INSCRIPTIONS

INDICES

PREFACE

The need for a supplemental volume to the original three volumes of *The Context of Scripture* became apparent as the final volume appeared in 2002. There were lacunae that demanded filling. For example, due to circumstances beyond our control, Prof. Hallo and I were compelled to complete the project at that time without having any Neo-Assyrian treaties included. With the happy discovery of the Tell Taʿyinat Esarhaddon Succession Treaty, a remedy in the form of a supplemental volume was further necessitated.

In addition, there were genres that had been overlooked in the devising of the original volumes. For example, no rituals for the cult image had been incorporated; the valuable literary work of Sargon II's Letter to the God was absent; etc. While these texts may not have as many direct biblical parallels as some other ancient Near Eastern texts – beside being important in their own right –, they provide the type of "silhouette" to the biblical material that Professor Hallo emphasized many times in his publications as crucial to comprehending the full context of the biblical texts.

Finally, over the last decade newly recovered inscriptions have been added to the corpus of ancient Near Eastern texts (e.g. the many hieroglyphic Luwian inscriptions). These afford scholars new insights and have been included. For these reasons, a supplemental volume was envisioned, and brought to completion – thanks to Brill's ongoing support (particularly manifested in Katelyn Chin).

The fivefold major linguistic divisions have been retained, with one important difference. The second division's title has been changed to "Anatolian" (rather than the former designation "Hittite"). This is a better reflection of the texts contained in this section. However, the threefold division of "Canonical Compositions," "Monumental Inscriptions" and "Archival Documents" has not been retained, due to pragmatic reasons in the production of this supplemental volume.

William W. Hallo (of blessed memory) – perhaps more than any other scholar – labored to find a controlled methodology for the integration of ancient Near Eastern texts and the Hebrew Bible. His resultant "Contextual Method" truly stands as a methodological watershed for such study. For those scholars who have truly put Hallo's balanced principles into practice, the reward is great. This fourth volume of *The Context of Scripture* contributes in a small way to his continued legacy.

On a personal note, I am greatly indebted to Professor Hallo. He was a wonderful mentor, teaching through the consistent implementation of his methodology. He was an especially congenial colleague in editorial work. However, he will be most remembered as the consummate gentleman.

K. Lawson Younger, Jr.
May 14, 2016

ABBREVIATIONS AND SYMBOLS

See earlier volumes of *The Context of Scripture* for additional abbreviations and symbols.

AASOR 16 — R. H. Pfeiffer and E. A. Speiser. *One Hundred New Selected Nuzi Texts*. AASOR 16. New Haven: American Schools of Oriental Research, 1936.

AdŠ — *Das Archiv des Šilwa-teššup*. 9 Volumes.

ARM 6 — J.-R. Kupper, *Correspondance de Bahdi-Lim, préfét du palais de Mari*. Archives royales de Mari 6. Paris: Impr. Nationale, 1954.

BAM — F. Köcher. *Die babylonisch-assyrische Medizin in Texten*. Berlin: De Gruyter, 1963–1980.

BBB — Bonner biblische Beiträge.

BiOr — *Bibliotheca Orientalis*.

CAL — S. A. Kaufman. Editor. *The Comprehensive Aramaic Lexicon* website = http://cal1.cn.huc.edu/.

CHANE — Culture and History of the Ancient Near East. Leiden: Brill.

CTU 1 — M. Salvini. *Corpus dei testi urartei. Vol. I: le iscrizioni su pietra e roccia – I testi*. Rome CNR, 2008.

DPS — M. Allotte de la Fuÿe. *Documents présargoniques*. 4 Volumes. Paris: E. Leroux, 1908–1913.

EN — *Excavations at Nuzi*. Designating volumes publishing texts from Nuzi in the HSS as well as in the series SCCNH.

ETSCL — Electronic Text Corpus of Sumerian Literature: http://etcsl.orinst.ox.ac.uk. Faculty of Oriental Studies, University of Oxford.

GHL — H. A. Hoffner, Jr. and H. C. Melchert, *A Grammar of the Hittite Language*. Languages of the Ancient Near East 1. 2 Volumes. Winona Lake, IN: Eisenbrauns, 2008.

HSS 9 — R. H. Pfeiffer, *Excavations at Nuzi II: The Archives of Shilwateshub, Son of the King*. HSS 9. Cambridge, MA: Harvard University Press, 1932.

HSS 15 — E. R. Lacheman, *Excavations at Nuzi* VI: *The Administrative Archives*. HSS 15. Cambridge, MA: Harvard University Press, 1955.

IM — Siglum for tablets in the collection of the Iraq National Museum, Baghdad.

JEN — *Joint Expedition with the Iraq Museum at Nuzi*.

JENu — Joint Expedition with the Iraq Museum at Nuzi, unpublished (object catalogued and kept in the Oriental Institute of the University of Chicago).

KADP — F. Köcher. *Keilschrifttexte zur assyrisch-babylonischen Drogen- und Pflanzenkunde*. Berlin: Akademie-Verlag, 1955.

KRI — K. A. Kitchen. *Ramesside Inscriptions, Historical and Biographical*. 5 Volumes. Oxford: Blackwell, 1970–1983.

LKU — A. Falkenstein. *Literarische Keilschrifttexte aus Uruk*. Berlin: Staatliche Museen zu Berlin, vorderasiatische Abteilung, 1931.

MH 1 — The Epigraphic Survey. *Medinet Habu I: Earlier Historical Records of Ramses III*. OIP 8. Chicago: University of Chicago Press, 1930.

MH 2 — The Epigraphic Survey. *Medinet Habu II: Later Historical Records of Ramses III*. OIP 9. Chicago: University of Chicago Press, 1932.

MH 8 — The Epigraphic Survey. *Medinet Habu VIII: The Eastern High Gate, with Translations of Texts*. OIP 94. Chicago: University of Chicago Press, 1970.

MRS — Mission de Ras Shamra.

NEA — *Near Eastern Archaeology*.

OIP — Oriental Institute Publications. The University of Chicago.

PNA — H. D. Baker and K. Radner. Editors. The Prosopography of the Neo-Assyrian Empire. 3 Volumes. Helsinki: Neo-Assyrian Text Corpus Project 1998–2011.

RIK 1 — *Reliefs and Inscriptions at Karnak*. Volume 1: *Ramses III's Temple Within the Great Inclosure of Amon, Part 1*, OIP 24. Chicago: University of Chicago Press, 1936.

RIK 2 — *Reliefs and Inscriptions at Karnak*. Volume 2: *Ramses III's Temple Within the Great Inclosure of Amon, Part 2*, and *Ramses III's Temple in the Precinct of Mut*, OIP 35. Chicago: University of Chicago Press, 1936.

RIK 3 — *Reliefs and Inscriptions at Karnak*. Volume 3: *The Bubastite Portal*, OIP 74. Chicago: University of Chicago Press, 1954.

RIK 4 — *Reliefs and Inscriptions at Karnak*. Volume 4: *The Battle Reliefs of King Sety I*, OIP 107. Chicago: University of Chicago Press, 1986.

SAA 3 — A. Livingstone. *Court Poetry and Literary Miscellanea*. State Archives of Assyria 3. Helsinki: Helsinki University Press, 1989.

SAA 4 — I. Starr. *Queries to the Sungod. Divination and Politics in Sargonid Assyria*. State Archives of Assyria 4. Helsinki: Helsinki University Press, 1990.

SAA 5 — G. B. Lanfranchi and S. Parpola. *The Correspondence of Sargon II, Part II: Letters from the Northern and Northeastern Provinces*. State Archives of Assyria 5. Helsinki: Helsinki University Press, 1990.

SAA 18 — F. Reynolds. *The Babylonian Correspondence of Esarhaddon*. State Archives of Assyria 18. Helsinki: Helsinki University Press, 2003.

SAOC — Studies in Ancient Oriental Civilization. Oriental Institute of the University of Chicago.

SCCNH — Studies on the Civilization and Culture of Nuzi and the Hurrians.

SBLWAW — Society of Biblical Literature. Writings of the Ancient World.

LIST OF CONTRIBUTORS

RICHARD E. AVERBECK
Trinity International University – Divinity School

MICHAEL DICK
Siena College, *emeritus*

F. M. FALES
University of Udine

ECKART FRAHM
Yale University

J. D. HAWKINS
University of London

RICHARD S. HESS
Denver Seminary

HARRY A. HOFFNER, JR. ‡
University of Chicago, *emeritus*

VICTOR HUROWITZ ‡
Ben Gurion University of the Negev

K. A. KITCHEN
University of Liverpool, *emeritus*

JACOB LAUINGER
The Johns Hopkins University

ANDRÉ LEMAIRE
École Pratique des Hautes Études, Paris-Sorbonne

ADAM E. MIGLIO
Wheaton College

DENNIS PARDEE
University of Chicago

JOACHIM-FRIEDRICH QUACK
University of Heidelberg

JOANN SCURLOCK
Elmhurst College, *emerita*

MATTHEW SURIANO
University of Maryland

EVA VON DASSOW
University of Minnesota

K. LAWSON YOUNGER, JR.
Trinity International University – Divinity School

‡ Deceased

EGYPTIAN INSCRIPTIONS

HIEROGLYPHIC COMPOSITIONS

THE TRIPLE TOPOGRAPHICAL LIST OF THUTMOSE III (4.1)
(1479–1425 BCE)

K. A. Kitchen

Thutmose III's topographical list is preserved at Karnak in the temple of Amen-Re at three locations: (List 1a) Pylon VI, on N. Tower, front (West) face; (List 1b) Pylon VII, on West Tower, front (South) face; and (List 1c) Pylon VII, on East Tower, rear (North) face. Lists 1a, 1b, each contain notionally 119 place-names overall of the Palestinian phase of the conquests of Thutmose III, but lack 4 names and 7 names respectively in these individual lists. List 1c is in two adjacent sections: that on the viewer's right is again the "Palestinian" series of 119 names (2 lacking), while the larger section at left is the list of northern Syrian names, notionally Nos. 120–359, of which 32 names at the end are destroyed, while 30 more names are lost in the upper two rows.[1] For all three lists together, an overall listing has been adopted, and is clearly set out in the edition by Simons 1937.[2] The common preserved text of all accessible names is given in sequence: A, the "Palestinian" (+ South Syrian) series (1–119); and then B, the "Syrian" series (120–359).

A. The "Palestinian" (+ South Syrian) Series

These are ostensibly the names of the places ruled by the chiefs whom Thutmose III took captive, when he conquered Megiddo, wherein they had taken refuge from his forces, in defeat. The list (1.–119.) runs as follows, ranging from Lebanon deep into Canaan.

1. Qadesh (modern Tell Nebi-Mend),	*a* Megiddo – Josh	13. Damascus,[13,b]
2. Megiddo (modern Tell el-Mutesillim),[3,a]		14. Atru,[14]
3. Khazi (modern Tell Hizzin),[4]	*b* Gen 14:15; 2 Chr 24:23; 2 Kgs 16:10	15. ʾUbil,[15]
4. Gi(n)ta-shuna,[5]		16. Ham(a)tu,[16]
5. Ain-Shawi,[6]		17. Aqidwa,[17]
6. D(u)bikhi,[7]	*c* 1 Chr 5:16	18. Shamana,
7. Bumaya (obscure),		19. Biʾarutu,
8. Kumidi,[8]		20. Madjana,[18]
9. Dothaim,[9]		21. Sharuna,[19,c]
10. Laban,[10]		22. Tubya,[20]
11. Qar(y)at Nazla,[11]		23. Badjan,[21]
12. Marom ("Height"),[12]		24. Imshan,[22]

1 See diagrams in Simons 1937:109–110. Older bibliography, see Porter, Moss, and Burney 1972:88 (235) for 1a; 170 (499) for 1b; and 167 end (497) for 1c.

2 Simons 1937:111–115, hieroglyphic text; 115–119, in modern transliterations with brief notes. See also conspectus and discussions by Helck 1971:121–153 (*passim*, but not in numerical order of the lists).

3 These first two names introduce the king's conquest of Canaan and Syria, respectively. See EA 234:19; EA 242:4; EA 243:11; EA 244:24, 42; and EA 245:26.

4 Helck 1971:130 and references. See EA letters 175:4; EA 185:43; EA 186:62 (convenient translations in Moran 1992).

5 Location uncertain; EA 177:2: "Gudda-shuna." See Helck 1971:130.

6 Shawi for *Shasi? see Helck 1971:130, refs.

7 Location not fixed, Helck 1971:130.

8 Modern Kamid el-Loz in the Beqaʿ Valley between the Lebanon and Anti-Lebanon mountain-ranges. See EA 116:75; EA 129:85; EA 132:49; EA 197:38; EA 198:5.

9 A northern "Dothaim," not the one in Samaria.

10 In EA 53, Lapana, along with Ruhizzi, appear near Baalbek (cf. Helck 1971:130). See also EA 54:27, 32.

11 Possibly old Nazala at el-Karyaten, northeast of Damascus (Helck 1971:130).

12 See Helck 1971:129, for a Merom (Josh 11:5, 7) and a Marum in Assyrian sources, in Galilee.

13 See EA 197:21 (2×); EA 53:63; EA 107:28.

14 Obscure. The suggested ʿAdra, East-Northeast of Damascus (so Abel 1933–1938, 2:8) begins with a sharp *ayin*, not a soft *aleph*, as here, hence is unlikely to fit here.

15 Location uncertain.

16 In the context, neither the Hamath on the Orontes River nor one south of Beth-Shan (cf. Helck 1971:129).

17 Location uncertain. Helck (1971:129) compares Katwa (up to 30 miles southeast of Damascus).

18 19. Biʾarutu and 20. Madjana may be in that area, but are not precisely identifiable.

19 See EA 241:4.

20 May be the Tubu of EA 205:3.

21 Unlikely to be Bashan (Zur-Bashan, Ziri-Bashani of EA 201).

22 Unlikely to be Imtan in the Jebel ed-Druze (as idenfied by Abel 1933–1938, 2:9) on phonetic grounds.

25. Masakha,[23]
26. Qanu,[24]
27. ʿAruna,[25]
28. ʿAstartu,[26,d]
29. Nurpi,[27]
30. Maquta,[28]

(Returning back west of the Jordan)
31. Lawisa,[29]
32. Hazor,[30,e] (then out of order)
33. Pahil,[31] (but more directly south of Hazor)
34. Kinneroth[f] (by Galilee's NW shore), (Slightly further south thence may then lie)
35. Shamana[32] (and likely)
36. Adamum,[33] (before reaching)
37. Qishon (and)
38. Shunem[34] (getting close to the Valley of Jezreel).

(The next segment involves the western Jezreel area and Mt. Carmel district)
39. Mishʾal,[g]
40. Aksaph,[35]
41. *Geba-Suman,[36]
42. Taʿanach,[37,h]
43. Ibleam,
44. Ginti-Ashna (at modern Jenin),[38]
45. ⟨*ʾE⟩lat-milku,[39,i]
47. Acco,[40,j]
48. Rosh-Qadesh ("Sacred height ['head']"),[41]
49. *Krymn*,[42]
50. Bira.[43]

(Much further north may lie)
51. Shamshatu,[44] and
52. Anakharoth,[45,k]
53. Greater Ophel,
54. Lesser Ophel,[46]
55. Khashabu,[47]
56. Tushultu,[48]
57. "Negeb,"[49]
58. Ashushkan,[50]
59. L/Raman.[51]

(A local South – North sequence)
60. Yurtsa,[52]
61. Makhasi,[53]
62. Joppa,[54,l]
63. Ginti/Gath,[55,m]
64. Lutan,[56]
65. Ono,[57]
66. Apheq,[58]
67. Socoh,[59]

d Josh 9:10, etc.
e Josh 11:1, etc.
f Kinnerot
g Josh 19:26; 21:30
h Taʿanach
i Josh 19:26
j Judg 1:31
k Josh 19:19
l Josh 19:46; 2 Chr 2:15 [Eng 2:16]; Ezra 3:7; Jonah 1:3
m Josh 19:45; 21:24; 1 Chr 6:54 [Eng 6:69]

23 May be the Mushikhuna of EA 182:4 (2×).
24 Most likely the Qani of EA 204:4. The closely-linked loyalist Amarna letters (EA 201–206) show solidarity among kinglets of this region: Zur-Bashan, Qanu, and T/Dubu (EA 201, 204, 205).
25 May well be the Khalunni of EA 197:14, being close to Bosra therein (with Helck 1971:129).
26 This is the well-known Ashteroth (Tell Ashtera), 20 miles east of the sea of Galilee. See EA 197:10; EA 256:21.
27 May be a little further north of 28. ʿAstartu. Rainey (2006:72) suggests for *-rpi*, cf. Deut 2:20 "(land of) Rephaim."
28 May be at Tell Miqdad, just over 12.5 miles (20 km) north of 28. ʿAstartu.
29 This is but a variant of biblical Laish (the later Dan) by the sources of the Jordan (Judg 18:7, 27, 29).
30 See EA 148:41; EA 227:3, 21; EA 364:18; and ARM 6, 78:15.
31 Classical Pella. See EA 256:8.
32 See EA 225:4.
33 Adami/Khirbet Damieh.
34 See EA 365:12, 21.
35 Tell Kisan in the plain of Acco. See EA 366:23; EA 367:1.
36 Location uncertain.
37 See EA 248:14 and Sheshonq number 14 (p. 16 below).
38 See EA 319:5.
39 Possibly the ʾAl-melek of Josh 19:26, possibly on south of Jenin.
40 EA 8:9; EA 233:5.
41 The neighboring ridge of Mount Carmel. See EA 264:18.
42 Location uncertain.
43 The name means "well." Thus a mere "well" is unlocatable. Note Judg 9:21 (Jotham, son of Gideon, fled to Beer, "well").
44 Location uncertain.
45 More than one place with this name is known.
46 The location of neither Greater or Lesser Ophel is known.
47 Khashabu is located at Tell Hashbe, about 10 miles WSW of the more famous Baalbek (cf. Helck 1971:130). See EA 174:8.
48 See EA 185:11; EA 186:13.
49 Negeb (Negev) is too vague to locate.
50 Obscure.
51 Obscure.
52 Located at Tell-Ful.
53 See EA 298:25.
54 EA 294:20; EA 296:33; EA 138:6.
55 This is understood as Gath(-rimmon), see Helck 1971, s.v. Rimmon. Likely located at Tell Jerishe. See EA 290:9, 28; EA 289:19.
56 The later Lydda.
57 Located at Kafr Ana.
58 Here written as Apqunu.
59 Sheshonq, number 38 (see below, p. 16).

68. Yehem,[60]
69. Khabisana,[61]
70. Gintu/Gath,[62,n]
71. Migdol (“fort”).[63]

(The list goes still further north)

72. ʾAptan,[64]
73. Shabtuna,[65]
74. Tayiʾa,[66]
75. Nawan,[67]
76. Hadid;
77. Har (“mountain”),[68]
78. Yaship-el,
79. Rughizzi,[69]
80. Karuru/Kalulu,
81. Har-ʾEl (“mount of God”),
82. Labiʾu,[70,o]
83. Numan,
84. Naʿaman,
85. Maromaim (“heights”),
86. ʿAyin (“spring”).

(Further groups also yield few secure identifications)

87. Rahbu,[71,p]
88. Aqal/r,[72]
89. Haikalayim (“Two temples”),[73]
90. ʾUbil (some stream?),[74]
91. ʾUtraʿa,[75]
92. ʾUbil (another stream?),
93. Ginti-ʾUta,[76]
94. Maqr/leput,[77]
95. “spring,”
96. K/Gur/lman,
97. Bitya,
98. Tipunu,
99. ʾUbil (another stream),
100. Yar/lutu,
101. Halkur,[78]
102. Yaʿqub-ʾEl,[79]
103. Qaputa,
104. Qadjiru,[80]
105. Rabitu,[81]
106. Maqr/latu,[82]
107. ʿEmeq (“valley”),
108. Sar/luta,
109. Beʾeroth (“wells”),
110. Beth-Shan,[83]
111. Beth-ʿAnath,[84]
112. Halqatu,[85,q]
113. ʿAyn-Qineam,[86]
114. Qebaʿu/Gebaʿu “hill,”[87]
115. Tsarar,[88]
116. Tsefat,[89]
117. B(u)rqana,[90]
118. Hum (or Hawam)
119. Aktamas.[91]

n Josh 11:22; 1 Sam 5:8; 7:14; 17:4, 52; 21:10–15; 27:6; 2 Sam 1:20; Amos 6:2; 1 Chr 18:1; 2 Chr 11:8; 26:6

o Num 34:7–9; Josh 13:5; 1 Kgs 8:65; 2 Kgs 14:25; Ezek 47:16

p Josh 19:26

q Josh 19:25

60 Located at Jemma. See Sheshonq, number 35 (see below, p. 16).
61 Obscure.
62 Philistine Gath; located at Tell eṣ-Ṣāfi. See Sheshonq, number 34 (see below, p. 16).
63 See refs., Helck 1971:121 end.
64 Obscure.
65 Shabtuna is Ribla on the route of Ramesses II’s advance north towards Qadesh-on-Orontes (Ramesses II, Battle of Qadesh, Bull. 7).
66 Obscure. However, see Alalaḫ texts (AT 85:2; 224:4; 330:6), and Amenhotep III (List B_N, 81).
67 Obscure.
68 See EA 74:20.
69 Not the same geographically as the Ruhizzi of the Amarna letters (cf. Helck 1971 and refs.).
70 This may be the Lebwe south of Qadesh-on-Orontes, 25 km northwest of Baalbek; biblical Lebo-(Hamath).
71 Probably Rehob south of Beth-shan.
72 Obscure.
73 Obscure.
74 Obscure.
75 Ambiguous: Edrei in Bashan; Edrei in Naphtali; or Derʿa by the Yarmuk; or some other?
76 Obscure.
77 Obscure.
78 May be a fortified place near Qadesh (cf. Helck 1971:128).
79 Remains unlocated.
80 Helck’s Gadara (1971:128) is unlikely. Rainey (2006:74) suggests Gazru (Gezer).
81 May well be the Rabute of EA 289:13; EA 290:11 (Helck 1971).
82 Obscure.
83 See EA 289:20.
84 Unknown location.
85 This is probably the Helqath south-east of Acco, now Tell Harbadj.
86 Probably biblical Yoqneam.
87 Unlocatable.
88 Possibly Tell Abu Sureq near Megiddo (cf. Helck 1971:126, with Abel 1933–1938, 2:28).
89 Tell Abu-Shusha. See Helck 1971:126.
90 Burkin, to the southwest of Jenin (cf. Helck 1971:126). See EA 250:14.
91 Remains wholly obscure.

B. The "Main Syrian" Series

This is List 1c, only on Pylon VII, East tower, North face. The first 17 place-names are destroyed, and thus are not included in modern numbering-systems, which (in sequence from lists 1a, 1b) continue as 120 ff., as here also below. Names not commented upon here rate as (at present) obscure, in both their onomastic and geographical identifications.

120. Pirati,
121. ʾAya,[92]
122. Amatu,
123. […]r/lazu,
124. Suka,
125. Tarmanan,[93]
126. L/rugaba,
127. Tunip,
128. [*lost*],
129. [*approximately 13 names lost here*],[94]
130. Zalabu,[95]
131. Sapkhash,
132. Niy,[96]
133. [*1 name, lost?*],[97]
134. Ara,[98]
135. Zapiziru,
136. Z/Sikaru?[99]
137. Zuluti?[100]
138. ʾUnama,
139. Arazikna,[101]
140. Khurikahhi?[102]
141. Zulasu,
142. Lulatiya,[103]
143. Sal/rakusha,[104]
144. [*lost*],
145. Unaya,
146. ʾUnafra,[105]
147. Yatakhab,[106]
148. Unuq,[107]
149. […]zina,
150. Sakuhiya,
151. Ubilalina,[108]
152. Zallawisu,[109]
153. Subqa,[110]
154. Paziru,[111]
155. Satikhebeg,
156. Amarsaki,[112]
157. Khalulasa,[113]
158. Nuraman/lanza,
159. Shawil/ranta,
160. Mararkhansa,
161. S/zigallu?[114]
162. [*lost*],
163. Kunlatu (> Kullatu),[115]
164. Til/riza,[116]
165. [*lost*],
166. Ulliza,[117]
167. Amr/lasa,
168. Khaziluzu(?),[118]
169. Arnira,[119]
170. Khatumiya,[120]
171. [*lost*],

92 Near Egypto-Hittite Syrian border?
93 Near Aleppo? Cf. refs., Helck 1971:140; Albright and Lambdin 1957:119, 15.
94 See Simons, 1937:119
95 See Helck 1971:140.
96 Well north of Hamath. See Helck 1971:140 and n. 88.
97 See Simons 1937:119.
98 Possible locations, cf. Helck, 1971:141.
99 Astour 1963:223.
100 Helck 1971:141.
101 See Alalaḫ texts; cf. Albright and Lambdin 1957:119, 16; Helck 1971:141.
102 Astour 1963:22, 223.
103 Astour 1963:223–224.
104 Helck 1971:141.
105 In Alalaḫ texts, Unapuri. See Albright and Lambdin 1957:119, 17.
106 In Alalaḫ texts, Yatkhapa. See Albright and Lambdin 1957:120, 18.
107 In Alalaḫ texts, Uniqa. See Albright and Lambdin 1957:120, 19.
108 In Alalaḫ texts, Ub/palali. See Albright and Lambdin 1957:120, 20.
109 Helck 1971:142.
110 Perhaps Sapiqiye, ca. 10 miles/15 km South of Aleppo. See Astour 1963:224.
111 Perhaps Basiri in the Ugaritic texts. See Astour 1963:224.
112 In Alalaḫ texts, Amarsaggi (also in Ramesses III's lists; Albright and Lambdin 1957:120, 21; Helck 1971:142).
113 In Alalaḫ texts, see Albright and Lambdin 1957:120, 22.
114 Helck 1971:142.
115 Albright and Lambdin 1957:120, 23; Helck 1971:142.
116 Cf. Tilishe (in Alalaḫ texts, Helck 1971:142); or Tirisa (in Assyrian texts, Astour 1963:225).
117 Helck 1971:142.
118 In Alalaḫ texts, Haziluhhe(?). See Helck 1971:142.
119 Cf. Annira in the Ugaritic texts, see Astour 1963:226.
120 In Alalaḫ texts, Khutame/ana. See Albright and Lambdin 1957:120, 24.

172. A[*p]urina,[121]
173. Z/Sunzaru,[122]
174. Kakham,
175. Al/rs/z[...],
176. Khazi[...],
177. Murarakhnas,
178. [.........]y,
179. Khur/l[...],
180. Wil[....],
181. Sa[..........].,
182. [*lost*],
183. [*lost*],
184. Nuban,[123]
185. Khatuma,[124]
186. Minnignasa,[125]
187. Tapkan(a)na,[126]
188. Susna/Zuzna,
189. Nirab,[127]
190. Tarab,[128]
191. Atugn/lari,
192. Ema[r],[129]
193. ʾUnt[...],
194. Sa[.........],
195. Sham(a)bu,
196. Nishapa,
197. ʾU/R/Lisakr/li,
198. Abita,[130]
199. Ziyurasa,[131]
200. ʾUtiyar,[132]
201. Natubi,[133]
202. Ziturasse,[134]
203. Ayatawa,
204. Sukawa,[135]
205. Tuʾub,[136]
206. Abilati,[137]
207. Shainalakiya,
208. ʾUri/ama,[138]
209. [...]tanaya,[139]
210. [...]ata,
211. Shailunagina,
212. Kaynabu,
213. Ali/asa,[140]
214. Nutana,
215. Azina,
216. Zitirasti,[141]
217. Turbinta,[142]
218. Muti/aya,
219. Na⟨n⟩api?[143]
220. Khaml/rul/ru,
221. Atura,[144]
222. Kal/rtimal/ruti,
223. Asiti,
224. Tanir/las,
225. Ienu,
226. Ati/abana,
227. Ashambu,
228. Ata/ikal/ra,
229. Tisita,
230. Atar/lnu,
231. Takamr/lasa,
232. Ubi/ata,
233. Ar/la[...],
234. Samar/lamr/lati,
235. ʾA/Unziqab,[145]
236. ʾAr/lasa,[146]
237. Ir(a)ta,[147]
238. ʾAti[...],
239. [*lost*],
240. Khal[...],
241. An/Un[...],
242. [*lost*],
243. Is/As[...],

121 Cf. Assyrian Apparazu. See Astour 1963:226.
122 Cf. Alalaḫ and Hittite Zuzzura/Zunzura. See Helck 1971:142.
123 Cf. Alalaḫ Nupan(n)i. Helck 1971:143.
124 For Khutamme at Alalaḫ, see Astour 1963:227.
125 Cf. classical Minnica and Minnig south of ʿAzaz, with Astour 1963:227.
126 In Alalaḫ texts, see Albright and Lambdin 1957:120, 26.
127 Modern Neirab, East-Southeast of Aleppo.
128 Later Ellitarbi/Litarbi? (Cf. Helck 1971:143).
129 On southern corner of Great Bend of Euphrates River.
130 Near Aleppo? Astour 1963:227.
131 In Alalaḫ texts, Ziurasse. See Albright and Lambdin 1957:120, 27.
132 In Alalaḫ texts, Utiyar. See Albright and Lambdin 1957:120, 28.
133 Perhaps Nitabi of the Alalaḫ texts. See Helck 1971:143.
134 Cf. Helck 1971:143; Astour 1963:227.
135 Sikawate of the Alalaḫ texts. See Astour 1963:227.
136 Perhaps Tu(u)ba of the Alalaḫ texts, with Helck 1971:144 and Albright and Lambdin 1957:120, 29.
137 Helck 1971:144.
138 In the Alalaḫ texts, Urima. See Albright and Lambdin 1957:120, 30.
139 Astour (1963:228) restores [A]tanaya, and references Assyrian Atinni.
140 Astour (1963:228) locates at Alasa, some 33 miles (51km) East-Northeast of Aleppo.
141 Cf. 202. above.
142 Identification with Turmitta is very uncertain. Cf. Albright and Lambdin 1957:120, 31.
143 If this is the correct reading, cf. Nanap in the Alalaḫ texts. Albright and Lambdin 1957:121, 32.
144 For an Aduri (as in EA 256), see Edel 1966:13, no. 8.
145 Anziqub(?) of the Alalaḫ texts, see Albright and Lambdin 1957:121, 33.
146 Helck (1971:144) offers Tell Arresh, on West bank of Euphrates between Carchemish and Meskene (uncertain).
147 Compare with Alalaḫian Irta, Albright and Lambdin 1957:121, 34.

244. A[...],
245. An[u?]n[u?],
246. Tar(a)bu,[148]
247. Fariwa,[149]
248. Sasban,
249. Katisha[...],
250. [*lost*],
251. [*lost*],
252. Sura,[150]
253. Papaʾa,[151]
254. Nuzina,[152]
255. Zimuka,[153]
256. [...]naya,
257. Kanu[..]askha,
258. [*lost*],
259. Sukiba/iki,[154]
260. Tarinu/Tarnu,[155]
261. Kamr/lu,
262. A/Itubi,
263. Atinni,[156]
264. Kir/lashawa,
265. R/Latima,
266. [...]sin-zi,
267–269. [*All lost*].
270. Carchemish,[157]
271. Djazkul/ra,
272. Murmar,[158]
273. Sata[...],
274–278. [*all lost*],
279. Khayatu,
280. Pidri,[159]
281. Ataritan,[160]
282. Mashawa,
283. An/lulak(ki?),
284. Napil/riyul/riwa,
285. Natikina,[161]
286. Atatima,[162]
287. Abarannu,
288/289. Ayal/ralu,
290. Anan/lam/ʿuya,
291. Taknu,
292. Tal/rukha,
293. ʾUr/lana,[163]
294. R/Lamanunaya,
295. [*lost*],
296. Papabi,
297. Ati[...],
298. Ar/lasha[...],
299. Mar/li[....],
300–305. [*all lost*],
306. Ebla (Ibla),
307. Kuramati,[164]
308. Ami/aku⟨n?⟩,[165]
309. Kazir/lu,
310. Umiya,[166]
311. Aleppo,
312. Piʾullu(?),
313. Uruma,[167]
314. Samʾalwa,
315. Ukam(a),
316. Purat,[168]
317. Sar/lur/lasu,[169]
318. Ar/lipankha,
319. [...]arizzi,
320. Puqiyu,
321. [...]u,
322. Tininura,[170]
323. Zir/lanasa,
324. Nul/ranassa,[171]
325–332. [*all lost*],
333. Wilima,[172]
334. Sin[...],
335. S/Tj[...],
336. A[...],

148 Possibly Taribu of Ugarit texts. See Astour 1963:228, from Nougayrol 1955:190, No. 11.800: 32.
149 Astour (1963:230) would place at Ferawan, some 6½ miles (20 km) East-Northeast of Maʿaret en-Noʿman.
150 Identity with Shuria (classical Sura) on Euphrates downstream from Emar is offered by Albright 1934:56, and by Astour 1963:230.
151 Astour (1963:230) locates at Fafin, some 3¾ miles (6 km) north of Aleppo.
152 Astour (1963:230) suggests it may be related to Greek Telanissos (Deir Semʿan), Northwest of Aleppo.
153 Astour (1963:230) suggests it was the Alalaḫian Shamuka (now Semka), some 12½ miles (21 km) East-Northeast of Maʿaret en-Noʿman.
154 Helck (1971:145) queries if it is the Shukewete of the Alalaḫ texts.
155 Cf. Astour 1963:230.
156 Helck (1971:145) offers tentative suggestions by Astour and Albright.
157 Modern Jerablus. See EA 54:51.
158 Suggestions, Helck 1971:146; Murmuriga the best one?
159 Assyrian Pitru (biblical Pethor) on the Euphrates, south of Carchemish (modern Tell Aushariye).
160 Astour (1963:231) would equate it with Alalaḫian Atrate.
161 Cf. Helck 1971:146, for tentative suggestions.
162 Astour (1963:231) compares Alalaḫian Atutamme.
163 Cf. Albright and Lambdin 1957:121, 35.
164 Possibly Qurumati on East Bank of Euphrates near Birejik (but Astour 1963:244, otherwise).
165 Cf. Albright and Lambdin 1957:121, 308.
166 Astour 1963:232: Alalaḫian Ummu, classical Imma, now Jeni-shehir.
167 Helck (1971:147) suggests it may be Urim, 12½ miles (20 km) Southwest of Aleppo.
168 Possibly Burat on East bank of Euphrates, about 7 miles (11 km) south of Carchemish.
169 Astour (1963:233) compares Alalaḫian Shurrashe or Shaurashe.
170 Two or three possible loci, see Helck 1971:147.
171 Cf. Astour 1963:234.
172 Cf. Albright and Lambdin 1957:121, 37.

337. Sha'lal/Mu(?)rar,[173]
338. Sisupa ("Tjitjupa"),
339. A[...],
340. [*lost*],
341. Zi[...],
342. Zir/lakha,[174]
343. Shusaran(a),[175]
344. ʾAzan(u)nu,
345. Abushatina,
346. Amuhar/l,
347. Timaqur/l,
348. "Ro-tep" (Egyptian "Mouth of the head"?)
349. Mur/liqa,[176]
350. Ir[...],
351–359. [*all lost*].

[173] Reading is uncertain. See Simons 1937:122. If reading is Sha'lal, then it is Albright's Shekhlal (1934:48); if the reading is Mu(?)rar, then one may cite Astour (1963:234) for Alalaḫian Murar or Mirar.

[174] Cf. Astour 1963:234, for Alalaḫian Zarahhe.

[175] Astour (1963:234) cites Alalaḫian Susula.

[176] Albright (1934:49) compared this item with Tell Muriq Northwest of Hamath, opposite Sinjar on the Orontes.

REFERENCES

Albright 1934; Albright and Lambdin 1957; Astour 1963; Edel 1966; Helck 1971; Moran 1992; Porter, Moss, and Burney 1972; Simons 1937; Tompkins 1893.

THE "SEA PEOPLES" RECORDS OF RAMESSES III (4.2)
(Monumental Records at Thebes)

K. A. Kitchen

In the early years of his reign (ca. 1183–1152 BCE), Ramesses III had to overcome three distinct assaults upon the vast Delta of northern Egypt by alien forces, would-be invaders from without. In Year 5 (1179/78), from the West by the Libyans and overseas allies; in Year 8 (1176/75), from the northeast, by a mixed group of "Peoples of the Sea," who had swept down the Mediterranean's east coast to attack the borderlands of Egypt, and in Year 11 (1173/72), again from the West, by Libyans and allies. It should be noted that the modern term "Sea-Peoples" derives in fact from the inscriptions of Merenptah, in his Year 5 (1209/08), whose scribes labelled the Libyans' exotic overseas-allies as "Foreign countries of the Sea," naming the non-Libyan foreigners as the Sherden, Shakalsha ("Shekelesh"), Aqaywasha, Lukku and Tursha (Karnak and Athribis stelae; in English, cf. Kitchen 2003:7, 19[twice]). Only the Shakalsha recur in the texts of Ramesses III, and the Tursha scarcely – new names then replace Merenptah's Aqaywasha and Lukku, seemingly vanished by Ramesses III's time.

Regrettably, the victory-inscriptions of Ramesses III are high on rhetorical praise of the valiant king, even if (more usefully) on statistics of the enemy slain and captured (with loot); but only rarely on campaign details. Put bluntly, they are 80–90% triumphant "waffle," while their allusions to the actual conflict and foreign groups involved are quite limited. For this reason, we give below the essential, more informative sections of these high-flown texts, rather than the endless reams of overblown heroics in praise of the pharaoh. But one must remember that he had to portray himself as being at least as valiant and victorious as his great namesake Ramesses II; so, through his able scribes, the louder he could shout the better!

Allusions to the Sea Peoples in Ramesses III's texts recur in several records in his temples at Thebes, which are therefore collected here; an additional *post-mortem* source (also included below) are the mentions of such foreigners in the historical summary in his honor in the great Papyrus Harris I, drawn up by his son and successor Ramesses IV, ca. 1151 BCE. It should be noted that in the actual war-scenes of the invading foreigners, curiously, their names almost never occur.

THE MEDINET HABU TEXTS

MH 1: *King receives prisoners and spoils after the sea-battle (abrégé): Episode (e:i), King's Speech* (MH 1, pl. 42, 43; *KRI* 5, 33) and *Episode (f:vi) Speech of foreign captives* (*KRI* 5, 34) [Earlier translations: Edgerton and Wilson 1936:42, 45; Kitchen 2008:28 (e:i), and 29 (f:vi)]

(e:i) King. Said by His Majesty to the King's Sons, the Grandees, King's Cupbearers and charioteers: "See for yourselves the vast might of my father Amen-Re! The foreigners that came from their (former) land, (even) from their isles amidst the Great Green (Sea) – they had set their course towards

Nile-Land, their spirits depending on their (strong) arms – but a net was set out for them, to entrap them! Caught(?) was whoever entered the Nile-mouths, (and) fell right into the trap, pinioned then and there, butchered, and their breasts shattered ...."

(f:vi) *Words of the captive chiefs*. Speech by the fallen grandees of the Sikilu ("Tjekkeru"), who are in His Majesty's grip, (while) praising this Goodly god, Master of the Two Lands, Usimare Meriamun: "Immense is your power, O Victorious King, Great Sun of Egypt. Greater is your sword than (even) a mountain of iron! Your renown is as that of (the god) Seth. Grant us (some) breath, (so) we can breathe it! Even the (very) life, that is in your grip forever!"

MH 2: *King leads three files of prisoners to Amun and the goddess Mut*: *(v) King's speech* (MH 2, pl. 44; *KRI* 5, 36), and *(vii–viii) Speeches by foreign captives* (*KRI* 5, 37) [Earlier translations, Edgerton-Wilson 1936: 47, 48; Kitchen 2008:31 (v), (vii–viii)]

(v) *King (abrégé)*. Said by the King of South and North Egypt, Usimare Meriamun: "You cause my fame to be mighty in the minds of their leaders ... I have carried-off their scouts, to present them ... to your spirit, my noble Father. My arm has brought down those who came to assert themselves – even the Philistines ("Pulasti"), the Danuna, and the Shakalsha ...."

(vii–viii) *Speeches of the Danuna and Philistine captives*. Spoken by the defeated Danuna: "Breath, breath, O goodly Ruler, mighty in strength like Montu who resides in Thebes!" Spoken by the defeated Philistines ("Pulasti"): "Grant us the (very) breath of our nostrils, O King, Son of Amun!"

MH 3: *Great Inscription of Year 8 – King's speech (abrégé)* (MH 1, pls. 45B, 46; *KRI* 5, 39:5–41:6). [Earlier translations, Edgerton and Wilson 1936:52–56; Kitchen 2008:34–35].

King's speech (the essentials). "Pay heed to me, O entire land, united as if in one place! Courtiers, King's Sons, and cupbearers of the Palace, (with) all citizens of Nile-land, (and) all of the able-bodied folk and the youth of this land! Pay heed to my pronouncements! So may you learn of my plans for sustaining you, and perceive the might of my noble father Amun, Kamephis, who created my excellence. His great, powerful sword is mine for strength, to lay every land prostrate under my sandals. He has decreed victory for me, his hand being with me, (and) so every transgressor of my frontier is slain in my grip. He chose and found me out from myriads, so that I am established on his throne in peace. Now, Egypt had been (as) a fugitive, having no (shep)herd, and they were afflicted because of the 'Nine Bows.'[1] But I surrounded her, and kept her firm by my valiant arm. I appeared like Re as King over Egypt, to defend her, and subdue the Nine Bows for her."

"(As for) the foreign countries, they made conspiracy/division(?)[2] in their regions ('isles'). Removed and dispersed in conflict were the lands (all) at one time. No country could resist their arms, beginning from Hatti (= Hittites), Qode (= Cilicia), Carchemish,[3] Arzawa (= W. Anatolia), Alasia (= Cyprus), cut off [all at once], in one place. Camp was set up(?) in one place, in Amurru; they cut off its people, and its land was as if it had never existed. They (= the invaders) came onward – a fire being (made) ready before them! – on towards Nile-land.

Their alliance was (of): the Philistines ('Pulasti'), Sikilu ('Tjekkeru'), Shakalsha, Danu⟨na⟩, (and) Washash, lands united. They laid hands on the lands as far as earth's outer rim, with hearts trusting and ready – 'Our plans will succeed.'"

"Now the mind of this god, Lord of the gods, was up and ready to ensnare them like birds. He granted me strength, my plans came to pass, and my [action(s)] went forward, flowing like some marvel. I organized my frontier in Djahy,[4] made ready before them, (with) the (local) chiefs, garrison-commanders and *maryannu*-warriors. I caused the mouths of the Nile to be made ready like a strong rampart, with large ships and (lesser) boats, made ready – these were manned, stem to stern with valiant warriors fully armed. The forces, of every (hand)-picked man of Nile-land, were like the lion roaring upon the mountain-peaks. The chariotry were (manned) by scouts, trained men(?), and every good and capable chariot-warrior. Their horses quivered all over, ready to trample the foreign landsmen under their hooves. I was very Montu (the war-god), valiant and steady before them, that they might behold the captives (taken) by my arms, – (even) the King of South and North Egypt, Usimare Meriamun, Son of Re, Ramesses III."

1 Traditional term for Egypt's foreign neighbors.

2 Sign is more V26 than F40 of Sign-list (Gardiner 1950:525 and 465 respectively), and as *ʿ*adutt(u)* rather than **shedtet* ("separated," as with Haider 2012:160, n. 42). The united "conspiracy" was then dispersed by Ramesses III – one could not so clearly disperse what was already (supposedly) separated! The seated-man determinative suits *ʿ*adutt(u)* perfectly; **shedtet* would require a striking man (or arm) determinative.

3 And a body of Philistines (as "Pa(las)tina," the later Pattina) overthrew Alalaḫ (west of Carchemish), and settled there, leading to a new local kingdom; cf. Hawkins 2009; Harrison 2009; Kohlmeyer 2009.

4 Term for the Levant, esp. coastal; in this case, probably for southern Canaan.

"I am the one who strides forth boldly, knowing his (own) strength, a hero who delivers his army on the day of conflict. (As for) those who reached my frontier, their seed exists no more, their heart and soul are finished forever and ever. Those who came unitedly upon the sea, the full flame was (ready) before them at the Nile mouths, while a barricade of lances surrounded them on shore – they were dragged-in, (boats) being capsized, and laid out on the beach, slain and turned into heaps, head over heel; their ships and property were as fallen into the waters."

"I made the lands turn back from (even) mentioning the Nile-land. (Should) they (even just) utter my name in their lands, then they are burnt up. Since I have sat on the throne of (Re)-Horakhty, and (the serpent-goddess) Great-of-Magic has settled on my head like Re, I have not allowed the foreign lands to (even just) look at Egypt's frontier, and to boast of themselves to the wider world ('Nine Bows')."

MH 4: *Medinet Habu, Temple of Ramesses III, South Rhetorical Stela, Year 12*: *Initial section* (MH 2, pl. 107 (cf. 128a); *KRI* 5, 73:3–11) [Earlier translations, Edgerton and Wilson 1936:130–131; Kitchen 2008:56–57]

King's speech (initial part). (Year 12, full titles of Ramesses III); he says: "Listen to me, O entire land, (you) citizens both young and old, of Nile-land! I am son of valor, offspring of a f[avored one], victorious of arm, mighty in strength as King of the Two Lands (united Egypt). I have brought down the level lands and hilly countries that infringed my frontier (ever) since I was affirmed as King upon Atum's throne. No land has survived to act aggressively in my presence, (while) I am affirmed like a bull, sharp-horned before them. I forced back the Asiatics who had trodden Egypt [...] dejected(?) through dread of me. They remember my name only as a (source of) terror in their lands, shuddering in contorted writhing at my battle-cry. I am a strong rampart, staunch in your time, a strong shade for your breasts."

"I have cast down the Sikilu ('Tjekkeru'), the land of the Philistines ('Pulasti'), the Danuna, the [Wa]shash, and the Shakalsha. I stifled the breath of the (Libyan) Meshwesh, ... [...] the Sibati-folk, [?ruin]ed and destroyed in their land. I am good at planning, able in [counsel(?) ...], (as) Lord(?), I [...] their mind(s), and I left them prostrate."

MH 5: Deir el-Medineh, Chapel C (behind Medinet Habu precinct), stela (*KRI* 5, 90–91, with references) [Earlier translation, Kitchen 2008:68–71, esp. p. 90, lines 10–12 (3rd stanza)]

"[A Lion] against Syria, he has trodden down the foreign lands;
the isles who sailed over his [boundaries(?), he looted them?]
[There sail]ed(?) the Philistines ('Pulasti') and Tursha, from the midst of the sea,
[then he reduced them to ruin?], as [...] his [...].,
(even the King of South and North Egypt, *etc., etc.*), ... Ramesses III."

MH 6: *Medinet Habu Temple, R. III, forecourt, on two pillar-bases* (MH 2, pl. 118:C, F; *KRI* 5, 102: 8, 11, at 118:C, F) [Earlier translations: Edgerton and Wilson 1936:146–147 and n. g; Kitchen 2008:118F (right), 118F (right)]

(Base 118C, right) The foreign lands of Philistia ("Pulasti"), whom His Majesty slew.
(Base 118 F, right) All plains and hill countries of D[anuna?, who are in His Majesty's grip].

MH 7: Medinet Habu Temple, East (front) High Gate, North Tower: Northern chiefs (MH 8, pls. 599, 600B; *KRI* 5, 104, 32: (b) ii) [Earlier translations: Edgerton and Wilson 1936:148; Kitchen 2008:80; 32]

(b: ii) *The 7 Northern chiefs*
I. The miserable Chief of Hatti as a prisoner.
II. The miserable Chief of Amurru.
III. Chief of the Sikilu ("Tjekkeru").
IV. Sherden of the Sea.
V. Chief of the Sha[su]-enemies.
VI. Tursha of the Sea.
VII. Chief of the Philistine ("Pulasti") enemies.

MH 8: *Papyrus Harris I (from a Deir el-Meineh pit, well behind Medinet Habu) in its "Historical Retrospect" section* (plate 76, lines 2 to 9) (Transcriptions of hieratic text: Erichsen 1933; new edition: Grandet 1994–1999)

My father Amun Lord of the gods, Re-Atum, and Ptah Fair-of-face caused me to appear as Lord of the Two Lands, in the place of my progenitor. (... *His acceptance as king* ...).

I organised Egypt in numerous categories (*or*: groups): cupbearers of the palace, great chiefs, infantry and chariotry, abounding by the hundred-thousands, (with) Sherden and Qeheq (personnel) without limit; minions by the ten-thousands – the manpower of Nile-land.

I extended the boundaries of Egypt on all sides, and I overthrew those who transgressed them, from their lands. I slew the Danuna from their isles, the Sikilu ("Tjekkeru") and Philistines ("Pulasti") (being reduced to ashes).

The Sherden and Washash of the Sea, they were reduced to what had never been, captured all together, and brought as captives to Egypt, like the sand of the seashore.

I settled them in forts, cowed by my name; their conscription was numbered by hundred-thousands. I provided all of them with garments and rations from the treasuries and granaries annually.

(Thereafter, the king reports warfare against the Seirites [= Edom], amid Shasu clans; official rock-face graffiti, etc., in this king's name indicate Egyptian activity out there, and in the copper-mines. Then follows a general account of his defeats of the Libyans and enslavement of his captives from their attacking forces.)

REFERENCES

MH I; MH 2; MH 8; *KRI* 5; Edgerton and Wilson 1936; Kitchen 2008; Erichsen 1933; Grandet 1994–1999.

THE LEVANT CAMPAIGN OF SHOSHENQ I (945–924 BCE) (4.3) KARNAK, TEMPLE OF AMEN-RE, BUBASTITE GATE

K. A. Kitchen

Late in his twenty-one year reign, the founder of the Libyan-origin 22nd Dynasty of Egypt, Shoshenq I, launched a military invasion into neighboring Iron-Age Palestine. But probably some time before that event, he had already opened up trade with Byblos in Phoenicia to secure timber-supplies in traditional fashion. Thus, Abibaal, king of Byblos, imported a statue of Shoshenq I for his own goddess Baʿalat-Gebal ("lady of Byblos") – upon which both this Phoenician dedication and the pharaoh's cartouches are engraved.[1]

Very different was the outwardly sudden outbreak of hostilities between Shoshenq I and his neighbors in Palestine. A damaged stela of Shoshenq[2] reports foreign intruders violating his north-east border, and slaying Egyptian army-personnel as far inland as the (east) shore of the East-Delta Bitter Lakes. He claims, "My [Maj]esty found … that [they] were killing [my soldiers? and] my army-leaders. My Majesty was (much) troubled about them …" This gave the pharaoh (in his own eyes) every excuse to pursue and expel the offenders, and then throw his forces into a sweeping campaign through Judah and Israel, their probably "alleged" zone of origin. Hence the brief but graphic narratives in 1 Kings 14:25–26 and 2 Chronicles 12:1–9. The biblical texts concentrate on Judah; but the geographical extent of the topographical list engraved as part of Shoshenq's victory record at the Karnak Temple of Amun in Thebes shows clearly that Shoshenq invaded both kingdoms, to impose vassal status upon them both. As did his victory-stela, set up in Megiddo.[3]

The date of the campaign comes from the Hebrew references in 1 Kings 14:25 and 2 Chronicles 12:2 as occurring in the 5th year of Rehoboam, king of Judah, which falls in 925 BCE, on the soundest, available chronology (closely linked to the well-established chronologies of Assyria and Egypt), as firmly established with minute care on proper Near-Eastern usage by Thiele 1986, in the final (3rd) edition of his work on Hebrew royal chronology.[4] Both on this basis and on cumulative figures for Egyptian reigns from 664 BC back to Shoshenq I, with all Near-Eastern links included, his accession stays at 945 BC.[5]

TRIUMPH-SCENE, BUBASTITE PORTAL, SOUTH FACE, THEBES, KARNAK TEMPLE OF AMUN

Introduction

In a grand version of the typical triumphal victory-scenes of the New-Kingdom pharaohs (within 1550–1100 BCE), Shoshenq I celebrated his Levant campaign. At the right, in traditional fashion, the King grasps the top-hair of a bunch of hapless, kneeling "Asiatic" prisoners, bending forward to smite them with his uplifted mace. At left, the god Amen-Re offers the sword of victory to the pharaoh, holds captive by cords, long rows of vertical, human-headed,

1 Translation and references, see Kitchen 1996:292, and Ritner 2009:219–220, No. 52.

2 Kitchen, 1996:294 and n. 287; and Ritner 2009:215–218, No. 50.

3 Kitchen, 1996:299, nn. 302–303; Ritner 2009:218–219, No. 51. Ḥor, a priest and scribe of Amun, mentions going on the "campaign into the foreign lands of Retenu" (= Palestine/Syria); Kitchen 1996:299, n. 304 and 575, § 510; Ritner, 2009:227–228, No. 54.

4 The date 962 BCE for the accession of Shoshenq I recently proposed (Schneider 2010:403) is based on false assumptions both about 22nd Dynasty royal reigns and dates and on improper dismissal of Near-Eastern synchronisms, too complex to present here. The speculations by Ben-Dor Evian 2011 are likewise of no merit, and her chronology improbable, in the full context of all our data for the period in both Egypt and the Levant. The so-called Bubastite Gate is simply the SE corner of the great court of Shoshenq I, and the only part largely completed by him, with the war-relief on the S. face, to "outshine" the neighboring such reliefs of Ramesses II.

5 Recent overall survey, Kitchen 2009:161–202, *passim*, and Kitchen 2013.

cartouche-shaped rings containing the names of places conquered during the king's campaign – the so-called topographical lists. Below, Amen-Re/Amun, the god who personified "Victorious Thebes" also holds cords with name-ring figures. (Below the King at left, is one final row of such name-rings, almost all now destroyed.) Around Amen-Re, is engraved his *threefold speech to the King*: (1) congratulations on his victory; (2) welcomes his building-plans [an item unique to this type of scene], and (3) endorses the King's successes.

The reference to Mitanni is merely a staple "flourish," to emphasize the "imperial" ranking of the scene and list, as was done by other pharaohs already in the New Kingdom from centuries before. Only Thutmose III (ca. 1479–1425 BCE) had actually seriously fought Mitanni on its own home ground, immediately east of the great bend of the River Euphrates (which he crossed in order to do). Later kings might reach Syria, but they did not cross over into Mitanni. But as "the back of beyond," Mitanni was included in their topographical lists simply to emphasize their imperial-conqueror status, even though they had never actually trodden its soil. Thus, it was included by both Ramesses II and Ramesses III in their lists (long after the Mitanni state had been destroyed by the Hittite king Suppiluliuma I and its territory swallowed up by Assyria). Shoshenq I's learned scribes simply took their cue on this detail from the neighboring lists of the mighty Ramesside kings, and included Mitanni in Shoshenq's list, so that it too would have "imperial" ambience. He and they were no more playing any deliberate anachronism-in-detail than the Ramessides were. A continuous set ideology, not anachronistic pseudo-history, was and is the keynote here.

A. Speech by Amen-Re

1. Amun hails the victorious King
"Welcome in peace, my dear Son, Lord who performs the rituals, King of Southern and Northern Egypt, **Hedjkheperre Setepenre**,[6] [...], Falcon-King, Strong Bull, Strong in Power! You have smitten the plains and hill-lands, you trod underfoot the tribal Nubians. Your sword vanquished the Mentyu-folk amid the sands, every moment, for your might triumphs (over) all lands.

You went forth in victory and returned in valor, and have united the [plains]. For you are offered up [all] the alien lands that knew not Egypt, daring to infringe your boundaries.

I sent their heads rolling, made your acts victorious, all plains and hills united [under] your sandals. Dread of you is far as the bounds of heaven's four pillars; Your Majesty's battle-cry echoes amid the Nine Bows (peoples). Fear of you has crushed the wills of the foreign lands, (even) as you are Horus, chief over the lands. I assigned to you all plains, all remotest reaches of (Nubian) Khent-hen-nufer. You circle in menace over your foes, and have crushed those in rebellion against you. Take to yourself the Sword, O Victorious King! Your mace has leveled the chiefs of the alien lands."

2. Amun lauds the Builder-King
Words spoken by Amen-Re, Lord of the Thrones of Both Lands, Presiding in Karnak, Lord of heaven, Ruler of Thebes:

"My heart is well pleased in beholding your victories, O my Son, **Shoshenq I, Beloved-of-Amun**,[7] whom I love! You came forth from me, to play the champion's role! I perceive your plans to be effective, and you have (already) wrought benefactions for my temple. You have affirmed my [City] of Thebes, Great Seat where my heart abides. You have begun to raise monuments in Thebes ('Southern On') and in Heliopolis ('Northern On'), and (for) every city likewise, (even) for each god in his province.

You have made my Temple of Millions of Years, the doorways to it in electrum, for my indwelling [Image]. Accordingly, may your heart be happy with the [leng]th of your lifespan, (for) the people are illumined, lit up, under your [*reign], (even as) I have established your seat beyond that of any other king."

3. Amun's endorsement of Shoshenq's victories
"With my sword have you felled all lands, by victorious deeds of valor. I have imposed [*dread] of you upon the Mentyu-folk of Asia; all foreign lands rage at your fiery blast against their backsides. They had attacked all lands, utterly (but) for Montu, you destroyed them, being mighty in crushing his foes. Your mace – it smote those rebellious against you, doomed (even) from faraway lands. Your uraeus-serpent seized them, and I set your boundaries at your (very) wish. I bring the Southerners in to you in submission, and the Northerners in the might of your power. You wrought great slaughter amidst their [*chiefs], beyond limit, fallen along their valleys.

Those who were many became as nothing, finally perishing, as if unborn. All foreign lands come, as if bound(?) – Your Majesty disposed of them in barely an instant. I lay low for you your opponents, I repress for you the militia of Mitanni, slaying them under your sandals.

6 The throne-name (in first cartouche) of Shoshenq I.
7 The personal name and epithet (in second cartouche) of Shoshenq I.

I am your father, Lord of the gods – (even) Amen-Re, Lord of the Thrones of Both Lands, unique Guide whose actions never fail. I will cause your valour (long) to be remembered, hereafter and for everlasting."

B. The Topographical List

1. The List proper, left half, Part 1. Rows of Name-rings, I–V, behind Amen-Re

(Row I) (a) The Nine Bows (Egypt's traditional potential foes)

1. The South.
2. The North.
3. The Nubian peoples.
4. Libya.
5. The Oases.
6. Tribesfolk of Asia.
7. Eastern desert-dwellers.
8. Upper (Southern) Nubia.
9. The Northern isles.

(b) *The Heading*. List of Asiatics.

(c) *The List*.

11. Ga[za?].
12. Ma[kkedah?]
13. Rubute.

(Row II)

14. Taanach.
15. Shunem.
16. Beth-Shan.
17. Rehob.
18. Hapharaim.
19. Adoraim.
20. [*lost*].
21. Shawadi.
22. Mahanaim.
23. Gibeon.
24. Beth-Horon.
25. "Qidatim" (for Qiryathaim?)
26. Ajalon.

(Row III)

27. Megiddo.
28. Adar.
29. "King's Monument" (*yad ha(m)melek*).
30. [....] r [..].
31. Hanim.
32. Aruna.
33. Borim.
34. Ginti-Padalla.
35. Yehem.
36. Beth-Olam(?)
37. "Kugaryu."
38. Socoh.
39. Berth-Tappuah.

(Row IV)

40. Abil.
41. [...]d. 42, 43, 44. [*all lost*].
45. Beth-Zoba(h).
46. Kik[kar?]. 47, 48, 49, 50. [*all lost*].
51. Sasadj[...].
52. [*lost*].

(Row V)

53. Penuel.
54. "New Town" (*Hadashat*).
55. "The ... Succoth."
56. Adamah.
57. Zemaraim.
58. Migdol.
59. [Ti]rzah(?)
60. [....]nr. 61, 62, 63, [*all lost*].
64. Ha(?)pin.
65. Pa-ʿemeq ("the Valley," *i.e.* of Jezreel).

Part 2. Rows of Name-rings VI–X, behind the goddess "Thebes"

(Row VI)

66. Ezem.
67. Anaru.
68. The Field[8] (of)
69. F(u)tayish.
70. El-Hallal.
71. The Field (of)
72. Abram.
73. The Spring
74. of Gabri.
75. The Spring (of)
76. Warkiyat.
77. The Field of
78. ʿAtsiyat.
79. Dad[..]ia.
80. Tsapiq.
81. Ma[...].
82. Tap[puah?]

(Row VII)

83. Ganat.
84. The Negev ("dry-land") (of)
85. ʿAtsihat.
86. Tashednau.
87. The Field (of)
88. Shanaya.
89. Haqa[q?]
90. The Negev (of)
91. Wahat-waruk.
92. The Negev (of)
93. Ashhati (for Shuhati?).
94. The Fort[9] (of)
95. Hanani.
96. The Fort (of)
97. El-Gad(?)
98. Admat ("Ground"?) (of)

8 Written *ḥql*, hence more "field" than "fort," cf. Ritner 2009:212, n. 40.

9 Written *hgr*, hence more "fort" (as Arabic *hajr*) than "field." Cf. (e.g.) Aḥituv 1984:109 and n. 244.

99. Hanani.
(Row VIII)
100. Adorem (*ai* > *e*?).
101. The Fort (of)
102. Tilwan/Tilon.
103. The heights (of)
104. Shal(a)lim(?)
105. The [he]ig[hts] (of)
106. David.[10]
107. Fields (of)
108. Arad.
109. (the) great(er), (and of)
110. Arad (of)
111. of the House (*bet*) (of)
112. Jeroham. 113, 114, 115, [*all lost*].
116. Ad[ar?].
(Row IX)
117. Adar (of?)
118. [*x*]biya.
119. [...]hagi(?)
120. [*X*]aryuka.
121. Falitimi.
122. Abil.
123. Beer-Luz.
124. Beth-ʿAnath.
125. Sharuhen.[11]
126. El-Mattan.
127. Goren.
128. Adummim (of?)
129. [*X*]rahat.
130. Ha[g/q?]ri, (off?)
131. Maru[...].
132. El-r[am?]
133. Yurtsa.
(Row X) Nos. 134–138. [*all lost*].
139. Jeroham (cf. 112 above).
140. ʾOnini.
141. [*lost*].
142. [?I]geb. 143, 144 [*both lost*].
145. Maʿ(?)akah?
146. Ad[....]. 147–148–149. [*all lost*].
150. "Jordan," (variant of a place *Yorda? – uncertain).

Part 3. Row of Name-rings(XI), at base of right half of scene, below the pharaoh
(Some 30 name-rings are completely lost, leaving only the last five as follows)
(Row XI) 1a. Sharu/ludad. 2a. Raphia. 3a. Laban. 4a. ʿAin-Goren. 5a. Ham.

[10] Here, "Davit," with de-voicing of the final voiced consonant (*d* > *t*) in Afro-Asiatic languages; many boys in Ethiopia & Eritrea are named Dawit < David; cf. likewise Canaanite *ḥereb*, "sword," > *ḥrp*, as a loanword in Egyptian (cf. long since, Burchardt 1910:36, No. 686, examples).
[11] The final three strokes are an error in hieratic for *na*; cf. Ahituv 1984:171, n. 499 after Müller.

Closing Observations on the List

The list is outwardly one of the longest and most detailed of its kind, rivalling the three other lists (and list-groups) of the preceding New-Kingdom era (16th–12th centuries BCE), namely the great triple list of Thutmose III (1479–1425 BCE), the grouped lists of Amenophis III (ca. 1390–1352 BCE), and large Medinet Habu lists of Ramesses III (ca. 1183–1152 BCE). The major lists of Thutmose III and Amenophis III are in both cases mainly original in content, and not just copies of earlier examples (leaving aside the commonplace "prologue" of the "Nine Bows"). The long Medinet Habu lists of Ramesses III by contrast include wholesale recopying of a large number of toponyms straight out of the great list(s) of Thutmose III (textual corruptions and all).

So, what is the nature of the Shoshenq list? A century or so ago, it was roundly dismissed by the well-known biblical critic Julius Wellhausen as probably a mere (second-hand) copy from some earlier list, hence of no historical value in itself or thus for biblical studies: "Er [= Shoshenq I] kann einfach eine ältere Liste eines seiner Vorgänger reproduziert haben" (= "He could merely have reproduced an older list of one of his predecessors").[12]

Unfortunately, neither he nor anyone else (it seems) has ever personally checked out this bold assertion. So, what are the facts? A close check-up reveals the following:

(1) Of the original 160 name-rings, only some 120 now survive for inspection;
(2) Out of the 120 still available for inspection (on the wall and/or in early fuller copies), many complete, but others in damaged state, *just 17* are *same* names (and, usually) places identifiable as such in the lists of both Shoshenq I and Thutmose III (our other biggest original repertoire). That is the quantifiable situation; the two lists have *little more than 10%* of names in common. They are, thus, virtually 90% independent of each other.
(3) And *what* names are in common? Mostly those that one would *expect* to find when Egyptian (or other) armies (and traders ...) ranged up and down the *usual routes* in Late-Bronze and Early-Iron Canaan. So, the 10% are ultimately non-significant, as everybody (independently) used them, anyway. Let us look at the seventeen:
  1. *ʿEmeq*. Sh(oshenq) 65. The Vale, par excellence: of Jezreel, from sea-coast to the Jordan. A general crossing-point for *all* armies and travellers between coast and inland routes.
  2. *ibr*. "stream." Sh. 34, 40, cf. 72. Too general to be of significance.
  3. *Yurtsa*. South of Gaza. Sh. 133. Simply part of the West coast zone and route, Egypt into the Levant.

[12] Wellhausen 1914: 68, n. 4.

4. *Iyrn*. "Ajalon." Sh. 26. In area of roads, from coast up to Jerusalem area.
5. *ᶜrn*. Aruna. Sh. 32. On northern part of a main road to and from Megiddo, through the coastal plain, south of Carmel range.
6. *Beth-ʿAnath* (*or ʿAnoth*). Sh. 124. Several possibilities, so no impact here.
7. *Beth-Shan*. Strongpoint in Vale of Jezreel, for all comers; cf. 1.
8. *Megiddo*. Sh. 27. A kingpin for *all* armies, imperial administrators, merchants, etc.!
9. *Negev-x*. Sh. 84, 90, 92. In area open to anyone seeking to dominate Negev zone.
10. *Laban*. Sh. 3a. On Egyptian (and general!) coast-route to the North, via Raphia, Gaza, etc.
11. *Rubute*. Sh. 13. On main route(s) from coast up to Jerusalem, etc.
12. *Raphia*. Sh. 2a. Unavoidable on the aforementioned general coast route!
13. *Rehob*. Sh. 17. Again, in the Beth-Shan W – E Jezreel (international) crossing-zone.
14. *Ham*. Sh. 5a. In area associated with SW zone, and so, open to its routes.
15. *Socoh*. Sh. 38. Again, on main (general) coastal route (between Megiddo and Gaza).
16. *Shunem*. Sh. 15. Yet again, in the Vale of Jezreel transit-region.
17. *Taʿanach*. Sh. 14. And again, same as just above.

(4) In short, (i) *no* invading armies coursing through Canaan/(Judah + Israel) or across the Jezreel vale, or pushing up into central Judea, or fanning into the Negev could have avoided contact with this particular body of over a dozen ever-present *key-points*, those actually reached depending on the routes taken in each instance. (ii) This "repetition" is *not* from a copyist recycling names from a temple wall, but is the *inevitable consequence* of all forces with the *same* basic aims being obliged to take over the *same* key-points, time and again in practice. (iii) Because most of these armies (be it of Thutmose III, or Sety I and Ramesses II, or of Shoshenq I) could only use the same key routes to hit various key-points, such key-points inevitably recur in the records of successive campaigners.

(5) In sharp contrast to such oft-visited key-points, major campaigners such as Thutmose III and Shoshenq I each in turn record innumerable "fresh" places in the course of (a) reducing sites that others had not; and/or (b) listing in greater detail more settlements of zones already known just generally. These more detailed records – in *both* cases! – confirm the originality and the authenticity of the actual campaigns of the two kings concerned. Both Thutmose III *and* Shoshenq I have left us *independent* detail-records from zones they each actually invaded; albeit, not the same terrain in each case: Thutmose went "big" in the northern Levant/Syria/Great Bend of the Euphrates; Shoshenq went "big" in western Palestine proper, and the Negev, with a short stab east of the Jordan. Their respective lists are in each case priceless documents for modern investigators, and cannot just be rubbished to feed an *a priori* prejudice. Wellhausen's dismissal of Shoshenq's list is wholly without any factual foundation; and was and is, alas, merely the illegitmate by-product of his anti-biblical biases.

REFERENCES

Full, definitive publication of the main scene and great topographical list by Shoshenq I at Karnak, see *RIK* 3 (1954); handbook version of the hieroglyphic texts, also in Jansen-Winkeln 2007:11–16, No. 20. Most recent translation of main texts and place-name list, see Ritner, 2009:200–213, No. 48D.

THE KAWA STELAE OF TAHARQA (YEARS 2–10, 689–680 BCE) (4.4)

K. A. Kitchen

From Nubia, the northern half of present-day Sudan, its rulers invaded Egypt, to establish a religiously "purer" regime, and their supremacy there constitutes ancient Egypt's 25th Dynasty, during 715–664 BCE; the four Nubian pharaohs were: Shabako (Nubia, 716; Egypt, 715–702); Shebitku (702–690); Taharqa (690–664); Tanutamun (664 in Southern Egypt, then only in Nubia). Fervent devotee of the Egyptian god Amun/Amen-Re, Taharqa built several temples to him in Nubia, including one at ancient Gem(pa)Aten, now Kawa, situated on the east bank of the Nile, about half-way between its 3rd cataract, and the arc of its great bend (out west of Gebel Barkal and the 4th cataract). Temples to Amun/Amen-Re were first built at Kawa during Egypt's New Kingdom (Empire period) by Amenophis III (ca. 1390–1353 BCE), then Amenophis IV/Akhenaten imposed his monotheistic Aten sun-cult (hence the name "Gem(pa)Aten," which stuck); and a lesser temple that we owe to Tutankhamun's reign.

It was over 630 years later that Taharqa "adopted" the main Kawa temple, a mainly brick structure and in poor state; he re-endowed its cult, and then rebuilt it entirely in stone, in his own name ("temple T" of modern publications). The five stelae translated here celebrate his works at Kawa: rebuilding-work, Year 6 (onwards), stelae IV, V; and re-dedication of the renewed temple in Year 10, stela VII. Then his successive endowments during his Years 2–8, 8–10 (stelae III, VI). The texts of these stelae were well published by Macadam (1949), but his invention of coregencies between the Nubian kings was a fallacy, as was his hypercriticism of "king" Taharqa in the biblical book of Kings.[1] It is nonsense, also, to damn "Tirhaqah *melek* Kush" ("Taharqa, Ruler of Kush") as an anachronism in 2 Kings 19:9 and Isaiah 37:9, that relate to the clash with Sennacherib in 701 BCE; Taharqa was then in fact ruler of Nubia ("Kush") and heir-apparent for Egypt under his brother Shebitku (ruling as overall king in Egypt). Both biblical passages (parallel texts) run straight down from 701 to the year 681 BCE, to the death of Sennacherib then, when Taharqa had been king over Egypt and Nubia for 9 years already (from 690). Incidentally, naming Taharqa as "king" in 701 by a writer acting in 681 is simply an identifying tag (or prolepsis) for his readers in his *own* time, 20 years later. It is precisely like anyone today remarking that "Queen Elisabeth II was born in 1926"; she was – but then *only* as princess Elisabeth, *not* queen. Not an "error," but simply an identifying tag for us readers of a later day. The texts are here presented in their proper (ancient) chronological order.

KAWA STELA IV, YEAR 6 (685 BCE) (4.4A)
(Macadam 1949:14–21, and pls. 7–8)

Lunette. Under the winged disc, Taharqa adores Amen-Re of Gem-Aten at the left, and the goddess Anuqet of the 1st Nile-cataract at the right.

Main Text. Dateline. (1)Year 6 under the Majesty of Falcon-King ("Horus"), Exalted-of-appearings; He of the Two Goddesses of North and South, Exalted-of-appearings; Golden Falcon, Protector of the Two Lands (i.e. Egypt), King of South and North Egypt. Nefertumkhure, Son of Re, Taharqa, living forever, the truly beloved of Maat, assigned (2)justice by Amun and living forever.

Prologue. Now, His Majesty was endowed with youthfulness, a uniquely valiant hero, – a powerful King, without his equal, Ruler like Atum, and love for whom (3)pervaded the lands (just) like Re at his risings in the sky – the Son of Re like (divine) Anhur, and his kingship (for) a million years, just like that of Tatonen.

(4)One wide-striding, broad-sandalled, sending his (swift) arrow so that he overpowers the great ones; one who tramples the mountains in (5)pursuit of his foe, battling with his scimitar, who slays myriads. At seeing him, every countenance just stares at him; all the folk rejoice when he appears with (6)fighting on his mind daily. He never tires, for it is his skill to provide for the conduct of war, with his fame ("name") traversing the plains and (7)highlands alike, so valiant is his brave arm.

Taharqa's concern for the Temple, as a Prince. Now, His Majesty was in Nubia as a fine youth, (and) as a King's Brother, dearly ("sweetly") loved. He travelled (8)north to Thebes, along with the (other) fine youths, whom His Majesty, King Shebitku, justified, had sent for, even from Nubia, so that he (Taharqa) (9)could be with him (Shebitku), – because he (Shebitku) loved him (Taharqa) more than all his brothers. (So), he (Taharqa) passed along by this District of Amun, even Gem-pa-Aten, and he paid homage at the temple's double doors, along with (10)His Majesty's army that had traveled north with him. He found that this temple had been built in mud-brick, and (that) the sand-drifts were up to its (11)roof, and covered with earth, at a time of year, when it was feared that rain might occur.

Taharqa as King, and Ancestral matters. So, His Majesty was most (12)disheartened over it – until His Majesty appeared as King, (even as) King of South and North Egypt, when the (Double Crown of) the Two Goddesses was established on his head, and his (prior official) name became Falcon-King ("Horus"), "Exalted-of-appearings." Then, he remembered this Temple (13)that he had (first) seen when a (mere) youth, – (but again now) in his 1st regnal year.

Then said His Majesty to his courtiers: "See, my intention is to (re)build the (14)Temple of my father Amen-Re (of) Gem-pa-Aten, because it had (only) been built of brick, and (got) covered in earth – no (15)good, in anybody's opinion. The deity was in this place, but what the rain had done was unknown. But it was he who had preserved this temple until I arose as King. For (16)he knew that I had (already) made monuments for him, (as) his son, even I, whom he had begotten.

Now, the (ancestral) mothers of my mother were committed to him (= Amun) by their (17)brother, the Senior (*or*: their 'Senior Brother'), the Sin of Re, (King) Alara, justified, (he having) said: 'O God who recognises one loyal to him, swift-striding (in) coming to whoever calls upon him! (18)Do look to me, concerning the womb(s) of my consorts(?) – may you establish their children upon earth! Deal with them, (just) as you have dealt with me, – so, may you grant them to attain to (19)prosperity!'

(Now), he (Amun) heeded what he (Alara) had said, concerning us. He (Amun) has set me up as King, just as he had said to him (Alara). 'How good, indeed, is it to act for him who acts – (20)(then)

[1] On the former, see the exemplary review-paper by Leclant and Yoyotte 1952; and on the latter, Kitchen 1996:157–161, 552–553, 557.

satisfied indeed is the heart of him (King) who acts for him (Amun) that acts for him (King)!' All you have said, it is true – his son, you (indeed) are, who refurbishes his (Amun's) monument."

Then His Majesty (21)dispatched his army to Gem-Aten, along with many work-teams, and goodly craftsmen beyond count, and a Chief of Works there, (22)with them, to direct the work n this temple, while His Majesty was (far north) in Memphis.

Then was this temple built of fine pale sandstone, (of) top (23)quality, hard, and wrought in everlasting work, facing to the west; the building (was) wrought with gold,[2] and the columns also with gold, and the insets(?) (24)thereof, of silver. Its pylon-towers were built, and its doorways erected, and engraved with the great names of His Majesty. Its abundant trees were planted in (25)the earth, and its pools excavated, along with providing its "House of Natron," and it being filled with its (equipment)-requirements, of silver, gold and (26)bronze beyond reckoning.

Then this god (Amun) was inducted within it, glorious ad splendid forever; (27)the reward for this being life and prosperity upon the throne of Horus forever.

2 Traces of gilding were found on wall-fragments in the excavations ("specks of gold leaf"). Cf. Macadam 1949:21, n. 52.

KAWA STELA V, YEAR 6 (685 BCE) (4.4B)
(Macadam 1949:22–32, and pls. 9–10)

Lunette. Under the winged disc, followed by Queen-Mother Abaru in each case, Taharqa offers to the god Amen-Re, of Gem-Aten on the left, and of Thebes ("Thrones of the Two Lands") on the right.

Main Text. Dateline. (1)Year 6 under the Majesty of Falcon-King ("Horus"), Exalted-of-appearings; He of the Two Goddesses of North and South, Exalted-of-appearings; Golden Falcon, Protector of the Two Lands (Egypt), King of South and North Egypt. Nefertumkhure, Son of Re, Taharqa, living forever, the truly beloved of Maat, assigned (2)justice by Amun and living forever.

Lo, His Majesty was a lover of Deity – (2)he spent his time by day and spent his nights (likewise) in seeking out benefactions (to do) for the gods: (re)building [their] temples that had fallen into decay, fashioning (again) their images as (they were) aforetime, (re)building their storage-magazines while furnishing (3)their altars, supplying them with sacred offerings of all kinds, while (also) making their libation-tables and vessels of electrum, silver and copper.

Now, His Majesty was pleased at heart in performing benefactions for them (= the gods) daily. This land has (had) (4)abundance, like it had been in the age of the Lord-of-All, everyone sleeping (through) till dawn, without (having to) say, "Oh that I had (this or that)!" Right-doing was introduced everywhere, and evil skewered into the ground.

(5)Wonders have happened in His Majesty's time, in Year 6 of his reign, the like of which have not been seen since the time of the ancestors – so greatly did his father Amen-Re love him. His Majesty had been (6)praying for a Nile-flood from his father Amen-Re, Lord of the Thrones of the Two Lands, so as to prevent famine from happening in his time.

Now, as for everything that passes the lips of His Majesty, his father Amun brings it to pass immediately. So, when the flood-season came along, (7)then it was flooding abundantly, daily; it spent many days in flooding, (rising) by a cubit each day. Thus, it reached even into the cliffs of Upper Egypt, and overtopped the mounds of Lower Egypt. The land became (even) as a primeval ocean, as a slumbering expanse – one could not distinguish between (8)land and river. It flooded up to 21 cubits, 1 palm and 2½ fingers, as at the quay of Thebes.[3]

His Majesty had the annals of the ancestors brought to him, (to) look up the inundation (level) as it happened in their times, but the equal ("like") thereof was not to be found. (9)And there was also a heavenly downpour in Nubia; and it made all the mountains sparkle. Every man in Nubia abounded in everything, and Egypt was in happy festival; so, they thanked His Majesty.

His Majesty was utterly joyful in heart at what his fat[her] (10)Amun had wro[ught for him], (he thus) proceeding to have sacred offerings presented to all the gods – so glad was his heart through what his father had done for him.

Yea, then said His Majesty, "My father Amen-Re, Lord of the Thrones of the Two Lands, has wrought for me these 4 glorious Wonders within a single year, even in Year 6 of my reign as King – never has the like been seen, (11)since the (age of) the ancestors of old!

3 See Macadam 1949:29, n. 25 with its nn. *a*, *b*. A river-rise (in round figures) of some 11 metres (about 32½ feet), roughly at 75 metres from a baseline of almost 64 metres on Karnak quay at Thebes.

(I) The Inundation came like a cattle-thief, when it wholly flooded the land; never has its like been found in writing, (even) from the time of the oldest kings! None have said, 'Oh! I have heard such (a case) from my father!'
(II) It caused for me, the entire (12)cultivated land to do well.
(III) It slew the rats and snakes in its midst, and kept it free of the locusts.
(IV) It did not allow the South winds to reap (it), (but) (13)I reaped the harvest, into the granaries, without limit thereof, of (both) Upper-Egyptian barley and Lower-Egyptian barley, and of every seed that grows upon earth."

I (originally) came down(stream) from Nubia, amidst the king's brothers, whom His Majesty (Shebitku) had summoned. (14)I stayed on with him, and he loved me more than (any other) of his brothers, or any of his (own) children; I was esteemed more than any of them, by His [late] Majesty. The hearts of the (ordinary) people turned to me, and love for me was with all the people.

(15)I assumed the crown in Memphis, after the Falcon [the late king Shebitku] had flown up to heaven. My father Amun decreed for me that all plains and every hill-country be placed under my feet – the South to Reteh-Qabet, and the North to Qebeh – (16)Hor; the East as far as the horizon, and the West as far as the sunset.

(Now), [she was] in Nubia, even the King's Sister, sweet of love, the King's Mother Abaru (may she live). Indeed, I had departed (17)from her while (I a was) a youth of 20 years (in age), when I came with His [late] Majesty to Lower Egypt. Thus, she came north to see me (in Egypt), after a (18)span of years.

She found me arisen upon the Throne of Horus, having received the crowns of Re, even (with) the Two Goddesses united upon my brow, and (while) all the (other) gods were the protection for my body.

She rejoiced with great (19)gusto, when she had beheld the beauty of My ("His") Majesty, just as Isis had beheld Horus arisen upon the throne of his father Osiris, after he (Horus) had been but a mere "youth within the nest" at Chemmis.

(20)(Thus) did the South and North (of Egypt), and every foreign land bow down to the ground before this Queen-Mother, celebrating with great joy – their elders along with their youngsters – and they acclaimed the Queen-Mother, (21)saying: "Isis (herself), when she had received her son Horus, was like the Queen-Mother, now she is reunited with her son!"

O King of South and North Egypt, Taharqa, living forever, beloved of the gods! May you (indeed) live for ever, even by the decree of your father Amun, the (22)excellent god, who loves him that loves him, and who recognises one who is loyal to him, and who has caused your mother to rejoin you in peace, that she may behold the benefits that he has wrought for you.

O Victorious King, may you live, may you be healthy, even as Horus did live for his mother Isis. You shall indeed appear upon the Throne of Horus forever and eternally.

KAWA STELA III, YEARS 2–8 (689–683 BCE) (4.4C)
(Macadam 1949:4–14, and pls. 5–6)

Lunette. Under the winged disc, small figures of Amen-Re of Gem-Aten (on right) and of the goddess Anuqet of the 1st Nile-cataract (on left) plus the vulture and serpent figures of the goddesses Nekhbet (right) and Wadjet (left) all offer the symbols of life and eternity to the Horus-Falcon and cartouche-titles of Taharqa ("Falcon-King, Exalted of appearings; Nefwrtumkhure, Taharqa," respectively).

Main Text (Recording donations by Taharqa to the Kawa temple, this is engraved in 25 vertical columns, reading from right to left, as follows) (1)Year (2) of the Falcon-King, Exalted of appearings; He of the Two Goddesses, Exalted of appearings; Golden Falcon, Protector of the Two Lands; King of South and North Egypt, Nefertumkhure, Son of Re, Taharqa, living forever. He has made as his monument for [his] fa[ther Amen]-Re, Lord of Gem-Aten, (the following gifts):

1 silver altar, worth ("at") (2)220 *deben*; 1 gold censer, at 12 *deben*; 1 gold *namzitu*-vase, at 10 *deben*, 5 *qite*; 1 gold *weneh*-stand(?) at ⟨1⟩ *deben*, 2 *qite*; 7 bronze *sha'am*-vessels; 50 rolls of *paqet*-linen; 38 of *shendjet*-linen; (3)12 of *rudj*-cloth; 20 of *menkhet*-cloth – making (a total of) 120 (items).

(Also): 1 lapis-lazuli figurine of Maat; 1,200 cyprus-seeds; ⟨1⟩ incense-tree; 1 drum; (4)1 harp – that he (= the King) may attain the gift of all life, all stability, all health, all joy, and the celebration of a million jubilee-festivals in profusion, having appeared as King of South and North Egypt upon the Throne of Horus, like Re forever.

(5)Year (3) of the King of South and North Egypt, Taharqa, living forever. He has made as his monument for his father Amen-Re, Lord of Gem-Aten, (these gifts):

1 silver *khawt*-vessel; 1 *khawt*-vessel cover; 50 *namzitu*-vessels with ram's face(s); 20 bronze *shu*-vessels; 20 large bronze *khawt*-vessels; 30 bronze (6)*denit*-vessels; 14 bronze *peshny*-vessels; 3 bronze ring-stands; 1 bronze *denit*-vessel with large rim(?); 1 bronze …(?); 1 bronze *aat*-vessel; 50 *deben* of wax; 20 *deben* of bitumen; 7 "loaves" of incense, and 5 of ladanum; 4 hour-priests; 2 (star)-transit instruments.

(7)Year (4) (of) the King of South and North Egypt, Taharqa, living forever. He has made as his monument for his father Amen-Re, Lord of Gem-Aten, (these gifts):

100 *deben* of gold; 5 silver ram's-face *namzitu*-vessels, at 8 *deben*; 1 silver *namzitu*-vessel at 15 *deben*; 1 gold ram's-face *heset*-vessel, at (8)7 deben; 1 gold ram's-face *namzitu*-vessel, at 3 *deben*, 5 *qite*; 1 bronze brazier-stand; 3 bronze *khawt*-vessels, (and) 3 bronze lotuses for *khawt*-vessels; 3 bronze ring-stands, at 9 *deben*; (and) 3 lamps – that he (= the King) may be granted all life, stability and dominion, all health, and all joy, forever.

(9)Year 5 (of) the King of South and North Egypt, Taharqa, living forever. He has made as his monument for his father Amen-Re, Lord of Gem-Aten, (these gifts):

1 gold *bbt* (= ?), at 21 *deben*, 6 *qite*; lapis-lazuli, amount 10 *deben*, 5 *qite*; real(?) tin(?), at 56 *deben*; turquoise, amount 61 *deben*; 10 rolls of linen; 5 of *shendjet*-linen; 5 of *rudj*-cloth; 20 of(?) *hrt*-cloth; making 40 (rolls).

(10)Year 6 (of) the King of South and North Egypt, Taharqa, living forever. He has made as his monument for his father Amen-Re, Lord of Gem-Aten, (these gifts):

1 gold lid, with the King's figure marked upon it, at 5 *deben*, 1 *qite*; (and) 1 silver and gold signet-ring – that he (the King) may be given all life, stability and dominion, (and) all health and all joy, like Re forever.

(11)Year 7 (of) the King of South and North Egypt, Taharqa, living forever. He has made as his monument for his father Amen-Re, Lord of Gem-Aten, (these gifts):

1 gold censer, shaped as the forepart of a lion; 1 gold falcon with a figure of the king in front, (both) upon a "Year"(-sign shaped) scepter; 1 gold ram's face sphinx along with the figure of a vulture, (both) upon (12)a "Year"(-sign shaped) scepter; a gold statuette of (the god) Khons, they (*sic*) being upon a "Year"(-sign shaped) scepter; a gold figure of Amen-Re, Lord of Gem-Aten, with two persea-trees at its end, and a figure of the King before it; (13)1 gold *meswut*-dish; 1 gold face of a ram, upon a pole-standard; ⟨1⟩ gold face of a ram over date-palms; 1 gold statuette of Amen-Re, Lord of [Gem]-Aten, over a date-palm; 1 gold figure of (the goddess) Isis, at (14)11 *deben*, 3½ *qite* of gold; 2 linen strips – which the Son of Re, Taharqa, dedicated to his father, Amen-Re, [Lord] of Gem-Aten, that he might be granted all life, all stability, all dominion, all health and all joy like Re forever.

(15)Year 8 (of) the King of South and North Egypt, Taharqa, living forever. He has made as his monument ⟨for his father⟩ Amen-Re, Lord of Gem-Aten, (these gifts):

1 bronze statue of the King, smiting foreign lands, and its 6 garments; 8 silver and gold unguent-jars.

The furnishings for the new temple that His Majesty had built:

1 gold broom; 1 gold *heset*-vessel; 1 gold *namzitu*-vessel; 2 gold *abesh*-vessels; 1 gold (17)trumpet; 1 gold incense-measure; 1 gold *shefdu*-vessel(?); 1 silver circular altar; 1 statue of the King, with gold face; 1 gold statue of the Nile-flood god, which is over it – making (18)10 gold articles, amounting to 51 *deben*, 4 *qite*.

1 silver offering-table; 15 silver *khawt*-vessels; 1 circular *ditto*; 1 silver censer; 1 silver *heset*-vessel; 1 silver incense-measure; 1 silver *shefdu*-vessel(?); 1 silver trumpet; 1 silver *maswut*-vessel; 1 silver *abesh*-vessel; 1 silver *qeby*-vessel; 2 silver *hemt*-vessels; 4 silver *weshem*-vessels; 1 silver cup; 1 silver (20)*peshny*-vessel; 1 silver *wedeh*-vessel; 1 silver casket for (the ceremony of) "Opening the Mouth" – its contents (being): 4 silver *deshret*-vessels, 2 silver torches, 2 silver *ʿaref*-vessels; 4 silver *rrm* (= ?); (and) 4 *ames*-scepters, (21)making 17 implements; 1 silver *hedj*-shrine(?), amounting to 1,891 *deben*, 1 *qite*; (also) 35 (sheets) of thin gold for engraving(?); and every kind of timber – acacia, cedar and persea.

He (the King) established the sacred (22)offerings (wine, bread, cattle, and fowl), victualed his altars, and furnished his workshops/magazines with servants, male and female, even the offspring of the Libyan chiefs.

(23)This temple was fully provided-for, that he (the King) had made for him (Amun), anew. So, he filled it with many chantresses (with) their sistra[4] in their hands, to play for his beautiful (24)countenance – that he (Amun) might reward him (the King) in these matters, by granting him all life, stability, prosperity, health and (25)joy from himself, that he (the King) may celebrate a million jubilees, by myriads, having appeared on the Throne of Horus of the living, and be glad in spirit like Re, forever and eternally.

4 I.e., their music.

STELA VI, YEARS 8–10 (683–681 BCE) (4.4D)
(Macadam 1949:32–41, and pls. 11–12)

Lunette. Under the winged disc, now wholly lost, the King (at right and left) makes offering to two forms of Amen-Re, probably those of Kawa and textually, only some portions of the customary and entirely mundane offering-formulae and benedictions remain.

Main Text (Recording further donations by Taharqa to the Kawa temple, now complete, this is again engraved in 25 vertical columns, reading from right to left, as follows) (1)Year 8 (of) the King of South and North Egypt, Nefertumkhure, Son of Re, Taharqa, living forever. He has made as his monument for his father Amen-Re, Lord of Gem-Aten, (the following gifts):

1 bronze offering-table; 11(?) bronze *kuihku*-vessels, (each) upholding two apes; 10 [+*x*? … *loss* …]; (2)54 [+ *x*? … *loss* …]; 50 bronze "millennium" ("1000-year") vessels; 15 bronze *denit*-vessels; 50 bronze knives; 5 bronze *ʿash*-vessels; 4 large bronze *qeby*-vessels; 10 bronze *irs*-vessels; 1 bronze sistrum; 1 bronze (3)[…]-vessel; 3 bronze *shefdu*-vessels; 3 bronze pairs of tweezers; 7 bronze *heset*-vessels; 1 bronze *djodja*-vessel; 5 bronze *gash*-vessels; 1 columnar support for a brazier-stand; (4)1 bronze smelting-brazier; 5 bronze lamps; 3 bronze *khawt*-vessels; 1 bronze *nehmet* (= ?); 1 bronze ring-stand; 1 bronze *ʿa*-vessel; 1 bronze *weshem*-vessel; 1 bronze ring-stand for an altar; 1 (5)bronze tool for chopping(?); 1 bronze hoe, amounting to 281 *deben* of bronze – making 7,815 *deben*.

8 *hrd*-rolls of cloth; 57 of *djat*-cloth; 2 of *tjetef*-cloth; (6)15 masts of date-palm wood; 4 (rolls of) *ifd*-cloth; 104 threads of yarn; 56 poles of zizyphus-wood; 15 (*x*-measures) of dried resin; 1 silver "arm" for enacting the rite of sprinkling; 2 bronze *st-mnt vessels*, making (7)1,515 *deben*; 550 *deben* of orpiment(?) – which the King of South and North Egypt, Taharqa, living forever, made over to his father Amen-Re, Lord of Gem-Aten, so that he may be granted all life, stability and dominion, all health, and all joy, like Re, forever and eternally.

(8)Year 9 (of) the King of South and North Egypt, Taharqa, living forever. He has made as his monument for his father Amen-Re, Lord of Gem-Aten, (the following gifts):

651 *deben* of gold; 1 golden fan(?) at 9 *deben*; 3,200 *deben* of silver; 1 silver (9)fan(?)-handle; 2 *shu*-vessels with gold rims; 1 silver *tef*, wrought in gold; 2 silver lamps; 1 silver palm-staff for a star-gazer; (10)1 silver and gold fan; 1 bronze *shu*-vessel; 1 bronze *qeby*-vessel; 10 bronze altars; 1 water-pot(?); 1,000 cypress-seeds; 13,456 *deben* (11)of bronze; 2 silver geese, at 200 *deben* of silver, and 4 *deben*, 4½ *qite*; 10 bronze *khawt*-vessels; ⟨1⟩ "lotus"-vessel; 147 *hnw*-vessels – that he might be granted life, stability and dominion like Re forever.

(12)Year 10 (of) the King of South and North Egypt, Taharqa, living forever. He has made as his monument for his father Amen-Re, Lord of Gem-Aten, (the following gifts):

15 *deben* of gold; 500 *deben* of *wesheb*; 106 *deben* of orpiment(?); 2,000 *deben* of blue stone for painting; 500 ⟨*deben*⟩ (of) (13)wax; 100 *deben* of *setjeh*; 10 faience *kr-t*-vessels; 100 cloths of *insy*-cloth; 200 cloths of *idmy*-cloth; 35 plaited(?) cloths with embroidered edges(?); 5 (14)"loaves" of ladanum; 60 (sheets) of *tgun*-gold for engraving; 300 *deben* of gold of its desert; and all timber in abundance, beyond reckoning – cedar, juniper and acacia.

His entire city was made to glitter, (15)with all manner of trees. For him (*or*: it = the temple), were appointed gardeners, of the best from Djesdjes (= Bahria Oasis), and likewise from the people of the Northland. His temple, after having fallen into ruin, was (now) (16)(re)built in good, hard sandstone, after His Majesty had found that it had been (previously) built (only) in brick, and that the sand-drifts had covered over its roof. (So), he built it for him (Amun) in stone, with workmanship the like of which had not (17)been seen from the (age of) the gods down to this (very) day. He (= King) wrought it in good, hard stone of excellence; its columns were erected, and overlaid with fine gold, and their inlays(?) wrought in silver. Its pylons were built (18)in goodly work, its doors were hung, (and) of real cedar, their bolts being of Asiatic bronze; and it (the temple) was inscribed in the great name of His Majesty, by all manner of skilled scribes, and engraved by excellent craftsmen (19)who rivalled what(ever) the ancients had achieved. Its storehouse was (well) stocked, and its altars supplied. He filled it with libation-tables of silver, gold and Asiatic bronze, and (with) every kind of genuine gemstone beyond counting. He filled ⟨it⟩ with (20)an abundance of servants; and he installed female servants for it, (drawn) from wives of chieftains of Lower Egypt.

Wine is trodden from this city's vintages ("vines"), even more abundant than from Djedjes; he appointed gardeners for them, even good gardeners (21)from (among) the Mentiu of Asia.

He filled this temple with priests – men who knew their rites ("spells"), from (among) the offspring of the grandees of every land. He filed his house with chantresses, to play before his beautiful countenance.

(22)His Majesty did all this, because so greatly did he love his father Amen-Re of Gem-Aten. For he (the King) recognized that he had excelled in his (Amun's) opinion, being swift of step in coming to him (Amun) that called him, because of the wonder that he had wrought for his mother in her womb, before she gave birth. For his own mother's mother was committed to him (Amun) by her brother, the Chief and Son of Re, Alara, (23)[justified], with the words, "O excellent god, one swift of step who comes to him that calls on you – may you look for me upon my sister, even a woman born along with me in the same womb. May you act for her, even as you acted for him who acted for you, for (it to be) a wonder unforeseen, and not (just) dreamt up by conspirators – for you did defeat for me, him that plotted evil against me, (24)and (you) did set me up as King. May you act for my sister likewise; and set up, for yourself, her children (also) in this land. May you grant that they ('he') attain felicity, and appearing as king, even as you have done for me!"

And he (Amun) heeded all that he (Alara) had said, without setting aside any of his words. And he has (now) appointed for himself even his very likeness, the Son of Re, Taharqa, living forever, King (25)[... *loss* ...] to com[memor]ate his name, to restore his monuments, to maintain his statues, to engrave his (Amun's) name upon the temple, to pronounce the name(s) of his (Taharqa's) female forbears, and to establish for them funerary offerings, and to assign to them abundant *ka*-servants, rich in everything. May he (Taharqa) attain to all life like Re forever.

KAWA STELA VII, YEAR 10 (681 BCE) (4.4E)
(Macadam 1949:41–44, and pls. 13–14)

Lunette. Under the winged disc, Taharqa adores Amen-Re of Gem-Aten at the left, and Amen-Re, Lord of the Thrones of the Two Lands (at Thebes) at the right.

Main Text. Dateline. (1)Year 10, 1st month of the Akhet-season, Day 1 (= New Year's Day), under the majesty of Falcon-King ("Horus"), Exalted-of-appearings; He of the Two Goddesses of North and South, Exalted-of-appearings; Golden Falcon, Protector of the Two Lands (Egypt), King of South and North Egypt. Nefertumkhure, Son of Re, Tah[arqa, given life like Re, forever].

(The text proper then follows in 14 vertical columns [2–15], almost half the area of which is now obliterated, leaving for us great gaps in the surviving text, which runs as follows)

(2)Setting-up, sprinkling, (and) handing-over the Temple to its (divine) Lord, (by) the King of South and North Egypt, Taharqa, living forever. He has made as his monument the temple of his father, Amun the Mighty, residing in Gem-Aten (Temple), built in (3)stone as a monument forever. The walls were built and the columns erected, abiding and firm eternally.

Now, His Majesty decreed that real (4)cedar of Lebanon be sent south, to erect its masts in this temple, which His Majesty had made for his father Amun, to be assigned to the pylon [of the temple] that His Majesty had constructed (5)for his father. Pools ("waters") were dug, (for) the altar-stands that please the heart of Amun the Mighty. He (the King) has made a storehouse for the sacred offerings that His Majesty has provided for his father, namely [the giving of?] his offering-bread.

(6)Now, indeed, as for His Majesty, he is a valiant king, of good counsel, and pleasing in actions. His father Amun has chosen him as [being an excellent] king, when he understood (7)that his aim was to (re)build the Temple, and to embellish sanctuaries (generally).

Now, His Majesty was at the to[wn of *X*, ... *large loss* ... addressing] his courtiers: "As for (8)that (matter) that My Majesty knows of, (even) this temple of my father Amen-Re of Gem-At[en, ... *large loss* ...], My Majesty has (now) made (anew) (9)the Temple (*pr*) of my father, Amun the Mighty, it being (re)built [in good stone, hard and lasting ...]."

[*All provision was then made, *etc.*, ...], under (the eye) of His Majesty, to abide and (10)endure, (a work) beloved of Ptah. [... *very large loss* ...] them(?), to do (11)according as His Majesty had begun [?to do, ... *huge loss* ...], causing the god to abide therein. (12)[... *all line lost, except* ...] forever, (but) built in brick, (13)[... *all lost, except* ...] alongside what had been in brick, of/for (14)[... *all lost, except* ...] a [so]n who champions his father, (and) who has acted for him that acted for him, (15)[... *all lost except* ...] ..., having appeared as King of South and North Egypt, upon the Throne of Horus forever.

REFERENCES

Full publication of the Kawa stelae, see Macadam 1949; and the extensive review-paper by Leclant and Yoyotte 1952; see now Jansen-Winkeln 2009:129–142, Nos. 73–77.

DEMOTIC COMPOSITIONS

THE SO-CALLED DEMOTIC CHRONICLE (4.5)

Joachim-Friedrich Quack

The composition is preserved on only one single papyrus (Paris, Bibliothèque Nationale 215 rt.), which, given that it lacks both the beginning and the end, seriously impedes interpretation. The papyrus is a palimpsest, i.e. the text in question was written after the preceding text inscribed on the papyrus was erased. It dates to the late 3rd century BCE and probably comes from the Memphite region. On the back of the same papyrus, a number of unrelated shorter texts were inscribed. They present a story about king Amasis who, suffering from a hangover, is distracted by means of a story about a sailor set in the time of king Psammetichus[1]; rules about Egyptian priests when they are sick; a tradition about the rules Cambyses set for the Egyptian temples as well as the compilation of Egyptian law by Dareios I[2]; and finally some fragmentary sections describing the dire condition of people working in the swamps.[3]

While there is an entrenched tradition of labelling the text of the recto as a "chronicle," it is by no means such a composition. An alternative proposal has been to call it an "oracle," but this also does not really fit. What we have in the preserved parts is basically an enigmatic text organized in chapters and concerned, among other things, with priestly service according to the lunar cycle, measures and weights. This is followed by an interpretation applying the basic statement to the political situation of Late-Period Egypt: beginning with the 28th dynasty and continuing until the 30th dynasty; the second period of Persian rule; and, in the last preserved parts, also the Greeks.[4] Sometimes further comments or even explanations for the interpretative framework are given, with the technique of the commentary having been compared to that of Jewish writings from Qumran.[5]

It is noteworthy that not only the period of foreign Persian rule is viewed very negatively, as a traumatic period, but that also most of the indigenous rulers of the 4th century BCE are seen quite negatively. Especially pronounced is the critique directed against Nektanebes I[6] and his son Teos. Given that parts of the text speak of a "future ruler" coming after them, there is some likelihood that the original composition was an instrument of political partisanship used by Nektanebos II who rebelled against Teos. Still, other parts of the text show knowledge of the length of the reign of Nektanebos II, as well as the second period of Persian rule and the Greek conquest. Therefore, these parts could not have been written before 332 BCE, i.e. the conquest of Alexander the Great, and were probably written quite a bit later, since a "long time" of Greek rule is mentioned.

Indeed, there are inconsistencies and fault lines which point towards a complicated redactional history preceding the text preserved on our only extant manuscript. Thus, what originally might have constituted a pamphlet in support of a specific (and ultimately successful) inner-Egyptian rebellion, became a vague hope of future independence from Greek rule.

The communication situation seems to be that of a court session at which king Nektanebes I is present, since he is addressed as "you" several times. The one who speaks and interprets the enigmatic is not identified anywhere in the preserved parts, but the way he addresses the king with harsh critique makes it likely that he must be somebody with independent authority. Perhaps the situation can be conceived as being somewhat similar to the biblical story of Daniel reading the writing on the wall for Belshazzar (Dan 5). It has been pointed out that the basic concept behind the text, that the length of a king's rule is related to the virtues and vices of that king, has strong similarities to the deuteronomistic history of the kings of Israel and Judah. It remains to be seen if this is due to genuine cultural borrowings or simply results from a similar situation of precarious political power.

The decipherment and translation of the text still pose some serious problems.[7] Furthermore, there are some indications that the copy transmitted to us is not free of writing faults and even serious omissions.

(1.1) [.........] the first shrine. (1.2) [.........] (1.3) [.........]		(1.4) [.........] (1.5) [.........] fear[8] (?), dust. (1.6) [.........] go to Heliopolis.

[1] The commonly used designation "Amasis and the skipper" is inaccurate and misleading as it combines a figure from the frame story with a figure from the main story.

[2] The priestly rules, as well as the records of decisions and law-collection are probably excerpts of a larger collection of rules and laws for the Egyptian temples of which a fragmentary Roman-period copy from Tebtunis is preserved (to be published by Fabian Wespi).

[3] Ever since the edition by Spiegelberg 1914, these passages have been assumed to be animal fables, but there is no positive evidence, and the bird names introducing them are likely to be simply an "alphabetic" organization, see Quack 2009a:172–173.

[4] For the relation of the data of the "Demotic chronicle" to other sources, see Johnson 1974.

[5] Daumas 1961.

[6] The name of this king is often erroneously given as Nektanebo(s) in modern publications.

[7] The translation given here is mainly based upon the German translation that I gave in Hoffmann and Quack 2007:183–191. Only points where I have changed my mind substantially are noted.

[8] I propose to read *snty(.t)*.

(1.7) [.........]
(1.8) [.........] the slaughtering[9] (?)
(1.9) [.........] the … which
(1.10) [.........]
(1.11) [.........] a man will reach them.
(1.12) [.........]
(1.13) [.........]
(1.14) [.........] in order to say it.
(1.15) [.........] the way
(1.16) [.........] …, and he will
(1.17) [.........] his sins
(1.18) [.........] That is [the] place of enquiry.
(1.19) [.........]
(1.20) [.........] Memphis. What they did
(1.21) [.........] together with him
(1.22) [.........]
(1.23) [.........] towards Egypt.
(1.24) [.........]

(2.1) May the last day of the month happen! The last day of the month will happen. That means: The completion of the enquiries, which will be done by the aforementioned gods, will come about.
(2.2) May the first day, second day, third day, fourth day, fifth day, six day of the month become full. May the ⟨first⟩ date become full. That means: Pharaoh Amyrtaios.[10] The second date. That means: Pharaoh Nepherites (I).[11]
(2.3) The third date. That means: Pharaoh Hakoris.[12] The fourth date. That means: Pharaoh Nepherites (II).[13] The fifth. That means: Pharaoh Nektanebes.[14]
(2.4) The sixth. That means: The king[15] Pharaoh Teos.[16] What they did is written down by Thoth when he revised their matters in Herakleopolis.
(2.5) May the seventh day be given to Ptah. He will name the ruler who will succeed him in order to revise the matters in Memphis, because what he will do – they will revise what he will do (2.6) in Memphis.
(2.7) End. The seventh chapter.
(2.8) The last day of the lunar cycle is correct in Pe[17] in the month of Mekhir. That means: The fulfillment of the generation is in accordance with what had been ordered in the month of Mekhir. That means: The fatality[18] will occur in it (2.9) because the last day of the lunar cycle is the fulfillment of the month.
(2.10) (The) beginning of (the) first day of the lunar cycle is in Dep[19] in the month of Pamenoth. That means: (The) beginning of rule which the one who will be ruler will do is in the month of Pamenoth, because (the) first day of the lunar cycle is (the) beginning of (the) month.
(2.11) The moon traverses the flood. The ruler will circulate around the entire land. That means: The ruler who will succeed them will leave Egypt.
(2.12) Left will be given in exchange for right. Right is Egypt, left is the land of Syria. That means: The one who will go to the land of Syria, which is the left side, (2.13) he will be replaced by the one who will be in Egypt, which is the right side.
(2.14) The one from Herakleopolis; the one from Hermopolis found him. The one from Herakleopolis is Aseph.[20] The one from Hermopolis found him. That means: When Thoth went to Herakleopolis, (2.15) enquiries about what he had commanded to Aseph concerning Egypt were what he made.
(2.16) Herakleopolis, Herakleopolis, Herakleopolis! That means: The one who went to Herakleopolis and abandoned the law, they enquired [about him] in Herakleopolis. (2.17) They had punishment dealt out against him. They had punishment dealt out against his son.
(2.18) End. The eighth chapter.
(2.19) (The) first phyle, may it push the bolt! That means: The future ruler in Egypt will push the bolts. This is that the king opens it.
(2.20) (The) second phyle, which has opened. That means: It is the second ruler who opens it.
(2.21) (The) third phyle, which has opened before the uraeus. That means: The third future ruler, they will be happy about his rule. The rest[21]: (The) third will be among the foreigners. (2.22) That is: Happiness on the part of the gods (because of) their rule.
(2.23) The smooth(-snake), she will come, she will bring the one of Herakleopolis in her apron. That means: The smooth(-snake), which is the uraeus, [she] will bring (2.24) the one from Herakleopolis,

9 For *ṯḥs* compare perhaps *Wb* V, 328, 4–7.
10 Amyrtaios (404/401–399 BCE), the only ruler of the 27th dynasty.
11 Nepherites I (399–393 BCE), the founder of the 29th dynasty.
12 Hakoris (393–380 BCE), a king of the 29th dynasty.
13 Nepherites II (380 BCE), the last king of the 29th dynasty.
14 Nektanebes (380–362 BCE), the founder of the 30th dynasty.
15 Only for this king does the scribe make use of a more archaic word for "king" besides the usual "pharaoh," perhaps marking that this is the actual living king.
16 Teos (364/62–360 BCE), a king of the 30th dynasty.
17 A place in the Delta in the region of Buto, strongly linked to Horus.
18 Probably the death of a king (Nektanebes I or Teos) is meant.
19 A "sister-city" to Pe, also in the region of Buto.
20 The name of this god (who is the main deity of Herakleopolis) is usually rendered as Harsaphes in modern scholarship, but Aseph comes closer to the forms attested in Greek administrative documents.
21 I.e. an explanation of the rest of the basic statement.

being content, in her apron to Pharaoh's palace. It is Aseph who will give orders to the future ruler. It is said: "It is a man of Herakleopolis who will rule after the foreigners (and) the Greeks."
(3.1) Now receive happiness, oh priest[22] of Aseph. That means: The priest of Aseph will be happy after the Greeks (have left). That is: A ruler manifests in Herakleopolis.[23]
(3.2) May he open the ovens, then I will give to him the fattened oxen. That means: The future ruler will open [the doors (?)] of the temples (3.3) and he will have offerings presented (to) the gods.
(3.4) Be valiant, be valiant, Herakleopolis! Be good, be good, Herakleopolis! That means: Much happiness will come about in Egypt in the time in question.
(3.5) May Ta-te-iy[24] go southwards, so that she opens. That means: The uraeus will go southwards and will open. That is a coming out of Upper Egypt and going to Lower Egypt.
(3.6) End. The ninth chapter.
(3.7) Month Athyr, pregnancy. That means: The future ruler in Herakleopolis will rebel in the month of Athyr.
(3.8) Month Khoiak, birth. That means: He will gather (troops) in the month of Khoiak.
Month Tybi, nourishment. That means: He will subsist[25] on weapons of war in the month of Tybi.
(3.9) "Call to me, then I will call to you" in the month of Mekhir. That means: A warrior will fight with his opponent in the month of Mekhir.
(3.10) A titular is mine in the month of Pamenoth. That means: He will be revealed, appearing with a crown of gold in the month of Pamenoth. That is: He rules in the month of Pamenoth.[26]
(3.11) They will give a seat in Pe. That means: They will place his eldest son upon his throne, namely (of) the future ruler. That is: To compare him with Harsiesis.
(3.12) They will give bread in Dep. ⟨That means⟩: They will give bread to those who are in Dep, for they are his army.
(3.13) The widow of the djed-pillar,[27] they received her sprout. That means: The widow of the djed-pillar, she has stopped mourning. That means: Isis will be (3.14) of joyful disposition towards the future ruler.
(3.15) Glad be her heart, that of the lady of Atfih! That means: (The) heart of the One, namely Isis who is the lady of Atfih. That is: Gladness of heart towards the (3.16) future ruler since he will not abandon the law.
(3.17) End. The tenth chapter.
(3.18) Yesterday is what has passed. That means: The first ruler who ruled after the foreigners, who are the Persians – pharaoh Amyrtaios. As (3.19) violations of the law were committed in his time (i.e. during his rule), he was made to do the walks of yesterday.[28] His son did not succeed him.
(3.20) Today is what has come about. That means: The second ruler who ruled after the Persians, namely Pharaoh Nepherites (I). As he carried out his occupations (3.21) with diligence, his son was allowed to succeed him. (However,) he himself was only given a short time span (i.e. rule) on account of (the) many sins that were committed in his time (i.e. during his rule).[29]
(3.22) Today is what has come about. That means: What is said today when ordering is what will happen because of it.
(4.1) First. If he says "first", it is ⟨concerning the first⟩ who ruled after the Persians. As he ordered injustice to be ⟨done⟩; one has seen the things that were done to him. His son was not allowed to succeed him. (4.2) Furthermore, he was deposed from his throne during his own lifetime.[30]
(4.3) The second one of the palm of the hand[31] (?). That means: The second ruler who followed the Persians, namely Nepherites (I). You have seen what has happened to him. (4.4) His son was allowed to succeed him. Of the palm of the hand(?).[32] He says it concerning the ruler of today, namely Nektanebes (I): He is the one who has given away the property of Egypt and all temples (4.5) in order to acquire wealth.[33] If he has said "palm of the hand (?)", which is a female name, as (the) name of Nektanebes, that is like saying that he was not male (?) in his time (i.e. during his rule).

22 The word used here is commonly translated as "prophet" which, however, might evoke the wrong associations because an Egyptian "prophet" is very different from a Hebrew one.
23 Literally "that is coming into existence by a ruler in Herakleopolis."
24 The exact reading is doubtful.
25 The word *stb* is to be understood as ancient *sḏb* (*Wb* IV, 381, 1–6).
26 Literally "ruling by him in the month of Pamenoth."
27 Written like this, but perhaps "the widow of Busiris" was intended. In any case, Isis as the widow of Osiris is meant.
28 Probably this means that he was made obsolete.
29 Nepherites I reigned for only 6 years.
30 This is about Amyrtaios who lost his throne to a revolt after a short rule.
31 I propose to connect the enigmatic word *ḥm3.t* with Coptic *hiōme* "palm of the hand" which would constitute a phonetic pun with *hime* "wife." In any case, this seems to be a derogatory designation for the family of the 29th and 30th dynasty.
32 The second part of the basic text is taken up again in order to receive a special explanation.
33 Nektanebes I imposed strenuous economic measurements in order to finance his war against the Persians, in particular the hiring of Greek mercenaries.

(4.6) Third. They gave him. That means: The third ruler who ruled after[34] the Persians. "They gave to him." That means: As he disregarded the law, he was replaced during his own lifetime.
(4.7) Fourth. He did not exist. That means: The fourth ruler who ruled after the Persians, namely Psammuthis.[35] That means: He was not on the path of the god. (4.8) He was not allowed to remain ruler.
(4.9) Fifth. He became full. That means: The fifth ruler who ruled after the Persians, namely Hakoris who repeated coronation.[36] He was allowed to fulfill his days of rule, (4.10) because he was beneficent to the temples. They ended. That means: He disregarded the law and no longer carried out inspections on account of his brothers.
(4.11) Sixth. He did not exist. That means: The sixth ruler, who ruled after the Persians, namely Nepherites (II). He did not exist. That means: It was not ordered that he should be allowed to exist,[37] (4.12) because the law had been disregarded under his father. They had punishment dealt out against his son after him.
(4.13) Seventh. A decade of days, add[38] (?) to it day 30. That means: The seventh ruler who will follow the Persians, namely Pharaoh Nectanebes. He will be granted 6 (+) 10 (=) 16 (4.14) years. They will give him day 30. That is the completion of the decades of days, [for] three months and three decades of days are what becomes three years, which are a surplus to 16, making 19, in order to let you know (4.15) his years of rule, those which he makes.
(4.16) The yardstick (?) of the builder, day 1. That means: The one who is on the way of building of his father. Day 1, that means: One year of rule is what he will be allowed to enact, (4.17) namely Pharaoh Teos, who will walk by the yardstick of his father.
(4.18) The balance of the stonemason, day 7. That means: The ruler who will succeed him, 18 years is what he will be allowed to make, because the balance of the stonemason (4.19) is the sword, which is (constituted of) five parts. Find[39] (?) (it), in order to say it: That is 6 (+) 7, makes 13; fill out with 5, making again 18 years.
(4.20) May the gates of the brewer (?) of a third of a *heqat*[40] be opened. The gates of duplicating[41] (?) the third of a *heqat*-measure will be opened. That means: (The) beginning of those who will succeed him, namely the Persians.[42] (4.21) That is: To open before the uraeus. That is: The foreign countries.
(4.22) Our lakes (and) our islands are full of tears. That means: The houses of the people of Egypt don't have people to live in them, namely in the time in question, (4.23) as if one says that the Persians will massacre them, they will take their houses and live there.
(5.1) "I love the first day of the month more than the last day." What he says is, namely: "The first year is better than the last year of the time which they, namely the Persians, will spend".
(5.2) Rain on the stone. The sky is clean. That means: They are massacring the people of Egypt while the sun sees them. That is the offering for the sun-god. (5.3) If he has said: "The sky is clean", that means: "The sun sees them." If he has said: "Rain upon the stone," that means: "They will cast (the) people to massacre." Water is man; (5.4) the stone is the massacre.
(5.5) End. The eleventh chapter.
(5.6) "I am clothed from my head to my feet." {namely} What you are saying[43] is namely: "I am appearing with the golden diadem; it will not be removed from my head." He only says it (5.7) about Pharaoh Nectanebes (I).
(5.8) "My cloak (?) is upon me." That means: "My processional garments are upon me, they will not be removed."
(5.9) "The sickle-sword is in my hand." What he is saying, is: "Are you perhaps saying by yourself[44]: "[The] office of (the) ruler is in my hand, it will not be removed (5.10) from me"?" The sickle-sword is the office of (the) ruler, which means to appear as a falcon, because "the sword of victory" is what should be said.
(5.11) He will act if you act. He will be strong if you are strong. That means: The god will act for you according to what you will do. If you make your heart strong, he will be stronger than you.
(5.12) Apis, Apis, Apis! That means: Ptah, the sun-god and Horus-son-of-Isis who are the lords of the office of (the) ruler. You have forgotten (i.e. forsaken) them when you were thinking of acquiring possessions. (5.13) His happiness has worked in the three cases. That means: The Apis-bull is the three gods which he has mentioned above. The Apis-bull

34 The manuscript has "among" which is obviously an error, given the parallel phrases in 4.1, 4.3, 4.7 and 4.9.

35 A rival king during the reign of Hakoris, probably about 393/92 BCE.

36 This epithet is connected to the fact that Hakoris repeated his coronation after crushing the revolt of Psammuthis, see Ray 1986.

37 Nepherites II was overthrown during the first year of his reign.

38 The reading is not clear, the group resembles a group for "sum, amount" which, however, is otherwise not attested as a verb.

39 The group looks most like *gmi*.

40 With all due reserve, I propose to analyze the sequence in question as first the word for "brewer" (CDD^c: 59–60), and afterwards, the sign for a third of the *heqat*-measure (for which see Zauzich 1987).

41 I propose to read *ḳb p3*, and then the group for the third of the *heqat*-measure.

42 The second period of Persian rule over Egypt (342–332 BCE).

43 This passage is particularly significant for understanding the reconstruction of the communicative setting, with the king being addressed directly by the interpreter of the enigmatic text.

44 Literally "speaking with your heart."

is Ptah, the Apis-bull is the sun-god, the Apis-bull is Horus-son-of-Isis.
(5.14) End. The twelfth chapter.
(5.15) The flocks (?) of the desert game have moved towards Egypt. That means: The foreigners who are in the east and the west of the land (i.e. of Egypt). They have moved (5.16) towards Egypt. They are the Persians.
(5.17) The crocodiles will catch them. What he says is that the god will take them to the places from which they came, namely the foreigners – they are the Persians.
(5.18) Gardener, carry out your work! That means: Pharaoh, carry out your work! He says it concerning Pharaoh Nektanebes (I), namely: His work of greed.
(5.19) Oh Chief gardener, raise up your hedge! He says it concerning him yet again. The rest of the other: To erect a hedge around his looted possessions.
(5.20) Give water to the small trees; let the large trees live! The rest of the other things which he has said is like saying: "Be wary of the covetous people!"
(5.21) Your one eye, there is no illness in it. That means: Your uraeus which is upon your head; it is not what is ill. (It is) like saying that (5.22) it does not have respect (?) for a ruler, namely, the one who will be charitable is the one whom she will love.[45] He says it concerning the white crown, which is the uraeus of Upper Egypt.
(5.23) There is opacity in it, in the other (eye), it is full of honey. ⟨That means:⟩ There is opacity in the uraeus, which is upon your head. That means: The red crown, which is full of loot. (5.24) That is honey, [namely possessions (?)] that are acquired by robbery.
(6.1) Mut is its medicaments, namely: (For) the one whom she will love. That means: Mut is the mistress of love.
(6.2) Mut, (the) cow, she was not provided for. She is hungry and implores Amun. That means: (The) uraeus is hungry; (6.3) she could not eat from your loot. She implores Amun, saying: "Provide the ruler who will be charitable!"
(6.4) The palette is reduced,[46] the tongs (?) are slackened, the rope is dangling.[47] He says it concerning Nektanebes, (6.5) namely: "Your palette, tongs and rope have ceased being covetous in Egypt."
(6.6) The profit (?) does not have measure. That means: The profit (?) which you have, does not have measure. We have accounted and (6.7) we know that it is the voice of the gods.
(6.8) The peasant is crying; his wife is beautiful. That means: The farmer will walk to the field, crying. ⟨…⟩[48] Barley and emmer are his way (6.9) of life. That means: The barley of the fields of Pharaoh never becomes full.
(6.10) The small children will go away to the … of (the) craftsman. He will give chaff to them. That means: The small children who are living in your (6.11) time (i.e. during your rule); they are hungry; they will go away. (The) craftsman is Memphis.[49] He will give chaff to them. That is something which does not constitute nourishment, (6.12) because it[50] exists upon the sycamore, whose name is Mut. And additionally, milk (i.e. sap) comes out of it, which again is fastened with ….[51]
(6.13) End. The thirteenth chapter.
(6.14) The great river (i.e. the Nile), may his origin be great in Elephantine, may it nourish the bakers. It is said concerning pharaoh (6.15) Nectanebes (I), namely: They will let the foreigners come to rule Egypt after you.[52] The water (i.e. inundation) will be high in his time (i.e. during his rule); (6.16) the bakers will live in the time in question.
(6.17) Rejoice, oh you serfs! You will be able to eat. That means: The small children who will live in the time in question; [they will] find bread to eat; (6.18) they will not starve like those who live in your time (i.e. during your rule).
(6.19) The small children who are (in) the streets; they will stand in the street (while) their … is with them. That means: It will happen again in the time in question (6.20) that it is the Greeks who will come to Egypt; they will exercise control over Egypt for a long time.
(6.21) May the dogs live! The big dog,[53] he will be able to eat; he will leave the weak ones (?).[54] They will rule in the time in question.
(6.22) End.
(7.1) The [fourteenth] chapter.[55]

45 This means that the uraeus-snake, as protector of the king, will not automatically help him, but decide her behavior according to his virtue.
46 This and the following verb are more likely to be qualitatives (with passive meaning) than infinitives.
47 Literally "dancing."
48 Something seems to be missing here, especially concerning the wife.
49 Probably this is related to the title of the high priest of Ptah of Memphis who was called "greatest of craftsmen."
50 Perhaps this refers to "nourishment."
51 The word *ḫṯ* (with tree-determinative) is of uncertain meaning.
52 The Egyptian text has the second person plural here, perhaps referring to Nektanebes and Teos, if both constitute the audience for the interpreter.
53 This might be a nickname for Alexander the Great, especially since a place in the Fayum which in Greek documents is called "The Island of Alexander" is rendered in Demotic as "The Island of the Dog." See Schentuleit 2008:158–159.
54 Perhaps read *gbe.w*.
55 Of column 7, only the beginnings of words are preserved, which cannot be translated in a meaningful way.

REFERENCES

Text: Spiegelberg 1914. Translations: Felber 2002; Hoffmann and Quack 2007: 183–191 and 353–354. Overview: Quack 2009a: 181–186 (with additional bibliography) and Quack 2015.

EGYPTIAN BIBLIOGRAPHY

Abel, F. M.
1933–1938 *Géographie de la Palestine*. 2 Volumes. Paris: J. Gabalda.

Aḥituv, S.
1984 *Canaanite Toponyms in Ancient Egyptian Documents*. Jerusalem and Leiden: Magnes Press and Brill.

Albright, W. F.
1934 *The Vocalization of the Egyptian Syllabic Orthography*. New Haven: American Oriental Society.

Albright, W. F., and T. O. Lambdin
1957 "New Materials for the Egyptian Syllabic Orthography." *JSS* 2:113–127.

Astour, M. C.
1963 Place-names from the Kingdom of Alalaḫ in the North Syrian List of Thutmose III: A Study in Historical Topography. *JNES* 22:220–241.

Ben-Dor Evian, S.
2011 "Shishak's Karnak Relief – More than Just Name-Rings!" Pp. 11–22 in *Egypt, Canaan and Israel. History, Imperialism, Ideology and Literature: Proceedings of a Conference at the University of Haifa, 3–7 May 2009*. Ed. by S. Bar, D. Kahn, and J. J. Shirley. CHANE 52. Leiden: Brill.

Burchardt, M.
1909–1910 *Die altkanaanäischen Fremdwörte und Eigennahmen im Aegyptischen*, I–II. Leipzig: J. C. Hinrichs'sche Buchhandlung.

Daumas, F.
1961 "Littérature prophétique et exégétique égyptienne et commentaires esseniens." Pp. 203–221 in A *la rencontre de Dieu. Mémorial Albert Gelin*. Bibliothèque de la Faculté Catholique de Théologie de Lyon 8. Le Puy: Mappus.

Edel, E.
1966 *Die Ortsnamenlisten aus dem Totentempel Amenophis III*. BBB 25. Bonn: Hanstein.

Edgerton, W. F., and J. A. Wilson
1936 *Historical Records of Ramses III. The Texts in Medinet Habu: Volumes I and II*. SAOC 12. Chicago: University of Chicago Press.

Erichsen, W.
1933 *Papyrus Harris I: hieroglyphische Transkription*. Bibliotheca Aegyptiaca 5. Bruxelles: Édition de la Fondation égyptologique Reine Élisabeth.

Felber, H.
2002 "Die demotische Chronik." Pp. 65–111 in *Apokalyptik und Ägypten. Eine kritische Analyse der relevanten Texte aus dem griechisch-römischen Ägypten*. Ed. by A. Blasius and B. U. Schipper. OLA 107. Leuven, Paris, Sterling: Peeters.

Grandet, P.
1994–1999 *Le papyrus Harris I (BM 9999)*. 3 Volumes. Bibliothèque d'étude 109/1–2. Cairo: Institut français d'archéologie orientale.

Haider, P. W.
2012 "The Aegean and Anatolia." Pp. 151–160 in *Ramesses III. The Life and Times of Egypt's Last Hero*. Ed. by E. H. Cline and D. O'Conner. Ann Arbor: University of Michigan.

Harrison, T. P.
2009 "Neo-Hittites in the 'Land of Palistin.'" *NEA* 72:174–189.

Hawkins, J. D.
2009 "Cilicia, the Amuq and Aleppo: New Light in a Dark Age." *NEA* 72:164–173.

Helck, W.
1971 *Die Beziehungen Ägyptens zu Vorderasien im 3. und 2. Jahrtausend v. Chr*. 2nd Edition. Ägyptologische Abhandlungen 5. Wiesbaden: Harrassowitz.

Hoffmann, F. and J. F. Quack
2007 *Anthologie der demotischen Literatur*. Einführungen und Quellentexte zur Ägyptologie 4. Berlin: Lit.

Jansen-Winkeln, K.
2007 *Inschriften der Spätzeit 2. Die 22.–24. Dynastie*. Wiesbaden: Harrassowitz Verlag.
2009 *Inschriften der Spätzeit. 3. Die 25. Dynastie*. Wiesbaden: Harrassowitz Verlag.

Johnson, J.
1974 "The Demotic Chronicle as an Historical Source." *Enchoria* 4:1–17.
1983 "The Demotic Chronicle as a Statement of a Theory of Kingship." *JSSEA* 13:61–72.
1984 "Is the Demotic Chronicle an Anti-Greek Tract?" Pp. 107–124 in *Grammata demotika. Festschrift für Erich Lüddeckens zum 15. Juni 1983*. Ed. by H.-J. Thissen and K. Th. Zauzich. Würzburg: Gisela Zauzich.

Kitchen, K. A.
1996 *The Third Intermediate Period in Egypt (1100–650 BC)*. 3rd edition. 1st edition 1973; 2nd edition 1986. Warminster: Aris and Phillips.
1999 *Poetry of Ancient Egypt*. Jonsered: Paul Aströms Förlag.
2008 *Ramesside Inscriptions Translated and Annotated. 5. Setnakht, Ramesses III, and Contemporaries*. Oxford: Blackwell.
2009 "Review of Jansen-Winkeln 2007." *BiOr* 66: 574–576.
2013 ?

Kohlmeyer, K.
2009 "The Temple of the Storm God in Aleppo during the Late Bronze and Early Iron Ages." *NEA* 72:190–219.

Leclant, J., and J. Yoyotte
1952 "Notes d' histoire et de civilization éthiopiennes propos d' un ouvrage récent." *Bulletin de l' Institut français d' archéologie orientale* 51:1–40.

Lippert, S. L.
2001 "Komplexe Wortspiele in der demotischen Chronik und im Mythus vom Sonnenauge." *Enchoria* 27:88–100.

Macadam, M. F. L.
1949 *The Temples of Kawa. Volume 1: The Inscriptions: Text, Plates*. Oxford: Published on behalf of the Griffith Institute by Oxford University Press.

MEYER, E.
1915 *Ägyptische Dokumente aus der Perserzeit*. SPAW 1915/16. Berlin.
MORAN, W.
1992 *The Amarna Letters*. Baltimore and London: Johns Hopkins University Press.
NOUGAYROL, J.
1955 *Le Palais Royal d'Ugarit. III: Textes accadiens et hourrites des Archives Est, Ouest et Centrales*. MRS 6. Paris: Imprimerie Nationale: Klincksieck.
PORTER, B., R. L. B. MOSS, and E. W. BURNEY
1972 *Topographical Bibliography of Ancient Egyptian Hieroglyphic Texts, Reliefs, and Paintings*, II. *Theban Temples*. 2nd edition. Oxford: Clarendon Press.
QUACK, J. F.
2009a *Einführung in die altägyptische Literaturgeschichte III. Die demotische und gräko-ägyptische Literatur*. 2nd Edition. Berlin: Lit.
2009b "Menetekel an der Wand? Zur Deutung der demotischen Chronik." Pp. 23–51 in *Orakel und Gebete. Interdisziplinäre Studien zur Sprache der Religion in Ägypten, Vorderasien und Griechenland in hellenistischer Zeit*. Ed. by M. Witte and J. F. Diel. FAT 2. Reihe. Tübingen: Mohr Siebeck.
2015 "As he disregarded the law, he was replaced during his own lifetime." On Criticism of Egyptian Rulers in the So-Called *Demotic Chronicle*. Pp. 25–43. In *Antimonarchic Discourse in Antiquity*. Ed. by H. Börm. Stuttgart: Steiner.
RAINEY, A. F.
2006 A. F. Rainey and S. Notley. *The Sacred Bridge. Carta's Atlas of the Biblical World*. Jerusalem: Carta.
RAY, J. D.
1986 "Psammuthis and Hakoris." *JEA* 72:149–158.
RITNER, R. K.
2009 *The Libyan Anarchy. Inscriptions from Egypt's Third Intermediate Period*. SBLWAW 21. Atlanta: Society of Biblical Literature.
SCHENTULEIT, M.
2008 "Toponyme und Lagebeschreibungen von Immobilien in demotischen Texten aus Soknopaiou Nesos." Pp. 158–167 in *Altägyptische Weltsichten*. Ed. by F. Adrom, K. and A. Schlüter. ÄAT 68. Wiesbaden: Harrassowitz.
SCHNEIDER, T.
2010 "Contributions to the Chronology of the New Kingdom and the Third Intermediate Period." *Ägypten und Levante* 20:373–409.
SIMONS, J.
1937 *Handbook for the Study of Egyptian Topographical Lists Relating to Western Asia*. Leiden: E. J. Brill.
SPIEGELBERG, W.
1914 *Die sogenannte demotische Chronik des Pap. 215 der Bibliothèque Nationale zu Paris nebst den auf der Rückseite des Papyrus stehenden Texten*. DemSt 7. Leipzig: J. C. Hinrichs.
THIELE, E. R.
1986 *The Mysterious Numbers of the Hebrew Kings*. 3rd revised edition. Grand Rapids: Zondervan.
TOMPKINS, H. G.
1893 "On the Topography of Northern Syria, with Special Reference to the Karnak Lists of Thothmes III." *Transactions of the Society for Biblical Archaeology* 9:227–254.
WELLHAUSEN, J.
1914 *Israelitische und jüdische Geschichte*. 7th edition. Berlin: G. Reimer.
ZAUZICH, K.-Th.
1987 "Unerkannte demotische Kornmaße." Pp. 462–471 in *Form und Maß. Beiträge zu Literature, Sprache und Kunst des alten Ägypten*. Ed. by J. Osing and G. Dreyer. Wiesbaden: Harrassowitz.

ANATOLIAN INSCRIPTIONS

HITTITE COMPOSITIONS

THE KUMARBI SERIES OF MYTHS (4.6)

Harry A. Hoffner, Jr.

The most important group of myths in the Hittite language is the Kumarbi Series. The earliest Kumarbi myths to be edited were the *Song of Emergence* (initially called *Theogony* or *Kingship in Heaven*) and the *Song of Ullikummi* (Forrer 1936; Güterbock 1946). Both were translated into English by Goetze 1955. A definitive edition of the *Song of Ullikummi* was prepared by Güterbock (1961). Until 1971, as can be seen both from Güterbock 1961 and Laroche 1971, only three fairly well-preserved compositions were attributed to this series: what was termed the *Kingship of LAMMA* (Text B), the *Theogony*, or *Kingship in Heaven* (Text A) and the *Song of Ullikummi* (Text E). Laroche (1971) identified further fragments which he thought belonged to this series. Siegelova (1971) demonstrated by means of new fragments, as well as new supplements to previously known pieces, that the so-called *Song of Ḫedammu* also belonged to the Kumarbi Series.

Hoffner (1988) reconstructed the myth about the personified Silver (Text C), demonstrating from its newly identified opening lines (§ 1.2) that this story too was a "song" belonging to the Kumarbi Series. We know from colophons that in the native terminology Text E was called the *Song of Ullikummi*, and Text A the *Song of Emergence*. The Silver myth's proemium contains the statement *išḫamiḫḫi* "I sing (of him, Silver, the excellent one)" (§ 1.2), which means that its colophon must have read SÌR KÙ.BABBAR "the Song of Silver." Hence, all parts of the Kumarbi Series except for the first member, the *Song of Emergence*, probably bore the names "Song of So-and-So" with the relevant name drawn from the central character in the piece. Most likely the scribes called Text B the *Song of LAMMA*, Text D the *Song of Ḫedammu*, and Text C the *Song of Silver*.[1]

The sequence of the stories is uncertain. It was usually assumed that the *Song of Emergence* (Text A) contains the beginning. This assumption was strengthened by Hoffner. He argued that only the *Song of Emergence* opened with a call to all the gods to hear the tale (§§ 1–2). All subsequent songs in the series opened, as do Silver and Ullikummi, with a description of a powerful adversary of Teššub whose name is given only at the end of the proem in the words "I am singing of So-and So" (see Text C §§ 1.1–1.2; Text E, § 1).[2] Also, once Corti (2007) discovered the true title of Text A as *Song of Emergence*, Text A distinguishes itself as the only member of the cycle whose native title did not contain the name of the chief character. This makes it unique and marks it as the beginning. Clues in the plots of the individual stories seem to favor the sequence: *Song of Emergence* (A), *Song of LAMMA* (B), *Song of Silver* (C), *Song of Ḫedammu* (D), and *Song of Ullikummi* (E).

The central theme of the entire series is the competition between Kumarbi and Teššub for kingship over the gods. As pointed out by Hoffner 1975:136–145, the sequence of divine rulers in the *Song of Emergence* is not a father, son, grandson, but an alternation of two competing lines. Alalu, driven from his throne by Anu, is the father of Kumarbi, who in turn drives Anu from his throne. Furthermore, when Kumarbi emasculates Anu to forestall his own removal by any descendant of Anu, he inadvertently makes his own belly the womb for Anu's seed, which produces Teššub, Tašmišu, the Aranzaḫ River, and several other gods. Although the end of the *Song of Emergence* is lost, everyone agrees that, since the *Song of Ullikummi* finds Teššub as king of the gods, he may have already attained that position by the end of the *Song of Emergence*. What has emerged from the recent reconstructions of Ḫedammu (Text D) and Silver (Text C) is that in all subsequent songs of the series Kumarbi seeks to depose Teššub by means of some offspring of his own. Ullikummi is Kumarbi's son by sexual union with a huge cliff (Text E, § 5). Ḫedammu is probably his son[3] by Šertapšuruḫi, the daughter of the Sea God (Text D introduction). Silver is his son by a mortal woman. It is not clear in what relationship the god LAMMA stands to Kumarbi. At one point we learn that Ea and Kumarbi had agreed to make him king of the gods. Certainly nothing excludes his being Kumarbi's son.

The two antagonists, Kumarbi and Teššub, are from opposite spheres. Kumarbi is a netherworld god, whereas Teššub is a celestial god. In the *Song of Emergence* (Text 14), Kumarbi's father Alalu is driven from the throne by Anu and takes refuge from Anu in the netherworld (the "Dark Earth"). Later, when Anu flees from Kumarbi, he heads for the sky.

When one assembles a list of the deities in these myths who give allegiance to one side or the other, the opposition of netherworld and sky is confirmed. In Kumarbi's camp are Alalu, Kumarbi's vizier Mukišanu, the great Sea God,[4] the Sea God's vizier Impaluri, the Sea God's daughter Šertapšuruḫi, Ḫedammu, Daganzipa (Earth), Silver, Ullikummi,

[1] We do not know how many "songs" originally made up the series. It is, possible that, in addition to the fragments listed by Laroche 1971 under CTH 346, we should consider CTH 350 (fragments naming *IŠTAR*/Šawuška) as belonging to the series. These pieces have not been included in this volume.

[2] Nevertheless, Beckman 2011:26, restores line 1 as "[I sing of Kumarbi, Father of the Gods.]" His restoration, though the right number of signs to fill the available space, is conjectural.

[3] That Ḫedammu is male is clear from Šawuška's enticing him sexually.

[4] There is a parallel with Ugaritic and Canaanite mythology here, in that Baʿal/Hadad (the storm-god of the sky) is perpetually at war with Mōt ("Death" the god of the netherworld) and Yamm ("Sea").

the *irširra-* deities, and probably Ubelluri (who lives under the earth and grows up to threaten the sky home of Teššub). Kumarbi's city is Urkeš,[5] while Teššub's is Kumme. In Teššub's camp are Anu, Tašmišu-Šuwaliyat, Ḫebat, Ḫebat's maidservant Takiti, *Šawuška-IŠTAR*, the divine bulls Šeri and Ḫurri, the Sun and Moon Gods, the War God Aštabi, Teššub's brother the Aranzaḫ River, the Mountain God Kanzura, KA.ZAL, and NAM.ḪÉ.

A third group of deities, generally unaligned, includes Ea, Ellil, LAMMA, Kubaba, the Primeval Deities (Nara-Napšara, Minki, Ammunki, Ammezzadu, Išḫara, etc.).

According to the proem of the *Song of Emergence*, the entire series of songs is addressed to the Primeval Deities. This epithet is sometimes translated "the Former Gods."

Ea, the Mesopotamian god of wisdom, occupies a special position in the developing narrative. In the *Song of Emergence* (Text A) he assists Kumarbi in ridding himself of the burden of Anu's seed. Toward the end of the *Song of Emergence* Teššub must be cautioned not to curse Ea, because there still was hope that he might be won over from Kumarbi's side. That Teššub was tempted to curse him shows that at this point he was aiding Kumarbi. In the Song of LAMMA, Ea and Kumarbi made LAMMA king (in the place of Teššub?). But by the time of the song of Ḫedammu, Ea has become troubled by the wasteful destructiveness of the quarrel between Teššub and Kumarbi and he scolds and warns both sides (Text D, fragment 6, § 2). In the Song of Ullikummi (Text E), which may be the latest "song" of those preserved for us, Ea helps Teššub's allies find the secret of Ullikummi's vulnerability.

The gradual transformation of Ea's loyalty from Kumarbi to Teššub may be one of the few remaining clues to the original sequence of the "songs." A second clue is in the behavior of Šawuška. In Ḫedammu she learns the effectiveness of sexual seduction against the monster Ḫedammu. But when she tries it again against Ullikummi, it fails because that creature is deaf and blind. This suggests that Ḫedammu preceded Ullikummi in the series.

The subsequent use of the *Song of Emergence* by Greek authors[6] is interesting in its own right, but is not directly pertinent to the interpretation of the Hurro-Hittite work.

REFERENCES

Haas 2006:130–133.

THE SONG OF EMERGENCE (4.6A)

§ 1 (A i 1–4) [. . .][7] the Primeval Gods who [are in the Dark Earth],[8] let the [those(?) Prime]val Deities, the weighty[9] ones, listen! Let Nara, [Napšara, Min]ki, (and) Ammunki listen![10] Let Ammezzadu [and . . .[11]], the father and mother[12] of [. . .] listen![13] § 2 (A i 5–11) Let [Anu(?)[14] and An]tu the father and mother of Išḫara, listen! EN.LIL and NIN.LIL, who [below] and above (are) weighty, mighty[15]

5 For the discovery of ancient Urkeš, see Buccellati and Kelly-Buccellati 1997.

6 Güterbock 1948; Dirlmeier 1955; Heubeck 1955; Steiner 1958; Walcot 1966; Haas 1975.

7 Cf. p. #, n. 2 above.

8 Restore [GE$_6$-*i* KI-*pí nu a-pé-e ka-ru-ú-i-l*]*i-iš*. Beckman (2011:26) accidentally transposes to KI-*pí* GE$_6$-*i*.

9 The term *daššu-* "weighty, important" figures often in the opening part of this myth; cf. i 6, 9, 16.

10 Probably one should emend *iš-ta-ma-aš-ki-id-di* to *iš-ta-ma-aš-kán!-du*.

11 This construction of the clauses is agreed upon by Pecchioli Daddi and Polvani 1990; Beckman, etc., but in none of the passages in which Ammezzadu occurs among sequences of deities is there a hint as to a female consort who might be the "mother." Polvani (2008:128, n. 3) suggest Tuḫuši. But in the only place where the two DNs are adjacent, Tuḫuši precedes Ammezzadu and ought to be the male in the pair. Haas (2006:134, n. 6) restores Alalu here, which agains runs into the contradiction of the gender pairings, since Alalu is clearly male and ought to precede.

12 The "father-mother" deity-pairs have a long history in ancient Mesopotamia, traced thoroughly by Haas 1994:108–115; cf. also Haas 2006:134; and van Dijk 1971:535, § 2 a. Cf. the similar situation in ancient Egyptian cosmogonies: "Der memphitische Hauptgott Ptah gilt ... als Schöpfer; er vereinigt in sich das Urgötterpaar Nun und Naunet (s. Achtheit) und den Lotosgott u. a. und wird Vater und Mutter des Atum genannt." (Helck and Otto 1956:405).

13 The sequence of Hurrian deities Nara, Napšara, Minki, Ammunki, and Ammezzadu occurs with minor spelling and sequence variants in ritual texts (cf. KBo 17.96 i 10; KBo 13.55 obv 6–10), as well as in lists of oath deities in New Hittite treaties (cf. KBo 12.134 obv 3–6).

14 So restored by Archi 1990:115, van Gessel 1998, 1:37 and Beckman 2011:26. But since Enlil follows in the next clause (i 5–6), some other divine pair must be here. In KBo 12.31 iv 12–13 the sequence Ammizzadu, Alalu, Anu, Antu, Apandu occurs immediately before Enlil. Therefore, I follow Siegelova 1971:29; Pecchioli Daddi and Polvani 1990:128, in restoring Anu and Antu.

15 Long ago E. Forrer read this correctly as *wa-al-li-u-ri-iš* "mighty," and collation confirmed this reading. The correctness of the unemended form is now clear from the Boğazköy Erim-ḫuš lexical text KBo 1.44 + KBo 13.1 + KBo 26.20 ii 27; cf. MSL XVII (1985) 107 with note on line 27′. The translation "proud" offered there is Güterbock's. The entry (Sum.) KA.ZAL = (Akk.) *mu-ti-el-lu* = (Hitt.) *wa-al-li-u-ra-aš* gives us the reading of the divine name ^{d}KA.ZAL-*aš* in Theogony: ^{d}Walliuraš. It is clearly an epithet rather than a name proper, "the Noble" (following the Akk. *muttallu CAD* M/2 306 f.) or "the Proud" (following Güterbock's translation in MSL XVII, based on Hitt. *walliya-* "to boast"). It is remotely possible that the DN occurs in the divine list: [*ḫantezzi pa*]*lši* ^{d}*Wa-al-li-ú*[*-ri* . . .] KUB 34.95:11′. One should ignore the nonsensical emendation *wa-ak!-tu!-u-ri-iš*, allegedly a variant of *uktūri-*, "eternal(?)," proposed by Goetze 1949:181, and followed by Pecchioli Daddi and Polvani 1990, García Trabazo 2002:162, and now also retained by Beckman 2011:26, and E. Rieken et al. (ed.), hethiter.net/: CTH 344 (TX 2012-06-08, TRde 2009-08-31).

deities, [...] and ...,[16] let them listen! Long ago, in primeval years,[17] Alalu was king in heaven.[a] Alalu was sitting[18] on the throne, and weighty Anu, the foremost of the gods,[19] was standing before him. He was bowing down at his[20] (Alalu's) feet, and was placing in his hand the drinking cups.[21]

§ 3 (A i 12–17) For a mere[22] nine years Alalu remained king in heaven.[b] In the ninth year Anu gave battle against Alalu,[23] and he defeated Alalu. He (Alalu) fled before him and went down to the Dark Earth. Down he went[24] to the Dark Earth, and Anu took his seat on his throne.[25] Anu was sitting on his throne, while weighty Kumarbi was giving him drink, bowing down at his feet, and placing drinking cups in his hand.

§ 4 (A i 18–24) For a mere[26] nine years Anu remained king in heaven.[c] In the ninth year against Kumarbi Anu gave battle. Kumarbi, Alalu's offspring,[27] gave battle against Anu.[28] No longer can he withstand Kumarbi's eyes, (can) Anu.[29] He wriggled loose from his (Kumarbi's) hands and fled, (did) Anu, and he[30] set out for the sky. (But) Kumarbi rushed[31] after him, seized Anu by the feet/legs, and dragged him down from the sky.

§ 5 (A i 25–29) (Kumarbi) bit off his (Anu's) genitals (*paršinuš*),[32] and his "manhood" united with Kumarbi's interior like bronze (results from the union of copper and tin). When Kumarbi had swallowed the "manhood" of Anu, he rejoiced and laughed out loud. Anu turned around toward him. To Kumarbi he began to speak: "Are you rejoicing with your belly[33] because you have swallowed my 'manhood?' "[34]

§ 6 (A i 30–36) "Stop rejoicing with your interior! I have placed a burden in your interior. First, I have impregnated you with the mighty(?) Storm God.[35] Second, I have impregnated you with the irresistible Tigris River. Third, I have impregnated

a Dan 4:37

b Exod 15:18; Ps 146:10; Luke 1:33; Rev 11:15; 22:5

c See note *b*

[16] *kulkulimma-* is a noun in the genitive. Haas (2006:134) claims *kulkulimma-* is "bright gleam." *CHD* Š 14 (*šā(y)e-* A a 1′ a′) "pantheon(?)" or aggregate of the gods. Beckman renders "[contented(?)] and quiet," without explanatory comment.

[17] On the time element here, see Polvani 2008:621.

[18] The verb "was king" (LUGAL-*uš ēšta*) is a simple preterite, setting the time frame for what follows, while the remaining four clauses in § 3 contain historical presents (*ēšzi, arta, ḫinkišketta, zikkezzi*), portraying vividly what transpired during that frame. All four clauses are asyndetic, contributing to the synchronicity of the picture. The correction GÌR.MEŠ-*aš-[š]a⟨-aš⟩* in line 10 is no exception, since it should either be read as the allative (GÌR.MEŠ-*a=šša* "to his feet") or corrected to GÌR.MEŠ-*aš-[š]a⟨-aš⟩* "at his feet" in accord with i 17 (see Rieken et al.).

[19] Although Alalu sits as king of the gods, it is Anu, the chief of the celestial deities who bears the title "the foremost (*ḫantezziyaš*) of the gods."

[20] See above in note 12.

[21] Parallel to §§ 2–3 in this text is a poorly preserved fragment KBo 22.87, which mentions the deity Eltara, also known from lists of these Primeval Deities in Hurrian religious contexts (Archi 1990; Haas 1994:112–115; van Gessel 1998 1:64; Haas and Bawanypeck 2003:571, 626; Taracha 2009:125–126). In this fragmentary piece Eltara also was king in heaven for a period of years, after which there was some sort of revolt. See Polvani 2008.

[22] Hittite *kappuwant-* "counted, few, mere." Pecchioli Daddi and Polvani 1990 "contati"; Beckman 2011 "only." For *kappuwant-* in the plural meaning "few" see KBo 10.2 ii17; KUB 14.1+ obv 52; KUB 38.12 ii 15; KUB 46.37 obv 37–38; KUB 30.10 obv 21. Only here and in line 18 is this adjective accompanied by a number, requiring us to translate "a *mere* nine years." On the possibilities of interpreting this phrase, see *GHL*, 167, n. 44.

[23] The repetitive style of this portion of the text is offset occasionally by deliberate variation. Here the indirect object Alalu precedes the subject Anu, while in the companion phrase in i 18–19 the reverse is the case.

[24] My translation seeks to reflect the style of the Hittite (which mirrors the Hurrian before it) in inverting the repeated clause. A somewhat similar inversion occurs in i 15–16.

[25] The same syntax is found in i 15–17 as described in note 12 above.

[26] See above in n. 16.

[27] Lit. "seed". This line makes it clear that the alternating usurpations are attempts by two competing lines to control the universe. As Alalu's son is Kumarbi, so Anu's son is Teššub. Cf. Hoffner 1975:138–139. Pecchioli Daddi and Polvani (1990:129, n. 10) add the thought that in Teššub, son of Anu and Kumarbi, the two lines merge. Perhaps so, but this certainly does not stop Kumarbi from seeking to restore his line to the throne through Ḫedammu, Ullikummi, Silver, etc.

[28] Note again the inversion of indirect object and subject in repeated synonymous clauses. Read ^{d}*A-nu-u-i* (dat. sg.) with the copy and Laroche, against Beckman's nominative ^{d}*A-nu-uš*.

[29] In this and the following sentence the subject Anu is placed after the verb at the end of the clause in what is called right displacement, a common feature of literary texts translated from Hurrian into Hittite. My translation tries to reproduce the effect, but is undeniably awkward.

[30] Given the right displacement in the preceding clause, there remains no nominal subject for this clause, if one reads MUŠEN-*aš ⟨i-wa-ar⟩* as is commonly done (see my WAW translation and Beckman). No simile is used in the corresponding clause in i 14–15, where Alalu escapes from Anu and flees down to the Dark Earth, and restoring the entire word *iwar* is not a trivial matter.

[31] Or "reached out" (see Beckman).

[32] For this noun, which means "loins" or "genitalia," see *CHD* P sub *parše/ina-*. The once proposed emendation *ge!-nu-uš-šu-uš* "knees" (as a euphemism for genitalia), which encounters gender difficulties anyway, is no longer necessary.

[33] Pecchioli Daddi and Polvani 1990 render the two identical occurrences of *PA-NI* ŠÀ-*KA* literally "before your belly" as "*alle*" and "*per le*". This expression is to be understood in the same way as to speak *PA-NI* ZI-*KA* "before (i.e., to) your mind." A kind of conversation or interchange is depicted here, in which Kumarbi celebrates with his belly. Cf. *CHD mema-* 9; *CHD peran* 1 c 1′ c′.

[34] I take this as a rhetorical question. The grammar permits taking it as a statement, see Pecchioli Daddi and Polvani 1990:130.

[35] The deity intended is the Hurrian Teššub, although the complementation of the logogram points to his Hittite name Tarḫunta.

you with the mighty(?) Tašmišu.[36] Two other[37] terrible gods I have placed in your interior as burdens. In the future you will end up striking the rocks of Mount Tašša with your head!"

§ 7 (A i 37–41) When Anu had finished speaking, he went up to the sky and hid himself.[38] K[umarbi,] the wise king,[39] spat from his mouth. He spat from his mouth spittle(?) [and semen] mixed together. With what Kumarbi spat up, Mount Kanzura[40] [...-ed[41]] the frightful (god) T[ašmišu(?)].

Having thus rid himself of one of the first three deities implanted by Anu's sperm, namely Tašmišu-Šuwaliyat, who will be born by Mt. Kanzura later, there remain of the initial three now the Storm-god and the Tigris River (Aranzaḫ).

§ 8 (A i 42–46) Kumarbi, ...-ing,[42] went to the city of Nippur. [(Someone) ...-ed] him to/at a lordly [......, and he] sat down, (namely,) Kumarbi. Not [...]. (Someone) counts [the months]. The ninth(?) month arrived, and inside of him the mighty [deities ...].

§ 9 (A ii 1–3) [...] Kumarbi [*accusative*]. From his [...] from the b[ody] come out! Or come out from his mind(?)! Or come out from his 'good place'!

§ 10 (A ii 4–15) The god A.GILIM within (Kumarbi's) interior began to speak words to Kumarbi: May you be living, O lord of the source of wisdom! If I were to come out, [...] he who [...] to Kumarbi ... which.... The Earth will give me her strength(?). The Sky will give me his valor. Anu will give me his manhood. Kumarbi will give me his wisdom. The primeval [...] will give [me ...]. Nara will give me his.... And (s)he gave ... Ellil will give me his strength(?), [...] his dignity, and his wisdom. And he gave ... to all hearts ... And ... of the mind ... [*Break.*]

§ 11 (A ii 16–22) (*Most of this paragraph is illegible.*) ... [...] Let the [...] stand [...]. Šuwaliyat [...]. When/if ... he gave to me, he [...] to me.

§ 12 (A ii 23–28) Anu began to rejoice.[43] ... come! ... to you ... I feared. You will [...] and what [...]-s I gave into [...], ... come! They will ... him like another woman. Come out in just the same way! ... come out by the mouth! ... come out! If you prefer,[44] come out by the "good place"!

§ 13 (A ii 29–38) Ea began to speak [words] to Kumarbi's interior. [...] ... place. If I come [out of the ...], it will snap me off like a reed.[d] If I come out ..., it/he will defile me there too, (namely, the ... deity); and it/he will defile me on the ear. If I come out through the 'good place,' a *tarškanza* woman will ... me upon my head. ... He chose it[45] from within. He split it like a stone, namely Kumarbi's skull, and KA.ZAL, the valiant ki[ng], came up out of[46] his skull.

§ 14 (A ii 39–54) As he went, (KA.ZAL) [took his stand] before Ea, [and he] bowed, and he fell down. Kumarbi, from [fear(?)/pain(?) his ...] changed (color?).[47] Kumarbi search[ed] for NAM.ḪÉ.[48] He began to speak to Ea: Give me (my) child (i.e., NAM.ḪÉ?), that I may eat him up.[e] Who [will ...]

d 2 Kgs 18:21; Isa 36:6; 42:3; Ezek 29:6; Matt 12:20

e Lev 26:29; Deut 28:53, 55, 57; Lam 2:20

[36] This god, whose Hittite name was Šuwaliyat, was the brother and partner of Teššub.

[37] Güterbock 1961:157 ("And two (other) terrible gods"), and Bernabé 1987 ("Otros dos ... dioses") recognized the need for the word "other/additional." This understanding is necessitated by the conjunction *-ya* "also" in 2! DINGIR.MEŠ-*ya-ták-kán*, and renders suspect the reading "3!" as a reference to the three deities just mentioned. I (Hoffner 1998a:43) therefore join with Bernabé; Pecchioli Daddi and Polvani 1990:130, n. 16, and García Trabazo 2002:168–169, in following the arguments of Forrer 1936, Güterbock, and others, and in rejecting the reading "3" earlier favored by Güterbock (1946), and followed by Goetze, Meriggi 1953; Haas 1994:84, and Beckman 2011. Cf. the works cited in Pecchioli Daddi and Polvani 1990:130, n. 16.

[38] The grammar doesn't permit the translation of Güterbock 1978:236 (followed by Bernabé) "... to the sky. But Kumarbi hid himself and spat from his mouth ...". Presumably Güterbock's understanding would refer to Kumarbi going into a kind of isolation during his "pregnancy."

[39] To this point no predecessor of Kumarbi as king of the gods has been called "wise," and the actions of these predecessors do not reflect either wisdom or cleverness. This quality is uniquely Kumarbi's, as shall be shown repeatedly in the individual "songs" that follow and make up the series.

[40] But in § 17 Kanzura is yet to be born from Kumarbi. This mountain, also called Kanturna, occurs also in the Song of Ullikummi III A ii 13–14. Whether or not true also in Hurrian, in the Hittite conception all mountains are male, and springs female. The divine biology in the Kumarbi series is counter-intuitive, since males become pregnant (cf. Kumarbi himself).

[41] García Trabazo 2002:168–169, "received," reading DINGIR-*an d*[*a-a-iš*] (sic!); other readings: AN an-d[a? (Meriggi); AN? AN? DA? (Laroche); ^{d}An-d[a?-...] (Güterbock); *na-aḫ-šar-an-ta-an* $^{(d)}$ ^{d}*Da*?-[*aš-mi-it ar-ma-aḫ-ḫa-*]*ta* "[became pregnant] with the terrible Tašmišu" (Beckman 2011:28) (*na-aḫ-šar-an-ti-it* would be required for this interpretation).

[42] Some (Bernabé 1987:148; Haas 1994:84) read *ša-u-wa-ni-ia-u-an-za* and take this word to mean "angry." Puhvel, *HED* E/I; Pecchioli Daddi and Polvani 1990:131, n. 23 read *i-ia-u-wa-ni-ya-u-an-za* (with Puhvel 1984:353–354) "recovering." But since Kumarbi's trip to Nippur is to handle the impending births of the terrible gods within him, he is hardly "recovering"!

[43] Reading *du-uš-ki-iš-ki-u-an* from the photo, against Meriggi's [*ḫu-k*]*i-iš-ki!-u-an* "to recite spells" (Meriggi 1953). Anuis happy that his sperm implanted in Kumarbi will now result in the births of these powerful opponents to Teššub.

[44] There is word play here, since "If you prefer" is literally "If it is good (*āššu*) to you."

[45] Possibly the head (*aršar* neuter, rather than the common gender variant *aršarna-*, assumed on the basis of nom. and acc. sg. complementation of SAG.DU; denied by *HED* Ḫ 189–190).

[46] Taking *tarnaššit* as an assimilated form of *tarnazšit* "from/through his skull"; cf. Hoffner 1977.

[47] García Trabazo 2002:172–173, "recovered [from a faint]."

[48] Güterbock 1982:38, n. 27, followed by Beckman 2011:30, n. 10, takes this to be an alternate name (or epithet) for Teššub, whom Kumarbi wishes to eat.

to me a woman, [so that] she may [...]? Who[49] [will ...] to me the Stormgod, that I may eat [him] up? I will smash him like a brittle reed. ... ... before ... ... Ea ... he deliberately(?) gathered him. ... Kumarbi (acc.) ... The heavenly Sun God saw him. ... Kumarbi began to eat. [The Basalt] [injured(?)] the teeth in Kumarbi's mouth. When it, namely [the Basalt Stone[50]], had injured his teeth, he began to weep.

§ 15 (A ii 55–70) Kumarbi [...-ed]. And words [he began to] speak. Who was I afraid of? Kumarbi ... like a ... [...-ed]. To Kumarbi he began to speak. Let them call [... a ...] stone! Let it be placed [...]! He threw the Basalt into the [...], (saying:) "In the future let them call you [...]! Let the rich men, the valiant lords, slaughter for you cattle [and sheep]! Let the poor men make sacrifice to you with [meal]!"[f] Not it ... Because [...-ed] Kumarbi from the mouth, no one [will ...] his [...]-*muwa* back. Kumarbi spoke [...]. A ... occurred to him ... they ... the lands above and below.

§ 16 (A ii 71–75) [The rich men] began to slaughter with cattle and rams. [The poor men] began to sacrifice with meal. [The ...-s] began to [...]. And his skull, like a garment, [they ...-ed. Like a ...] they mended(?) together Kumarbi's skull. The heroic Stormgod came out through the [good] place.

§ 17 (A ii 76–86) [...] the Fate Goddesses. And [they closed up(?)] his good place like/as (they would mend a torn) garment.... second place [...] ... [...] came out. They brought him to birth, [did the Fate Goddesses,] like a woman of the childbed. When [they had brought(?)] Kumarbi to Mount Kanzura, [they helped] her to give birth, (namely,) Mount Kanzura. [And Šuwaliyat,] the hero, came [out].[51] [...] he came out through the good place. Anu rejoiced(?) too, [as/because(?)] he beheld [his sons(?)]. [*Rest of column ii broken off.*]

§ 18 (A iii 2–21) [...] we will destroy [...]. Anu [...] Furthermore we will destroy [... also]. [...] him in their midst [...] we will destroy NAM.ḪÉ like a [......]. When [Kumarbi ...], what words you/he spoke [...], will you destroy[52] Kumarbi [...]? [...] on my throne [...] Kumarbi [accusative]. Who [will] destroy Teššub for us? And when he comes to maturity(?), they will make someone else [...]. [...] will indeed leave [...]. Abandon him! [...] Ea, lord of the source of wisdom. Make [...] king! [...] word(s) [...] ... [...]. When Teššub [heard these words], he was displeased.[53] [Teššub ...] said to (his) bull, Šeri:

§ 19 (A iii 22–29) "[Who] can come[54] against [me any more] in battle?[55] [Who can] defeat[56] [me now]? Even Kumarbi [cannot(?)] arise [against me(?)]! Even Ea [...] the son, and the Sun God [...]. I drove [Kumarbi(?) from his throne(?)] at the time [of ...]. I cursed him [...].[57] I cursed the War God too, and brought him to the town Banapi. So who now can do battle[58] any more against me?"[g]

§ 20 [*In what follows Teššub's bull Šeri warns him of the danger of cursing certain other deities and cautions him against overconfidence.*] (A iii 30–39) The bull Šeri replied to Teššub: "My lord! Why are you cursing them, [... the ...] gods? My lord, why [are you cursing] them? Why are you cursing Ea also?"[59,h] Ea will hear you [...] with.... Is it not so? [His ...] (is) great. (His) intelligence is as big as the land. Powerful(?) for you [is ...]. [...] will come. You will not be able to lift [your(?)] neck(?). [...] speaks. [...] wise(?) is he. [...] Ea. [*Break of about twenty-five lines.*]

§ 21 (A iii 64–66) "... of the hand [...] May he loose ...! [May he ...] eyebrows! May he make ... (of) silver (and) gold!"

§ 22 (A iii 67–72) When Ea heard the words, he was displeased in (his) heart. And he began to speak words back to the god Tauri(?): "Do not speak curses to me! He who cursed me curses me [at great risk to himself(?)].[i] You who repeat to me [those curses(?)] are yourself cursing me! Under the pot [a fire is placed(?)], and that pot will boil over(?)."[60,j]

f Lev 5:7; 12:8; 14:21; Exod 30:15

g 1 Sam 2:3; 1 Kgs 20:11; Ps 75:4; Prov 27:1; Obad 1:12

h Exod 22:28

i See note *h*

j Jer 1:13

[49] This passage is problematic, since a neuter pronoun (*kue*) should not serve as subject to a transitive verb. Yet the verb to be restored must be transitive, since it takes a direct object (*-an* ... ᵈIŠKUR-*an*). Something other than *ku-e-ia* should be read from the traces, perhaps this is a scribal slip for intended *ku-iš* or *ku-i-e-eš*?

[50] Restoring [*ku-un-ku-nu-zi-iš*] or [ᴺᴬ⁴*ŠU-U-zi-iš*] in ii 54. Beckman reads (53) ... *iš?-tar?-x x-x-ta* (54) [*iš-tar-ni-ik-ta*].

[51] The emerging (*parā uwa-* "to come forth, emerge,") of these gods and goddesses at birth is the theme of this myth and gave to it its title, the "Song of Emerging" (Corti 2007).

[52] Or: you will destroy.

[53] Teššub is sad to hear that his opponents have made another deity (perhaps ᵈLAMMA) king. Yet he is confident that he can handle this pretender. Thus the words which he speaks in lines 22 ff. are confident, even boastful.

[54] Pronoun and verb are plural.

[55] So following the restoration suggested by Laroche 1969 on the basis of line 29.

[56] The verb is singular.

[57] As previously (i 27 ff.) Anu had cursed him.

[58] Pronoun and verb are plural.

[59] The point of the question may be that Ea is not at this time in the camp of Kumarbi and should not be antagonized needlessly, or it may be that Šeri considers Ea a particularly dangerous opponent.

[60] The meaning is that although the fire underneath burns the bottom of the pot, it will be extinguished by its contents, when the pot boils over. Tauri is merely repeating the curses of Teššub which he has heard. But since those curses are extremely unpleasant to Ea, he warns his messenger that he too may "get burned!"

[End of column iii. First fifty lines of column iv broken away. The first preserved lines mention a wagon, which is personified in what follows.]

§ 23 (A iv 6–16) When the sixth month passed, the Wagon[61] [......] The Wagon's "manhood" [... ed] the Wagon back [to ...] contrived a plan. Ea, [lord of the source of] wisdom [......]-ed. The Earth Goddess set out for Apzuwa, (saying:) "Ea, [lord of the source of] wisdom, knows what to do." He (Ea?) counts (the months): The first, the second, the third month passed. The fourth, the fifth, the sixth month passed. [The seventh], the eighth, the ninth month passed. And the tenth month [arrived]. In the tenth month Earth [began to] cry out in labor pains.

§ 24 (A iv 17–27) When Earth cried out in labor pains, [...] she bore sons. A messenger went (to tell the king of the gods). And [the god ..., the king], on his throne approved. [...] drove(?) the fine word. [...] Earth has borne two sons/children. [... When] Ea [heard] the words, [he ...] orally(?) a messenger [... And the god ...], the king, [...] a gift.[62] (The king gives) a fine garment for him/her [...] an *IPANTU*-garment[63,k] trimmed with silver for [...] wraps [...].

§ 25 (*Colophon*: A iv 28–35) Tablet one of the *Song of Emergence*,[64] not complete(?). Written by (literally, "hand of") Ašḫapa, son of [...]-taššu, grandson of LAMMA.SUM, ⟨great⟩ grandson of Waršiya, student of Zita. Since the tablet I copied from was worn, I, Ašḫapa, recopied it under the supervision of (the supervisor) Zita.

k Exod 25:7; 28:6; 35:9

61 The "wagon" referred to here is the deified and personified constellation we call the Big Dipper.

62 The "king" is the same god who in iv 18–19 from his throne approved of the birth of Earth's two sons. He now gives gifts either to the two sons or to their mother Earth.

63 Cf. Old Assyrian *epattum* (from **epadtum*), an expensive garment (Hoffner 1996; Corti 2007:113; Collins 2007:221; skeptical: Schwemer 2005:227).

64 Newly restored from join made by Corti 2007, whose study makes plausible the rendering of SÌR GÁxÈ.A as Hittite *parā pawaš* "of going forth," an approximate match to the verbal complex *parā uwa-* "to come forth" used to describe the theogonies, the births of the gods from Kumarbi's interior. Corti even suggests that *parā pāwar* in this myth title may approximate the idea of "genesis."

REFERENCES

Text: CTH 344; A. KUB 33.120+33.119+36.31+48.97 + KBo 52.10. B. KUB 36.1 (= A iii 26ff.). *Transliteration*: Forrer 1936; Güterbock 1946:6–12; Otten 1950:513; Meriggi 1953:110–157; Laroche 1969:153–161; Otten and Rüster 1973; García Trabazo 2002:155–175; Corti 2007; Beckman 2011; E. Rieken et al. (ed.), hethiter.net/: CTH 344 (INTR 2009-08-12). *Translation(s)*: Forrer 1936; Güterbock 1946:6–12; Meriggi 1953:110–157; Goetze 1955:120–121; Güterbock 1961:155–161; Vieyra 1970:539–546 (translation of A i 1–42); Kühne 1975; Kühne 1978:153–155; Güterbock 1978:234–236; Wilhelm 1982 (translation of A i 7–36); Bernabé 1987:139–155; Hoffner 1990:40–45 (rev. ed. 1998); Pecchioli Daddi and Polvani 1990:115–131; Prechel 1996:97, n. 189 (translation of A i 5–6); Beckman 2011. *Studies*: Güterbock 1948; Otten 1949; Lesky 1950; Steiner 1958; Walcot 1966:1–26; Perry 1966:145–149; DeVries 1967:23–31; Vieyra 1970:520–522, 539–546; Güterbock 1978:211–253; Bernabé 1989; Haas 1994:72–78, 82–85, 106–116; Buccellati and Kelly-Buccellati 1997; Singer 2002; Beckman 2005; Haas 2006:133–143; Corti 2007; Polvani 2008; Hoffner 2009b; Beckman 2011.

THE SONG OF THE GOD LAMMA (4.6B)

The beginning of the text is broken away. When it begins to be readable, a battle is taking place. Šawuška addresses her brother Teššub as "my brother" and "younger brother."

§ 1 (A i 2–12) ... While Šawuška was [speak]ing[65] [to her brother Teššub], the arrow of LAMMA [sped], and it pierced(?)[66] Šawuška in her breast. A second arrow of LAMMA [sped]. They [...]-ed the chariot to [...], [but LAMMA's arrow] pierced [...], so that [...] could no longer ... they could no longer set out.[67]

§ 2 (A i 13–20) LAMMA decided on [...]. He took [...] and [...] it behind Teššub. The stone [went(?)] after Teššub. It struck the sky, and [the sky] was shaken/torn [like an empty garment],[68] so that [Teššub] fell down [from the sky]. LAMMA [...-ed], and took the reins and the [whip] out of Teššub's hand.

§ 3 (A i 21–31) Teššub turned back and began to speak [to LAMMA[69]]: "The reins [and whip] which you took from [my] hand and [took them into your own] hand, those reins ... [When] they will [summ]on you to the *kallištarwa*-house, may the reins [...] for/from you. Let a woman[70] not eat of the sheep they sacrifice to the reins. A man [..., and ...] he holds"

The text breaks for about thirty or forty lines, which probably told how Ea appointed LAMMA to be king of the gods.

65 I restore [*me-mi-i*]*š-ke-et*.

66 *šal-wa-a-et*, cf. *CHD* Š 107–108.

67 For a different reconstruction of the text and translation, see Rieken et al. (ed.), hethiter.net.

68 See *CHD* Š 264 with support from CTH 345. Differently Rieken et al. (ed.), hethiter.net ("erhob sich").

69 So Meriggi.

70 So Meriggi read the traces: MUNU[S]-*za*? *l[e]-e*.

§4 (A ii 1–7) Now [when] LAMMA [heard] Ea's words, he began to [rejo]ice[71] within himself. [He … ed], he ate and drank, and went up to heaven [to kingship(?)]. […] up to heaven […].

§5 (A ii 8–27) For nine years LAMMA was [king] in heaven. And in those years unfavorable weather,[72] wolves, and thieves did not exist. In place of[73] the unfavorable weather, it was …ing BA.BA.ZA-flour. In place of (ordinary) rain, it was [ra]ining *tawal*-beer and *walḫi*-drink.[74] What in the night […] takes, takes butter, [and] what […] he keeps placing […], places […]. At the gate […]. And he [… s] … [The mountains(?)] flowed [with] "beer-wine."[l] The valleys [and …] flowed [with …] poured out. Man [… was well off(?)], and he was fully […]. And in what [… he … ed], there he [… ed]. No one began to […] to/for him. In(to) the city of [… he …]ed. [*The end of column ii is broken away.*]

§6 (A iii 1–18) […] the deity […] lifted up [her eyes …] and she [… ed, and] she saw […] coming toward her three DANNA-s away. [The goddess Kubaba(?)] began to say [to LAMMA:] "First [I have seen] the great gods, the elders, your forefathers. Go to meet them and bow to them" LAMMA began to reply to the goddess Kubaba: "The Primeval Gods are great. They have arisen. Where […] to them […] not […] bread in the mouth […]. On what paths do the w[inds] go and come on?[m] Shall I, LAMMA, king of heaven, bow to the gods?"[75] The tempestuous(?) winds brought LAMMA's harsh words to Ea (while he was) on his way.[76] Ea began to [sp]eak to Kumarbi: "Come, let us go back. This LAMMA whom we made king in heaven, just as he himself behaves improperly(?),[77] so he has made the countries improper(?), so that no one any longer gives bread or drink offerings to the gods."

§7 (A iii 19–30) Ea and Kumarbi turned [their faces]: Ea [went] to Apzuwa, but Kumarbi went away to Tuttul. Ea made a messenger stand up in front [of himself] and undertook to dispatch him to LAMMA (saying): "Go, speak these words to [LAMMA]: 'Why did we make you king in heaven? […] never made/did […]. He[78] did [not] summon anywhere.'" [*The end of the speech is fragmentary.*] The messenger departed and recounted [Ea's words] just so.

§8 (A iii 31–38) When […] had heard [… words], he began to […] to himself. Ea began to [sa]y to Izzummi, [his vizier]: "Go down to the Dark [Earth], and tell the words which I am speaking to you to Nara-Napšara, my brother, (saying): 'Take my speech and hearken to my words. [LAMMA] has made me angry, so I have deposed him from the kingship in heaven'"

§9 (A iii 39–46) "'That LAMMA whom we made king in heaven, just as he himself behaves improperly(?), so he has made the countries improper(?), so that no one any longer gives bread or drink offerings to the gods. Now, Nara, my brother, hear me. Mobilize[79] all the animals of the earth. Mt. Našalma […], and unto his head [… '"].

[*Gap of undetermined length.*]

§10 (A iv 8–16) […] began to [speak to …] before […] who placed the burden [in …]. […] began to speak […]. Hear my words. [Hold your ear] inclined [to …]. […] wagon […]. His *ikdu* (a body part) from his back […] under 700 […].

§11 (A iv 17–22) [As] Teššub (and) NINURTA, his vizier, […-ed], they made LAMMA the same way. They spread/trampled(?) […], [they …-ed] LAMMA […]. They cut up(?) […] from his back. They cut up […] his *ikdu*.

§12 (A iv 23–30) LAMMA [spoke] back to Teššub: "Teššub, my lord! Long ago […]. To me […]!" Teššub spoke (back) to LAMMA: "Let them proceed to […] (to/from) you. [Let them …] (to) me. [Let them …] the cup from you quickly(?). I […] it to you"

Seven more lines too fragmentary for translation. Then tablet ends. Only one sign of the colophon remains.

l Exod 3:8, 17; Lev 20:24; Num 16:13; Deut 6:3; Jer 11:5; 1 Sam 14:26.

m John 3:8

71 I restore [… *du-uš-ki-iš-k]i-u-wa-an*. Rieken restores [… *me-mi-iš-k]i-u-wa-an da-a-i[š]* "began to say," although nothing follows as a quote.

72 *CHD* Š 246–247 ("unfavorable weather conditions such as a violent storm or a blizzard").

73 Rieken correctly observes that NOUN-GENITIVE + acc. *pedan* is not the normal way one wrote "in place of" in Hittite, but rather *pedišši*. Yet it seems to be the best option for translating this passage.

74 Tentative and problematic translation; see Reiken et al. (ed.) hethiter.net.

75 My earlier translation ("I allot to them"), which is also that of HED 3:356, is unlikely, since there is no resumptive pronoun for "them." The verb *ḫink-* would seem to be intransitive here, hence "bow." But since LAMMA's words make Ea angry (§8), I prefer to understand this last statement as a rhetorical question, implying that LAMMA acknowledges the greatness of the other gods, but refuses to bow to them because of his position as king of heaven.

76 Variant adds the words "When Ea heard LAMMA's words."

77 Melchert, CLL s.v.; *CHD* L–N 460.

78 Although one would like to take "you" as the subject of these clauses, Rieken is right that *ḫalzaiš* is nowhere attested as a "you" form. Perhaps the subject was a singular collective representing humankind, since Ea has complained that LAMMA's unfriendliness was copied by the countries.

79 Or "Stir up," cf. *CHD* L–N 5–6, s.v. *nini(n)k-*.

REFERENCES

Transliteration: CTH 343; Laroche 1969:145–152; E. Rieken et al. (ed.), hethiter.net/:CTH 343.1 (TX 2012-06-08, TRde 2009-08-30). *Translation*: Güterbock 1961:161–164; Bernabé 1987:203–207; Hoffner 1990 [also 1998a]:46–47; E. Rieken et al. (ed.), hethiter.net/: CTH 343.1 (TX 2012-06-08, TRde 2009-08-30). *Studies*: Forrer 1936; Meriggi 1953; Güterbock 1978; Haas 1994:97–99; 2003; 2006:143–147. *Online sources*: E. Rieken et al. (ed.), hethiter.net/: CTH 343.1 (INTR 2009-08-12).

THE SONG OF SILVER (4.6C)

1. *Fragment 1: Introduction* (HFAC 12)
§1.1 […], the Sun God of the Sky, …, […] … […] no one does/makes [… like him(?)],[80] [his] intelligence [is greater(?) than their(?) intelligences]. His word [is greater(?)] than [their(?)] words, his wisdom [is greater(?)] than [their(?)] wisdom, his battle [and his] glo[ry(?) are greater(?) than theirs, and their(?)] *ḫandatar*-s [are not(?) greater(?)] than his *ḫandatar*-s.
§1.2 I sing of him, Silver the Excellent One […]. Wise men [……] to me [the[81] … of] the fatherless [boy(?)]. It did not exist. Long ago Silver's [… ……]. And his [gl]ory[82] they do not know. […(?)] men ran/run into battle. […(?)] did not exist. And grain […(?)]. […] hungry(?) […]

2. *Fragment 2: The Birth of Silver?*
[*Fragment 2 reports a birth. And since Silver is the principal character of this story, as well as the son of Kumarbi, it seems probable that it is his birth which is described.*]
§2.1 … went.
§2.2 […] fire […] of alabaster […] his eyes […] they gave it [.… The first, second, third, and] fourth months passed; the fifth(?), [sixth, seventh, eighth, and ninth months passed; and the tenth month] arrives.
§2.3 … [His/her tears] flow [like streams] ….

3. *Fragment 3: Silver and the Orphan Boy*
In this passage Silver is described as a wannumiyaš DUMU, a child whose father is either dead or missing. Although many translate this as "orphan," since Silver's mother is still with him, he is not an orphan in the usual sense. There is just a hint that his fatherless condition could be regarded as shameful.[n] *This hint is not strong enough to justify a translation "bastard." Silver's consternation at being told by the fatherless boy that he too was fatherless need not mean that he was discovering this for the first time. It is unlikely that another child in the community would have more information about this than he. Rather he finds it humiliating to be reminded by others that he too was abandoned by his father. This leads him to inquire further about his father from his mother, which he proceeds to do in fragment 4.*

n Judg 11:1–3

o Exod 22:22; Deut 24:17; 27:19; Job 29:12; 31:21; Jer 22:3

§3.1 ….
§3.2 Silver [struck] a fatherless boy [with] a stick. The fatherless boy spoke a harsh word to Silver: "My Silver, why [are you hitting us]? Why are you striking[83] us? You are fatherless like us."[o] [Now when Silver heard these words], he began to weep. Weeping, Silver went into his house. Silver began to repeat the words to his mother: "The boys I struck in front of the gate are berating/defying(?) me."
§3.3 "I struck a boy with a stick, and he spoke a [harsh] word back to me. Hear, O my mother, the words which the fatherless boy said to me: 'Why are you [hitting us? Why are you striking] us? [You are fatherless] like [us.]"'

4. *Fragment 4: Silver's Quest for Kumarbi*
Without context we are left without a clue as to why Silver threatened his mother with a stick. The sequence: "O Silver! Do not strike me! The city(?) [you inquire about] I will tell/describe it to you" shows that the speech that follows is by the person threatened, and "[Silver] listened to his mother's words" indicates that the speaker was Silver's mother. The description of Silver's father as "father of the city Urkeš" identifies him as Kumarbi, which makes Silver one more of the sequence of kings of heaven who descend from Kumarbi and who eventually oppose Teššub. Teššub can be described as Silver's brother, although he sprang from Anu's sperm, because the "womb" from which he was born was Kumarbi's interior (see the Song of Emergence).

[*First three lines too fragmentary to translate.*]
§4.1 [His mother(?)] took the stick away from [him …. His mother] turned around [and] began to reply [to Silver, her son]: "Do [not hit me], O Silver! Do not strike me! The city(?) [you inquire about] I will tell/describe it to you.[84] [Your father is Kumarbi],

80 In Hoffner 1988 and Hoffner 1990, I ventured a guess at how these opening lines might be restored, but since the evidence is so slight I have left the text unrestored here.

81 Presumably a neuter noun that is referred to by "it" ([N]U.GÁL-*at ēšta*) in the following clause.

82 Restoring [*ma*]-*iš-ta-aš-ša-an-na*; from the noun *maišt-/mišt-* "brilliance, luster, glory," related in root **miš-* to the adj. *mišriwant-* "brilliant, glorious"; cf. Rieken 1999:137–139. The similarly spelled word with the wool determinative (*CHD* L–N 119) has a different meaning.

83 The verb *kuwaškeši* could also mean "(why) are you killing (us)," assuming that Silver has used his stick before and with lethal effect.

84 From what follows it is clear that what the mother tells Silver is his family, using the city of Urkeš as a point of departure.

He is the Father of the city Urkeš.[85] [He ...-s], and he resides in Urkeš. [...] the lawsuits of all the lands he [satisfactorily resolves(?)]. Your brother is Teššub. He [is kin]g in heaven. And he is ki[ng] in the land. Your sister is Šawuška, and she is queen in Nineveh. You should [not] fear any [deity(?)]; [...] deity [....] He [stir]s up(?) the enemy land(s), and the wild animals. From top to bottom [he ...-s]. From bottom to top [he ...-s." [When Silver] had listened to his mother's words, he set out for Urkeš. He arrived in Urkeš, but he did not find [Kumarbi] in his house. He (Kumarbi) [had] gone to roam the land(s). He wanders about up(?) in the mountains. [*Text of col. ii breaks off.*]

5. *Fragment 5: Tašmišu and Teššub*
It is presupposed in this fragment that Silver has displaced Teššub as king of the gods. Teššub's brother Tašmišu, who is also his vizier, seems to taunt him for being timid and afraid of Silver.

§ 5.1 (A iii 3–8) ... [His vizier began] to speak to Teššub: "[Is it] not [possible(?)] for you to thunder? Do you [not] know [how to ...]? On(?) the ... [Silver(?)] has become king, and [now] he dr[ives(?)] all the deities with a goad(?) of pistachio wood."
§ 5.2 (A iii 9′–18′) Teššub [began to] speak (back?) to his vizier: "Come, let us go and eat [...]. Our father, [Kumarbi(?)], did not defeat [Silver(?). But we(?) will] now [defeat(?)] Silver!" They took each other by the hand, [the two brothers, and to ...] they set out. In one stage they made [the trip]. At the city [of ...] they arrived. They [...-ed]. On a noble/powerful[86] [...] Silver is sitting like a [shaft(?). They/he] fear[ed(?) him, the ...], the violent [god ...].

p Gen 37:9; Ps 148:3

§ 5.4 (A iii 19′–20′) Teššub [and Tašmišu arrived in ...]. He saw him and [...]. [*The text of A col. iii breaks off here.*]

6. *Fragment 6: About Old Men*
§ 6.1 (2 B iii 19–30) [...] the old [men ...] ... began to [...]. The tree which we will cut for ourselves, you ... will ... it up too. What ox you [...] in the midst of the vegetable garden, you, O ... [will ...] was of the heart. [...] by means of whose meadow [...] the owner of the meadow [...] and they [...] the old men [...].

7. *Fragment 7: Silver Threatens the Sun and Moon*
This episode could be placed either before or after Silver's becoming king of the gods, although the words "what [lands] you [govern]" are more appropriate to the latter period. It serves to show his great power.

§ 7.1 (4 A 1′–4′) [...] sent: "Go down [to the Dark Earth and ...] him [with] a goad(?)" [...] began to [...].
§ 7.2 (4 A 5′–12′) [...] he closed up his [...] with [...] judged [...]. And all the gods [...] they come/see(?). Silver [seized(?)] power with his hands. Silver seized the spear. He dragged the Sun and Moon down from heaven. The Sun and the Moon did reverence. They bowed to Silver.*p* The Sun and the Moon began to speak to Silver:
§ 7.3 (4 A 13′–17′, B 11′–12′) "[O Silver, our lord], do not kill us! We are the luminaries [of heaven] and [earth]. We are the torches of the [lands] you [govern. If you kill us], will you proceed to govern the dark lands personally?" [Silver's] soul within [him was filled with] love. [He had] pity on [...].

[85] If this myth reflects the genealogy of the Kumarbi Series, the real father of the Storm God was Anu. But since Anu's seed was implanted in Kumarbi, there is a sense in which his father was Kumarbi. Apparently, Silver was the son of Kumarbi by a mortal woman and the stepbrother of Teššub, Šawuška, and of Tašmišu through the common father Kumarbi.
[86] Hittite *nakki-*; cf. *CHD* L–N 364–368.

REFERENCES

Text: CTH 364. *Transliteration and Translation* (Edition): Hoffner 1988. *Translation*: Hoffner 1990:48–50; Bernabé 1987:209–214; Hoffner 1998a:48–50. *Studies*: Kammenhuber 1976; Haas 1994:96–97; Wilhelm 2003; Beckman 2005:260–261; Haas 2006:148–151.

THE SONG OF ḪEDAMMU (4.6D)

In this Song Kumarbi raises up yet another opponent to challenge Teššub and his allies. See earlier discussion in the Introduction to the Kumarbi series (4.6 above). Once again it is a monster whom Kumarbi himself fathers. Kumarbi takes as wife Šertapšuruḫi, the daughter of the Sea God. By her he engenders a monster named Ḫedammu. The monster is a sea serpent with an enormous appetite for all kinds of creatures. The first of Teššub's allies to discover the monster's existence is his sister Šawuška (written as Ishtar in the Kumarbi cycle), Queen of Nineveh. In fragment 5 she reports the bad news to Teššub, which drives him to tears of despondency. Apparently a struggle ensues in which both sides cause injury, and wreak havoc among mortals, for in fragment 6 the peace-making god Ea, "King of Wisdom," admonishes first Teššub's party (called just "the gods" in § 6.1) and then Kumarbi, reminding them all that the destruction of human worshipers means disaster for all the gods, since mortals serve and support them. § 6.1 seems to be addressed to Teššub's followers, since they alone would be troubled by the prospect of Teššub, Šawuška and Ḫebat rather than Kumarbi – being reduced to manual labor. In Fragment 7 Kumarbi is displeased that Ea has rebuked him in the assembly. This may mark the beginning of the progressive estrangement of Ea from Kumarbi, which eventually leads him to offer his counsel also to Teššub in the Song of Ullikummi. In Fragment 9 Mukišanu,

Kumarbi's vizier, is sent to the Sea God. Since his mission is secret, he is instructed to take a subterranean route, and to instruct the Sea God to come to Kumarbi by the same route. Once the Sea God has arrived, Kumarbi instructs his vizier to bolt the door so that no one will interrupt or overhear them as they make their plans. In Fragment 11 Teššub's sister Šawuška forms a plan to defeat Ḫedammu, using her own feminine charms. She washes and anoints herself with fine perfumed oil, enhancing her already seductive qualities. After she instructs her two maidservants, Ninatta and Kulitta, to accompany her with music, she goes down to the sea to entice Ḫedammu. Fragments 12 through 15 are too broken to yield more information than that Šawuška and Ḫedammu engage in conversation. In Fragment 16 Šawuška sedates Ḫedammu with a love potion. She displays her naked body to him and arouses him sexually. No extant fragment explicitly states that Šawuška succeeds in killing Ḫedammu, but the overall plot line of the Kumarbi cycle implies that each opponent of Teššub is eventually defeated. All that we possess of this myth are fragments, the ordering of which is that of the latest edition by Siegelova (1971). Because the translation is based upon an eclectic text, we dispense with the column and line count.

(Fragment 1)

§ 1.1 ... [The Sea God(?)] heard, and his mind within [rej]oiced(?). He [propped(?)] his foot on [a stool(?)]. They put a rhyton in the Sea God's hand. The great [Sea God began to] reply to Kumarbi: "Our matter is settled,[87] Kumarbi, Father of the Gods. Come to my house in seven days,[q] and [I will give you] Šertapšuruḫi, my daughter, whose length is [...] and whose width is one mile. [You will drink(?)] Šertapšuruḫi like sweet cream."[r] When Kumarbi heard (this), his [mind] within him rejoiced. Night fell. [...] They brought the great Sea God out of Kumarbi's house accompanied by (the music of) bronze *arkammi*- and *[galgaltu]ri*-instruments and with bronze rhytons, and they escorted him to his house. In [his house(?)] he sat down on a good chair made of [...]. The Sea God waited seven days for [Kumarbi(?)].

§ 1.2 Kumarbi [began] to speak [words] to his vizier: "Mukišanu, [my vizier! Listen carefully to] the words which [I speak] to you! [...]" [...]

q Judg 14: 12, 17

r Song 2:3

(Fragment 2)

[*In the first badly preserved lines the cities of Kummi(ya) and Tuttul are mentioned. It is possible, but not certain, that the words "They raise up Ḫedammu against [Teššub(?)]" in lines 5–6 indicate that he, like Ullikummi, is Kumarbi's surrogate. No account of Ḫedammu's birth is preserved, but it is likely that he is the offspring of Kumarbi's union with the Sea-god's daughter, Šertapšuruḫi. This fragment describes the serpent Ḫedammu's voracious appetite for a wide variety of creatures.*]

[......] The put him/it in oil. [...] They put him/it in water. [They(?) protect(?)[88]] him/it like an apple tree be[fore] the cold [......] They give him two thousand oxen [and horses(?)] to eat. The goat kids and lambs that they [give] him [to eat are beyond] counting. He eats [oxe]n and horses by the thousands. [...] snails(?) and frogs. [His tongue(?) shoot]s forth like a lance,[89] and it [spears(?)] them [in] the water: fishes of the field (and) dogs of the river.[90] He eats them by the thousands. He swallows [...] like honey. He licks up [...] like [...].

(Fragment 5)

§ 5.1 [KBo 19.112] "... Šawuška, [Queen of Nineveh], comes. [Let them set up a chair for her to sit in]. Let them spread a table for her to eat at." [While they were thus speaking], Šawuška reached them. They set up a chair for her [to sit in], but she didn't sit down in it. They decked [a table for her to eat at], but she didn't reach out to it. [They gave her a cup], but [the Queen of Nineveh] didn't put her lip to it. [...][91] began to speak: "Why do you not eat or drink, my lady?[92,93] [Is it because you don't know how to do it, namely,] eating. It is because [you] don't know how to do it, drinking? [Have] they [incited(?) ...] and [the great(?)] Sea God against the gods, so that he [...]-ed in sky and earth? And what surrogate/usurper shall I [...] describe in the Sea?" He kept speaking [...] about Ḫedammu [...], and Šawuška [...-ed] him.

§ 5.2 [...] heard Šawuška, [and became sad. His ...] ...-s. His [tears flow] forth [like] streams. [...]

87 Lit., "To us is a settled/genuine matter/word," which in context I take to refer to a marriage agreement.

88 So restored by Pecchioli Daddi and Polvani 1990.

89 Although Siegelová 1971 followed the Assyriological evidence available at the time in translating "drawbar, singletree" (German "Deichsel"), we now know that this word also had the meaning "spear, lance" (Civil 1987, cf. also Güterbock 1989:311; Starke 1990:414, n. 1488), which fits admirably its use to designate the royal bodyguard (LÚ.MEŠ *MEŠEDI*, *cf.* Hoffner 1987; Herbordt 1998:313, 318 "magnus hastarius"; Heinhold-Krahmer 2001:195 with notes).

90 These otherwise nonsensical combinations may be kennings, or simply deliberately impossible combinations intended to imply the indiscriminate character of Ḫedammu's diet ("any-old creatures").

91 Unfortunately, we do not know the identity of this deity who acts as host to Šawuška.

92 Lit., "my lord" (*išḫā-mi*).

93 *HED* E/I 264 (following Siegelová 1971?) ends the question here, and restores the following as Šawuška's reply: "Because I don't know how to eat or drink." In many ways this interpretation is satisfying, but it faces the problem that after this speech (in line 15) Šawuška is introduced as a new actor/speaker. If it is the host who continues to speak the following clauses, they must be questions, perhaps rhetorical ones. For a similar situation see the Song of Ullikummi, § 25 (Tablet I A iv 41–48).

(Fragment 6)[94]
§ 6.1 (II 1′–7′)[95] [Ea], King of Wisdom,[96] spoke among the gods. [The god Ea] began to say: "Why are you (*plural*) destroying [mankind]? They will not give sacrifices to the gods. They will not burn cedar as incense to you (*plural*).[s] If you (*plural*) destroy mankind, they will no longer [worship] the gods. No one will offer [bread] or libations to you (*plural*) any longer. Even Teššub, Kummiya's heroic king, will himself grasp the plow. Even Šawuška and Ḫebat will themselves grind at the millstones."[97,t]
§ 6.2 (ii 9′–16′)[98] [Ea], King of Wisdom, said to Kumarbi: "Why are you, O Kumarbi, seeking to harm mankind? Does [not] the mortal take a grain heap and do they not promptly offer (it) to you, Kumarbi? Does he make offering to you alone, Kumarbi, Father of the Gods, joyfully in the midst of the temple? Do they not (also) offer to Teššub, the Canal Inspector[99] of Mankind? And don't they invoke me, Ea, by name as King? [...] you (Kumarbi) are putting wisdom behind [the ...] of all [...]. [...] the blood and tears of mankind [...] Kumarbi [...]." [*Breaks off.*]

(Fragment 7)
§ 7.1 Kumarbi [began to speak] words to [his own mind:] "[Why] would [you] rash[ly[100] ... at] me, Kumarbi, like a [...], in the place of assembly?[101] Why would you strike me, Ea, [...], King of Wisdom? [Why] would you [...?] Why would [you defend(?)] mankind, [...] and Ea, foremost [among the gods]?"
§ 7.2 Kumarbi [spoke] (words) before his mind: "[...] me, Kumarbi, son of Alalu(?). But [...] me to the god Ammezzadu." In the midst of the gods Kumarbi [raised up Ḫedammu(?)] like a [...] as a surrogate against Teššub.
The heroic [......] to Teššub [......] [*Breaks off.*]

(Fragment 9)[102]
§ 9.1 [... "... Make your journey] under [river] (and) earth! [Don't let the Moon God], the Sun God or the [gods] of the Dark Earth [see you!] Come up to Kumarbi from beneath [river and] earth!"
§ 9.2 [Mukišanu] heard the words and [promptly] arose. He made his journey under river and earth. [Neither] the Moon God, the Sun God or the gods of the Dark Earth saw him. He went down to the Sea God.
§ 9.3[103] Mukišanu spoke Kumarbi's words to the Sea God: "Come! The Father of the Gods, Kumarbi, is calling you. The matter for which he calls you is urgent. So come promptly! Come away below river and earth! Don't let the Moon God, the Sun God, or the gods of the Dark Earth see you!" When the great Sea God heard the words, he promptly arose and made his journey under river and earth. He traversed (the distance) in one (stage) and came up below Kumarbi's chair from/by ... and earth. They set up a chair for the Sea God to sit in, and the great [Sea God] sat down in his chair. They placed a table for him set with food. The cupbearer gave him sweet wine to drink. Kumarbi, Father of the Gods, and the great Sea God sat eating and drinking.
§ 9.4[104] Kumarbi spoke words to his vizier: "Mukišanu, my vizier! Listen carefully to the words I speak to you! Bolt the door! [...] Throw the latch(?). [Let not the ...] like an aroma(?) (or: like a drop(?)) [...]. 'Poor men' [will ... us(?)] like a...."
§ 9.5[105] Mukišanu [heard] the words, and quickly [arose]. He began to [throw] the latch(?) and the [...]. And [...] bronze [...].

(Fragment 10)[106]
[...] a blow [...]. The lightning flashes and the [...]-s of Teššub and Šawuška have not yet gone away from us with the water (i.e., rain?). We have not yet come [...]. Our knees tremble [beneath] us. Our head spins like a potter's wheel.[u] Our little family(?)[107] [... s] like ...

(Fragment 11)[108]
§ 11.1 (Teššub speaks to Šawuška:) [...] we (i.e., Ḫedammu and I) will engage in [conflict(?). And ...] Ḫedammu [accusative]. [...] If [I ...]

s Gen 6:8; 8:20–22; 1 Sam 15:22; Pss 40:6–8; 50:9–11; Isa 1:11–13; Hos 6:6

t Matt 24:41

u Jer 18:3

[94] Pecchioli Daddi and Polvani 1990, episode 6.
[95] Rieken et al., § 6″:52–61.
[96] Here, as in Mesopotamian mythology, Ea, the king/lord of wisdom (Akkadian *bēl nēmeqi*), is the god who sympathizes with humans and pleads their case.
[97] This is a typical theme in Mesopotamian mythology: that mortals were created in order to spare the gods the labor of producing food for themselves.
[98] Rieken et al., § 7′:62–71.
[99] LÚ.PA$_5$ (Labat, *Manuel*, sign 60) = Akk. *gugallu*, supervisor of irrigation and canal maintenance, a title usually borne by the god Adad in Mesopotamia (*CAD* G 121–122).
[100] Cf. *CHD* L–N 185 sub *marri* adv.; reading *mān* ... [*kuwat* ...]; cf. *mān* ... *kuwat* "why would ...?" in next clause. This *mān* is a variant spelling of *man*, the potential particle (cf. *CHD* L–N 139–143; *GHL* §§ 23.13–16).
[101] Since Kumarbi's words are addressed to Ea, one is reminded of Ea's words to Tauri at the end of Text 14 (A iii 67–72) about his own anger boiling over like a pot on those who curse him.
[102] Pecchioli Daddi and Polvani 1990, episode 8. See Fragment 28, not translated here, for a related text.
[103] Rieken et al., CTH 348.I.1 § 10:81–99.
[104] Rieken et al., CTH 348.I.1 § 11:100–109.
[105] Rieken et al., CTH 348.I.1 § 12:110–115.
[106] Rieken et al., CTH 348.I.1 § 13:116–121.
[107] Or perhaps: "our goat kid."
[108] Pecchioli Daddi and Polvani 1990, episode 9.

Ḫedammu, [it will …]. But if Ḫedammu [… s], then it is my fault.
§ 11.2 [Now when Teššub(?)] finished speaking, [he went] away. [But Šawuška] went to the bath house. [The Queen of Nineveh] went there to wash herself. She washed herself. She […]ed. She anointed herself with fine perfumed oil. She adorned herself. And (qualities which arouse) love ran after her like puppies.
§ 11.3[109] [Šawuška] began to say [to Ninatta and] Kulitta: "Take [an *arkammi*-instrument], take a *galgalturi*- instrument. At the sea on the right play the *arkammi*, on the left play the *galgalturi*. […] to kingship […]. Perhaps [Ḫedammu(?)] will hear our message (i.e., song). […] let us see how […]."
§ 11.4 […] Ninatta and Kulitta […].

(Fragment 12)[110]
§ 12.1 […] Šawuška […] Ḫedammu […] in the deep waters […].
§ 12.2 When Ḫedammu […]s, […]. And Ḫedammu […]. [He raised(?)] his head from the watery deep. He spied Šawuška. Šawuška held up her naked members before Ḫedammu.
§ 12.3 Ḫedammu began to speak words to Šawuška: "What deity are you, that [you] do not […?] You […], and in/to the sea […] …" And [Šawuška …-ed] to him as to a bull. […] doesn't know […].

(Fragment 13)
§ 13.1 [… to] Ḫedammu [in(?)] the sea […] Šertapšuruḫi […].
§ 13.2 [… to(?)] Ḫedammu […] began to [say: "…] heroic [..] he fills […] my mother […] you (*nominative*) […]"

(Fragment 14)
Ḫedammu [began] to say to Šawuška: "You […] unlike a(ny other) woman. So I will eat you up. [The …-s] are angry, and they […] to me. […]."

(Fragment 15)[111]
§ 15.1 Ḫedammu spoke words to Šawuška: "What kind of woman are you?"[112] Šawuška replied to Ḫedammu: "I am an angry(?)[113] girl. [Before(?)[114]] me the mountains [hold down(?)] (their) greenery as (before) a violent storm(?)."[115] Šawuška speaks flatt[ery(? …] to Ḫedammu, pra[ises(?)][116] him with words and intoxicates him.
§ 15.2 Ḫedammu said to Šawuška: "What kind of woman are you, that […] a name […]? I am […]." [*Only bits of the rest of Ḫedammu's speech are preserved.*]

(Fragment 16)[117]
§ 16.1 (lines 3–10) […] in the sky clouds […] with/from […] waters […] he/she made. When [Šawuška], Queen of Nineveh, had approved [the …], she filled a love potion(?) – *šaḫiš*- and *parnulliš*- wood in "strong" waters and smelled(?) the love potion, the *šaḫiš*- and *parnulliš*- wood, in the waters. Now when Ḫedammu had tasted the aroma, namely, the beer, [sweet] sleep overcame the mind of the valiant Ḫedammu. He was dozing like an ox (or) ass.[118] He recognizes no […] he keeps on eating frogs and snails(?).
§ 16.2 [Šawuška] said to Ḫedammu: "Come up again. [Come(?)] from the strong waters. Come through the midst of […]" [Ḫedammu …-s] 90,000 […]. He levels(?) a […] place from the earth. Šawuška holds out [her naked members toward Ḫedammu]. Ḫedammu [sees(?) the beautiful goddess], and his penis springs forth. His penis impregnates […]s. He […]-ed 130 cities […]. [He …-ed] 70 cities with his belly. […] came to an end. […] heaped up piles of heads.
§ 16.3 Šawuška, Queen of Nineveh, was struck […] on/at the …. At the second […] she came down [to] Ḫedammu, and Šawuška, [Queen] of Nineveh, walked before him. Šawuška came [down to him], and after her Ḫedammu, like a …, pours out […]. They […] it on the earth [like(?)] frightful floods. The valiant Ḫedammu came down from his throne, from the sea. He came out onto the dry land […].

109 Siegelova's edition needs to be augmented here with KBo 22.51.
110 Pecchioli Daddi and Polvani 1990, episode 10.
111 Pecchioli Daddi and Polvani 1990, episode 13.
112 Lit., "Who of woman are you?"
113 Hittite *ḫarša*[*lanza*], from *ḫaršalant*- (*HED H*, 185–186; *HEG A-H*, 183); Pecchioli Daddi and Polvani 1990:142 "una fanciulla adirata."
114 Restoring *peran* in the lacuna immediately before the verb.
115 The word is *šarāwar*, which also occurs in Song of the god LAMMA, § 5, and note 72. See *CHD* Š 246–247; following Goetze, Friedrich, Kronasser, and Siegelová (see *CHD* Š s.v.), Pecchioli Daddi and Polvani (1990) and Bernabé (1987:168) take *šarāwar* to mean "anger." Both also incorrectly take *laḫḫurnuzzi* as the subject, although neuter nouns cannot serve as subjects to transitive verbs; the *CHD* article too makes this mistake.
116 Restoring *wa*[*lliyazi*] or *wa*[*llāi*], from *walla-/walliya*- "to praise, boast about" (*HWb* 242; Laroche 1964:27–29; Hoffner 1982:135, n. 13; Tischler 2001:193; Haas 2006:297).
117 Pecchioli Daddi and Polvani 1990, episode 14.
118 Perhaps meaning that he slept standing up.

REFERENCES

Text: CTH 348. Current listing of component texts is available online in ttp://www.hethport.uni-wuerzburg.de/hetkonk/CTH 348, and in E. Rieken et al. (ed.), hethiter.net/: CTH 348. *Transliteration and Translation* (Edition): Friedrich 1949; Siegelová 1971; E. Rieken et al. (ed.), hethiter.net/: CTH 348. *Translation*: Bernabé 1987:157–170; Pecchioli Daddi and Polvani 1990:131–141; Hoffner 1990:50–55; Haas 1994:86–88. Studies: Komoróczy 1973; Kammenhuber 1974; 1976; Haas 1994:86–88; Wilhelm 2003; Haas 2006:153–156.

THE SONG OF ULLIKUMMI (CTH 345) (4.6E)

The final clause of §19 summarizes the overarching theme of the Kumarbi Cycle: Kumarbi, who ironically is "host/parent" for Anu's seed, which becomes Teššub, attempts in each succeeding song of the cycle to raise up someone (Ullikummi, Ḫedammu, Silver, and LAMMA) to supplant Teššub as king of the gods. Clever Kumarbi devises a plan to dethrone Teššub. He proposes to raise up an "Evil Day" in the form of a "hostile man", an unbeatable opponent. The stone monster he eventually raises up is in fact called a "man" in §36. Kumarbi leaves his home city, Urkeš, and travels to a place called Cold Lake, where he finds a great rock, here conceived as female and a potential sexual partner for Kumarbi. Its enormous size, three miles long and [one] and a half miles wide, encourages Kumarbi to suppose that the offspring he could engender from such a rock would surely be able to overcome Teššub. Sexually excited, Kumarbi impregnates the rock. Before the rock gives birth (§10 and following), Kumarbi confers with his old ally, the Sea God (§§6–9). Attending the birth are the Fate Goddesses and Mother Goddesses, who present the newborn to its father Kumarbi to legitimate it formally by holding it on his knees, and to give it a fitting[119] name.[120] Kumarbi chooses the name Ullikummi on the basis of the child's desired destiny: to destroy Kumme, the city of Teššub, and to dethrone Teššub (§12). The accumulation of similes ("like chaff," "like an ant," "like a brittle reed," "like birds," "like empty pottery bowls") in §12 is appropriate, since Kumarbi enforces his predictive wish by means of the language of analogic magic. See Hoffner 1998a, text no. 2 ("The Disappearance of Telipinu") §§10–14. Fearing for the newborn's safety until it has grown large enough to ward off attacks, Kumarbi entrusts it to the *irširra*- goddesses to take it to the nether world and deposit it on the right shoulder of the Hurrian Atlas, Ubelluri (§§13–20). There it will remain hidden until it has grown powerful. When, by its daily growth of a cubit, Ullikummi has grown so tall that it meets the sky and the temples of the heavenly gods, it can be ignored no longer. The Sun God, an ally of Teššub, sees it first (§23). Going to the sea for a closer look (§24), the Sun God shows his amazement, horror and anger through the gesture of holding his hand to his forehead. Quickly, the Sun God goes to warn Teššub. In a stereotypical scene of a messenger arriving with a message so urgent that he refuses to eat before delivering it (§§26–28) the Sun God refuses food, drink and a chair to sit on.[121] After delivering his message, the Sun God accepts the hospitality of Teššub (§31), and eventually returns home to the sky. Teššub forms a clever plan in his mind and sets out with Tašmišu, his vizier. The two are joined by Teššub's sister, Šawuška, and go up to Mt. Hazzi, from which to see Ullikummi in the distance (§32). When he sees the monster, Teššub in anger and despair, asks a series of rhetorical questions (§33). As she had done in the earlier Song of Ḫedammu (Text D, §12.2), Teššub's sister Šawuška tries to help him by using her feminine charms against his opponent (§35–37). This fails because Ullikummi is deaf to her music and blind to her naked beauty. It is not clear if Ullikummi was born deaf and blind or has become so through some event not preserved in the earlier parts of the composition. In §23 the text informs us that the Sun God saw Ullikummi, and "Ullikummi saw the Sun God of the Sky." Perhaps the words in §23 are for literary symmetry and not intended to be taken literally. Ullikummi is really incapable of seeing. The great wave that explains the situation to Šawuška urges her to go quickly to warn Teššub to attack promptly before the monster grows even larger and stronger. Šawuška does so, and §§38–48 tell of the preparations for battle and the first fight between Teššub's group and Ullikummi, which the latter wins. Tašmišu advises the defeated Teššub to seek the help of Ea (§49). Ea discovers the secret of Ullikummi's power which is his sure footing on the right shoulder of Ubelluri (§§60–62). Ea and the Primeval Gods use the primeval copper cutting tool once used to cut apart heaven and earth to sever Ullikummi from his secure footing on Ubelluri's shoulder. Having now made it possible for Teššub to destroy Ullikummi, kindly Ea expresses sadness at the prospect of so many souls being dispatched to the gloomy realms of the dead (§65). The rest of the preserved text describes the second battle of Teššub against Ullikummi, which he apparently will win.

(Tablet I)

§1 [*The first part of the opening paragraph is broken away in all the copies of the story.*] (A i 1–4) [...] In whose mind is [there ...]? [... who] forms [a clever plan]? It is Kumarbi, Father of All Gods, of whom I sing.[122]

§2 (A i 5–8) Kumarbi forms in his mind a clever plan. He[123] raises an "Evil Day" in the person of a

[119] See n. 15 below.

[120] On birth and name-giving among the Hittites, see Hoffner 1968, 1998b.

[121] See Gen 24:33, where Abraham's servant likewise refuses the customary comforts of a guest until he has discharged his obligation to his master and delivered his message.

[122] The Song of Silver (Text C) provides another example of this opening. Its significance is explained in Hoffner (1988b).

[123] Copy B: "It is he who raises ..."

hostile man. He seeks hostile plans against Teššub. He raises a supplanter against Teššub.[124]

§ 3 (A i 9–10) Kumarbi [forms] a clever plan in his mind and aligns it like a bead (on a string).[125]

§ 4 (A i 11–16) When Kumarbi [had formed] a clever plan [before his mind], he promptly arose from his chair. In his hand he took a staff; [on his feet] he put the swift winds [as shoes]. He set out from the city Urkeš and arrived at Cold Lake.[126]

§ 5 (B i 13–20) Now in Cold Lake there lies a great rock: its length is three miles and its breadth is [...] and a half miles. His mind leaped forward upon what it has below[127] [...], and he slept with the rock. His penis [thrust(?)] into her. He "took" her five times; [again] he "took" her ten times. (*About thirty to thirty-five lines lost.*)

§ 6 (A ii 1–8) [On the ...] Kumarbi, Father of the Gods, is sitting. [...] saw Kumarbi and set out for the sea [...].

§ 7 (A ii 9–13) Impaluri began to speak words to the Sea God: "Because my lord [has ...-ed] me, [I went(?)] to the side of the sea. I saw [...] Kumarbi, the Father of the Gods, is sitting [...[128]]."

§ 8 (A ii 14–19, C ii 7–21) [When the Sea God] heard the words of Impaluri, the Sea God replied to Impaluri: "Impaluri, [my vizier]! [Hold] your ear [inclined] to [my words which I shall speak] to you. [Go] speak these weighty [words before Kumarbi]. Go speak to Kumarbi: 'Why have you come against my house in anger? Trembling has seized the house. Fear has seized the servants. In anticipation of you, cedar has already been broken (for fragrance). In anticipation of you, food has already been cooked. In anticipation of you, the musicians hold their ISHTAR-instruments in readiness day and night. Arise and come back home to my house.'" So Kumarbi arose, and Impaluri went before him. But Kumarbi [...[129]].

v Gen 27:35–36; Matt 1:21

So Kumarbi set out and went into the Sea God's house.

§ 9 (C ii 22–37) And the Sea God said: "Let them set a stool for Kumarbi to sit on. Let them set a table before him. Let them bring him food and drink. Let them bring beer for him to drink." The cooks brought cooked dishes. The cupbearers brought him sweet wine to drink. They drank once, twice, three times, four times, five times, six times, seven times, and Kumarbi [began] to say to Mukišanu, his vizier: "Mukišanu, my vizier! Give ear to the word that I shall speak to you. In your hand take a staff; [on your feet] put on shoes, and go [...]. In the waters [...] [Speak(?) these] words before the waters. [...] Kumarbi [...]". [*Break of about twenty lines.*]

§ 10 (A iii 1–9) [...] when from the dark [...] the watch arrived [...]. ... [...-ed] the stone. [They(?)] made her (i.e., the great rock) give birth [...]. The rock [...] the son of Kumarbi [was] glo[rious(?)].[130]

§ 11 (A iii 10–14) [The ...[131]] women made her give birth. The Fate Goddesses and the Mother Goddesses [lifted the child] and cradled [him] on Kumarbi's knees. Kumarbi began [to amuse] that boy, and he began to clean(?)[132] him, and he gave [to the child(?)] a fitting[133] name.[v]

§ 12 (A iii 15–25)[134] Kumarbi began to say to himself: "What name [shall I put on[135]] the child whom the Fate Goddesses and Mother Goddesses have given to me? He sprang forth from the body like a shaft. Henceforth[136] let Ullikummi be his name. Let him go up to heaven to kingship. Let him suppress the fine[137] city of Kummiya. Let him strike Teššub. Let him chop him up fine like chaff.[138] Let him grind him under foot [like] an ant. Let him snap off Tašmišu like a brittle reed. Let him scatter all the gods down

124 Copy B: "He who raises an 'Evil Day,' makes hostile plans against Teššub." This paragraph's four clauses form the structure A B A′ B′.

125 Possibly this line in the proemium gives a clue to the structure of the series. Each of the individual compositions (the "songs") is like a bead (Hittite *kunnan*) lined up (*išgareške-*) on a string (= the series). The imperfective (*-ške-*) form is appropriate for the action of threading beads one after the other on a string. Translating the verb as "to pierce, set" (so Puhvel, *HED* E/I 416–419, and García Trabazo 2002), masks what is intended here. See [*and*]*a-ma anturyaš* LÚ.MEŠ EN.NU.UN *kiššan išgariške* "Line up the interior guards as follows!" KUB 26.9+ i 13–14.

126 For this Cold Lake (*ikunta lūli*), see Singer 2002.

127 A reference to the rock's genitals.

128 García Trabazo (2002) restores "on a throne" here.

129 Goetze 1949, 182, restores: "[went forth] from [his house]," followed by García Trabazo 2002.

130 *la-lu-k[i?-...].*

131 Güterbock restores conjecturally *ḫašnuppalleš* "midwives."

132 Hitt. *kunkeške-*, the imperfective of *kunk-*. Translation guessed from this context.

133 Hitt. *šanezzi-* "first-class, fine, apt, fitting" (*CHD* Š 177 *šanezzi-* 2 d). The name is fitting, because *via* popular etymology from the Hurrian it could mean "enemy of (Teššub's city) Kummiya." Cf. "Let him suppress the fine city of Kummiya. Let him strike Teššub" (§ 12). On name-giving at birth see Hoffner 1968 and Hoffner 1998b.

134 This is a typical name-giving scene, on which see the comprehensive study of Hoffner 1968 and the updated summary in Hoffner 1998b. Hoffner compares biblical name-giving scenes in Genesis and elsewhere.

135 The verbal complex *laman dāi-* "to put a name" (*CHD* L–N 32 *laman* c 1′ a′) is common Indo-European stock for name-giving, found in Sanksrit, Greek and Slavic tradition (Watkins 2000:xxiii "nŏmen- dhē-").

136 For this force of *paiddu* (lit., "let him go") in phraseological constructions, see Hoffner 1968:202, n. 42; DeVries 1967:195, n. 134; and van den Hout 2003:201.

137 It is appropriate that in giving Ullikummi a "fitting" (*šanezzi-*) name (iii 14), the speaker should use the same adj. *šanezzi-* (in the sense of "fine") of the city he will suppress.

138 The use of similes ("let him/it ... like ...") is common in predictions, curses, and magic formulae in general; cf. *CHD* L–N 100 ff. (*maḫḫan* "like, as"), 145–146 (*mān* 1 "like").

from the sky like flour/meal.[139] Let him smash them [like] empty pottery bowls."[140],[w]

[*After the name-giving and associated predictions or spells, Kumarbi turns to the question of how to protect the infant "monster" from Teššub until he is grown enough to be safe.*]

§ 13 (A iii 26–36) When Kumarbi had finished saying these words, he said to himself: "To whom shall I give this child? Who will [take] him and treat him like something sent?[141] [Who ...? Who will carry the child] to the Dark Earth? The Sun God of [the Sky and the Moon God] must not see him.[142] Teššub, the heroic King of Kummiya, must not [see him] and kill him. Šawuška, the Queen of Nineveh, the one of the ... woman, must not see him and snap him off like a brittle reed."[x]

§ 14 (A iii 37–45) Kumarbi began to say to Impaluri: "Impaluri, give ear to my words, the words which I speak to you. In your hand take a staff; on your feet put shoes like the swift winds. Go to the *irširra*-deities[143] and speak before the *irširra*- deities these weighty words: 'Come! Kumarbi, Father of the Gods, is calling you to the house of the gods. [You do not know[144]] the matter about which he calls you. So come quickly." '

§ 15 (A iii 46–48, C iii 4–8) " 'The [*irširra*- deities] will take the child and [carry] it to the [Dark] Earth. The *irširra*- deities [...], the powerful ones(?).[145] But he [will] not [...[146]] to the great [*god*]s." ' And [when] Impaluri [heard these words, he took] a staff in his hand, he put [shoes on his feet]. Impaluri [went forth] and came to the [*iršir*]*ra*- deities.

w Cf. Ps 2:9; Isa 30:14

x Exod 2:1–10; Matt 3:13–23

§ 16 (C iii 9–19) [Impaluri] began [to speak] words to the *irširra*- deities: "Come. Kumarbi, Father of the Gods, [is calling] you. You do not know the matter about which [he is calling] you. So come quickly." So when the *irširra*- deities heard the words, [they hastened] and hurried. They [rose from their chairs], made the trip in one stage, and arrived where Kumarbi was. Then Kumarbi began to speak to the *irširra*- deities:

§ 17 (C iii 20–27) "Take this [child] and treat it like something sent.[147] Carry it to the Dark Earth. Hasten, hurry. Place it on Ubelluri's[148] right shoulder. Each day let it grow one *AMMATU* higher. Each month let it grow IKU higher.[149] Whatever stone strikes(?) its head, may it do it no harm(?)."[150]

§ 18 (A iv 6–12) Now when the *irširra*- deities heard [these] words, they took [the child] from Kumarbi's knees. The *irširra*- deities lifted the child and pressed [it] to [their] breast as close as (their) garment. The *ir*[*širra*- deities(?)] lifted it, (namely,) [the chil]d and cradled it on Ellil's knees. Ellil lifted his eyes and saw the child. It was standing before the god, its body made of basalt stone.

§ 19 (A iv 13–19) Then Ellil began to say to himself, "Who is he, this child whom the Fate Goddesses and Mother Goddesses have raised again?[151] Who can [any longer[152]] behold[153] the intense struggles of the great gods? This evil (plot) can only be Kumarbi's. Just as Kumarbi raised Teššub,[154] so (now) he has raised against him this Basalt as a supplanter."

---

139 The scribe of copy A has erased something and written the word "birds" over it. Later in the Song of Ullikummi (§ 69) this phrase occurs with the word "meal" (*memal*) instead of "birds." The usual object of the verb "scatter" (*išḫuwa-*) is dry particulate material like flour or meal.

140 Cf. the use of curses involving destroying cups and other objects in the Hurrian myth "The Song of Release" (Hoffner 1998a:68–73). Biblical: Ps 2:9; Isa 30:14.

141 The idea behind *uppeššar* "something sent" here is a valuable item that is committed to another to keep safe and eventually return, i.e., a charge. Haas (2006:162) uses a nice phrase "ihn als ein Gepäckstück tarnen," i.e. disguise him as a harmless bit of baggage!

142 These negative imperatives (Hitt. *lē* rendered here "must not") can be seen as part of the father's protective spells pronounced over the child at name-giving. They do not merely express a faint hope, but rather represent something akin to a protective prophecy: the words are intended to prevent Šawuška from seeing the child prematurely, while he is still small and "snapping him off like a brittle reed," whereas the earlier prediction assures that Ullikummi will snap Tašmišu like a brittle reed (see § 12).

143 The *irširra*-deities seem to be divine wetnurses and custodians of children. The name is an agent noun based on the verb root *irš-* "to suckle" + agent-forming suffix *-iri-* + pl. definite article *-na* (Haas 1994, 309; 2006, 162 n. 51).

144 Restored from § 16 C iii 13.

145 Restoring [... UR.]SAG-*li*ḪI.A-*uš*, i.e., *ḫaštaliuš*; cf. § 36 (Tablet II B ii 15) and n. 145.

146 Restoring "be visible" (García Trabazo 2002:197).

147 Copy C iii 20 mistook the word for *šuppeššar* "something sacred," but B iii 10 preserves the correct form *uppeššar* "something sent"; cf. § 13 n. 141.

148 We are introduced here to the god Ubelluri, the Hurrian Atlas, who lives under the earth and sea and bears heaven and earth on his shoulders, and takes no notice of what transpires above him. He is considered unaligned and impartial in the struggle between the partisans of Kumarbi and Teššub (Haas 2006:132). On this character see von Schuler 1965:206 s.v. It stands to reason that, since heaven and earth were constructed to rest upon Ubelluri's shoulders, he must be one of the oldest of the divine beings.

149 This suggests a 1:30 ratio between the *AMMATU* and the IKU. The absolute value of these units is currently disputed.

150 The meaning is uncertain. The Hittite is literally translated: "Whatever stone is struck upon its head, may it be clothed upon its eye(s)."

151 It is possible that the word "again" alludes to an earlier "song" in the Kumarbi series where the Fate Goddesses and the Mother Goddesses raised another offspring of Kumarbi. See the introduction to the Hurrian myths.

152 *nam-ma* restored here on the basis of Tablet II B i 32′ (§ 33).

153 Lit., "see" (Hitt. *uškezzi*).

154 Actually, as we know from the *Song of Emergence*, he was forced to give birth to him, but did not "raise" (*šallanu-*) him in the same sense that he does these later beings.

§20 (A iv 20–21) When Ellil [finished speaking these] words, [they placed(?)] the child on Ubelluri's right shoulder [like a shaft[155]].
§21 (A iv 22–26) The Basalt kept growing. The strong [god]s(?)[156] kept raising it. Each day it grew one *AMMATU* higher; each month it grew one IKU higher. Whatever stone struck(?) its head did it no harm(?).[157]
§22 (A iv 27–32) When the fifteenth day arrived (and the Basalt had grown to a height of half an IKU), the Stone was high: it was standing like a shaft with the sea coming up to its knees. The Stone protruded from the water. In height it was like a [...]. The sea reached to the place of its [...] belt like a garment. The Basalt was lifted up like a ....[158] In the sky above it meets temples and a *kuntarra*-shrine.[y]
§23 (A iv 33–36) The Sun God looked [down] from the sky and saw Ullikummi. Ullikummi saw[159] the Sun God of the Sky. The Sun God began to say to himself, "What quickly growing deity [stands] there in the sea? His body is unlike that of all the other gods."
§24 (A iv 37–40) The Sun God of the Sky turned his rays and proceeded to the sea. When the Sun God reached the sea, he held his hand to his forehead.[160] [He got a] close [look] at Ullikummi. From anger his appearance changed.
§25 (A iv 41–48) When the Sun God of the Sky saw the god E[llil], he turned his rays around again and proceeded to where Teššub was. [Tašmišu] saw the Sun God coming and said to Teššub, "Why is the Sun God of the Sky, [King] of the Lands, coming? On what business does he come? The matter must be [important]. It must be something [not] to be disregarded. The struggle must be severe. The battle must be severe. It must entail uproar in heaven and famine and death in the land."
§26 (A iv 49–50) Teššub said to Tašmišu, "Let them set up a chair for him to sit in; let them lay a table for him to eat from."

y Gen 11:1–9

z Gen 24:33

§27 (A iv 51–54) And while they were speaking thus, the Sun God approached them. A chair was set up for him to sit in, but he wouldn't sit down. A table was set for him to eat from, but he wouldn't touch a thing. A cup was offered to him, but he wouldn't put his lip to it.[161,z]
§28 (A iv 55–58) ...[162] Teššub began to say to the Sun God, "Is it because the chamberlain set up the chair so badly, that you will not sit down? Is it because (my) table man who set the table is so bad, that you will not eat? Is it because the cupbearer offered you [the cup] so badly, that you will not drink?"
§29 (Colophon) "Tablet one of the Song of Ullikummi [...]."

(Tablet 2)
§30 [*The beginning is broken. Apparently after explaining why he will not observe the amenities of hospitality until he has delivered his urgent message, the Sun God tells Teššub the bad news about Ullikummi.*]
§31 (B i 1–13) [When] Teššub heard [these words], his appearance changed because of his anger. But [to the Sun God of the Sky] Teššub said, "Let [the food on the table] become appealing[163] [to you] and eat [your fill]. Let [the wine in the cup] become appealing [to you] and drink your fill. [Then get up] and go up to the sky." [When] the Sun God of the Sky heard [these words], [he] rejoiced. [The food on the table] became appealing [to him], so that he ate. [The wine in his cup] became appealing [to him], so that he drank. [The Sun God] got up and went up to the sky.
§32 (B i 14–28) After (the departure) of the Sun God of the Sky, Teššub formed a plan in his mind. Teššub and Tašmišu joined hands and went out of the *kuntarra*-shrine and the temple. Šawuška too came from the sky, looking formidable. Šawuška said to herself, "Where are my two brothers running to?" Boldly(?) Šawuška approached. She came up

155 Restored from §22 and other passages in this text. The word *šiya(t)tal* (Starke 1990:200–205 would read *šietri-*) denotes a shaft or javelin (*CHD* Š, 3:339–340). As the *CHD* notes: "The translation "javelin" for *š.* satisfies most of the demands posed by the several Hitt. contexts as well as those of word formation. The comparison of the stone monster Ullikummi (a) and mountains (b) along with the Akk. parallels for describing mountains as 'standing up like the sharpened blades of swords' or 'spear-heads' as pointed out by Güterbock, JCS 6:36, fits that meaning without any problem."

156 Read A.ḪI.A "waters" (Goetze 1949:182; García Trabazo 2002), or [DING]IR.M[EŠ]-*e*?-*e*[*š*?] (Güterbock 1946). For Goetze's reading to be correct, one would have to read *da-aš-sa-mu-uš* A.ḪI.A[*-an-te-eš*] for which there is no space on the line. A.ḪI.A would have to cover an ergative **widananteš* instead of the normal neuter pl. *widār*. For a neuter noun cannot serve as subject of a transitive verb according to Hittite grammar. With no phonetic complement possible, it is unlikely that this is the reading.

157 Thus Kumarbi's prophecy of §17 (C iii 20–27) begins to be fulfilled.

158 Hittite/Luwian *maldani-*. Cf. *CHD* L–N 135 "(meaning unknown)"; *HEG* L–M, 110–111. All sorts of guesses have been made: "tower" (Goetze, *ANET* 123; Haas 2006:163), "mushroom/toadstool" (Hoffner 1967:60), "sledgehammer/grindstone" (Puhvel 2004:28 sub *malatt-*), "siege ramp" (Stefanini 1988:251–252), but without further clear references it is impossible to know the meaning. Of the two possible contextual clues, in view of Ullikummi's being called the "swiftly rising god" (*nu-*[*ut-t*]*a-ri-ia-an* DINGIR-*LIM-in*, §60), I prefer identifying the *maldani-* as something that grows tall quickly, like the beanstalk of *Jack and the Beanstalk*.

159 See introduction to Text E.

160 A gesture of dismay.

161 Cf. Gen. 24:33 and n. 3 above.

162 The two signs cannot be read [*n*]*a-aš*! (so García Trabazo), since (EGIR-*pa*) *memiškiwan daiš* does not take third person subject clitics (*-aš, -e, -at*), cf. GHL 280–283 (§§18.13–18.19).

163 Again our *Leitmotif* word *šanezzi-* "fine, appropriate."

to her brothers. Then they all joined hands and went up Mount Hazzi. (Teššub), the King of Kummiya, set his eye. He set his eye upon the dreadful Basalt. He beheld the dreadful Basalt, and because of anger his appearance changed.

§ 33 (B i 29–41) Teššub sat down on the ground, and his tears flowed like streams. Tearfully Teššub said, "Who can [any longer] behold the struggle of such a one? Who can go on fighting? Who can behold the terrors of such a one any longer?" Šawuška said to Teššub, "My brother, he doesn't have even a little intelligence,[164] but battle prowess has been given to him tenfold. And you do not know the intelligence of the child whom [the ...-s] will bear to them. [...] we are in the house of Ea. If I were a [...] man(?), you would be [...]. But I will go [and ...]." [*Text breaks away here until the end of the column.*]

§ 34 (B ii 1–4) [*Preserves only beginning of the lines.*] "They who [...], as the watery d[eep(?) ..., so] let the [... s] be [... ed]."

§ 35 (B ii 5–12) [Šawuška(?)] dressed and ornamented herself [with ...]. From Nineveh she [came to the sea(?). She took(?)] the BALAG.DI and the *galgalturi*- instruments in her hand. Šawuška set out. She fumigated with cedar. She struck the BALAG.DI and the *galgalturi*. She shook the "gold things,"[165] and she took up a song, and heaven and earth sang along with her.

§ 36 (B ii 13–25) Šawuška keeps singing and putting on herself seashells and pebbles (as adornment). A great wave(?) ⟨arose⟩ out of the sea. The great wave(?) said to Šawuška, "For whose benefit are your singing? For whose benefit are you filling your mouth with wind? The man (*meaning Ullikummi*) is deaf: he can[not] hear. He is blind in his eyes: he cannot see. He has no feelings. So go away, Šawuška, and find your brother before he (*Ullikummi*) becomes really powerful,[166] before the skull of his head becomes really terrifying."

§ 37 (B ii 26–30) When Šawuška heard this, she extinguished [the burning cedar]; she laid down [the BALAG.DI and *galgalturi*- instruments], and [she stilled] the "gold things." Tearfully she set out [for ...]. [*Two or three more lines badly damaged.*]

§ 38 [*Ten lines at the beginning of column iii are very badly damaged. Teššub is addressing Tašmišu*:] (B iii 3–14) "Let them mix fodder. Let them [bring] fine oil and anoint the horns of the bull named Šerišu.[167] Let them plate with gold the tail of the bull named Tella. Let them turn the axle(?). On the inside let them move their strong things. On the outside let them release strong stones for the ... Let them call forth the stormy weather. Let them summon the rains and winds which break the rocks at ninety IKU's, which cover eight hundred. Let them bring forth from the bedchamber the lightning that flashes terribly.[aa] Let them put forward the wagons. Afterward (you) prepare and ready them, and bring me back word."

aa Psa 135:7; Job 38:22; Jer 10:13; 51:16

bb Isa 13:13; Ezek 38:20; Hag 2:6, 21; Matt 24:29

§ 39 (B iii 15–24) Now when Tašmišu heard the words, he hurried and hastened. [He drove] the bull Šerišu [here] from the pasture. [He drove] the bull Tella [here] from Mount Imgarra. [He tied them up] in the outer gate complex. He brought fine oil and [anointed the horns] of the bull Šerišu. He [plated with gold] the tail of the bull Tella. [He turned] the axle(?). [On the inside] he [moved their strong things]. On the outside he released [the strong] stones [for the.... He called forth the stormy weather. He summoned the rains and winds] which [break the rocks for a distance of ninety IKUs]. [*The rest of column iii is broken away.*][168]

§ 40 [*In the few broken lines which remain of column iv the first battle between Teššub and Ullikummi seems to be described.*] (B iv 1–14) [...] at five hundred meters (Teššub) approached for battle. He held a weapon and wagons. He brought forth clouds from the sky. Teššub set his eye upon the Basalt and saw it. In height it was [...]. But subsequently it tripled its height.

§ 41 (B iv 15 ff.) Then Teššub said to Tašmišu, "[...] wagons [...] let them go [...] summon [...]" and he went [...] words [...]. [About twenty lines lost.]

§ 42 (Colophon) Tablet two, incomplete, of the Song [of Ullikummi].

(Tablet 3)

§ 43 [*Beginning thirty lines lost.*] (A i 2–24) When the gods heard the word, they prepared the wagons and assigned [...]. Aštabi sprang [upon his wagon like a ...] and [...-ed on] the wagon. [...] he arrayed the wagons, [...] Aštabi thundered [...], and with thunder Aštabi [...] let go down to the sea. They drew [water with a ...]. And Aštabi [...-ed]. Seventy gods seized [...]. But still [...] was not able. And Aštabi [...], and the seventy gods [fell(?)] down into the sea. [...] the Basalt, (his) body [...] and he shook the sky, he [...]-ed [...]. [...] shook out the [sky][bb] like an empty[169] garment. The Basalt grew [...] tall. Before him the height was 1,900 and ... DANNAs. It stands below on the Dark Earth. The Basalt is lifted up like a ....[170] It meets the *kuntarra*-shrine and the temples. Its height is (now) 9,000 DANNAs. The Basalt [...]. Its width

---

164 Hittite *māl* (*CHD* L–N, 124–125; Rieken 1999:49–51; *HED* M 20–21) means "intelligence, wits, wisdom." It is contrasted here with physical prowess and strength.

165 Some kind of rattle used to accompany singing and dancing.

166 Hitt. denominative verb *ḫaštališzi*, based on the adj. *ḫaštali*- "valiant, heroic, powerful."

167 Šeri (or Šerišu) is the name of one of Teššub's twin bulls, the other being Tella.

168 All of the foregoing describes the preparations for Teššub to go into battle on his bull-drawn cart (or chariot).

169 Or: "unornamented."

170 Cf. n. 40 above.

is (also) 9,000 DANNAs. It took its stand before the gates of the city Kummiya (Teššub's city) like a shaft. The Basalt penned up Ḫebat in the temple, so that Ḫebat no longer hears the message of the gods, nor does she see Teššub or Šuwaliyat with her eyes.

§ 44 (A i 25–29) Ḫebat spoke these words to Takiti: "[...] I do not hear the important word of Teššub [my] lord. Nor do I hear the message of Šuwaliyat and all the gods. Perhaps that Ullikummi, the Basalt, of whom they speak, has overcome my husband, the mighty [Storm-god(?)[171]]."

§ 45 (A i 30–33) Again Ḫebat said to Takiti, "Hear my words. Take a staff in hand; put shoes on your feet like the winged winds. Go [to ...]. Perhaps the Basalt has killed [my husband, Teššub, the] mighty king. [Bring] me [back] word."

§ 46 (A i 34–37) [When Takiti heard the words], he hastened and hurried. [He ...] drew forth [...] goes. But there is no road [...] to Ḫebat [he came(?)].

§ 47 (A i 38) [Takiti said to Ḫebat], "My lady, [...]" [*About twenty lines to the bottom of column i lost.*]

§ 48 (A ii 1–16) When Tašmišu heard Teššub's words, he quickly arose, [took] a staff in hand, put shoes on his feet like the winged winds, and went up on the high watchtowers (of his castle). He took [his place] facing Ḫebat (and said), "[...] me to the Little Place[172] until he fulfills the years which have been decreed for him." Now when Ḫebat saw Tašmišu, she almost fell down from the roof. Had she taken a step, she would have fallen down from the roof. But her female attendants seized her and didn't let go of her. And when Tašmišu had finished speaking the word, he came down from the watchtowers and went to Teššub. Tašmišu said to Teššub, "Where shall we sit down there upon Mount Kandurna? [If(?)] we sit down on Mount Kandurna, another(?) will be sitting on Mount Lalapaduwa. Where will we transport [...]? Up in heaven there will be no king."

§ 49 (A ii 17–26) [Tašmišu] spoke again to Teššub, "[Hear] my words, my lord Teššub. Give [ear] to the words that I speak to you. Come, let us go to Apzuwa, before Ea [...]. Let us ask for the tablets containing the ancient words. [When] we come before the gate of the house of Ea, we will bow [five times] at Ea's door and [again] five times at Ea's inner door(?). [When] we come [before] Ea, we will bow fifteen times before Ea. Perhaps [it will become pleasant] to Ea by means of ...; perhaps Ea [will listen(?)] and have pity on us and show us [the tablets containing] the ancient [words]."

§ 50 (A ii 27–32) [When Teššub] heard the words [of Tašmišu], he hastened [and hurried]. He quickly arose from his chair. [Teššub and Tašmišu] joined hands and made the trip in one stage, and they [arrived] at Apzuwa. [Teššub] went to the house of Ea. [He bowed five times] at the first [door], he bowed five times at the inner door(?). [When] they arrived before Ea, he bowed [fifteen times before Ea].

[*Seven lines of very fragmentary text follow and then the text is completely lost.*]

§ 51 (A ii 3–6) [...] began to speak [...] to me the word [...]. You, O Teššub, [...] before me. Let [...] stand up before [...]. And wor[d(s) ...].

§ 52 (A ii 7–12; aggregate line count 50′–55′) When Tašmišu [heard] the words, he ran forth [from ...], he [kissed(?)] him on the knees three times; he kissed him on the soles of his feet(?) four times. He fought/struggled, and [...] to him [...] while to him [...] to the Basalt death(?) on the right [shoulder ...].

§ 53 (A ii 13–19) Ea spoke to Tašmišu, "[...] on Mount Kandurna [...] on Mount Lalapaduwa [...] on the Dark Earth [... the ancient], fatherly, grandfatherly [tablets, and bring] forth the copper cutting tool, and [cut] off [Ullikummi, the Basalt], under his feet. [...]"

§ 54 (A ii 20–23) [When] Ea [finished speaking] the words, [he ...] in Mount [Kandurna ..., ... in] Mount Lalapaduwa [... said] to himself [...]

§ 55 (F i? 1–11) [*In a short and broken fragment Teššub meets Ea, and the latter is angered by his presence.*]

§ 56 (A iii 1–10) [...] joined hands [...] while [...] came forth from the assembly [... Ellil(?)] began to weep [and said], "May you live, Ea! [...] who comes back before [...] the aroma(?) of the gods [...]. Why did you/he(?) cross it? [...]"

§ 57 (A iii 11–18) Ea [said] to Ellil, "[Don't you know, Ellil? Has no one brought] you word? [Do you not know him whom Kumarbi created] as a supplanter against Teššub? [The Basalt which] grew [in the water is 9,000 DANNAs] in height. He is lifted up like a ... [...] against you [...] primeval [...")].

§ 58 (A iii 19–22) [*Five more fragmentary lines, which mention the "sacred temples."*]

§ 59 (A iii 24–29) When Ea [finished speaking] the words, [he went] to Ubelluri. [...] Ubelluri [lifted] his eyes [and saw Ea]. Ubelluri [spoke words] to Ea, "May you live long, O Ea!" [Ea stood] up [and spoke] a greeting to Ubelluri: "[May you] live, [Ubelluri, you] on whom the heaven and earth are built!"

§ 60 (A iii 30–39) Ea spoke to Ubelluri, "Don't you know, Ubelluri? Has no one brought you word? Do you not know the swiftly rising god whom Kumarbi created against the gods, and that Kumarbi is ... planning death against Teššub, and is creating against him a supplanter? Do you not know the

171 Text: x[o]x-*an*; perhaps ^{D}U-*an* or ^{D}IŠKUR-*an*?

172 That is, he must leave his throne.

Basalt which grew in the water? It is lifted up like a ....[173] It has blocked heaven, the holy temples, and Ḫebat. Is it because you, Ubelluri, are remote from the Dark Earth, that you are unaware of this swiftly rising god?"[174]

§ 61 (A iii 40–44) Ubelluri spoke to Ea, "When they built heaven and earth upon me, I was aware of nothing. And when they came and cut heaven and earth apart with a copper cutting tool, I was even unaware of that. But now something makes my right shoulder hurt, and I don't know who this god is."

§ 62 (A iii 45–47) When Ea heard those words, he went around Ubelluri's right shoulder, and (there) the Basalt stood on Ubelluri's right shoulder like a shaft.

§ 63 (A iii 48–55) Ea spoke to the Primeval Gods, "Hear my words, O Primeval Gods, who know the primeval words. Open again the old, fatherly, grandfatherly storehouses. Let them bring forth the seal of the primeval fathers and with it reseal them. Let them bring forth the primeval copper cutting tool with which they cut apart heaven and earth.[cc] We will cut off Ullikummi, the Basalt, under his feet, him whom Kumarbi raised against the gods as a supplanter (of Teššub)."

cc Gen 1

§ 64 [*The first twenty-six lines of column iv are broken away.*] (A iv 4–8) Tašmišu [. . .] bowed down [. . .] began to say [. . .]. In his body the [. . .]s have been changed. On his head the hairs changed their appearance.

§ 65 (A iv 9–12) Ea spoke to Tašmišu, "Go away from before me, my son. Do not stand up before me. My mind within me has become sad/angry, for with my eyes I have seen the dead, seeing the dead in the Dark Earth, and they are standing like dusty and . . .[175] ones"

§ 66 (A iv 13–20) Ea spoke to Tašmišu, "First I routed [. . .] Ullikummi, the Basalt. Now go fight him again. Don't let it stand any longer in the gate(s) of the . . . like a shaft" Tašmišu heard and rejoiced. He clapped three times, and up in the sky the gods heard. He clapped a second time, and Teššub, the valiant King of Kummiya, heard. Then they came to the place of assembly, and all the gods began to bellow like cattle at Ullikummi.

§ 67 (A iv 21–22) Teššub leaped up into his wagon like a . . . and with thunder came down to the sea. Teššub fought the Basalt.

§ 68 (A iv 23–24)[176] The Basalt spoke to Teššub, "What can I say to you, Teššub? Keep attacking. Be of good courage, for Ea, King of Wisdom, stands on your side"

§ 69 (A iv 25–28) "What can I say to you, Teššub? I held [counsel(?)], and before my mind I lined up wisdom like (a string of) bead(s) as follows: 'I will go up to heaven to kingship. I will take to myself Kummiya, [the gods'] holy temples, and the *kuntarra*-shrine. I will scatter the gods down from the sky like flour."

§ 70 (A iv 29–39) Ullikummi spoke again to Teššub, "[Behave] like a man again [. . .]. Ea, the King of Wisdom, stands on your side [. . .] he takes away. And let them go [. . .] to the mountains. Let them [. . .] in the land the high [. . .]. My liver and lung [. . .] let them go. In the land [. . .] those who [. . .]ed up, [. . .] let them [. . .]" [. . .] said, "Long ago [. . .] me [. . .]. What name [shall I give] to him, [. . .]?" [*Rest broken away.*]

§ 71 (An unplaced fragment, III E2 iii 1–5) [. . .] the Basalt [. . .] he performs [. . .] Teššub, . . . the god Ea, king [of wisdom, . . .] joined your side [. . .]

§ 72 (E2 iii 6–13) I spoke wisdom to myself [. . .] took wisdom into [. . .] mind [. . .] spoke as follows: ["'. . .] let him go up to heaven; [let him take] Kummiya, [the fine city; let him strike Teššub, heroic King] of Kummiya; [let him scatter] the gods [down from the sky like flour.]" [*The rest is broken away.*]

173 Cf. n. 40 above.

174 Cf. n. 40 above.

175 The word bears the gloss marker wedges, which may indicate it is Luwian: *:gullušiuš*. The meaning is unknown.

176 In §§ 68–69 Ullikummi, the basalt monster, speaks to Teššub during the fight. His words are half mockery ("Why are you worried? You have Ea on your side!") and half bravado ("I will . . ., I will ......"). This is the kind of speech that typically precedes battlefield engagements. For the extra-biblical picture, see Glück 1964 and Liverani 2001:113, cited by Hoffner 2009a:79 (commentary on text 2.1, an Old Hittite letter). For many biblical examples, see those cited in Revell 1997.

REFERENCES

Text: CTH 345; complete apparatus in Pecchioli Daddi and Polvani 1990:142–143; García Trabazo 2002:176; and online at http://www.hethport.uni-wuerzburg.de/hetkonk/; and E. Rieken et al. (ed.), hethiter.net/: CTH 345.I.1 (TX 2009-08-31, TRde 2009-08-29). *Transliteration and translation*: Güterbock 1946; 1952; Meriggi 1953; Korolëv 1999; García Trabazo 2002:176–251; E. Rieken et al. (ed.), hethiter.net/: CTH 345.I.1 (TX 2009-08-31, TRde 2009-08-29). *Translation*: Goetze 1955:121–125; Güterbock 1961:164–171; DeVries 1967:31–37, 56–58; Vieyra 1970:522–524, 546–554; Komoróczy 1973; Jakob-Rost 1977:43–58; Kühne 1978:151–152; Güterbock 1978:211–253; Haas 1982:149–160; Bernabé 1987:171–199; Hoffner 1990:55–65; Pecchioli Daddi and Polvani 1990:142–162; Ünal 1994. *Studies*: Güterbock 1948; Otten 1949; Güterbock 1961:164–171; DeVries 1967:31–37, 52–147, 168–178; Komoróczy 1973:21–45; Hoffner 1975:138–139; Salvini 1977:73–91 (comments on the Hurrian sources); Güterbock 1978:237–241; Burkert 1979; Polvani 1992; Haas 1994:88–96; Popko 1995:124–126; Giorgieri 2001; Janda 2001; Haas 2006:156–175; Gane 2008 (compares with the Little Horn of the biblical Book of Daniel); Alaura 2011.

HIEROGLYPHIC LUWIAN COMPOSITIONS

KARKAMIŠ A11b+c (4.7)

J. D. Hawkins

This pair of stone slabs ("orthostats") formed the inscribed door-jambs of the building, the dedication of which they describe. This was erected by Katuwa, the last of a four-generation line of "Country Lords," the House of Suhi (I), who seem to have dominated Karkamiš throughout the 10th century BCE. Katuwa was the most active builder in the area of the city so far revealed by excavation. These two door-jambs originally belonged in the gatehouse of the building entered between the two lines of reliefs, the Warriors' Procession and that of the women and gazelle bearers (the "Processions of Karhuha and Kubaba" described in the text), but they were removed by the later ruler Yariri in the course of his remodeling of the entry by the addition of the "Royal Buttress" with the inscription of KARKAMIŠ A6 (4.12, see below). He re-used them face down as the threshold slabs in the "King's Gate" where they were found by the excavators.

§1. I am Katuwa the Ruler, loved by the gods, Country Lord of the city Karkamiš, son of Suhi the Country Lord, grandson of Astuwalamanza[1] the Country Lord.
§2. This city of my father and grandfather was (in the hand) of Ni(?)nuwi.[2]
§3. He reached out in vain.
§4. and him together with Uratarhunda's grandsons[3] I *exiled*(?),
§5. and from them my SAPALALI city Ipanisi, also my SAPALALI *domains*(?) of the city Muziki [I took].
§6. and I (re)built it.
§7. In the year that I *carried off*(?) the chariot(ry) of the city Kawa[4]
§8. – to those territories my fathers, grandfathers and *ancestors* had not marched,
§9. but me my lord Tarhunza, Karhuha and Kubaba loved for my rule,
§10. and for me they sat on the HUHURPALI,[5]
§11. and they marched before me,
§12. and I ravaged those countries,
§13. and I brought in the *spoils*(?),
§14. and victorious I came up from those countries
§15. – these upper stories[6] in that year I built.
§16. I conceived my lord Karhuha's and Kubaba's procession.
§17. and I set them up on this plinth.
§18a. The blood offerings for them are this:
b. together with the gods: annual bread;
c. for Karhuha: one ox and a sheep;
d. for Kubaba: one ox and one sheep;
e. for the god Sarku: one sheep and a *lamb*(?);
f. one sheep for the male gods;
g. [one shee]p for the fe[male gods ...].
§19. [He wh]o approaches these [gods?] with evil,
§20. or approaches these upper stories with evil,
§21. or if they shall pass down to one
§22. who shall ... them,
§23. and shall [...] these orthostats in their place,
§24. or shall erase my name on these orthostats,
§25. against him may Tarhunza, Karhuha and Kubaba, and the Storm-God of Mount Arputa and the gods of the river-land of the river Sakur litigate!
§26. From him may they sever(?) virility,
§27. and from her may they sever(?) femininity,
§28. from him may they not accept male issue(?),
§29. and from her may they not accept female issue!
§30. Since I took away for myself this city from Uratarhunda's grandsons by force,
§31. and since I did not exile(?) it,
§32. let these gods be heard!
§33. As timber became available to me for these upper stories,
§34. these upper stories of the gatehouse[6] for Ana my dear wife with love in that year I built.

1 Name formerly read Astuwadamanza.

2 Name (first syllable, reading uncertain) of person understood to be the leader of the group referred to as "Uratarhunda's grandsons."

3 The earliest Karkamiš inscription known at present is a stele of Uratarhunda entitled "Great King, Hero, king of the land of Karkamiš," set up for him by the Country Lord Suhi (I). From this we may understand §2–5 as recording a struggle for control of Karkamiš between the competing lines of great Kings and Country Lords, in which the latter were ultimately victorious.

4 I formerly suggested an identification with Que, the Cilician plain, but this is now seen on ÇINEKÖY (see 4.19 below) to have been written Hiyawa.

5 Suggested to have been part of a war chariot (Melchert 1988).

6 The "upper stories (of the gatehouse)" (§§15, 33–34) would typically have been built in wood on a ground floor of mud-brick with orthostat facings to the lower walls. The gatehouse is shown as a pictogram to be a towered structure entered through an arch, above which is a first-floor window of the wooden women's quarters.

REFERENCES

Hawkins 2000:101–108, pls. 14–17.

KARKAMIŠ A6 (4.8)

J. D. Hawkins

This inscription stands on the "Royal Buttress," accompanying the sculptures of that monument: in the center the author Yariri leading the young ruler Kamani, followed on the right by rows of children in two registers and a nurse holding a baby and leading an animal; and round the corner to the left, a row of beardless armed guards. The figures of Kamani, Yariri, the children and the baby are identified by name in adjoining epigraphs. The Royal Buttress was a later, modifying addition, ca. 800 BCE, to Katuwa's monumental gatehouse flanked by the relief processions of Karhuha and Kubaba. Katuwa's inscribed doorjambs had been removed and re-used by Yariri (see 4.11 see above).

Yariri was not himself a paramount ruler, but apparently a guardian of his deceased lord's heir and children. He describes his fame, his guardianship of the heir Kamani, for whom he built the structure ("seat"), and his siblings, and lays the building under a protective curse.

§1. I am Yariri the Ruler,[1] the … … Prince, far famed in the West and the East, the Prince loved by the gods.
§2. My name because of my rule the gods – Tarhunza and Tiwaza[2] – made pass to the sky,
§3. my name the gods made pass abroad,
§4. and for me they heard it on one side in Egypt,
§5. and on another side they heard it in Babylon
§6. and on another side they heard (it) among the Musa, the Muska and the Sura.[3]
§7. To every king I reconciled the subjects.
§8. When I built this seat for Kamani my lord's[4] son,
§9. he marched to this precinct,
§10. I set him up on high,
§11. and he mounted above everyone,
§12. as he was a child.
§13. With him I made his brothers
§14. and those who were of *fighting*(?)[5]
§15. with honor to them I thereupon put knuckle-bones(?)[5] in the hand,
§16. and those among them who were of *ploughing*(?)[6]
§17. with honor to them I thereupon put *spinning-tops*(?)[6] in the hand.
§18. As Kamani was a child,
§19. I will stand him … three-four times,
§20. and I will raise (him) up before Tarhunza, Tiwaza and Kubaba, also all the gods,
§21. and I will make (him) say:
§22. "O Kubaba, you will make them grow in my hand!"
§23. As he marched to this precinct,
§24. I built this seat for him.
§25. If this seat will pass down to any king
§26. who will take it …,
§27. – let him not take a stone from these stones,
§28. nor take away a stele for a stele –
§29. or who erases my name,
§30. or who takes away one from these children or from these eunuchs,[7]
§31. (for) him may Nikarawa's dogs eat up his head!

1 "Ruler" (*tarwani-*) is a title which may be borne by one ruler subordinate to another, in this case Yariri's "lord," apparently deceased, for whom he is acting as regent (see n. 4, below). It has been speculatively suggested from the somewhat strange way in which Yariri is depicted that he might have been a eunuch minister acting as regent and guardian (see n. 6).

2 Tiwaza – the Sun-God.

3 The Musa, Muska and Sura are probably to be identified as Anatolian peoples: The Lydian (Musioi), the Phrygians (Muski) and perhaps the Urartians (Sura).

4 The "lord" is Astiruwa, named below in 4.13, §16, who may be understood to be deceased.

5 Some of the children are shown holding knuckle-bones, used widely in antiquity as a children's game. The passage §§14–15 may best be understood if the word guessed to mean "knuckle-bones" (*katuninzi*) is the same stem as the word for "fighting" (*katunas*). These children would be marked either symbolically or punningly to become warriors.

6 Other children hold spinning-tops, and as above, it may be that the word for "spinning-tops" (*tarpunanzi*) resembled the word for "ploughing" (*tarpunas*), so these children would be marked for farmers.

7 In the context of this curse, "taking away one of the children" may easily be understood as damaging one of their images. Likewise, in the case of the eunuchs (as this word *wasinasi-* has been argued to mean), see Hawkins 2002. This may be understood to refer to the beardless guards depicted on the left side of the Royal Buttress.

REFERENCES

Hawkins 2000:123–128, pls. 31–33.

KARKAMIŠ A15b (4.9)

J. D. Hawkins

This inscription is preserved on the side of a cylindrical stone base, of which half is lost, taking with it the end of line 1, the beginning and end of lines 2 and 3, and the beginning of line 4. A separate part of the inscription ran in a circle around the flat top; half of this too is lost and the surviving part is worn and difficult to read, but appears to deal with the erection of the monument. A square mortise hole cut in the top would probably have served to support a statue, perhaps the one referred to in §10.

In the text as preserved, Yariri boasts his ascendancy in Karkamiš (line 1), his irrigation and building works (line 2), his guardianship of his lord's heir Kamani and the other children (line 3), and extraordinarily his skill in literacy and language (line 4).

§1. I am Yariri the Ruler loved by Tarhunza, Kubaba, Karhuha and Tiwaza.
§2. Me the gods made strong and exalted over Karkamiš,
§3. and I strengthened Karkamiš,
§4. and I [rais]ed up my lord's [ho]use,
§5. and Karkami[š ...]
§6. [...] ... I made the river pass,
§7. ... here I made the river pass,
§8. and here I made the river pass.
§9. I built the temple of the Harmanean god,
§10. I made my person a stone ...,[1]
§11. and Kubaba will receive me placed at her foot.
§12. I brought up Kamani the heir,
§13. and as I *showed*(?) skill exceeding over kings,
§14. I brought up his younger brothers,
§15. I *admitted*(?) (them?) to the *brotherhood*(?),
§16. and to them, to my lord Astiruwa's children I extended *protection*(?).
§17. Me the gods [...]
§18. [...] in the writing of the City, the writing of Sura, the writing of Assur, and the Taimani writing.[2]
§19. And I knew twelve languages,
§20. and my lord *gathered*(?) to me every country's son by travelling for the sake of language,[3]
§21. and he taught me every skill.

1 This seems to refer to Yariri's erection of his own statue, of which we have only the inscribed base.

2 A passage that has aroused much interest and speculation. The "writing of the City" is doubtless Hieroglyphic Luwian, and the "writing of Assur" Assyrian Cuneiform. The "writing of Sura" (or perhaps "Zura") has been suggested to be Urartian or alternatively Tyrian, i.e. Phoenician. The "Taimani writing" could be Aramaic or possibly South Arabian (Teman). [Editor's note: see now the discussion in Younger 2014]

3 A remarkable statement: apparently Yariri's lord Astiruwa introduced him to speakers of many languages for language tuition!

REFERENCES

Hawkins 2000:130–133, pls. 36–37.

TELL AHMAR 6 (QUBBAH STELE) (4.10)

J. D. Hawkins

This amazingly preserved stele was reported to lie in the River Euphrates in June 1999, and was successfully removed from the river in July by the team of the Tell Ahmar Archaeological Project, who has been excavating at Tell Ahmar from 1988 under the direction of Dr. Guy Bunnens. It was taken to the Museum of Aleppo, where it has been excellently restored.

The stele is one of a series found at Tell Ahmar and in its environs and bears the longest and best preserved inscription. Most are the work of Hamiyata, the ruler of the city known to the Assyrians as Til-Barsib, renamed Kar-Shalmaneser after its conquest by that king in 856 BCE. The native name however is seen from the inscriptions to have been Masuwari. From these inscriptions we may see a power struggle in the city between two competing families extending over four-five generations. This must approximately have taken place during the 10th century BCE.

In his inscriptions, Hamiyata records his military deeds, first in his father's reign, then after his succession by divine favor in his own. He acknowledges as his special patron the Storm-God "Tarhunza of the Army," whose manifestation is represented by the figure on the front of the stele. He concludes with a colorful curse to protect his stele.

§1. I am Hamiyata the Ruler, the king of Masuwari[1] city, the servant of Tarhunza.
§2. Me the *firstborn*(?) son the gods loved: celestial Tarhunza, Ea, the Grain-God, the Moon-God, the benevolent Sun-God, the Stag-God, Karhuha, Kubaba, Hiputa, Sauska of the Army, the Mighty God, Sarruma, the Heaven, the Earth, the gods ..., the gods ...[2]
§3. And they gave me my father's succession.
§4. While my father was alive,
§5. I destroyed my father's enemies, those of the east in the east,
§6. and those of the west I destroyed with my Lord's support,
§7. this Tarhunza of the Army[3] marched before me.
§8. But when my father died,
§9. these gods loved me in full measure.
§10. They did not look down on my father's name,
§11. they raised it up.
§12. I *revealed* a way to the gods,
§13. I established a full ritual for them.
§14. For man and boy I exalted the soul and the head.
§15. I *turned* to the first of ... (?).
§16. I *closed*(?) the frontiers,[4]
§17. but this Tarhunza of the Army loved me,
§18. and he made me his own in vision and in HUSALAHIT-
§19. and he marched before me.
§20. I extended the frontiers,
§21. and I destroyed my enemies.
§22. To me the god-inspired one[5] said:
§23. "Set up Tarhunza of the Army!"
§24. In the year that I went to the River ...[6] with Tarhunza's support with 500 wagons ... and with a ... army,
§25. when I went forth,
§26. this Tarhunza of the Army in that year I set up.
§27. And when the chariot(ry) ...s with ...
§28. I will always give to this Tarhunza of the Army nine oxen (or "a ninth [part]").
§29. He who erases Hamiyata's name,
§30. or who desires evil for Hamiyata's posterity,
§31. for him may this Tarhunza of the Army become a lion,
§32. may he swallow down his head, wife and child;
§33. for him let him not USALALI the ...,
§34. and let him not go to the land Anaita[7] to *supplicate*(?) this Tarhunza of Hamiyata!

1 Masuwari, the Luwian name of Tell Ahmar/Til-Barsib.

2 Longest and best preserved god-list of the Hieroglyphic Luwian inscriptions. To the basic Luwian pantheon of the celestial Storm-God (Tarhunza), the Sun-God (Tiwaza), the Moon-God (Arma), the Stag-God (Runtiya), Heaven and Earth, it adds the old Hurrian deities Ea, the Grain God (Kumarbi/Kumarma), Hiputa (Hebat), Sauska (of the Army), the Mighty God (Tisupa/Teššub) and Sarruma, also the gods of Karkamiš – Karhuha (normally syncretized with the Stag-god) and Kubaba. It ends with three groups of unidentified gods.

3 The Storm-God of the Army, known already in the Hittite pantheon, is here explicitly given as the title of the figure on the front of the stele.

4 Although not precisely understood, this clause seems to stand in contrast to "extending the frontiers" (§20).

5 Apparently an inspired prophet of a type appearing intermittently throughout the ancient Near East, who gave unsolicited communications from the deity.

6 The river name is written with unread signs, so cannot be identified.

7 The country Ana(ita) mentioned also in other TELL AHMAR inscriptions, may be identified as ʿAna(t) on the middle Euphrates. Bunnens suggests from the contexts that the toponym might have chthonic connotations of "underworld."

REFERENCES

Hawkins 2006; Bunnens 2006.

ALEPPO 6 (4.11)

J. D. Hawkins

The Syro-German mission excavating on the citadel of Aleppo since 1996 has progressively revealed the ancient and famous temple of the Storm-God, one of the most important cult centers of the ancient Near East, dating back at least to the early 3rd millennium BCE. Archaeologically consecutive phases of construction and rebuilding have been identified, including a north "pedestal" wall of 26 relief sculptures of different periods assembled as a single structure at a late phase. In 2003, the east wall was uncovered, revealing a central scene of Storm-God and king, flanked by alternating "false windows" and bull-men. The king is accompanied by the well preserved Hieroglyphic Luwian inscription ALEPPO 6. In 2004–2005, the south entrance of the cella was excavated, on the west side of which the portal figures, a fish-man, lion, sphinx and a second lion were preserved. The last two bore parts of a broken inscription ALEPPO 7 by the same king as ALEPPO 6. It is hoped that further excavation may recover further parts of this.

In his inscription, the king gives his name and title as "King Taita, Hero, Palistinean[1] King"; records his mutually beneficial relationship with the Storm-God; and ends up with injunctions for future offerings to the deity. The inscription is provisionally dated to the 11th century BCE. This agrees with the excavator's stylistic dating of the figure, as well as with the C14 dating of the wood from the temple floor.

A "Taita, Hero, King of the Walistinean[1] land" was already known from the inscriptions MEHARDE and SHEIZAR (4.16 and 4.17 below), and it was originally thought that this should be the same as the king author of ALEPPO 6. However, dating criteria for the inscriptions now suggest that MEHARDE and SHEIZAR are significantly later than ALEPPO 6 and 7, thus probably 10th century BCE. An assumption that Taita II of MEHARDE-SHEIZAR was grandson of Taita I of ALEPPO 6 would allow for a suitable lapse of time.

The kingdom of Palistin/Walistin[1] is suggested by other evidence to be centered at Tell Tayinat in the Amuq plain. A connection has been proposed for this kingdom's name with the Philistines, whose characteristic pottery is seen to spread from Anatolia to Cilicia, Cyprus and the Levant from the early 12th century BCE.

§1. King Taita am I, the Hero, Palistinean[1] King.
§2. For my lord the Halabean[2] Storm-God I honored the wish,[3]
§3. and the Halabean Storm-God did (that) of my wish.[3]
§4. He who comes to this temple to celebrate the god
§5. if he is a king,
§6. let him sacrifice an ox (and) a sheep.
§7. On the other hand, if he is a … king's son,
§8. or he is a country lord,
§9. or he is a river country lord,
§10. let him too sacrifice a sheep.
§11. On the other hand, if he is an inferior man,
§12. (there shall be) bread, oblation and …

1 Toponym formerly read PaDAsatin-/WaDAsatin-, but evidence has appeared that the sign DA should actually be read *la* or *li*.
2 Halab is the ancient name for modern Aleppo.
3 Lit., "person, soul"; hence "desire, wish."

REFERENCES

Kohlmeyer 2009; Hawkins 2011.

MEHARDE (4.12)

J. D. Hawkins

The upper part of this stele in the Aleppo Museum is registered as coming from the village Meharde near the point where the Hama-Qal'at el Mudiq road crosses the Orontes River. More recently the lower part has appeared on the antiquities marker.

The front of the stele shows a large, frontally rendered female figure in a long dress standing on the back of a couchant lion. On her left, a small figure facing right stands on the lion's head. The large figure must represent the "divine Queen of the Land" named in the inscription. The monument was erected by Taita entitled "the Hero, King of the Walistinean[1] land," thus bearing the same name and titles as the author of ALEPPO 6 (4.15 above), but dating criteria for the script suggest that MEHARDE was significantly later. The identification of this author as Taita II, grandson of an earlier Taita I, would seem to fit the time-scale. Placing ALEPPO 6 and 7 approximately in the 11th century BCE, we would envisage for MEHARDE a date of late 11th or early 10th centuries BCE.

§1. This monument is (of?) the divine Queen of the Land.
§2. Taita made (it) for her, the Hero, the King of the land Walistin[(1)].
§3. He who against this monument […]
§4. […]
§5. But he who will …
§6. for him may the divine Queen of the Land be the prosecutor!
§7. But he who overturns this monument in its place,
§8. may the divine Queen of the Land destroy his …!
§9. Ahu(?)za the scribe carved it.

1 Formerly read *Wa*DA*satin*-, but the sign DA has been re-read *la* or *li*: see 4.15 above, n. 1 on the reading *Palistin*-. It can hardly be doubted that the two toponyms refer to the same country, which is found also on a fragment from Tell Tayinat in the Amuq, suggesting that this was the center of the kingdom. The P/W alternation suggests a hesitation in the rendering of the initial consonant.

REFERENCES

Hawkins 2000:415–416, pls. 225–226.

SHEIZAR (4.13)

J. D. Hawkins

This stele is also in two parts, the upper in the Beirut Museum to which it was presented in 1974, the lower in Hama Museum, where the provenance is registered as Sheizar, a medieval castle on a height above the village of Meharde. The actual provenance of both stelae is presumably an ancient site in the vicinity.

The inscription identifies the stele as the funerary monument of the wife of Taita II. If, as she claims, she lived to one hundred years old, her monument could easily be as much as fifty years later than the inscription of her husband, thus perhaps mid-10th century BCE.

§1. I am Kupapiya, wife of Taita, the Hero of the land Walistin.
§2. Because of my righteousness, I *lived* 100 years.
§3. My children … placed me on the *pyre*(?),
§4. and this monument for me my grandchildren, great-grandchildren and great-great-grandchildren caused to …
§5. Among my [posterity?] he who is my grandchild, great-grandchild, great-great-grandchild, or great-great-great-grandchild,
§6. he who […]s […][1]
§7. for him may the divine Queen of the Land be the prosecutor!
§8. Pedantimuwa the scribe carved it,
§9. and as servant to him […] *was present*(?).

1 Presumably, we should understand the curse to be directed against anyone who harms the posterity.

REFERENCES

Hawkins 2000:416–419, pls. 227–228.

HAMA 4 (4.14)

J. D. Hawkins

This inscription along with HAMA 1–3 was one of the earliest Hieroglyphic Luwian monuments observed (1812), recovered (1872) and published (1873). It is a door-jamb bearing two separate inscriptions, A on its broad side face, B on its narrow front face. To the left of Side A, the inscription must have continued on another element now lost, which has carried away the continuation of lines 1 and 2 and the ends of lines 3 and 4; and line 4 in fact is the continuation of B line 4.

As the inscription makes clear, this doorjamb belonged to the temple of Pahalati (= Semitic Baʿalat "Lady"), which has been identified as Bâtiment III on the excavated citadel of Hama. Its author Urhilina has been identified with "Irhuleni the Hamathite," named as an opponent by Shalmaneser III in the years 853–845 BCE. In his inscription, Urhilina records his building and endowment of the temple.

A.
§1. I am Urhilina, Parita's son, Hamathite King.
§2. […]
§3. and men and women walked […]
§4. In my [days?] I myself was … king …
§5. For every single god I made his own seat,
§6. and this seat for Baʿalat I built,
§7. and I put Baʿalat's and my name (on it).
§8. He who takes away Baʿalat's and my name from this seat,
§9. him Tarhunza […]

B.
§1. Baʿalat's temple in my father's and grandfather's times *lacked*(?) *income*(?)
§2. and they did not *burn*(?) the *burnt*(?) sacrificial (ox) to the deity up (and) down.

§3. But in my own times it did not *lack*(?) *income*(?).
§4. I established ritual and libation for her forever.
§5. and the burnt(?) sacrificial ox [...]
§6. (*erasure*) perpetual bread, also libation and ritual.

REFERENCES

Hawkins 2000: 403–406, pl. 213.

ÇINEKÖY (4.15)

J. D. Hawkins

In 1997 in a field near the village of Çineköy some 30 km. south of Adana, a colossal limestone statue of the Storm-God with a basalt base in the form of his cart drawn by two bulls was discovered and taken to the Adana Museum. The base bears a bilingual inscription in Hieroglyphic Luwian and Phoenician: The Hieroglyphic text began on the block's right side between the legs of the bull, continued across the back and left side between the legs of the other bull and on to the front between its fore-legs, and ended on the horizontal surface between its hooves; the Phoenician text occupying much less space was placed on the front of the block between the two bulls.[1]

The author of the inscription is Warika son of [...], "grandson" of [Muk]sa, king of Hiyawa (Phoenician W[RYK, son of ...], descendant of MPŠ, [king of the DNNYM]). This bilingual, although much shorter than the KARATEPE bilingual, is clearly closely related to it, since most of its phraseology reappears there.

Warika, king of Hiyawa, is clearly the same man as Awariku king of Adana (Phoenician ʾWRK king of the DNNYM), who in turn is identified with Urikki king of Que attested in the inscriptions of Tiglath-pileser III and Sargon II of Assyria in the period 738–710 BCE.

ÇINEKÖY must be earlier than KARATEPE, which narrates the affairs in Adana after the reign of Awariku. A surprise from this new inscription is the warm relations with Assyria and its king. The Assyrian monarch is more likely Tiglath-pileser III, with whom Warika/Urikki may have enjoyed a client relationship, than to Sargon who may have annexed Que as an Assyrian province.

Another surprise is that the Hieroglyphic equivalent of Phoenician DNNYM (the Danunîm) is not Adana as in KARATEPE, but Hiyawa. This is clearly the Hieroglyphic form of Assyrian Que, the country of the Cilician plain rather than its capital city Adana. It is also probable that Hiyawa is the Iron Age reflection of Late Bronze Age Ahhiyawa, the designation found in the Hittite texts of Boğazköy for the Mycenaean Greeks of western Anatolia. We may suppose that the name came to Cilicia with the Mycenaean expansion and population movements at the end of the Bronze Age. Such a migration is associated in the Greek tradition with the name of the hero Mopsos (alias Moxos), who was said to have led colonists from western Anatolia to Pamphylia and Cilicia, founding cities en route. KARATEPE already attested the presence in Cilicia of the "house of Mopsos" (Hieroglyphic: *Muksa*; Phoenician: MPŠ), and ÇINEKÖY now make clear that the royal house of Cilicia claimed him as founding father. These 8th century references lend a degree of historicity to the Greek traditions of the 12th century BCE.

§1. [I am] Wari[ka, ...'s] son, [Muk]sa's grandson, king of Hiyawa, Tarhunz[a's] se[rvant].[2]
§2. I, Warika, extended the plain of [Hi]yawa by (the help of) Tarhunza and my father's gods.[3]
§3. And I made horse upon horse,[4]
§4. and I made army upon army.[4]
§5. So the (As)syrian[5] king and all the (As)syrian[5] house became fat[her and mother][6] to me,
§6. and Hiyawa[7] and (As)syria became one house.

[1] For the Phoenician text, see *COS* 4.16 below.
[2] Cf. KARATEPE, §I 5–6, where Azatiwada has the same title.
[3] Cf. KARATEPE, §V.
[4] This equates with KARATEPE, §§VIII–IX.
[5] "Assyria" is written Hier. *Sura* = Phoen. *ʾšr*, the latter guaranteeing the interpretation *Assur*, which is otherwise written in Hier. *Asura*.
[6] Cf. KARATEPE, §III.
[7] The equation here, Hier. Hiyawa = Phoen. DNNYM confirms that ÇINEKÖY replaces KARATEPE's *Adana* with *Hiyawa*, the former being the city, the latter the country.

§ 7.	So I smote[8] fortresses, from the east ... eight, and from the west seven fortress(es).	§ 9.	I by myself made lands,
§ 8.	So in places which[9] were great *marshes*(?)[10] of the river Sapara	§ 10.	and sett[led] towns.
		§ 11.	[... Tarhunza] the highly blessed.

[8] Cf. KARATEPE, § XXV, where Hier. "I smote" = Phoen. ʿN ʾNK. Here Phoen. BN ʾNK, "I built" (KARATEPE, §§ XIX, XXIII) is clearly a mistake for ʿN ʾNK.

[9] Correct the editor's *za-ia*, "these", to REL-*ia*, "which"; cf. KARATEPE, § XXXIII, 172–173.

[10] Written with the logograms "great-pool-stone." The context appears to be one of draining marshes.

REFERENCES

Tekoğlu and Lemaire 2000.

ANATOLIAN BIBLIOGRAPHY

ALAURA, S.
2011 "Aspekte der Gesten- und Gebärdensprache im 'Ullikummi-Lied.'" Pp. 9–24 in *Hethitische Literatur: Überlieferungsprozesse, Textstrukturen, Ausdrucksformen und Nachwirken. Akten des Symposiums vom 18. bis 20. Februar 2010 in Bonn*. Ed. by M. Hutter and S. Hutter-Braunsar. Münster: Ugarit-Verlag.

ARCHI, A.
1990 "The Names of the Primeval Gods." *Or* 59:114–129.

BECKMAN, G. M.
2005 "Hittite and Hurrian Epic." Pp. 255–263 in *A Companion to Ancient Epic*. Ed. by J. M. Foley. Oxford: Blackwell.
2011 "Primordial Obstetrics." Pp. 25–33 in *Hethitische Literatur: Überlieferungsprozesse, Textstrukturen, Ausdrucksformen und Nachwirken. Akten des Symposiums vom 18. bis 20. Februar 2010 in Bonn*. Ed. by M. Hutter, and S. Hutter-Braunsar. Münster: Ugarit-Verlag.

BERNABÉ, A.
1987 *Textos literarios hetitas*. Madrid: Alianza Editorial.
1989 "Generaciones de dioses y sucesión interrumpida. El mito hittita de Kumarbi, la 'Teogonía' de Hesíodo y la del 'Papiro de Derveni.'" *AuOr* 7:159–180.

BUCCELLATI, G., and M. KELLY-BUCCELLATI
1997 "Urkesh: The First Hurrian Capital." *BA* 60:77–96.

BURKERT, W.
1979 "Von Ullikummi zum Kaukasus: Die Felsgeburt des Unholds. Zur Kontinuität einer mündlichen Erzählung." *Würzburger Jahrbücher für die Altertumswissenschaft* NF 5:253–261.

BUNNENS, G.
2006 *A New Luwian Stele and the Cult of the Storm-God at Til Barsib-Masuwari*. Tel Ahmar 2. Louvain: Peeters.

CIVIL, M.
1987 "Hh VI dans Nuzi SMN 2559 et Emar VI/2 540 et 730." *RA* 81:187–188.

COLLINS, B. J.
2007 *The Hittites and Their World*. Archeology and Biblical Studies 7. Atlanta: Society of Biblical Literature.

CORTI, C.
2007 "The So-called 'Theogony' or 'Kingship in Heaven.' The name of the Song." Pp. 109–121 in *VI Congresso Internazionale di Ittitologia Roma, 5–9 settembre 2005*. Ed. by A. Archi and R. Francia. Rome: CNR – Istituto de Studi sulle Civiltà dell'Egeo e del Vicino Oriente.

DEVRIES, B.
1967 The Style of Hittite Epic and Mythology. Ph.D. Dissertation, Brandeis University.

DIRLMEIER, F.
1955 "Homerisches Epos und Orient." *Rheinisches Museum* 98:18–37 (= *Ausgewählte Schriften zu Dichtung und Philosophie der Greichen*, Heidelberg, 1970, 55–67).

FORRER, E.
1936 "Eine Geschichte des Götterkönigtums aus dem Hatti-Reiche." *Annuaire de l'Institut de Philologie et d'Histoire Orientales et Slaves* 4:687–713.

FRIEDRICH, J.
1949 "Der churritische Mythus vom Schlangendämon Hedammu in hethitischer Sprache." *ArOr* 17:230–254.

GANE, R. E.
2008 "Hurrian Ullikummi and Daniel's 'Little Horn.'" Pp. 485–498 in *Birkat Shalom: Studies in the Bible, Ancient Near Eastern Literature, and Postbiblical Judaism Presented to Shalom M. Paul on the Occasion of His Seventieth Birthday*. Ed. by C. Cohen. Winona Lake, IN: Eisenbrauns.

GARCÍA TRABAZO, J. V.
2002 *Textos religiosos hititas. Mitos, plegaries y rituales*. Biblioteca de Ciencias Bíblicas y Orientales 6. Madrid: Editorial Trotta.

GIORGIERI, M.
2001 "Die hurritische Fassung des Ullikummi-Lieds und ihre hethitische Parallele." Pp. 134–155 in *Akten des IV. Internationalen Kongresses für Hethitologie. Würzburg, 4.–8. Oktober, 1999*. Ed. by G. Wilhelm. Wiesbaden: Harrassowitz.

GLÜCK, J. J.
1964 "Reviling and Monomachy as Battle-Preludes in Ancient Warfare." *Acta Classica* 7:25–31.

GOETZE, A.
1949 "Review of H. G. Güterbock, *Kumarbi. Mythen vom churritischen Kronos aus den hethitischen Fragmenten zusammengestellt, übersetzt und erklärt*." *JAOS* 69:178–183.
1955 "Hittite Myths, Epics, and Legends." in *ANET*.

GÜTERBOCK, H. G.
1946 *Kumarbi: Mythen vom churritischen Kronos*. Zürich: Europa Verlag.
1948 "The Hittite Version of the Hurrian Kumarbi Myths: Oriental Forerunners to Hesiod." *AJA* 52:123–134.
1952 *The Song of Ullikummi: Revised Text of the Hittite Version of a Hurrian Myth*. New Haven: American Schools of Oriental Research.
1961 "Hittite Mythology." Pp. 139–179 in *Mythologies of the Ancient World*. Ed. by S. N. Kramer. New York: Doubleday.
1978 "Hethitische Literatur." Pp. 211–253 in *Neues Handbuch der Literaturwissenschaft*. Band 1. Ed. by W. Röllig. Wiesbaden: Akademische Verlagsgesellschaft Athenaion.
1982 *Les hiéroglyphes de Yazılıkaya: A propos d'un travail récent*. Institut francais d'études anatoliennes Paris: Editions Recherche sur les civilisations.
1989 "Marginal Notes on Recent Hittitological Publications." *JNES* 48:307–311.

HAAS, V.
1975 "Jason's Raub des goldenen Vliesses im Lichte hethitischer Quellen." *UF* 7:227–233.

1982 *Hethitische Berggötter und hurritische Steindämonen: Riten, Kulte und Mythen. Eine Einführung in die altkleinastiatischen religiösen Vorstellungen*. Kulturgeschichte der Antiken Welt 10. Mainz: Philipp von Zabern.
1994 *Geschichte der hethitischen Religion*. Handbuch der Orientalistik I/15. Leiden: Brill.
2003 "Betrachtungen zu CTH 343, einem Mythos des Hirschgottes." *AoF* 30:296–303.
2006 *Die hethitische Literatur: Texte, Stilistik, Motive*. Berlin: Walter de Gruyter.

HAAS, V., and D. BAWANYPECK
2003 *Materia Magica et Medica Hethitica. Ein Beitrag zur Heilkunde im Alten Orient*. Berlin: Walter de Gruyter.

HAWKINS, J. D.
2000 *Corpus of Hieroglyphic Luwian Inscriptions*. Volume 1: *The Hieroglyphic Luwian Inscriptions of the Iron Age*. UISK 8.1. Berlin and New York: Walter de Gruyter.
2006 "The Inscription." Pp. 11–31 in *A New Luwian Stele and the Cult of the Storm-God at Til Barsib-Masuwari*, G. Bunnens. Tell Ahmar 2. Louvain, Paris and Dudley, MA: Peeters.
2009 "Cilicia, the Amuq, and Aleppo: New Light in a Dark Age." *NEA* 72:164–173.
2011 "The Inscriptions of the Aleppo Temple." *AnSt* 61: 35–54.
2013 "The Luwian Inscriptions from the Temple of the Storm-God of Aleppo." Pp. 493–500 in *Across the Border: Late Bronze-Iron Age Relations between Syria and Anatolia. Proceedings of a Symposium held at the Research Center of Anatolian Studies, Koç University, Istanbul, May 31–June 1, 2010*, ed. K. A. Yener. ANESSup 42. Leuven: Peeters.

HEINHOLD-KRAHMER, S.
2001 "Zur Diskussion um einen zweiten Namen Tutaliyas IV." Pp. 180–198 in *Akten des IV. Internationalen Kongresses für Hethitologie. Würzburg, 4.–8. Oktober, 1999*. Ed. by G. Wilhelm. Wiesbaden: Harrassowitz.

HELCK, W., and E. OTTO
1956 *Kleines Wörterbuch der Ägyptologie*. Wiesbaden: Harrassowitz.

HERBORDT, S.
1998 "Seals and Sealings of Hittite Officials from the Nişantepe Archive, Boğazköy." Pp. 306–318 in *Acts of the IIIrd International Congress of Hittitology. Çorum, September 16–22, 1996*. Ed. by S. Alp, and A. Süel. Ankara: Grafik, Teknik Hazırlık Uyum Ajans.

HEUBECK, A.
1955 "Mythologische Vorstellungen des Alten Orients im archaischen Griechentum." *Gymnasium* 62:508–525.

HOFFNER, H. A., Jr.
1967 *An English-Hittite Glossary*. Revue hittite et asianique 25, Fasc. 80. Paris: Librairie C. Klincksieck.
1968 "Birth and Namegiving in Hittite Texts." *JNES* 27:198–203.
1975 "Hittite Mythological Texts: A Survey." Pp. 136–145 in *Unity and Diversity: Essays in the History, Literature, and Religion of the Ancient Near East*. Ed. by H. Goedicke, and J. J. M. Roberts. Baltimore-London: The Johns Hopkins University.
1977 "Hittite Lexicographic Studies 1." Pp. 105–111 in *Studies Finkelstein*.
1982 "The Milawata Letter Augmented and Reinterpreted." *AfO* Beih. 19:130–137.
1987 "Hittite Note on Mešedi, Mešettu(m)." *RA* 81:188–189.
1988 "The Song of Silver." Pp. 143–166 in *Documentum Asiae Minoris Antiquae: Festschrift für Heinrich Otten zum 75. Geburtstag*. Ed. by E. Neu, and C. Rüster. Wiesbaden: Harrassowitz.
1990 *Hittite Myths*. SBLWAW 2. Atlanta: Scholars.
1996 "Hittite Equivalents of Old Assyrian *kumrum* and *epattum*." *WZKM* 86:151–156.
1998a *Hittite Myths* (2nd rev. ed.). SBLWAW 2. Atlanta: Scholars.
1998b "Name, Namengebung. C. Bei den Hethitern." *RlA* 9:116–121.
2009a *Letters From the Hittite Kingdom*. SBLWAW 15. Atlanta: Society of Biblical Literature.
2009b "Schöpfung, Schöpfungsmythos. B. Bei den Hethitern." *RlA* 12:67–73.

JAKOB-ROST, L.
1977 *Das Lied von Ullikummi: Dichtungen der Hethiter*. Leipzig: Insel Verlag.

JANDA, M.
2001 "Trace indoeuropee nel mito di Ullikummi." Pp. 193–204 in *Anatolisch und Indogermanisch/Anatolico e Indoeuropeo. Akten des Kolloquiums der Indogermanischen Gesellschaft Pavia 22.–25. September 1998*. Ed. by O. Carruba, and W. Meid. Innsbruck: Institut für Sprachwissenschaft der Universität Innsbruck.

KAMMENHUBER, A.
1974 "Historische-geographische Nachrichten aus der althurrischen Überlieferung, dem altelamischen und den Inschriften der könige von Akkad für die Zeit vor dem Einfall der Gutäer." *Acta Antiqua Academiae Scientiarum Hungaricae* 22:157–247.
1976 "Neue Ergebnisse zur hurrischen und altmesopotamischen Überlieferung in Boghazköy." *Or* 45:130–147.

KOHLMEYER, K.
2009 "The Temple of the Storm God in Aleppo during the Late Bronze and Early Iron Ages." *NEA* 72/4:190–202.

KOMORÓCZY, G.
1973 "'The Separation of Sky and Earth': The Cycle of Kumarbi and the Myths of Cosmogony in Mesopotamia." *Acta Antiqua* 21:21–45.

KOROLËV, A. A.
1999 "Hittite Texts: New Readings, Joins, and Duplicates." *Studia Linguarum* 2:281–290.

KÜHNE, C.
1975 "Hethitische Texte." Pp. 169–204 in *Religionsgeschichtliches Textbuch zum Alten Testament*. Ed. by W. Beyerlin. Göttingen: Vandenhoeck und Ruprecht.
1978 "Hittite Texts." Pp. 146–184 in *Near Eastern Religious Texts Relating to the Old Testament*. Ed. by W. Beyerlin. Philadelphia: The Westminster.

LAROCHE, E.
1964 "La prière hittite: vocabulaire et typologie." *Annuaire École pratique des Hautes Études* (Ve section) 8–29.
1969 *Textes mythologiques hittites en transcription*. Paris: Librairie C. Klincksieck.
1971 *Catalogue des textes hittites*. Études et Commentaires 75. Paris: Librairie C. Klincksieck.

LESKY, A.

1950 "Hethitische Texte und griechischer Mythos." *Anzeiger der phil.-hist. Klasse der Österreichischen Akademie der Wissenschaften* 87:137–160.

LIVERANI, M.

2001 *International Relations in the Ancient Near East, 1600–1100 B.C.* New York: Palgrave.

MERIGGI, P.

1953 "I miti di Kumarpi, il Kronos currico." *Athenaeum* 31:101–157.

OTTEN, H.

1949 "Vorderasiatische Mythen als Vorläufer griechischer Mythenbildung." *Forschung und Fortschritte* 25:145–147.

1950 *Mythen vom Gotte Kumarbi: Neue Fragmente.* Veröffentlichungen der Deutschen Akademie der Wissenschaften zu Berlin, Institut für Orientforschung 3. Berlin: Akademie Verlag.

OTTEN, H., and C. RÜSTER

1973 "Textanschlüsse und Duplikate von Boğazköy-Tafeln (21–30)." *ZA* 63:83–91.

PECCHIOLI DADDI, F., and A. M. POLVANI

1990 *La mitologia ittita.* Testi del Vicino Oriente Antico 4.1. Brescia: Paideia Editrice.

PERRY, J. W.

1966 *Lord of the Four Quarters: The Mythology of Kingship.* New York: G. Braziller.

POLVANI, A. M.

1992 "Su alcuni frammenti mitologici ittiti." Pp. 445–454 in *Hittite and Other Anatolian and Near Eastern Studies in Honour of Sedat Alp.* Ed. by H. Otten, E. Akurgal, H. Ertem, and A. Süel. Ankara: Türk Tarih Kurumu Basımevi.

2008 "The god Eltara and the Theogony." Pp. 617–624 in *VI Congresso Internazionale di Ittitologia Roma, 5–9 settembre 2005.* Ed. by A. Archi, and R. Francia. Rome: CNR – Istituto de Studi sulle Civiltà dell'Egeo e del Vicino Oriente.

POPKO, M.

1995 *Religions of Asia Minor.* Warsaw: Academic Publications Dialog.

PRECHEL, D.

1996 *Die Göttin Išara: ein Beitrag zur altorientalischen Religionsgeschichte.* ALASP 11. Münster: Ugarit-Verlag.

PUHVEL, J.

1984 *Hittite Etymological Dictionary.* Volumes 1–2: *Words Beginning with A, E, I.* Trends in Linguistics. Documentation 1. Berlin: Mouton de Gruyter.

2004 *Hittite Etymological Dictionary.* Volume 6: *Words Beginning with M.* Trends in Linguistics. Documentation 22. Berlin: Mouton de Gruyter.

REVELL, E. J.

1997 "The Repetition of Introductions to Speech as a Feature of Biblical Hebrew." *VT* 47:91–110.

RIEKEN, E.

1999 *Untersuchungen zur nominalen Stammbildung des Hethitischen.* StBoT 44. Wiesbaden: Harrassowitz.

SALVINI, M.

1977 "Sui testi mitologici in lingua hurrita." *SMEA* 18:73–91.

SCHULER, E. VON

1965 "Kleinasien: Die Mythologie der Hethiter und Hurriter." Pp. 141–215 in *Wörterbuch der Mythologie 1.* Ed. by H. W. Haussig. Stuttgart: Ernst Klett Verlag.

SCHWEMER, D.

2005 "Lehnbeziehungen zwischen dem Hethitischen und dem Akkadischen." *AfO* 51:220–234.

SIEGELOVÁ, J.

1971 *Appu-Märchen und edammu-Mythus.* StBoT 14. Wiesbaden: Harrassowitz.

SINGER, I.

2002 "The Cold Lake and its Great Rock." Pp. 128–132 in *Sprache und Kultur. Tbilisi: Staatliche Ilia Tschawtschwadse Universität Tbilisi für Sprache und Kultur.* Institute zur Erforschung des westlichen Denkens.

STARKE, F.

1990 *Untersuchung zur Stammbildung des keilschrift-luwischen Nomens.* StBoT 31. Wiesbaden: Harrassowitz.

STEFANINI, R.

1988 "Alcuni problemi ittiti, lessicali e sintattici." Pp. 251–256 in *Studi di Storia e di Filologia Anatolica dedicati a Giovanni Pugliese Carratelli.* Ed. by F. Imparati. Florence: Edizione Librarie Italiane Estere (ELITE).

STEINER, G.

1958. Der Sukzessionsmythos in Hesiods "Theogony" und ihren orientalischen Parallelen. Ph.D. Dissertation, Üniversität Hamburg.

TARACHA, P.

2009 *Religions of Second Millennium Anatolia.* Dresdner Beiträge zur Hethitologie 27. Wiesbaden: Harrassowitz.

TEKOĞLU, R. and A. LEMAIRE.

2000 "La bilingue royale louvito-phénicienne de Çineköy." *CRAIBL*: 961–1006.

TISCHLER, J.

2001 *Hethitisches Handwörterbuch.* Innsbrucker Beiträge zur Sprachwissenschaft 102. Innsbruck: Institut für Sprachen und Literaturen der Universität Innsbruck.

ÜNAL, A.

1994 "Hethitisch-altanatolische Mythen, Legenden, Epen und Märchen aus dem Staatsarchiv von Hattuscha." Pp. 802–865 in *Mythen und Epen II.* Ed. by O. Kaiser. Gütersloh: Gütersloher Verlagshaus Gerd Mohn.

Van Den Hout, T. P. J.
2003 "Studies in the Hittite Phraseological Construction. I. Its Syntactic and Semantic Properties." Pp. 177–204 in *Hittite Studies in Honor of Harry A. Hoffner, Jr. on the Occasion of His 65th Birthday*. Ed. by G. M. Beckman, R. H. Beal, and J. G. McMahon. Winona Lake, IN: Eisenbrauns.

Van Dijk, J.
1971 "Gott A. Nach sumerischen Texten." *RlA* 6:532–543.

Van Gessel, B. H. L.
1998 *Onomasticon of the Hittite Pantheon*. Parts 1–3. Handbuch der Orientalistik I/33. Leiden: Brill.

Vieyra, M.
1970 "Les textes hittites." Pp. 459–566 in *Les religions du Proche-Orient asiatique*. Ed. by R. Labat, A. Caquot, M. Sznycer, and M. Vieyra. Paris: Fayard/Denoel.

Walcot, P.
1966 *Hesiod and the Near East*. Cardiff: University of Wales.

Watkins, C.
2000 *The American Heritage Dictionary of Indo-European Roots*. Boston: Houghton Mifflin.

Wilhelm, G.
1982 *Grundzüge der Geschichte und Kultur der Hurriter*. Darmstadt: Wissenschaftliche Buchgesellschaft.
2003 "König Silber und König Hidam." Pp. 393–395 in *Hittite Studies in Honor of Harry A. Hoffner, Jr. on the Occasion of His 65th Birthday*. Ed. by G. M. Beckman, R. H. Beal, and J. G. McMahon. Winona Lake, IN: Eisenbrauns.

Younger, K. L., Jr.
2014 "The Scripts of North Syria in the Early First Millennium: the Inscription of Yariri (KARKAMIŠ A15b) Once Again." *Transeuphratène* 46: 169–183 (= *Volume d'hommages pour André Lemaire*), eds. Jean-Marie Durand and Josette Elayi. Paris: Gabalda.

WEST SEMITIC INSCRIPTIONS

PHOENICIAN COMPOSITIONS

THE PHOENICIAN INSCRIPTION OF ÇINEKÖY (4.16)

André Lemaire

In 1997, a monumental limestone statue of the Storm God and a basalt bull-drawn chariot were accidentally discovered near Çineköy some 30 km south of Adana (Cilicia). A partly preserved Luwian-Phoenician bilingual inscription was carved on the bull-drawn chariot. The Phoenician palaeography dates it slightly earlier than the Karatepe inscriptions (i.e., the second half of the 8th century BCE). King Warika/Urikki, offspring of Muksas/*Mpš*/Mopsos and identical with Awariku of Karatepe and with Urikki of the Neo-Assyrian sources, praises the excellent relations between Assyrians and Danunians/Hiyaweans. The translation given here is based on the Phoenician inscription engraved between the two bulls, with references to the parallel Luwian inscription (see 4.15 above).

(1) I am Wa[rika *son of ...?....*] (2) offspring of Mopsos[1] [*king of the Danunians?*[2]] (3) blessed by Baal[3] who [*enlarged*[4]] (4) *the house/kingdom*[5] of the land of the plain of [Adana[6] thanks to] (5) Baal[7] and thanks to the go[ds[8] and] (6) I also acquired horse [upon horse *and* ar](7)my upon army.[9] The king of [*Ashur and*] (8) all the house of Ashur became for me a father [and] (9) a mother.[10] And Danunians[11] and Assyrians (10) became one house.[12] And I built[13] fortres[ses:] (11) eight-VIII at the rising of the sun and at the set(12)ting of the sun seven-VII, and *thus* XV. (13) *And in the place(s)* [......][14] (16) (*those that are*) *oppressed/cramped for room, I have them to live t*[*here. Ma*]*y Baal* (17) Kur[15] [*give?*] tranquility, safety, abundance and [*all?*] good (18) to this king and *also in this* [*...?....*]

[1] The dynasty of the Cilician kings was called *bt mpš* "house of Mopsos" (Karatepe A I,16; II,14–15; III,11).

[2] See Luwian: "Hiyawean king." For the restoration *mlk dnnym*, see Karatepe A I, 2.

[3] *Hbrk bʿl*. Compare Karatepe A I, 1.

[4] For this restoration, see the Luwian text and Karatepe A I, 4.

[5] *Bt* could also be the end of [*yrḥ*]*bt*, restored in the lacuna (Lipiński 2004).

[6] *ʾrṣ ʿmq ʾdn*: see Karatepe A I, 4; II, 15–16.

[7] Luwian: "Tarhunza."

[8] Luwian: "the gods of my father."

[9] Compare Karatepe A I, 6–8. For *bʿbr bʿl wʾlm*, see Karatepe A I, 8; II, 6; III, 11.

[10] Compare Karatepe A I, 3.

[11] Luwian: "*Hiyawa*." Compare Hittite *Aḫḫiyawa* and Greek *(Hyp-)akhaioi* (Herodotus VI, 91). This appellation of Cilicia can also be compared to Assyrian *Qaue/Quwe* and to Neo-Babylonian *Ḫume*.

[12] *Bt ʾḥd*. Compare Akkadian *bītum ištēn* to express an alliance.

[13] Luwian: "I stroke." Was there a confusion BN/ʿN in Phoenician? Compare Karatepe A I, 13, 18.

[14] Lines 13–16 are almost illegible. See at the end, Luwian: "(that were) ... of the river Sapara, I made lands ... founded? towns ... [Tarhun]za?, the blessed one" (Hawkins 2005).

[15] *Bʿl kr* is also attested in the Cebelireis Daği inscription (5B) (see *COS* 3:55). For the deity Kur(ra), see Younger 2009b.

REFERENCES

Bremmer 2008:136–143; Hawkins 2005; Lanfranchi 2005, 2009; Lemaire 2006; Lipiński 2004:127–128; Oettinger 2008; Singer 2009; Tekoğlu and Lemaire 2000; Younger 2009b.

HEBREW COMPOSITIONS

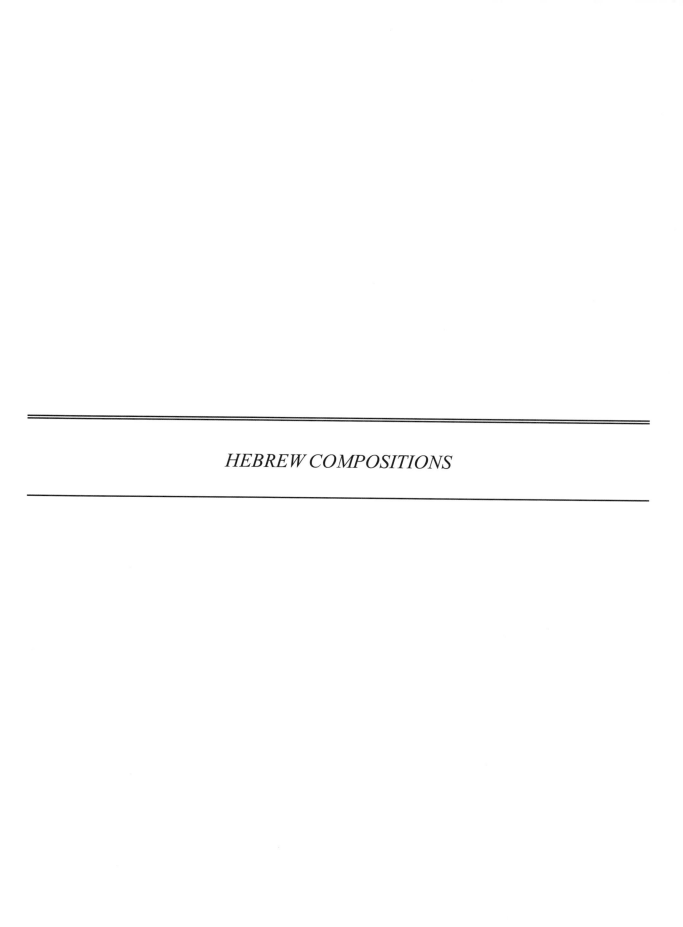

BARLEY ORDER (4.17)

Matthew Suriano

The text referred to as the "Barley Letter" is an incised Hebrew ostracon that was discovered in the Joint Expedition to Samaria in 1932 and labeled by the excavator Ostracon C 1101 (Sukenik 1933). The extant writing is beautifully incised on a sherd of red burnished ware. The fragmentary nature of the ostracon, however, makes its reading and interpretation speculative (Lemaire 1972). Nonetheless, recognizable vocabulary and the use of hieratic numerals suggest that the text recorded a business transaction. The Barley Order is unrelated to the administrative dockets known as the Samaria Ostraca, which were discovered in a different area and date to an earlier phase of the city. The paleography and archaeological context of the Barley Order places it in the second half of the eighth century (see Dobbs-Allsopp, Roberts, Seow, and Whitaker 2004:389), with a *terminus ante quem* of 722 BCE.

Baruch, greetings[1] […]
Baruch, the shepherds have been attentive […]
He will apportion[2] 3(?)[3] measures of barley […]

---

[1] The first word *brk* can be read as the passive participle, "blessed." The appearance of the same form at the beginning of line two, however, suggests that the word here is a personal name. The second word, *šlm*, is read by some as a verb ("paid" or "completed") or as a personal name Shillem or Shallum. These possibilities allow for multiple combinations in translating the first line: "Blessed by Shallum …" or "Baruch [son of] Shallum" (Albright 1936 and ANET). For the various renderings of the second word as a verb, see KAI 185; Lemaire 1972, 1977; Lipiński 1977:86; Dobbs-Allsopp, Roberts, Seow, and Whitaker 2004:389–390. The translation here takes these words as an opening address, reading *šlm* as the standard greeting (lit. "peace"). For an alternative reconstruction of the first line, see Galling 1961:173–185.

[2] Some have read the first word of the third line as a proper noun, Imnah (Gen 46:17; see Albright 1936:212–213). In light of the numbers that follow, however, the word *ymnh* is translated here as a prefix verb from *mnh* meaning "apportion" (*Piel*).

[3] There are three hieratic numbers clearly visible at the end of the extant line, however a marking before the three dashes could be an additional number and some have read it as a 10 for a total of 13 (Albright 1936:212).

REFERENCES

Text, translations and studies: Aḥituv 2008; Albright 1936, and in *ANET*; Avigad 1993; Dobbs-Allsopp, Roberts, Seow, and Whitaker 2004; *KAI*; Gibson *SSI* 1; Gogel 1998; Lemaire 1972, 1977; Sukenik 1933; Renz 1995.

SAMARIA OSTRACA (4.18)

Matthew Suriano

The Samaria Ostraca represent an archive of 107 inscribed potsherds that were discovered by George Andrew Reisner and Clarence Stanley Fisher in 1910 during Harvard University's initial season of the excavation at Sebastiye, ancient Samaria (Reisner, Fisher and Lyon 1924).[1] The ostraca, written in a northern form of Hebrew (with Hieratic numerals), are lists of wine and olive oil that were shipped to the royal capital from the outlying area. Discovered in the remains of Samaria's acropolis, the ostraca typically record the source of the shipment, the products shipped, and the individuals responsible for shipping and receiving the wine and oil. Although laconic, these administrative texts provide valuable historical and cultural information for understanding the northern kingdom during the Iron Age IIB. Archaeologically, the ostraca come from the leveling fill of the so-called "Ostraca House," thus, they are not contemporary with this structure, as scholars had previously thought (see Kaufman 1966; and Tappy 2001:496–503). The excavated remains from the general area of the Ostraca House, on the other hand, indicate that this part of the compound had earlier served as a place for receiving shipments (Sebastiye's Summit Strip S4 and Strip S7). Thus, the associative context of the ostraca is significant, even if their secondary deposit makes their precise dating difficult.

The original excavator noted that several of the ostraca were written on potsherds from the same vessel. Thus, they were apparently written in Samaria, where the shipments were received. The fluid style of writing (in black ink) and the multiple hands noted by epigraphers indicate that the ostraca were recorded by a group of scribes, recording shipments as they were being received within the royal compound. Historically, the ostraca are dated to the second quarter of the eighth century BCE based on a combination of factors that include paleography (Rollston 2010),

[1] George Andrew Reisner published 63 of the 113 inscribed objects discovered in 1911. Ivan Kaufman (1966) re-examined and photographed using infrared technology 109 of these ostraca in Istanbul, listing four as missing. André Lemaire (1977) renumbered the ostraca in Kaufman's work, following Reisner's original order (see Dobbs-Allsopp, Roberts, Seow and Whitaker 2004:339). The translation here follows this system of numbering.

chronological data contained in the text of the ostraca (Rainey 1988), and the archaeological dating of Samaria's remains (Tappy 2001). The texts, in most cases, are dated either to the "ninth year" or "tenth year" (spelled with an ordinal number), or to "year 15" (written with hieratic numerals). Scholars divide the corpus into two categories based on the different systems of dating, Types I and II respectively (Kaufman 1982; 1992). Ostraca that list wine shipped from vineyards, without a stated recipient, belong in a third category (Renz 1995). The few ostraca of this third group probably represent records of wine from royal vineyards shipped directly to the king (Suriano 2016). The dates in all of these texts refer to the year of the king's reign, although the ruler's name is never specified. Archaeological and historical factors suggest a king from Jehu's dynasty: either Jehoash or Jeroboam II. The different dates and dating methods that separate Type I from Type II may indicate an administrative change during the reign of a single king. Conversely, the variant years could indicate that the ostraca belong to two different kings, which would suggest either a concurrent date (under a co-regency) or consecutive dates. In the latter case, postulating two different kings would require a gap of eleven years at the minimum, and twenty-five years maximum. In the former case, the co-regency of two kings would explain why the two types of ostraca were discarded together in the fill of the Ostraca House. Those who advocate co-regents for the two dating systems have suggested that Year 15 belonged to Jehoash and the ninth and tenth years were those of his son, Jeroboam II (Rainey 1988; and Dijkstra 2000). Most scholars, however, assign the ostraca to a single ruler, most likely Jeroboam II (786–746 BCE), which would require a seven-year span between the ninth year and year 15.

Although the Samaria Ostraca are verb-less texts, their contents offer rare insight into the language, culture, and landscape of Israel during the eighth century. Lexical and philological studies have shown that several of their linguistic peculiarities are indicative of northern Hebrew (Sarfatti 1982). The products listed, "washed oil" and "aged wine," are prestige items that most likely represent cultural equivalents to forms of oil and wine mentioned in the Hebrew Bible (Sasson 1981; Briquel-Chatonnet 1992a–b; and Suriano 2007; cf. Sivan and Schniedewind 1990). In other words, neither product is mentioned in biblical literature or epigraphic sources from Judah (though aged wine is referred to in the Mishnah), but cultural considerations indicate that they were northern equivalents to products known from southern sources (Stager 1983). The word for "year," is an isogloss known from Phoenician and Moabite (Garr 2004), but it is unique from all other forms of Hebrew. Furthermore, the orthography of the ostraca seems to reflect a contracted diphthong, notably in the consistent spelling of the word "wine" (Cross and Freedman 1952). Finally, the Yahwistic theophoric-element in the spelling of personal names, *-yāw*, differs from the way that it is written in the onomastica of biblical and southern (Judahite) epigraphic sources. In addition to the Yahwistic names, the ostraca list several personal names with Baʿal-theophoric elements. Most of the ostraca contain reference to a person, whose name is marked with a preposition. The interpretation of the Samaria Ostraca and their function rests largely on whether this person (the so-called *lamed*-man) is understood as an owner of the shipped products (Yadin 1959 and 1962; Cross 1975; Kaufman 1966 and 1982), or the recipient (Rainey 1962, 1970, 1979, 1988; Aharoni 1962 and 1979; Lemaire 1977). A combination of factors favors the recipient theory, thus the basic syntax of the ostraca should be rendered: "from Gath Pirʾan, to Shemaryaw" (using number 14 as an example). The meaning of the shipments, and the exact nature of the *lamed*-men, however remains unclear. Some have suggested that these individuals are members of the king's court who have received royal land grants (Rainey 1970 and 1979; Dearman 1988; Schloen 2001; see 2 Sam 9:7), while others see them as representatives in the capital of the rural countryside (Niemann 2008).

The place names, from which the wine and oil are sent, provide valuable information for reconstructing the landscape surrounding the northern capital (Lemaire 1977; B. Mazar 1986:183–186; Aharoni 1979). In the Type I ostraca, the sources of the shipment are villages, which reflect a ~13 km radius surrounding Samaria. Because the Hebrew Bible/Old Testament only describes the boundaries of Ephraim and Manasseh, the place names in the Samaria Ostraca help us fill out the territory of these tribes. A change occurs in the year 15 ostraca, where the shipments are sent from clans rather than villages. The clan names correspond to the genealogy of Manasseh in Josh 17:2–3; Abiʿezer, Ḥeleq, Asriʾel (spelled Saraʾel without the prosthetic *aleph*), Shechem, and Shemidaʿ. In place of Ḥepher are two daughters of his son Zelopheḥad (cf. Num 27:1–11; and 36:1–12): Noʿa and Ḥoglah (Lemaire 1971).

SAMARIA OSTRACON 1 (4.18A)

In the tenth year[2] to Shem-
aryaw[3] from Beʾerayim a jar[4] of
aged [wine].[5]
Garaʿ (son of) Elisha, 2
Uzzaʾ (son of) Qa[d]bes, 1
Eliba (son of) N] […,1
Baʿalaʾ (son of) ʾElîš[a] 1
Yadaʿyaw 1

---

[2] This is the longest of the Samaria Ostraca, at eight lines, and one of the few that lists multiple people and numbered quantities (see also Samaria Ostracon 2 [4.18B].

[3] The name is found in the Hebrew Bible (2 Chr 11:19 and Ezra 10:32) in the form *šᵉmaryāhû* (see 1 Chr 12:5 [Hebrew]). The northern form *šmryw* (as it is written in the Samaria Ostraca) appears also at Kuntillet Ajrud and in seal impressions from Samaria (*WSS*:159 no. 377) and Dothan (Barkay 2005:171).

[4] The vessel of shipment used throughout the Samaria Ostraca, *nēbel*, appears also in the Hebrew Bible. It is uncertain, however, whether it refers to a wineskin or a ceramic vessel. The latter case would suggest further that the *nēbel* was a small vessel and not a storage jar (M. Aharoni 1979:96). Rather than representing a fixed quantity, in biblical literature the term seems to signify a special quality within socially embedded forms of exchange (Nam 2012:157–158; citing 1 Sam 1:24; 10:3).

[5] The product, *yn yšn*, is found also in the Mishnah (Paul 1975; and Sarfatti 1982:76). It is probably a semantic parallel to the biblical Hebrew term *šᵉmārîm mᵉzuqqāqîm* "refined aged wine" in Isa 25:6 (Suriano 2007:30–31).

SAMARIA OSTRACON 2 (4.18B)

In the tenth year,
to Gaddiyaw
from Azzah.
Abibaʿal, 2
Aḥaz, 2
Shebaʿ, 1
Meribaʾal, 1

SAMARIA OSTRACON 3 (4.18C)

In the tenth year, to [Aḥim]aʿ
from Shemidaʾ,[6] a jar of …
aged [wine]. To Baʿalaʾ s[on of …]

---

[6] The name Shemidaʾ, which is a clan of Manasseh (Num 26:32), is found prominently among other Manassite clans in the Type II (Year 15) texts.

SAMARIA OSTRACON 4 (4.18D)

[In the] ninth year, from Qo[ṣoh]
to Gaddiyaw, a jar
[of aged wine.]

SAMARIA OSTRACON 8 (4.18E)

[In the] ninth [year], from Geb-
[aʿ, to Abino]ʿam, a jar of
[aged w]ine.

SAMARIA OSTRACON 10 (4.18F)

In the ninth year, from
Yaṣit, to Abinoʿa-
m, a jar of
aged wine.

SAMARIA OSTRACON 12 (4.18G)

In the ninth year,
from Siptan, to Baʿal-
zamar, a jar of
aged wine.

SAMARIA OSTRACON 14 (4.18H)

In the nin[th] year, from Gath Pirʾan, to Shemaryaw,
a jar of aged wine.

SAMARIA OSTRACON 16 (4.18I)

In the tenth year, from Se-
pher to Gaddiyaw, a jar
of washed oil.[7]

7 There are two lines of thought regarding this product. The first is that it represents a cosmetic product for bathing (Diringer 1934:37–38; Demsky 2007:333–336; Amar 2009:18–26). According to this interpretation, *rḥṣ* is a Qal active partiple (*rāḥāṣ*), analogous to "waters of ablution" (*mê niddā* in Num 19:13) and "bathing waters" (*mê rāḥāṣ*) in 1QS 3:5 (Israel 1975:17–20; Lipiński 1977:85–86). The second, which is followed in this translation, is that the participle is a Qal passive, **šamn rāḥūṣ* (Lemaire 1977:46–47; *SSI* 1:8; Briquel-Chatonnet 1992b:236; Renz 1995:83, ns. 2–3). Understood as such, the participle is descriptive of its mode of production and semantically equivalent to the biblical Hebrew term "crushed oil" (*šemen kātît* in 1 Kg 5:25; see Sasson 1981:1–5; Stager 1983:241; Suriano 2007:29).

SAMARIA OSTRACON 18 (4.18J)

In the ninth year, from Ḥaṣerot
to Gaddiyaw, a jar of
washed oil.

SAMARIA OSTRACON 19 (4.18K)

In the tenth year,
from Yaṣit, a jar
of washed oil to
Aḥinoʿam.

SAMARIA OSTRACON 23 (4.18L)

In year 15, from Ḥeleq,
to Asaʾ [son of] Aḥimelek.
Ḥeleṣ, from Ḥaṣerot.

SAMARIA OSTRACON 28 (4.18M)

In year 15, from Abiʿezer,[8] to Asaʾ
[son of] Aḥimelek.
Baʿalaʾ of Elmattan

8 A well-known clan from the Hebrew Bible (Josh 17:2; Judg 6:34 and 8:2; cf. Iezer in Num 26:30), Abiʿezer also appears as a source of shipment a Type I text from the tenth year.

SAMARIA OSTRACON 44 (4.18N)

[In year] 15,[9] from Shechem,[10]
[to]]…[
[…] the wine …

---

[9] A few of the Type II ostraca such as this one have a direct article attached to the Hieratic numerals, written: *h*-10 5. Despite this, the translations of all Type II texts will consistently render the year as a cardinal number.

[10] This is the most recognizable place name in the Samaria Ostraca. Shechem (identified with Tell Balaṭah in modern Nablus) is well known from the Hebrew Bible (Gen 12:6; Josh 24:1; Judg 9:1; 1 Kg 12:1, 25) and ancient sources such as the Amarna letters. In biblical literature, as well as in the Samaria Ostraca, Shechem appears as both the name of a city as well as a clan-name (Num 26:31; Josh 17:2). The appearance of Shechem along with Shemida᾿ and Abiʿezer (all listed as kindred clans, belonging to Manasseh) among the toponyms of the Type I ostraca (in addition to the clan names of the Type II texts) indicates that there was considerable overlap between kinship groups and settlement names (Schloen 2001:162–165).

SAMARIA OSTRACON 53 (4.18O)

In the tenth year, wine of
the vineyard of the Tell in a jar[11] of
washed oil.

---

[11] In the ostraca from the vineyard of the Tell, the wine shipment is ambiguously associated with a jar of washed oil through an attached preposition: *yn bnbl šmn rḥṣ*. The preposition could indicate a form of exchange, "for a jar of washed oil" (Reisner, Fisher, and Lyon 1924, 2: 230), "instead of …" (Schloen 2001:158), or type of value (Kaufman 1966:145, n. 52). Another possible reading is be "with a jar of washed oil" (Renz 1995:103). It is translated here as indicative of its mode of shipment, "in a jar of washed oil" (Diringer 1934:35; Lemaire 1977:36), which may indicate a specialized type of wine (Suriano 2016). A less likely possibility is that the preposition is the result of scribal error (so *SSI* 1:13; Aḥituv 2008:306), since it occurs in other ostraca.

REFERENCES

Text, translations and studies: Aḥituv 2008; Aharoni 1962, 1979; Albright in ANET; Dijkstra 2000; Dobbs-Allsopp, Roberts, Seow, and Whitaker 2004; *KAI*; Gibson *SSI* 1; Gogel 1998; Kaufman 1966, 1982, 1992; Lemaire 1971, 1977; B. Mazar 1986; Nam 2012; Niemann 2008; Rainey 1962, 1967, 1970, 1979, 1988; Reisner n.d.; Reisner, Fisher, and Lyon 1924; Renz 1995; Sasson 1981; Schloen 2001; Stager 1983; Suriano 2007; 2016; Tappy 2001; Yadin 1959, 1962.

MOABITE COMPOSITIONS

THE EL-KERAK/KEMOSHYAT INSCRIPTION (4.19)

Dennis Pardee

Acquired for the Jordan Archaeological Museum in 1958 and published in 1963 (Reed and Winnett; palaeographic table and discussion in van der Kooij 1987:117, 120; new copy and photograph in Rollston 2008:81, 112), this Moabite inscription is reported to have been discovered in the course of trenching for the foundations of a new construction in the town of el-Kerak. It is a small fragment (height 14 cm, width 12.5 cm) of a basalt block that bears the central part only of three lines of text. It is difficult to say whether the original inscription consisted of only these three lines. There is an uninscribed space above the first line and, below the third line, remnants of a decorative carving. The editors compared one of the Aramaic stelae from Neirab (*KAI* 225), where a section of the skirt in the representation of the author was smoothed to receive four lines of writing, these lines being separated from the beginning of the text by a wide space (*ANEP* 280); this approach has been developed convincingly by Parker and Arico 2015. The principal importance of this text in Moabite studies has been to supply the widely accepted restoration of the patronym in the first line of the Mesha inscription (*KAI* 181), where the last two signs have disappeared, as {kmšyt}. The principal points of discussion have been: (1) whether the name Mesha is to be restored before that of Kemoshyat in line 1, making of this another Mesha inscription (Freedman 1964; Timm 1989: 277)[1]; (2) the etymology of the second element of the author's name (Reed and Winnett 1963 identified this element as ŠT "to put," but most scholars since H. L. Ginsberg's oral suggestion reported by Reed and Winnett [1963:8, n. 20a] have proposed to see here an abbreviated form of NTN "to give"); (3) the meaning of {mbʿr} in line 2 (whether derived from a basic meaning of "burn" or of "destroy"; in the first case, whether the cultic sense of "altar" or the more general "brazier"). The uncertainty regarding the meaning of this last term and the small extent of the preserved text make it impossible to identify the literary type of the inscription: votive, victory, or yet another type?

(1) [... K]emoshyat, king of Moab, of D[YBN ...]
(2) [...] Kemosh to/for MBʿR, because [...]
(3) [...] I did [...]

---

1 Miller (1992:87) has expressed doubt regarding the legitimacy of the restoration *kmšyt* in the Mesha inscription and hence regarding the identification of this personage of the el-Kerak inscription as the father of Mesha (cf. Gaß 2009:68).

REFERENCES

Aḥituv 2005:355–357; 2008:387–389; Braslavi 1964; Freedman 1964; Gaß 2009:66–69; Gibson 1971:83–84; *KAI* 306; Miller 1992:78, 87; Naveh 1965:66–67; Reed and Winnett 1963; Routledge 2004:140–141, 238–239, n. 16; Schiffmann 1965; Swiggers 1982a, b; Teixidor 1967:169–170; Timm 1989:269–277; van der Kooij 1987:113, 117, 120; Vera Chamaza 2005:35–36; Weippert 1964:169–172; 1966: 328–330.

THE NEW MOABITE ROYAL INSCRIPTION (4.20)

Dennis Pardee

A new Moabite inscription was brought to the attention of the scholarly world in 2003 when Aḥituv published an edition complete with photographs, a hand-copy (by Ada Yardeni), transliterations into Roman and square Hebrew characters, a translation, and a commentary. Nothing is known of its discovery, for Aḥituv gained access to it when it was placed in the Israel Museum, Jerusalem, on long-term loan by private owners. The text is inscribed on four facets of an original octagonal column which has been truncated horizontally, cutting through the first and last lines of the inscription as preserved, and vertically so that only five facets are (partially) preserved. Though the date of this re-cutting is unknown, it seems clear that it was done for utilization of the stone in a construction of some sort, for the editor reported the presence of mortar on the lower edge of the stone in its present state. As with any unprovenanced object, the question must be raised of its authenticity – but, in this case, the modern forgers would have to have been expert in ancient epigraphy, had experience cutting and carving stone, and been wily enough to inflict serious damage on their work once completed.[1] It appears necessary, therefore, to ascribe the similarities between this text and the famous Mesha inscription to Moabite royal rhetoric. Because the name of the royal figure who dictated the inscription is not preserved, the principal dating criterion is palaeographic; the number of Moabite inscriptions is, however, too small for this sub-discipline of Northwest-Semitic palaeography to have been established on a firm basis, so all that one can say with any confidence is that the text was probably produced after the Mesha inscription,

1 Emerton (2005:293) and Dearman (2009:97–98) have explicitly raised the question of authenticity, the latter in more detail and with the assessment that "The balance of probability is that of authenticity ..." (p. 97).

some time during the eighth century (Dearman 2009:98). The one historical event that may be deduced from the text is a battle between Moab and Ammon that resulted in Ammonite prisoners being put to forced labor in Moab. Because of the absence of other clear references to such conflict between the two polities, any historical dating is just as problematic as is the palaeographic dating.

(1′) [...] [...]
(2′) [...]many prisoners[2] [ ][3]
(3′) [...]I [b]uilt BT HRʾŠ,[4] and with Ammonite prisoners[5]
(4′) [...]excavation, a mighty gate.[6] Flocks of sheep and goats and herds of cattle
(5′) [...]The Ammonites saw that there was sickness[7] throughout
(6′) [...] [ ]
(7′) [...]

2 The mention of prisoners (here and in the following line) is reminiscent of Mesha's use of Israelite prisoners for his building projects (*KAI* 181, lines 25–26), particularly for excavating *mkrtt* (see here below, line 4′).

3 Two signs are preserved, after this long break, {lk}, and some reconstruction including the word *mlk*, "king," is plausible.

4 Lit., "house of the head," reference unknown: *hrʾš* could be a common noun ("house of the high point") or the phrase *bt hrʾš* could be a toponym of some sort, town, fortress, or temple (see the detailed discussion in Dearman 2009).

5 It has been claimed that the absence of a word-divider in the phrase *bny ʿmn* makes of the six signs a single word and thus that the {y} represents a preserved /ay/-diphthong or an historical spelling (Aḥituv 2003:6; Becking 2009:5). Hebrew usage shows, however, that the name was perceived as consisting of two words. It is far more plausible, therefore, to see the absence of a word-divider as simply reflecting the compound nature of the phrase – few inscriptions, from Ugaritic on, show absolutely consistent use of the word-divider – and to identify the {y} as a final *mater lectionis* (for /ê/ < /ay/, as in the preceding word, *ʾsry*, "prisoners of"; cf. *ʾsry yšrʾl*, "prisoners of Israel," in the Mesha inscription [*KAI* 181, lines 25–26], there with a word divider between the two words).

6 The phrase is *mkrt šʿr ʾdr*. The first word is probably the singular of *mkrtt*, attested as a plural in the Mesha inscription (*KAI* 181, line 25); *krty*, "I excavated," is the verb used by Mesha – in the new inscription, the reconstruction at the beginning of the line is complicated by the uncertain syntax of the preserved words. Comparison of the three forms in the two inscriptions allows for the conclusion that the root is KRT "to cut," and that the presence of only one {t} in the verbal form and in the singular noun is owing to the proximity of root letter /t/ and an additional morpheme with /t/: /karattī/ < /karat + tī/ and /mikrat/ < /mikrat + t/ (some have preferred to analyze *krty* as from KRH "to dig"). Nevertheless, because of the lacuna at the beginning of the line, the structure of the phrase *mkrt šʿr ʾdr* is uncertain. The editor took the "mighty gate" as being constructed for the *mkrt*, reconstructing *bnty l* "I have built for," in the lacuna (Aḥituv 2003; 2008; so Becking 2009:4), whereas others have seen here a so-called construct chain ("an excavation of a gate, a mighty one"). Aḥituv's interpretation reflects the fact that "a mighty gate" is indefinite in the Moabite, whereas others have translated the phrase as though it were definite (Lemaire 2005:98, 100; Gaß 2009:77; 2012:48). Against Aḥituv's interpretation, it may be observed that the *mkrtt* in the Mesha inscription were dug "for" another installation (the *qrḥh*), not the other way around. As regards the narrow meaning of *mkrt*, some have proposed that the term designates some kind of water installation (Aḥituv 2003; Emerton 2005; Kallai 2006), others a protective moat (Lemaire 2005, reconstructing *krty* in the lacuna, "I have excavated a moat for the mighty gate"; so Gaß 2009; 2012). In the first case, one wonders why a mighty gate would have been constructed for a water installation; in the second, why a moat would have been dug for a gate (a moat normally surrounds all of a site or, at least, that part of a site that is not protected by a natural declivity); also against the latter interpretation must count the indefinite formulation "a mighty gate." One wonders, then, if the phrase refers simply to the excavation necessary for the installation of a new gate, either an entirely new one or a replacement gate of larger dimensions than its predecessor.

7 The writing {ḥlh} indicates that the subject is singular, apparently indefinite ("one was sick" = "people were sick"). If *ḥlh* is a noun (Gaß 2009:81; 2012:56), the Moabite pattern was different from that of Hebrew, where the masc. sing. noun was /ḥᵒlī/, with {y} *mater lectionis* in the absolute and construct forms, consonantal {y} in suffixal forms. At least in Biblical Hebrew, the term always refers to physical illness, whether literal or metaphorical (e.g., sick with love), and it appears unlikely that the term refers here to political weakness (Aḥituv 2003:5 "... the Ammonites saw that they were weakened," citing Samson's weakness in Judg 16:7, 11).

REFERENCES

Aḥituv 2003; 2004; 2005:373–377; 2008:419–423; Becking 2009; Dearman 2009; Emerton 2005; Gaß 2009:76–83; 2012:47–60; Kallai 2006; Lemaire 2005.

THE INCENSE ALTAR FROM KHIRBET EL-MUDIYINEH (4.21)

Dennis Pardee

Discovered in regular excavations (Dion and Daviau 2000) and hence of doubtless authenticity, the date, the linguistic identification, and the interpretation of this text have nevertheless all been matters of debate in the scholarly literature. The text consists of two lines inscribed vertically on an incense altar of complex form that stands nearly a meter high. Date: the editors placed the archaeological context at *ca.* 800 BCE (Dion and Daviau 2000:3, 5), but the possibility of a date as much as a century later has been proposed (Routledge 2003), as has a palaeographic dating of *ca.* 725 +/- 50 years (Rollston 2004:69, n. 33). Linguistic identification: without placing a specific linguistic tag on this text, the editors pointed out that *ʾš* as a relative pronoun (line 1) occurs only in Phoenician (Dion and Daviau 2000:11); others have stressed that the verb ʿŚ(Y) "to make," is not Phoenician, but Moabite and Hebrew; Rainey joined the two observations in proposing that the author was a Northern Israelite somehow influenced by

Phoenician (2002:86). Interpretation: the three principal words of the second line, which reads *lysp bt ʾwt*, have all received varying interpretations, *ysp* as either a personal name or a verb ("to add, augment"), *bt* as the word for either "daughter" (*bat*) or "house" (*bêt*), and *ʾwt* either as a personal name or as a common noun meaning "sign, oracle" (the first alternative was proposed in all three cases by the editors and accepted by Gaß; the second was proposed by Rainey and accepted by Aḥituv and by Lipiński). Against Rainey's revised version must count the fact that one expects the verb YSP to be followed by a prepositional complement (as in the parallel from the Mesha inscription, *KAI* 181, line 21 "to add X to the land of DYBN"): the English translation "to augment X" finds no good parallel. Hence the editors' interpretation may be preferred – they made it clear that the preposition *l* would not designate the dedicatee of the altar, but the individual on whose behalf the scribe/artisan prepared the cultic object for the temple in which it was discovered (Dion and Daviau 2000:10). The uncertainty regarding date is compounded by the relative paucity of Transjordanian inscriptions on stone, but the script is neither Phoenician nor Israelite (Rollston 2004:69 n. 33). Though there has been debate regarding the form of the relative pronoun in Ammonite (e.g., Rainey 2002:83; Gaß 2009:72), recent epigraphic research has shown the only certainly attested form to be *š* (Richelle 2012:139), and, as is well known, that particle in Moabite is *ʾšr*. Any obvious linguistic ascription is thus presently unknown, though the identification as a Transjordanian dialect is favored by the features that appear to preclude a Phoenician or Israelite origin.

(1) Incense altar that Elishamaʿ made
(2) for (= on behalf of) YSP, daughter of ʾWT.

REFERENCES

Aḥituv 2005:377–379; 2008:423–426; Dion and Daviau 2000; Gaß 2009:72–74; Lipiński 2004:139–140; Rainey 2002; Rollston 2004:69–70, n. 33; Routledge 2003.

MARZEAḤ PAPYRUS (4.22)

Dennis Pardee

The two-line inscription on papyrus mentioning a *mrzḥ* is of unknown provenance; one of the photographs on which the first publication was based show it in what is purported to be the form in which it was found, that is, folded and sealed by a bulla (Bordreuil and Pardee 1990: pl. VIII 2). As with any unprovenanced object, the plausibility of authenticity must be assessed, but, by their very nature, such considerations may never rule out a modern origin (see Gaß 2009:86–87 for discussion and bibliography on this question). The editors proposed a Transjordanian origin, in part because of what they took for a place name on the bulla ({l mlk | ʾkʿtʿ[n]} "(Belonging) to the king of *ʾktn*," to be compared with modern Tell Iktanu).[1] Though the text is very brief, the most obvious interpretation is as the record of a property settlement established by divine decree.[2] The language of the text is a matter of debate, as it does not match in all attested features with any of the presently known Transjordanian languages.[3]

(1) Thus say the gods to Saraʾ:[4] Yours are the *mrzḥ*,[5,a] the grindstones, and the
(2) house; Yišʿaʾ is excluded[6]; Milkaʾ is the guarantor.[7]

a Jer 16:5; Amos 6:7

[1] Cross (1996:316–317) has rejected this reading of the seal, preferring to attach the *alif* at the beginning of the second line to the signs of the first line, giving the name *mlkʾ*, found in the principal text. Cross offered no cogent interpretation of the following signs, but Botta (2009:134) suggests "scribe" (i.e., kʿtʿ[b]), though he cites no parallels.

[2] Rather than as a settlement of a dispute over leadership of the *mrzḥ* (Aḥituv 1999).

[3] The editors expressed doubt that the perfect linguistic match with Mishnaic Hebrew constituted sufficient grounds for declaring the text a forgery (Bordreuil and Pardee 1990:68; cf. Pardee 2005:196–197; 2008:65).

[4] On the reading of this name with {s} rather than {g}, see Bordreuil and Pardee 2000.

[5] *mrzḥ* is a West-Semitic term of uncertain etymology but attested from the second half of the third millennium (Ebla) down into Rabbinic times (McLaughlin 2001). It designates a social group of males numbering a dozen or so whose meetings were typified by the consumption of wine (O'Connor 1986). Each such group had a tutelary deity, but bloody sacrifice was not practiced by such groups – though there is no reason to doubt that, in keeping with the principal activity, the meetings may have included the offering of libations to the divine patron. The *mrzḥ* is thus not a cultic association in the narrow sense of the word, and the places in which such groups met may not properly be described as a temple or a sanctuary (Pardee 1996). The term itself "may denote the social entity in question, its human membership, or the place where the group meets" (Pardee 2005:197) – the association here with a set of grindstones and a house indicates the last meaning in this text.

[6] The phrase is *wyšʿʾ rḥq mhm*, lit. "and Yišʿaʾ (must be) far from them." On the legal use of RḤQ, see Botta 2009.

[7] *hšlš*, lit. "the third." The use of *šālīš* for a neutral third party to whom the legal decision was entrusted for arbitration in case of a later dispute is attested in Mishnaic Hebrew.

REFERENCES

Aḥituv 1999; 2005:379–383; 2008:427–431; Bordreuil 1992:188–189; Bordreuil and Pardee 1990; 2000; Botta 2009:133–134; Cross 1996/2003; Gaß 2009:84–87; McLaughlin 2001:35–36; Pardee 2005:196–197; 2008:64–65; Routledge 1996:367–368.

ARAMAIC COMPOSITIONS

THE KTMW INSCRIPTION (4.23)

Dennis Pardee

The site of Zincirli has furnished a significant body of epigraphic material, in Phoenician, in a dialect of Aramaic attested only from this area known as Samalian, and in standard Old Aramaic. During the 2008 campaign of the renewed excavations by the Oriental Institute of the University of Chicago, a new inscription came to light that appears to represent a somewhat different linguistic usage, a dialect situated typologically between Samalian and standard Old Aramaic. It contains motifs present in the Samalian inscriptions, principally that of the author's "soul" being depicted as eating and drinking after death, but, unlike the Samalian inscriptions, it was dictated by a non-royal personage. The author refers to himself by name, KTMW in consonantal script, a name that is certainly of Luwian origin though the precise etymology of the KT-element and hence the pronunciation are uncertain.[1] He describes himself as a servant of a king named Panamuwa, probably the second known king of Yʾ DY by that name, which permits dating the inscription to the third quarter of the eighth century.[2] The stele, with its inscription and depiction of KTMW seated at a banquet table in raised relief, is well preserved.[3] Only the top of the stele has undergone any serious damage, but even there the remains of a winged sun disk are visible. The result of this remarkable state of preservation is that the readings are clear, the only epigraphic ambiguity arising from the similarity of the signs {d} and {r}, for these two signs were insufficiently differentiated to permit certain readings in the cases of previously unattested words with no obvious etymology, in particular the word for the place where the stele was set up ({syr/d}) and two of the divine names ({hdd . qr/dpd/rl } and {ngd/r . ṣwd/rn}). These ambiguities, as well as the author's reference to his "soul" (*nbš*) as destined to be "in" the stele (*bnṣb zn*) have already sparked several publications.

(1) I am KTMW, servant of Panamuwa, who commissioned for myself (this) stele while (2) still living. I placed it in my eternal chamber[4] and established a feast[5] (at) (3) this chamber: a bull for Hadad Qarpatalli,[6] a ram for NGD/R[7]

1 The second element, {mw} /muwa/, is well known and expresses "abundance/might." Younger (2009a:159–166) has proposed that the first element has to do with "fighting" and that the entire name expresses might in battle and is to be pronounced Katamuwa, Katimuwa, or Katumuwa.

2 The two inscriptions on which the kings named Panamuwa are the principal figures (*KAI* 214, 215) refer to them as "king of Yʾ DY (vocalization unknown)," whereas the later king Bar-Rakib, who describes himself as voluntarily submitting to Assyrian hegemony, gives his own title as "king of Samʾal" (*KAI* 216, 217). On the history and significance of the two names, see Schloen and Fink 2009:6–7. The name of the Aramaean kingdom is also attested as *Bīt Gabbāri* in Akkadian, "House of Gabbār," named after the first ancestor in the dynastic list enumerated by the ninth-century king Kulamuwa in his inscription composed in Phoenician (*KAI* 24; cf. Niehr 2010:267–284).

3 See Schloen and Fink 2009; Struble and Herrmann 2009; Herrmann 2014a and 2014b.

4 The Aramaic phrase is {syr/d ʿlmy}, where the second term expresses the desired perennity of the mortuary construction (compare, in Phoenician, *KAI* 1:1), while the reading and interpretation of the first are uncertain. The editor preferred the reading {syr} and suggested a connection with SR 'turn aside', as a reflection of the act of attending the feast (Pardee 2009:60). Since, it has been proposed that the correct reading is {syd} and that the basic meaning was "gathering/gathering place" (Mazzini 2009); a connection with Old South Arabian *mswd*, designating a part of a construction, including a section of a tomb, was posited (Nebe 2010: 320–321, cites the same data but comes to the interpretation "Kultdistrikt/Kultakt"). The architectural connection with Old South Arabian *mswd*, as argued in more detail by Sanders (2012; 2013), makes this suggestion very appealing. The differing forms rule out an explanation by direct contact between the two linguistic communities. But the general etymological link appears plausible, and it opens up new vistas on the similarities between the two cultures that led to the derivation of very different forms from a hollow root to designate part or the entirety of a mortuary construction. It is important, nevertheless, to note that the construction at Zincirli was not a tomb, for no burial remains were discovered there: the "eternal chamber" was apparently intended for the stele, which certainly was not buried, and for the "soul" of the author, which continued its being in the stele (see note below to *nbš*).

5 The verb is *ḥggt*, plausibly with a connotation of travel involved in attending the feast, for words derived from ḤGG often carry a notion of "pilgrimage." The D-stem verb appears to express the act of establishing such a feast, plausibly by enacting it for the first time. The second part of the inscription deals with the obligation of carrying on the feast in the future. One of the enigmas of the inscription is what it was in KTMW's profile as a servant of the king of Samʾal that led to the use of a term connoting pilgrimage. Since preparing the commentary in the edition of this text, I have come across a reference to the use of the D-stem of ḤGG in an Old North Arabian inscription (Dadanitic) of a not dissimilar type (see the recent study by Hidalgo-Chacón Diez 2009) – there it is the offerings that are the formal object of the verb, here the offering-chamber.

6 Following Yakubovich (2010:396), who explains {qr/dpd/rl} as a Luwian term for "companion" (**ḫarpatalli*).

7 According to Masson (2010:53), {ngd/r} should be read {ngr}, taken as representing the deity "Nikarawas/Nikaruhas." She also cites the fact that this divinity was a dog-owner as an indication that {ṣwd/rn} should be read as {ṣwdn}, which she interprets as "hunter."

(4) ṢWD/RN, a ram for Šamš, a ram for Hadad of the Vineyards,
(5) a ram for Kubaba,[8] and a ram for my "soul" that[9] (will be) in this stele.[10]
(6) Henceforth, whoever of my sons or
(7) of the sons of anybody (else) should come into possession of
(8) this chamber, let him take from
(9) the best (produce) of this vineyard (as) a (presentation)-offering[11]
(10) year by year.[12] He is also to perform the
(11) slaughter (prescribed above) in (proximity to) my "soul"
(12) and is to apportion
(13) for me a leg-cut.[13]

8 On the spelling of this name as {kbbw}, see Younger 2009a:166–179.

9 An additional isogloss (missed by the editor) separating the dialect of this inscription from Samalian: the relative pronoun with a feminine antecedent is here {zy}, over against {ʾzh} in *KAI* 215:2 (Nebe 2010:323).

10 The term is *nbš*, the regional equivalent of the more widely attested *npš*, conventionally translated "soul" but with a wide spread of functional values across the Semitic languages. I indicate the conventional nature of the translation by the quotation marks around this term. The two references to the *nbš* in this text (here and in line 11) make it clear that the author considered that his *nbš* would continue in a form capable of eating and drinking and that it was enshrined behind the depiction in stone of the author's human form. Since no trace has been found either of the inhumation here of the author's corpse (Herrmann 2014a; 2014b) or of a cremation urn that would have contained his ashes, the *nbš* was apparently considered capable of continuing its being in the stele, with no attachment to the author's corporeal remains. The statements in this inscription are more explicit as to how his successors are to go about nourishing the *nbš* than were similar statements in the Samalian inscriptions *KAI* 214 and 215. Some interpreters have seen in this usage of *nbš* a sign of the Luwian (and more generally Indo-European) concept of the soul as separable from the body (Pardee 2009:62; Schloen and Fink 2009:10–11; Masson 2010:53–56; Melchert 2010; Hays 2011:128–129) while others lean towards a more specifically Semitic interpretation (del Olmo Lete 2011:308, n. 3; Suriano 2014) or have attempted to come up with an integrated view of the two (Sanders 2012).

11 The Aramaic term is written {šʾ}, but it is of uncertain origin and meaning. It is here translated as from NŚʾ "to lift, bear." Hardly "ram" (Nebe 2010:324–326), for not only does this interpretation not fit the context, but the word derived from Ṯʾ denoting an ovid is elsewhere morphologically and lexically marked for feminine gender, i.e., "ewe" (Ugaritic *ṯảt*, standard Old Aramaic *šʾh*, later *tʾtʾ*, Arabic *ṯaʾwat-*). This word for "ewe" has nothing to do with the Semitic word for "sheep," e.g., Ugaritic *š* (contra Nebe 2010:325) which is cognate with Hebrew *śe*[h] and is unrelated to the feminine word *ṯảt*. Lemaire's view (2012:132, 135), though not stated explicitly, appears to be that {šʾ} in this text is the masculine form of the feminine forms just cited; but the broad attestation of the explicitly feminine forms argues against that analysis. Since the Standard Aramaic post-positive article {-ʾ} is elsewhere unattested in this inscription, it is also unlikely that we have here the masculine word corresponding to Hebrew *śe*[h] in a definite form. It is equally unlikely that demonstrative *znn* here precedes the noun it modifies (Nebe 2010:325), as occurs in later dialects, or that a sheep would have been included among the "best (products) of this vineyard" (Lemaire 2012:134).

12 {ywmn lywmn}, lit. "days to days" (compare *miyyāmîm yāmîmā*[h] designating an annual pilgrimage in 1 Sam 1:3). In an attempt to rescue the identification of the language of this text as Samalian, Lemaire proposes to explain the phrase as something other than the repeated plural of *ywm*, "day," i.e., the final {-n} as something other than the consonantal element of the plural morpheme (Lemaire 2013), and thereby to remove the most striking isogloss with Old Aramaic. The parallel with 1 Sam 1:3 is striking while the other explanations that Lemaire proposes are unconvincing (the {-n} would represent either an adverbial morpheme or afformative /-ān/, which would have a particularizing function – one that is common in East Semitic, but not in West Semitic). Equally unconvincing is his attempt to reject the identification of {krmn}, the second element of the divine name "Hadad of the Vineyards" in line 4, as another Aramaic plural in favor of the analysis as a place name, for a "Weather Deity of the Vine" is attested in Luwian (Pardee 2009:62; Masson 2010:53).

13 Because of the presence of the verb HRG "to kill, slaughter," in lines 10–11, identifying the word written {šq} as corresponding to Hebrew *šōq*, "upper part of the leg, thigh," appears preferable to taking it as derived from ŠQY and meaning "libation" (Nebe 2010:318, 326; Coogan 2013:158).

REFERENCES

Coogan 2013: 146, 157–158; del Olmo Lete 2011; Hays 2011:128–129; Lemaire 2008–2009:17–18; 2012; 2013; Masson 2010; Mazzini 2009; Melchert 2010; Nebe 2010; Niehr 2010:282–284; Pardee 2009a; 2009b; Sanders 2012; 2013; Suriano 2014; Younger 2009a.

SAMʾALIAN FUNERARY STELE: ÖRDEKBURNU (4.24)
(Istanbul Archaeological Museum, Number 7696)

André Lemaire

This stele was pointed out to von Lushan (1888) in Ördekburnu, 18 km south of Zincirli, but its interpretation and language was very uncertain for more than a century after the detailed study of the inscription by Lidzbarski who reluctantly proposed to consider it an Anatolian inscription in Aramaic script. Because of this proposition, it was not included in *KAI* and Tropper 1993, even though several epigraphers (Bowman, Landsberger) proposed to consider it a West Semitic inscription. After a new detailed study of the inscription, Lemaire and Sass, showed that this only partially legible inscription is written in Samʾalian, the Aramaic dialect of the kingdom of Samʾal (Zincirli). Above the inscription, the iconography of this stele may be compared to contemporary funerary steles and reveals that the deceased was probably a woman, since she holds spindles. In front of her, the standing man is represented higher and holding a mace. At the top of the stele, the presence of three symbols of deities may be compared to those in Kulamuwa and Barrakib. Thus they might indicate a member of the royal family, which seems to be confirmed in the inscription by the mentions of "kingship/succession," Rakib᾽il, and a royal necropolis. Line 10 was engraved vertically on the left side of the stele. The inscription dates to the end of 9th – early 8th century BCE.

(1) I?[1] [*am PN*] … (2) … *my* sons *in* … *and* in (the) kingship/succession[2] (3) … *he will affirm*[3] … *on this. Let him* (4) *do good for the na*[*me*][4] … *by the sword.*[5] *And my sons* (5) … (be) he to Rakib᾽il the/my god[6]; (6) agreeable and *gracious/well placed* (be) he to Kubaba[7] *of Aram*.[8] Let him (7) *present an offering*: for Rakib᾽il two sheep[9] (8) for the Day,[10] and for Kubaba two sheep for the Day, (9) and in the royal necropolis ("[resting] place[11] of the kings") two sheep for me.[12] (10) And he who will do good for the name of *Piya-X*[13] *let his* "soul" *be* …

[1] The reading of the first four lines is very uncertain.
[2] *Ḥlbbh* is the only clear word of the first four lines. Compare Hadad 3, 9, 10, 12, 13, 19.
[3] *Ys῾d*: compare *wys῾d ᾽brw*, "and he will affirm his power," in Hadad 15 and 21.
[4] *Yhny ᾽š*[*m*]: this uncertain reading may be compared to the same formula, line 10.
[5] *Bḥrb*: compare Hadad 25.
[6] Rakib᾽il is the dynastic god, *b῾l b(y)t*, in Kulamuwa 16 and Panamuwa 22. His mention as the first deity is probably an indication that this inscription aims at a member of the royal family of Sam᾽al.
[7] Kubaba, the great goddess of Carchemish, is also mentioned in Katumuwa 5 and in a fragmentary stone inscription from Tell Sifr (Michelini Tocci 1962).
[8] Alternatively *᾽rmly* is interpreted "lunar" by Lipiński (2000:234, n. 9).
[9] *Š᾽yn*: dual, compare Aramaic dual on an 8th century BCE inscribed weight.
[10] *Ym* "the day" is probably here the day of the annual celebration of the mortuary rites (compare Akkadian *kispu*).
[11] *Mqm*: compare Hadad 14.
[12] For sacrifices offered to the deceased after those offered to the gods, compare the end of Katumuwa.
[13] The name of the deceased is partially illegible; its uncertain beginning would fit a Luwian name.

REFERENCES

Bowman 1948:71, n. 27; Landsberger 1948:48, n. 124; 64, n. 166; Lemaire and Sass 2012; 2013; Lidzbarski 1915; Lipiński 2000:233–234, n. 6; von Luschan 1911:329–330; Tropper 1993.

THE INSCRIPTION OF NINURTA-BĒLU-UṢUR/INURTA-BĒL-UṢUR (4.25)

K. Lawson Younger, Jr.

At ancient Ḫadattu (modern Arslan Taş) about 30 km east of the Euphrates near the Turkish border, a trilingual inscription on monumental gate lions was discovered.[1] It was written in Neo-Assyrian cuneiform, Aramaic, and hieroglyphic Luwian (Younger 2007c). It belonged to Ninurta-bēlu-uṣur/Inurta-bēl-uṣur, the provincial governor of Kār-Shalmaneser (Kār-šulmānu-ašarēd/Til-Barsib). This man was also a eunuch of the Assyrian *turtānu*, Šamšī-ilu. The inscription appears to date to around 780 BCE.

A pair of basalt lions were at the east gate of the city and a pair were at the west gate. The east gate lions both have an incised nine-line Assyrian, a nine-line Aramaic and a four-line hieroglyphic Luwian inscription (Galter 2004a, 449, and fig. 6; 2004b). All three texts were written on the surface of the lion facing the wall. The Akkadian and Aramaic inscriptions record that Ninurta-bēlu-uṣur/Inurta-bēl-uṣur (^{md}MAS.UMUN.PAB; Aramaic: *᾽nrtblṣr*) constructed Ḫadattu's wall and gates, in which the lion colossi were stationed. The Luwian text has been published (Hawkins 2000, 246–248), and appears to be somewhat independent of the Assyrian and Aramaic texts (the personal name at the beginning of the inscription is not preserved), although it reports on the building activity of the "country lord" of the city of Masuwari (Luwian name for Til-Barsib) in the city of Hatata (= Ḫadattu). While the Aramaic text is poorly preserved, it follows that of the Assyrian (Röllig 2009).

There can be no doubt as to who was the underling, this "eunuch of Šamšī-ilu."[2] Röllig (2009:277) rightly points out that the long and complicated emphasis on the origin of (N)inurta-bēlu-uṣur stands out, which seems to underline the legitimacy of this process; yet, at the same time because there is the absence of any filiation, it is reasonable to

[1] Thureau-Dangin et al. 1931. For recent excavations and study, see Cecchini and Venturi 2012.
[2] Galter 2004b, 175–176; Röllig 2009, 276; RINAP 1:162.

assume that this governor is a parvenu,[3] who was moreover of Aramean origin (note the reference to the *bīt abīya* / *byt ʾby*), although he does not bear an Aramaic name. His name (N)inurta-bēlu-uṣur "O Ninurta, protect the lord!" seems to have been characteristic of the second level provincial officials, particularly in this period.[4] Consequently, one might suggest that it was an assumed name when he took the office.[5]

THE AKKADIAN TEXT (4.25A)[6]

[I, Ninurta-bēlu]-uṣur, provincial governor (EN.NAM = *bēl pīḫāti*) of the city of Kār-Shalma[neser], erected solid basalt [lions …] … (which are) in the gate[s of] the city of Ḫadattu.

Ninurta-bēlu-uṣur (mdMAŠ-EN-PAP) of the city of Ṣiranu, which is (in the area of) the city of Ḫalaḫḫu, which is in front of the city of Lipapan in the mountains, the city of the house of my father; at that time, I created, built, (and) completed the city of Ḫadattu.

(As for) a future ruler who repairs its dilapidated section(s but) erases my inscribed name and inscribes his (own) name (in its place), may (the god) Aššur, the great lord, in the assembly of the gods verily order his destruction … and his name ….

(Lacuna)

[3] In other words, a person of obscure origin who has gained wealth, influence, or celebrity.

[4] Galter 2004a:450. A few examples of this pattern are: Aššur-bēlu-uṣur; Nabû-bēlu-uṣur; etc. For the name Ninurta-bēlu-uṣur, see Baker 2000g.

[5] It is doubtful that Ninurta-bēlu-uṣur was from a native local dynasty (contra Bunnens 2009:78–79). Moreover, there is absolutely no proof of the existence of a continued political entity called "Masuwari," as Makinson (2002–2005) speculates; only that the city continued to exist and that that name was used by Luwian speakers, where Aramean and Assyrian speakers used Til-Barsib or Kār-Shalmaneser. Not only is there is no evidence that the political entity Masuwari survived the Assyrian conquest of the region, there is no clear evidence that the designation was used to describe a political entity that existed at the time of the Assyrian conquest!

[6] For a complete discussion of all the Akkadian inscriptions, see RINAP 1:161–163, Text 2001; Galter 2004a; 2004b; 2007.

THE ARAMAIC TEXT (4.25B)[7]

… and I built fortifications (?) [in (?)] Ḥadattu (*ḥdš* = *ḥdt*)[8] to set (my?) name: Inurta-bēl-uṣur (*ʾnrtblṣ?r?*), the one who (is) of/from the town of Ṣiranu (*Ṣrn*) which (is) (in) the area of Ḥalaḫḫu (*ḥlḥ*)[9] that (is) before Lilaban (*llbn*), the town of the house of my father (*qryt . byt . ʾby*).

In my days, I made Ḥadattu (*ḥdš* = *ḥdt*) and I built it and I brought it order(?) Its …. and the gates of his … I made good (?). Four (?) lions (?), I had erected in its gates.

[7] Röllig 2009 (Aramaic Text A). I have not included the curse formulation since it is very fragmentary and adds little to the discussion.

[8] For discussion, see Röllig 2009:275.

[9] This is not the Ḫalaḫḫu district in the Assyrian heartland (an area where some Israelites were deported, 2 Kgs 17:6), but another place of the same name in the northwestern Jezirah.

THE LUWIAN TEXT (4.25C)[10]

… x … -tas Masuwarean Country-Lord (*ma-su-wa/i+ra/i-za-sa*(URBS) REGIO-*ni*(-) DOMINUS-*ia-sá*).

I founded the city of Hatata (= Ḫadattu) in one year;

and for me the gods … (?) he/they will buy.
But he …
… I […]ed.
… who with ox(en) …[11]

[10] Hawkins 2000:246–248. Line 1 is longer than lines 2–4, and there are approximately a half-dozen signs at the beginning of line 1 that are very difficult to make out. Hawkins' drawing (2000:pl. 104) does not accurately represent this (compare with pl. 105). While one would have expected the inscription to begin with EGO (*amu*) "I (am)," this cannot be read, nor can the name of the author of the inscription. Hawkins (2000:247) suggests that the word ending in *-tas* may be the ending of a title. While Luwian *Masuwarizas*(URBS) REGIO-*ni*(-)DOMINUS-*ias* ("Masuwarean Country-Lord") clearly corresponds to Akkadian EN.NAM URU.*Šulmān-ašarēd*, it is still not clear that the two inscriptions are by the same author (see Hawkins 2000:247). However, the placement of the hieroglyphic Luwian inscription is such that it appears to be integral with the Akkadian and the Aramaic – all three are contained in the same prepared surface area on the lion (see Hawkins 2000:pl. 105; Galter 2004a:449, fig. 6).

[11] The latter parts of line 2 through line 4 are very difficult. The translation follows Hawkins' discussion (2000:247–248).

REFERENCES

Galter 2004a; 2004b; 2007; Röllig 2009; RINAP 1:162; Hawkins 2000:246–248; Younger 2007.

TELL SHIUKH FAWQANI (TSF 46) (4.26A)

F. M. Fales

The *editio princeps* is found in F. M. Fales (Fales *et al.* 2005:653–655, color photography, hand-copy, transliteration, translation). This version will be followed here, with some updatings. The tablet was retrieved in 1995 during a salvage excavation by a French-Italian archeological team at Tell Shiukh Fawqani on the Upper Euphrates (cf. Bachelot and Fales 2005, esp. pp. 616ff.). It is of brittle dark-grey clay with some missing central fragments, with 10 lines incised in large-sized Aramaic alphabetic script, of rectangular shape and with a "vertical" orientation (= length–width approx. 2::1 in size, written along the shorter edge) which is amply attested for contemporaneous Neo-Assyrian (NA) texts (deeds, letters, etc.). The nature of the text is a legal document of the "contract" type (Fales 1986:15–16), recording a pledge of an individual or a loan of silver (see below), with three persons as the receiving party; their three stamp seals are impressed on the upper edge of the tablet. No date is given, but since the creditor, Šê'-'ušnî, also recurs in TSF 47, the hypothetical date of the latter (after 672 BCE) may be applied to this text as well.

(Obverse)
(1) Ḥamanin,[1] [ ]*lḥ* (and) Šibâ[2]
(2) from Burmar'ina[3] [...] *a man*[4]
(3) against(?) eight shekels,[5] to
(4) Šê'-'ušnî[6] [....]

(erasure of 1 line)
(5) three minas.[7]
(6) Witness: P [x] L;
(Reverse)
(7) and Š [x x]LN[8];

[1] Line 1. *ḥmnn* is presumably a personal name, for which the cuneiform parallel is represented by *Ḫamanini* from Tell Halaf (PNA 2/1:446a); he is the first of the parties named at the beginning of this deed.

[2] Line 1. After the small break following *ḥmnn*, the number of graphs on the line makes it likely that two further names were given: the presence of three stamp seals on the upper edge would also justify positing three individuals as counterparts to the creditor Šê'-'ušnî.

[3] Line 2. This line contains the indication of the toponym (*brmrn*) which should represent the ancient name of Tell Shiukh Fawqani itself: its identification stems from the single attestation of an URU*Burmar'ina* in the annals of Shalmaneser III, and is commonly accepted as such (cf. Bagg 2007:55). Early on in the second campaign of this ruler (857 BCE) the Assyrian army proceeded against the Aramaic kingdom of Bit-Adini, led by the insubmissive chief Aḫuni, sacking the town of La'la'tu. The Assyrians thereupon attacked Til Barsib (the present-day site of Tell Aḥmar), and, having defeated Aḫuni in pitched battle, shut him up in his fortified city. In the next passage, the king states: "moving on from the city Til Barsib I approached the city Burmar'ina which belonged to Aḫunu, the man of Bit-Adini. I besieged the city, captured it, and felled 300 of their fighting men with the sword. I erected a tower of heads in front of his city. In the course of my advance, I received tribute from Habinu of Til-Abnâ, from Ga'uni of Sarugi and from Giri-Dadi of Immerina. Moving on from the city Burmar'ina I crossed the Euphrates in rafts (made of inflated) goatskins. I received tribute from Qatazilu of Kummukh" (RIMA 3:15, lines 33–37). Now, the location of Tell Shiukh Fawqani with regard to Tell Aḥmar/Til Barsib is some 18 km northwards (i.e. less than one day's march of the Assyrian army) on the same eastern bank of the Euphrates. Further, the cities of Til-Abnâ, Sarugi and Immerina – whence the local rulers came to Burmar'ina with a pacifying tribute for the Assyrian ruler – are commonly placed in the area between Urfa and the Euphrates, i.e. as adjoining inland states to the N-NE of Burmar'ina itself (see Bagg 2007, s. v.). And finally, after crossing the Euphrates at Burmar'ina, Shalmaneser claims to have reached the area of Kummukhean political influence, i.e. he directed his march towards the north, in the direction of the great eastward loop of the western bank of the river centering on Samsat. Of course, the Tell Shiukh Fawqani text presented here refers to a Burmar'ina of some two centuries later: this was now a sleepy town on the Euphrates which had, already long hence, come to form part of the provincial organization of the Assyrian empire, and which depended from the nearby administrative and military center of Til Barsib. As for the toponym itself, its second element seems to point to the Aramaic noun **mr'*, "lord", with pronominal suffix of the 1st person plural. As for the first element, it may well be asked whether a divine name **Būr* should not be taken into account here, following a suggestion already offered in 1895 by A.H. Sayce, and more recently by R. Zadok (1977:65), thus yielding a nominal sentence name "*Būr* is our lord." The recently published Assyrian and Aramaic evidence from Tell Šēḫ Ḥamad concerning many personal names built with the divine element *Būr* at ancient Dūr-Katlimmu, and which points to a cult of this deity spread in the region between Harran and Hindanu on the middle Euphrates (Radner 2002:16), lends additional probability to this interpretation.

[4] Line 2. The break at the center of the line only allows a tentative restitution of the contents, and thus of the nature of the contract. The final letter might have been preceded by an *aleph*, thus yielding [']*š*: whether actually "a man" was meant here (as in TSF 47, q.v.), or rather the semantically wider *'š*, "everyone, each," is however open to question. In the latter case, the expression could refer to each of the three named individuals who were in debt with the creditor named in line 4 – i.e. the text would not represent the record of a pledge (as in TFS 47), but merely a debt-note of sorts, and the sum might indicate the amount that each of the three debtors was responsible for.

[5] Line 3. *ktmnt šqln*. The initial *k* is a preposition of comparative value: "as, in accordance with" (*DNWSI*, 482). The following sum of "8 shekels" is again identical to that of TSF 47; but cf. the previous line.

[6] Line 4. *š''šny* = *Šê'-'ušnî. The name of this individual, who also appears in tablet Tell Shiukh Fawqani no. 47, means "the god Se' is my strength", with the predicate constituted by a nominal formation from the Aramaic verb *'ṬN, already attested in Aramaic-Assyrian texts (cf. Fales 1986:190–191). The subject element presents the divine name *Se' (= *š'* in alphabetic script, with the standard graphemic cross-shift *š*::*s* between alphabetic and cuneiform realizations), which is a local form of the name of the Moon-god Sîn, particularly well attested in NW Mesopotamia, i.e. in the area of the major temple of the deity at Harran and adjoining regions (see Lipiński 1994:171–192). Šê'-'ušnî is clearly the creditor in the present deed.

[7] Line 5. The function of this further quantification is unclear, possibly because of the preceding break in line 4 and of the subsequent erasure: did each of the three debtors have to put up one mina (of silver) each, by way of interest, in case of non-restitution of the sum loaned? Or was this the redemption price for the pledged "man" of line 2?

[8] Rev. line 7. The name might have been a largely Akkadian formation, again compounded by the local name of the Moon-god, *Se', a middle element which is lost in the break, and the predicative *ln* = *ilāni*, e.g. *Se'-šar- ilāni, "Se' is the king of all the gods" or the like.

(8) and *Na*[*suḫ*]-manānī,[9] (9) from [x]..HNQ[10];	(10) and [...-]apla-iddi[na].[11]

9 Line 8. The suggestion here is that of a name compounded with the DN *nsḥ*, although admittedly the *samekh* is ill preserved, and the *ḥeth* is entirely lost. As for the predicative element, *-mʾnny* seems the most reasonable solution, although the *mem* is not entirely clear as such, due to the adjacent break. The DN *nsḥ* = cuneiform *Našuḫ / Našḫu* (see above, Obv. line 4, for the cross-shift *š*::*s*) is a rendering of the DN *Nusku, well attested in NW Mesopotamia, and again specifically at Harran and adjoining regions (since Nusku was the divine son of the Moon-god); an individual named Našuḫ-manānī is in fact attested in cuneiform from the "Harran census" (PNA, 936b).

10 Line 9. This line should contain an unidentified place-name.

11 Line 10. The Akkadian onomastic elements *-aplu/a-iddina*, "has given a son," should have been preceded by the name of the deity granting birth, which is lost in the break.

REFERENCES

Fales 2005.

TELL SHIUKH FAWQANI (TSF 47) (4.26B)

F. M. Fales

The *editio princeps* is Fales 1996 (photograph, hand-copy, transliteration, translation, commentary). Re-edition can be found in Lemaire 2001:123–125 (no. 4), for which also see *CAL ad* no. 13300; and by F. M. Fales in Fales *et al*. 2005:655–660 (with color photography, hand-copy, transliteration, translation, commentary). All prior versions will be taken into account here, with some updatings, mainly regarding onomastic data. The tablet, in compact yellowish clay, is incised in small-sized Aramaic script for the remarkable total of 21 lines, almost entirely complete. It is of rectangular shape and with a "vertical" orientation (see TSF 46). The nature of the text is a legal document of the "contract" type (Fales 1986:15–16), recording a pledge of a slave against a loan of silver; the creditor is the same individual as in TSF 46, Šê'-'ušnî, while the debtors are three members of the Assyrian armed forces, albeit bearing Aramaic personal names. The tablet also bears three ovoidal stamp seal impressions, with field dividers crossing them at their center, placed on the Reverse after the end of the text, side by side. Inscriptions in Aramaic (but so faded as to be illegible) lie on the bottom fields in the first two impressions from the left. No date is given, but the formula on the "loyalty oath" in Obv. line 12 points to a date following 672 BC (see below).

(Obverse) (1) [Seal[1] of Ša]'il[2] and Meya'[3] and Palṭî,[4] (2) men of the king's army[5]	(3) from Bit-Zamāni,[6] who are giving a man, (4) by the name of Nasuḥâ/Pasḥâ,[7] as pledge to Še'-'ušnî,

1 Line 1. The restoration of *ḥtm* – the term for the seal identification of the three debtors – is based on parallels from many other contemporaneous Aramaic texts on clay tablets from Syria and Mesopotamia (Fales 1986; Lemaire 2001; Röllig 2014).

2 Line 1. Considering the integration acceptable, the name would be an Aramaic participial form of the verb *šʾl*, "to ask": see PNA, 1063b–1064b for the cuneiform attestations of the name Sa'ilu and its variants (cf. *ad* TSF 46 for the graphemic cross-shift *š*::*s*).

3 Line 1. In cuneiform, a name Meiaʾ (possibly a hypocoristic based on **mî*, "Who?") is attested, with explicit reference to the Aramaic attestation here, PNA 747a.

4 Line 1. The name is a West Semitic hypocoristic, "My deliverance [is DN]"; cf. line 19, below.

5 Line 2. *gbrn zy kṣr. mlkʾ*. The expression refers to "men, belonging to" the particular branch of the army which depended directly from the Assyrian ruler, with a loan-translation from Akkadian *kiṣir šarri*. Cf. most recently Fales 2009:**75–76**.

6 Line 3. *Bīt Zamāni* was a former Aramean territory on the upper course of the Tigris (near present-day Diyarbakir) which was (re)-conquered by the Assyrians in the 9th century and became an Assyrian province, also named *Amedi*: cf. Radner 2006–2008:49. The local station of the three military, instead, is not given outright, but may be deduced from the place of origin of four witnesses named on the Reverse, who were present on their behalf, and who are described together as *mn trbšyb*, "from Til Barsib" (line 19). We are thus informed of a military contingent stationed in the nearby provincial capital: this is not surprising, in view of other contemporaneous textual clues which tie this city and the surrounding territory to the direct governorship of the "Commander-in-chief" (*turtānu*) at least until the early 7th century (Ibid., 48).

7 Line 4. The reading of the PN as *nsḥʾ* (Nasuḥâ), i.e. as a hypocoristic formed with the name of the god *Našuḫ/Našḫu*, had been already brought forth as an option (Fales 1996:93), and appears to be the more reasonable of the two interpretations. The following *šmh*, agreeing with Lemaire (and CAL) presents many difficulties, esp. as regards the initial *š*, but certainly would make good sense.

(5) against eight shekels of silver (on edge: II?).[8]
(6) And there will be nothing outstanding, incumbent upon Še'-'ušnî.[9]
(7) If he (= any debtor) redeems the man, the sum
(8) will be of one mina, but (as for) the share, its interest will be (only) of one-half.[10]
(9) But if the man has worked for Še'-'ušnî,
(10) he (= any debtor) will give in accompaniment (only) two-thirds of his (= the man's) capital.[11]

(11) Whoever will open his mouth[12] – the life of the king
(12) and his loyalty oath[13] will hold him responsible.[14]
(13) If they actually give back the sum,[15]
(14) they will take away the man.[16] Whoever gives
(15) a sickle at the harvest will ...[17]
(Reverse)
(16) Witness: Hadad-remanni (...);[18]
(17) and witness: Šin-zabad, the boatman;[19]
(18) and Namum(?)-marî[20] and Še'-'izrî,[21]

[8] Line 5. Two right-slanting vertical traces are incised after the text at the end of the line. They would seem to be number symbols, as in the Tell Šēḫ Hamad text D 19, l. 3, but their relation to the preceding numerical lexeme "eight" is unclear.

[9] Line 6. *wl š?ʾr ʿm šʾʿšny*. This is a difficult line. Lemaire and CAL corrected the reading in Fales 1996 to *wršʾ bdn šʾʿšny*, "and Šê'-'ušnî has power in justice," although considering this rendering quite uncertain. A further paleographical examination showed that the key lexeme should be *š?ʾr*, "remainder, something outstanding," well known from business contexts of later date (cf. *DNWSI*, 1098–1099) followed by an *ʿm* denoting incumbency of the named person (*DNWSI*, 869, for parallels). Thus, the present clause would be of an introductory legal nature, implying that the acquisition of the man as a pledge on the part of Šê'-'ušnî had "no strings attached."

[10] Lines 7–8. *hn yn?q* (eras.)*h ʾš kspʾ / bmnh wmntʾ rbh bplgh*. This is the first of a series of hypothetical clauses, introduced by *hn*, "if," regarding the possibility that specific juridical conditions should apply (cf. also lines 9 and 13). An in-depth examination of the script gave a reading of a verbal form *ynq*(eras.)*h*, from **nqy*, which in the D-stem means "to clear" (cf. *DNWSI*, 757). In line 8, *mntʾ* should derive not from *mnh*, "mina," present at the beginning of the line, but from a further *mnh*, "share" (*DNWSI*, 657). The whole clause thus implies that, if anyone of the debtors wanted to redeem the pledged man, the cost would be one mina; on the other hand (notice the adversative *w*), the redeemer's share of the original interest rate on the 8 shekels of silver owed by the three military would be reduced to/by one-half. However, it is not clear whether the *plg* should be understood as an absolute figure, i.e. equals to a 50% interest rate, or to a relative one (a reduction by 50% of an unspecified rate). The former solution seems, intuitively, more probable.

[11] Lines 9–10. This clause records a further hypothetical case: if the man had performed work for Šê'-'ušnî, anyone redeeming or buying him – or getting him back when the capital sum plus interest were paid back in full – would obtain a discount in relation to the man's work for the creditor, corresponding to one-third of the capital itself. The key item in line 9 is the verb *plḥ* as a probable loan-translation from Akkadian *palāḫu* in its specific meaning for work-obligations in Neo-Assyrian contracts of pledge (see already Fales 1996:97; *contra*, Lemaire 2008:82); in line 10, the initial *k!lwʾ* should go back to a root *lwy*, "to accompany," which is hardly at all attested epigraphically (*DNWSI*, 569), but is well known as a component of Aramaic PNs written in cuneiform, e.g. as in Se'-lawā(nī), "Se' has accompanied (me)" (cf. PNA, 1102).

[12] Line 11. *mn ywmh pmh*. The verb should derive from *ymʾ*, "to swear, to take an oath" (cf. *DNWSI*, 459–460). In this specific instance, it should refer to a possible formal protest regarding the validity of the present contract.

[13] Lines 11–12. *ḥyy mlkʾ / wʿdwh*. This clause refers to two elements ("the life of the king" and "his loyalty oath") which were equally considered as endowed with a divine quality or essence emanating from the god Aššur through the persons of the Assyrian rulers; they are occasionally found together in Neo-Assyrian contracts, with powers of retaliation and punishment in their own right as in the present case. Specifically, the "loyalty oath" (*ʿdy* = Assyrian *adê*) attained the status of a religious-institutional "reality" within the Assyrian empire in 672 BCE, when Esarhaddon imposed a binding agreement, sworn before the gods of Assyria, to all "the people of Assyria, great and small, from the Upper Sea and the Lower Sea" for the succession of his son Assurbanipal (see most recently Fales 2012 for the reconstruction of the relevant text and its ceremonial context). This date may thus be considered to be the *terminus post quem* for the present text (cf. Fales 1996:99–100).

[14] Line 12. *y?bʿmh! bydh*. Lemaire 2001 and CAL here prefer to read *ybʿwn bydh*, a further form of the verb **bʿy* which, however, is not easy to reconcile with the available sign-shapes. For the entire clause as a loan-translation of Akkadian *ina qāti bu'û*, "to hold responsible," cf. the examples referring to the *adê* quoted in *CAD* B, 364–365, and especially Watanabe 1987.

[15] Line 13. The form *htwn* should be a causative of the prefix-conjugation in the (relatively rare) "long imperfect" form, preceded by *l*, probably of asseverative value ("if they actually give back ..."). The same form may be found in an Assyro-Aramaic text from Guzana/Tell Halaf (Fales 1986: no. 35).

[16] Line 14. *ypw?g?n. ʾš*. The suggestion by Lemaire to read *ypdyn* is, by the French author's own admission, complicated by an unexpected *yod*, which is harder to explain than a *hapax legomenon*-loan from the Assyrian verb *puāgu*, "to take away" (cf. Fales 1996:102).

[17] Lines 14–15. The exhortation of the prophet in Joel 3:13, "Put ye in the sickle, for the harvest is ripe," may be recalled here. This last provision, unfortunately fragmentary and not attested elsewhere in Assyro-Aramaic, might have some relation with the so-called "harvester clause," i.e. the condition that the debtor should provide a given number of harvesters to assist at the harvest of the creditor's field (Postgate 1976:44–45) to be found in loans of barley: cf. Fales 1986:136 and *passim*, and see D 19 from Tell Sheikh Hamad below.

[18] Line 16. *hdrmn* should correspond to Assyrian **Adad-rēmanni*, a very common name (cf. PNA, 34b–35b).

[19] Line 17. Cf. PNA, 1150b, for this onomastic formation as unique in this period: however, the variant Se'-zabadi, equally going back to the Moon-god, and to the Aramaic verb "to grant," is known in cuneiform. The profession of this man, *mlḥ*, "boatman," appears totally compatible with the location of the site of Tell Shiukh Fawqani – as well as Tell Aḥmar further south – on the Euphrates riverbank (see already Fales 1996:105).

[20] Line 18. The reading *nmmrʾ* is undisputable; and the second element is quite likely as Aramaic **mareʾ*, "(my) lord." Lemaire (2001:124) renders *Nemumarâ*, with no explanation.

[21] Line 18. The cuneiform variant of this Aramaic name ("Se' is my help"), with ⟨d⟩, Se'-idrī, is clearly attested; cf. PNA, 1101a (with quote of the present text).

(19) and Ḥasan[22] and Palṭi-'el[23] from Tarbušibi,[24]
(20) (and) Mulleš-ibni,[25] (and) Ma'šē[...],
(21) (and) Ḥanan,[26] (and) Aplad-śagib,[27] son of Sās-ili.[28]

22 Line 19. The cuneiform attestation Ḫašānu (PNA, 464a–b) provides a good counterpart to this Aramaic name, meaning "the strong one."

23 Line 19. This West Semitic name has parallels in cuneiform Palṭi-il, "My deliverance is god/the god El", as well as in the Old Testament; cf. PNA, 982b–983a, with explicit reference to the Aramaic attestation here. See also line 1, above.

24 Line 19. *mn trbšyb* sums up the place of origin of the last four witnesses (lines 18–19), if not of all the ones previously named. Cf. Fales 2014:35, for this particular version of the place-name *Til-Barsib/p; and see *ad* l. 3, above, for the presence of a military garrison in this town.

25 Line 20. This Akkadian name presents the DN of the spouse of the god Aššur, *mlš*, cuneiform Mullissu, "Mullissu has created": cf. PNA, 766b, with quote of the present text.

26 Line 21. The cuneiform attestations of this Aramaic name, as Ḫanana and Ḫanani, are plentiful: cf. PNA 449b–450a.

27 Line 21. "(the god) Aplad(ad) is exalted": cf. PNA, 114b, with quote of the present text. The god Apladad was especially revered in the Middle Euphrates region.

28 Line 21. The complex *ss* represents a local rendering **Šāš* for the divine name **Śamaš*, known also from Ma'allanate and Tell Sheikh Hamad (where a precise correspondence between cuneiform *Šamaš-aḫu-uṣur and alphabetic *ssḥṣr* is attested in Radner 2002: no. 35).

REFERENCES

Fales 1996; 2005; Lemaire 2001.

TELL AḤMAR (T 11) (4.27)

F. M. Fales

The *editio princeps* is Bordreuil and Briquel-Chatonnet 1996–1997:100–107 (photograph, hand-copy, transliteration, translation, commentary). There is a re-edition in Lemaire 2001:126–128, no. 6. The tablet is squarish (4.3 × 4 × 2.1 cm) of light brown color, with breaks both on top and at the bottom; it appears crudely fashioned, with bulges in some points and extremely wide margins; cf. Fales *et al.* 2005:609 for a labeling of this particular tablet typology, which finds a few parallels in the Tell Shiukh Fawqani Aramaic archive, as a "cake-slice" form. From its extant formulae and fragmentary data, the text may be made out as a loan-document of silver.

(Obverse)
(beginning lost)
(1) [....] and KL, horse trainers (?)[1]
(2) [....] ... for twenty shekels[2]
(3) of silver; whoever will return in suit against someone else,[3]
(4) [...].... or he will [gi]ve (as) substitute[4]
(5) silver, four minas.
(6) Witness: Še'-'uš[nî?],[5]
(lower edge)
(7) and witness: Gabbar,[6]
(Reverse)
(8) and witness: 'Abbah;
(9) witness: the son of Gira',
(10) and witness: Rapû,[7]
(11) and witness: Nabî
(12) and witness: Arah/Urah.
(one line(?) lost)

1 Line 1. The *editio princeps* had the reading *pršn* here, understood as "horses," but Lemaire's version presents the reading *rkšn*, which might represent a secondary loan-translation from the Neo-Assyrian professional term *raksu*, "horse-trainer" (cf. Fales 2013). A military profession at Til-Barsib would certainly tally with the presence of armed forces in the city, as also attested in TSF 47.

2 Line 2. The reading *b ʿšrn šqln* was established by Lemaire (2001:127) against *b ʿšr lšqln* of the *editio princeps*.

3 Line 3. This formula, misunderstood in the *editio princeps*, was restored as *mn ʿl mn yšb* by Lemaire (2001:127); it also appears in a Tell Shiukh Fawqani text (no. 45; Obv. 3′: Fales *et al.*, 2005:652).

4 Line 4. [ ]x *y. w[yt]n bdl*[ ]. Lemaire (2001:127) understands *bdl* as "tin." However, the term *bdl* should be rather taken as "substitute" on the basis of the Aramaic texts from the ancient site of Ma'allanate, kept in the Brussels Museum; while the editor of these texts, E. Lipiński (2010) continues to render *bdl* as "tin," the argument for a more realistic translation with the term "substitute" in juridical meaning had been already made by Fales 2000:112–113.

5 Line 6. Lemaire (2001:127), tentatively restores the name of the first witness as *šʾʿš[ny]*: could this man have perchance been the same person as the businessman known from texts TSF 46 and TSF 47, which were made out and witnessed some 18 km away?

6 Line 7. The reading *gbr* (Lemaire 2001:128) is to be preferred to *grd*, which has no parallels.

7 Line 10. *rpw* (or *rpd*) is Lemaire's reading (2001:128).

REFERENCES

Bordreuil and Briquel-Chatonnet 1996–1997:100–107; Lemaire 2001:126–128.

TELL ŠEḪ ḤAMAD (TSH D 19 = *KAI* 313) (4.28A)

F. M. Fales

The *editio princeps* is Röllig 1997:367–370 (photograph, hand-copy, transliteration, translation, commentary). Text is in transliteration (Hebrew font) in *KAI* 313 (re-edition in Lemaire 2001:147–148, no. 3; Röllig 2014:58–59). The tablet was retrieved in 1995 by the German archaeological expedition to Tell Sheikh Hamad on the lower basin of the river Habur, an affluent of the Euphrates in NW Mesopotamia. This site, which yielded written materials of both Middle Assyrian and Neo-Assyrian age, was known as Dūr-Katlimmu in the second millennium, but took on the additional name *Magdalu in the Neo-Assyrian phase. The text is of the "docket" type, where it may be presumed that the clay surface was modeled around a string and thereupon inscribed, prior to being attached to some surface or goods (Postgate 1976:5; Radner 1997:27). In this case it is of triangular shape, which is the most common one in this period for loans or debt-notes. A number of fingernail-marks may be observed on the top edge of the tablet.

(Obverse)
(1) Seal of Ḥuzir,[1] son of
(2) Hadad-gabar[2] (concerning) silver
(3) – 8 shekels –[3]
(4) belonging to Barruq,[4] debited against him.
(5) By one-third (will the interest accrue).
(6) Month VIII,[5]

(Reverse)
(7) eponymy of Kanūnāyu.[6]
(8) Witnesses: Salmānu-ʻizrî,[7]
(9) Nādin, Na'id-Hadad,
(10) Aplad-ʻazar,[8]
(11) Salmānu-taqqin,
(12) Ḥuzir.[9]

1 Line 1. *ḥzr*. For a witness of this name, cf. D 15, line 5. In cuneiform texts, the name Ḫuzīru is attested at Tell Sheikh Hamad as applied to a house-owner (Radner 2002: no. 31, 19 and *ibid*., no. 125, Rev. 9); for other occurrences in the NA written record, cf. PNA, 484b.

2 Line 2. This Aramaic name means "Hadad is strong," see PNA, 45a for cuneiform parallels.

3 Line 3. The number is given symbolically, with 8 right-slanting vertical lines, slightly spaced in three distinct groups (3-3-2).

4 Line 4. The name of the debtor could be either Akkadian or Aramaic: cf. PNA, 271–271. One *Barruqu* is known from the cuneiform texts of Tell Sheikh Hamad (Radner 2002: no. 104, line 1).

5 Line 6. The text has *yrḥ smnh*, "the eighth month."

6 Line 7. *knny* = Kanūnāyu refers to a post-648 BCE eponym, who was governor of Dur-Šarrukin, attributed to 624 BCE: cf. PNA, 604a–b, no. 63. The eponym *knny* is also known from Ma'allanate.

7 Line 8. Names compounded with the DN Salmānu, Akkadian or West Semitic predicative elements, are quite frequent at Tell Sheikh Hamad (see also line 11, below): for a *Salmānu-idri* in the contemporaneous cuneiform texts, cf. Radner 2002: nos. 41, 67.

8 Line 10. For the god Aplad(ad), see TSF 47, above. In this name, the West Semitic root *ʻzr, "to help" follows the DN.

9 Line 12, As noted by Röllig (2010:58), this second occurrence of the name *ḥzr* should refer to a further individual; the lack of the patronymic could be telling in this respect.

REFERENCES

Röllig 1997; 2014; *KAI* 313; Lemaire 2001:147–148.

TELL ŠEḪ ḤAMAD (TSH D 15 = *KAI* 314) (4.28B)

F. M. Fales

The *editio princeps* is Röllig 2014:50–51 (photograph, hand-copy, transliteration, translation, commentary). Text is found in transliteration (Hebrew font) in *KAI* 314. The tablet was retrieved in 1995 by the German archaeological expedition to Tell Sheikh Hamad. This text is also of the triangular "docket" type (cf. D 19), relevant to a loan of barley (seed).

(Obverse)
(1) Seal of QŠʻR.[1]

(2) (concerning) barley, 2 (homers?),[2] belonging to
(3) Salmānu-ērеš.[3] Debited against QŠʻR.

1 Line 1. This name is known in a further text of the Tell Sheikh Hamad Aramaic archive as a witness, but has no parallels in the cuneiform texts from the site. Its etymology and overall meaning uncertain: the signs *qš* might refer to the Edomite DN *Qaus/Qôs, which appears in PNs in the cuneiform texts of this age as Qaus- as well as Qauš-; cf. PNA, 1011a–b.

2 Line 2. Two slanted vertical marks stand for the number, as in other texts here. The unit of measure is not given, and may only be inferred.

3 Line 3. *šlmnrs* appears as Salmānu-ērеš in two contemporaneous Assyrian texts from Tell Sheikh Hamad, albeit with different patronymics (Radner 2002: nos. 69, 120), Cf, also PNA, 1078.

(4) (it will increase) by one-half of them,[4] and 2 harvesters.[5] (Reverse)	(5) Witnesses: Ḥuzir,[6] (6) ʼSLN,[7] Zēru-ukīn,[8] (7) Aḫu-larīm.[9]

4 Line 4. "of them" (*-hn*) refers back to the 2 homers of line 2.

5 Line 4. *ḥṣdn II*. This is the "harvester clause," by which the debtor is obliged provide a given number of harvesters to assist at the harvest of the creditor's field, as an element of the interest rate for the loan of barley seed. In this case, the two "harvesters" are to be added to a 50% increase (*bplg*, "by one-half") in the amount of barley to be given back at the following harvest.

6 Line 5. The name occurs also in D 19 (*q.v.*), lines 1, 12.

7 Line 6. This name has no parallels in the Assyro-Aramaic corpus, as noted by Röllig 2014:50.

8 Line 6. *zrkn*. One Zēru-ukīn is well attested in the cuneiform archives of Tell Sheikh Hamad; cf. Röllig 2014: *l.c.*, for the attestations.

9 Line 7. *ʾḫlrm*. The name Aḫu-larīm is well attested in the cuneiform texts of the age: cf. PNA, 64a. In the Assyrian texts from Tell Sheikh Hamad, a man of this name appears as witness in the deed of sale of a plot of land (Radner 2001: no. 37), and might be the same person as the one named here.

REFERENCES

Röllig 2014:50–51; *KAI* 314.

THE ASSUR OSTRACON (4.29)

F. M. Fales

The so-called "Assur ostracon" is a thick sherd, found in numerous joining pieces, albeit with various intermediate gaps, with a glossy surface covered by 21 lines of Aramaic cursive alphabetic script in reddish ink. It is at present still unique as a testimonial of epistolography in Aramaic from the Neo-Assyrian period. The Assur ostracon was discovered (as perhaps secondarily fallen) in a grave chamber within a private house to the SW of the New Palace of the city of Assur by the German archaeological expedition led by W. Andrae (cf. Pedersén 1986:113–114, *ad* house no. 81). First published by Mark Lidzbarski (1921:5–15), it has been further tackled a number of times (cf. Fitzmyer and Kaufman 1992:42; see also CAL *s.v.*), but among Semitists (where it is known with the descriptor *KAI* 233, from its number in the 1968 edition by Donner and Röllig) is perceived as a document of difficult interpretation and which yields only partial sense. See however most recently Lindenberger 2003:18–20; and Fales 2010:194–199, where the text is examined in the light of the basic "rules" which apply to contemporary Assyrian epistolography, and specifically to the small sub-group of private correspondence from this age, with the result of a more adequately comprehensible version, which is reproduced here with small changes.

(1) [... To my broth]er,[1] Pirʾ-Amur(ru),[2] (from) your	brother Bel-eṭir.[3] M[any] greetings.[4]

1 It appears quite likely that this text painted on a sherd represented the preliminary draft of an epistolary message in Aramaic (see below, n. 3). This draft should have been subsequently recopied on a pliable scroll and sent to its intended addressee(s). It is much harder to believe that the Assur ostracon could have circulated as such, due to its length and (consequently) size: cf. the discussion on ostraca as epistolary media somewhat similar to the modern "telegram" by Schwiderski 2000:237–238. On the other hand, a final copy of the text (presumably enclosed within a container or sealed shut, on whatever medium) was surely destined for circulation, as may be made out from the mention of a messenger in line 19

2 Line 1. *prwr*: for the equivalence of the name of the addressee with *Pirʾ-Amurru (although the latter is not attested as such in the Neo-Assyrian text corpus), cf. PNA, 995b. The second element (*-wr*) in this construct-state PN is the same as in the compound divine name *ʾlwr* in the Aramaic inscription of Zakkur, line 1. For the god Amurru as subject-element in West Semitic PNs in cuneiform script, cf. PNA, 109a.

3 Line 1. *blṭr*. Cf. PNA 299b–300a, for the attestations of Bel-eṭir; he is known from contemporary texts in cuneiform as a military, and specifically as a cohort commander (*rab kiṣir*) of king Assurbanipal, active in southern Mesopotamia, presumably during the years in which the Assyrian ruler was engaged in warfare against his brother, Šamaš-šumu-ukin, king of Babylonia (645–640 BCE). An Assyrian letter indicates that the king had dispatched 200 horsemen under Bel-eṭir and Arbayya – who is also mentioned in the ostracon (line 2), in the region of Uruk (see line 3), to assist the local pro-Assyrian governor, Nabû-ušabši –, who might be the same person as the Nabû-zer-ušabši mentioned in line 19 of our text. While Bel-eṭir, at the time of the writing of the ostracon, seems to have resided – perhaps after retiring from the battlefield – in his hometown (?) Assur (and maybe in or near the very house where the text was retrieved), his former army crony Pirʾ-Amur(ru) was still located in the southern Mesopotamian region. Thus the letter was written to be sent from north to south; but since the ostracon was in fact retrieved in Assyria, it can only have represented a first draft on which a further text was (meant to be) based. See also n. 1, above.

4 Line 1. For this *salutatio*, cf. most recently Contini 1995:61. The expression *šlm l[śgʾ]* clearly parallels the *šulmu adanniš* to be found in contemporaneous Assyrian letters. A crucial point to be underscored here is that (as specified above) the ostracon was written by and to individuals also known in the contemporary Neo-Assyrian correspondence as officials of the Empire; due to their rank, these people must have absolutely been expected to speak/read Assyrian on official matters, but this private letter was thought out and written in Aramaic. We are not dealing here with a family letter, in which private ideas were exchanged among members of a tight-knit foreign community – as, e.g., in a number the letters in Aramaic from Achaemenid Egypt – but with a letter traded between officers in the Assyrian armed forces. These people chose to chew the fat, to set forth their private problems, and to ask for support, in the vernacular, not in the official language of "work." On the relations between Assyrian and Aramaic, cf. the recent overviews in Beaulieu 2006; Fales 2007.

(2) [*When*] you were with me in Babylonia,[5] and I and Arbayya[6] and M[...],
(3) [... and I was going] from Uruk[7] with Ger-Ṣapunu[8] and with Ugammar-A[*ššur*][9]
(4) I [...] Bit-Amukanni. They were four: a letter from the king of Babylon
(5) was in their hands. [*They were going to*] Bit-Amukanni. In Ḥapirû, in the open countryside,[10] we caught them, [and ...]
(6) them. [I ... and I w]rote[11] to the king my lord.[12] Then we took [...] from the *riv*[*er*]
(7) and I came [...] before the [k]ing my [lord ...]: "They were placed with the infantry;[13] (but) the king my lord will give them to me."
(8) On this matter, the king my lord said to me: "They are [yours], and they will not *serve* him." And he ordered thus. *Into an inheritance portion of the hou*[*sehold of my father I turned* (?)][14] them, [these *men from*]
(9) Bit-Amukanni; their hands I inscribed,[15] and I established before me. They had deserted, you see? They were in Bit-Amukanni. From [their] hands ...

[5] Line 2. The central matter on which Bel-eṭir's letter hinges from here onward, regards facts which occurred in the "old days," when he and Pir'-Amurru were fighting together in southern Mesopotamia ("[*When*] you were with me in Babylonia"). For *mtkdy* = *Māt Akkadê* (as the Babylonian region was commonly called), cf. the parallel attestation *mt 'kdh* in the so-called "Beirut decree" from approx. 600 BCE (Fitzmyer and Kaufman 1992:25).

[6] Line 2. *'rby*. Arbayya/u was, with Bel-eṭir, a further cohort commander in Babylonia, as known from some Assyrian letters: cf. PNA, 127b–128a. The name might mean "the Arab," as this alphabetic attestation suggests.

[7] The city of Uruk (present-day Warka) where the writer of the letter and his cronies were based, is located at 31°19.3′N, 45°38.4′E. This and other geographical data are based on Parpola and Porter 2001, *passim*.

[8] Line 3. As noted in PNA, 426b, the name of this further army man is linguistically Canaanite, and specifically Phoenician ("client of the [god/mountain] Ṣapunu"). No attestation for an individual bearing this name is given in the NA epistolary corpus.

[9] Lines 4–5. *3+1 hmw 'grt mlk bbl / bydh*[*ym*]: "They were four: a letter from the king of Babylon / was in their hands." In the course of an action in the southern countryside, the group of Assyrian military had intercepted and captured four deserters, coming up from the Chaldean territory of Bit-Amukanni, who were bearing a secret letter from the enemy king (*mlk bbl*). To be noticed is that this is the most ancient attestation for *'grt* as "letter," in conformity with the usage of the term in later Egyptian Aramaic (cf. *DNWSI*, 12), while in Assyrian Aramaic the term means "contract," or even more generally "legal document." On the other hand, *egirtu* in Neo-Babylonian is well attested in the meaning "letter."

[10] Line 5. The location of *ḥpyrw* is unknown, but since the four men were proceeding from Babylon (32°32.14′N, 44°26.41′E) southward to Bit-Amukanni, it should be located in the Euphrates catchment area, in the "open countryside" or "steppe" (*mdbr*) possibly not far to the northwest from the point of arrival. Uruk, from which the Assyrian patrol originated, is not very far to the east of the reconstructed territory of the Bit-Amukanni tribal confederation.

[11] Line 6. Lit.: "I sent" (*cf. DNWSI*, 477), but see Fales 2010:196, n. 35 for the justification of this translation.

[12] Line 6. This must have been Assurbanipal himself; for the well-known Assyrian policy of directly addressing the king through written entreaties on specific matters vital to the subjects' interests, cf. Fales 2001:179–180.

[13] Line 7. *'m klby' śmn*: this has always been, and still remains, an extremely tricky passage. Following Lidzbarski (1921:11, 14), *KAI* 2:283 translated "mit den Hunden *waren sie eingesperrt*" (cf. also Gibson 1971:103: "... had been put with the dogs"; Lindenberger 2003:19: "they were put with the dogs"). However, this interpretation does not tally in full with the *wlṭḥnw lh* of the following line, which implies that a specific person was responsible for these POWs – and this person cannot be identified with the Assyrian king, since it would have been redundant (as well as disrespectful) to say that the POWs did not work for him anymore, after he himself had graciously given them over to Bel-eṭir. Further, *pace* Lidzbarski and all the others, there is no record of POWs being placed with the dogs in the Assyrian epistolary corpus: the quotes brought forth on this count – from Assyrian royal inscriptions of Esarhaddon and Assurbanipal – refer in point of fact to the dire punishment of formerly rebellious kings, who were tied up with dog chains and made to stand guard at the city gates, also as examples for the populace (cf. *CAD* K 69b). But, of course, these kings were not also expected to work for the Assyrian ruler in their "free" time! In the light of these arguments, it seems reasonable to seek other interpretations for the expression *'m klby' śmn*. The suggestion that here, as well as in the Elephantine text AP 30, line 16, *klby'* should be taken as a loanword from Assyrian *kallābu*, "footsoldier" has been suggested and defended in Fales 1987:469; 2009:88–91, and 2010:196 n. 36.

[14] Line 8. *bzyt b*[....]. The form *bzyt* was analyzed by *KAI* 2:284–285 as deriving from *bzh*, "to despise" or from *bzh* "to divide." Other hypotheses are *ḥ!zyt* by Gibson 1971:103, 107, and Lindenberger 2003:19: *ḥzyt b*[*'ynyn zyly mn*], "I have seen with my own eyes," while the CAL (*s.v.*) refers the form back to *bzz*, "to despoil." In an attempt to endow the overall complex of lines 8–11 with a coherent sense, it is suggested in the present version that *zyt* be understood as a hitherto unattested loanword from the Akkadian legal term *zittu*, "part, portion," and the following words be integrated as *b*[*yt 'by*], thus translating "into (*b*) a(n inheritance) portion of the hou[sehold of my father]" followed by a verb with the object "them." In other words, Bel-eṭir should be relating the fact that, after the king had given him the men as his property, he passed them over to his father's estate, albeit reserving them for his own inheritance portion. This solution would *per se* clarify the function as "my father" of the individual dubbed *'by* in line 10, and who was understood by all previous interpreters as a personal name, Abay or similar – with the effect of introducing a further unknown protagonist in this already muddled tale.

[15] Line 9. The branding of slaves on the hands with the names of their owner is referred to here; see also line 12, below. On the practice, cf. Dandamayev 1984:229–231.

(10) My father spoke thus: "Of (the four) – *i.e.* Śam-hayqar, Nabû-zer-ukin, Aḫḫešay, and Walūl –, Upaqa-ana-Arbail[16] is to take into cust[ody] Nabu-zer-ukin and Aḫḫešay,
(11) and [he ...] (also) Walūl and Śam-hayqar." And my father w[*rote*]: "When Upaqa-ana-Arbail comes to Assur, immediately he will make them return. For Upaqa-ana-Arbail."[17] And in case
(12) Apil-Ešarra should ask: are these words really true? Bel-eṭir, my own name, is inscribed on their hands. Call them, and ask them (if)
(13) these words are really true. They are my slaves, they had deserted. They [...] are from Bit-Amukanni. Now, I have sent Na'di-Marduk as your help before you.
(14) [...] them; I want to see them. Send us a message. Further:[18] (as for) the son of NM[... Za]ban, and the son of B[...]Zaban, Zaban-iddina and Nabû-ušallim, from Bit-Adini,[19]
(15) [*list*]*en* further: Tiglath-pileser[20] took captives from Bit-Amukanni, and Ululayu[21] [took] captives from Bit-Adini, and Sargon took captives from Dur-Sin,
(16) and [Senn]acherib[22] took cap[tives] from Kšw[... All the kings of] Assyria seiz[ed *people, but year*] after year they escaped,[23] and they used to pursue them. But constantly, the kings [of Assyria]
(17) *in the treaty documents*[24] [wrote ...], saying: Do not look for the escapees; *who*[*ever has sinned/rebelled against*] Assyria, the fire will consume them! But the king my lord has appointed [*PN*]
(18) in *GN*, [*and again*] they are pursuing the escapees from Assyria.
(19) For Nabû-zer-ušabši,[25] [*my brother*]:[26] behold, I am sending you my messenger Ug[ammar-DN]. Are you mad at me? The wrath of the god which ....
(20) Why are [you] mad at me? And now, ... Opis, in ... when you will see him [in] Opis; and he ... a year (ago) we sent it to him [...]

16 Line 10. For the name Upaqa-ana-Arbail, see PNA, 1388b. The individual thus named seems to have had the task of bringing at least two of the four POW-slaves to Bel-eṭir's father in Assur.

17 Line 11. This seems to be a straightforward quote from a message, which was included *verbatim* within the body of Bel-eṭir's letter. Possibly the order to Upaqa-ana-Arbail was part and parcel of what the addressee Pir'-Amurru was supposed to look after personally – i.e., it represented the actual reason for the letter sent by his old army buddy Bel-eṭir.

18 Lines 14–18. Here a further problem, similarly dealing with POWs or deserters, but linked to a different Chaldean tribe, is tackled by Bel-eṭir, presumably still for the benefit of Pir'-Amurru. It is however less clear what the sender requires from the addressee regarding these further 4 individuals.

19 Line 14. Bit-Adini refers to the Chaldean tribe of that name, which was a clan or subdivision of the major tribal confederation of Bit-Dakkuri and not to the homonymous tribal state on the bend of the Euphrates in NW Mesopotamia – which had been conquered in the 9th century by Shalmaneser III. The same place name occurs in the next line, in connection with Shalmaneser V's conquests. Bit-Adini is further known from Sennacherib's annals as one of the groups fighting against the Assyrians at the battle of Halulê, in 691 BCE (cf. Lipiński 2000:163).

20 Line 15. The reference is of course to Tiglath-pileser III (745–727 BCE). The presence of a historical reminiscence on a specific theme, going back to the very beginnings of the Assyrian empire, is not unique to this text, but appears here and there also in the Neo-Assyrian epistolary corpus: cf. the following passage in a letter addressed to Sin-šar-iškun, son of Assurbanipal, from Babylonia (SAA 18, 187:5–15), "Ever since the reign of Tiglath-pileser, king of Assyria, my fathers have kept the surveillance for (lit., "the watch of") the kings of Assyria. Bel-šuma-iškun, my grandfather, whom Sennacherib and your father appointed, provided the [...]s for the repairs. He kept the surveillance of Sennacherib and Esarhaddon, and set up a fine household in [...]. During the revolt of Šamaš-šumu-ukin, just as Assurbanipal remembered those favors which my grandfather had rendered ... (*rest fragmentary*)."

21 Line 15. This is the well-known sobriquet of the Assyrian king known with the dynastic name Shalmaneser V (727–722 BCE). The name *Ulūlāyu* is not only attested in two Babylonian kinglists, but also in a number of Nimrud letters which he authored as Crown Prince, reporting to his father on a number of tasks performed for the royal palace and the capital city. Ulūlāyu was thus quite surely not a secondary dynastic name, as long believed, but a given name, either a birthname or a familiar byname. Cf. Fales 2014:221.

22 Line 16. Had the prosopographical details concerning Bel-eṭir under Assurbanipal not been available, the mention of Sennacherib (704–681 BCE) would have in any case acted as *terminus post quem* for our ostracon.

23 Line 16. The problem of fugitives in the Assyrian empire is treated in various epistolary texts and in the treaty-documents/oaths (*adês*) stipulated by the Assyrian kings: cf. most recently Hipp 2015 for a survey of the relevant material and an overview of the historical question.

24 Line 17. *b*[ʿ]*dyn*, "*in the treaty documents*." The sequence *b*[ʿ]*dyn* may be made out from Lidzbarski's attempts, where an *ʿayin* is noted as possibility in second position; CAL has *b*[.]*dyb*, but the last *beth* is not indicated among Lidzbarski's possibilities. As noted in the previous footnote, the Assyrian *adês* devote a certain space to the problem of fugitives: however, the possibility of a variation in the relevant policies (punishment or all-round curse by the gods) as might be indicated here, is not confirmed by the Assyrian sources as such.

25 Line 19. For Nabû-zer-ušabši, *cf.* PNA, 912a, with reference to the Assur ostracon; for Nabû-ušabši, governor of Uruk ca. 661–649 BCE, *cf.* PNA, 901b–902a. The two individuals might have been one and the same.

26 Lines 19–21. One may ask whether these three final lines should be considered as pertaining to one and the same epistolary text as the previous one (i.e. as a message within a message), or rather to a totally different letter. The fact that both addresses were linked to the Uruk region must be underscored, possibly in favor of the first solution; on the other hand, if the ostracon just held rough copies of outgoing epistolary texts, the second solution might be subscribed as well.

(21) in Bit-Diblā, … Šumu-iddina … [*the one*] who made you bitter, who caused … is Šumu-iddina[27] of Bit-Diblā."[28]

[27] Line 21. For the name, and this attestation, cf. PNA, 1292b.

[28] A final note may regard the particular Aramaic dialectal traits of the Assur Ostracon, which are to some extent unique, connecting it, interestingly enough, less to Assyrian Aramaic than to later varieties (*cf.* already Fales 1996:42), although some conservative traits are present as well. For the latter, notice the following: in phonology, *ḏ is consistently realized as *z*, "ḍ" is realized as *q* (cf. qrqw) in lines 9, 13), *ṯ is always *š* except in the haphel *yhtb* (line 11); in morphology, the infinitive *lʾmr* (lines 8, 10, 17), and the pronoun *ʾt* (lines 2, 19, [20], 21) link the ostracon with Old Aramaic. As for innovative traits, the *m* > *w* shift (*e.g.* in the PN *šwdn* for Šum-iddina, or in the GN *byt ʾwkn* for Bit-Amukanni) is attested regularly in Aramaic from Neo-Babylonian (NB) times; the independent pronoun *zly* (line 13) is known from NB Neirab and Egyptian Aramaic; the interjection *ʾrh*, "behold!" (line 19) is attested at Hermopolis; the independent pronoun *hmw* is used as the direct object of a finite verbal form (line 7: *yhb hmw ly mrʾy mlkʾ*) as in Egyptian Aramaic; and finally, the conjunction *ʾzy* (lines 6, 14 [2]), and the adverb *mn ʿqb* (line 11) are *hapax legomena* for Aramaic (cf. *DNWSI*, 25, 881, resp.). Thus, in practice (*cf.* already Folmer 1995:747), only some lexical items and basic features of syntax (OV word order and *zy*- phrases) connect the Assur Ostracon to the remainder of the Assyrian Aramaic material.

REFERENCES

Beaulieu 2006; Contini 1995; Dandamayev 1984; Fales 1987; 1996; 2007; 2009; 2010; 2014; Folmer 1995; Fitzmyer and Kaufman 1992; Hipp 2015; *KAI* 233; Lidzbarski 1921; Lindenberger 2003; Lipiński 2000; Parpola and Porter 2001; Pedersén 1986; Schwiderski 2000.

ARAMAIC INSCRIPTION OF THE XANTHOS TRILINGUAL STELE (4.30)

André Lemaire

In 1973, the excavations of Xanthos, directed by H. Metzger, brought to light a late Persian Period monumental stele dating to 337 BCE. Sometimes referred to as the Letoon Trilingual Stele, its three inscriptions are in Aramaic (in the front), in Lycian (on the left side), and in Greek (on the right side). Both Greek and Lycian texts seem practically identical and are a kind of civic version presenting the decision from the point of view of the city while the Aramaic text is a satrapic version presenting the final decision of the satrapic authority in a kind of promulgation (lines 6–18). This decree is followed by the indication of the one responsible for the engraving and by the usual maledictions to protect this cultic decree. The two final maledictions (19b–23 and 24–27) were probably added by the priest who put his property under the protection of his gods and of the great gods of the main sanctuary where the stele was erected.

(1) In the month of Siwan, year one (2) of King Artaxerxes,[1] (3) in the fortified city of Orna,[2] Pixodaro(s) (4) son of Katamno(s), the satrap (5) in Caria and Lycia, said[3]:

(6) "The 'citizens' of Orna[4] have contemplated (7) *making an altar/chapel*(?)[5] to the god Kandawats[6] (8) Caunian and his colleagues.[7] (9) And they made Simias (10) son of Koddorosi priest. And there is a *property* (11) which the 'citizens' of Orna gave[8] (12) to the god Kandawats.

Year after (13–15) year a (mi)na and a half of silver will be given by the country. For the new moon, this priest sacrifices a sheep (16) to the god Kandawats, and he *sacrifices* (17) every year an ox.

And this domain, (18) which is his own, is freed."[9]

(19) The property-holder[10] has written this decree.[11]

Furthermore, (20) if ever *someone takes (this domain?) back*[12] (21) from the god Kandawats or from (22) (*t*)*his* priest, *let him be* taken back by the god Kandawats (23) and his colleagues. (24–26) And whoever takes back from the god(s) Leto, Artemis, Ḫshatrapati and *others*,[13] these gods (27) will seek[14] (for it) from him.

[1] Arses apparently took the throne name Artaxerxes (IV) (Badian).

[2] Orna is the local ancient name of Xanthos.

[3] *ʾmr*: here with the nuance of promulgating, issuing a decree.

[4] *Bʿly ʾwrn*.

[5] The reading and meaning of *krpʾ* is uncertain. The Greek version reads "altar" and the Lycian one "sanctuary."

[6] This Caunian/Carian name means "king" (compare Luwian *hantawati* and Greek *basilei*). Here it is used as the personal name of a god.

[7] Aramaic *knwth* "his colleagues," corresponds to Greek *Arkesimai* and to Lycian *ArKKazuma*, and might be a translation of this last name.

[8] *Yhb* "to give," appears also in line 13 and specifies the endowment of the new cult.

[9] The domain is exempt of taxes.

[10] The Greek text shows that Simias and his heirs were to be the true owners of the domain: they were interested to have this decree publicized.

[11] *Dth* may be translated "law," "decree". Here it concerns a new cult.

[12] The verb *hnṣl* "to take (back)," "to reclaim" (also line 23) is the opposite of *yhb* "to give" (lines 11, 13).

[13] Proposed corrected reading: *wʾḥwrn*⟨ʾ⟩*yš*. Alternatively Kottsieper proposes reading *ʾḥwd?nyš* interpreting it as the unattested Carian name of the "Nymphs."

[14] *Ybʿwn*: compare the inscriptions of Gözneh (lines 2–3) and Keseçek Köyü (line 5).

REFERENCES

Badian 1977; Briant 1998; Dupont-Sommer 1979; *KAI*[5] 319; Kottsieper 2002; Lemaire 1996; Teixidor 1978, 1986:339–341, 379, 453–454.

WEST SEMITIC BIBLIOGRAPHY

AḤITUV, S.

1999 “A Divine Verdict: A Judicial Papyrus of the Seventh Century BCE.” Pp. 1–4, 226* in *The Frank Moore Cross Volume*. Ed. by B. A. Levine, A. Biran and H. Geva. ErIs 26. Jerusalem: Israel Exploration Society (Hebrew).

2003 “A New Moabite Inscription.” *Israel Museum Studies in Archaeology* 2: 3–10.

2004 “*ktwbt mlkwtyt ḥdšh mmw ʾb*.” *Qadmoniot* 128: 88–92.

2005 *hktb whmktb. ʾwspt ktwbwt m ʾrṣ-yśr ʾl wmmmlkwt ʿbr hyrdn mymy byt-r ʾšwn*. Jerusalem: Bialik Institute.

2008 *Echoes from the Past. Hebrew and Cognate Inscriptions from the Biblical Period*. Jerusalem: Carta.

AHARONI, M.

1979 “The Askos: Is it the Biblical Nēbel?” *Tel Aviv* 61–62: 95–97.

AHARONI, Y.

1962 “The Samaria Ostraca – an Additional Note.” *IEJ* 12 (1962): 67–69.

1979 *The Land of the Bible: A Historical Geography*. Trans. by A. F. Rainey. Ed. A. F. Rainey. Revised and enlarged edition edition. Philadelphia: Westminster.

ALBRIGHT, W. F.

1936 “Ostracon C 1101 of Samaria.” *PEQ* 68: 211–215.

AMAR, Z.

2009 “ŠMN RAḤUṢ.” *PEQ* 141: 18–26.

AVIGAD, N.

1993 “Samaria (City).” Pp. 1300–1312 in *NEAEHL*.

BACHELOT, L. and F. M. FALES (Editors)

2005 *Tell Shiukh Fawqani 1994–1998*. 2 Volumes. Padova: S.A.R.G.O.N.

BADIAN, E.

1977 “A Document of Artaxerxes IV?” Pp. 40–50 in *Greece and the Eastern Mediterranean in Ancient History and Prehistory. Studies presented to Fritz Schachermeyr*. Ed. by K. H. Kinzl. Berlin and New York: Walter de Gruyter.

BAGG, A. M.

2007 *Die Orts- und Gewässernamen der neuassyrischen Zeit. Teil 1: Die Levante*. Répertoire Geographique des Textes Cunéiformes 7.1. Wiesbaden: Ludwig Reichert.

BARKAY, G.

2005 “Iron II Seal Impression.” Pp. 171–172 in *Dothan: Remains from the Tell (1953–1964)*. Ed. by D. M. Master. Winona Lake, IN: Eisenbrauns.

BEAULIEU, P. A.

2006 “Official and Vernacular Languages: The Shifting Sands of Imperial and Cultural Identities in First Millennium B.C. Mesopotamia.” Pp. 187–216 in *Margins of Writing, Origins of Cultures*. Ed. by S. L. Sanders. Chicago: OIP.

BECKING, B.

2009 “Exile and Forced Labour in Bêt Haro ʾš: Remarks on a Recently Discovered Moabite Inscription.” Pp. 3–12 in *Homeland and Exile. Biblical and Ancient Near Eastern Studies in Honour of Bustenay Oded*. Ed. by G. Galil, M. Geller, and A. R. Millard. Leiden: Brill.

BORDREUIL, P.

1992 “Vingt ans d' épigraphie transjordanienne.” *SHAJ* 4: 185–189.

BORDREUIL, P. and F. BRIQUEL-CHATONNET

1996–1997 “Aramaic Documents from Til Barsib.” *Abr-Nahrain* 34:100–107.

BORDREUIL, P., and D. PARDEE

1990 “Le papyrus du marzeaḥ.” *Semitica* 38: 49–68, pl. VII–X.

2000 “Nouvel examen du «papyrus du marzeaḥ».” *Semitica* 50: 224–226.

BOTTA, A. F.

2009 *The Aramaic and Egyptian Legal Traditions at Elephantine: An Egyptological Approach*. Library of Second Temple Studies 64. London: T&T Clark.

BOWMAN, R.

1948 “Aramaeans, Aramaic, and the Bible.” *JNES* 7: 65–90.

BRASLAVI, J.

1964 “kmšyt ʾby myšʿ mlk mwʾb. lktwbt hmwʾbyt hḥdšh.” *Yediot* 28: 250–254.

BREMMER, J. N.

2008 *Greek Religion and Culture, the Bible and the Ancient Near East*. Jerusalem Studies in Religion and Culture 8. Leiden and Boston: Brill.

BRIANT, P.

1998 “Cités et satrapes dans l' empire achéménide: Xanthos et Pixôdaros.” *CRAIBL*: 305–340.

BRIQUEL-CHATONNET, F.

1992a “Hébreu du nord et phénicien; étude comparée de deux dialectes cananéens.” *OLP* 23:89–126.

1992b *Les relations entre les cités de la cote phénicienne et les royaumes d' Israël et de Juda*. Leuven: Peeters.

BUNNENS, G.

2009 “Assyrian Empire Building and Aramization of Culture as seen from Tell Ahmar/Til Barsib.” *Syria* 86: 67–82.

CECCHINI, S. M. and F. VENTURI

2012 “A Sounding at Arslan Tash. Re-Visiting the ‘Bâtiment aux ivoires.’” Pp. 325–341 in *Proceedings of the 7th International Congress on the Archaeology of the Ancient Near East (London 12 April–16 April 2010)*. Ed. by R. Matthews and J. Curtis. Wiesbaden: Harrassowitz.

CONTINI, R.

1995 “Epistolary Evidence of Address Phenomena in Official and Biblical Aramaic.” Pp. 57–67 in *Studies Greenfield*.

COOGAN, M. D.

2013 *A Reader of Ancient Near Eastern Texts. Sources for the Study of the Old Testament*. Oxford: Oxford University Press.

Cross, F. M., Jr.

1996 "A Papyrus Recording a Divine Legal Decision and the Root *rḥq* in Biblical and Near Eastern Legal Usage." Pp. 311–320 in *Texts, Temples, and Traditions. A Tribute to Menahem Haran*. Ed. by M. V. Fox, V. A. Hurowitz, A. Hurvitz, M. L. Klein, B. J. Schwartz, and N. Shupak. Winona Lake: Eisenbrauns. Reprint: pp. 63–69 in F. M. Cross, *Leaves from an Epigrapher's Notebook. Collected Papers in Hebrew and West Semitic Palaeography*. HSS 51. Winona Lake, IN: Eisenbrauns, 2003.

1975 "Ammonite Ostraca from Heshbon. Heshbon Ostraca IV–VIII." *AUSS* 13: 1–20.

Cross, F. M., Jr., and D. N. Freedman

1952 *Early Hebrew Orthography: A Study of the Epigraphic Evidence*. New Haven: American Oriental Society.

Dandamayev, M.

1984 *Slavery in Babylonia from Nabopolassar to Alexander the Great, 626–331 B.C.* Dekalb, IL: Northern Illinois University Press.

Davies, G. I.

1991 *AHI*.

Dearman, J. A.

1988 *Property rights in the eighth-century prophets: the conflict and its background*. Atlanta: Scholars Press.

2009 "Moab and Ammon: Some Observations on Their Relationship in Light of a New Moabite Inscription." Pp. 97–116 in *Studies on Iron Age Moab and Neighbouring Areas in Honour of Michèle Daviau*. Ed. by P. Bienkowski. ANESSup 29. Leuven: Peeters.

Del Olmo Lete, G.

2011 "KTMW and His 'Funerary Chapel.'" *AuOr* 29: 308–310.

Demsky, A.

2007 "*šmn rḥṣ* – Bath Oil from Samaria." Pp. 333–336 in *"Up to the Gates of Ekron." Essays on the Archaeology and History of the Eastern Mediterranean in Honor of Seymour Gitin*. Ed. by S. W. Crawford and A. Ben-Tor. Jerusalem: W. F. Albright Institute of Archaeological Research and Israel Exploration Society.

Dijkstra, M.

2000 "Chronological Problems of the Eighth Century BCE: A New Proposal for Dating the Samaria Ostraca." Pp. 76–87 in *Past, Present, Future: The Deuteronomistic History and The Prophets*. Ed. by J. C. de Moor and H. F. Van Rooy. Leiden and Boston: Brill.

Dion, P., and P. M. M. Daviau

2000 "An Inscribed Incense Altar of Iron Age II at *Ḫirbet el-Mudēyine* (Jordan)." *ZDPV* 116: 1–13.

Diringer, D.

1934 *Le iscrizioni antico-ebraiche palestinesi*. Firenze: F. Le Monnier.

Dobbs-Allsopp, F. W., J. J. M. Roberts, C. L. Seow, and R. E. Whitaker

2004 *Hebrew Inscriptions: Texts from the Biblical Period of the Monarchy with Concordance*. New Haven: Yale University Press.

Dupont-Sommer, A.

1979 "Troisième partie: l' inscription araméenne." Pp. 129–178 in *Fouilles de Xanthos VI: La stèle trilingue du Letôon*. Ed. H. Metzger and P. Demargne. Paris: Klincksieck.

Emerton, J. E.

2005 "Lines 25–6 in the published title of the Moabite Stone and a Recently-Discovered Inscription." *VT* 55: 293–303.

Fales, F. M.

1986 *Aramaic Epigraphs on Clay Tablets of the Neo-Assyrian Period*, Roma.

1987 "Aramaic Letters and Neo-Assyrian Letters: Philological and Methodological Notes." *JAOS* 107:451–469.

1996a "Most Ancient Aramaic Texts and Linguistics: A Review of Recent Studies." *Incontri linguistici* 19:33–57.

1996b "An Aramaic Tablet from Tell Shiukh Fawqani, Syria." *Semitica* 46:81–121 (Introduction by L. Bachelot, Appendix by E. Attardo), pls. IX–X.

2000 "The Use and Function of Aramaic Tablets." Pp. 89–124 in *Syria in the Iron Age*. Edited by G. Bunnens. Louvain, Paris and Sterling, VA: Peeters.

2001 *L'impero assiro: storia e amministrazione (IX–VII sec. a.C.)*. Roma and Bari: Laterza.

2007 "Multilingualism on Multiple Media in the Neo-Assyrian Period: A Review of the Evidence." *SAAB* 16:95–122.

2009 "The Assyrian words for '(Foot)soldier.'" Pp. 71–94 in G. Galil *et al.* (Eds.), *Studies ... Bustenay Oded*, Leiden: Brill.

2010 "New Light on Assyro-Aramaic Interference: The Assur Ostracon." Pp. 189–203 in *CAMSEMUD 2007. Proceedings of the 13th Italian Meeting of Afro-Asiatic Linguistics held in Udine, May 21–24, 2007*. Ed by F. M. Fales and G. F. Grassi. Padova: S.A.R.G.O.N.

2012 "After Ta'yinat: the New Status of Esarhaddon's *adê* for Assyrian Political History." *RA* 106:133–158.

2013 "On רכש, *rakkasu*, and *raksu*." Pp. 71–88 in *In the Shadow of Bezalel. Aramaic, Biblical, and Ancient Near Eastern Studies in Honor of Bezalel Porten*. Ed. by A. F. Botta. Leiden: Brill.

2014a "The Two Dynasties of Assyria." Pp. 201–238 in G. Gaspa *et al.* (Eds.), *Studies ... Giovanni Battista Lanfranchi*, Münster: Ugarit-Verlag.

2014b "Til-Barsib. A. Philologisch." *RlA* 14:34–37.

Fales, F. M., K. Radner, C. Pappi, and E. Attardo

2005 "The Assyrian and Aramaic Texts from Tell Shiukh Fawqani." Pp. 595–694 in *Tell Shiukh Fawqani 1994–1998*. 2 Volumes. Edited by L. Bachelot and F. M. Fales. Padova: S.A.R.G.O.N.

Folmer, M. L.

1995 *The Aramaic Language in the Achaemenid Period. A Study in Linguistic Variation*. Leuven: Peeters.

Fitzmyer, J. A. and S. A. Kaufman

1992 *An Aramaic Bibliography. Part I: Old, Official, and Biblical Aramaic*. Baltimore and London: Johns Hopkins University Press.

Freedman, D. N.

1964 "A Second Mesha Inscription." *BASOR* 175: 50–51.

Galling, K.

1961 "Eine Ostrakon aus Samaria als Rechtsurkunde: Erwängung zu C1101." *ZDPV* 77: 173–185.

Galter, H.

2004a "Militärgrenze und Euphrathandel. Der sozio-ökonomische Hintergrund der Trilinguen von Arslan Tash." Pp. 444–460 in *Commerce and Monetary Systems in the Ancient World: Means of Transmission and Cultural Interaction. Proceedings of the*

Fifth Annual Symposium of the Assyrian and Babylonian Intellectual Heritage Project Held in Innsbruck, Austria, October 3rd–8th 2002. Edited by R. Rollinger and Ch. Ulf. Melammu Symposia 5. Stuttgart: Franz Steiner Verlag.
2004b "Der Himmel über Hadattu. Das religiöse Umfeld der Inschriften von Arslan Tash." Pp. 173–188 in *Offizielle Religion, lokale Kulte und individuelle Religiosität. Akten des religionsgeschichtlichen Symposiums "Kleinasien und angrenzende Gebiete vom Beginn des 2. bis zur Mitte des 1. Jahrtausends v. Chr." (Bonn, 20.–22. Februar 2003)*. Edited by M. Hutter and S. Hutter-Braunsar. AOAT 318. Münster: Ugarit-Verlag.
2007 "Die Torlöwen von Arslan Tash." Pp. 193–211 in *Festschrift für Hermann Hunger zum 65. Geburtstag gewidmet von seinen Freunden, Kollegen und Schülern*. Edited by M. Köhbach, S. Procházka, G. J. Selz, and R. Lohlker. Wiener Zeitschrift für die Kunde des Morgenlandes 97. Vienna: Selbstverlag des Instituts für Orientalistik.

Garr, W. R.
2004 *Dialect Geography of Syria-Palestine, 1000–586 B.C.E.* Winona Lake, IN: Eisenbrauns.

Gaß, E.
2009 *Die Moabiter – Geschichte und Kultur eines ostjordanischen Volkes im 1. Jahrhundert v. Chr.* ADPV 38. Wiesbaden: Harrassowitz.
2012 "New Moabite Inscriptions and Their Historical Relevance." *JNSL* 38: 45–78.

Gibson, J. C. L.
1971 *SSI*. Volume 1.

Gogel, S. L.
1998 *A Grammar of Epigraphic Hebrew*. Atlanta: Scholars Press.

Hawkins, J. D.
2000 CHLI 1.
2005 "Die Inschrift des Warikas von Hiyawa aus Çineköy." Pp. 155–156 in *TUAT*. NF 2.

Hays, C. B.
2011 *Death in the Iron Age II and in First Isaiah*. FAT 79. Tübingen: Mohr Siebeck.

Herrmann, V. R.
2014a "The Architectural Context of the KTMW Stele from Zincirli and the Mediation of Syro-Hittite Mortuary Cult by the Gods." Pp. 73–87 in *Contextualising Grave Inventories in the Ancient Near East. Proceedings of a Workshop at the London 7th ICAANE in April 2010 and an International Symposium in Tübingen in November 2010, both Organised by the Tübingen Post-Graduate School "Symbols of the Dead."* Qaṭna Studien Supplementa 3. Ed. by P. Pfälzner, H. Niehr, E. Pernicka, S. Lange, and T. Köster. Wiesbaden: Harrassowitz.
2014b "The KTMW Stele from Zincirli: Syro-Hittite Mortuary Cult and Urban Social Networks." Pp. 153–181 in *Redefining the Sacred: Religious Architecture and Text in the Near East and Egypt 1000 BC–AD 300*. Contextualizing the Sacred 1. Ed. by E. Frood and R. Raja. Turnhout: Brepols.

Hidalgo-Chacón Diez, M. del Carmen
2009 "Neuarbeitung der dadanischen Inschrift Abū l-Ḥasan 197." *AuOr* 27: 43–56.

Hipp, K.
2015 "Fugitives in the State Archives of Assyria." *SAAB* 21:47–77.

Israel, F.
1975 "L'olio da toeletta' negli ostraca di Samaria." *RSO* 49: 17–20.

Kallai, Z.
2006 "Note on J. A. Emerton: Lines 25–6 in published article of the Moabite Stone and a Recently-Discovered Inscription." *VT* 56: 552–553.

Kaufman, I. T.
1966 "The Samaria Ostraca: A Study in Ancient Hebrew Paleaography." Th.D. Dissertation, Harvard University.
1982 "The Samaria Ostraca: An Early Witness to Hebrew Writing." *BA* 45: 229–239.
1992 "Samaria (Ostraca)." Pp. 921–926 in *ABD* 5.

Kottsieper, I.
2002 "Zum aramäischen Text der 'Trilingue' von Xanthos und ihrem historischen Hintergrund." Pp. 209–243 in *Ex Mesopotamia et Syria Lux. Festschrift für M. Dietrich*. Ed. by O. Loretz, K. Metzler and H. Schaudig. AOAT 281. Münster: Ugarit-Verlag.

Landsberger, B.
1948 *Sam'al. Studien zur Entdeckung der Ruinenstätte Karatepe*. Veröffentlichungen der Türkischen Historischen Gesellschaft 7. Num. 16. Ankara: Türk Tarih Kurumu.

Lanfranchi, G. B.
2005 "The Luwian-Phoenician Bilingual of Çineköy and the Annexation of Cilicia to the Assyrian Empire." Pp. 481–496 in *Von Sumer bis Homer. Festschrift für Manfred Schretter*. Ed. by R. Rollinger. AOAT 325. Münster: Ugarit-Verlag.
2009 "A Happy Son of the King of Assyria: Warikas and the Çineköy Bilingual (Cilicia)." Pp. 127–150 in *Of God(s), Trees, Kings, and Scholars. Neo-Assyrian and Related Studies in Honour of Simo Parpola*. Ed. by M. Luukko, S. Svärd and R. Mattila. Studia Orientalia 106. Helsinki: Finnish Oriental Society.

Lemaire, A.
1971 "Le "Pays de Hépher" et les "Filles de Zelophehad" à la lumière des ostraca de Samarie." *Semitica* 22: 13–20.
1972 "L'ostracon 1101 de Samarie: Nouvel essai." *RB* 79: 565–570.
1977 *Inscriptions hébraïques*. Paris: Cerf.
1995 "The Xanthos Trilingual Revisited." Pp. 423–432 in *Solving Riddles and Untying Knots. Biblical, Epigraphic, and Semitic Studies in Honor of Jonas C. Greenfield*. Ed. by Z. Zevit, S. Gitin and M. Sokoloff. Winona Lake, IN: Eisenbrauns.
2001 *Nouvelles tablettes araméennes*. Genève: Droz.
2005 "Essai d'interprétation historique d'une nouvelle inscription monumentale moabite." *CRAIBL*: 95–108.
2006 "La maison de Mopsos en Cilicie et en Pamphylie à l'époque du Fer (XIIe–VIe s. av. J.-C.)." *Res Antiquae* 3: 99–107.
2008 "Remarks on the Aramaic of Upper Mesopotamia in the Seventh Century B.C." Pp. 77–92 in *Aramaic in its Historical and Linguistic Setting*. Edited by H. Gzella and M. L. Folmer. Wiesbaden: Harrassowitz.
2008–2009 "Philologie et épigraphie hébraïques et araméennes." *ÉPHÉ SPH* 141: 16–18.
2012 "Rites des vivants pour les morts dans le royaume de Sam'al (VIIIe siècle av. n. è.)." Pp. 129–137 in *Les vivants et leurs morts. Actes du colloque organisé par le Collège de France, Paris, les 14–15 avril 2010*. Ed. by J.-M. Durand, T. Römer, and J. Hutzli. OBO 257. Fribourg: Academic Press; Göttingen: Vandenhoeck & Ruprecht.

2013 "Le dialecte araméen de l' inscription de Kuttamuwa (Zencirli, VIIIe s. av. n. è.)." Pp. 145–150 in *In the Shadow of Bezalel. Aramaic, Biblical, and Ancient Near Eastern Studies in Honor of Bezalel Porten*. Ed. by A. F. Botta. Leiden: Brill.

LEMAIRE, A. and B. SASS
2012 "La stèle d'Ördekburnu: vers la solution d' une énigme de l' épigraphie ouest-sémitique." *CRAIBL*: 227–240.
2013 "The Mortuary Stele with Samʾalian Inscription from Ördekburnu near Zincirli." *BASOR* 369: 57–136.

LIDZBARSKI, M.
1915 "VI. Die Stele von Ördek-burnu." Pp. 192–206 in *ESE* 3.

LINDENBERGER, J. M.
2003 *Ancient Aramaic and Hebrew Letters*. SBLWAW 4. Atlanta: Scholars Press.

LIPIŃSKI, E.
1977 "North-West Semitic Inscriptions." *OLP* 8: 81–117.
1994 *Studies in Aramaic Inscriptions and Onomastics, II*. Leuven: Peeters.
2000 *The Aramaeans. Their Ancient History, Culture, Religion*. OLA 100. Leuven: Peeters.
2004 *Itineraria Phoenicia*. OLA 127. Leuven: Peeters.
2010 *Studies in Aramaic Inscriptions and Onomastics, III: Ma'lana*. Leuven: Peeters.

LUSCHAN, F. VON
1911 *Ausgrabungen in Sendschirli 4*. MOS 14. Berlin: Reimer.

MAKINSON, M.
2002–2005 Muṣru, Maṣuwari and *MṢR*: From Middle Assyrian Frontier to Iron Age City. *SAAB* 14:33–62.

MASSON, É.
2010 "La stèle mortuaire de Kuttamuwa (Zincirli): comment l' appréhender." *Semitica et Classica* 3:31–51.

MAZAR, B.
1986 *The Early Biblical Period: Historical Studies*. Jerusalem: Israel Exploration Society.

MAZZINI, G.
2009 "On the Problematic Term *syr/d* in the New Old Aramaic Inscription from Zincirli." *UF* 41: 505–507.

MCLAUGHLIN, J. L.
2001 *The* marzēaḥ *in the Prophetic Literature: References and Allusions in Light of the Extra-Biblical Evidence*. VTSup 86. Leiden: Brill.

MELCHERT, H. C.
2010 "Remarks on the Kuttamuwa Inscription." *Kubaba* 1: 4–11.

MICHELINI TOCCI, F.
1962 "Un frammento di stele aramaica da Tell Sifr." *Oriens Antiquus* 1: 21–22.

MILLER, J. M.
1992 "Early Monarchy in Moab?" Pp. 77–91 in *Early Edom and Moab. The Beginning of the Iron Age in Southern Jordan*. Ed. by P. Bienkowski. Sheffield Archaeological Monographs 7. Sheffield: Collis.

NAM, R.
2012 "Power Relations in the Samaria Ostraca." *PEQ* 144: 155–163.

NAVEH, J.
1965 "ktwbwt knʿnywt wʿbrywt (1960–1964)." *Lešonenu* 30: 65–80.

NEBE, G. W.
2010 "Eine neue Inschrift aus Zincirli auf der Stele des Kutamuwa und die hebräische Sprachwissenschaft." Pp. 311–332 in *Jüdische Studien als Disziplin – Die Disziplinen der Jüdischen Studien. Festschrift der Hochschule für Jüdische Studien Heidelberg 1979–2009*. Ed. by J. Heil and D. Krochmalnik. Heidelberg: Universitätsverlag Winter.

NIEHR, H.
2010 "Götter und Kulte in den Königreichen der Aramäer Syriens." Pp. 210–316 in *Religionen in der Umwelt des Alten Testaments* II: *Phönizier, Punier, Aramäer*. By C. Bonnet and H. Niehr. Stuttgart: Kohlhammer.

NIEMANN, H. M.
2008 "A New Look at the Samaria Ostraca: The King-Clan Relationship." *Tel Aviv* 35: 249–266.

O'CONNOR, M.
1986 "Northwest Semitic Designations for Elective Social Affinities." *JANES* 18: 67–80.

OETTINGER, N.
2008 "The Seer Mopsos (Muksas) as a Historical Figure". Pp. 63–66, in *Anatolian Interfaces. Hittites, Greeks and Their Neighbours*. Ed. by B. J. Collins. Oxford: Oxbow Books.

PARDEE, D.
1996 "*Marziḥu*, *Kispu*, and the Ugaritic Funerary Cult: A Minimalist View." Pp. 273–287 in *Ugarit, Religion and Culture. Proceedings of the International Colloquium on Ugarit, Religion and Culture, Edinburgh, July 1994. Essays Presented in Honour of Professor John C. L. Gibson*. Ed. by N. Wyatt, W. G. E. Watson, and J. B. Lloyd. UBL 12. Münster: Ugarit-Verlag.
2005 Review. *JNES* 64: 196–199.
2008 Review. *JNES* 67: 63–67.
2009a "A New Aramaic Inscription from Zincirli." *BASOR* 356: 51–71.
2009b "Une nouvelle inscription araméenne de Zincirli." *CRAIBL*: 799–806.

PARKER, H. D. D., and A. F. ARICO
2015 "A Moabite-Inscribed Statue Fragment from Kerak: Egyptian Parallels." *BASOR* 273:105–120.

PARPOLA, S. and M. PORTER
2001 *The Helsinki Atlas of the Near East in the Neo-Assyrian Period*. Casco Bay and Helsinki: The Neo-Assyrian Text Corpus Project.

PAUL, S.
1975 "Classifications of Wine in Mesopotamian and Rabbinic Sources." *IEJ* 25: 42–44.

PEDERSÉN, O.
1986 *Archives and Libraries in the City of Assur*. Part II. Uppsala: University of Uppsala.

POSTGATE, J. N.
1976 *Fifty Neo-Assyrian Legal Documents*. Warminster:

Radner, K.
1997 *Die neuassyrischen Privatrechtsurkunden als Quelle für Mensch und Umwelt*, Helsinki:
2002 *Die neuassyrischen Texte aus Tall Šēḫ Ḥamad*, Berlin.
2006–2008 "Provinz. C. Assyrien." *RlA* 11:42–68.
Rainey, A. F.
1962 "Administration in Ugarit and the Samaria Ostraca." *IEJ* 12: 62–63.
1967 "The Samaria Ostraca in Light of Fresh Evidence." *PEQ* 99: 32–41.
1970 "Semantic Parallels to the Samaria Ostraca." *PEQ* 102: 45–51.
1979 "The *Sitz im Leben* of the Samaria Ostraca." *Tel Aviv* 6: 91–94
1988 "Towards a Precise Date for the Samaria Ostraca." *BASOR* 272: 69–74.
2002 "The New Inscription from Khirbet el-Mudeiyineh." *IEJ* 52: 81–86.
Reed, W. L., and F. V. Winnett
1963 "A Fragment of an Early Moabite Inscription from Kerak." *BASOR* 172: 1–9.
Reisner, G. A.
n.d. "Israelite Ostraca from Samaria." Boston: Unpublished Report of the Harvard University Palastinian Expedition.
Reisner, G. A., C. S. Fisher, and D. G. Lyon
1924 *Harvard Excavations at Samaria, 1908–1910*. 2 Vols. Cambridge: Harvard University.
Renz, J.
1995 *Handbuch der althebräischen Epigraphik*. Ed. by J. Renz and W. Röllig. 3 vols. Darmstadt: Wissenschaftliche Buchgesellschaft.
Richelle, M.
2012 "Notes épigraphiques sur l'ostracon numéro 3 de Tell el-Mazar." *Semitica* 54:127–146.
Röllig, W.
1997 "Aramaica Haburiensia II. Zwei datierte aramäische Urkunden aus Tall Šēḫ Ḥamad." *AoF* 24:366–374.
2009 "Inschriften des Ninurta-bēlu-uṣur, Statthalters von Kār-Salmānu-ašared. Teil 1." Pp. 265–278 in *Of God(s), Trees, Kings, and Scholars: Neo-Assyrian and Related Studies in Honour of Simo Parpola*. Edited by M. Luukko, S. Svärd, and R. Mattila. Studia Orientalia 106. Helsinki: Finnish Oriental Society.
2014 *Die aramäischen Texte aus Tall Šēḫ Ḥamad/Dūr-Katlimmu/Magdalu*. Berlin.
Rollston, C. A.
2004 "Non-Provenanced Epigraphs II: The Status of Non-Provenanced Epigraphs within the Broader Corpus of Northwest Semitic." *Maarav* 11: 57–79.
2008 "The Dating of the Early Royal Byblian Phoenician Inscriptions: A Response to Benjamin Sass." *Maarav* 15: 57–93.
2010 *Writing and Literacy in the World of Ancient Israel: Epigraphic Evidence from the Iron Age*. Archaeology and Biblical Studies. Leiden and Boston: Brill.
Routledge, B.
1996 *Intermittent Agriculture and the Political Economy of Iron Age Moab*. Thesis, University of Toronto. Ann Arbor: University Microfilms International.
2003 "A Comment on A. F. Rainey's 'The New Inscription from Khirbet el-Mudeiyineh.'" *IEJ* 53: 192–195.
2004 *Moab in the Iron Age: Hegemony, Polity, Archaeology*. Philadelphia: University of Pennsylvania Press.
Sanders, S. L.
2012 "Naming the Dead. Funerary Writing and Historical Change in the Iron Age Levant." *Maarav* 19: 11–36.
2013 "The Appetites of the Dead: West Semitic Linguistuc and Ritual Aspects of the Katumuwa Stele." *BASOR* 369: 35–55.
Sarfatti, G.
1982 "Hebrew Inscriptions of the First Temple Period: A Survey and Some Linguistic Comments." *Maarav* 31:55–83.
Sasson, V.
1981 "*šmn rḥṣ* in the Samaria Ostraca." *JSS* 26: 1–5.
Schiffmann, I.
1965 "Eine neue moabitische Inschrift aus Karcha." *ZAW* 77: 324–325.
Schloen, J. D.
2001 *The House of the Father as Fact and Symbol: Patrimonialism in Ugarit and the Ancient Near East*. Studies in the Archaeology and History of the Levant 2. Winona Lake, Ind.: Eisenbrauns.
Schloen, J. D., and A. S. Fink
2009 "New Excavations at Zincirli Höyük in Turkey (Ancient Sam'al) and the Discovery of an Inscribed Mortuary Stele." *BASOR* 356: 1–13.
Schniedewind, W. M., and D. Sivan
1997 "The Elijah-Elisha Narratives: A Test Case for the Northern Dialect of Hebrew." *JQR* 87:303–338.
Schwiderski, D.
2000 *Handbuch des nordwestsemitischen Briefformulars*. Berlin and New York: De Gruyter.
Singer, I.
2009 "The Luwian-Phoenician Bilingual from Çineköy and its Historical Implications." Pp. 147–152, 287* in *Ephraim Stern Volume*. Ed. by J. Aviram. ErIs 29. Jerusalem, Israel Exploration Society.
Stager, L. E.
1983 "The Finest Olive Oil in Samaria." *JSS* 28: 241–245.
Struble, E. J., and Herrmann, V. R.
2009 "An Eternal Feast at Sam'al: The New Iron Age Mortuary Stele from Zincirli in Context." *BASOR* 356: 15–49.
Sukenik, E. L.
1933 "Inscribed Hebrew and Aramaic Potsherds from Samaria." *PEQ* 65: 152–156.
Suriano, M. J.
2007 "A Fresh Reading for 'Aged Wine' in the Samaria Ostraca." *PEQ* 139: 27–33.
2014 "Breaking Bread with the Dead: Katumuwa's Stele, Hosea 9:4, and the Early History of the Soul." *JAOS* 134: 385–405.
2016 "Wine shipments to Samaria from Royal Vineyards." *Tel Aviv* 43:99–110.

Swiggers, P.
1982a "Note sur le nom moabite Kmšyt." *AION* 42: 305–306.
1982b "The Moabite Inscription of el-Kerak." *AION* 42: 521–525.

Tappy, R. E.
2001 *The Archaeology of Israelite Samaria, Volume II: The Eighth Century BCE*. HSS 50. Atlanta: Scholars Press.

Teixidor, J.
1967 "Bulletin d' épigraphie sémitique." *Syria* 44: 163–195.
1978 "The Aramaic Text of the Trilingual Stele from Xanthos." *JNES* 37: 181–185.
1986 *Bulletin d' épigraphie sémitique (1964–1980)*. BAH 127. Paris: Geuthner.

Tekoğlu, R. and A. Lemaire
2000 "La bilingue royale louvito-phénicienne de Çineköy." *CRAIBL*: 961–1006.

Thureau-Dangin, F. et al.
1931 *Arslan-Tash*. 2 vols. Paris: Libraire Orientaliste Paul Geuthner.

Timm, S.
1989 *Moab zwischen den Mächten. Studien zu historischen Denkmälern und Texten*. ÄAT 17. Wiesbaden: Harrassowitz.

Töpelman, J.
1921 *Altaramäische Urkunden aus Assur*. Leipzig:

Tropper, J.
1993 *Die Inschriften von Zincirli*. ALASP 6. Münster: Ugarit-Verlag.

Van der Kooij, G.
1987 "The Identity of Trans-Jordanian Alphabetic Writing in the Iron Age." *SHAJ* 3: 107–121.

Vera Chamaza, G. W.
2005 *Die Rolle Moabs in der neuassyrischen Expansionspolitk*. AOAT 321. Münster: Ugarit-Verlag.

Watanabe, K.
1987 *Die adê-Vereidigung anlässlich der Thronfolgeregelung Asarhaddons*, Berlin: Gebr. Mann.

Weippert, M.
1964 "Archäologischer Jahresbericht." *ZDPV* 80: 150–193.
1966 "Archäologischer Jahresbericht." *ZDPV* 82: 274–330.

Yadin, Y.
1959 "Recipients or Owners: A Note on the Samaria Ostraca." *IEJ* 9: 184–187.
1962 "A Further Note on the Samaria Ostraca." *IEJ* 12: 64–65.

Yakubovich, I.
2010 "The West Semitic God El in Anatolian Hieroglyphic Transmission." Pp. 386–398 in *Pax Hethitica. Studies on the Hittites and Their Neighbours in Honour of Itamar Singer*. Ed. by Y. Cohen, A. Gilan, and J. L. Miller. StBoT 51. Wiesbaden: Harrrassowitz.

Younger, K. L., Jr.
2007 "Some of What's New in Old Aramaic Epigraphy." *NEA* 70:138–146.
2009a "Two Epigraphic Notes on the New Katumuwa Inscription from Zincirli." *Maarav* 16: 159–179.
2009b "The Deity Kur(ra) in the First Millennium Sources." *JANER* 9: 1–23.

Zadok, R.
1977 *On West Semites in Babylonia during the Chaldean and Achaemenian Periods. An Onomastic Study*. Jerusalem.

AKKADIAN INSCRIPTIONS

NUZI TEXTS

TEXTS FROM NUZI (4.31)

Eva von Dassow

Introduction

Nuzi was a city in the land of Arrapḫe, which lay northeast of the Tigris between the Little Zab and the tributaries of the Radānu, flowing from the Zagros foothills. During the 15th and early 14th centuries BCE, Arrapḫe was a kingdom subordinate to Mittani.[1] Its seat of kingship was the city of Arrapḫe, also called Āl-ilāni, "City of the Gods," located at present-day Kirkuk. Toward the end of the 19th century CE, cuneiform tablets dug clandestinely from the ancient mound in Kirkuk began to circulate on the antiquities market. This site, being inhabited, could not be excavated, so archaeological prospectors settled on a nearby mound called Yorġan Tepe where tablets had also turned up, and excavations were conducted there from 1925 to 1931. Yorġan Tepe proved to be the site of a city called Gasur in the late third millennium BCE, which at some point, over centuries of occupation, acquired the name Nuzi. The excavations produced a broad exposure of Late Bronze Age Nuzi (Stratum II), which met with destruction in the mid-14th century, and yielded a wealth of finds that include approximately five thousand tablets.[2] These are mostly legal and administrative records forming institutional and family archives. Other sites in the region have also been investigated, including Tell al-Faḫḫar, where several hundred tablets contemporaneous with those from Nuzi were found during excavations in the late 1960s. Tell al-Faḫḫar was identified as the site of Kurruḫanni, a town mentioned in the Nuzi tablets, until Rafał Koliński demonstrated that it could not be this town and was instead a settlement of the type called a *dimtu* (see below, 4.31D); he proposed identifying it as the *dimtu* Makunta.[3] The tablets from Nuzi, Arrapḫe, and Tell al-Faḫḫar are written in a Middle Babylonian dialect of Akkadian that is heavily influenced by Hurrian, the principal language of the Mittani Empire and evidently the language spoken by most of the population of Arrapḫe.

The Late Bronze Age city of Nuzi comprised a citadel, or fortified inner town, surrounded by an outer town (Hurrian *kirġe* and *adašši*, respectively).[4] Within the inner town were a palace, a double temple thought to be dedicated to Ištar (Hurrian Šawuška) and the storm-god Teššub, and densely-built residential quarters, all provided with a citadel-wide drainage system. Tablets were found in many, but by no means all, of the houses in the inner town, as well as in the palace and temple. Residences excavated in the outer town include the mansion of Prince Šilwe-teššub and the houses of wealthy landlords like Teḫip-tilla, son of Puḫi-šenni, and his sons, which yielded multi-generational family archives. These archives provide the basis for a relative chronology of Nuzi, and thus the kingdom of Arrapḫe, during this period. While the scribes of Nuzi always recorded their names on the legal records they wrote, they made use of no system for dating the documents. Thus the internal chronology of the corpus has to be reconstructed on the basis of prosopography – the identities and relationships of the people attested in the tablets. The framework of this reconstruction is built from the five attested generations of three families: a prolific scribal family descended from Apil-Sin; the family of Teḫip-tilla, son of Puḫi-šenni (attested from Teḫip-tilla's parents to his great-grandson); and the family of Prince Šilwe-teššub (a contemporary of Teḫip-tilla's sons and their offspring).[5] Šilwe-teššub may have succeeded to the throne of Arrapḫe during the last generation before the kingdom's fall, according to a recent study by Diana Stein (2010).

During the mid-14th century the kingdom of Mittani began to fracture under the pressure of conflict with Ḫatti, complemented by internal strife that cleft the royal house in two.[6] One faction, under the rule of Artatama II and then his son Šuttarna III, made a pact with Ḫatti and cultivated the alliance of Assyria, erstwhile subject to Mittani. The other, under the rule of Tušratta, kept up diplomatic relations with Egypt and conflict with Ḫatti, until Tušratta was assassinated. His son Šattiwaza fled and sought refuge first at the Babylonian court, where he was repulsed, and then at the feet of Suppiluliuma I, king of Ḫatti, who gladly took the Mittanian prince as his protégé. Hittite forces did battle against the Hurrian forces mobilized by Šuttarna III, who was defeated, and Suppiluliuma installed Šattiwaza as king of Mittani, now subordinated by treaty to Ḫatti. In the meantime, Assur-uballiṭ, king of Assyria, used the conflict besetting Mittani to his advantage: his kingdom recovered its independence, he commenced diplomatic relations with Egypt, his forces besieged Waššukanni, capital of Mittani – and they beset Arrapḫe, too, which lay

[1] On Arrapḫe in relation to Mittani, and the empire's political structure, see von Dassow 2014.

[2] A succinct introduction to the site of Nuzi, the excavations, and the finds is provided by Stein (1997). The excavation results were published by Starr (1937; 1939).

[3] See Koliński 2001, ch. III.1, also published as a separate article (Koliński 2002).

[4] The fortifications, part of which Starr excavated, are described in a tablet published by Lion (2010). On the buildings in Nuzi, see Novak 1999, and for the locations where tablets were found, Lion 1999a.

[5] For this framework see Friedmann 1987; the anchor to absolute chronology is corrected by Stein (1989; see further the introduction to HSS IX 1, below). Maidman (2010:xxvi) adds the genealogy of the family descended from Kizzuk, reconstructed by Dosch and Deller (1981).

[6] The story of Mittani's demise is derived primarily from the historical prologues to the two versions of the treaty between Suppiluliuma and Šattiwaza (Beckman 1999 nos. 6A and 6B), supplemented by elements from other sources; see Podany 2010:291–301; and Wilhelm 2012.

just east of Assyria. Assyria won the war, conquered Arrapḫe, and destroyed Nuzi, as well as other towns and village settlements like the *dimtu* Tell al-Faḫḫar, probably sometime in the 1330s BCE.[7] That is when the archives end.

Out of the five thousand tablets found at Nuzi, nine are presented here.[8] They are a selection of documents representing local and superordinate governance, as well as legal transactions and processes between individuals. One tablet is a letter from the king of Mittani to the king of Arrapḫe (4.31A), and two are documents issued by the king of Arrapḫe (4.31C and 4.31I). A tablet recording a gift of property to Šilwe-teššub (4.31B), a tablet recording the settlement of a long-running court case over title to the *dimtu* of Kizzuk (4.31D), and two documents deriving from the archives of Teḫip-tilla, son of Puḫi-šenni (4.31E and 4.31F) are included. Two tablets (4.31G and 4.31H) sample perhaps the most colorful of the Nuzi dossiers: the litany of charges against the mayor Kušši-ḫarbe, whom citizens accuse of multifarious deeds of abuse and corruption. His case has sporadically achieved notoriety beyond Assyriology, for the same charges are echoed periodically in our own age – whichever age it may be – since the same abuses are reliably committed by persons in power from time to time.

In the legal practice of Arrapḫe, scribes recorded the principal elements of transactions or court proceedings in the form of direct speech uttered by the participants, a practice that gives the documents a certain immediacy, even vivacity, for the present-day reader. The ostensible utterances are not however quotations. In the first place, they are rendered into the Hurrianized form of Akkadian in which the documents were written, which is fundamentally a language of writing, not of speech; it was what scribes of Arrapḫe learned when they learned to write cuneiform. Most of the people whose statements the documents record probably spoke Hurrian, while no doubt other languages were spoken in Arrapḫe as well, hence what they said had to have been translated by the scribes. In the second place, their statements are generally rendered into standard legal forms (in the case that such existed), and they are formulated from the retrospective of the completed transaction or proceeding. What we are reading, then, contrary to the impression given by formulas like "thus (said) so-and-so … and they asked him … and he declared as follows," are digests, not transcripts, which reduce the reality of speech and action to a succinct record containing all the elements necessary for its legal formulation and only those. The like is true, to some extent, of letters as well.

1. LETTER FROM THE KING OF MITTANI TO ITḪI-TEŠŠUB, KING OF ARRAPḪE (HSS IX 1: "Sauštatar Letter") (4.31A)

This tablet, found in the house of the prince Šilwe-teššub (in Room A26), is a letter from "the king" (of Mittani) to Itḫi-teššub, king of Arrapḫe, whose name is given in the hypocoristic form Itḫiya. It came to be known as the "Sauštatar Letter" because it bears the seal of Sauštatar, son of Parsatatar, king of Mittani, and it was long considered a chronological anchor for the Nuzi archives and the stratum in which they were found. However, not only Sauštatar but subsequent kings of Mittani used Sauštatar's seal (see Stein 1989; Sallaberger, Einwag, and Otto 2006:85–86), and incongruities result from using this letter as a reference point for synchronizing Nuzi with other sites, if Sauštatar is assumed to have been its author. Therefore, it should be attributed to one of his successors, though to which one is uncertain. The letter is at least two generations older than its archaeological context (Stein 1989:48). It informs Itḫi-teššub that the king of Mittani, who had assigned a town to Amminaya, now assigns a(nother?) town to one Ukke. Amminaya was the wife of Ḫešmi-teššub, who (probably) succeeded Itḫi-teššub as king of Arrapḫe, and the mother of Šilwe-teššub, in whose archive this tablet was found.[9]

Notwithstanding its simplicity of expression, the text is not altogether clear – what town did the king of Mittani give to Ukke? Since Šilwe-teššub retained property interests in Paḫḫarašše, it would seem that this town was not taken from his mother during the reign of his grandfather. Perhaps the king of Mittani had reassigned Paḫḫarašše from Ukke to Amminaya, and this is what he means by telling Itḫi-teššub, "your town in his territory I have given to Amminaya" (lines 21–22); on this account he now reassigns a town from Amminaya to Ukke (lines 5–6).

7 Maidman (2010:16–20, and more extensively Maidman 2011) reconstructs the course of Assyria's war on Arrapḫe and shows that, contrary to previous opinion, only Assyrian and not also Babylonian forces were involved. His prolix argument for a date earlier in the reign of Assur-uballiṭ (2011, esp. 121–126) is flawed and will have to be addressed elsewhere.

8 The spelling of names employed herein differs on some points from that which has become conventional in the study of texts from Nuzi and Arrapḫe, insofar as Hurrian names are rendered in accord with the principles of Hurrian phonology and orthography (see, in brief, Wilhelm 2004:98–99), thus: consonants are voiceless in initial position, in medial position when long (K, -kk-, P, -pp-, T, -tt-), and in contact with another non-sonorant consonant (thus, e.g., -tḫ-), while consonants are voiced in final position, in medial position when short, and in contact with a sonorant (-g-, -b-, -d-; -nd- instead of -nt-, etc.); sibilants, fricatives, and laryngeals follow partly similar rules. Consonantal phonology is not however fully realized here for the sake of leaving the names recognizable.

9 Stein 1993 (vol. 8: 27) outlines Šilwe-teššub's genealogy, with reference to the evidence from which it is derived, and provides a diagram of his family tree, illustrated with members' seals (1993 vol. 9, fig. 39).

(lines 1–2) To Itḫiya, speak; thus (says) the king. (lines 3–6) The town of Paḫḫarrašše,[10] which I gave to Amminaya – now I have given a town from her area to Ukke. (lines 7–11) Now, I have sent to Saušsatti, the district governor of the town of Atilu,[11] to survey their territories,[12] and I have instructed Saušsatti thus: (lines 11–18) "Determine[13] the territory of Amminaya. Ukke shall not encroach upon the territory of Amminaya, and Amminaya shall not encroach upon the territory of Ukke."[14] (lines 19–23) And no one shall encroach upon the territory of Amminaya. Your town in his territory I have given to Amminaya, and may you know this. (seal of Sauštatar, impressed on the reverse of the tablet)[15]

[10] Paḫḫarrašše, a town in the kingdom of Arrapḫe, is attested almost exclusively in the archives kept in the house of Šilwe-teššub; references are collected in Fadhil 1983: 128–135.

[11] A town Atilu is otherwise unattested in the Nuzi archives (Fadhil 1983: 129; Fincke, RGTC 10: 63). The term rendered "district governor" is the Hurro-Akkadian word *ḫalṣuḫlu*, on which see von Dassow 2014: 20, with n. 27; see also 4.31I, line 25, with n. 58, below.

[12] The word *pāṭu* (written ZAG) means "border," but also the territory within it, as Zaccagnini (1979: 19, n. 21) argues regarding its usage in Arrapḫe; see the introduction to 4.31I, below.

[13] The quoted instruction must correspond to what the preceding lines say the king sent Saušsatti to do, but the words written are not the same: Saušsatti is sent to *šu-ú-li-i* in l. 9, and the king tells him *šu-ú-ma*(*-mi*) in l. 12. Wilhelm (2006: 102) translates both words "festlegen"; Fadhil (1983: 129) argues that *šu-ú-li-i* must represent the scribe's mis-hearing of *šulwî*, "to survey" (infinitive); Speiser, the text's first translator, took *šu-ú-ma* as an imperative of *šâmu*, "to determine" (1929: 272), which it is not, so subsequent translators have tended to prefer the interpretation Speiser rejected and to take the form as a pronoun with enclitic *-ma* (followed by quotative *-mi*). The present translation follows Fadhil's interpretation of the first word and Speiser's (as well as Wilhelm's) understanding of the second, while bracketing the analysis of the forms.

[14] The quoted speech ends where the use of the quotative particle *-mi* does.

[15] The sealing is Stein 1993 no. 711, discussed and illustrated in vol. 8: 18–19, 60, 92, and vol. 9:72, 528–529.

REFERENCES

Text: HSS IX 1 (SMN 1000) = AdŠ 685. *Editions and translations*: Speiser 1929; Lewy 1942:33–34; Fadhil 1983:129; Koliński 2001:111; Wilhelm 2006:102.

2. ḪAŠIYA DONATES REAL ESTATE TO PRINCE ŠILWE-TEŠŠUB (HSS IX 35) (4.31B)

This tablet, found in the same room (A26) as the preceding one, records the declaration of Ḫašiya, son of Algi-teššub, that he has donated real estate to Šilwe-teššub, the prince, as a "gift." He says he has in turn received his "gift" from Šilwe-teššub, but without specifying what it was he received. One suspects that some other kind of transaction underlies this one. Ḫašiya is elsewhere attested as a debtor of Šilwe-teššub (see n. 1 below); perhaps through his donation of property he resolved accumulated debts. The property Ḫašiya donated is described as "houses" within Āl-ilāni, the capital city, which were surrounded on two sides by "houses" already belonging to the prince. The donated houses could have been buildings of any size or type, even mere shacks. In any case, this property was subject to *ilku*, the service obligation owed by free subjects of the realm based on tenure of real property within its territory.[16] With his acquisition of Ḫašiya's property, Šilwe-teššub acquires the *ilku*-duty incumbent on it (lines 19–22), just as nowadays one's purchase of a house entails assuming the obligation to pay property taxes assessed on it.

Unusually, Šilwe-teššub also acquires the obligation to clear claims against the property that may emerge (a duty normally incumbent on the alienating party), except from Ḫašiya himself, who would incur a prohibitive penalty should he try to reclaim the houses. The prince's acquisition is further protected by the document's final clause, stating that it has been written "after the new edict." This likely refers to a decree of debt remission (Akkadian *andurāru*, Hurrian *kirenzi*), which would have the effect of annulling outstanding non-commercial debts so that (inter alia) real property alienated in distress would revert to its original owners.[17] The formula stating that a tablet was "written after the (new) edict," often appended to transactions in real property, affirmed that the transaction was not subject to the most recent such decree. Since the tablets are undated, one wonders how anyone would know, later on, whether that was true. Evidently this logical gap was filled by the plain fact of having it in writing, on clay, sealed by witnesses and by the party who gave up property rights.

(lines 1–2) Thus (says) Ḫašiya, son of Algi-teššub:[18] (lines 2–11) "The houses within Āl-ilāni, north and west of houses of Šilwe-teššub the prince, south of houses of Wandiya, son of Algi-tilla, east of the

[16] On *ilku* in relation to property and citizenship, see von Dassow in press.

[17] On *andurāru* (or *kirenzi*) in the kingdom of Arrapḫe, see Lion (1999b), who also remarks on the formula "written after the edict" (*ina arki šūdûti šaṭir*) and points out that the edicts from Nuzi whose contents are known – two of which are included here (HSS XIV 9 and HSS XV 1) – do not have to do with *andurāru* (*ibid.*: 319–320, with references). While of course edicts of other kinds were also issued, only *andurāru* decrees would have definite relevance for transactions involving the alienation of property rights.

[18] Ḫašiya, son of Algi-teššub, also appears in the following tablets (all from Šilwe-teššub's archives): HSS IX 18 lists him as a witness; in HSS IX 90 (Wilhelm 1992, no. 228), he and a co-debtor borrow grain from Šilwe-teššub, which they are to repay in its principal amount after the harvest; his role in the fragmentary HSS XIX 35 is unclear to me.

road to Nuldaḫḫe, which I once received in exchange from Urḫi-tilla, son of Aštar-tilla,
(lines 12–19) Now I have given those houses, together with their tablets, to Šilwe-teššub the prince, as a gift.[19] And I have received my gift from Šilwe-teššub."
(lines 19–22) Šilwe-teššub bears the *ilku* of the houses; Ḫašiya does not bear it.
(lines 22–28) If Ḫašiya reclaims the houses,[20] he shall pay tenfold compensation to Šilwe-teššub. If the houses have a claimant, Šilwe-teššub shall clear (the claim).
(lines 28–30) (This) tablet was written in Āl-ilāni after the new edict.

(lines 31–38). Seal of Arikkani, son of Šeḫurni, witness;
Seal of Šipki-teššub, son of Šukriya;
Seal of Šipiš-šarri, son of Utḫaptae;
Seal of Muš-teššub, son of Nai-teššub;
Seal of Urḫiya, son of Muš-teššub;
Seal of Nigriya, son of Šurgip-šarri;
Seal of Šar-tilla, scribe, son of Iliya;
Seal of Ḫašiya, owner of the houses.

(seals impressed on reverse, upper edge, and left edge of the tablet)[21]

19 The word used for "gift" in these lines, *magannu* along with the abstract *magannūtu*, is probably the Akkadianized form of a Hurrianized loanword from an Indo-Aryan language (Mayrhofer 2006:86, with references), rather than a noun derived from the Semitic root *mgn, "give" (O'Connor 1989), though such nouns also exist. The original Indo-Aryan stem would be *maghá-* (in its Vedic reflex), provided with the Hurrian derivational suffix *-nni*, the vocalic ending of which is then replaced by the Akkadian case marking, following a pattern applied to several other Hurrian words formed from Indo-Aryan stems. In the Hurrian-language context of the Mittani Letter, *maganni* behaves morphologically like a Hurrian word (see Giorgieri and Röseler 1996), and it is not impossible that two near-homophones with concordant meaning entered Near Eastern vocabularies by different linguistic paths (and then converged).
20 Lit., "calls after the houses," with the legal meaning of suing to reclaim them.
21 For these eight seal impressions, see Stein 1993, vol. 9: 49.

REFERENCES

Text: HSS IX 35 (SMN 133) = AdŠ 554. *Edition*: Maidman 2010:182–185 (text 80).

3. ROYAL ORDER CONCERNING *ILKU* DONE IN THE ROYAL CITY (HSS XIV 9) (4.31C)

In this somewhat fragmentary tablet, the king issues an order that men who perform *ilku*-duty in the "city of the king" do not also do it in their places of residence; whoever takes a man away from *ilku* in the royal city is to be fined two oxen. The order thus protects the men from double taxation. As mentioned in the introduction to the preceding text, *ilku* was a duty owed by free citizens based on tenure of property. This duty, which encompassed both labor and military service, was assessed on citizens according to their place of residence, and could often be performed there as well. In the present case, men have been levied for duty in the royal city, so it is forbidden to levy them in their home towns at the same time; perhaps complaints about such excess levies prompted the issuance of this order. Which king issued it the tablet does not say. However, it was sealed by Agiya the minister (*sukkallu*), who is attested by both his name and seal impression in numerous other tablets, including text 4.31D (JEN 321) below. These tablets show that he was a contemporary of Šilwe-teššub the prince (Stein 1993, 9:348–349).

The phrase "city of the king" (or "royal city") probably refers to the city of Arrapḫe, where the king resided. The tablet, however, was found in Nuzi, more specifically in one of the paired temples in the middle of town (G29). This find context unfortunately indicates nothing about the tablet's functional or archival context. The tablets found in the temple constitute a miscellaneous assemblage of diverse family and administrative dossiers, and no clear reason why they should have been stored where they were found emerges from the textual or archaeological evidence.

(lines 1–3) Thus the king has announced [(regarding)] the men who [have go]ne up into the [royal ci]ty.[22]
(lines 3–4) Thus (speaks) the king:[23]

(lines 5–9) "The men who [have go]ne up into the [royal ci]ty and bear *ilku*, [they shall not do *ilku*] in the place they reside; their *ilku* is that of the r[oyal c]ity, and none other."

22 The reading and translation presented here generally accord with Lion, HSS LXV, no. 63 (Lion and Stein in press), following Müller (1968:138–139), on all but one significant point: whereas Lion translates the verb she restores as *ītelû* (lines 2, 5) as "they have departed," I translate it as "have gone up"; the verb *elû*, "to go up," can carry either meaning, and the choice really depends on whether the preposition *ina* is taken as "into" or "out of" (both of which it means). Maidman's very divergent rendering of the text proceeds from his refusal to restore URU LUGAL, "city of the king," where the words are incompletely preserved (lines 2, 5, 8), and to assign the two words to different syntactic units where the phrase is preserved intact (lines 11, 15), on the grounds that a "city of the king" does not occur elsewhere in the Nuzi texts (2010:175–176, with n. 54). But it does. Müller identifies several attestations of "city of the king" in the Nuzi texts, and discusses them at length, concluding that the city of the king must have been Arrapḫe (1968:91–105).
23 This phrase introduces the quotation of the king's order, using the quotative particle *-mi*. My division of the text is based on understanding the first sentence (lines 1–3) as well as the stipulation of a fine (lines 10–15) as, respectively, introductory and supplementary to the communication of the king's order by (evidently) Agiya the *sukkallu*.

(lines 10–15) Anyone who causes a man of the royal city to go out from the *ilku* of [the royal city] shall pay two oxen to the [...](-official) of the royal city.

(seal of Agiya)[24]
(line 16) Seal of Agiya, the minister.
(lines 17–18) [Ha]nd of Akkulenni, the scribe.

[24] The seal of Agiya, son of Nai-teššub, the *sukkallu* (which was also used by another administrator) is Stein 1993, sealing no. 404; also Stein, HSS LXV, sealing no. 267 (in Lion and Stein in press).

REFERENCES

Text: HSS XIV 9 (SMN 3626). *Editions and translations*: Müller 1968:89–174; Koliński 2001:117 (transliteration only); Maidman 2010, no. 76; Lion, HSS LXV, no. 63 (in Lion and Stein in press).

4. JUDICIAL RESOLUTION OF DISPUTE OVER *DIMTU* OF KIZZUK (JEN 321) (4.31D)

This document, a tablet that was enclosed in a clay envelope sealed by the scribe who wrote it, records the final settlement of a lawsuit over title to a *dimtu* settlement and its fields. The winner was Kel-teššub, son of Ḫudiya, descendant of Kizzuk, after whom the *dimtu* was named. Tenure of the property had passed into other hands, among them those of Wandari, son of Ukkuya, the defendant in this lawsuit. Several tablets recording various stages in the legal proceedings, which were commenced by Kel-teššub's father Ḫudiya against other tenants of the *dimtu*'s lands, were kept in the archives of his family in their house, located not far from the mansion of Šilwe-teššub the prince in the outer town of Nuzi.[25] The dossier is incomplete, preventing full understanding of the dispute, which the tablets would not provide anyway: the settlement of a lawsuit was always recorded from the standpoint of its outcome, i.e., of the winner, so the resulting document is nothing like a transcript of the proceedings. In this instance, however, the dossier Kel-teššub kept (what survives of it) includes records of what we might call the discovery phase of the case, which went before the king of Arrapḫe. Ḫudiya had sued to recover possession of the property from several defendants, who claimed rights to it on various grounds: they acquired the fields through adoption (on this mechanism for property transfer, see below, 4.31E, [JEN 160]); the town belonged to the palace; and besides, it is named Ṭāb-ukur, not Kizzuk, whose descendant Turi-kintar stole it (JEN 325 and 388).[26] Two officials, Ḫudib-abu the district governor and Agiya the minister – the same Agiya who sealed the royal order conveyed in 4.31C above (HSS XIV 9) – were charged with inquiring about the disputed *dimtu* with neighboring towns, to determine whose title claim was valid. Their inquiry discovered that the men of neighboring towns agreed that the *dimtu* was named for Kizzuk, although the defendants, who at this point were Wandari and one Keliya, still maintained that it was named for Ṭāb-ukur (JEN 135).

The Akkadian term *dimtu*, in the usage of Arrapḫe, had a series of related meanings besides its primary meaning, "tower": it also denoted a rural dwelling compound, fortified with perhaps one or more towers; the settlement at such a compound; and the lands of that settlement.[27] Here the rural compound with its associated settlement and cultivable lands is at issue. The judicial process focuses on determining the settlement's name because it took its name from its original title-holder, whose descendants have an inherent right to the property – even if it had been alienated through sale, or by some other means, their right was in principle recoverable.[28] In the present document, then, once the court has ascertained that the *dimtu* was named for Kizzuk, that it was held by patrimonial right, and that they do not know Wandari (i.e., recognize his right to the property), Kel-teššub's title is vindicated. Even the fact that Wandari inherited the property from his father and does the *ilku* duty incumbent on it (on which see the introduction to 4.31B [HSS IX 35] and 4.31C [HSS XIV 9] above) does not count against this determination, since Wandari can bring no one to testify to his title. One can only guess what the background was – had Ḫudiya been captured in war, so that, in his absence, Wandari's father Ukkuya acquired his lands and paid duty on them, until Ḫudiya was redeemed from captivity and could get back home to redeem his property? Such a situation is envisioned and provided for in the Laws of Hammurabi, § 27 (*COS* 2.131).

[25] The tablets belonging to this dossier are presented, in their probable chronological sequence, by Maidman (2010, Ch. 3): JEN 644 (his no. 55), 388 (no. 56), 325 (no. 57), 512 (no. 58), 135 (no. 59), 184 (no. 60), and 321 (no. 61), the present document, which evidently concluded the case. The archives of this branch of the Kizzuk family were kept in the rooms numbered 11 and 12 in the excavation area labeled "T" (for Teḫip-tilla, son of Puḫi-šenni); some tablets, including this one, were dispersed into room 13 in the house next door (see Deller 1983: 20; Lion 1999a:45).

[26] In a fragmentary passage, JEN 388 also records the testimony of one of the defendants to the effect that Ukkuya had given as bridewealth fields he had acquired (lines 25–28); presuming that this Ukkuya is the father of Wandari, whom Kel-teššub sues, the passage does not indicate how the land had come into Ukkuya's possession.

[27] See Koliński 2001; note especially his diagram of the compound of the *dimtu* Šelwuḫu based on the description of it in HSS XIII 363 (p. 9, Fig. 1), and his plans of the excavated compound at Tell al-Faḫḫar, which he shows to correspond to the description of a *dimtu* (Figs. 3 and 4).

[28] One document pertaining to the case of the *dimtu* of Kizzuk makes clear that rights to the settlement and its lands were not exclusive: in JEN 644, five men grant Ḫudiya fields and the *dimtu*, and if Hudiya wins his case, he may take one share in those fields and *dimtu*.

(Envelope) [Seal] of Urḫi-Teššub, scribe[29]
(Tablet)
(lines 1–4) Kel-teššub, son of Ḫudiya, appeared before the judges in a case against Wandari, son of Ukkuya. Thus (said) Kel-teššub:
(lines 4–15) "Wandari is holding by force my *dimtu*, that of Kizzuk, which is on the other (river)bank, with my fields. I have sued him for it. I have appealed to the king, and he sent to Ḫudib-abu the district governor, saying, 'Inquire of the towns on the right and on the left of the *dimtu* of Kizzuk, and return a report.' Ḫudib-abu the district governor inquired of the towns, he wrote their words on a tablet, (and) the seals of the men of the towns are rolled on the tablet."[30]
(lines 16–20) The judges asked Wandari; thus (said) Wandari: "My father held the *dimtu* of Kizzuk with its fields. I hold it after my father, and it is I who do the *ilku* (duty) for those fields and that *dimtu*."
(lines 21–23) And Kel-teššub produced the tablet of the towns that Ḫudib-abu the district governor wrote; he read it out, as follows:
(lines 24–34). "Thus the men of Kumrima,
Thus the men of Wuldukuriya,
Thus the men of Ezira,
Thus the men of Kuluttuwe,
Thus the men of Šimerunni,
Thus the men of Edeššenni,
Thus the men of Ašuri,
Thus the men of Tilli-ša-kakki,
Thus the men of Ḫašluniya,"
So, thus (say) the nine towns on the right and on the left of the *dimtu* of Kizzuk:[31]
(lines 35–37) "'The *dimtu* which is "of Kizzuk," with its fields, belongs to Kizzuk, as patrimonial (property).[32] And as to Wandari, we do not know.'"
(lines 38–41) The judges said to Wandari, "Now, nine towns count for testimony[33] for Kel-teššub. So bring men of yours testifying for you."
(lines 42–43) Thus (said) Wandari, "There are no men testifying for me."
(lines 43–50) Since the tablet of Ḫudib-abu the district governor was read before the judges, the nine towns count for testimony for Kel-teššub, the seals of the men of the nine towns and of Ḫudib-abu are rolled on the tablet, and there is no one testifying for Wandari, the judges made a judgment in accord with the tablet. Kel-teššub prevailed in the case.
(lines 50–56) Kel-teššub took the *dimtu* of Kizzuk, together with the fields west of the border of (the town) Eteššenni, north of the border of (the town) Ezira, (and) east of the *dimtu* of Ulluya.
(line 57) Hand of Urḫi-teššub, scribe.
(lines 58–72). Seal of Tiltaššura, the minister; seal of Agiya, the minister,
Seal of Arib-abu, son of Teḫib-abu,
Seal of Niḫri-teššub, son of Pui-tae,
Seal of Šurgi-tilla, son of Agiptašenni,
Seal of Waḫri-tae, son of Tarmi-teššub,
Seal of Ḫudanni, son of Tarmi-tilla,
Seal of Teḫip-tilla, son of Ḫašuar,
Seal of Turar-teššub, son of Eḫli-teššub,
Seal of Šur-teššub, son of Tantea,
Seal of Zilib-abu, son of Šurgum-adal,
Seal of Arnunti, scribe,
Seal of Enna-muša, son of Kannabu,
Seal of Šar-teššub, son of Utḫap-tae,
Seal of Ḫudib-abu, son of Tarmi-tilla,
Seal of Muš-teššub, son of Pilmašše,
(line 73) Hand of Urḫi-teššub, scribe.

29 No one who has examined this tablet and its envelope seems to have recorded the sealings it bears. I thank Diana Stein (personal communication) for helping to investigate the matter.

30 This may have been more than one tablet in reality. JEN 512 records the names and bears the sealings of thirteen men from four of the nine towns listed in the present document (their testimony as reported on that tablet, however, does not quite match what Kel-teššup reports; see Maidman 2010:251–252, nn. 41–42). JEN 184 records the declaration of men from the same nine towns as in the present document, who say the *dimtu* is named for Kizzuk and there is no other name; the tablet is sealed by nine men, perhaps one representative per town (though none of the names corresponds to any of the thirteen recorded in JEN 512).

31 In recording the statement with which Kel-teššub introduces his report of the men's testimony, the scribe provides the *dimtu*'s name with the Hurrian genitive ending *-we*, thus Kizzukwe, "of Kizzuk"; he does the same in recording the first phrase of the men's testimony ("the *dimtu* which is Kizzukwe"), thus specifying that according to the report the *dimtu* is (named) "of Kizzuk."

32 Here the scribe writes *ša Kizzuk-ma* (not Kizzukwe), using the Akkadian relative pronoun *ša* to signify possession and appending the enclitic *-ma* for emphasis. The word used to specify that the property is "patrimonial" is Hurrian *attiġe*, provided with the Akkadian nominative ending *-u*.

33 The word here and in l. 45 is *pa-la-aḫ-ḫi*, which has received translations dependent on deriving it from Akkadian *palāḫu*, "to fear, respect, serve" (e.g., Maidman 2010:141, with n. 57). Not only does the meaning suit the context poorly (hence the diverse contorted translations), the spelling with double *-ḫḫ-* would be anomalous if it were this verb. Perhaps it is a Hurrian word formed of the stem *pal-*, "know," with the derivational vowel *-a-* and the suffix *-ḫḫe* (which forms derivative adjectives, often used as substantives), thus "attesting," or the like.

REFERENCES

Text: JEN 321 (= JENu 191a, 191b). *Editions and translations*: Lewy 1942:344–347; Hayden 1962:120–123 [*non vidi*]; Jankowska 1969:260–261; Maidman 2010, no. 61.

5. DECLARATION OF NO CONTEST BY HOLDERS OF TITLE ALIENATED THROUGH REAL-ESTATE ADOPTION (JEN 160) (4.31E)

A legal practice peculiar to Arrapḫe, though not without parallel elsewhere in the ancient Near East, was the use of adoption as a mechanism for transferring title to real property. In a contract for real-estate adoption, one party "adopts" another party and gives the "adoptee" a piece of real estate as an "(inheritance) share" while receiving in exchange a "gift" of consumable goods. Such contracts often stipulate that the "adopter" who alienates title continues to bear the *ilku* duty incumbent on the property; meanwhile, they include none of the stipulations that characterize real adoptions, such as obligations of care. Real-estate adoption was a legal instrument whereby a property owner obtained financing by ceding to the financier a title claim on his or her property, as in a mortgage. The question why such transactions were formulated in terms of adoption has been answered with divergent proposals, most of which are ruled out by the evidence of the documents they mean to explain. Leaving aside the more bizarre hypotheses, most explanations turn on the idea that there was a prohibition, emanating from either family or state, on alienating real property; the idea of a prohibition in law is premised on the assumption that land subject to *ilku* was held by royal grant. But clearly there was no such prohibition, and more specifically, there was no prohibition on alienating property subject to *ilku*, which was not in fact generally held by royal grant. The state enforced these contracts, with the participation of family members of the parties alienating title; the state can hardly be supposed to have enforced an illegal subterfuge. Nor does real-estate adoption reflect some odd custom that immigrating Hurrians brought in, for not only had Hurrian-speakers immigrated about a millennium earlier, this legal instrument was evidently developed in Arrapḫe during the period of the Nuzi archives. Instead, real-estate adoption is to be explained by the state's issuance of *andurāru* edicts that provided for the remission of debts and the restoration of persons or property alienated through debt. Family members had an inherent right to recover patrimonial property thus alienated. Thus, if one mortgaged one's family home and lost it in foreclosure, one could recover it when a debt-remission edict cancelled one's mortgage, while the mortgagee would lose the title claim he or she obtained through providing financing. Conversely, if one "adopted" one's financier, his or her title to the property one "bequeathed" was protected under the very same principle.[34]

One of the most prolific financiers in Nuzi was Teḫip-tilla, son of Puḫi-šenni, from whose archives this tablet derives.[35] Teḫip-tilla and some of his descendants dwelt in the outer town of Nuzi, next door to the Kizzuk family whose lawsuit to recover their *dimtu* is documented in the preceding text (4.31D); since his is the fourth generation before the end of the Nuzi archives, Teḫip-tilla can be dated very broadly around 1400 BCE. More than a thousand tablets were found in the houses belonging to Teḫip-tilla and his sons, a number that would multiply were the houses of family members who dwelt elsewhere discovered. The family amassed vast landholdings through many methods, including especially real-estate adoption. Teḫip-tilla alone was "adopted" by hundreds of people, and one of them was ᶠMattiya, daughter of Ḫašiya, a member of the Kizzuk family. Her filiation and descent are known from tablets recording her cession to Teḫip-tilla of rights to real estate through adoption (JEN 18 and 405; see Dosch 1993:134–135). The present tablet attests that she had herself acquired title to that property through adoption by one Uida. It records a declaration by Uida's son and two other potential claimants (presumably members of his family) that Uida had given ᶠMattiya the property in adoption, she had given it to Teḫip-tilla in adoption, and they will not seek to claim the property from Teḫip-tilla – although they still pay property tax, i.e., do the *ilku* incumbent on it. That they continue to bear *ilku* on property to which their family had ceded title, even one generation and one further cession of title later, shows that, first, real-estate adoption was not a legal instrument through which full and final property transfer was accomplished (i.e., it was not a sale); and further, that it was a means of ceding title that would not divest the original property owner of his *ilku* duty.

(lines 1–7) [Declara]tion of Eḫli-teššub and Unap-tae, sons of Wandiya, and declaration of Pui-tae, son of Uida; before the judges and before the *ḫalṣuḫlu* they spoke as follows:
(lines 7–14) "A field in the *dimtu*(-settlement) of Kubiya, (measuring) 5.8 homers by the large measure of the palace; within this field is a *dimtu*(-compound) and garden; within the garden is a well lined with baked bricks – this field Uida gave to ᶠMattiya, and adopted her.[36]
(lines 14–18) And ᶠMattiya has adopted Teḫip-tilla, son of Puḫi-šenni, and she gave the field, *dimtu*, well, and garden to Teḫip-tilla as his share.
(lines 19–20) But it is we who bear the *ilku* of this field."[37]

---

34 For a comprehensive discussion see von Dassow in press. On *andurāru* in Arrapḫe, see above, text 4.31B, n. 17; on *ilku*, see 4.31B–D. Note that *ilku* is not mentioned in text 4.31A above, one of the few texts from Arrapḫe that attest royal grants of land.

35 On the Teḫip-tilla family's archives, and scholarship on them, see Lion 1999a:44–45.

36 The disagreement between the 3ms. pronominal suffix *-šu* and its referent, the woman ᶠMattiya, is normal in the Hurrianized Akkadian written in Arrapḫe, for gender is not grammatically marked in Hurrian.

37 The statement *ilka ... nīnu-ma našânu*, using the 1cpl. pronoun *nīnu*, suffixed with *-ma*, when the predicative *našânu* is already marked 1cpl., is phrased to emphasize that "it is we who bear the *ilku*" (notwithstanding that someone else has now alienated the field).

(lines 20–22) "From this day (onward), we shall not sue Teḫip-tilla on account of this field."
(lines 23–24) Hand of Šumu-libši, scribe, son of Itti-Nabû.

(lines 25–27). [Seal of Teš]šuya, the prince,
[Seal of Tarmi-t]eššub, son of Eḫli-teššub,
[Seal of Paya], son of Pui-tae.[38]

[38] Diana Stein confirms the presence of the sealings, based on the notes Edith Porada made when preparing her dissertation (published as Porada 1947); I am grateful to Stein for consulting Porada's notes and providing information about the sealings (personal communication).

These three men appear as judges in other documents; sometimes two of them co-occur. For example, JEN 711 and 753 were sealed by three judges, including Teššuya the prince (using the seal Porada 1947 no. 632) and Tarmi-teššub, son of Eḫli-teššub (editions: Maidman 1994:142–144; 288–290); Tarmi-teššub, son of Eḫli-teššub – who, incidentally, used three different seals (Porada 1947 nos. 361, 492, and 793) – also sealed JEN 682 and 740 (editions: Maidman 1994:40–43; 237–239), together with Tarmiya, son of Unap-tae, the third judge in JEN 711 and 753. Paya, son of Pui-tae, sealed the real-estate adoption JEN 720 with one seal (Porada 1947 no. 937; edition of JEN 720: Maidman 1994:170–173), sealed HSS V 47 as judge with another seal (Porada 1947 no. 1006), and was listed as judge in HSS V 48; he also sealed several of the tablets in the Kušši-ḫarbe dossier (on which see the introduction to text 4.31G).

REFERENCES

Text: JEN 160 (= JENu 601). *Edition*: Dosch 1993:134.

6. CONVICTION OF OXHERD ON ACCOUNT OF OX THAT GORED ITS FELLOW OX (JEN IV 341) (4.31F)

Like the preceding text, this tablet derives from the archives of the wealthy Teḫip-tilla, son of Puḫi-šenni. Here he successfully sues Taya, an oxherd in his employ, because one ox injured another while in his charge.[39] Since Taya cannot produce witnesses to this event that happened out in the field, he loses the case and must replace the defunct ox. The ox at fault presumably inflicted injury by goring, which would make this tablet a unique record of an actual legal case corresponding to the laws about goring oxen, as noted by J. J. Finkelstein (1981). Finkelstein also observes that Taya was very likely telling the truth about what happened – and how could there have been any witness? – so that this case is also an instance of the tendency for law to serve the interests of power, not necessarily justice.

(lines 1–5) Teḫip-tilla, son of Puḫi-šenni appeared before the judges for a lawsuit against Taya, son of Warad-aḫi, (saying that) Taya was an oxherd of Teḫip-tilla and he had injured one ox.[a]
(lines 6–7) Thus (said) Taya: "An ox injured its fellow ox in the field."
(lines 8–11) And the judges said to Taya, "Bring your witnesses that it injured its fellow ox in the field."
(lines 12–13) Thus (said) Taya: "I have no witnesses."
(lines 13–14) Thus (said) the judges: "Give an ox in place of the one you injured."
(lines 15–19) Teḫip-tilla prevailed in the lawsuit, and they sentenced Taya to (compensate) Teḫip-tilla for one ox of the herd.[b]
(lines 20–24). Seal of Šagarakti, son of Ar-tirwi,
Seal of Ninu-adal, son of Arib-abu,
Seal of Tanni-muša, son of Imbi-ilu,
Seal of Nai-šeri, son of Kabutta.[40]
(line 25) Hand of Itḫabiḫe, scribe.

a Exod 21:35–36
b Deut 19:15

[39] The verb used is the D-stem of *šebēru*, "break"; here it must denote an injury severe enough to cause the ox's death.
[40] Diana Stein confirms the presence of the sealings on the basis of Edith Porada's notes (4.31E, n. 5).

REFERENCES

Text: JEN 341 (= JENu 504). *Edition*: Finkelstein 1981:21, n. 5.

7–8. THE CRIMES OF KUŠŠIḪARBE, EX-MAYOR OF NUZI (4.31G–H)

One of the most remarkable groups of texts found at Nuzi is the dossier of tablets recording the testimony of citizens against Kuššiḫarbe, a former mayor of Nuzi who was a contemporary of Teḫip-tilla, son of Puḫi-šenni. Twenty-four tablets and fragments belonging to this dossier have been identified, all originating from one or two rooms in the palace.[41] Each tablet records a series of accusations against Kuššiḫarbe and his henchmen, some of whom eventually turned informer on Kuššiḫarbe. The charges are presented as quotations of what the accusers said, and then the accused is quoted rebutting the accusation or giving his version of events. This makes for a lively back-and forth that one can readily envision playing out in court before the participants, the rapporteur who took their statements down on clay, and the judges who sealed the tablets. The charges are the stuff of tabloid journalism – and have indeed been featured in the popular press.[42] Kuššiḫarbe and his accomplices are accused of (*inter alia*) swindling the government

[41] See Maidman 2010:13, with n. 40. Maidman assembles and edits all these tablets and fragments, arranging them in their likely chronological order, *ibid.*, Ch. 2.
[42] See Speiser 1951:88–89, in *The National Geographic Magazine*, and Kuntz 1998, in *The New York Times*.

and expropriating the property of citizens, of kidnapping, assault, battery, and extortion, of taking bribes, of failing to fulfill the requests the bribes were paid for, and even of procuring women for sex. What the extant records do not tell us, however, is the outcome of the proceedings, which transpired only after Kuššiḫarbe had been succeeded as mayor by two other holders of the office. Was he convicted, and if so how was he punished? Apparently the verdict was issued elsewhere – probably in the city of Arrapḫe, perhaps by the king – and the documentation we have was for some reason not forwarded to the superior court but left behind in Nuzi, to be excavated millennia later, so that we can write the rest of the tale in our imaginations.

Curiously, while he was in office Kuššiḫarbe also featured in another context, namely a kind of date formula: a handful of contracts were "dated" to his mayoralty, a practice so far attested for only one later mayor of Nuzi (see Cassin 1982:110–111). Unfortunately, the scribes did not indicate in which year during the mayor's tenure of office the contract was made, and they did not systematically develop the practice of dating documents by magistracies as had been done centuries earlier in Assur. The reference to the mayor was not, then, a true date formula, but had some other significance that has escaped our understanding so far.

7. EXPROPRIATION OF MATERIALS AND *ILKU* LABOR, BREAKING AND ENTERING, FAILURE TO PERFORM UPON FEE PAYMENT (AASOR 16, 1 + EN 10/2, 70) (4.31G)

(lines 1–2) Thus (said) Turari: "Thirty (pieces of) [fire]wood[43] were placed in the city gate, and Kuš[šiḫarbe took them]."
(line 3) Thus Kuššiḫarbe: "I did not take [them]."
(lines 4–7) Thus Turari: "Thirty men enlisted for *ilku* from the *dimtu*(-settlement)s [take?] grain from the palace, and they [cultivate] sesame[44] and millet for Kuššiḫarbe, and they collect firewood."
(lines 8–12) Thus Kuššiḫarbe: "I sent Zilip-tilla; thus I (said): 'Cultivate sesame and millet – there is one homer of sesame and millet that is planted (?) – and collect firewood.' But the thirty men enlisted for *ilku* from the *dimtu*(-settlement)s, I don't know (about) them."
(lines 13–17) Thus Palteya: "Forty (pieces of) *šaššugu*-wood [belonging to the palace] – Ḫudiya the carpenter took them, and he [mad]e a door for Kuššiḫarbe. And the door [he made] was for Kuššiḫarbe's house in Anzugalli. [And I] transported those (pieces of) wood."
(lines 18–20) Thus Kuššiḫarbe: "The wood was mine, and I did give it to make a door, but I did not give wood belonging to the palace to make a door."
(lines 21–26) Thus Ḫudiya the carpenter: "The door I made, Šaḫlu-teššub gave me wood from Anzugalli, and the rest of the wood he gave was from Nuzi. And I knew that wood belonged to the palace, but I made it into a door for Kuššiḫarbe."
(lines 27–32) Thus Ḫašib-abu: "Šaḫlu-teššub [assi]gned (?) me (to do) two pairs of *saddinni* and two *ušpaḫḫe* (cords?).[45] Thus he (said): 'Thus Kuššiḫarbe: "Collect oil from the men in your charge and do the *saddinni*."' So I collected oil from the men in my charge, and I did them."
(lines 33–36) Thus Šaḫlu-teššub:[46] "[I gave] two pairs of *sa*[*ddinni*] belonging to Kuššiḫarbe to Ḫašib-abu to weave. And thus I (say): 'You yourself said "Weave! Collect oil from the men in your charge and do (it)!'"
(lines 37–39) Thus Kuššiḫarbe: "I did not tell Šaḫlu-teššub, 'Collect oil for the *saddinni* and the *ušpaḫḫe* from the town!"
(lines 40–42) Thus Ḫašib-abu: "The palace personnel sealed the houses, and Kuššiḫarbe broke the seals and raided (?) the houses."[47]
(lines 43–44) Thus Kuššiḫarbe: "Ḫašib-abu himself broke the seals [of the houses] and [raided] his house."
(lines 45–52) Thus Ḫašib-abu: "Teḫup-[šenni] and Unap-tae stole a fattened pig, and before the judges [...]. And Kuššiḫarbe [...] Zilip-tilla [...], according to Turari [...] and his fee[48] [...] and the criminals[49] who [...] Kuššiḫarbe to[ok]."

[43] The Hurrian word *ambanni* has been derived from the stem *am*-, "to burn" (augmented with -*b*), and accordingly translated "firewood" (see Richter 2012:20). This would not be a particular kind of wood, however, and the occupational term *ambannuḫlu* would denote no special occupation (nothing one does with wood destined to burn is a specialized activity), so the translation "firewood" is not beyond question here.

[44] As shown by Powell (1991), Akkadian *šamaššammū* must denote not flax but sesame, after all (cf. Maidman 2010:95).

[45] What exactly these two Hurrian or Hurrianized words designate is not certain. *CAD* S:17 gives "(a cloth and a garment)" for *saddinni* and "(cord)" for *ušpaḫḫu* (*CAD* U/W: 303), but why quantities of oil would have to be collected to produce such items is mysterious, notwithstanding the use of oil in textile production (Abrahami 2014:298, citing this text). Moreover, the next passage indicates that the *saddinni* already existed – they were Kuššiḫarbe's, and Šaḫlu-teššub gave them to Ḫašib-abu – yet the latter is to "weave" them (*maḫāṣu*); meanwhile one does not "weave" cords. Accordingly the text's first editor, E. Speiser, rendered the words in question very differently, translating *maḫāṣu* as "apply."

[46] The segmentation and interpretation of the nested quotations follows that of Maidman (2010:95).

[47] The verb is *mašāru*, which in context must mean something like "strip" (as Speiser rendered it) or "rob" (as suggested in *CAD* M 1:359).

[48] The word *ṭātu* may mean "bribe," but also "gratuity" or "fee"; which nuance is appropriate depends on the circumstances, which in this fragmentary passage are unknown to us.

[49] Reading $^{\text{lú.meš}}$*sà-ru-ti*, thus *sarrūti*, "criminals," with *CAD* S:183 (cf. Maidman 2010:95).

(lines 53–54) Thus Kuššiḫarbe: "Teḫup-šenni and Unap-tae – I did not t[ake] their fee from them!"

(lines 55–56). Seal of Partasua
Seal of Biriaššura[50]

[50] To my knowledge the sealings on tablets belonging to the Kuššiḫarbe dossier are unstudied, though the same individuals and their seals also appear elsewhere; for example, Partasua's sealing is Stein 1993, no. 709 (see the list of attestations, vol. 9:526–527).

REFERENCES

Text: AASOR 16, 1 + EN 10/2, 70 (= SMN 285+1647). *Editions and translations*: Pfeiffer and Speisor, AASOR 16, 1; Maidman 2010, no. 37.

8. PROCURING SEX AND DENYING IT (AASOR 16, 4) (4.31H)

(lines 1–8) Thus (said) Zilip-tilla: "Last year ᶠPizatu permitted ᶠḪumerelli (to go), and Šimi-tilla and I went by night and called for her, and we brought her to Kuššiḫarbe's place and he had sex with her."[51]
(lines 9–10) Thus Kuššiḫarbe: "No! Not at all! That's not the story! I did not have sex with her!"
(lines 11–15) Thus Palteya: "I summoned ᶠḪumerelli (and) brought her into the *ḫurizade*-house[52] of ᶠTilunnaya, and Kuššiḫarbe had sex with her."
(lines 16–21) Thus Kuššiḫarbe: "(May I be cursed) if Palteya brought ᶠḪumerelli into the *ḫurizade*-house of ᶠTilunnaya and I had sex with her!"
(lines 22–24). Seal of Ariḫamanna
Seal of Teḫip-šarri
Seal of Partasua
(line 25) Hand of Ak-dingira.

[51] The verb in the text, Akkadian *niāku*, is correctly translated by an English verb that is likewise active-transitive and that is generally considered too crude to print, hence the circumlocution "have sex with."
[52] Various meanings, none very well grounded, have been suggested for the Hurrian word *ḫurizade*, which should probably be separated from *ḫurizu* as suggested by Richter (2012:171).

REFERENCES

Text: AASOR 16, 4 (= SMN 13). *Editions and translations*: Pfeiffer and Speisor, AASOR 16, 1; Maidman 2010, no. 53.

9. ROYAL ORDER CHARGING LOCAL AUTHORITIES WITH RESPONSIBILITY FOR TERRITORY AND POPULATION (HSS XV 1) (4.31I)

This tablet communicates an order, apparently issued by the king (but the word is missing in a break), charging mayors and *dimtu* chiefs to protect the territory and inhabitants under their authority. The first 20 lines convey the order to mayors, then lines 25–30 introduce the order to be distributed to *dimtu* chiefs ("lords of *dimtu* settlements"), which occupies the remainder of the text. The order must have been issued in many copies, one per mayor, for dozens of towns in the realm, just as lines 25–30 prescribe that tablets are to be issued to each *dimtu* chief. This copy, though addressed to the mayor of Tašuḫḫe, was found at Nuzi, among 160 tablets belonging to a family archive kept in a house across the street from the temple (in Room C28; see Starr 1939:234, with pl. 13; Lion 1999a:52, with nn. 37–38). The tablet is sealed by one Mušteya, whom some have read as the king of Arrapḫe under whose authority the order was issued; if so, he, not Šilwe-Teššub, would have succeeded Ḫešmi-Teššub as king. However, the evidence that there was a king named Mušteya is exiguous, and not unequivocal (see n. 62 below, on line 48). More likely this Mušteya was an official executing documents issued by the king, who perhaps was Šilwe-teššub by now, if the tablet indeed dates to the last years of Arrapḫe.[53]

In specifying the areas of a mayor's responsibility, the text differentiates between the town's *pāṭu* and its *limītu* ("limit"; line 4), between *dimtu* settlements located in the *ṣēru* and ones located in the town's *pāṭu* (lines 5–6 vs. 20–21), and thus between *pāṭu* and *ṣēru* ("open country"). Accordingly, as Zaccagnini explained (1979:19–20), *pāṭu* in the usage of this text cannot mean "border" (since that is its *limītu*) and must instead mean "territory," beyond which is the "open country" (*ṣēru*).[54] Settlements may be located either within a town's territory – *pāṭu* in the sense of Greek *chōra*, as the territory of a *polis* – or beyond it, up to the limit of another town's area. How such limits or borders were known and marked is hard to tell, but what is clear is that this order means to leave no no-man's-land between the area of one town and the next, no space in the kingdom over which no one is in charge. As Koliński pointed out (2001:17), in the case of inhabited *dimtu* settlements, their chiefs are responsible, while responsibility for whatever happens in abandoned ones devolves to the mayor.

The references to "enemies" who kill and rob suggest the historical context of the last years before Arrapḫe was conquered by Assyria, when the kingdom was subjected to Assyrian raids. Numerous tablets from Nuzi and the city of Arrapḫe attest the mobilization of troops to defend against Assyrian attack, and there are tablets documenting

[53] This is the context in which Maidman places it (2010:30), but perhaps on invalid grounds (see immediately below).
[54] So also Cassin (1982:101–102) and Koliński (2001:3); cf. Maidman 2010:30, with n. 79.

losses in war, too.[55] However, the responsibilities with which mayors and village heads are charged in this text do not sound different from those that local authorities are normally expected to fulfill in much of the Middle East today (especially in rural areas) – a comparison that should not evoke the image of a "timeless Orient," but rather the pragmatics of delegating and exercising supervision over the population under one's jurisdiction. So it may not be correct to interpret the order conveyed by HSS XV 1 as an element of Arrapḫe's preparations for war.

(line 1) [. . .], mayor of Tašuḫḫe,[56]
(line 2) [The king] has issued them an order, (to wit):
(lines 3–5) Every mayor shall guard the territory of his town, up to its very limit.[57]
(lines 5–7) If there is a *dimtu* (settlement) that is abandoned, even in the open country of his town, the mayor shall guard it.
(lines 8–10) And in the territory of his town, let there be no robbery that (anyone) commits, let there be no enemies who kill or who seize.
(lines 10–14) And if in the territory of his city there is (anyone) who commits a robbery, or enemies who seize or who kill, the mayor bears responsibility.
(lines 15–19) If there is a refugee of Arrapḫe who flees from the territory of that town and enters another land, the mayor bears responsibility.
(lines 20–24) If there is a *dimtu* (settlement) that is abandoned, within the territory of that town, the mayor bears responsibility.
(lines 25–30) And the district governor[58] shall give tablets to each of the lords of *dimtu* settlements, and thus he shall issue them the order:
(lines 31–38) "If there is anyone who gets away from that *dimtu* having (committed?) his plunder,[59] or there are enemies who kill or who seize, the lords of that *dimtu* are caught in a crime and I shall take the *dimtu*."
(lines 39–44) "You shall approach me, and you yourselves shall tell me, (that) that man [shall not escap]e (?) [fro]m the edict.[60] And the enemies [. . .] enemies [. . .]."
(lines 44–47) "And if there is (anyone) [who e]scapes from [the edict, you shall se]ize him, and he shall come to the palace."[61]
(line 48). Seal of Mušte[ya]
(seal impressed on left edge)[62]

55 See Maidman 2010:15–20, with texts 13–30.

56 Most editions restore *kīnanna*, "thus," at the beginning of line 1, but the partly-preserved sign at the end of the break does not resemble *n*]*a*; moreover, lines 1–2 would then mean something like "The mayor of Tašuḫḫe [. . .] has issued them an order, as follows" which is incongruent with the restoration LUGAL in line 2. (Hence Maidman [2010:31–32, with nn. 80 and 83] restores *kīnanna ana*, for which there is not enough space, in line 1.) An alternative restoration could be [*ṭuppu š*]*a*, "tablet of the mayor of Tašuḫḫe," but the sign in question does not resemble *š*]*a* either. I propose that what was written here was the name of the mayor of Tašuḫḫe, so the first line of the tablet serves as a heading indicating to whom this copy of the order was addressed.

57 The text's syntax is rather awkward, often using "extra" conjunctions (*u* and enclitic *-ma*) and relative pronouns (*ša*). Taking these features as meaningful, I have preserved the awkward syntax in translation (though not at the price of acceptable English), where possible rendering the conjunctions with words that seem to capture the sense. In line 4, enclitic *-ma* affixed to *limītu* is rendered "very"; in line 6, the conjunction *u* preceding *ina ṣēri* is rendered "even."

58 The term rendered here as "district governor" is written [lú]GAR KUR, *šakin māti*. In texts from Arrapḫe, as well as elsewhere in Mittani (and then in Assyria), a district is called *ḫalṣu* and the governor of one is called *ḫalṣuḫlu*, which may therefore be the equivalent of *šakin māti* in Mittanian usage (as suggested by Deller [1983:22] and later Koliński [2001:16, with n. 16; cf. Fadhil 1972:109). See also text 4.31A, lines 7–11 (above) with n. 11.

59 According to the copy of the tablet, the text reads (31) *šum-ma iš-tu* A[N.Z]A.GÀR-*ma* (32) *ša-a-šu ki-i la ḫ*[*u-u*]*b-ti-šu* (33) *ša ú-uṣ-ṣú-ú ša i-ba-aš-ši-i*; finding that *ki-i la ḫubtīšu* makes no sense, scholars have emended it to *ša*! *i-na*! *ḫubtīšu*, which still makes too little sense to yield a consensus translation of the sentence (compare the editions cited below). Without offering a new reading, my translation attempts to convey what seems to be the sense, namely that if someone "gets away with" plundering in a *dimtu* – or killing or kidnapping – those in charge of it are guilty of letting him.

60 These orders are in the second person plural, with the pronoun *attunu* added for emphasis (line 39). What the orders mean is not entirely clear, given the breaks in the text and its inherent ambiguities – are the *dimtu* lords to come and accuse (or defend) one of their number who has evaded the edict (or not)? Their collective responsibility is in any case demanded.

61 Since it is assumed that the transgressor should be remanded to the authorities, É ("house") is emended to É⟨.GAL⟩ ("palace").

62 In some editions the seal caption is restored to read NA_4 *Mu-uš-te*[-(*i*)*a* LUGAL], on the assumption that the tablet must have been sealed by the king who issued the order it conveys. This restoration would find support in a royal letter found at Tell al-Faḫḫar bearing the seal of *Mu-uš-te-ia* LUGAL, as read by Fadhil (1972:108–109, text no. 30 [= TF_2 628]), who compares the royal letter JEN 494, also sealed by Mušteya (evidence that goes unmentioned in subsequent editions of HSS XV 1); unfortunately, Fadhil does not remark on the seal impressions themselves. Müller (1969:239) had already observed that both JEN 494 and HSS XV 1 were sealed by someone named Mušteya, but not with the same seal. Deller (1983) re-studied all three tablets, obtaining comments on the seal impressions on JEN 494 and HSS XV 1 from Diana Stein; based on a cast of the Tell al-Faḫḫar tablet, he affirmed Fadhil's reading ˹LUGAL˺, but found the traces of the seal impression too faint to discern. (Deller also commented on TF_2 628's IM number, given variously as 73271, 73272, and 73273; ibid.: 27, n. 43.) Subsequent collation of the Tell al-Faḫḫar tablet in Baghdad, however, disconfirmed the reading LUGAL in the seal caption (Wilhelm 1993–1997). Therefore, these three tablets appear to attest more than one Mušteya, none of whom may have been king.

REFERENCES

Text: HSS XV 1 (SMN 3126). *Editions and translations*: Müller 1968:195–239; Jankowska 1969:273–275; Zaccagnini 1979:17–19; Cassin 1982:114–117; Koliński 2001:16–17; Maidman 2010, no. 8.

RITUAL FOR THE CULT IMAGE

THE MESOPOTAMIAN "WASHING OF THE MOUTH" (*MĪS PĪ*) OR "OPENING OF THE MOUTH" (*PĪT PĪ*) RITUAL (4.32A–C)

Michael Dick

Introduction

"O great gods, with whom does the creation of gods and goddesses appropriately belong? You have you been constantly entrusting me (by oracle) with this difficult task (to be done) in a taboo place." (Leichty 2011:107, Text 48, line 66).

Could any Israelite prophet have put the theological issue more bluntly than the Assyrian King Esarhaddon cited above? Although the Hebrew Bible has many prohibitions against the worship of cult statues,[1] most of the icon polemics focus on iconoplasty, the making of that divine image. The prophets attack the cult image as a mere "product of human hands."[2] Forms of this argument have played an important role in the history of religions and have formed the basis for iconoclastic movements within Judaism, Christianity, and Islam. Although parodied by works such as Second Isaiah,[3] Jeremiah,[4] or the Apocryphal Letter of Jeremiah, the Mesopotamian ritual translated here gives an emic voice to the very iconodule about his/her own theology concerning the cult statue. These Mesopotamian texts address precisely those very points that polemics in the Hebrew Bible considered most vulnerable for the iconodule: the human making of the divine image, iconoplasty. The *mīs pî* "Mouth Washing" ritual represents the most complete such text from antiquity and thus is of clear interest to specialists in both Mesopotamian studies and in the study of ancient religions in general.[5]

The Cult Image

A priori archaeologists have difficulties determining a statue as a divine cult image. Definitions of our term "cult statue" would be helpful. Berlejung (1998:6) defines an "image" as: "... the tangible and describable appearance of a deeper based reality, the manifestation of an unseen actuality. Such an image makes the unseen visible and leads the observer directly into the hidden truth." The adjective "cult" adds a consideration of the functionality of this image. In distinction to votive images or images of the monarch, the cult image[6] was the focus of public *latreia* and marked the official presence of that deity, around which the deity's ceremonies revolved. Certain artistic canonical principles have evolved: size (relative and absolute), large eyes, flounced skirt or garment, horned crown, particular weapon or other symbol (*šurinnu*, *miṭṭu* or *kakku*) associated with a specific deity (Hallo 1983:4–5). We also should not expect many such cult images to have survived, since texts tell us that they often had a perishable core of wood plated with gold and were clothed in precious attire (*šukuttu*) that would have been stolen long ago (Sauren 1969:118).

The Relationship between the Cult Statue and the Deity

How did the Mesopotamians regard the relationship between the cult image and the deity? The answer is not simple and probably differed on both diachronic and synchronic axes; that is, it changed through time and in different regions. The issue needs further study.[7] In the past, some have used the analogy of the Roman Catholic Theology of the "Eucharistic Presence."[8] To Orthodox and Roman Catholics, the bread and wine during the Eucharistic ritual become the real presence of the Divine Jesus, while still subsisting under the appearance of bread and wine. Obviously, the Eucharistic species are not coterminous with Jesus, so that for the Believer, the Eucharistic Presence can be found simultaneously in Churches throughout the world. Nor would the destruction of the consecrated bread and wine entail the destruction of Jesus.

This analogy from a contemporary religious practice can help us understand the theology of the ancient Near Eastern cult image. By a cultic ritual (*mīs pî*), the "work of human hands" became for the iconodule the real presence of the

[1] Exod 20:5; 23:34; 34:14; Deut 4:3; 5:9; Hos 5:11.

[2] Exod 20:4; 34:17; Isa 2:8; Hos 14:4; Mic 5:12.

[3] Isa 40:18–20; 41:6–7; 44:9–22.

[4] Jer 10:3–5. Cf. also Judg 17:4–5.

[5] For complete abbreviations and references, see *CAD*.

[6] It is important to realize that the *mīs pî* ritual was not limited solely to anthropomorphic "statues," but could also be used for other objects that were considered to embody the divine, such as a lunar disk or cult implements (Berlejung 1998:181).

[7] Both Mettinger (1995:20–23) and Berlejung (1998:6–11) apply contemporary studies of the philosophy of symbol to the cult image. Mettinger uses C. S. Peirce and Berlejung, H. G. Gadamer.

[8] Dick 2005.

deity.[9] Offerings are brought before Marduk himself in the Esagila not before the statue of Marduk. We can sense this in Kabti-ilāni-Marduk's 8th century BCE theological masterpiece, the Erra Epic. The sorry fate of the Marduk *statue* with its soot-covered visage and deteriorated clothing happens to *Marduk himself*, who can only appreciate his sorry state when the conniving god Erra points it out.

> What happened to your attire (*šukuttu*), to the insignia of your lordship, magnificent as the stars of the sky? It has been dirtied! What happened to the crown of your lordship, which made Eḫalanki as bright as Etemenanki? Its surface is shrouded over! (I 127–129)[10]

The Erra Epic makes it clear that if a statue's appearance corrupts, then the deity can abandon his image. Erra reassures Marduk that he shall rule in his stead while Marduk leaves during his statue's restoration.

> Erra opened his mouth and spoke to Prince Marduk, "Until you enter that house, Prince Marduk, and Girra purifies your garment and you return to your place, till then I shall rule in your stead' (I 180)."[11]

Likewise, in 689 BCE, Sennacherib brought the Marduk *statue* from Babylon to Assur. In reality, this marked the *god* Marduk's exile in Assyria, as we learn in the theologically significant *Marduk's Ordeal*, first edited by Zimmern (Livingstone 1986:208–235); here we read that Marduk lost a lawsuit (a *rîb* like Psalm 82) brought against him by the god Aššur and was deported to Assyria. As the *Akītu Chronicle* records: "For 8 years of Sennacherib, 12 years of Assurbanipal, for 20 years, Bel stayed in Aššur (Grayson 1975:127, Chronicle 14, lines 31–32)."

The Autogenesis of the God/Statue

The approval for the very existence of a cult statue rested with the god.[12] The physical appearance of the statue was likewise a godly prerogative. Mari letter M.7515 talks about an oracle to determine the appearance of the image of the deity Lāgamāl. Even as late as Seleucid times, the making of a cult image needed divine approbation (McEwan 1981). In the text of Ash. 1923.749 (Uruk), the gods Šamaš, Marduk, Zababa, and Sadarnunna were asked to indicate *via* augury approval for the appearance of the cult statue for the carpenter and goldsmiths.

The *rites de passages* – to use hesitantly van Gennep's nomenclature (van Gennep 1960) – from a product of human artifice to the god were effected by the consecration of the ritual called *mīs pî "Washing of the Mouth."* This ritual was made up of a ritual tablet that included the actions to be performed (*dromena*) as well as the beginning line of incantations to be recited (*legomena*) while performing that action. This ritual tablet would then be either preceded by or followed by multiple tablets containing the complete incantations.

For the *mīs pî* ritual, the ritual tablet survives in two exemplars: The Babylonian version complete in one tablet (BM45749) and the Nineveh version, which C. Walker and M. Dick (2001) assembled from numerous overlapping fragments of Ashurbanipal's Nineveh library. There were approximately 6–8 incantation tablets, depending on the arrangements of the text on tablets, i.e. dual- or single-column tablet.

At present, there are few extant source materials for the reconstruction of the *mīs pî* ritual and its accompanying incantations from the 3rd or 2nd millennia BCE. Most of the available sources for reconstructing both the ritual tablet and for the accompanying incantations are of Neo-Assyrian or Neo/Late-Babylonian date (8th–5th centuries BCE, but 2nd century for some fragments from Uruk). They come from Nineveh, Assur, Ḫuzirīna (Sultantepe in Turkey), Hama (Syria), Babylon, Sippar, Nippur, Kalḫu (Nimrud), and Uruk. The large majority of the texts come from Nineveh and date to the 7th century BCE; many of the incantation tablets have colophons that mark them as belonging to the royal library of Assurbanipal.

V. A. Hurowitz's list (2003:150) shows how this rite effects the divine birth of the statue:

[9] Berlejung (1998:177, n. 932) is correct that in a real sense the statue was already a god prior to the *mīs pî* by virtue of its supernatural origins. Boden (1998) stresses that the image starts out as "material" and then becomes a god. Both may be correct, in that in rituals the goal of a liturgy may be proleptically reached from the beginning.

[10] Translation from Cagni 1977. See *COS* 1:407 (Text 1.113). Cf. Judg 8:27; 17:5; 18:14–20.

[11] *COS* 1:408 (Text 1.113).

[12] Hurowitz (2003:150, etc.) aptly refers to the "autogenesis" of the god/statue.

THEOLOGOUMENON	EFFECTIVE RITUAL TEXTS
The Ritual disassociates the statue from human artisans Human craftsmen have their hands ceremoniously cut off	NR 179–186 BR 52; IT 3: 83ab–86ab
The gods are the real craftsmen who created the statue	IT 3: 58ab–69ab, 87–91; 17ab–19ab
The statue is born of and nurtured by the gods	IT 4: A 23ab–33ab
Autogenetic birth of the god/statue in Heaven	Incantation Tablet (IT) 1/2, STT 199:1–5 "In Heaven it is born of itself; on earth it is born of itself"
Introducing statue to Ea, its father	NR 61–63, BR 4
Counting the statue among its brother gods	NR 89, 165; IT 3 C 6–10
The wood for the statue originated in a sacred forest	IT 1/2 STT 199:13–31[13]
The tree from which the statue is made is considered a World Tree/*Weltbaum*	IT 1/2, STT 199:30–31
The gods really perform the ritual	IT 1/2 C:15–93

NR = Niveveh Ritual; BR = Babylon Ritual; IT = Incanation Tablet; STT = Sultantepe Tablet.

Both the Babylonian Ritual tablet and the Nineveh version appear below, as well as two of the most important incantations.

NINEVEH RITUAL TABLET (4.32A)

The First Day

(A) *Preparation in the City, in the "Countryside," in the Garden, and in the Temple*[14]
(1) When you wash the mouth of a god,
(2) on a favorable day[15] at dawn you go into the countryside,[16,a] to a garden[17] on the bank of a river,[18] and
(3) you observe sunrise; you set up a marker stone.[19]
(4) You return to the city and inspect the designated materials.[20] At the first hour of daylight, you return to the countryside and
(5) you take a load of reeds,
(6) tie reed bundles,[21] arrange them up in a circle, and

a Lev 16:22

[13] See Hurowitz 2006; Dietrich 1992.

[14] This division of the ritual into sections is indebted to the perspicacious analysis of the rite by Berlejung 1998:434 ff.

[15] See Labat 1965:91, number 31. This menology lists the propitious times for renewing (*ú-diš*) a statue: "If during the month of Nisan (from the first to the thirtieth) a man restores the deteriorated statue of his god or goddess, then this man will live a long life and his god will speak favorably of him. If during the month of second Nisan DITTO, then death (?) will be in the house of that man." "It (the *bīt mummu*) was the place where the statues and ornaments of the gods and the equipment and ornamental work of their temples were made or restored; the place where the newly made images of the gods were magically animated and where the damaged images were reanimated by restoring them and by performing the prescribed rituals … We may therefore call the *bīt mummu* the workshop of the temples; the expression is synonymous with the *bīt mārē ummâni*, 'the house of the craftsmen' … It was most likely a workshop and a technical training school (Heidel 1948:103)." For a study of these craftsmen, see Verderame (2008). The *bīt mummu* was probably identified with the Apsû as we see in the Sumerian Enki and the World Order (lines 194–196) where Ea/the Apsû is addressed: UMUN$_2$-ZI KI DINGIR Ù-TU-ZA AN-GIN$_7$ ŠU NU-TE-GÁ "in your special workshop, the place where gods are born, ungraspable as heaven …" (unpublished translation of J. Cooper).

[16] The *midbār* in the Hebrew Bible can serve a similar role in Lev 16:22. This is not a mere topographic observation, but rather a theological observation. The *ṣēru* "wilderness" outside the city represents chaos and the uncreated. As the threshold to the underworld, it represents transition from death to life. See the diagram in Pongratz-Leisten 1994:36, 18–19; Berlejung 1997:53–54. Rituals of purification were often conducted here so that the impurities could be sloughed off into the area of the wilderness (Maul 1994:124; Wright 1987:255–256).

[17] The logograms here GIŠ.SAR and elsewhere in the ritual can mean either garden or orchard. On orchards and rituals, see Berlejung 1997:50 and Glassner 1991:11.

[18] For rituals done on the bank of a river, see Maul 1994:48, n. 4. Thanks to the research of A. R. George (George 1992) on Babylonian temple typography, we can actually trace the steps of the priests in Babylon south from the Esangila to the river bank temple of Ea, the Ekarzaginna, through the two gates named "the River God" and "the Garden of the Apsû, where the mouths of the gods are opened" (BM 35046, lines 26–27).

[19] This marks the direction of sunrise towards which the statue will face (line 97).

[20] These are the materials to be used in the following ritual (lines 5–53), perhaps even including the reeds. They have to be inspected for ritual purity. They were not taken out earlier because the celebrant had to get up in the dark to go out in time to observe sunrise, so it would have been too dark for him to make the proper inspection.

[21] The *urigallu* were bundles of reeds grouped in a circle to enclose sacred space (Wiggermann 1992:70–71). We see an example of such a reed enclosure in Collon 1987:173, seal 803.

(7) make reed-huts for Ea, Šamaš and Asalluḫi.[22]
(8) You recite [three tim]es each the incantations "Pure reed, long reed, pure node of a reed"
(9) (and) "Asari[23] saw your pure clay in the Apsû"
(10) to the reed-huts.

(11) You establish [reed-huts] for Kusu,[24] Ningirima[25] (and) Dingirmaḫ[26] [...]
(12) Around/alongside the chapel of that god[27] ...
(13) you arrange tamarisk branches, date-palm-heart (and) cedar.
(14) with colored yarn [you ...] the chapels, [...]
(15) [... you recite] the incantation "Reed grown from the Apsû" to the reed [hut?];
(16) [... you recite] the incantation "Reed whose heart is pure and good" to the reed [hut?];
(17) [You recite] the incantation "Flour nobly poured out" to the magical circle of flour ..."

(18) You go [to] the river, and throw *maṣḫatu*-flour[28] into the river. [You libate][29,b] barley beer.[30]
(19) You lift up your [hand];[31] and you recite [three times each in fro]nt of the river the incantations "Apsû-temple, to determine fates ...,"
(20) "Quay of the Apsû, pure quay ...,"
(21) (and) "shining quay, quay of En[ki] ...,"
(22) and [you dr]aw water (for) seven holy-water-basins.[32]
(23) You return (to the city); and in the chapel of Kusu at night [you fill][33] the holy-[water-basin]
(24) [for mouth-washing] with tamarisk-branches, [the *alkali*-plant, date-palm-heart,]

b Num 28:3–5; 29:31

(25) seven palm-shoots, *šalālu*-reed, marsh-reed, sweet-reed,
(26) ..., salt, ce[dar, cypress, juniper,]
(27) ["horned *alkali*"], *sikillu*-plant, tree resin(?),

(Probably no gap here, but in K 6324+, lines 8–27 are written as lines 8–33; to judge by BM 45749, 18 "line 34" should follow directly after "line 27," so there is some overlap here.)

(34) [lode]stone, [x-stone ...]
(35) *muššaru*-stone, carnelian, lapis-lazuli, *pappardilû*-ston[e, *papparminu*-stone,][34]
(36) quartz, silver, gold, copper, and ir[on],[35] and then
(37) oil, first class oil, perfumed(?) oil, cedar oil, syrup and ghe[e you set up.]
(38) [You bind] white wool, red wool (and) blue wool[36] around its (holy water basin's(?)) neck.
(39) You cover the opening (of the holy water basin) with a small *saḫḫaru*-bowl.[37] As you cover it,
(40) you recite the incantation, "The king in heaven drew (water) in a pure place."
(41) You move the censer (and) torch alongside the holy-water-basin,[38]
(42) you purify the area; you sweep the ground;[39] you sprinkle pure water.
(43) You set in place a censer of juniper; you libate beer.
(44) You set up three heaps of meal over the holy-water-vessel.[40]

22 The trinity of Ea, Šamaš, and Asalluḫi (the triad of white magic) is very common in purification rituals. The position of Šamaš in the middle is probably intentional, for this deity will play the central role in the ritual (on the second day). Ea (Sumerian Enki) is the primary deity of purification rituals in which water plays such an important role, because he is the main god of "holy water" (*RlA* 2:376). The waters used in the mouth-washing ceremony are called "the waters of incantation (a NAM-ŠUB/*mē šipti*)" in 4 R^2 25 iv.52–53. Ea is also the god of Apsû and of the city of Eridu (see *RlA* 2:378). Ea is likewise the patron deity of the craftsmen, in which role he enjoys the epithet ^{d}NU-DÍM-MUD "Image fashioner" (see Jacobsen 1976:111, n. 157). Asalluḫi was later identified with Marduk. On the naming of Marduk as Asalluḫi in the *Enūma Eliš*, see Jacobsen 1976:182. Asalluḫi was the patron of exorcism (EN *a-ši-pu-ti*) who purifies heaven and earth (*mullil šamê u erṣeti*).

23 Asari, originally an independent god, became identified with Marduk as early as the *Enūma Eliš* 7:1.

24 For the purification goddess Kusu, see Michalowski 1993:158–159; Conti 1997:256–257.

25 Very ancient religious texts from the third millennium already mention her as the goddess of purification, with aqueous associations (Apsû): Cunningham 1997:16–17; Michalowski 1993:159. She is especially related to the *egubbû* holy water basin and thus is mentioned in the central position in the triad (Berlejung 1998:212).

26 Dingirmaḫ is the Sumerian equivalent of Bēlet-ilī the "birth goddess."

27 In the actual performance of the ritual, the name of the deity whose statue was being consecrated would have been invoked rather than *ilu šuāti* "that god." This reference in line 12 must be to another reed-hut established for the deity. Perhaps "around the chapel (intended) for that god ..."

28 *Maṣḫatu*-flour is a perfumed flour used in burnt offerings.

29 For libation offerings (*nesek*) in the Hebrew Bible, see Num 28:3–5. In Num 29:31 the libation accompanies a grain offering (*minḥah*), as in this passage NR 18.

30 *Miḫḫu*-beer often appears in offerings to the river (Maul 1994:52, n. 86).

31 See Gruber 1980:60–84 for a discussion of this idiom for the posture "to lift the hand" for praying.

32 In the NR the *egubbû* are prepared here, although they will not be used until the second day (see STT 200: 49–62). The BR places this preparation at a later point in the ritual. For a description of this container, see Maul 1994:41 ff.

33 The verb appears at the end of line 37. Though missing now, it was probably ŠUB/*nadû* "to set up."

34 These are all semi-precious stones used for necklaces, cylinder seals, etc.

35 Placing these items (plant and mineral) in the holy water basin was common to many purificatory rituals (e.g. Namburbi). These ingredients seem to increase the cleansing properties of the water in the basin.

36 Many rituals used colored wool bands.

37 This *saḫḫaru* bowl was used for syrup (*dišpu*), flour (*siltu*), groats (*dulīqāte*), etc.; it covered the mouth of the *egubbû* as a paten covers a chalice in some Christian rituals.

38 Purificatory rites frequently use these three (torch, censer, and holy-water basin), Maul 1994:94–97; Conti 1997:253 f. See lines 59 and 151.

39 For sweeping as purification, see Maul 1994:48.

40 Perhaps the *zidubdubbû* "heaps of flour" are placed on the *saḫḫaru* bowl that covers the *egubbû* holy water basin.

(45) You recite the incantation, "Mountain, forest of cedar-incense," three times.
(46) You recite the incantation, "Holy-water-vessel of Kusu and Ningirima,"[41]
(47) three times [before] the holy-water-vessel.
(48) You recite [the incantation, "...] Nidaba,"[42] three times.
(49) [...] Before the holy-water-vessel you set up the offering-arrangements.[43]
(50) You sacrifice a ram; you set up a censer of juniper.
(51) You libate beer; you raise your hand, and
(52) you recite three times the incantation, "Pure water which runs in the Tigris,"
(53) before the holy-water-vessel and prostrate yourself.
(54) You return to the storehouse (for designated cultic materials);[44] and you inspect the *paṭiru*-altar[45] for use at the river.[46]

(B) *In the House of the Craftsmen*
(55) In the house of the craftsmen, where the god was created,[47]
(56) you sweep the ground; you sprinkle pure water. For Ea, Asalluḫi and that god,
(57) you set up 3 censers of juniper; you libate beer.
(58) On that god you perform Mouth-Washing (and) Mouth-Opening.[48]
(59) You bring the censer (and) torch past him (the god); you purify him with the holy-water-basin.
(59a) You recite three times [the incantation, "In heaven] by your own power you emerge."
(60) You speak as follows to that god:

(61) "From today you go before your father Ea.[49]
(62) Let your heart be pleased, let your mind be happy.
(63) May Ea, your father, be full of joy with you."
(64) You speak it three times[50] and prostrate yourself, and

(C) *Procession from the House of the Craftsmen to the River*
(65) you take the hand of that god and make a ram accompany (?)[51] him.
(66) You recite the incantation, "As you go out, as you go out, great ...," (going) from the house of the craftsmen
(67) as far as the river in front of the god with a torch.

(68) As many of the craftsmen as [approached] that god
(69) and their equipment together with that god [process(?)] to the country.

(D) *At the River Bank*[52]
(70) You place ⟨them⟩ [in the or]chard on the river bank.
(71) You seat [that god] on a reed mat[53] and set up reed-huts.
(72) You place the offering-table [for] Ea and Asalluḫi.
(73) You scatter [date]s and meal;[54]
(74) [you set in place] a [confec]tion of syrup and ghee;
(75) you set in place a [censer of junip]er; you sacrifice the ram.
(76) You libate [*mazû*-be]er and prostrate yourself.[55]
(77) [...] you set in place [a censer of ju]niper; you libate best beer.[56]
(78) [You place ...] an axe, a nail, a saw,
(79) [a tortoise and turtle] of silver and gold into the thigh of the ram;

---

41 While most of the incantations are in Sumerian, this one is in Akkadian.

42 The goddess Nidaba (or Nisaba) represented wheat.

43 The *riksu* "offering arrangements" means the complex of *paṭiru*-altar, the offerings on it and all the ceramic containers with offerings at its base (Maul 1994:66, n. 74).

44 The celebrant has exhausted the stock he took out in line 4 and comes back for the materials he will need in lines 55–108 (but note he does not go back again in line 109, and the BR does not mention the *isḫu* at all).

45 For a description and a picture of a *paṭiru*-altar, see Maul 1994:48, 58.

46 The *bīt isḫi* was first mentioned in line 4. The *CAD* I/J 190a understood here "a model of the river" because they saw the location as the *bīt mummu* and because they read *šá* as GAR (*tašakkan*). Cf. Berlejung 1998:214, n. 1153. However, *tašakkan* "you place" is usually rendered GAR-*an* with the phonetic complement. The point is that in the chapel of Kusu, and later in the god's own temple, you expect to find an altar already installed, but at the riverside, you do not. Moreover, indeed the only place in the remainder of the text where the *paṭīru* is mentioned is in line 72 where you set up the altar for Ea and Asalluḫi in the orchard at the riverbank. This *paṭiru*-altar is to be taken to the river and set up for offerings to Ea and Asalluḫi at line 72.

47 In some sense, the statue was already a "god" from the beginning, contra Dietrich 1992:36.

48 This is the first mouth washing (MW) of the ceremony.

49 This accompanies the "god's" procession to the river, the threshold to Ea's Apsû. This prayer is in Akkadian.

50 The threefold repetition of incantations is very common in rituals (Hurowitz 1989:66, n. 87).

51 The same unknown root appears in BR line 5.

52 Since historical texts concentrate on "mouth-washings" at the river bank, this must constitute the heart of the ritual. This is the threshold of the Apsû, where the "god" is ritually separated from the human and incorporated into the world of the god Ea, his father.

53 For the role of the reed-mat in insulating the cult image, see Berlejung 1997:55, n. 46; *TUAT* 2:235, line 16.

54 For the scattering of dates and *sasqû*-meal, see Maul 1994:51–52. One passage lists the quantities of these two as 2 SILA/*qû* (ca. a liter) each. These ingredients were mixed into the *mirsu*-confection (Maul 1994:51, n. 68).

55 See Gruber 1980:238–254 for a treatment of *šukēnu*.

56 For an illustration of the arrangement of all of these offerings, see Maul 1994:58–59.

(80) [you bind it up and] throw it [into the river.][57]

(Gap of some lines)[58]

(87) [...] ...
(88) [... the ⟨Akkadian⟩ incantation, "He who comes, his mouth is washed;
(89) [... with] his brothers let him be counted;
(90) [... the axe,] the nail (and) the saw of the craftsmen,
(91) [as many as work]ed on him, take away in its[59] body!
(92) [...] that god, oh Ea, his mouth is washed;
(93) [... with] his brothers count him."
(94) You recite (this) three times, and before Ea you dismantle the offering-arrangements.

(E) *Procession from the River into the Garden*
(95) [You take] the hand of [the god];

(F) *In the Garden in the Circle of Reed Huts and Reed Standards*
(95) and in the garden in the midst of the reed-huts and reed-standards
(96) you seat that god on a reed mat on a linen cloth.[60]
(97) You set his eyes towards sunrise;[61] and alongside that statue
(98) in the midst of the reed-huts and reed-standards you lay down the equipment for the god, all of it,
(99) and the equipment of the craftsmen; and you withdraw.

(100) For the gods Anu, Enlil, Ea,[62] Sîn,[63] Šamaš,[64]
(101) Adad, Marduk, Gula[65] (and) Ninsianna[66]
(102) you set up 9 censers towards the evening-star;[67] and you set up an offering arrangement;
(103) you sacrifice a ram; you libate best beer,
(104) you perform Mouth-Washing[68] (and) Mouth-Opening. You dismantle the offering-arrangements, and

(105) for Dingirma, Kusu, Ningirima, Ninkurra,
(106) Ninagala, Kusigbanda, Ninildu, Ninzadim and that god[69]
(107) you set up 9 censers to the gods of the night; you invoke their names;
(108) You sacrifice a ram; you perform Mouth-Washing and Mouth-Opening.[70]

The Second Day

(109) In the morning in the midst of the reed-huts for Ea, Šamaš and Asalluḫi
(110) you set three thrones. You spread out a red cloth;[71] you hang a linen cloth before it.[72]
(111) You set up three tables; you sprinkle dates and meal.
(112) You set in place a confection of syrup and ghee.
(113) You fill an *adagurru*-vessel[73] with *našpu*-beer.
(114) You cut sweet reed and its pulp; and when you set the tables,
(115) you fill 6 *kukkubu*-jars[74] with best beer; and you set them in a row next to each other (?).

57 Ea reclaims his tools, since in reality he and the craft-deities had worked on that god.

58 Berlejung suggests that mouth-washings took place in this gap and at the gap at the end of NR so that the number of mouth-washings would correspond with those in BR. This would yield seven mouth-washings of the statue (Berlejung 1998:234).

59 "Its" refers to the sheep thrown into the river in line 80.

60 Judging from an incantation to the *tapsû* in Borger 1973:171, it was a sign of divinity (ME-TE-NAM-DINGIR-RA); according to Borger's commentary on p. 176, it was a head covering.

61 Sunrise signifies revivification and re-animation (Maul 1994:125). Berlejung has a good treatment of the importance of this transition (from night to day) from the point of view of van Gennep's (1960) rites of passage (Berlejung 1998:221–222). Berlejung 1997:57 "The exposure of the image to the stars could be interpreted as a *rite d'agrégation* connecting the image with the cosmos and its divine counterparts." Also, see Maul 1994:45.

62 Anu, Enlil, and Ea do not represent individual stars, constellations, or planets, but the entire sky; they represent the "paths of Anu, Enlil, and Ea" which are the three segments of the horizon over which the stars rise (Reiner 1995:5–6).

63 The male Moon god Sîn is the father of both Šamaš and Venus/Ištar.

64 Šamaš is significant placed in the middle of these nine deities; this prepares us for the centrality of the sun god on the second day of the ritual.

65 Gula, the goddess of healing, is represented by the constellation of the Goat (now Lyra; see Reiner 1995b:53).

66 The planet Venus (Reiner 1995:67, 68, 73). On the genders of Venus, see Reiner 1995:6, n. 14.

67 For the role of these astral deities in the rite, see Reiner 1995:140–141.

68 This is the second MW in the preserved text of NR; the parallel place in the BR mentions the fourth MW.

69 These craft, birth, and purification deities are also so listed in Borger 1956:89, § 57. As Berlejung (1998:228) indicates, this second group of nine deities, whose censers were arranged to the south/right (BR 26) of the statue, symbolizes the origin of the cult image. The first group of nine (the stars of the night), whose censers were positioned to the north/left (BR 27) of the statue, symbolized its destiny.

70 This is the third MW.

71 These actions (setting up divine thrones and covering them with red cloths) are briefly described in Maul 1994:49. Apparently, statues, standards or symbols of the three gods of white magic would have been seated on thrones covered with a red cloth. See Mayer 1976:152–153.

72 Following *CAD* K 475; *CAD* Š 1:22. Berlejung (1998:444) seems to understand it as a carpet ("Teppich") rather than a curtain.

73 The *adagurru*-vessel is defined more by function than ceramic type. It was any vessel used for libations and thus is almost exclusively mentioned in ritual texts. For a description and references to pictures, see Maul 1994:53; Sallaberger 1996:110.

74 A *kukubbu* is a tankard with a lip (Salonen 1966:218; Sallaberger 1996:113) which would hold from 0.8 to 3.3 liters. It could be used for libations (Maul 1994:53).

(116) You set in place a censer of juniper. You set three cups of blood[75] in a row.
(117) You lay down choice plants;[76] you lay out 3 white fattened sacrificial sheep.
(118) you provide in splendid abundance the fruit of the orchard; sifted "large-grained" barley
(119) behind the choice plants you scatter.
(120) You set in place white wool, red wool, combed wool, red-dyed-wool,
(121) blue wool, various(?) wools, fleece;[77] … and retire.
(122) […] Ninagala[78]
(123) […] Ninzadim
(124) […] the craftsmen …
(125) […] you lay down
(126) […] …
(127) […] a torch
(128) […] you purify.

(129) […] blaze?
(130) […] … you heap
(131) you scatter juniper.
(132) You raise […] cedar in your hand and
(133) you recite [the incantation, "Born in heaven by] his own power";
(134) you recite [the incantation, "Šamaš], great lord of heaven and earth,"
(135) [(and) the incantation, "Water of life, the river] rising in flood"; and
(136) you give(?) […].
(137) you recite three times [the incantation, "The flood, its divine task is unique, is holy"; and]
(138) you sacrifice/libate […].
(138a) […] …
(139) […] …
(140) […] you … the purification ritual
(141) […] tamarisk,
(142) date-palm-"heart" … he/you lay down and raises his hand; [and]
(143) he[79] recites [the incantation], "Šamaš, exalted judge of heaven and earth,"[80]
(144) (and) the ⟨Akkadian⟩ incantation, "Ea, Šamaš and Asalluḫi."
(145) Thus(?) he recites before Šamaš.

(146) You set in place [for] Kusu, Ningirima, Ninkurra,
(147) Ninagala, Kusigbanda, Ninildu,
(148) (and) Ninzadim a censer of juniper.
(149) You sacrifice a ram; you libate best beer;
(150) you perform [Mouth]-Washing[81] (and) Mouth-Opening;
(151) you move [a censer (and) a to]rch over him.
(152) [You purify] him [with a holy-water-vessel], (and) you retire, and

(153) […] x x [x]
(154) […] ? x
(154a) [… x [x]

(If K 6324+ and K 8656 are continuous, there is no gap)

(155) [… g]hee [x x]
(156) […] x you set up a libation vessel [x].
(157) You set in place […]; you sacrifice a ram (and)
(158) you present the [shoulder], the fatty tissue, and the "roast";[82]
(159) you libate syrup […]. The *āšipu*-priest stands beside that god;[83]
(160) You recite the [incantation, "On the day when the g]od was created,"[84] and you prostrate yourself and
(161) you perform Mouth-Washing[85] and Mouth-Opening.
(162) [Afterwards] you recite the incantation, "Pure statue, suited to the great 'ME.'"[86]
(163) Cleansing rite[87] and whispered prayer.[88]

(164) [Into the ear(s)] of that god you speak as follows:

[75] Blood is rare in Mesopotamian rituals. It is unclear what its role here is, since it is not mentioned again.

[76] These "choice plants" (Ù.BAR) must be the equivalent of the U.GIŠ.KIRI discussed in Maul 1994:62 f. These plants, which are especially mentioned in prayers to Šamaš, Ea, and Asalluḫi, purify objects placed on them by conducting their impurities into the earth/Underworld. It is even possible that these plants include those placed in the holy water basin *egubbû* in lines 24–27 (Maul 1994:45, n. 94).

[77] For similar offerings to Šamaš of various wools, see the Sultantepe, Nineveh, Boğazköy bilinguals in Cooper 1972:69–81. These incantations are particularly relevant because they contain many of the offerings catalogued in this section of the NR: throne, table, red cloth, linen cloth, most of the wool types listed in NR, "large grain," syrup, ghee, ripened dates, meal, "best beer," and "*našpu*-beer." The Sultantepe text (STT 197) would even appear to be a *Mīs Pî* text (Cooper 1971:9).

[78] These were the craft deities, different forms of Ea.

[79] Since the verb is rendered as a logogram ŠID-*nu*, it could be normalized as either the 2nd person "you" or 3rd person "he." Most verbs that are phonetically written are in the 2nd person "you"; however, the suffix ŠU-*su* (line 142) might suggest a change to 3rd person here.

[80] This is a *ki'utukku* prayer to Šamaš.

[81] This is the fourth MW of the NR.

[82] For a description of these three offerings and illustrations of their placement on the *paṭiru*-altar, see Maul 1994:54–55, 58–59.

[83] K 2969 (Incantation Tablet 3 line 47) says the priest stands at the left side of the deity. See Maul 1994:66.

[84] This is the first of five *šu-illa* "Lifting of the Hand" prayers and marks the high point of the ritual. For this prayer genre, see Mayer 1976:7–8, 32, n. 63.

[85] This is the fifth MW of the NR. If there were a MW in the gap of lines 82–87 and at the end of NR, which has been lost, then there would have been altogether seven MW, corresponding to the fourteen of BW. Because of the importance of the number seven, this seems likely (Berlejung 1997:62, n. 73).

[86] The second of the *šu-illa* prayers. On the concept of Sumerian ME, see Berlejung 1998:20–25.

[87] On the *takpirtu* cleansing rite, see Wright 1987:296–298; this ritual removal of contamination could involve disposal of the "choice plants" mentioned in line 117.

[88] The content of the "whispered prayer (*liḫšu*)" follows (lines 167–171).

(165) "You are counted [among] your brother [gods],"
(166) you whisper [into his right ear.]

(167) "From today may your destiny be counted as divinity;
(168) [with your brother gods] you are counted;
(169) approach [the king who knows your voice;]
(170) approach [your temple …];
(171) [to the land where you were created] be reconciled,"
(172) you whisper [into his left ear].

(173) [You retire; and] you position al[l the (human) craftsmen] involved with that god
(174) [before (?) Ninkurra], Ninagala, Kusigbanda,
(175) [Ninildu] (and) Ninzadim;[89] and
(176) […]
(177) […]
(178) [……] x […]

(179) "(I swear) I did not make (the statue) […];
(180) Ninagala, who is Ea […]."
(181) "I did not make (the statue); (I swear) I did not [make (it);]
(182) Ninildu, who is Ea the god of the carpenter [made it …]";
(183) I did not make (the statue), (I swear) I did not make (it)," […];
(184) Kusigbanda, who is Ea the god of the goldsmith [made it …];
(185) Ninkurra, who is Ea the god of […];
(186) Ninzadim, who is Ea the god [of … made it].

(187) The priest before that god[90] […]
(188) ⟨recites⟩ the incantation, "As you emerge, as you emerge, great …,"[91] […],
(189) the incantation, "Statue born in a pure place …,"[92] […]
(190) the incantation, "Statue born in heaven …,"[93] […]
(191) the incantation, "Ninildu, great carpenter of Anu …," […]
(192) the incantation, "Exalted garment, *lamahuššu*-garment of white linen …,"[94] […]
(193) the incantation, "Exalted crown, crown [endowed with] great awe, … […]"
(194) the incantation, "Holy throne, which Ninildu, gre[at carpenter of Anu …," …]

(195) You recite the incantation, "Go, do not tarry,"[95] […];
(196) [you recite] the second incantation, "Go, do not tarry";
(197) you enter the magic circle[96] […];
(198) you recite the third incantation, "Go, do not tarry"; and
(199) (The performance of) "Wher[ever] Šamaš goes."

(200) First you dismantle the offering-arrangements of that god;
(201) afterwards you dismantle the offering-arrangements of the gods of the craftsmen;
(202) afterwards you dismantle the offering-table of Kusu and Ningirima;
(203) afterwards you dismantle the offering-arrangements of the great gods.

(204) […] x x
(Continuation Lost)

89 These are all various craft gods connected with Ea: the stone-carver god, the carpenter-god, the goldsmith god, the metal smith god, etc. They are said to have created their divine "brother," not the human artisans, who all swear an oath that they did not craft the god/statue. The statue is truly "unmade by human hands."

90 Up to this point, the priest had only stood at the side of the god/statue, whose incorporation into the divine community is complete; the priest now assumes the position *before* the deity (Berlejung 1997:63).

91 The third of the five *šu-illa* prayers.

92 The text of the fourth *šu-illa* prayer is not preserved on Tablet 4.

93 The fifth *šu-illa* prayer.

94 Now the ritual focuses on the divine paraphernalia.

95 This is a *ki'utukku* prayer and thus the imperative verb addresses Šamaš and not to the divine statue. Thus, it is *not* an appeal for the god of the new statue to descend (Berlejung 1997:65, n. 80). For the *ki'utukku* (KI.^{d}UTU.KAM) genre, see Mayer 1976:31, n. 63.

96 See comments on line 57 of the BR. The "you" here probably refers to the *āšipu*-officiant who is now to enter the magical/ritual circle. On entering the sacred space after the gods have partaken of the sacrificial meal, see Maul 1994:61.

THE BABYLONIAN VERSION OF THE "OPENING OF THE MOUTH" RITUAL (BM 45749) (4.32B)

The First Day

(A) *In the House of the Craftsmen*

(1) When you wash the mouth of a god, on a favorable day in the *bīt mummi*, you set up two holy-water-vessels. (‖ 1, 55)[97]

(2) (You place) a red cloth in front of the god and a white cloth to the right of the god. You set up offering arrangements for Ea and Asalluḫi. You perform Mouth-Washing (‖ 58)
(3) on that god, and you set up an offering arrangement for that god. You raise your hand; and you

97 represents Nineveh Ritual (NR) parallels.

recite the incantation, "Born in heaven by your own power,"[98]
(4) three times. Before that god, you recite three times the incantation, "From today you go before your father Ea," and (‖ 61–64)

(B) *Procession from the House of the Craftsmen to the River*
(5) you take the hand of the god and lead? a ram. You recite the incantation, "As you grew up,[99] as you grew up from the forest," while (going) from the house of the craftsmen (‖ 65–66)
(6) with a torch in front of the god to the riverbank. (‖ 67–71)

C. *At the River Bank*
(6) And seat (him) on a reed-mat, and
(7) you set his eyes towards sunset. You set up a reed-hut. For Ea, Asalluḫi, and that god you set up offering arrangements. (‖ 72)
(8) You libate *mazû*-beer;[100] you open the thigh of a ram; and you place inside an axe, a chisel, a saw, (‖ 77–78)
(9) a tortoise, and turtle of silver and gold; you bind it up and throw it into the river. (‖ 79–80)
(10) You pronounce before Ea three times, "King, lord of the deep," and raise your hand and recite three times the incantation, "Enki, king of the Apsû," and (‖ 81?)
(11) you libate beer, milk, wine and syrup. You perform Mouth-Washing; and you pronounce three times the incantation, "He who comes, his mouth is washed," (‖ 87–88)
(12) and (then) you dismantle the offering arrangements. (‖ 94–96)

(D) *Procession from the River into the Garden*
(12) You take the hand of that god, and

(E) *In the Garden in the Circle of Reed Huts and Reed Standards*
(12) you seat him in the garden in the midst of the reed-standards on a reed-mat
(13a) on a linen cloth. You set his eyes towards sunrise. (‖ 96–99 18)
(13b) You go to the river and throw *maṣḫatu*-meal into the river.
(14) You libate *miḫḫu*-beer. You lift up your hand; and you recite three times each in front of the river the incantation, "Apsu-temple,[101] where fates are determined," (and) the incantation, "Quay of the Apsu, pure quay"; (‖ 18–20)
(15) and you draw water (for) seven holy-water-basins, and you place it in the chapel of Kusu.[102] (‖ 22)
(16) You throw into the holy-water-basin of Mouth-Washing[103] tamarisk, *maštakal*, date-palm-"heart," seven palm-shoots, *šalalu*-reed, *apparu*-reed, (‖ 24–25)
(17) sweet reed, …, sulphur, …, salt, cedar, cypress, juniper, (‖ 26)
(18) ["horned *alkali*"], *sikillu*-plant, tree resin(?), lodestone, *zalāqu*-stone, (‖ 27, 34)
(19) […] *muššaru*-stone, carnelian, lapis-lazuli, *pappardilû*-stone, *pappardildilû*-stone, *dušu*-stone, (‖ 35–36)
(20) [silver, gold,] tin, iron, oil, salve-oil, perfumed? oil, cedar oil, syrup (and) ghee. (‖ 36–37)
(21) you lay down and arrange […] of the offering arrangements (and) their aromatics. You fill a trough of tamarisk wood with the waters of the holy-water-basins;
(22) and you throw into the trough carnelian, lapis-lazuli, silver beads, gold beads, juniper (and) *ḫalṣu*-oil, and
(23) [you set …] the holy-water-basins on the brick of Dingirmaḫ
(24) you set up [……] the holy-water-basins, and perform Mouth-Washing.[104] You dismantle the offering arrangement.

(25) You set up 9 offering arrangements for Anu, Enlil, Ea, Sîn, Šamaš, Adad, Marduk, Gula (and) Ishtar, the stars (‖ 100–101)
(26) [……], towards the north. You recite the incantation, "Tamarisk, pure wood," and you perform Mouth-Washing.[105] (‖ 102, 104)

(27) You set up towards the south 9 offering arrangements for Ninmaḫ, Kusu, Ningirima, Ninkurra, Ninagal, (‖ 105–106)
(28) Kusigbanda, Ninildu, Ninzadim and that god, *ditto*.[106] (‖ 107–108)

[98] This, the first incantation in BR, apparently named the series in Nimrud and Sultantepe. It would have been the first line in the series, since the ritual tablet was the last tablet.
[99] Sumerian È is translated by Akkadian *šâḫu* "to grow up" in the bilingual versions of this incantation.
[100] *Erimḫuš* V 166 LÙlu-luLÙ = *bu-ul-lu-lu* (MSL XVII 74). *šikar rēštî mazâ* for KAŠ.SAG LÙ.LÙ. See *CAD* M 1:439: KAŠ LÙ.LÙ.A = *mazû* (a type of beer).
[101] This temple ÈŠ.ABZU is treated in George 1993:83, n. 264.
[102] According to Krecher (1966:133–134), there are two deities named Kusu (dKÙ-SÙ); the first is a female grain goddess, while the second – the one referred to here – was a god of exorcism and prayers. He was known as "the chief exorcist of Enlil (*šangammaḫu ša dEnlil*)" and as the "expert in ritually pure waters (*ša mê ellūti īdû*)." See Tallqvist 1938:344. However, the three gods Kusu, Ningirim, and Nisaba, are all gods of reeds and grasses and according to Jacobsen (1976:10) are "restorers of divine images." These three are associated in several liturgies.
[103] In the NR, the *egubbû* had already been prepared before the actual beginning of the ritual proper.
[104] This is the third MW.
[105] The fourth MW.
[106] This is the fifth MW, since the *ditto* refers back to the MW of line 26.

(29) You set up 2 offering arrangements for Jupiter and Venus, *ditto*.[107]

(30) You set up 2 offering arrangements for the Moon and Saturn, *ditto*.[108]

(31) You set up 3 offering arrangements for Mercury, Sirius (and) Mars, *ditto*.[109]

(32) You set up 6 offering arrangements for the Scales (Libra) (which is) the star of Šamaš, the Plough (Triangulum/Andromeda), "ŠU.PA" (Boötes),
(33) the Wagon (Ursa Major), Erua (Coma Berenices), the She-Goat (Lyra), *ditto*.[110]

(34) You set up 4 offering arrangements for the Field (Pegasus/Andromeda), the Swallow (Pisces), Anunitum (Pisces) (and) the Furrow (Virgo), *ditto*.[111]

(35) You set up 4 offering arrangements for the Fish(?), the Giant (Aquarius), Eridu (and) the Scorpion, *ditto*.[112]

(Reverse of the Tablet)

(36) You set up 3 offering arrangements for the (stars) of Anu, the (stars) of Enlil and the (stars) of Ea, *ditto*.[113]

The Second Day

(37) In the morning you set up within the reed-hut three thrones for Ea, Šamaš and Asalluḫi. (‖ 109–110)
(38) You spread out a red cloth; you stretch out a linen (cloth) in front. You set up three tables; you sprinkle ripened dates (and) meal. (‖ 110–111)
(39) You set in place a confection of syrup (and) ghee. You set up a libation-vessel. You set in line 6 *kukkubu*(?)-jars; (‖ 112–115)
(40) you lay down choice grasses. You provide in splendid abundance the fruit of the orchard. You stretch out(?) … (‖ 115–118)
(41) You scatter sifted barley; you sprinkle juniper on a censer; you raise cedar in your hand, and (‖ 118–132)
(42) you recite three times the (Sumerian) incantation, "Born in heaven by his own power";[114] [you recite] the incantation, "Šamaš, great lord of heaven and earth," (‖ 133–134)
(43) the (Sumerian) incantation, "Water of life, the river rising in flood …," [and] …… you give(?). (‖ 135–136)
(44) You recite the incantation, "The flood, its divine task is unique, is holy," and you libate ……; you sprinkle on a censer; (‖ 137–138)
(45) you place *masḫatu*-flour on the forehead of a ram and sacrifice (it); you complete the offering arrangement.

(46) The *āšipu*-priest stands on the left side of that god, before Ea, Šamaš and Asalluḫi, and recites the incantation, "Šamaš, exalted judge." (‖ 143)
(47) He recites three times the incantation, "Ea, Šamaš and Asalluḫi." He recites the incantation, "On the day when the god was created," and you perform Mouth-Washing.[115] (‖ 144, 160–161)
(48) Afterwards you recite the incantation, "Pure statue, suited(!) to the great 'ME' "; you perform a Cleansing Rite; (‖ 162–163)
(49) you recite a Whisper Prayer. You retire; and [you position] all of the craftsmen who approached that god (‖ 172–173)
(50) and their equipment […… before(?)] Ninkurra, Ninagal, Kusigbanda, (‖ 173–174)
(51) Ninildu (and) [Ninzadim], and you bind their hands with a scarf; (‖ 175)
(52) and cut (them off) with a knife of tamarisk wood … You make (them) say: "I did not make him (the statue), Ninagal (who is) Ea (god) of the smith made him." (‖ 179–180)
(53) You open the eye of that god. The *āšipu*-priest recites before that god … the incantation, "As you grew up, as you grew up." (‖ 187–188)
(54) He recites the (Sumerian) incantation, "Statue born in a pure place," the incantation, "Statue born in heaven," (‖189–190)
(55) the (Sumerian) incantation, "Ninildu, great carpenter of Anu," the incantation, "Exalted garment, *lamaḫuššu*-garment of white linen," (‖ 191–192)
(56) the (Sumerian) incantation, "Exalted crown," (and) the incantation, "Holy throne"; and before [that god] he recites the incantation, "Go, do not tarry"; (‖ 193–195)

---

107 For a treatment of the astrology here, see Reiner 1995:140–143. The *ditto* recounts the sixth MW.
108 The seventh MW.
109 The eighth MW.
110 The ninth MW of the BR.
111 The tenth MW of the BR.
112 The eleventh MW of the BR.
113 The twelfth MW of the BR.
114 This incantation was already recited on line 3.
115 This is the thirteenth MW in the BR.

(57)[116] the second version he recites and he enters the ritual circle; the third version he recites; performance of "Wherever Šamaš goes …"[117] First you dismantle the offering arrangement (‖ 196–200)
(58) of that god; afterwards you dismantle (the offering arrangement) of Kusu and Ningirima; afterwards you dismantle (the offering arrangement) of the gods of the craftsmen; (‖ 200–202)
(59) Afterwards, you dismantle the offering arrangement of the great gods. (‖ 203)

(F) *Procession from the Garden to the Temple Gate*
(59) You take the hand of the god; and you recite the incantation, "May the foot which bestrides the ground [bestride the pure place"] (and) the incantation, "As he walked through the street," all the way to that god's temple.

(G) *At the Temple Gate*
(60) At the door of that god's temple, you make an offering.

(H) *Procession from the Temple Gate to the Cella*
(60) You take the god's hand and make him enter; and you recite the incantation, "My king, to your heart's content,"
(61) (going) to the sanctuary.

(I) *In the Cella*
(61) You seat the god in his cella; and you recite in his cella the incantation, "The celestial evening meal," and the incantation, "Fit for the august throne-dais."
(62) On the right of the sanctuary, you set up a reed-hut; you set up an offering arrangement for Ea and Asalluḫi; you complete the offering arrangement, and
(63) you perform Mouth-Washing[118] on that god, and for that god you set up an offering arrangement. With water (from) the trough you purify that god and

(64) You recite seven times the incantation, "Asalluḫi, son of Eridu"; and bring near the trappings of divinity;
(65) at night you set them (upon him).

(J) *To the Quay of the Apsû*
(65) You go to the Kār-Apsî, and stay there; you perform a Cleansing Ritual all the way to the Kār-Apsî.

(K) *Colophon*
(66)[119] The initiate may show it to the initiate. The uninitiated may not see it. Taboo of the great Enlil, Marduk.
(67) According to the wording of a tablet, the copy of a red-burnt tablet of Nabû-etel-ilāni,
(68) the son of Dābibi, the incantation-priest(?). Iddina-Nabû, the son of Luḫdu-Nabû,
(69) the *āšipu*-priest, for the life of his soul and for the prolonging of his days, has written (it) and
(70) set it in Esangila.

116 There are three different versions of this incantation in Incantation Tablet 4 of the series: lines 66–72 (version one); lines 73–B6 (second version); lines B7–19 (third version). The first of these has the rubric KA.INIM.MA KI-dUTU-KAM.

Some authors have suggested that the god of the statue is here invited to enter the "form" of the statue whereby it can become the divine presence (Winter 1992:23). The beginning of the Nabû-apla-iddina text given above (III:19) refers to the finding of a model/form of the statue (*uṣurat ṣalmi*) of Šamaš, which is the same word translated here as "form." However, if we read the Sumerogram GIŠ.ḪUR.ME as the Akkadian *gišḫuru*, then it is the "magic circle" used in rituals (see *CAD* G 102a and note association with Šamaš).

117 C. Walker and I (2001) understand this phrase to be a form of Sumerian rubric which accompanied at least the first incantation "Go, do not tarry" (Tablet 4 line 72) and to be an indication that the appropriate performance accompanied all three incantations. Compare NR 200.

118 The fourteenth and final MW in the BR.

119 See Hunger 1968, § 151 for a treatment of this colophon.

IMPORTANT INCANTATIONS (4.32C)

The following bilingual incantation (Sumerian and Akkadian) AN-NA NÍ-BI-TA TU-UD-DA-ÀM appears by incipit in BR 3, 42 and in NR 133. This incantation appears either in incantation tablet 1 or 2. It perfectly encapsulates the Mesopotamian theology of the cult image:

(1–2) [Incantation: in Heaven] it is [born] of itself;[120]
(3–4) on earth it is born of itself.[121]
(5) In Heaven it is complete; on earth it is complete.[122]
(6) I am the purificatory-priest; I have washed my mouth,
(7) I have washed my hands, I have washed my feet,[123]
(8) May the clean earth become clean(?) …
(9–10) May it become pure, may it become clean, may it become bright.
(11) May the evil the evil tongue stand aside.

120 The Akkadian translation is: "the heavens were created of themselves." Note the singular form *ibbani*, where plural *ibbanû* is expected.

121 The Akkadian translation is: "the earth was created of itself."

122 The Akkadian, "Heaven is my spring, earth is my spring," reading the Sumerian TIL as IDIM, must have meant that heaven and earth were the sources of the water for the priest's washing.

123 The Akkadian translation is, "I am the purificatory-priest whose mouth is washed; my hands are pure; my feet are clean."

This next bilingual incantation comes from tablet 4 of the incantations; it clearly stresses that, *pace* Second Isaiah and Jeremiah, this image was born of the gods themselves. It was not a product of human hands!

(23ab) Incantation: Statue born in heaven,[124]
(24ab) in/from the mountain, a pure place …
(25ab) The Tigris, the Mother of the Mountain,
(26ab) carried within her(?) the pure waters.
(27ab) Bēlet-ilī,[125] the mother of the Land,
(28ab) raised you on her(?) pure lap,
(29ab) Ninzadim, the great stonecutter of Anu,
(30ab) with his pure hands cared for you.[126]
(31ab) The goddess LÀL,[127] creatress of limbs,
(32ab) has placed you in a pure place,
(33ab) and has poured the water of incantation over you.
(34ab) By the rites of purification the *apkallu*-priest of Ea has raised up your head.
(35ab) May Šamaš heed your true decision.
(36ab) […] may you be endowed with the proper overpowering brilliance.
(37ab) May you be …
(38ab) May you be its *ušumgallu*-dragon, and may its word fill the land!
(39ab) May you be gloriously enthroned!
(40ab) May you dwell in your cella of brilliant light!
(41ab) May the temple where you walk be open!
(42ab) May the temple of your …!
(43ab) May your … be of heartfelt joy!
(44ab) May your [herd?] be of abundant cattle and abundant sheep!
(45ab) May the house where you dwell be one of every purity!
(46ab) In your exalted shrine, may nothing ever cease!
(47ab) May the house of your name be a house of well considered decisions!
(48ab) Tarry therein with abundant repasts![128]
(49ab) In your shining cattle pens, may cow and calf constantly low!
(50ab) May you be one whose ewes bear healthy lambs!
(51ab) May you be one whose yellow she-goats bear yellow kids!
(52ab) May you be one whose orchard is abundant with syrup and wine!
(53ab) May the mountains, which bear produce, bear you produce!
(54ab) May the plain (and) field, which bear produce, bear you produce!
(55ab) May the fruit-orchard, which brings produce, *ditto*!
(56ab) May the net that produces fish (and) birds, *ditto*![129]
(57ab) May the abundance of the Mountains and the fullness of the sea, which bear produce, *ditto*!
(58ab) On the pure lap of your Mother Nintu[130] …
(59ab) Lie on a pure linen cloth!
(60ab) May you be the good protective deity of your temple!
(61ab) In the sanctuary of your temple, may you be established!
(62ab) In your place, the abode of rest, take up your dwelling forever!
(63ab) May Sîn,[131] your beloved, love you!
(64ab) Let the heart of Enki and Ninki be calm towards you!

124 Akkadian: "Statue which Anu created."
125 The mother goddess; she is the same as Mother Nintu in line 58ab.
126 The statue was not a product of human artisans but rather of craft gods.
127 This otherwise unknown goddess must be Lalḫurgalzu, another name for the Mother Goddess.
128 *CAD* M 1:123.
129 See *CAD* S 161b for translation.
130 The goddess Nintu is the Mother Goddess.
131 The Moon god.

REFERENCES

Text: Walker and Dick 2001; Dick 1999. Studies: Berlejung 1996; 1997; 1998; Blackman 1924; Boden 1998; Borger 2005; Cassin 1986; Clifford, 1980; Curtis 1990; Dietrich 1992; Hallo 1983; 1988; Holter 1995; Hurowitz 1989; 2003; 2006; Jacobsen 1987; Levtow 2008; Meier 1937–1939; Mettinger 1995; Pongratz-Leisten 1994; Porter 1993; Renger 1981; Smith 1925; Thureau-Dangin 1921; Trimborn 1984; Walker 1966; Winter 1992.

NEO-ASSYRIAN TREATIES

TREATY OF ŠAMŠI-ADAD V WITH MARDUK-ZAKIR-ŠUMI, KING OF BABYLON (4.33)

Jacob Lauinger

Šamši-Adad V of Assyria (823–811) inherited an empire in chaos from his father Shalmaneser III. According to the new king's own inscriptions, his brother Aššur-da''in-apli had incited a total of 27 cities, including Aššur and Nineveh, to revolt. Although the inscription laconically attributes success in subduing the revolt to Šamši-Adad V alone, the existence of this treaty between the king and Marduk-zakir-šumi, king of Babylon, suggests that Šamši-Adad V received support from the Babylonian king much as the Babylonian king himself had been helped by Šamši-Adad V's father in the face of a revolt on his accession to the throne some decades earlier.

The terms of the treaty, as preserved, reflect Marduk-zakir-šumi's position of advantage over his Assyrian treaty partner:

> one can see that Akkad [i.e., Babylonia] precedes Assyria in the enumeration of the countries, that the Assyrian king is not given any royal title, that he is obliged to surrender fugitives from Babylonia, that he must promise to report a certain Marduk-rimanni if the latter plots against Babylonia, and that the treaty oath is sworn by Babylonian gods alone (Brinkman 1968:204).

As Brinkman observes, the one-sided nature of the treaty implies that "Shamshi-Adad saved his throne, but probably lost face in the process" (1968:204–205 with n. 1267, although see Parpola and Watanabe 1988:xxvi for a different opinion).

The treaty was excavated by Hormuzd Rassam at the Assyrian capital of Nineveh (the precise find spot is unknown) and is unusual because it is the only extant Neo-Assyrian treaty carved into stone, being "the lower left half of a polished black stone tablet measuring 4.4 × 12.5 × 8.6 cm" (Parpola and Watanabe 1988: xliii). The script is Babylonian, not Assyrian as with the other extant Neo-Assyrian treaties, and Weidner (1932–1933b:27) suggested that this stone tablet was originally the Babylonian copy of the treaty that was at some point brought back to Assyria as booty (perhaps by Šamši-Adad V on one of his two campaigns in Babylonia?). Given the historical background to the treaty, it seems equally possible that the treaty tablet was composed and carved in Babylonia and thereafter presented to Šamši-Adad V to be stored and even perhaps displayed at his court or in a temple (cf. Noth 1961:143 n. 73). In this regard, the treaty deserves comparison with Esarhaddon's Succession Treaty, as these two treaties represent the only extant "treaty tablets" (i.e. official and not archival copies) found in first-millennium Assyrian contexts, and one speculates that the difference in material (stone as opposed to clay) might reflect Babylonian and Assyrian practices (the medium of clay being necessary for the divine seals of Aššur to be impressed upon the surface of the Assyrian treaty, see the Introduction to Esarhaddon's Succession Treaty, 4.36). Note also the appearance at the end of this treaty of curses known also from the Code of Hammurabi (see COS 2.131 and the comments in general of Altman [2012:191–192]).

(1′–2′ not translated)
(3′–5′) [...] when a provincial governor [... ...] has sent troops (but) the king [... no]thing [...], he (Šamši-Adad V) shall trust[1] [... in the stea]dfastness of their hearts.
(5′–6′) He shall not deport [...] Akkad and Assyria.
(6′–7′) If [...] are seized,[2] (or) if [...] to forts to/for [...], [he shall ...].

[1] Brinkman (1990:110) notes that the construction *šumma ... lā ittaklu*, and the similar constructions that follow that "apparently deal with a series of conditions for the treaty." Accordingly, he translates the negation particle before the verb here and throughout the text, e.g. "he has not trusted." Since the mood of these verbs is subjunctive, however, we might expect not a straightforward conditional clause but rather that "special linguistic formulation used in all kinds of solemn, oath bound statements" (Parpola and Watanabe 1988:xxxix, cited in Brinkman 1990:110) in which positive vows are expressed with negation and vice versa. Cf. the translation of SAA 2.1 and see Parpola and Watanabe 1988:xxxix for the perfect tense as a feature of Middle and Neo-Babylonian negative promissory oaths (although note that the perfect tense is used in this text for positive promissory oaths as well, *contra* their chart). Brinkman's translation perhaps stems from a desire to account for the shift in tense from perfect to present at the end of the obverse, see note 5 below and 4.36, n. 27.

[2] *Contra* SAA 2.1 and most recently Kitchen and Lawrence 2012 1:936, traces visible in the published photograph support the reluctance of Brinkman (1990:108), who collated the text from the original, to read the beginning of the line as [*i*]*ṣ*- for *iṣṣabtu*, "he shall not seize." I understand simply a 3 m.pl. stative in the indicative introduced by *šumma* which governs both a conditional clause and introduces a "solemn statement" (on which double function, see Watanabe 1987:30 and Parpola 1987:173). The subjunctive verb of the "solemn statement" is understood to have originally been at the beginning of 8′.

(8′–10′) Šamši-Adad (V) shall not heed the evil word(s) that Marduk-remanni,[3] [the x?], has spoken [about the ...] of the king, namely: "Kill, blind, seize [the ...] of King Marduk-zakir-šumi!"
(10′–14′) [He] shall [(not) ...], nor [shall he ...] eyes, feet, or *ext[ended]* finger [in/to ...] and his land nor give back the booty/captives [*from GN*(?)], nor shall fugitives [*from GN*] flee here.[4]
(14′-le 2) May the king not (need to) instruct him. [*He who*] violates [*the oath and acts* contrary to his duty,[5]
(le-r 1) May Marduk, the great lord, whose command takes precedence, decree [...], his ill health, and the scattering of his people. May he pour out his life like water. [*May he destroy*] his land. May he strike down his people [with starvation] and famine. May he lead him [*into* ...].
(r 1–2) May Nabû, the exalted heir, [who ...] evil demons, not spare his life.[6]
(r 3) May [Anum, fat]her of the gods, break his scepter.
(r 3–5) [May] Enlil, the lord, determiner of fates, [*whose command is not overt*]*urned*, determine for him a reign of hardship, few days, (and) years of sca[rcity as his fate].
(r 5–7) May Ninlil,[7] the great mother, whose command [is honored] in the [Ekur, not inter]cede [for him] before Enlil in the place of judgment and decision.
(r 7–8) [May] Ea, sage of the gods, the one who knows everything, dam [his] rivers [at the source].
(r 8–9) May Šamaš, the great judge of heaven and earth [... the lord of tru]st, reject his rule, (and) may he not [judge] his case.
(r 10–13) [May Sîn, *the lord of heaven*, who]se *appearance*[8] is proclaimed among the gods [impose a heavy penalty, a] great [punishm]ent which will not be removed from his body. [May he cause the days, months, and years] of his [rei]gn to end in moaning and [groaning].

[3] The identity of Marduk-remanni is unknown, see Mattila 2001. According to the interpretation offered here, he was likely a Babylonian (as indicated by his name) who had exhorted violence to the [troops?] of the Babylonian king and consequently whom Šamši-Adad was adjured not to heed. SAA 2.1 offers a different translation, "Šamši-Adad shall not say (any) evil words about Marduk-rimanni [... to] the king (viz.): 'Kill, blind, or se[ize him', nor] shall King Marduk-zakir-shumi listen to him (should he say such things)," which Kitchen and Lawrence (2012 1:936) follow. The difference between the two interpretation lies in the analysis of *ša ... iqtabû* in lines 8′–9′, which I understand to be the relative *ša* followed by a subjunctive verb; these words are not connected syntactically in SAA 2.1, being a determinative *ša* ("words about Marduk-remanni") and the verb of a "solemn statement." Cf. also the cautious translation of Brinkman (1990:109): "if Shamshi-Adad [has heard] a plot of/which Marduk-rimanni ... [the k]ing (...) has spoken, namely: 'Kill, blind, capt[ure] ....' ... king Marduk-zakir-shumi has heard/listened to him."

[4] Restoring the verb at the beginning of line 14′ as [*it-t*]*a-bi-tu-ni* for *ittābitūni*, the N perfect 3 m.pl. with ventive of *abātu* with *mun-nab-t*[*u*] (13′) in the (Babylonian) nominative plural as its subject. Presumably, the verb continues a sequence of "solemn statements," the beginning of which, in line 11′, is now lost. Following an original suggestion of Borger (1965:168), the verb is restored in SAA 2.1 as [*in-n*]*a-bi- tu-ni* (according to the the photograph, the partially preserved sign fits [*t*]*a* or *n*]*a* equally well, and cf. Brinkman's reading cited below), and the sentence, extended to encompass the remainder of line 14′, is translated as: "The king shall indicate to him the fugitives who fled [*from Assyria to Babylonia*]." There are a number of difficulties with this translation, which is followed in its essentials by Kitchen and Lawrence (2012 1:937): Given the case ending, it is difficult to take *mun-nab-tu* as a plural direct object, whether the dialect in question be Assyrian or Babylonian; the Object-Subject-Verb word order is atypical and unexpected; and in the absence of vowel syncope, [*in-n*]*a-bi-tu* should be analyzed as present/durative not preterite/punctual. Cf. Brinkman's minimalist rendering of these same lines: "fugitive ... [*fl*]*ed* ...."

[5] The verbs in these lines, *iqabbâš*[*šu*] and *iḫaṭṭû* are no longer introduced by *šumma* and stand in the present tense, not the perfect tense as previously. This parallelism implies that the clause containing *iqabbâššu* needs to be understood together with *iḫaṭṭû*, not with what comes before ("The king shall indicate to him the fugitives [who] fled ...," Parpola and Watanabe 1988:4, so also Kitchen and Lawrence 2012 1:937). Brinkman's (1990:109) translation "(he) shall say to him ... offend" moves in this direction of this parallelism and interprets the first verb as a positive promissory oath. But if this is the case, how do we account for the absence of the expected *šumma* before *šarru*? For this reason, I hesitantly analyze *lā iqabbâš*[*šu*] as a prohibitive and *iḫaṭṭû* as a subjunctive verb following a relative pronoun or perhaps subordinate conjunction now lost from the beginning of line le 1, e.g. [*ša ina adê*] *iḫaṭṭû lā illakšu* [*illaku*]. The translation "contrary to his duty" attempts to render the negation particle *lā* before the substantive *ilkašu*. Parpola and Watanabe (1988:4) followed by Kitchen and Lawrence 2012 1:937, read *-nu* coming out of the break in line le 2′, but this reading is not supported by the collation of Brinkman (1990:108).

[6] As noted by Borger (1965), these curses are an abridged version of curses found in the epilogue of the Code of Hammurabi (McCarthy 1981:109, n. 12 lays out the parallel passages and see Kitchen and Lawrence 2012 2:94 for a table providing a partial comparison of the language; see Roth 1997 for the standard edition of the Code). Kitchen and Lawrence suggest that "Shamshi-Adad's scribes [or better, Marduk-zakir-shumi's? – JL.] abbreviated the full versions of the curses (as given by Hammurabi) to suit the proportional space available on the stone tablet" (2:93). Their subsequent conclusion that the quotations in the treaty of curses from the Code of Hammurabi represent "an explicit linking of the treaty tradition with that of law" must remain speculative; the quotations could equally be interpreted as recourse by Babylonian scribes to a learned tradition of curses from which the curses of both the treaty and the Code are derived. In this regard, Brinkman's warning in reference to the reconstruction of the curses in light of the spacing of the lines is apt: "Though one could envisage shorter writings ... one must also reckon with the possibility of a slightly different version of the text (1990:111, cf. also Borger [1965:169])."

[7] Reading the divine name ^{d}NIN.LIL$_2$ as Ninlil and not Mulliltu in light of the fact that the text's prevailing dialect is Babylonian and not Assyrian, so also Brinkman 1990:110 and Kitchen and Lawrence 2012 1:937.

[8] The word *šēressu*, "his *appearance*," is obscure, mostly appearing in personal names of the late third and early second millennium outside of the relevant passage in the Code of Hammurabi and this quotation, see *CAD* Š/2 s.v. *šērtu* D (Roth [1997:138 with 142, n. 53] emends the parallel text of the Code to *te*!*-ret-su* for *têressu*, "his oracular decision," agreeing with the interpretation found in earlier volumes of the *CAD*). Alone among previous translations, SAA 2.1 understand the word to be the homophonous word *šērtu*, "punishment," (*CAD* Š/2 s.v. *šērtu* B) which occurs as the object of Sîn's action in the following line of the curse.

(r 13–16) [May Adad take away from him the rai]n from the skies (and) the seasonal floods from the springs. May he dest[roy his land with famine and starvation. May he thunder furiously over his city. May he turn] his [land] into [a ruined tell].

(r 16) [*May Zababa ... who goes ...*]

(Remainder of the reverse is not preserved)

REFERENCES

Parpola and Watanabe 1988 (SAA 2.1); Weidner 1932–1933b.

TREATY OF AŠŠUR-NERARI V WITH MATI᾿-ILU, KING OF ARPAD (4.34)

Jacob Lauinger

This treaty between the Assyrian king Aššur-nerari V (754–745) and Mati᾿-ilu, the king of the Syro-Anatolian city-state of Arpad, was made during a period of general decline in Assyria's centralized control in the first half of the eighth century. Nonetheless, Parpola and Watanabe (1988:xxvii) suggest that the treaty "was probably concluded in Aššur-nerari's very first year and it seems to have been duly observed by Mati᾿-il, since, while Arpad was the target of an Assyrian campaign in 754, the city does not figure in Assyrian sources later in Aššur-nerari's reign." Mati᾿- ilu is also famously known from the three Sefire treaties, written in Aramaic on stone stelae in which the king of Arpad swears an oath of loyalty to a certain Bar-ga᾿yah of KTK (see *COS* 2:213–217 for a translation and bibliography).

Unlike the Sefire treaties, however, which were inscribed on stone and publically presented, Mati᾿-ilu's treaty with Aššur-nerari V is known from a single clay tablet found at Nineveh. The tablet, which originally comprised six columns, is badly damaged: Just the bottom third of the tablet remains, and Parpola and Watanabe (1988:xliii) estimate that less than 31% of the total composition (149 of about 485 lines) are preserved. Nonetheless it seems likely from the rotation of the tablet and the arrangement of the columns on the reverse that the tablet was not an official "oath tablet" (*tuppi adê*, see 4.36) but rather was written by the Assyrian chancellery for its own use, as seems also to have been the situation with the other Neo-Assyrian treaties found at Nineveh (Radner 2006:373).

Aššur-nerari's treaty with Mati᾿-ilu also provides us with the earliest known occurrence in Akkadian of *adê*, a word that is conventionally translated as "treaty" in the titles of these translations. Indeed, some scholars deny that the word should be translated as "treaty" at all. As famously articulated by Gelb (1962:161), an *adê* is "a pact or agreement *imposed* by one party upon another and sworn to by the obligated party *only*. It is not a pact between equals" (emphasis in the original). Gelb's view is weakened, though, by instances known from letters where rulers swear *adê*-oaths to each other.[1] In defense of a broader conception of the word, Parpola and Watabane 1988:xv point out the texts' function as "unquestionably bilateral agreements between rulers and hence treaties by the modern definition." More recently, Altman (2012:189–190) distinguishes between *adê*-oaths that "regulate proper behavior" to the current monarch and those that concern another individual (i.e., Esarhaddon's Succession Treaty), considering only the former category to be treaties, and see now Lauinger 2013.

There has been a strong tendency to conceptualize the *adê*, in the words of Tadmor (1982:147), as an "originally western form" that "must have answered the needs of the Assyrian monarchy, and thus in the eighth to seventh centuries ... emerged as a powerful tool in the service of the monarchy." However, as Radner (2006:352) stresses, *adê* replaces Akkadian words, notably the cognates *riksu* and *rikiltu*, in designating the "bond" created between two parties when one or both swears an oath to the other. Consequently, the appearance of the *adê*-oath in eight-century Akkadian texts, needs to be understood as a terminological innovation, not a conceptual one. Attempts to argue for the *adê* as an intrinsically "western form" on the basis of chronology or etymology meet with difficulty as well, see Radner 2006:352–353 for a cogent summary of the debate, citing previous literature.

Obverse

(beginning of column not preserved – at least 30 lines lost[2])

(i.1′–9′) [... may Mati᾿-ilu], his sons, his daughters, [his] mag[nates, (and) the people of his land ...] as much as [...]. [May ...] his land as severely as

[1] E.g., "After listening carefully to each other, the king of Elam and the king of Assyria made peace with each other by Marduk's command. Each has sworn an *adê*-oath to the other (lit. they have turned into the owners of each other's *adê*, Akk. *a-na* EN.MEŠ *a-de-e šá a-ḫa-meš it-tu-ra*)" (SAA 18.7 obv. 3–7).

[2] This estimate of missing lines and the estimates that follow derive from Parpola and Watanabe's (1988:xliii–xlvi) reconstruction of the original tablet.

a wasteland. When [he] st[ands, *may*] the ground [*be*] as [*narrow*] as a brick.[3] When his sons, [his] daughters, [his magnates, (and) the p]eople of his land want to stand, may it (the ground) disappear. [May] Mati᾿-ilu, [his sons], his [dau]ghters, his magnates, (and) the people of his land [be ....] like limestone. May he be cr[ushed][4] like gypsum together with the people of his land.

(i.10′–20′) This spring lamb has not been brought here from out of its pen for sacrifice, nor has it been brought here for a banquet[5] nor has it been brought here for purchase nor has it been brought here for (divination about) a sick person nor has it been brought here for slaughtering (it) in orde[r that …]. It has been br[ought here] in order to establish the *adê*-oath of Aššur-nerari, king of [Assyria], with Mati᾿-ilu. If Mati᾿-ilu [violates] the *adê*-oath, th[is] sworn agreement,[6] just as this spring lamb has been brought here from its pen (but) will not return to its pen [nor behold] its pen (ever again), so alas, may Mati᾿-ilu [disappear][7] from his land together with hi[s] sons, [his magnates], (and) the people of his land. He will not return to his land, nor will he [behold] his land (ever again).

(i.21′–28′) This head – [it] is not the head of a spring lamb. [It] is the head of Mati᾿-ilu. [It] is the head of his sons, his magnates, (and) the people of [his] l[and]. Mati᾿-ilu sh[all] not [violate t]his *adê*-oath, (or else) just as this head of a spring lamb has been torn [off], (and) its knuckle has been placed in its mouth (and) […], so may the h[ea]d of Mati᾿-ilu be torn off and his son[s (…)] be […] in/by a […].[8]

(i.29′–35′) This shoulder – [it] is not the shoulder of a sp[ring lamb]. It is the shoulder of Mati᾿-ilu. It is the shoulder of [his] s[ons, his magnates], (and) the people of his land. Mati᾿-[ilu] shall not violate this [*adê*-oath, (or else) ju]st as [this] shou[lder of a spring lamb] has been torn off (and) […] in/by […],[9] so may the sh[oulder of Ma]ti᾿-ilu, [his] sons, [his magnates] (and) the peo[ple of his land] be torn off (and) […] in/by […].

(ii not preserved) …[10]

(beginning of column iii not preserved)

(iii.1′–3′ not translated) (iii.5′–10′) [… *the king*]*s*[11] of the land of Hatti [… …] an Urartian […] you shall seize […] you shall send (him?) *to me*. (break of unknown length)

(iii.11′–18′) [… … y]ou shall not violate […] you shall not violate it/do him wrong […] *you shall not kill him* […] *you shall (not) go* [*to* …][12] these […].

(iii.19′–28′) [… …] or a chariot fighter or a cavalry-

[3] Reiner (1969:532) reads line i. 5′ as 1 KÙŠ ("may his soil be [as narrow] as a brick of one cubit"), in which she is followed by Watanabe (1987:198). Borger (1982–1985:155) suggests *ina ú*-[*zu-zi-ša*] restoring a 3 f.s. possessive pronominal suffix referring back to *libittum*, "brick" ("wie ein aufgerichteter Ziegelstein"). The present translation follows the suggestion of Watanabe and Parpola (1988:8) to restore instead a 3 m.s. suffix referring back to Mati᾿-ilu as *ina u*-[*zi-zi-šú*]. The suggestion is attractive in light of the same verb appearing in reference to Mati᾿-ilu's children and subjects in the immediately following line and has been adopted by other recent editors; e.g., *CAD* U/W s.v. *uzuzzu* mng. 1a and Kitchen and Lawrence 2012 1:940. On the curse, cf. § 63 of Esarhaddon's Succession Treaty.

[4] Restoring either *lip-p*[*ar-ri-ir*] with Parpola and Watanabe (1988:8) or *lip-p*[*i-᾿i-iṣ*] with von Soden (1991:188; cited in *AHw* 1581a).

[5] Following Reiner 1969:532 in reading *qí-ni-ti*, "banquet," so also Borger 1982–1985:155 and Parpola and Watanabe 1988:8, against Weidner's (1932–1933a:18–19 with n. 9) reading *ki-ni-ti*, ("*kinîtu*-Fest"), but see the objections of Deller (1991:346, n. 7).

[6] Reading *ina a-de-e ta-mi-ti an*-[*ni-ti i-ḫa-ṭu*], adapting the suggestion of Watanabe 1987:11, so also Parpola and Watanabe 1988:8. Weidner (1932–1933a:18) restores *ina a-de-e ta-mi-ti* DINGIR.[MEŠ *i-ḫa-ṭi*], so also Reiner 1969:532, Borger 1982–1984:155, and *CAD* T s.v. *tāmītu* mng. 1a, "an agreement sworn by the gods (lit. a sworn agreement of the gods)" But, as written, *tāmīti* should not be in the construct state.

[7] Various treatments of the final verb are *li*-[*iš-te-li*], "möge M. … [heraufgebracht werden]" (Weidner 1932–1933a:18–19); "M. [will be ousted]" (Reiner 1969:532), "soll M. … [herausgeholt werden]" (Borger 1982–1985:155); *li*-[*iḫ-liq*], "may M. … [be ousted]" (Parpola and Watanabe 1988:8); *li*-[*iḫ-liq*], "may M. … [be removed]" (Kitchen and Lawrence 2012 1:940–941).

[8] The end of the curse has been variously interpreted: Weidner 1932–1933a:18–19: *mârê*[MEŠ-*šu* …] *ina b*[*ît*]*i lu ka*-[…], "[*Seine*] *Söhne* […] im *H*[*aus*]*e* fürwahr"; Borger 1982–1985:155 with note to line 28′ omits the sign read DUMU in 27′ and suggests restoring the end of the line as: *lu ka*-[*ia-an*]?, translating "in […] *standig vorhanden sein*"; Parpola and Watanabe 1998:9: DUMU.[MEŠ-*šú* GAL.MEŠ-*šú*] *ina* ˹É˺ *lu ka*-[*ar-ru*], "may his sons [and magnates] be thrown into […]," reading É with Weidner but not translating the word (cf. Kitchen and Lawrence 2012 1:941: "(may) [his] son[and nobles] be th[rown] into a house(?)"). The logic of the action done to the spring lamb seems to be that the punishment meted out to the sons (and magnates, if such are to be restored at the end of i.27′) is represented by the placement of the lamb's knuckle in the mouth of its decapitated head. A stative of *karāru* at the end of the line could fit this logic, but other verbs do also, for example, *katāmu*, "to cover," e.g. "May his son[s] be co[vered over (in dirt)] in the house." While ˹É˺ fits the traces of the second sign in line 28′, from the published photograph other signs are epigraphically possible. Perhaps DUMU.[MEŠ-*šu*] *ina* ˹SAḪAR˺ *lu ka*-[*at-mu*], "may his sons be buried." On the curse in general, cf. § 69 of Esarhaddon's Succession Treaty.

[9] At the end of i.33′, Parpola and Watanabe (1988:9) restore [*šak-na-tu-ni*], "(just as the shou[lder of this spring lamb] is torn out, and) [is placed] in […]," so also Kitchen and Lawrence (2012 1:942).

[10] Lines iii.1′–10′ are known from a fragment identified and published by Millard (1970). The placement of the fragment follows Parpola and Watanabe (1988).

[11] It is also possible to read [*citi*]*es*, as Millard (1970:174) points out, observing further that this stipulation prohibiting Urartian influence (line iii.8′) "agrees with the known history of Arpad."

[12] Lines iii.16′–17′: [… x]x GAZ-*šú* / […] *ta-lak-ni*. So little text remains that it is not certain that these verbs should be understood as "solemn statements." Weidner (1932–1933a:18) transliterates the end of iii.16′ as -*n*]*i* GAZ-*šú*, and the photograph of the tablet seems to confirm that the traces of the sign before GAZ do not fit LA, so if the lines are "solemn statements," then the positive formulation requires a translation in the negative. If a solemn statement, the following verb *ta-lak-ni* shows syncope of the subjunctive marker -*u*, "[t]he most common type of defective writing" (Luukko 2004:36) in the NA dialect (cf. iii.23′).

man [...]. You shall not conceal (him or) offer (him) protection. You shall not send (him) to another land. Mati᾽-ilu[13] shall be loyal to Aššur-nerari. Your heart shall be devoted to Aššur-nerari, king of Assyria. Yo[u], your son⟨s⟩, (and) the people of yo[ur] land [shall not s]eek *ev*[*il*[14] ...]. (remainder of column, about 12 lines, not preserved).

Reverse

(iv.1–3) [If the Assyrian army] marches to war by the command of Aššur-nerari, Mati᾽-ilu shall set out on march wholeheartedly together with his magnates, his troops, (and) [his] cha[riotry].

(iv.4–7) (Or else) may Sîn, the great lord who resides at Harran, cover Mati᾽-ilu, his magnates, (and) the people of his land in leprosy like a cloak. May they roam the steppe.[15] May he (Sîn) show them no mercy. May there be no "dung" of oxen, donkeys, sheep, and horses in his (Mati᾽-ilu's) land.[16]

(iv.8–16) May Adad, the canal inspector of heaven and earth, bring to an end both the land of Mati᾽-ilu and also the people of his land by means of famine, starvation, and a shortfall. May they (the people of his land) eat the flesh of their sons and daughters, and may it please them as if it were the flesh of male (or) female spring lambs.[a] May they be deprived of Adad's thunder, so that rain becomes taboo for them. May dust be their food, pitch be their ointment, donkey urine be their drink, (and) papyrus be their clothing. May their bed be in a pile of garbage.[17]

(iv.17–26) Mati᾽-ilu, his sons, (or) his magnates ⟨⟨who⟩⟩ shall not violate the *adê*-oath of Aššur-nerari, king of Assyria, (or else) may his farmer not call out a work song in the countryside.[18] May steppe grass not burst up to see the sun. May the women who draw water draw none from the springs. [May ... be] their [f]ood. [May ... be] their [dr]ink. [... ... ...] (break of unknown length)

(iv.27′–28′) [... as they say "Alas!" a]nd "[We v]iolated the oath [of Aššur-nerari, king of Assyria!]"[19]

(iv.29′–33′) [Mati᾽-ilu shall not violate this *adê*-oath of Aš]šur-nerari, king of Assyria. He shall look at [.... ...] and Nineveh: Ditto. [...] the people of his land [...] *you shall be deported.*[20]

(v.1–7) Our death shall be your death (and) our life shall be your life.[21] Just as your own life, that of your sons, (and) that of your magnates *are che*[*ri*]*shed*,[22] you shall seek[23] (what is good for) the life of Aššur-nerari, his sons, (and) his magnates, (or else) may Aššur, father of the gods, who grants kingship turn your land into a desert, your people into victims of devastation, your cities into heaps, (and) your house into ruins.

(v.8–15) If Mati᾽-ilu violates this *adê*-oath of Aššur-ne[ra]ri, king of Assyria, may Mati᾽-ilu become a prostitute (and) [his] soldier[s] become women. May they receive [*a gif*]*t* in the square of their city like a prostitute. May one land *push* them

[a] Lev 26:29; Deut 28:53–57; Jer 19:9; Ezek 5:10; 2 Kgs 6:28–29; Lam 2:20; 4:10

[13] Following Parpola and Watanabe (1988:10) in reading [ᵐKI.M]IN (lit. "Mr. Ditto," i.e. Mati᾽-ilu, by which convention Mati᾽-ilu is typically referenced in the text) at the end of line iii 23′, although the subject of the sentence is translated in SAA 2.2 as "you." Note that the reading [ᵐKI.M]IN results in a switch to the 3rd person in a section otherwise entirely in the 2nd person.

[14] Following the suggestion of Parpola and Watanabe (1988:10, n. to line 26) to restore [*lum*]-*nu* at the end of the line.

[15] Cf. § 39 of Esarhaddon's Succession Treaty.

[16] Reading the first three signs of line iv.7 as *ka-bu-ut* after the collation of Borger (1982–1985:156, n. 7a), so also Parpola and Watanabe (1988:11) and Kitchen and Lawrence (2012 1:942). Given the context, the reference is likely not to animal excrement but to stones used for magico-medicinal purposes that were named after animal dung; see *CAD* K s.v. *kabû* A usage b.

[17] Cf. § 47 of Esarhaddon's Succession Treaty.

[18] The orthography departs here from the rest of the text, as preserved, in spelling the word *šumma* with which the stipulations begin as BAD(=*šum*$_4$)-*ma* and not *šúm-ma*.

[19] The text of these lines comes from the small corner fragment published by Millard (1970), while the restoration derives from lines v.14–15 below. The present lines have the variant *tāmītu*, "oath," in place of *adê*, "loyalty-oath," and spell *nihtiṭi* with -*ṭí* and not -*ṭi*.

[20] Following Millard (1970) and later editors in understanding the verb to be a 2 m.s. form of *galû*. The switch from third to second person evidently anticipates the phraseology of the following stipulation.

[21] Despite the absence of the subjunctive marker -*ni* on the infinitive *mu᾽ātka*, "your death," the clause is taken as a "solemn statement" because it is clearly parallel to *balāṭkani*, "your life," in the following line which is marked in the subjunctive.

[22] Weidner (1932–1933a:20) restores *l*[*u-ut-tu*]-*ni*, translating "fürwa[hr erstreb]en." Reiner (1969:533) does not translate the word. Borger (1982–1985:156) translates the word as "suchst" (using the same translation for the verb in v.4) but with no indication of how he reads either. Watanabe and Parpola (1988:13) read and restore *ku-*[*nu*]-*ni*, not translating the word but indexing it under *kuānu*, "to be firm" (p. 92). Kitchen and Lawrence follow Parpola and Watanabe's reading and (lack of) translation. I tentatively read *ku-*[*nu*]-*ni* as well but take *kunnûni* as a D stative 3 m.pl. + subjunctive of *kunnû*, "to cherish."

[23] The reading of the verb as *tú-*[*b*]*a-᾽u-u-ni* follows Parpola and Watanabe 1988:12. I understand the sense of the verb in parallel to § 21 (line 231) of Esarhaddon's Succession Treaty.

to another.[24] [May] Ma[ti᾽-ilu]'s life[25] [be that of] a mule (i.e. childless due to male infertility). May his wives be extremely old (i.e. no longer able to conceive children). May [Ištar, the lad]y of men (and) the mistress of women, take away their 'bow'.[26] May she establish their *shame*.[27] May [their] wee[ping] be bitter as they say "Alas!" and "We violated the *adê*- oath of Aššur-nerari, king of [Assyria]!"

(v.16–19) If Ma[ti᾽-ilu violates thi]s [*adê*-oath] of [Aššur-nērā]rī, king of Assyria [....] (Break of unknown length.)[28]

(v.20′–23′) [...] before the kings [...] *treachery of the gods*[29] [...] each other [....]

(v.24′–27′) If Mati᾽-ilu [violates this] *adê*-oath [...] may his gate be blocked up, and [may] bandits [...] the door(s) of [his] people [...] may they (i.e. the people) sleep[30] [...].

(vi.1–5) [May a swarm of locusts[31] ar]ise and devour his land. [...], and may he gouge out their eyes. May a [city of[32]] one thousand houses turn into (a city of) one house. May one thousand tents turn into one tent. May (only) one man survive within the city in order to sing my praise.

(v.6–26) You are sworn by Aššur, king of heaven and earth. By Anu (and) Antu: Ditto. By Enlil (and) Ninlil:[33] Ditto. By Ea (and) Damkina: Ditto. By Sin (and) Ningal: Ditto. By Šamaš (and) Aya: Ditto. By Adad (and) Šala: Ditto. By Marduk (and) Zarpanitu: Ditto. By Nabû (and) Tašmetu: Ditto. By Ninurta (and) Gula: Ditto. By Uraš (and) Ninegal. By Zababa (and) Baba: Ditto. By Nergal and Laṣ: Ditto. By Madanu (and) Ningirsu: Ditto. By Humhummu (and) Išum: Ditto. By Girra (and) Nusku: Ditto. By Ištar, lady of Nineveh: Ditto. By Ištar, lady of Arbela: Ditto. By Adad of Kurbail: Ditto. By Adad of Aleppo: Ditto. By Palil, who marches in front: Ditto. By the heroic Seven (i.e. the Pleiades): Ditto. By Dagan (and) *Muṣuruna*:[34] Ditto. By M[elqart (and) Esh]mun: Ditto. By Kub[aba (and) Kar]huha: Ditto. By Adad, [DN], and Ramanu of [Damascus: Ditto.] By Za-[...: Ditto.]

(Remainder of column, approximately 50 lines, not preserved)

---

24 Following Parpola and Watanabe (1988:12) in understanding the verb as a precative of *daḫu*, a sparsely attested verb, so also Kitchen and Lawrence 2012 1:944. Weidner (1932–1933a:22, n. 35) suggests *ṭehû*; cf. Pomponio (1990:53): "Il paesi contro il paesi si accosti (ostilmente)." Reiner (1969:533) does not translate the verb. Borger (1982–1985:157, n. 10a) suggests *lid-din-?*

25 Following Parpola and Watanabe (1988:12) in reading TI as *balāṭu*, "life," so also Kitchen and Lawrence 2012 1:944, though note that in the previous section *balāṭu* is written logographically as TI.LA. Weidner (1932–1933a:22) takes *-ti* with the previous signs to form a Babylonian 3 m.pl. accusative suffix, otherwise unattested in this text, which is in general in the Assyrian dialect. Reiner (1969:533) seems to agree with Weidner as she supplies an antecedent to *ša*, translating "(seed) of M," so also Borger (1982–1985:157): "(Der Same)" and the reading in *CAD* K s.v. *kudānu* usage b-3′ ([... *-š*]*u* ANŠE.GÌR.NUN.NA[sic!], "let his [seed] be a mule's"). Cf. also the translation of Pomponio (1990:53): "Lo stesso (sia) un mulo." Parpola and Watanabe (1988:12) translate "may Mati᾽-ilu's (sex) life be that of a mule," so also Kitchen and Lawrence 2012 1:944, but it is difficult to find a precise parallel for this use of *balāṭu*. Perhaps the comparison to a mule is meant to invoke less "(sex) life," i.e. a life in which sex does not lead to procreation, and more the "lifetime" of a mule, i.e. a lifetime spent without children. In any event, the point of the curse is clearly male infertility; cf. the parallel in § 66 of Esarhaddon's Succession Treaty, as noted by Watanabe (1987:199).

26 Watanabe (1987:194) cites this line as a parallel to § 48 of Esarhaddon's Succession Treaty ("May Ištar, lady of battle and war, smash your bow in the thick of ba[ttle]"). However, in the Mati᾽-ilu treaty, the verb is not *šebēru*, "to break," but *ekēmu*, "to deprive," and *qaštu*, "bow," is better understood here as a euphemism for the penis, so already *CAD* E s.v. *ekēmu* usage e, and see Biggs Šaziga 37 No. 18:3 cited *CAD* Q s.v. *qaštu* mng. 1f for a parallel ("May the quiver not be empty, may the bow not be slack"). A euphemistic use of "bow" is supported both by Ištar's epithets in the immediate passage and by the larger context of the curses, and cf. a similar use of "bowstring" in Esarhaddon's Succession Treaty (4.36).

27 Tentatively reading the direct object as [*l*]*a*[?] ⸢*bal*⸣*-tu-šú-nu*. Weidner (1932–1933a:22) reads the object of *liškun* as [*n*]*a-pal-tu-šu-nu*, translating "Vernichtung," but observing that (22, n. 41) "[*pa*]*p-pal-tu*, 'Sperma' würde besser in den Zusammenhang passen; nach Meissner dann vielleicht zu übersetzen: 'ihr Sperma möge sie hinlegen' (so dass es nicht wirken kann)." However, I do not know a form of that noun with the feminine *-t*, it being attested to my knowledge only as *papallu*. Reiner (1969:533) translates "their [ster]ility," but does not give any indication of how she is reading the signs in question. Borger (1982–1985) does not translate the word. Parpola and Watanabe (1988:12) read [x]x *bal-tú-šú-nu*. Von Soden (1991:188) suggests reading [*n*]*a*[!]*-pùl-tú-šú-nu*, translating "[Issar] moge ihr Leben (zur Ausloschung) 'hinlegen'!" My suggestion to read the first damaged sign as [*l*]*a*[?] goes against Weidner's copy (1932–1933a:25), which shows the tail of a Winkelhaken coming out of the break, but does not seem impossible according to the traces of the sign visible in the published photograph.

28 The following two sections are known from a fragment published by Parpola and Watanabe (1988:123).

29 The syntactic relationship, if any, between *sarti* and DINGIR.MEŠ is presumably genitival, cf. Parpola and Watanabe's (1988:12) translation, "a divine punishment," so also Kitchen and Lawrence 2012 1:945. Their translation "punishment" seems to derive from NA legal documents in which *sartu* designates a penalty or guarantee, see Radner 1997:175–176, but it is questionable whether that context is appropriate here.

30 Understanding the final *-a* on the verb as the 3 f.pl. suffix (the subject being *nišu*, "people," in the preceding line). Cf. Parpola and Watanabe (1988:13), who translate "may he sleep," taking the *-a* as the ventive, so also Kitchen and Lawrence (2012 1:947).

31 Following the restoration of Reiner (1969:533), so also Parpola and Watanabe (1988:13) and Kitchen and Lawrence (2012 1:946).

32 Following the restoration of Parpola and Watanabe (1988:13), so also Kitchen and Lawrence (2012 1:946). The restoration of a word at the beginning of the line is required by the line spacing.

33 Or *Mullissu* if the name is normalized into the Assyrian dialect, as done by Parpola and Watanabe (1988:13). But the Babylonian form *tummâtūnu* may suggest that the Babylonian dialect is more appropriate here.

34 Parpola and Watanabe (1988:13 note to line v.21) observe that "The determinative actually does look more like UR[U] as copied by Weidner, but the reading ⸢d⸣ also seems within possibilities and has been adopted in view of the continuation. The next sign is either [*m*]*u* or [*š*]*e*. Watanabe suggests that the name be connected with KUR *mu-ṣu-ru-na*," a mountain probably near the Phoenician coast (Bagg 2007:180). Cf. Lipiński (2000:613) who reads UR[U *M*]*u-ṣur-u-na*, understanding a qualification of the preceding divine name, i.e. "Dagan of (the city of) Muṣuruna."

REFERENCES

Parpola and Watanabe 1988; Weidner 1932–1933a.

ESARHADDON'S TREATY WITH BAAL, KING OF TYRE (4.35)

Jacob Lauinger

Esarhaddon's treaty with the Phoenician king Baal of Tyre was most likely established in or around the year 677 BCE. In that year, Esarhaddon's inscriptions narrate how, the Assyrian ruler gave two erstwhile Sidonian cities to Baal, the king of Tyre in the wake putting down a rebellion by the king of Sidon (RINAP 4.1, iii.15–17). The favorable trade concessions that Baal receives in this treaty acquire greater significance when understood to be at Sidonian expense, and thus it is likely that the Tyrian king swore the *adê*-oath at this time even if no extant inscriptions mention the event (Parpola and Watanabe 1988:xxix). In 671 with the aid of the Kushite king Taharqa, Baal attempted to throw off the Assyrian yoke and was defeated (RINAP 4.31, r.1′–11′ and 34, 12′–18′; on the career of Baal of Tyre, see Lipiński 1999).

This particular *adê*-oath is unique among the extant examples for its stipulations concerning commerce. These stipulations reflect, of course, the famed mercantile abilities of the Phoenicians. Esarhaddon's treaty with Baal of Tyre, then, demonstrates that the Assyrian kings might impose *adê*-oaths particular in their substance to individual oath takers as well as more general oaths of loyalty that could be imposed upon any given client king or even the entire populace (e.g. Esarhaddon's Succession Treaty, 4.36; cf. McCarthy 1981:121, n. 51).

The text of the treaty is known from a single four-column tablet found at Nineveh. The tablet is poorly preserved, with only its upper third remaining; Parpola and Watanabe (1988:xlvii) estimate that 75%–80% of the text is now missing. Having an arrangement of columns and lines similar to Aššur-nerari V's treaty with Mati᾿-ilu (4.33), it is clear that the tablet is not an official "*adê*-tablet" (see *ṭuppi adê* in the introduction to Esarhaddon's Succession Treaty, 4.36), but rather a copy of such a text written by the Assyrian chancellery and stored at Nineveh. A notation on the tablet's upper edge describing its contents as "Tablet of an *adê*-oath that was established. Made by (lit. that of) Baal, the Tyrian" (see n. 16 below). This description implies that the tablet originally contained the entire text of Baal's *adê*-oath and not an excerpt.

(Col. i)
(i.1–4) [The *ad*]*ê*-oath of Esarhaddon, k[ing] of Assyria, son of [Sennacherib, also king of Assyria with Baa]l, king of Tyre, with [PN, *his son, and his other sons and grandsons*, (and) with al]l [Tyrians, men of his hands], great and small [...].[1] (Break of unknown length.)
(i.5′–8′) [...] or [...] or [...] or with [...] not [...]. If [you/he do/does] not[2] [...].
(i.10′–12′) If Ass[yria ...] you[r ... ...]
(Remainder of column not preserved)

(Col. ii)[3]
(7 lines missing)
(ii.8–12) [... ... a]ccording to [...] may [... ...].
(ii.13–14) [... concer]ning the exe[mpt ....]
(Remainder of column – at least 20 lines – note preserved)

(Col. iii)
(iii.1′–6′) [... ...] their [...]s, Esarhaddon, king of As[syria ... ... Ty]re concerning [....] Neither send nor dis[patch ... to th]ese [...]s (or) these cities which I destroyed [... ... (and) to which] they will come.
(iii.6′–14′) [If the royal deputy whom] I have appointed [o]ver you [...]s something to/for you in [...], (and) the elders of your land [...] *when*

[1] The restoration of these lines derives from the opening of Esarhaddon's Succession Treaty, as seems likely from the preservation of TUR GAL, literally "small (and) great" in line 3. A significant difference between the two openings, however, lies in the presence of the determinative for male personal names following Baal of Tyre's name in line 2 (see already the translation of SAA 2.5, "... [with Baa]l, king of Tyre, with [..., *his son, and his other sons and grandsons*]"). The presence of this sign means that Baal's name was followed by the name of another person, most likely the Tyrian king's heir, in contrast to the various tablets of Esarhaddon's Succession Treaty from Nimrud, which identify only the individual Median city lords by name and leave their sons and grandsons anonymous.

[2] Akk. *šúm-ma la* [...], but likely not a "solemn statement," as positive stipulations are formed in this text by statements in the present indicative and negative stipulations by prohibitives. This stipulation and the one that follows are from Sm. 964, a "small chip." For the identification and placement of fragment, see Parpola and Watanabe 1988:xlvii and 24 note to the lines although the reasoning for its placement is not explicit. The notation (+) signifies that a physical join is lacking.

[3] The estimation of missing lines and the readings of individual signs in this column follow the collations of Parpola and Watanabe (1988:24).

[*giving*] *advice*,[4] (then) the royal delegate will [sit] with them. [...] of the boats [... ...] of [.... If ...] which comes before you,[5] do not listen to it. If without the royal delegate [...],[6] and do not open (it) a letter that I send to you without the royal delegate. If the royal delegate is not on hand, you will wait for him (and then) open (the letter) or a messenger [...].[7]

(iii.15′–17′) If there is a ship of Baal or of the people of Tyre that is shipwrecked in the land of Philistia or the entire territory of Assyria, everything that is on the ship belongs to Esarhaddon, king of Assyria. But none of the people who are on the ship may be harmed! They will return *to their land*.[8]

(iii.18′–22′) These are the ports and roads (for trade) which Esarhaddon, king of Assyria, assi[gned] to his servant Baal:[9] (The roads) to Akko (and) Dor; al[l] (the ports) in the district of the land of Philistia; and al[l] (the ports) in the cities of the territory of Assyria which is seacoast; and (the port) in Byblos; (as for) Mount Lebanon, all of the cities which are in the mountains, as many cities [that Esa]rhaddon, king of Assyria (has), Baal [may enter] the cities.

(iii.23′–28′) According to that which Esarhaddon gave [to him (i.e. Baal)], the Tyrians are (i.e. remain) in their boats. All who enter[10] [and ...] in the settlements of [PN], (that is) his cities, his villages, (or) his ports which are for raising [...],[11] no matter how many are his associates,[12] just as in the past, [they will be .... Although] they will be denounced,[13] nobody may [do] a wrong (and) injure [the people] on their ships.

(iii.28′–30′) In the la[nd of *Baal*],[14] in his districts (and) his villages, just as in the past, the Sido[nians ...]

(Remainder of column not preserved)

(Col. iv)

(iv.1′) [May Mullissu who dwells in Nineveh bind a flaming iron sword to you.]

(iv.2′) [May] Ištar who [dwells in Arbela not look mercifully or favorably a]t you.

---

4 Akk.: *ina mil-˹ki˺* [...]. Parpola and Watanabe (1988:25) translate "the elders of your country [*convene to take*] counsel," so also Kitchen and Lawrence (2012 1:959), but it seems difficult to construe a sense of purpose with *ina*. I understand the preposition to have a temporal sense, but cf. Borger's translation, "mit *Rat*" (1982–1985:158).

5 Because of the verb (*ta-lak-an-ni*), the antecedent of the relative pronoun and subject of "come" must be feminine. Parpola and Watanabe look back to the mention of ships in line 9′ in their translation "[You may not ... any ship ...] which comes to you" (1988:25, so also Kitchen and Lawrence 2012 1:959). Or possibly *egirtu*, "letter"? Cf. line 13′.

6 Akk. *˹šúm˺-ma ba-la-at* ^{lú}*[*qe*]*-e-bi* [x x x x], with the estimate of missing signs following Parpola and Watanabe 1988:25. The syntax is difficult. As the text does not formulate stipulations with *šumma*, we should have a straightforward conditional statement. The estimated four signs missing at the end of the line would seem then to comprise an apodosis that is coordinated with line 13′ (is *balāt qēpi* then repeated for emphasis?).

7 Borger (1956:108) first read *ú-la-a ina lìb(?)-bi(?)* x x, similarly Weidner (1932–1933c:31), but later translated only "oder [...]." Reiner (1969:534) seems to understand a prohibitive, translating the end of the line with the preceding verbs as "wait for him and then open it, [do] not ...." Parpola and Watanabe (1988:25) read the final four signs after *ú-la-a* as ^{lú}*A.˹KIN x˺. As, according to their collation, there is room for only one sign at the end of the line and we expect a verb following *ūlā*, read perhaps ˹DU˺ for *illak*?

8 Following Parpola and Watanabe (1988:25) in reading the end of line as *˹i-na* KUR˺*-šú-nu ú-sa-ḫu-˹ru˺*, so also Kitchen and Lawrence (2012 1:958). For *suḫḫuru* with the preposition *ina*, cf. LUGAL *be-lí ina*^{uru}*ku-me lu-sa-ḫi-ir-šú-nu*, "Let the king, my lord, return them (Kummaean scouts) to Kumme" (*SAA* 5.105, obv. 24–25).

9 In the lines that follow, the geographical areas are preceded by either the preposition *ana* ("to") or *ina* ("in"). I understand *ana* to indicate Tyrian access to roads *to* various urban centers (the *ḫūlu* of line iii.18′) and *ina* to indicate their access to ports *in* various urban centers (i.e. both prepositions refer back to the "ports and roads" mentioned in the section's opening line). This interpretation is supported by the specification in line iii.20′, where the preposition *ina* appears, that the relevant Assyrian cities are on the seacoast.

10 Akk. *e-˹rab˺-u-ni*, following the collation of Parpola and Watanabe (1988:27), so also Kitchen and Lawrence (2012 1:960). Borger (1956:107) reads *e(?)-bur(?)-u-ni*, translating "hinüberfahren," see also Reiner's (1969:534) translation "cross over." The expected form is *ebbiruni*, however, and Borger (1982–1985:159, n. 24′a) later suggested *iš(?)-pur-u-ni*, translating "(so viel wie) er *geschickt hat*."

11 Parpola and Watanabe (1988:27) estimate that seven signs are lost at the end of this line, enough for both a noun in the genitive following *ana naše*, "for raising" and a second verb in the subjunctive governed, like *errabuni*, by *ammar*, "All who" (line 24′). Parpola and Watanabe suggest restoring [*toll*] as the object of "to raise," but this restoration goes against the sense of the stipulation as I understand it: Baal has been granted the right to trade with the settlements of [PN], but his men are to stay on the ships while they are docked and are not to enter the settlements. Cf. the episode at Dor in *The Report of Wenamun* (see *COS* 1.41)

12 Following Reiner (1969:534, n. 1) in reading the beginning of the line as *am-mar a-ḫi-ta-te-šú-nu-u-ni*. Reiner understands the plural form of *aḫītu* to signify the "outskirts of a city" (*CAD* A/1 s.v. *aḫītu* mng. 4b), and so translates "as many as lie in the outlying regions," referring to the preceding "cities, villages, (or) ports," so also Parpola and Watanabe (1988:27) and Kitchen and Lawrence (2012 1:961). But, as the previous line ended with a clause-final subjunctive verb (no longer preserved, see the previous note), this line should begin a new clause. Therefore, it seems better to translate *aḫītu* with the sense of "persons attached to a group" (*CAD* A/1 s.v. *aḫītu* mng. 5) and understand the word to refer to the Tyrians who violated the stipulation by leaving their ship while in port.

13 Taking *in-na-˹ga˺-ru-u-ni* as an N present (durative) of *nagāru*. Borger (1956:109), *AHw*/1 16a, and Parpola and Watanabe (1988:27) take the verb as an N present of *agāru*, but this interpretation does not fit the context, as the Tyrians are explicitly stipulated to remain *on* their boats so as to not interact with the local populace; cf. *CAD* M/1 s.v. *magāru* discussion which sees "an irregular form of *magāru* (for *immaggaruni* or the like) or of *nagāru*, q.v. rather than the passive of *agāru*, 'to hire,' cf. also *CAD* N/1 s.v. *nagāru* usage b. Kitchen and Lawrence (2012 1:960–961) opt for *magāru* but their translation "as in the past they agreed" obscures the text missing from the end of line 26′. Because the verb is in the subjunctive, we expect the final signs of line 26′ to provide a subordinating conjunction if it is not governed by *kī ša* appearing earlier in that line (so Kitchen and Lawrence [2012 1:961]). Perhaps restore at the end of the line [... *a-ki*]?

14 Restoring *ina* ŠÀ K[UR ^{m}*ba-a-lu*] at the end of line iii.28′, cf. *ina* ŠÀ URU.MEŠ *šá* ^{m}˹x x x˺ (iii.24′), "in the cities of [PN]." As lines iii.23′–28′ seem to stipulate the behavior of Tyrian merchants abroad (in Sidon?), so do lines iii.28′–30′ (+ additional lines now lost) seem to stipulate Tyrian behavior toward Sidonian merchants in Tyre.

(iv.3′–4′) [May] Gula, the [great] physician [place sickness (and) fatigue in yo]ur [heart (and) a persistent sore on you[r] body. Bathe in [blood and pus as if in water]!
(iv.5′) May the Seven (i.e. the Pleiades), the heroic gods, [devastate y]ou with their [terrible] weapons.
(iv.6′–7′) [May] Bethel (and) Anath-Bethel [deliver y]ou into the paws of a devouring lion.[15]
(iv.8′–9′) May the great gods of heaven and earth, the gods of Assyria, the gods of Akkad, and the gods of "Across-the-River" (i.e. Syria) curse you with a curse than cannot be lifted.
(iv.10′–13′) May Baal Shamem, Baal Malage, (and) Baal Saphon raise an evil wind against your ships. May it (i.e. the wind) loosen their moorings. May they (i.e. the gods) rip up their mooring post. May a mighty wave sink them (i.e. the ships) in the sea. May a fearful swell surge over you.
(iv.14′–17′) May Melqart (and) Eshmun hand over your land to destruction (and) your people to deportation. [May] they [tear] you from your land. May they destroy the food in your mouth, the clothing on your body (and) the oil when you anoint yourself.
(iv.18′–19′) May Astarte break your bow in a dangerous battle. May she place you at the fee[t of your enemy]. May some foreign enemy distribute [your] possess[ions] (i.e. among his troops as plunder).
(iv.20′–21′) Tablet of an *adê*-oath that was established. Made by (lit. that of) Baal, the Tyrian.[16] In/when [...].

[15] The restorations of the curses here and above in this column derive from Esarhaddon's Succession Treaty (§ 50–55), in which the same curses appear in the same order (although note that curses found there invoking Aramis, Addu and Šala of Kurba'il, Šarrat-Ekron, and Kubaba and Karhuha of Carchemish are absent here). Undoubtedly, at least some of the curses in the immediately preceding sections of Esarhaddon's Succession Treaty occupied much of the approximately 50–60 lines that are missing from column iv. Note that the curses preserved here are directed against a plural object (i.e. the 2 m.pl. suffix *-kunu* is used) despite the fact that the stipulations in column iii are in the singular (i.e. "you (s.) must not ...").

[16] Akk.: 20′ *ṭup-pi a-d*[*e*]*-e kun-nu šá* {m}*ba-a-lu* KUR *ṣu*[*r-ra-a-a*] 21′ (uninscribed space) *ina* [x x x] (line 21′ was identified by Parpola and Watanabe after collation during the preparation of their 1988 edition, and so the line does not appear in earlier treatments). The word *kunnu* should not be a Babylonian verbal adjective of *kunnu* modifying *adê*, eg. "tablet with the established (text of the) sworn agreement with Baal (the ruler of Tyre)" (*CAD* K s.v. *kunnu* adj), because it does not agree in number with *adê* (for the Babylonian dialect elsewhere in the curse section, note the D precative *liza''iza* in the previous line). An adjective *kunnu* could modify *ṭuppi* but the resulting translation makes little sense. I understand it to be a Babylonian stative in the subjunctive for an asyndetic relative construction with *adê*. The phrase *ṭup-pi a-d*[*e*]*-e kun-nu*, "tablet of an *adê*-oath that was established" may have served as a descriptive label on this chancellery copy with the following phrase *ša Ba-a-lu* KUR *Ṣu*[*r-ra-a-a*] designating the oath-taker and a final phrase (preserved only as *ina* [...] in our text) designating the time or place of the oath.

REFERENCES

Parpola and Watanabe 1988 (SAA 2.5); Weidner 1932–1933c.

ESARHADDON'S SUCCESSION TREATY (4.36)

Jacob Lauinger

In early May 672 BCE, Esarhaddon, king of Assyria, (680–669 BCE) required all the subjects of the Assyrian empire – not just those living in Assyria and its provinces but also the subjects of its client kingdoms – to swear an *adê*-oath promising to uphold the succession of his son Aššurbanipal to the throne of Assyria (and, in somewhat more muted fashion the succession of Aššurbanipal's brother Šamaš-šumu-ukin to the throne of Babylonia). The oath itself was most likely sworn by the various officials, governors, and client kings on behalf of their subject populaces, but the oath ceremony was still probably a lavish affair lasting a number of days. The decision to undertake this massive enterprise may have been motivated by the king's ill health or by memories of his own troubles succeeding to the throne of his father, especially as his new heir was, as Esarhaddon himself had been, a younger son. Or the Assyrian king may simply have been following a standard protocol.

Among the extant Neo-Assyrian *adê*-oaths, the so-called Esarhaddon's Succession Treaty (also known as the "Vassal Treaties of Esarhaddon") is noteworthy for several reasons. One is simply the text's length and state of preservation. Consisting of approximately 670 lines and almost completely preserved, our access to Esarhaddon's Succession Treaty underscores what a small percentage of text remains of the other Neo-Assyrian *adê*-oaths.

A second noteworthy feature is that the text is known from multiple manuscripts (mss). Most of these come from Max Mallowan's excavations at the Assyrian city of Nimrud (ancient Kalhu), where in 1955 the excavators discovered over 350 cuneiform fragments in the throne room of the Temple of Nabu (see Wiseman 1959 for the *editio princeps*). These fragments have been reconstituted into eight or nine original manuscripts,[1] all of which record the

[1] On this question, see the discussion of Farber (1990:163).

adê-oaths of client kings who ruled in an area of Assyria's eastern periphery associated with Media in antiquity (hence these client kings' conventional moniker of "Median vassals" in the literature). Three other fragments of the text come from Walter Andrae's early excavations at the city of Assur, with detailed information on their find-spots unfortunately lacking (see Weidner 1939 for an edition of one and now Frahm 2009: No. 70–71 for editions of the other two). It is unclear whether these three fragments derive from one, two, or three mss. Finally in 2009, the Tayinat Archaeological Project under the direction of Timothy Harrison discovered another copy of Esarhaddon's Succession Treaty together with a small group Mesopotamian scholarly texts lying *in situ* on a raised platform in the inner sanctum of a temple at Kunulua, (modern Tell Tayinat), capital of the Neo-Assyrian province of Pattina/Unqi (see Lauinger 2012 for an edition of the text and Harrison and Osborne 2012 for the tablet's archaelogical context).

The third noteworthy feature of Esarhaddon's Succession Treaty is that the copies from Nimrud and Tayinat (those from Assur are too fragmentary for conclusions) are not copies of the Assyrian chancellery like the other extant *adê*-texts but rather are *ṭuppi adê*, the "*adê*-tablet(s)" on which each oath-taker had his *adê*-oath officially inscribed. All of these tablets are sealed with three divine seals of the Assyrian national god Aššur, one dating to the Old Assyrian period, the second to the Middle Assyrian period, and the third to Esarhaddon's father, Sennacherib. This third seal in particular bears a caption describing it as the Assyrian national god Aššur's Seal of Destinies. Because the *ṭuppi adê* were sealed with this seal, they actually became Tablets of Destinies and the stipulations inscribed on them now transformed into the oath takers' immutable destiny (George 1986).

Unusually for cuneiform tablets, which are typically rotated along the horizontal axis, the *ṭuppi adê* need to be rotated along the vertical axis, like turning the pages of a book, in order for a reader to move from the obverse to reverse. Watanabe (1988) has observed that if one of these tablets was positioned in an upright fashion, this arrangement would allow them, at least in theory, to continue to read the text by walking around the tablet. And, indeed, the tablet from Tayinat seems to confirm Watanabe's suggestion as it "was found face down on the podium with its reverse facing up … and was aligned with the temple's north and west walls, only a short distance from the north wall. These circumstances suggest a scenario in which the oath tablet was originally displayed in an upright position on its lower edge in front of the temple's northern wall only to topple forward during the temple's destruction" (Lauinger 2011:12).

Historical circumstances suggest that Judah, like the Median client kingdoms, was required to swear an *adê*-oath to Esarhaddon or another Assyrian king, and the influence of Esarhaddon's Succession Treaty on the Book of Deuteronomy has been felt since the paradigmatic early studies by Frankena (1965) and Weinfeld (1972). For a more recent discussion citing much earlier literature, see Levinson 2010; for a counterbalancing view, see Holloway 2007.

The different manuscripts of Esarhaddon's Succession Treaty contain hundreds of textual variations, including many of a minor orthographic (e.g. UŠ-*ti* = *ridûti* against UŠ-*te* = *ridûte*) or lexical (e.g. *ṭābtu*, "pleasant" against *damiqtu*, "good") nature. While such variants have the potential to greatly aid our understanding of the circumstances in which the text was composed and transmitted, such potential can only be realized by systematic study both within and across mss. In the notes to the translation below, I restrict my comments to those variants that are in my opinion of more immediate significance.

(Caption):[2] The unalterable seal of Aššur, king of the gods, lord of the lands, the incontestable seal of the great prince, the father of the gods.

§1 The *adê*-oath of Esarhaddon, king of Assyria, son of Sennacherib, king of Assyria, with the governor of Kunalia, with the deputy, the majordomo, the scribes, the chariot drivers, the third men, the village managers, the information officers, the prefects, the cohort commanders, the charioteers, the cavalrymen, the exempt, the outriders, the specialists, the shi[eld bearers (?)], the craftsmen, and with [all] the men [of his hands], great and small, as many as there are – [wi]th them and with the men who are born after the *adê*-oath in the [f]uture, from the east to the west, all those over whom Esarhaddon, king of Assyria, exercises kingship and lordship, concerning Aššurbanipal, the great crown prince designate,[3] the son of Esarhaddon, king of Assyria, on whose behalf he established the *adê*-oath with you,[4]

2 The caption is written in a single horizontal line across the very top of the obverse. It identifies the seal impressions with which the tablets are sealed (see the Introduction to the text).

3 The translation of Aššurbanipal's title follows that of Watanabe and Parpola 1988, itself an adaptation of Reiner 1969. Literally, the title translates as "great crown prince of the House of Succession." The House of Succession was the name given to the palace in which the heir to the Assyrian throne resided and helped administer the kingdom for his father.

4 The Nimrud mss featuring the Median city lords have a somewhat different opening, e.g. "The *adê*-oath of Esarhaddon, king of Assyria, son of Sennacherib, king of Assyria, with Ramataya, city lord of Urakazabanu, with his sons (and) grandsons, (and) with the all the men of his hands, great and small, as many as there are" before continuing as in ms T. Note, however, that only one ms from Nimrud includes the specification also in ms T at the end of the section (lines 11–12) that the *adê*-oath specifically concerns Aššurbanipal. In these two mss the lines in this section are also ordered somewhat differently than in those mss that lack the concluding statement.

§ 2 (which) he confirmed, made, and established with you[5] before Jupiter, Venus, Saturn, Mercury, Mars and Sirius, before Aššur, Anu, Enlil,[6] Ea, Sin, Šamaš, Adad, Marduk, Ninlil, Šerua, Belet-ili, Ištar of Nineveh, Ištar of Arbail, the gods who dwell in heaven and earth, the gods of Assyria, the gods of Sumer and Akkad, and the gods of all the lands.

§ 3 Swe[ar one by one] by Aššur, father of the gods, lord of the lands![7] Ditto: By Anu, Enlil, and Ea! Ditto: By Sin, Šamaš, Adad, and Marduk! Ditto: By Nabu, Nusku, Uraš, and Nergal! Ditto: By Ninlil, Šerua, and Belet-ili! Ditto: By Ištar of Nineveh and Ištar of Arbail! Ditto: By all the gods of the Inner City! Ditto: By all the gods of Nineveh! Ditto: By all the gods of Kalhu! Ditto: By all the gods of Arbail! Ditto: By all the gods of Kilizi! Ditto: By all the gods of Harran! Ditto: By all of the Assyrian gods! Ditto: By the gods of the cities of Babylon, Borsippa, and Nippur! Ditto: By all of the Sumerian and Akkadian gods! Ditto: By all the gods of the lands! Ditto: By all the gods of heaven and earth! Ditto: By all of the [go]ds of his land and his district![8]

§ 4 (This is) the *adê*-oath which Esarhaddon, king of Assyria, established with you before the great gods of heaven and earth concerning Aššurbanipal, the great crown prince designate, son of Esarhaddon, king of Assyria, your lord, who called his (i.e. Aššurbanipal's) name and appointed him as the designated crown prince:

When Esarhaddon, king of Assyria, passes away, you shall seat Aššurbanipal, the great crown prince designate, on the throne of kingship.[9] He shall exercise the kingship and lordship of Assyria over you. You shall guard him in both country and town. You shall do battle concerning him,[10] and you shall die (if necessary). You shall speak with him from the truth of your heart. You shall provide him with good advice wholeheartedly. You shall establish a good path for his feet. You shall not remove him from office. You shall not install (one) of his brothers, older or younger, in his place on the throne of Assyria in his place. You shall not change (nor) alter the word of Esarhaddon, king of Assyria. Aššurbanipal, the great crown prince designate of Esarhaddon, king of Assyria[11] – this is the one you shall obey. He shall exercise the kingship and lordship of Assyria over you.

§ 5 You shall protect Aššurbanipal, the great crown prince designate, whom Esarhaddon, king of Assyria, appointed for you and ordered for you, and concerning whom he confirmed and established an *adê*-oath with you. You shall not do him wrong. You shall not raise your hands for evil against him. You shall not undertake machinations, a revolt, (or) anything malicious and harmful. You shall not remove him from the kingship of Assyria. You shall not help (one) of his brothers, older or younger, take the throne of Assyria in his place. You shall not place a different king (or) a different lord over yourselves. You shall not swear an oath to a different king (or) a different lord.

§ 6 If you hear something harmful, ugly (or) inappropriate about the exercise of kingship – (some-

---

5 Despite the ruling separating this section from the previous one, the three verbs *udanninuni iṣbatu iškununi* are subordinate to the relative pronoun *ša* in line 1, cf. Parpola and Watanabe 1988:xxxvi. Ms T confirms the existence of three not two verbs, as in Parpola and Watanabe (1988:29), *contra* the earlier reconstruction of the end of the section by Watanabe (1987:59 and 178). For a discussion of uses of the derived adjective of the first verb, *danānu*, in connection to oaths, see Watanabe (1987:179), and note in particular the Neo-Assyrian locution *uppu dannutu*, lit. "strong tablet," used to designate a valid legal document. The final verb *šakānu* seems to be the standard Neo-Assyrian verb used to designate the conclusion of an *adê*-oath and thus the creation of the bond between the two parties, while the second verb *ṣabātu* is the Neo-Babylonian equivalent of Neo-Assyrian *šakānu* in this context (Parpola and Watanabe 1988:29 note to line 24). Note in particular that this verb is written in the Babylonian dialect without the Assyrian subjunctive marker *-ni* found on the other two verbs.

6 In this section, I render divine names conventionally instead of providing their Neo-Assyrian equivalences, e.g. Illil for dEN.LÍL or Mullissu for dNIN.LÍL.

7 Akk. *dAš-šur* AD DINGIR.MEŠ EN KUR.KUR *ti-t[am-ma-a]*. Frankena (1965:127) suggests restoring *tam-[mu]* at the end of this line for the Assyrian D stative 3 mpl of *tamû*, "you are sworn," in which he is followed by Reiner (1969:534). This interpretation depends on Wiseman's (1959:31) original interpretation of the sign *-ti* that immediately precedes *tam-* as a phonetic complement to KUR.KUR, i.e. KUR.KUR-*ti* for *mātāti*. However, Borger (1961:176) observes that logographic writings of *mātāti* are not written in the text with a phonetic complement, implying that the sign TI is better taken with the following *tam-*. Watanabe (1987:178) develops this point, suggests restoring *ti-tam-[ma-a]* for a Gtn imperative 2 cpl of *tamû*, with the Gtn stem having a distributive sense, and this restoration is followed here, so also Parpola and Watanabe (1988:30) and Kitchen and Lawrence (2012 1:964). Though one recalls the stative form *tummâtunu* in a similar context in line vi.6 of Aššur-nerari V's treaty with Mati᾽-ilu of Arpad (4.34), the limited space available here seems to rule out the restoration of a stative form *ti-tam-[ma-tu-nu]* or *ti-tam-[ma-ku-nu]* in the Babylonian or Assyrian dialects, respectively.

8 The final injunction, with its interesting pairing of a 2 ms possessive pronominal suffix with the 2 cpl imperative, is present only in two of four extant mss. The order of the final five injunctions also diverges among the mss.

9 Stipulations are rendered here as "solemn statements" consisting of the negation particle + present tense subjunctive verb for a positive statement (with the negation particle removed for a negative statement following the logic of the formula, see Parpola and Watanabe 1988:xl and note especially the variant mss cited there in which e.g. the solemn statement *lā tušaṣbatāni* is replaced by the indicative verb *tušaṣbatā*).

10 The verb *ta-ma-ḫaṣ-a-ni*, "to strike, battle," can also be read *ta-ma-qut-a-ni* "to fall," and the signs are so read by Borger (1982–1985:161); Parpola and Watanabe (1988:30); and Kitchen and Lawrence (2012 1:967). But note the parallel line 230 where the variant *la ta-ma[ḫ-ḫaṣ-a-ni]* appearing in one of the fragments from Assur seems to establish that the verb in question is *mahāṣu* (Watanabe 1987:178).

11 Two of five extant mss add the verb *ukallimukanuni* after "Esarhaddon, king of Assyria," which transforms the *ša* following "Aššurbanipal, the great crown prince designate" from a determinative pronoun into a relative pronoun, i.e. "Aššurbanipal, the great crown prince designate whom Esarhaddon, king of Assyria, appointed for you."

thing) which is inappropriate and malicious with regard to Aššurbanipal, the great crown prince designate – whether from the mouth of his brothers, his uncles, his cousins, (or) his family, the seed of his father's house, or from the mouth of the magnates (or) governors, or from the mouth of bearded courtiers (or) eunuchs, or from the mouth of the scholars or from the mouth of anyone at all, you shall not conceal (it). You shall come and tell (it) to Aššurbanipal, the great crown prince designate.

§ 7 If Esarhaddon, king of Assyria, should die while his sons are young,[12] you shall help Aššurbanipal, the great crown prince designate, take the throne of Assyria. You shall install Šamaš-šumu-ukin, his *beloved brother*,[13] the crown prince designate of Babylon, on the throne of kingship of Babylon. You shall put the kingship of Sumer and Akkad, of Karduniaš[14] in its entirety under his control. He shall take all the gifts that Esarhaddon, king of Assyria, his father, gave to him. You shall not hold one thing back.

§ 8 You shall be loyal and sincere with Aššurbanipal, the great crown prince designate, whom Esarhaddon, king of Assyria, appointed for you, and with his brothers, sons of the great crown prince designate Aššurbanipal's mother, on whose behalf Esarhaddon, king of Assyria, established the *adê*-oath with you. You shall always serve them with righteousness and propriety. You shall speak with them from the truth of your heart. You shall protect them in both country to town

§ 9 You shall not wrong Aššurbanipal, the great crown designate whom Esarhaddon, king of Assyria, ordered for you, (or) his brothers, sons of the great crown prince designate Aššurbanipal's mother, concerning whom he (i.e. Esarhaddon) established the *adê*-oath with you. You shall not raise your hands for evil against him. You shall not undertake machinations, a revolt, (or) anything malicious.

§ 10 If you hear something malicious, harmful (or) ugly – (something) [*which*][15] is inappropriate and malicious concerning Aššurbanipal, the great crown prince designate, son of Esarhaddon, king of Assyria, your lord – whether from the mouth of his enemy or the mouth of his friend or from the mouth of his brothers, his uncles, his cousins (or) his family, the seed of his father's house, or from the mouth of your brothers, your sons, (or) your daughters, or from the mouth of a prophet, an ecstatic, (or) an interpreter of oracles,[16] or from the mouth of anyone at all, you shall not conceal (it). You shall come and tell (it) to Aššurbanipal, the great crown prince designate.

§ 11 You shall not do (something) malicious (or) harmful to Aššurbanipal, the great crown prince designate, whom Esarhaddon, king of Assyria ordered for you. You shall not seize and kill him. You shall not give him to his enemy. You shall not remove him from the kingship of Assyria. You shall not swear an oath to another king (or) another lord.

§ 12 If anyone speaks to you of a revolt (or) rebellion in which Aššurbanipal, son of Esarhaddon, king of Assyria, your lord, concerning whom he (i.e. Esarhaddon) established the *adê*-oath with you, is to be killed, (…), murdered, (or) eliminated, or if you hear (such talk) from anyone's mouth, you shall seize the instigators of the rebellion. You shall bring (them) before Aššurbanipal, the great crown prince designate. If you are able to seize and kill them, you shall seize and kill them. You shall eliminate their name and seed from the land. If you are unable to seize and kill them, you shall inform Aššurbanipal, the great crown prince designate. You shall stand by him. You shall seize the instigators of the rebellion and you shall kill (them).

[12] On the question of Aššurbanipal's age on his appointment as crown prince and, consequently, the practical relevance of this stipulation, see Parpola 1983: 139–140, discussing a letter that mentions Aššurbanipal's infant son and is probably to be dated to 669 BCE, and Parpola 1987:168.

[13] As this section makes clear, Esarhaddon bypassed Aššurbanipal's older brother Šamaš-šumu-ukin when the king appointed Aššurbanipal to be his successor to the throne of Assyria. However, he did appoint Šamaš-šumu-ukin to succeed to the throne of Babylonia. Šamaš-šumu-ukin is qualified here by the Akkadian word *talīmu*, a word whose "precise connotations, as opposed to *ahu*, 'brother,' are not clear," (*CAD* T s.v. *talīmu* discussion), cf. the translations of the word by Reiner (1969:535) as "dear brother," Parpola and Watanabe (1988:32) as "equal brother," and Hecker (2004:92) as "*älteren* Bruder." The inscriptions of Aššurbanipal and Šamaš-šumu-ukin employ the word as part of a deliberate rhetorical strategy, "to be understood in the light of Esarhaddon's domestic policy propagating the notion of a full (albeit cosmetic) equality between Assyria and Babylonia," according to Parpola (1987:169). For a treaty in which Šamaš-šumu-ukin himself swears an *adê*-oath to Aššurbanipal, see the Zakutu Treaty (4.37). In 652 BCE, 17 years after swearing that oath of loyalty, Šamaš-šumu-ukin led Babylonia in rebellion against his brother's authority, a rebellion that lasted until Aššurbanipal destroyed Babylon in 648.

[14] Karduniaš is a toponym originally used by the Kassites in reference to Babylonia; i.e., to Sumer and Akkad.

[15] Restoring the relative pronoun *ša* seems required by the syntax, and traces of this sign may be visible in one ms (otherwise, no extant ms preserves the transition from *lā banītu* to *ina muhhi Aššur-bāni-apli*). Cf. the syntax in § 6 (l. 74).

[16] Following most translators in understanding the profession, literally "a member of those who inquire into the word of the god" (DUMU *ša-'i-li a-mat* DINGIR) to refer more generally to an interpreter of oracles than specifically to a dream interpreter, as does Reiner (1969:535). While a specialist designated as *šā'ilu* is associated with the interpretation of dreams (see the reference cited under *CAD* Š/1 s.v. *šā'ilu* mng. 1b), other references associate the *šā'ilu* with different means of divination (notably incense; see the other references cited under *CAD* Š/1 s.v. *šā'ilu* mng. 1 and the discussion section) and there is no compelling reason to restrict the responsibilities of the specialist to dream interpretation in this passage. On the sequence "a prophet, an ecstatic, (or) an interpreter of oracles," see Nissinen 1998:160–161.

§ 13 If *you come into contact with*[17] the instigators of a rebellion, be they few or many, and you hear anything, good or bad, you shall go to Aššurbanipal, the great crown prince designate, son of Esarhaddon, king of Assyria. Your heart shall be given over entirely to him. You shall not swear (oaths) to each other whereby (statues of) gods are installed and an *adê*-oath is established before (those) gods by means of an arrangement on an offering table, drinking from a cup, lighting a fire, water, oil, (or) seizing the breast. You shall go and tell Aššurbanipal, the great crown prince designate, son of Esarhaddon, king of Assyria, your lord. You shall seize and kill the instigators of the rebellion and the guilty troops. You shall eliminate their name and seed from the land.

§ 14 Whether an Assyrian or someone subservient to Assyria, whether a bearded courtier or a eunuch, whether a citizen of Assyrian or of another land, if anyone at all has besieged Aššurbanipal, the great crown prince designate, in either country or town and has rebelled or revolted against him, you shall stand by Aššurbanipal, the great crown prince designate. You shall protect him. You shall wholeheartedly kill the troops who are rebelling against him. You shall rescue Aššurbanipal, the great crown prince designate, and his brothers, sons of his mother.

§ 15 You shall not become an ally with someone who rebels against Aššurbanipal, the great crown prince designate, son of Esarhaddon, king of Assyria, your lord, who, established the *adê*-oath with you concerning him. If they should seize you by force, you shall escape. You shall come before Aššurbanipal, the great crown prince designate.

§ 16 You shall not hold in your heart a malicious thought about Aššurbanipal, the great crown prince designate, whether [*on*] *military service ... or* [*at*] *rest*,[18] not when you reside within the land and not when you enter a tax-collection center. You shall not revolt against him. You shall not undertake machinations, rebellion, (or) anything malicious.

§ 17 Aššurbanipal, the great crown prince designate, the son of Esarhaddon, king of Assyria, your lord – he shall be your king and your lord when Esarhaddon, king of Assyria, your lord, should pass away. He shall humble the mighty and raise the humble. He shall kill those to be killed and spare those to be spared. Whatever he commands, you shall obey, and you shall act in accordance with his commands. You shall not seek another king (or) another lord against him.

§ 18 If anyone in the palace should revolt against Esarhaddon, king of Assyria, either during the day or night, either on the road or within the land, *do not obey him*![19] If a messenger from the palace should come before the prince at an unusual time during the day or night and say: "Your father has summoned you, may the lord come," do not listen to him and do not let him go free! (Not only) must he must not to go, but you will strengthen his guard. Not until one among you who loves his lord and worries about the house of his lords goes and inspects the health of the king, his lord, in the palace will you go to the palace with the prince, your lord.

§ 19 You shall not establish an assembly. You shall not bind each other with oaths. You shall not give kingship to one among you.

§ 20 You shall not help (someone) from among his brothers, his uncles, his cousins, (or) his family, the seed of his father's house, either persons who are in Assyria or who fled to another land, take the throne (and then) give him the kingship and lordship of Assyria, not (someone) in an inner or outer royal *area* nor (someone) from among (other) *work groups*, great (or) small,[20] not (someone) from among the old (or) young, not (someone) from among the well-off or less fortunate, not a bearded courtier or a eunuch, not (someone) from among the (house-born) slaves to the purchased ones, not (someone) from among the citizens of Assyria or another land, not anyone at all, not even one of you. Rather, you shall help Aššurbanipal, the great crown prince designate, take the throne of Assyria. He shall exercise the kingship and lordship of Assyria over you.

§ 21 You shall do battle[21] concerning Aššurbanipal, the great crown prince designate son of Esarhaddon, king of Assyria, your lord, and you shall die (if necessary). You shall seek out and do that which is pleasing to him. You shall not do anything malicious to him. You shall not give bad advice to him. You shall not set him on an unwholesome course. You shall always serve them with righteousness and propriety.

---

17 The translation tentatively follows Parpola and Watanabe (1988:34). The phrase *issišu šakānu* typically means "to ally with, to make common cause with someone" (see *CAD* Š/1 s.v. *šakānu* mng 5b s.v. *itti* for references), and is used with this meaning in § 15 and § 22 of this text.

18 The translation "*or* [*at*] *rest*," derives from the restoration of Parpola and Watanabe (1988:36) *lu in*[*a u -m*]*e*? *ra-qi*, lit. "on a day of being available." For *ḫurādu* as "military service," see their note to the line.

19 The verbal form, written *la taš-me-a-šú* in both extant ms, is understood as a prohibitive in light of the parallel form *la ta-*[*šam-a-šú*] extant in one ms later in the section.

20 On the words *kalzi* and *kalzāni*, tentatively translated here as "(royal) *area*" and "*work groups*," see Watanabe 1987:184 and Parpola and Watanabe 1988:37 note to line 217, and cf. *SAA* 15.233.

21 On the translation "do battle" and not "fall," see note 10.

§ 22 If Esarhaddon, king of Assyria, should pass away while his sons are young, and either a bearded courtier or a eunuch should kill Aššubanipal, the great crown prince designate, and assume the kingship of Assyria, you shall not be his. You shall not become his servant. You shall resist and be his enemy. You shall turn all the other lands against him and incite rebellion against him. You shall seize and kill him, and you shall help a son of Aššurbanipal, the great crown prince designate, take the throne of Assyria.

§ 23[22] You shall wait for a pregnant woman of Esarhaddon, king of Assyria, or a wife of Aššurbanipal, the great crown prince designate, (to give birth). When (a son) is born, you shall raise (him). You shall help him take the throne of Assyria. You shall seize and kill the instigators of the rebellion. You shall eliminate their name and seed from the land. You shall shed blood for blood. You shall avenge Aššurbanipal, the great crown prince designate. You shall not cause Aššurbanipal, the great crown prince designate, the son of Esarhaddon, king of Assyria, your lord, to eat or drink a deadly plant, nor anoint him with one. You shall not perform sorcery. You shall not make gods and goddesses angry with him.

§ 24 You shall love Aššurbanipal, the great crown prince designate, son of Esarhaddon, king of Assyria, your lord, like your (own) lives. You shall not slander his brothers, the sons of his mother before Aššurbanipal, the great crown prince designate. You shall not say anything malicious. You shall not lift your arms against their houses. You shall not wrong them. You shall not appropriate any gift that their father gave to them (or) something that they themselves acquired. Gifts (such as) fields, houses, orchards, people, equipment, horses, mules, donkeys, oxen, (or) sheep that Esarhaddon, king of Assyria, gave to his sons, shall be at their disposal. You shall say good things about them before Aššurbanipal, the great crown prince designate. They shall have access to him and be united with you.

§ 25 You shall tell this *adê*-oath which Esarhaddon, king of Assyria, confirmed and established with you, making you swear an oath concerning Aššurbanipal, the great crown prince designate, and his brothers, sons of the great crown prince designate Aššurbanipal's mother, to your sons and your grandsons, to your seed, and to the seed of your seed who are born in future days after the *adê*-oath and you shall instruct them as follows:

Guard this *adê*-oath! Do not break this *adê*-oath! Do not destroy your lives! Do not hand your land over for destruction and your people for deportation! This matter which is pleasing to the gods and humanity – may this same matter be pleasing and gratifying to you. May Aššurbanipal, the great crown prince designate, be protected for the lordship of the land and the people. Afterwards, may his name be called for kingship. Do not place another king (or) another lord over yourself!

§ 26 If anyone should make a rebellion (or) revolt against Esarhaddon, king of Assyria (and then) sit on the throne of kingship, you shall not rejoice in his kingship. You shall seize and kill him. If you are unable to seize and kill him, you shall not consent to his kingship. You shall not swear an oath of servitude to him. You shall revolt against him and battle him wholeheartedly. You shall turn other lands against him. You shall rob and murder him. You shall eliminate his name and seed from the land. You shall help Aššurbanipal, the great crown prince designate, take the throne of his father.

§ 27 If (someone) from among his brothers, his uncles, his cousins, from among the seed of the house of his father, from among the seed of previous kings, from among the magnates,[23] governors (or) eunuchs, from among the citizens of Assyria (or) from among the citizens of another land tries to get you to conspire and orders you as follows: "Slander Aššurbanipal, the great crown prince designate, in front of his father! Say something malicious, something harmful toward him!" you shall not cause conflict between him and his father. You shall not set them up to hate each other.

§ 28 Speak as follows to the envious person who would instruct you and who would have you make (him) detestable[24]:

Where are those brothers or servants who made (a son) detestable to his father because they slandered

[22] I follow most previous translations against *SAA* 2.6 in understanding § 23 to begin here as all extant mss have the horizontal ruling by which sections are conventionally distinguished after line 248. Parpola and Watanabe (1988:38–39) suggest a new section begins only with the stipulation that begins "You shall not cause Aššurbanipal, the great crown prince designate, the son of Esarhaddon, king of Assyria, your lord, to eat or drink a deadly plant ..." (line 259). While this organization into sections makes good sense in terms of content, a ruling is absent in all extant mss.

[23] Of the five mss preserving this line, two have "magnate(s)" (Akk. *rabî*, written GAL) and three have "prince(s)," (Akk. *rubê*, written NUN-e). I translate "magnate" as the title in question appears in the context of members of the Assyrian administration.

[24] Although in the one attestation of *nazāru* in the Š-stem outside of this text that is known to me, the pronominal suffix functions as the object of G transitive verb (lit. "he made me be cursed," SAA 16.78, rev. 3), it is unclear to me why a "causative translation ... is out of the question" (Parpola and Watanabe 1988:42 note to line 329), so that we cannot understand the pronominal suffix in this instance to be the object of causation and the subject of the G transitive verb (lit. "he caused you to curse [someone];" cf. Reiner 1969:537, n. 10, Borger 1982–1985:168, and Watanabe 1987:159).

him before his father? Was the opposite[25] of what Aššur, Šamaš, and Adad ordered [concerning hi]m (i.e. a father) true? Did your father …[26] without Aššur and Šamaš? Honor your brother and protect your lives!

§ 29 If someone tries to get you to conspire and orders you – (someone) from among his brothers, his uncles, his cousins, his family, the seed of the house of his father, or a eunuch, or a bearded courtier, or a citizen of Assyria or the citizen of another land or anyone at all orders you as follows: "Slander his brothers, sons of his mother, in front of him! Cause a fight between them! Cut his brothers, sons of the same mothers, off from him!" you shall not listen. You shall not say anything malicious about his brothers in front of him. You shall not cut him off from his brothers. You shall not let the one who spoke like this to you go free. You shall come and tell Aššurbanipal, the great crown prince, designate as follows: "Your father established the *adê*-oath with us concerning you, and he caused us to swear it.[27]"

§ 30[28] You shall not look at Aššurbanipal, the great crown prince designate, (or) his brothers without reverence or submission. If someone does not protect (him), you shall fight them as if fighting for yourselves. You shall cause to enter frightful *terror* into their hearts as you say: "Your father wrote (it) in the *adê*-oath. He established (the oath), and he caused us to swear it."

§ 31 When Esarhaddon, king of Assyria, your lord, has passed away, and Aššurbanipal, the great crown prince designate, has sat on the throne of kingship, you shall not say anything malicious about his brothers, sons of his mother, in front of their brother. You shall not make (them) detestable (and then) say (to Aššurbanipal): "Lift your hand against them for evil!"[29] You shall not alienate them from Aššurbanipal, the great crown prince designate. You shall not give a report harmful to them in front of their brother. (As for) the offices to which Esarhaddon, king of Assyria, their father, assigned them, you shall not make a statement before Aššurbanipal, the great crown prince designate, (to the effect that) he removes them from their offices.

§ 32 You shall anoint neither your faces nor your hands nor your throat[30] with the SAR-BU which is *against* the gods of the assembly.[31] You shall not bind (it) in your lap. You shall not do anything that undoes an oath.

§ 33 You shall neither retract nor dissolve the oath. You shall not think up and carry out any *šingāti*[32] of retraction (or) dissolution. You and your sons yet to be born are sworn for now and ever by this oath to Aššurbanipal, the great crown prince designation, son of Esarhaddon, king of Assyria, your lord.

§ 34 As you stand at the place of this oath, you shall not swear the oath with your mouth only. You shall swear it wholeheartedly. You shall teach the *adê*-oath to your sons who are born afterwards. You shall not claim to be sick with an unclean disease. You shall enter into the *adê*-oath of Esarhaddon, king of Assyria concerning Aššurbanipal, the great crown prince designate. For the future and forever, Aššur is your god and Aššurbanipal, the great

[25] I follow Watanabe (1987:102) in emending ⟨*a-bu-tu*⟩ after *lā* in light of the need for a feminine subject for the 3 fs verb *takūn*. I understand the sentiment to be a rhetorical question regarding to filial piety.

[26] Watanabe's (1987:186) reading of the problematic signs at the end of the line as UDU.TI-*ú* ŠID for *udutilû imnu*, "he recited (the incantation) 'live sheep,'" has not been adopted in later translations nor taken up by *CAD* U/W s.v. *udutilû*.

[27] Watanabe (1988:160) suggests that the final verb *ú-tam-ma-na-a-[ši]*, preserved in two mss from Nimrud, was perhaps an error for *uttammināši*, i.e. "to cause to swear" and should be in the perfect and not in the present tense. The suggestion was reasonable in light of the immediately preceding verb *issakan* (perfect tense) and the lack of any guidance from the parallel verb at the end of § 30, which is poorly preserved in the Nimrud mss (*ú-ta*[*m* …], one ms). But the appearance of the form *ú-tam-ma-na-a-ši* at the ends of both § 29 and 30 in ms T implies that the present tense is the intended form. Perhaps the *adê*-oath continued to be sworn on successive occasions after its initial establishment or the durative aspect of the present tense is of significance here.

[28] The text of this section follows ms T, in which it is best preserved. In what seems to be an emphatic example of dittography, the section is written twice in ms T, although with different line breaks and orthography; see Lauinger 2012:116.

[29] Following previous translators in understanding the verb – written *ú-bíl* in two mss and *ub-bíl* in one – as an irregular imperative of *abālu*, see Watanabe 1987:187 for disussion.

[30] The phrase found in one ms, "nor your throat" (*lu na-pul-ta-ku-nu*) is replaced in the two other extant ms with "your clothing" (*lu-bul-ta-ku-nu*) in what seems to be an ocular elision of *-na-*. Note that one of these ms introduces the word with TÚG, the determinative placed before words signifying textiles.

[31] The passage is difficult, in part because the ambiguity of the prepositional phrase *ina muḫḫi ilāni* obscures the nature of SAR-BU, as Parpola and Watanabe (1988:43 note to line 373ff.) observe. They note also that previous interpretations of the direct object as *sarbu*, "tallow," (Watanabe 1987:187–188) or, dividing the wedges differently, as *šaršerru*, "red paste," (Reiner 1969:537, n. 13 and *passim* in the *CAD*) are unlikely because whatever SAR-BU signifies must also be able to be bound (*rakāsu*, "to bind," in the subsequent clause).

[32] A translation of *šingāti* as "*stratagems*" is proposed by Reiner (1969:538) without comment but has not been generally accepted; see e.g. Watanabe (1987:161), Parpola and Watanabe (1988:44), Kitchen and Lawrence (2012 1:983), and *CAD* Š/3 s.v. *šingu* B ("mng. uncert."), and see also Watanabe's note to line (1987:188). (*CAD* T s.v. *turtu* A mng, 2a cites the passage omitting *šingāti* from the quoted text with ellipses but including "some stratagem" in its translation.) The reading of the three following signs as *me-me-né* in place of [*ina* IG]I-*ni* found in earlier editions is clear now from ms T.

crown prince designate, is your lord. May your sons and your grandson fear his sons![33]

§ 35 Whoever changes, neglects, violates (or) voids the oath of this tablet, transgresses against the father, the lord, and the *adê*-oath of the great gods, breaches their entire oath, and discards this *adê*-tablet, a tablet of Aššur, king of the gods, and the great gods, my lords, (or) discards the statue of Esarhaddon, king of Assyria, the statue of Aššurbanipal, the great crown prince designate, or the statue(s) of his brothers and his heirs *which are (set) around him* —[34] you shall guard like your god this sealed tablet of the great ruler on which the *adê*-oath of Aššurbanipal, the great crown prince designate, son of Esarhaddon, king of Assyria, your lord, is written, which is sealed with the seal of Aššur, king of the gods, and which is set up before you.

§ 36 You shall not discard (it). You shall not consign (it) to fire. You shall not drop (it) into water. You shall not bury it in dirt. You shall not destroy (it) or make (it) disappear or efface (it) by any ingenious device.[35]

§ 37 (or else) may Aššur, king of the gods, decreer of fates, decree and evil an unpleasant fate for you![36]

§ 38 May Mullissu, his wife, his beloved, make his speech[37] evil! May she not intercede for you!

§ 38A[38] May Anu, king of the gods, rain down sickness, weariness, the *di'u*-disease,[39] sleeplessness, moaning, and unhealthy flesh on all of your houses!

§ 39 May Sin, moonlight of heaven and earth, clothe you with leprosy! May he forbid your entrance before the gods and the king! Roam the steppe like an onager (or) a gazelle!

§ 40 May Šamaš, sunlight of the heavens and earth, not hand down a just judgment for you! May he take away your eyesight! Walk around in darkness!

§ 41 May Ninurta, foremost of the gods, fell you with his ferocious arrow! May he fill the steppe with your blood! May he feed your flesh to the eagle and the vulture!

a Lev 26:29; Deut 28:53–57; Jer 19:9; Ezek 5:10; 2 Kgs 6:28–29; Lam 2:20; 4:10

§ 42 May Venus, brightest of the stars, cause your wives before your eyesto lie down before your eyes in the lap of your enemy! May your sons lose control over your estate! May a foreign enemy divide up your possessions!

§ 43 May Jupiter, the exalted lord of the gods, not show you Bel's entrance into the Esaggil! May he destroy your life![40]

§ 44 May Marduk, the first-born son, decree a grievous punishment and an irremovable curse as your fate!

§ 45 May Zarpanitu, who grants both name and seed, eliminate your name and seed from the land!

§ 46 May Belet-ili, mistress of progeny, bar offspring from your land! May your wet nurses be deprived of the cries of children and infants in the street and square![41]

§ 47 May Adad, the canal inspector of heaven and earth, bar rain showers from your land! May your fields be deprived of grain! May he submerge your land in a severe flood for no good end! May the locust which reduces the land devour your harvest! May the clamor of the grindstone and oven be absent from your houses! May the grain that you grind disappear! Instead of grain, may your sons and daughters grind your bones! May (not even) a joint of your finger sink into dough! May the *quqānu*-insect eat the dough out of your bowls! May a mother shut the door against her daughter! Eat the flesh of your sons out of hunger! May a man eat the flesh of another man out of hunger and want![a] May a man wear the skin of another man! As for your flesh, may dogs and pigs eat it! May your spirit have no caretaker, no one to pour it libations!

§ 48 May Ištar, lady of battle and combat, break your bow in a tight battle! May she bind your arms! May she place you below your enemy!

§ 49 May Nergal, warrior-hero of the gods, end to your life with his merciless sword! May he put slaughter and disease among you!

---

33 The object "sons" (*a-na* DUMU.MEŠ-*šú*) is clear in ms T, against earlier readings of the fragmentary Nimrud mss such as *a-de-e-šú* (Watanabe 1987:110) or *a-na šá-*[*a*]*-šú* (Parpola and Watanabe 1988:44).

34 The anacoluthon is marked by the fact that its verbs occur atypically with the Babylonian subjunctive while in the remainder of the section the verbs occur in the Assyrian dialect more typical of this text; see Watanabe 1988:43 and 190. The section is most fully preserved in ms T.

35 Parpola and Watanabe (1988:410) depart from translating the construction *šumma* + subjunctive verb as a "solemn statement" in this section and treat the clauses as conditional. However, I cannot explain the subjunctive mood other than as signaling a solemn statement.

36 One of the three extant mss adds the injunction "May he not give you a long-lasting old age and the attainment of extreme old age!" following the translation of Parpola and Watanabe (1988:45).

37 According to one extant ms. The other extant ms has "your speech."

38 The section is conventionally designated as such because it is omitted from ms 27, the best preserved of the Nimrud mss that is typically used as a "master" text against which other mss are compared. As the section is included in all four other extant mss, ms 27 is the outlier.

39 Perhaps a fever caused by an intestinal infection; see Scurlock and Anderson 2005:59–60.

40 Only two mss preserve the transition between the two curses. The other ms includes the direct speech marker and so attributes the second curse to Jupiter, i.e. "May Jupiter, the exalted lord of the gods, not show you the entrance of Bel into the Esaggil, saying to you: May he (i.e. Bel) destroy your life!"

41 On a parallel to this curse in the Erra Epic, see Watanabe 1983.

§ 50 May Mullissu who dwells in Nineveh tie a burning sword to you.

§ 51 May Ištar of Arbaʾil have no mercy (or) compassion for you.

§ 52 May Gula, the great Chief Physician, put weariness in your heart and a weeping wound in your body! Bathe in blood and pus as if in water!

§ 53[42] May the Seven (i.e. the Pleiades), warrior-heroes of the gods, devastate [you with their] furious [weapons]!

§ 54 May Aramis, lord of the city and land of Qarnê, lord of the city and land of Azaʾi,[43] fill you with bile!

§ 54A[44] May Adad and Šala of Kurbaʾil create piercing pain and ill health everywhere in your land!

§ 54B May Šarrat-Ekron[45] make a worm fall from your insides!

§ 54C May Bethel and Anath-Bethel deliver you to a devouring lion!

§ 55 May Kubaba and Karhuha[46] of Carchemish give you a severe case of *rimṭu*-disease![47] May your blood drip away onto the ground like raindrops!

§ 56 May the great gods of heaven and earth who dwell in the world and are named in this tablet smite you! May they regard you with anger! May they curse you terribly with a grievous curse! May they tear you from the world of the living up above! Below in the underworld, may they deprive your ghost of water! May shade and sunlight constantly chase you away! May you not find refuge even in a hidden corner! May bread and water take their leave from you! May famine, want, hunger, and plague not loosen their hold on you! Before your eyes, may dogs and pigs drag the teats of your young women and the penises[48] of your young men back and forth through the squares of Aššur! May the earth not receive your corpses, but rather may the stomach of dogs and pigs be your grave! May your days be gloomy and your years be dim! May a never-brightening darkness be your fate! May your life end in weariness and sleeplessness! May a flood, an irresistible deluge from the earth, rise up and devastate you! May something good be forbidden to you! May something grievous be your lot! May your food be bitumen and pitch! May your drink be donkey piss! May your salve be naptha! May your cloak be river weeds! May the *šēdu*-demon, *utukku*-demon, and evil *rābiu*-demon choose your houses!

§ 57 May these gods witness (the following oath): We shall not start a rebellion (or) revolt against Esarhaddon, king of Assyria, our lord or against Aššurbanipal, the great crown prince designate, or his brothers, sons of the great crown prince designate Aššurbanipal's mother, or the other sons who are the offspring of Esarhaddon, king of Assyria. We shall not form an alliance with his enemy. If we hear of sedition, instigation, the whisper of an evil, malicious, or ugly matter, or some criminal and disloyal speech concerning Aššurbanipal, the great crown prince designate, or his brothers, sons of the great crown prince designate Aššurbanipal's mother, we shall not conceal (it). We shall tell it to Aššurbanipal, the great crown prince designate. As long as we, our sons, and our grandsons live, Aššurbanipal, the great crown prince designate, shall be our king and our lord. We shall not place another king (or) the son of another king over us, our sons, and our grandsons. May all the gods who are named here hold us, our seed, and the seed of our seed, accountable.

§ 58 You shall not violate this *adê*-oath which Esarhaddon, king of Assyria, your lord, established with you concerning Aššurbanipal, the great crown prince designate, and his brothers, sons of the great crown prince designate Aššurbanipal's mother, and the other sons who are the offspring of Esarhaddon, king of Assyria, your lord (or else) may Aššur, father of the gods, strike you down with his furious weapons!

§ 59 May Palilu, the lord at the forefront, cause the eagle and vulture to eat your flesh!

42 This section is omitted from ms T.

43 Some sparse onomastic evidence fits well with the dominion attributed to Aramis here and provides some further support for understanding him to have been the head of a local Syrian pantheon; see Lauinger 2012:119.

44 No ms from Nimrud preserves an unbroken transition from the previous curse invoking Aramis to that invoking Bethel and Anath-Bethel § 54C (according to the numbering here). Accordingly, it was not known until the discovery of ms T that two additional curses invoking the pair Adad and Šala of Kurbaʾil and Šarrat-Ekron follow immediately after the curse invoking Aramis. These curses are now designated § 54A and § 54B, so that the curse invoking Bethel and Anath-Bethel (formerly § 54A) is now § 54C.

45 Undoubtedly, the goddess is to be identified with *Ptgyh*, the Lady of Ekron known from the Ekron inscription; see Lauinger 2012:199 for a brief discussion of the divine name and reference to some previous literature. For the Ekron Inscription, see also *COS* 2:164.

46 The divine name of this city god of Carchemish is preserved only in ms T. Previous editors read the traces of ᵈ*kar* preserved in the sole extant Nimrud ms as ᵈ[5], for "goddess" as a qualification of Kubaba.

47 To my knowledge, the word is a hapax. Parpola and Watanabe (1988:49) suggest the word designates a venereal disease and suggests restoring [urine] as subject of following verb (so also Scurlock and Andersen 2005:107), but this suggestion seems less likely now that ms T has shown the subject to be "blood."

48 Lit. "bowstrings" (*matnātu*), following Parpola and Watanabe (1988:49 note to line 481f., so also Kitchen and Lawrence 2012 1:989). Cf. the note to line v.13 of Aššur-nerari's treaty with Matiʾ-ilu of Arpad (*COS* 4:34).

§ 60 May Ea, king of the Abzu, the lord of the spring, give you water of death to drink![49] May he fill you with dropsy!

§ 61 May the great gods of heaven and earth make water and oil forbidden to you!

§ 62 May Girra, the one who provides food to the great gods, torch your name and your seed!

§ 63[50] May all the gods who are named in this *adê*-tablet shrink the ground to the size of a brick for you! May they make your land like iron so that nothing sprouts from it!

§ 64[51] Just as rain does not fall from a sky of bronze, so may rain and dew not visit your fields and meadows. Instead of rain, may charcoal fall in your land!

§ 65 Just as lead cannot withstand fire, so may you not withstand your enemy! May you not grasp your sons and your daughters in your hands!

§ 66 Just as a mule has no offspring, so may your name and seed and the seed of your sons and your daughters vanish from the land!

§ 67[52] Just as a shoot [..], and a seed and beer yeast are placed within, and just as these seeds do not sprout, and the beer yeast does not turn back to its …, so may your name, your seed, and the seed of your brothers and sons vanish from the face of the earth!

§ 68 May Šamaš overturn your city and your district with an iron plough![53]

§ 69 Just as this ewe is cut open, and the flesh of her child is placed in her mouth, so may you be forced to eat the flesh of your sons and daughters out of hunger![54,b]

b Lev 26:29; Deut 28:53–57; Jer 19:9; Ezek 5:10; 2 Kgs 6:28–29; Lam 2:20; 4:10

§ 70 Just as young male and female sheep and male and female spring lambs are cut open, and their intestines wrap around their feet so may the intestines of your sons and daughters wrap around your feet!

§ 71[55] Just as the snake and mongoose will not enter a single burrow and lie down (together) but plot only to cut each other's throats, so may you and your women not enter the same house and lie on the same bed! Plot only to cut each other's throats!

§ 72 Just as bread and wine is entering your intestines, so may this oath enter your intestines and the intestines of your sons and daughters!

§ 73 Just as you propel water from a tube, may you, your women, your sons, and your daughters be propelled! May the waters of your rivers and springs flow backwards!

§ 74 May bread be exchanged for gold in your land![56]

§ 75 Just as honey is sweet, so may the blood of your women, your sons, and your daughters be sweet in your mouth!

---

49 Both extant Nimrud ms have the verb as *šaqû*, "to give s.t. drink," while ms T has *šutēšuru*, "to keep in order." While this verb appears in other texts in connection with gods and spring, it "does not seem to fit the context of the curse … and perhaps represents an inadvertent substitution of another word commonly written with *nagbu*" (Lauinger 2012:120).

50 Several of the preserved mss begin this curse and many of those that follow with the cuneiform signs KI.MIN or KI.MIN KI.MIN, indicating the repetition of the stipulation that introduces § 58 (occasionally made explicit in subsequent curses) that the oath-takers shall not violate the *adê*-oath lest they be cursed (though, *contra* Reiner [1969:539, n. 24]. KI.MIN does not also specify the subject of the curse as "all the gods who are named in this *adê*-tablet." This subject is stated *after* KI.MIN in § 63 of all extant mss and so cannot be meant by KI.MIN there or in subsequent appearances, see also §§ 69, 75, 80, 92, 99). There does not seem to be any consistency to when the notation KI.MIN is employed or in which mss, and I do not indicate its presence in the translation.

51 I follow scholarly convention in distinguishing the following lines as a new section but only to keep section numbers in accordance with previous literature. As Watanabe (1987:198) points out, only in one of seven extant mss does a horizontal ruling separate § 63 from § 64, so the two sections' curses comprised a unit in antiquity.

52 The translation derives from ms T, in which the section is better preserved than in the Nimrud mss. Some details remain unclear, but "[e]vidently, the curse refers to the method by which the germination of barley is halted during the malting process" (Lauinger 2012:120; see this reference also for some literature on whether *sikkatu*/*sikkitu* signifies beer yeast or a plant).

53 In place of "district" (*nagû*), found in the two extant Nimrud ms, the Tayinat ms has "land" (*mātu*).

54 The verb is *lušākilūkunu*, an Assyrian Š precative 3 mpl of *akālu* (written *lu-ša-kil-u-ku-nu* in one Nimrud ms; the other mss from Nimrud and Tayinat either contain defective writings or scribal errors). The subject of this 3 mpl form and many others that follow is not explicit and open to interpretation. In earlier translations, the preferred subject is "they," understanding the subject to be unnamed gods. This interpretation is supported by the occasional specification of "all the gods who are named in this *adê*-tablet" as the subject of a curse (e.g. § 77 where three of five extant mss specify the subject, cf. § 92 where two of eight do so). However, the same verbal forms that lack any explicit subject may also be interpreted as impersonal uses of the 3 mpl, a typical locution for the passive in Neo-Assyrian (see Hameen-Anttila 2000:88), and this interpretation is supported by § 90 where different mss variously have the final verb as a stative (*lū raḫ at*), N precative (*lirrah ā*) or Š precative (*lušarhi ū*), cf. on this point Parpola and Watanabe 1988:xl. With regard to the other 3 mpl forms, the scribes themselves may have not been sure whether to take "the gods" as the subject or to understand an impersonal construction, hence the lack of consistency across mss in appearance of the phrase "all the gods who are named in this *adê*-tablet" the subject of a curse. For the purposes of this translation, I take 3 mpl forms as impersonal constructions unless a majority of extant mss explicitly name the gods as the subject or the context requires them to be such.

55 One of the five extant mss begins the curse with the stipulation: "You shall not violate this [*ad*]*ê*-oath of Esarhaddon, king of Assyria, [concerning Aššurbanipal, the great crown prince desig]nate, (or else)."

56 The translation renders two different verbs: *lušālikū* (lit. "may they cause to eat") in the one extant Nimrud ms; and *lilqû* (lit. "may they take") in the Tayinat ms.

§ 76 Just as the worm eats cheese, so may the worm eat your own flesh and the flesh of your women, your sons, and your daughters while you are still alive!

§ 77 May all the gods who are named in this *adê*-tablet break your bow! May they place you below your enemy! May they remove the bow from your hands and cause your chariots to move backwards!

§ 78 Just as a stag is hunted down and killed, may you, your brothers, your sons, and your daughters be hunted down and killed![57]

§ 79 Just as a caterpillar does not see and will not return to its cocoon, so may you not return to the women, sons, and daughters in your houses!

§ 80 Just as a bird is seized in a snare, so may you, your brothers, and your sons be placed in the hands of your killer![58]

§ 81 May your flesh and the flesh of your women, your brothers, your sons, and your daughters, turn black like pitch, bitumen, and naptha!

§ 82 Just as a *ḫaʾeparušhi*-beast is caught in a trap you, so your brothers, your sons, and your daughters should be seized by your enemy!

§ 83 May your flesh, the flesh of your women, your brothers, your sons, and your daughters be used up like the flesh of a chameleon!

§ 84 Just as holes pierce a honeycomb, so may holes pierce your flesh and the flesh of your women, your brothers, your sons, and your daughters while you are still alive!

§ 85 Just as with the locust, the *barmu*-insect, the *louse*, the larva, and the caterpillar, may your cities, your land, and your district[59] be devoured!

§ 86 May you be made like a fly in the hands of your enemy! May your enemy crush you!

§ 87 Just as this bug stinks, so may your breath stink before the god, king, and mankind!

§ 88 May you, your women, your brothers, your sons, and your daughters, be strangled with a cord!

§ 89 Just as this wax figure is consumed by fire, and this clay one is dissolved in water, so may your image burn in fire and be submerged in water!

§ 90[60] Just as this chariot is soaked in blood up to its floorboards, so may your chariots be soaked[61] with your blood in the midst of your enemy!

§ 91[62] May you be spun around like a spindle. May you be made like a woman before your enemy!

§ 92[63] May you, your brothers, your sons (and your daughters) be made to run around backwards like a crab!

§ 93 May you be surrounded with something malicious and harmful like fire!

§ 94 Just as the oil is entering your flesh, so may the oath be made to enter your flesh and the flesh of your brothers, your sons, and your daughters!

§ 95 Just as the *Cursers* wronged Bel,[64] and he cut off their hands and feet and *blinded*[65] their eyes, so may you be finished off! May they make you bend like a bed of reeds in the water! May your enemy pull you out like a reed from a bundle!

§ 96 You shall not abandon Esarhaddon, king of Assyria, your lord, or Aššurbanipal, the great crown prince designate, or his brothers, sons of the great crown prince designate Aššurbanipal's mother, and the other sons who are the offspring of Esarhaddon, king of Assyria. You shall not go to the north or the south.[66] May swords devour him who goes to the north, and may swords also devour him who goes to the south![67]

---

57 The translation follows ms T. One extant ms from Nimrud adds the qualification *ina* ŠU^{II} EN [ÚŠ-*ku*]-*nu*, "by [your kil]ler," while the other has EN [ÚŠ-*ku-nu*], "[your kil]ler" as the subject of the curse. Does this variation between the three mss derive in some way from the appearance of the phrase "in the hands of your killer" in § 80 of the Nimrud mss?

58 Translating "in the hands of your killer" (*i-na* ŠU^{II} EN ÚŠ-*ku-nu*) with all five extant Nimrud mss. Ms T has *i-na* ŠU^{II} ^{lú}KÚR-*ku-nu*, "in the hands of your enemy."

59 The two extant Nimrud ms having "district" (*nagû*) while the ms from Tayinat has "fields" (*eqlēti*).

60 One of seven ms begins the curse with the general stipulation against violating the oath, see note 55 above.

61 See note on the impersonal use 3mpl verbal forms in n. 54 above.

62 Two of seven extant mss specify the subject of the curse: "May all the gods who are named in this *adê*-tablet."

63 Two of eight extant mss specify the subject of the curse: "May all the gods who are named in this *adê*-tablet."

64 For *a-ra-ru* as *Arrāru*, a *nomen professionalis* construed as a proper noun, "Cursers," see Watanabe 1987:206, where the curse is understood to refer to a now-lost mythological work, so also Parpola and Watanabe (1988:57) and Kitchen and Lawrence (2012 1:999). Wiseman (1959:77) and Reiner (1969:540) read the divine name Bel (^{d}EN) as DINGIR EN, "god and lord," with Reiner "tak[ing] the expression *arāru haṭ û* … to be synonymous with *ḫīṭa ḫaṭû*" (n. 27) and translating "those who blaspheme against the god or the lord." Note that in all six extant mss, the verb *haṭû* takes its direct object with *ana* and not with *ina* as otherwise in this text.

65 The verb *gullulu* is obscure, and its translation derives from the context; cf. Reiner 1969:540, n. 26 and Watanabe 1987:206.

66 Literally "You shall not go to the right or the left." For "right" and "left" as "north" and "south," see Parpola 1983:117. As Parpola and Watanabe (1988:57, note to line 634 f.) observe, "The implication is … 'anywhere.' "

67 One of the six extant mss qualifies the swords as "iron" (AN.BAR).

§ 96A[68] May you, your women, your brothers, your sons, and your daughters be felled like a young lamb or goat!

§ 97 Just like the call of these doves, so may you, your women, your sons, and your daughters neither rest nor sleep! Your bones will not be near each other!

§ 98 Just as the inside of a hole is empty, so may your hearts be empty!

§ 99 When your enemy stabs you, may the honey, oil, ginger, and cedar resin that you are accustomed to put in your stab wound vanish!

§ 100 Just as bile is bitter, may you, your women, your sons, and your daughters be bitter towards each other!

§ 101 May Šamaš, spread a bird net of bronze over you, your sons, and your daughters! May he cast you into an inescapable trap! May he not let you come out alive!

§ 102 Just as this water skin has been cut open and its water spilled out, so may your water skin break in a place of severe thirst and dehydration! Die from thirst!

§ 103 Just as this sandal has been cut up,[69] may your sandals be rent[70] in a place of thorns and "cutters"[71]! Crawl on your belly!

§ 104 May Enlil, master of the throne, cause your throne to overturn!

§ 105 May Nabu, bearer of the tablet of destinies of the gods, erase your name! May he eliminate your seed from the land!

§ 106 May the door before you be soaked (in blood?)! May your doors not open!

§ 107: Colophon Month II, day 18,[72] eponymy of Nabu-belu-uṣur, prefect of the land of Dur-Šarrukku (i.e. 672 BC). The *adê*-oath which Esarhaddon, king of Assyria, established concerning Aššurbanipal, the great crown prince designate of Assyria, and concerning Šamaššumu-ukin, crown prince designate of Babylon.[73]

68 As with § 38A (see note 38) the section is omitted from ms 27 but is present in all other extant mss (six in this instance).

69 The sole Nimrud ms to preserve the verb has *šalqatuni*, as in the previous curse. Ms T has the synonymous verb *batqatuni*.

70 The sole Nimrud ms to preserve the verb has *lipparmā*, the N precative of *parāmu*, "to rend," while ms T has *libtuqū*, repeating the verb *batāqu* now in the form of a precative.

71 The word *ga-zi-ri* is preserved only in ms T and is understood to be a loanword from the West Semitic root **gzr*, "to cut." It is to my knowledge a hapax and may designate a sharp stone; see Lauinger 2012:122.

72 Two extant mss from Nimrud are dated to the 18th day while a third is dated to the 16th day. (Unfortunately, the relevant signs in the ms from Tayinat are damaged, and the text could be dated any time from the 16th–19th.) The difference in date between the Nimrud mss is likely not because of scribal error. For instance, in the Rassam Cylinder, the date of Aššurbanipal's succession is the 12th day (Streck 1916: 2 I 12), and several scholars have suggested that various dates refer to different portions of the ceremony that were conducted on different days or to different times at which the respective tablets were copied, see Wiseman 1959:5; Cogan 1977:99, and Watanabe 1987.

73 This longer version of the colophon is preserved in one only ms. Three other extant mss from Nimrud as well as the ms from Tayinat have a shorter colophon that omits mention of Esarhaddon, i.e. "the *adê*-oath that was established concerning Aššurbanipal …."

REFERENCES

Borger 1982–1985; Frahm 2009; Lauinger 2012; Parpola and Watanabe 1988; Pomponio 1990; Reiner 1969; Watanabe 1987; Weidner 1939–1941; Wiseman 1958.

THE ZAKUTU TREATY (4.37)

Jacob Lauinger

This *adê*-oath is remarkable among the extant Neo-Assyrian treaties for being imposed by someone other than an Assyrian king. The dominant party in this oath is the dowager queen of Assyria, Zakutu (an Akkadian rendering of the West Semitic name Naqia), the wife of Sennacherib (704–681), the mother of Esarhaddon (680–669), and the grandmother of Aššurbanipal (668–627). Although she imposed this oath of loyalty upon Aššurbanipal's brothers (two of whom are mentioned by name), royal officials, and the Assyrian populace in general, Zakutu was not the recipient of the oath. Rather, the recipient was her grandson Aššurbanipal, on whose behalf the previous king Esarhaddon had also imposed an oath of loyalty (see Esarhaddon's Succession Treaty 4.36). The fact that this oath is imposed by Aššurbanipal's grandmother and by Esarhaddon or Aššurbanipal "fit[s] only one historical situation, the short period of time between Esarhaddon's death (Arahšamna 10 = November 1, 669 B.C.) and the accession of Assurbanipal the next month" (Parpola 1987:168). As Melville (1999:86–87) observes, although Zakutu's role has been taken as evidence of her extraordinary influence at the Assyrian court or obstacles to Aššurbanipal's succession, the dowager queen may simply have been fulfilling a task assigned to her by her son Esarhaddon before that monarch's death; cf. Parpola's (1987:168) remarks that Zakutu's actions are "in line with the common praxis according to which a widow with no grown-up sons would manage her household until her oldest son had become of age."

Our single extant copy of Zakutu's treaty was found at Nineveh and is a product of the court chancellery. Unlike the large multi-column tablets that extend to hundreds of lines whether they be the actual "*adê*-tablets" that oath-takers were sworn to protect (such as Esarhaddon's Succession Treaty, see 4.36) or files of the court chancellery (such as Aššur-nerari V's treaty with Mati᾽-ilu, see 4.34), Zakutu's treaty is written on a small single column tablet in only 56 lines. And unlike other Neo-Assyrian *adê*-oaths, the text does not conclude with a series of curses but simply ends on a stipulation. The stipulations themselves are curiously restricted in nature being entirely concerned with speech: The obverse is concerned solely with traitorous speech, while the reverse is concerned solely with reporting such speech made by others. Nowhere, for instance, does the text contain a stipulation against actually harming Aššurbanipal! Given the structure and content as well as the format of the tablet, it seems likely that this manuscript of Zakutu's treaty is an extract from or even a partial draft for a much longer *adê*-oath that is no longer extant; cf. *SAA* 2.3 and 2.12, other tablets from Nineveh that contain extracts of *adê*-oaths, and see Parpola and Watanabe 1988:xlvi–xlvii and l. This observation may help explain the numerous errors and omissions that are found in the text (omission are indicated in the translation below while emended readings of individual signs are not, for which see Parpola's [1987] transliteration).

Obverse

(1–9) [The *ad*]*ê*-oath of Zakutu, the wife of Senna[cherib], [kin]g of Assyria, the mother of Esarhaddon, king of Assyria,[1] with Šamaš-šumu-ukin, his (i.e. Aššurbanipal's) *beloved brother*,[2] with Šamaš-metu-uballiṭ[3] and the rest of his brothers, with the king's progeny, with the magnates, the governors, the bearded officials, the eunuchs, (and) the courtiers, with the exempt and all those who enter the palace, (and) with the Assyrians, great and small.

(9–12) Whoever in this *adê*-oath that Zakutu, the wife, established with all the people of the land concerning Aššurbanipal, her favorite grandson,[4]

(12–15) whoever of you[5] deceitfully spread [...] something evil, [wi]cked, or about a revolt [concerning Aššurbanipal, king of Assyria, your lord;[6]

(16–19) (whoever of you) construct in your heart an evil [sch]eme (or) [a wic]ked plot concerning Aššurbanipal, king of Assyria, [your lord] (and then) [speak (it) alo]ud;

(19–22) (whoever of you) [off]er in your heart evil *instructions*[7] (and) wicked counsel advocating revolt and rebellion concerning Aššurbanipal, king of Assyria, your lord (and then) speak (it) aloud;

(23–24) (whoever of you) discuss killing [Aššurbanipal, king] of Assyria, your lord, [with] another [*person*]:

(25-le 2) [May Aššur, Sin, Šamaš], Jupiter, Venus, [Satu]rn, [Merc]ur[y, Ma]r[s, Sirius ...].

(Two lines not preserved)[8]

1 Parpola 1987:165–166 emends the text by adding "⟨and the mother of Assurbanipal, king of Assyria⟩" here, noting that "The words supplied within angle brackets are required by the suffix *-šu* ["his"] in line 3, which can only refer to Assurbanipal" (p. 169). The emendation does not appear in Parpola and Watanabe 1988:62.

2 On Šamaš-šumu-ukin and his qualification here, see Esarhaddon's Succession Treaty 4.36, n. 13.

3 Šamaš-metu-uballiṭ may be mentioned here by name because he was third in line to succeed the throne of Assyria after Esarhaddon's death, behind Aššurbanipal and Šamaš-šumu-ukin, see Baker and Gentili 2011 for discussion and previous literature.

4 Parpola 1987:169, pointing to parallels, observes, "This passage looks like an anacoluthon for *mannu ša ina libbi adê ... iḫattûni*" ("whoever sins against the *adê*- oath"). Cf. the language supplied in parentheses in the translations of Parpola and Watanabe (1988:62), so also Kitchen and Lawrence 2012 1:1007: "Anyone who (is included) in this treaty which Queen Zakutu has concluded with the whole nation concerning her favourite grandson [Assurba]nipal"; and Hecker (2004:92): "(und) wer da ist, der in diesem Vertrag (genannt ist), den die Palastdame Zakūtu bezüglich ihres Lieblingsenkels Assurbanipal mit den menschen des gesamten Landes schloß."

5 The Akkadian construction *mannu ša* ("whoever") followed by verbs in the 2 c.pl. is difficult. Parpola (1987:169) describes it as "unique" and observes that it "seems an anacoluthon for *mannu atta/attunu ša* and the like."

6 Parpola (1987:167) translates "who should [...] fabricate and carry into effect an ugly and evil thing or a revolt," so also Parpola and Watanabe 1988:62 and Kitchen and Lawrence 2012 1:1007. I understand the verbs *tasalli᾽āni teppašāni* as hendiadys; cf. Hecker (2004:92): "Wer von euch ... lügnerisch ausübt," and cf. also *CAD* S s.v. *salā᾽u* B v. usage a-2′: "whoever (among you) who makes up and spreads untruths and seditious lies." Accordingly, *lā de᾽iqtu*, *lā ṭābu* and *nabalkattu* all should qualify *abutu* with the *u* coordinating them, and so I understand *nabalkattu* as an accusative of respect. This stipulation, then, like the others that follow on the obverse, concerns evil thoughts and speech not evil acts. For another opinion on this stipulation, see Parpola 1987:169–170.

7 Following Parpola 1987:167, the word translated here as "*instructions*," Akk. *ussuktu* is understood to derive from *esēḫu*, "to assign, instruct," so also Parpola and Watanabe 1988:62, Kitchen and Lawrence 2012 1:1007, and Hecker 2004:92 ("Absicht").

8 The restoration and the estimate of missing lines follows Parpola 1987:165. The restoration derives from § 2 of Esarhaddon's Succession Treaty where the planets and Sirius are met in the same order; so also Hecker (2004:92, n. 346), although, as Parpola (1987:170) observes, "the context and space considerations in line 25 [of the Zakutu treaty] imply that the passage is a curse section, not an enumeration of gods witnessing the treaty" as with the parallel passage in Esarhaddon's Succession Treaty. Similarly, Hecker points out in the note cited above that the missing two lines most requested some sort of punishment from the aforementioned gods. Most likely the curse ended on r 1 where a dividing line separates the two groups of stipulations. Parpola and Watanabe (1988:62–63) read and translate the traces in the final line of the curse as: [x x x x Z]AG ⸢*ù*⸣ [KAB x x], "*sou*]*th and* [*north*]," so also Kitchen and Lawrence 2012 1:1006–1007.

Reverse
(r 1) [...]
(r 2–7) From this day, [if] you ⟨hear⟩[9] an evil word which is spoken about revolt and rebellion [concerning] Aššurbanipal, king of Assyria, your lord, you shall come, (and) you shall [inf]orm Zakutu, his (grand-)mother, or Aššurbanipal, [king of Assyria], your [l]ord.
(r 7–12) And if [yo]u hear about the killing or removal [of Aššur]banipal, king of Assyria, your lord, [you] shall come, (and) [you shall in]form Zakutu, [his mother], or Aššurbanipal, king of Assyria, your lord.
(r 12–17) And if you hear [*that*] *someone is constructing an evil* [*schem*]*e*[10] concerning Aššurbanipal, king of Assyria, your lord, you shall come, (and) you shall declare (it) before Zakutu, his mother, and before Aššurbanipal, king of Assyria, your lord.
(r 18-le 2) And if you hear and know (someone) saying, '(These are) the men inciting violence and making plots who[11] are among you!' – whether you hear and [know] (of them) from among the bearded officials or among the eunuchs or among his (i.e. Aššurbanipal's) brothers or among the royal seed or among your brothers or among your friends – you shall seize (them) and kill (them). *You* [*shall bri*]*n*[*g (them) to Zakutu, his mother, or to Aššurbanipal, king of Assyria, your lord*].[12]

9 For the emendation, proposed by Parpola (1987:166) and followed as well by Parpola and Watanabe (1988:63), Hecker (2004:92), and Kitchen and Lawrence (2012 1:1006), cf. lines rev. 9, 15, 18, and 23 of this text.

10 No subject is explicit for the verb, which is written *i-nak-kil-an-ni* and is parsed as a G present + ventive + subjunctive *-ni* (following [*kī*], restored at the beginning of line rev. 13, although conceivably from concord following the embedding of a conditional clause within the solemn statement as in line r 5). We do not expect the subject to be [*nikl*]*u*, "[*schem*]*e*," for that word typically appears as a cognate accusative with *nakālu* and the verb is transitive in the G-stem. Nor can *i-nak-kil-an-ni* be a defective writing for 3 mpl verb used impersonally for we would expect the form of the ventive to be *-ni*(*m*). Cf. the various translations: *CAD* N/1 s.v. *nakālu* mng 1a: "If you hear of someone planning an evil plot"; Parpola 1987:167: "should you hear of an ugly [scheme] being elaborated," so also Parpola and Watanabe 1988:64 and Kitchen and Lawrence 2012 1:1008; Hecker 2004:92: "wenn ihr hört, daß ungute Arglist ... ersonnen wird."

11 Parpola (1987:166, so also Parpola and Watanabe 1988:64), deletes the relative pronoun *ša*, translating "If you hear and known that there are men instigating armed rebellion or fomenting conspiracy in your midst," cf. Hecker (2004:92–93): "Und wenn ihr hört oder wißt, daß unter euch Leute sind, die zum Kampf verleiten (oder) aufwiegeln." (Kitchen and Lawrence [2012 1:1008] confusingly *restore* [ša] but omit it from their translation in what is seemingly a misreading of the conventions of SAA 2 where [[ ]] indicates text present on the tablet but removed by the editors, i.e. ⟨⟨ša⟩⟩ as the emendation is more conventionally rendered.) However, the text has the direct speech marker *mā* not *kī*, "that," after "if you hear and known" so that what follows is a quotation of direct speech, presumably from a hypothetical informant who would be identifying the conspirators to the oath taker.

12 le 1–2: The restoration follows Parpola (1987:166), so also Parpola and Watanabe (1988:64), Hecker (2004:93), and Kitchen and Lawrence (2012 1:1008). As Parpola (1987:170) observes, the stipulation has a parallel in Esarhaddon's Succession Treaty § 12. He also remarks that "After rev. 27 [= ue 2] the edge is uninscribed and the curse section normally closing Assyrian treaties is definitely missing."

REFERENCES

Hecker 2004:92–93; Parpola 1987:165–170; Parpola and Watanabe 1988:62–64.

OATH OF LOYALTY TO ESARHADDON (4.38)

Jacob Lauinger

This small fragment of a cuneiform tablet from Nineveh was identified by Simo Parpola in the Kuyunjik collection of the British Museum. Whether the fragment is in fact an *adê*-oath cannot be established without question because so little text remains, but the probable presence of the "solemn statement" construction (*šumma* + subjunctive verb) together with its vocabulary (e.g. *ina gu-m*[*ur-ti*] in line rev 5′; note the Babylonian dialect) make such quite possible. Parpola (1987:175) suggests that the mention of incense (*qutāru*) in line obv. 9′ "may indicate that this treaty dates from 670 B.C., since the unsuccessful coup d'etat of 670 coincided with a worsening of the king's condition."

Obverse
(beginning of obverse not preserved)
(1′–2′) [...] to a/the ci[ty[1] ...]
(3′) to Esarh[addon, king of Assyria ...]
(4′–6′) If a [...] is available,[2] [...] his seed and fa[mily ...]

1 The sign taken here as a logogram may perhaps be used here as a determinative before a specific, named city.

2 Lines 4′–5′ read 4′ *šum-ma* LÚ.[...] 5′ *iz-za-zu-u-n*[*i* ...]. I understand the verb *izzazzuni* to belong to a conditional clause embedded with a solemn statement in the subjunctive mood because of concord (4.37, n. 10). It seems likely that the sign LÚ is a determinative before a profession that is now lost.

(7′–10′) You shall[3] [… If …] sacrificed [… fo]r you[4] […] incense […] you shall … […] (11′–12′) the king of Assyria […] (remainder of obverse not preserved) *Reverse*	(beginning of reverse not preserved) (1′–2′) […] not[5] […] (3′) you sh[all (not) …] (4′) that which yo[u …] (5′–6′) wholeheart[edly … …] (remainder of reverse not preserved)

3 Parpola (1987:174) read originally *la tu-šal-l*[*a*?-], "you will *res*[*cue*]," while Parpola and Watanabe (1988:59) read the SAL sign as *-raq-* suggesting (note to line 7, 10) the restoration *la tu-raq-q*[*a-qa-ni*], "you shall *flat*[*ten out*" or "*ref*[*ine*." Or perhaps restore *la tu-raq-q*[*a-ni*] for a form of *ruqqû*, "to make perfumed oil," in light of the fact that its appearances frame mentions of sacrifice and incense?

4 Following Parpola (1987:175) in understanding the verb *iq-qu-u-ku*[*n-u-ni*] as *naqû* + 2 mpl accusative/dative suffix. See his remarks for near parallels to the "unusual" orthography of *-kunu* + subjunctive *-ni*.

5 Or the negation particle *lā* may indicate here a positive stipulation constructed as a "solemn statement."

REFERENCES

Parpola 1987:174; Parpola and Watanabe 1988:59.

LATE NEO-ASSYRIAN ROYAL INSCRIPTIONS

ESARHADDON'S THOMPSON PRISM (Nineveh A) (4.39)

Victor Avigdor Hurowitz

One of the most important sources for the reign of Esarhaddon is the fully preserved hexagonal prism known for many years as the Thompson Prism, and eventually classified by Borger as Nineveh A.[1] This text, written in the king's eighth year (673 BCE) has been the subject of recent scholarly interest[2] because of the light it sheds on Esarhaddon's reign until slightly after his failed Egyptian campaign, and before his victorious war with Šubria[3]; but especially for the king's "apology," in which he explains his selection as heir to Sennacherib and his subsequent struggle with his siblings to realize his own appointment to the throne. The apology was written not at the time of the events, in the king's first year, but several years later, retrospectively and in connection with his own selection of Assurbanipal to succeed him. The king wished to assure that the challenges he faced upon his accession to kingship will not befall his chosen heir. The overall thematic structure of the text is:

- I. Introduction (i.1–ii.39)
  - A. Identification of the building (with royal titles) (*ekal* RN) (i.1–7)
  - B. Apology (i.8–ii.11)
  - C. Divine Appointment of the King (titles, pedigree, divine blessings) (ii.12–39)
- II. Foreign relations/ historical survey (*ina ūmišuma*) (ii.40–iv.77)
  - A. Campaign nearest to home: Rebellion of Nabû-zēr-kitti-līšir (ii.40–64)
  - B. Western Campaigns (ii.65–iii.42)[4]
    1. Sidon and environs: Abdi-Milkutti (ii.65–iii.19)
    2. Kundi and Sissû – Sanda'urri[5] (iii.20–38)
    3. Arzâ and king Asuḫili (iii.39–42)
  - C. Northern Campaigns (iii.43–61)
    1. Land of Hubušna[6] and Teušpâ, the Cimmerian (iii.43–46)
    2. Cilicia and Hittites (iii.47–55)
    3. Tīl-Ašuri/Pitânu and Barkaneans (iii.56–58)
    4. Manneans and Išpakâ, the Scythian (iii.59–61)
  - D. Southern Campaigns (iii.62–iv.31)
    1. Bīt-Dakkuri and Šamaš-ibni (iii.62–70)
    2. Gambula and Bēl-iqīša, son of Bunanu (iii.71–83)
    3. Adumutu and Ḫaza'ilu[7] (iv.1–31)
  - E. Eastern Campaigns (iv.32–52)
    1. Media[8] (iv.32–45)
    2. Patušarri of Media and Sidir-parna and E-parna (iv.46–52)
  - F. Farthest Campaign: Bāzu[9] (iv.53–77)
  - G. Hymnic Coda and summary of foreign activities (iv.78–v.25)
  - H. Sequel – Elamites and Gutians[10] (v.26–32)

[1] Thompson 1931; Borger 1956:36–66. This text is known from the Thompson Prism itself and thirty-four additional duplicates. For the history of Esarhaddon's reign see Grayson 1991a; Brinkman 1984:67–84; Frame 1992:64–101; Porter 1993; Leichty 1995; Radner 2007.

[2] Tadmor 1983 (with previous bibliography); 1999; 2004; 2006:57–76 and 77–91; and Eph'al and Tadmor 2006.

[3] See recently Eph'al 2005; Eph'al and Tadmor 2006. Eph'al, on the basis of the use of direct speech and proverbs in Thompson Prism and the Letter to the Gods about the Shubrian campaign, suggests they were written by the same author.

[4] Cogan 2008:131–137.

[5] For identification of Sandaurri as the cuneiform form of the well-known (hieroglyphic Luwian) Azatiwata of Karatepe, see Hawkins 1979:153–157. He has also been identified with *sndwr* mentioned in the Aramaic "Adon Papyrus" from Egypt. See Green 2004.

[6] See Medvedskaya 1997:205.

[7] See Eph'al 1982:125–130; Rainey 1993:152–157.

[8] Leichty 2008.

[9] See Eph'al 1982:130–137. The Land of Bâzu is apparently in Arabia and in the Heidel Prism it is mentioned after Adumatu, but here it has been moved so as to end the review of campaigns far from home (see Tadmor 2004:270–272). This campaign is enveloped by a chiastic inclusio *māt Bâzu nagû* (iv.53) // *nagê Bâzi* (iv.76). The depiction of the Land of Bâzu as *120 bêru qaqqar bâṣi* (iv.55) may involve a play on words (see Tadmor 1999:59). A similar word play can be found in the famous "Letter to the God" describing Sargon's Eighth Campaign where immediately after reaching the mountains Sinahulzi and Biruatti the king says he had traversed *šadê bērūti*, "remote mountains" (l. 28; see Foster *BM*, 793, n. 2). In the Thompson Prism itself, another example of a word-play on a topographical designation although not a city name per se may be iii.80, 83: *Ša-pî-Bēl āl dannūtīšu dannassu udannin* ... *kīma dalti ina pān māt Elamti ēdilšu*, "Šapî-Bēl, his fortress city I fortified its fortification ... like a door in front of the Land of Elam I locked it." In iii.43–46 we find a play on an ethnic name where *Teušpâ Gimmirraja ummān-manda*, "Teušpâ the Cimmerian who is an Ummān-manda" is beaten by weapons *adi gimir ummānīšu*, "to the last of his troops."

[10] The reference here can hardly be to the historic Gutians of the end of the Sargonic Period, but, rather to the mountainous area east of the Tigris past Elam. The archaic name may also bear legendary connotations of a barbaric people.

III. Transition passage from military campaigns to building activities (*ultu*) (v.33–39)
IV. Building Report (*ina ūmišuma*) (v.40–vi.53)
V. Closing Prayer (vi.54–64)
VI. Blessings for restoring the building (*ana arkât ūmē*) (vi.65–73)

(i.1–7) The palace of Esarhaddon, great king, mighty king, king of totality, king of the land of Assyria, governor of Babylon, king of Sumer and Akkad, king of the four quarters, true shepherd, favorite of the great gods, who, from his youth, Aššur, Šamaš, Bēl, and Nabû, Ištar of Nineveh, (and) Ištar of Arbela called his name for kingship of the land of Assyria.

(i.8–14) Of my older brothers, I am their young brother. By command of Aššur, Sîn, Šamaš, Bēl and Nabû, Ištar of Nineveh, (and) Ištar of Arbela, (my) father who created me, in the assembly of my brothers, truly raised up my head (selected me), saying: "This is the son who is my successor!" Šamaš and Adad he asked by (means of) divination, and a firm "yes" they answered him, saying: "He is your replacement (successor)!"

(i.15–19) Their honored word he attended to, and the people of the land of Assyria, small and great, my brothers, seed of my father's house, he gathered together. Before Aššur, Sîn, Šamaš, Nabû, (and) Marduk, the gods of the land of Assyria, the gods who dwell in heaven and earth, in order to guard my succession, he made them (the people assembled) say (in adjuration) their (the gods') honored name.

(i.20–25) In a favorable month, (on a) propitious day, according to their exalted command, into the *bīt-rīdûti* (House of Succession/Crown Prince's Palace), a frightening place where imposing kingship is found in its midst, I joyously entered; but persecution and envy poured out upon my brothers, and they abandoned (the command) of the great gods, and in their own insolent actions they trusted, and they plotted evil.

(i.26–28) Evil tongue, slander, deception not in accord with the heart of the great gods, upon me they made up incorrect lies; behind me (my back) they constantly spoke enmity.

(i.29) The appeased heart of my father, not in accordance with the gods, they angered towards me.

(i.30–34) Down below in his heart love (for me) possessed him, and so that I should perform kingship his eyes were directed. With my heart I spoke and pondered in my innards, saying: "Their actions are insolent, and in their own designs they trust, and that which is against the heart of the gods, what will they do?"

(i.35–40) Aššur, King of the Gods, (and) merciful Marduk for whom calumny is an abomination, in blessing, supplication, and obedience (pressing the nose) I prayed to them and they accepted my words. According to the design of the great gods, my lords, in face of the evil acts, they seated me in a secret place, and their sweet protective shadow they extended over me, and guarded me for kingship.

(i.41–47) *Afterwards*, my brothers went berserk, and whatever for the gods and mankind was not good they did, and they plotted evil. They rebelled, and (with) weapons, inside Nineveh, without the gods, in order to exercise kingship, they butted with each other like billy goats. Aššur, Sîn, Šamaš, Bēl, Nabû, Ištar of Nineveh, (and) Ištar of Arbela viewed badly the deeds of the rebels which were done not according to the gods, and they did not stand at their sides.

(i.48–52) Their (my adversaries) force they (the gods) reduced to idiocy (assigned to the wind), and below me they (the gods) made them (my enemies) crouch. The people of the land of Assyria, who the loyalty oath (*adê*), the oath of the great gods, to guard my kingship, had sworn to by water and oil, did not go to their (the rebels') aid.

(i.53–57) I, Esarhaddon, who by trust in the great gods, his lords, in the midst of battle his breast did not turn away, their wicked deeds, quickly I heard; and "Woe!" I said, and my princely garment I ripped, and I wailed laments. Like a lion I raged and my innards burned.

(i.58–65) In order to exercise kingship of the house of my father, I clapped my hands. To Aššur, Sîn, Šamaš, Bēl, Nabû and Nergal, Ištar of Nineveh, (and) Ištar of Arbela I raised my hand (in prayer), and they accepted my word. With their firm "yes" they sent me again and again trustworthy entrails, and "Go! Do not hold back! We shall go by your side, and we will kill your enemies." One day, two days, I did not hesitate. The face of my troops I did not inspect. The rear (of my troops) I did not see. The census of horses, bound to the yoke, and equipment for my battle I did not muster. Supplies for my campaign I did not pile up.

(i.66–68) Snow, cold of the month of Šabāṭu, the strongest cold, I did not fear. Like a flying eagle, to knock over my enemies I opened my hands.

(i.69–77) The road to Nineveh exhaustingly and rapidly I traveled, and in front of me, in the land of Ḫannigalbat, all of their exalted warriors held up the front of my battle (camp), they sharpened their weapons. The fear of the great gods, my lords overwhelmed them, and they saw the mighty onslaught of my battle, and they became like crazed women.

Ištar, mistress of battle and war, lover of my high-priesthood, stood at my side, and broke their bows. Tightly ranked battle lines she opened, and in their assmbly they said, thus: "This is our king!"

(i.78–86) At her august command, they came over to my side and stood behind me. Like lambs they gamboled, they beseeched my lordship. The people of the Land of Assyria which the loyalty oath (*adê*) sworn by the name of the great gods before me had pronounced, came up unto me, and kissed my feet; while they – the rebels, who did rebellion and revolt, who heard the progress of my campaign, and abandoned the armies in which they confided, and fled to an unknown land – I captured; and at the quay of the Tigris, at the command of Sîn (and) Šamaš, the gods, lord of the quay, I made my entire army, jump over the wide Tigris as if it were a ditch.

(i.87-ii.2) In the month of Addaru, a favorable month, on the eighth day, the *eššešu* festival of Nabû, in the midst of Nineveh, the city of my lordship, I entered joyfully, and sat goodly on my father's throne.

(ii.3–11) For me blew a south wind, a breeze of Ea; a wind who's blowing is good for exercising kingship; and good signs in heaven and on earth came to me. They (the gods) constantly arranged for me the messages of ecstatic (prophets), messengers of the gods and Ištar; they made me trust in my heart. The troops, the sinners, who to exercise kingship of the land of Assyria my brothers had caused to plot evil, all of them (their assembly), as one I examined, and I imposed upon them heavy punishment, and I destroyed their progeny.

(ii.12–24) I, Esarhaddon, king of totality, king of the land of Assyria, heroic male, first and foremost of all kings, son of Sennacherib, king of totality, king of the land of Assyria, son of Sargon, king of totality, king of the land of Assyria, creation of Aššur (and) Mullissu, beloved of Sîn and Šamaš, elevated by Nabû (and) Marduk, acceptable to Ištar the queen, desired by the great gods, expert puissant, knowledgeable wise man, the one whom the great gods had elevated to kingship for the restoration of the (statues of the) great gods and the perfection of the sanctuaries of all the holy cities; builder of the Temple of Aššur, constructor of Esaggil and Babylon, restorer of the (statues of the) gods and goddess which are in its (Babylon's) midst, the one who returned the plundered gods of the lands from the midst of (the city) Aššur to their places, and seated (them) in restful dwellings.

(ii.25–29) Until I completed the temples, and had seated their gods in their daises in eternal dwelling, by their great encouraging oracle from the rising of the sun (east) to the setting of the sun (west) I walked dominantly again and again; and I have no equal. The rulers of the four quarters (of the earth) I made bow at my feet; they (the gods) assigned to me the land which had sinned against Aššur.

(ii.30–39) Aššur, father of the gods, placed in my hands (assigned to me) abandoning and resettling, expanding the border of the land of Assyria; Sîn, lord of the diadem, determined as my destiny masculine might, courage; Šamaš, the torch of the gods, had issued for prominence the call of my honored name; Marduk, king of the gods, caused the fear of my kingship to sweep over the lands of the quarters (of the earth) like a heavy cloud; Nergal, the almighty of the gods, had given me as a gift fury, splendor and radiance; (and) Ištar, mistress of battle and war, had presented me as a present a mighty bow, a fierce arrow.

(ii.40–51) At that time, Nabû-zēr-kitti-līšir, son of Merodach-baladan, governor of the Sealand, who does not keep the loyalty oath (*adê*), who does not heed the treaty of the land of Assyria, forgot the good of my father, and in the disturbances in the land of Assyria he called up his troops and his camp; and he surrounded with a siege Ningal-iddin, governor of Uruk, the servant who sees my face; and he took hold of his exit (from his city). After Aššur, Šamaš, Bēl and Nabû, Ištar of Nineveh, (and) Ištar of Arbela, had sat me, Esarhaddon, for good on the throne of my father, and had given me lordship of the lands – he did not fear, he was not slack, he did not release my servant; and, he did not send to me his own rider, and he did not inquire after the well being of my kingship. His wicked deeds I heard of in the midst of Nineveh, and my heart was angry, my innards burned.

(ii.52–57) My officer/eunuch, the provincial governor of the borders of his land, I sent to him, and he, Nabû-zēr-kitti-līšir, the rebel, the insurgent, heard the movement of my troops, and he fled to Elam, like a fox. Because of the oath of the great gods, which he transgressed, Aššur, Sîn, Šamaš, Bēl and Nabû inflicted upon him a great punishment, and in the midst of Elam they killed him in battle.

(ii.58–61) Naʾid-Marduk, his brother, saw the deed which Elam had done to his brother, and from Elam he fled to me; and to perform service to me, he came to the land of Assyria, and he beseeched my lordship.

(ii.62–64) The Sealand, in its entirety, the domain of his brother, I made see his face (I subjugated to him). Yearly, without ceasing, with his heavy visitation offerings he comes to me to Nineveh, and kisses my feet.

(ii.65–70) Abdi-milkutti, king of Sidon, who does not fear my lordship, does not listen to the utterance of my lips, who trusts in the rolling sea, and threw off the yoke of Aššur, Sidon, the city in which he trusts, which is founded in the middle of the sea, I swept over like a flood; I ripped up its wall and its settlement, and I cast it into the middle of the sea, and the place where it had been found I destroyed.

(ii.71–82) Abdi-milkutti, its king, fled from before my weapons into the midst of the sea. By command of Aššur, my lord, I hunted him like a fish from the middle of the sea, and I cut off his head. His wife, his sons, his daughters, the people of his palace, gold, silver, possessions, belongings, precious stones, clothing of multi-colored material and linen, hides of elephants, tusks of elephants, ebony, boxwood, whatever its name is, treasure of his palace, very much, I plundered. His vast people who have no number, oxen, sheep and goats, very much I led off. I gathered it to the midst of the land of Assyria, and the kings of Hatti (Syria-Palestine) and the coast of the Sea, all of them, in another place I had them make a city, and I called its name the city of Kār-Aššur-aḫḫe-iddina (Port Esarhaddon).

(iii.1–19) The city of Bīt-Ṣupūri, the city of Sikkû, the city of Giʾ, the city of Inimme, the city of Ḫildūa, the city of Qartimme, the city of Biʾrû, the city of Kilmê, the city of Bitirume, the city of Sagû, the city of Ampa, the city of Bīt-Gisimea, the city of Birgiʾ, the city of Gambūlu, the city of Dalaimme, the city of Isiḫimme, the cities of the environs of Sidon, a place of grazing and watering, his stronghold, which by the encouragement of Aššur, my lord, my hands had conquered, the people, captured by my bow from the eastern mountain and from the sea, I settled inside, and I turned that region into the territory of the land of Assyria. I took it anew. I placed over them my eunuchs/officers as provincial governors; and I imposed upon it more tax and tributes than before. From among those cities of his I assigned into the hands of Baʾali king of the city of Tyre the city of Maʾarubbu (and) the city of Ṣarepta. I added to the tribute of my lordship more than his earlier annual giving, and made it permanent on him.

(iii.20–27) Moreover, Sanduʾarri, king of (the cities of) Kundi and Sissû, a dangerous enemy, who does not fear my lordship, who had abandoned the gods and confided in difficult mountains, he (and) Abdi-Milkutti, king of Sidon, joined together to help each other; and by the name of their gods, swore an alliance with one another; and trusted in their own strength.

(iii.28–31) I trusted in Aššur, Sîn, Šamaš, Bēl and Nabû, the great gods, and I surrounded him by siege, and like a bird from the heart of the mountains I hunted him, and I cut off his head.

(iii.32–35) In Tašritu, the head of Abdi-milkutti; in Addaru, the head of Sanduʾarri. In a single year I cut them off; and the first one I did not delay, and the last one I was quick.

(iii.36–38) In order to reveal to people the might of Aššur my lord, I hung them around the necks of their eunuch/courtiers, and with singers and lyres, I passed back and forth in the squares of Nineveh.

(iii.39–42) The city of Arzâ in the territory of the Brook of Egypt I plundered for myself, and Asuḫili, its king, I placed in fetters, and I led him to the land of Assyria. At the edge of the city gate, in the middle of the city of Nineveh, I seated him, bound up with a bear, a dog and a pig.

(iii.43–46) Moreover, Teʾušpâ, the Cimmerian (*gimmirāya*), an Ummān-manda, whose place is remote in the land of Ḫubušna, along with his entire (*gimir*) army, I struck with weapons.

(iii.47–51) I trampled the necks of the people of the land of Cilicia (Ḫilakku), mountaineers who live in the difficult mountain ranges of the vicinity of the land of Tabala; wicked Hittites, who trust in their mighty mountains, and since ancient times do not submit to a yoke.

(iii.52–55) Twenty-one of their mighty cities, and many small cities, which are around them, I surrounded, I captured, I plundered their plunder, I destroyed, I tore down, and I burnt in fire. The rest of them, who did not have any sin or crime, I imposed upon them the heavy yoke of my lordship.

(iii.56–58) I threshed the wicked Barnakians, who dwell in the land of Tīl-Ašurri, which in the mouths of people of the land of Miḫrannu, is called the land of Pitānu.

(iii.59–61) I scattered the Mannean people, the uncontrollable Gutians, and its army. I killed by a weapon Išapakaja, the Asguzian, a reinforcement who does not save him.

(iii.62–70) I plundered the land of Bīt-Dakkuri, which is in the midst of the land of Chaldea, an enemy of Babylon. I captured Šamaš-ibni, its king, a criminal rogue, who does not fear the command of the Lord of Lords, who carried off by force the fields of the sons of Babylon and Borsippa, and turned (them) into his own. Because I knew the fear of Bēl and Nabû, I returned those fields, and I entrusted (them) to the sons of Babylon and Borsippa. I seated Nabû-Šallim, son of Balasi, on his throne; and he (now) pulls my harness.

(iii.71–83) Bēl-iqīša, son of Bunnannū, the Gambulian, whose dwelling is situated at a distance of twelve double hours march over land in water and marsh, by the command of Aššur, my lord, fear fell upon him, and following his (own) sense, he took for me tax and tribute, perfect large oxen (and) a team of white mules from the land of Elam, and he came to Nineveh before me, and kissed my feet. I had mercy on him, and I instilled trust in his heart. The city of Ša-pī-Bēl, his fortress city, I strengthened its foundation, and he, along with his archers, I brought inside, and I locked it like a door in the face of Elam.

(iv.1–16) The city of Adumatu, the fortress city of the Arabs, which Sennacherib, king of the land of Assyria, the father who created me, had captured, and its possessions, its property, its gods, along with Apkallatu, queen of the Arabs had plundered, and had taken to the land of Assyria – Ḫazzaʾilu (Hazael), king of the Arabs, along with his heavy visitation offerings, came to Nineveh, the city of my lordship, and kissed my feet. He prayed to me to give (him the idols of) his gods, and I had mercy on him, and Atar-samayin, Dāya, Nuḫāya, Ruldayawu, Abirillu, Atar-qurumâ, the gods of the Arabs, their ruins I renewed, and I wrote on them the mighty deeds of Aššur, my lord, and an inscription of my name; and I gave them back to him. (The lady), Tabuʾa, who was raised in the palace of my father, I placed as ruler over them, and I returned her to her land with her gods.

(iv.17–22) I added sixty-five camels and ten donkeys, more than the previous tribute, and I imposed (it) upon him. Ḫazzaʾilu (Hazael), fate carried him off (he died), and Iatāʾ, his son, I seated on his throne; and I added ten mina of silver, 1,000 choice stones, 50 camels, 100 bags of aromatics, above the tribute of his father, and I imposed on him.

(iv.23–31) Afterwards, Uabu, in order to exercise kingship over the Arabian (people), incited all of them to rebel against Iatāʾ; but I, Esarhaddon, king of the land of Assyria, king of the four quarters, who loves truth, and for whom falsehood is an abomination, sent troops of war to the assistance of Iatāʾ, and they trampled the Arabian (people), all of them, and Uabu, along with the troops who were with him, they cast into chains, and brought to me, and I put on them a neck-stock, and I tied them to the side of my city gate.

(iv.32–37) Uppis, the city chief of the city of Partakka, Zanasana, the city chief of (the city) of Partukka, Ramateya, the city chief of (the city) of Urakazabrana, Medes, whose place is distant, who in (the time of) the kings, my fathers had not crossed the border of the land of Assyria, and had not trampled its ground, the fear of the radiance of (the god) Aššur, my lord, overwhelmed them.

(iv.38–45) Large war horses, a block of lapis lazuli, broken off (quarried) from his mountains, they brought to me to Nineveh, city of my lordship, and they kissed my feet. Because of the (other) city-chiefs who had raised hand against them, they beseeched my lordship and requested my assistance. I sent with them my officers (eunuchs), provincial governors of the area of their land, and the people dwelling in those cities they trampled and caused to bow at their feet. Tax and tribute of my lordship I imposed upon them.

(iv.46–52) The land of Patušarri, a region at the edge of the "Salt House" (salty desert), which is in the midst of the distant land of Media, of the area of the land of Bikini, the mountain of Lapis lazuli, which in (the time of) the kings, my fathers, no one had trampled the land of their mountain, Šidirparna (and) E-parna, mighty city chiefs, who were not submissive to the yoke, they, along with their men, horses of their riders, cattle, sheep, (Bactrian) camels, their heavy plunder I plundered; (and took) to the midst of the land of Assyria.

(iv.53–70) The land of Bāzu, a region whose place is remote, a dry wilderness, a land of salt, a place of thirst, 120 double-hour marches of land of sand (*baṣṣi*), thorns and "gazelle-tooth" stones, a place where snakes and scorpions fill the field like ants, twenty double hours of (Mount) Ḫazû, a mountain of *saggilmud*-stone, I left behind me; and I crossed over that region, which from days of yore no king before me had gone. At the command of Aššur, my lord, I went dominantly again and again in its midst. Kīsu, king of the city of Ḫaldisu, Akbaru, king of the city of Ilpiatu, Mansaku, king of the city of Magalani, Yapāʾ, queen of the city of Diḫrāni, Ḫabisu, king (of the city of) Qabadāʾ, Niḫaru, king (of the city of) Gāʾuani, Baslu, queen (of the city of) Iḫilum, Ḫabaziru, king (of the land of) Pudāʾ, eight kings from the midst of that region, I killed. Like malt I spread out the bodies of their heroes.

(iv.71–77) I plundered (the idols of) their gods, their property, and their possessions, and their people, (and sent) to the midst of the land of Assyria. Layalē, king of the city of Yadiʾ, who had fled before my weapons, fear fell upon him, and he came to the city of Nineveh before me, and kissed my feet. I had mercy on him, and that region of Bāzu I made see his face (serve him).

(iv.78–v.14) By strength of Aššur, Sîn, Šamaš, Nabû, Marduk, Ištar of Nineveh, (and) Ištar of Arbela I conquered all the arrogant enemies. At the mention of their divinities enemy monarchs sway in the wind like reeds, kings who dwell in the sea, whose walls are the sea, and the waves are their outer walls, which ride on ships as if they were chariots, to which boatmen are hitched as if they were horses, fearfully they are repeatedly reduced to hard straits, their hearts pound, and (v.1) they vomit gall. There is no rival, unequal are my weapons, and among the chieftains who go before me none can be compared to me. Anyone who despised the king my father, and answered with enmity, by the command of Aššur, my lord, they were delivered into my hands. Their hard stone walls, I crumble like a potter's vessel. The corpses of their heroes, I fed to the vultures without burial. I plundered their stored up possessions to the land of Assyria. The gods in whom they trust, I count as plunder. Like sheep I lead their luxuriant people. Whoever, in order to save his live, flees into the midst of the sea, does not escape my net, and does not save his life. The speedy one (lit. "open of knees") who takes hold of the ledges of distant mountains, like a bird from the midst of the mountain, I hunt him, and tie his arms. Their blood, I made flow like the breech of (water) in the gully of the mountain.

(v.15–18) The Suteans, who dwell in camps, whose place is far away, like the fury of the onset of a storm I ripped up their roots. He who placed the sea as his fortress, and the mountain as his strength, no one escaped from my net.

(v.19–25) In taking flight they cannot flee. He of the sea – to the mountain! And he of the mountain – to the sea! I commanded their dwelling. By command of Aššur, my lord, who will compete with me for kingship? And among the kings my fathers, whose lordship is made great like mine? From the midst of the sea, my enemies thus said to me, saying: "The fox, before the sun, whither shall he go?"

(v.26–39) Elamites (and) Gutians, arrogant chieftains who answered the kings, my fathers, with enmity, heard the might of Aššur, my lord, which he exercised among all the foreigners, and dread and fear was poured out over them; and in order not to trespass the boundaries of their lands, they sent to Nineveh before me their messengers of good and well-being, and the name of the great gods they pronounced (swore by oath). After Aššur, Šamaš, Bēl, Nabû, Ištar of Nineveh, (and) Ištar of Arbela, caused me to stand in victory over my enemies, and I accomplished whatever filled my heart – in capturing the widespread enemies, which with the encouragement of the great gods, my lords, my hand captured, I had the temples of the holy cities of the land of Assyria and the land of Akkad built; and in silver and gold I plated them; and I made them as bright as the day.

(v.40–53) At that time, the Palace of Muster of Nineveh, which the kings who went before me, my fathers, had made – for mustering the camps, counting the warhorses, mules, chariots, military equipment, weapons of war, and the plunder of enemies, everything, whatever be its name, which Aššur, king of the gods has given me as my royal portion, for the horses to run wild, (and) for the procession of chariots, that place was too small. People of the lands, captured by my bow, I made them carry hoe and brick basket, and they molded bricks. That small palace I razed in its entirety, and much land as an addition, I cut out of the midst of the swamp, and I added to it. With strong limestone from the mountains I filled up the foundation platform.

[a] 2 Kgs 21:1–18; 2 Chr 33:1–20

(v.54-vi.1) I called up kings of the land of Hatti and the other side of the Euphrates, Baʾalu, king of (the city of Tyre), Manasseh,[a] king of the city of Judah, Qaʾuš-gabri, king of the city of Edom, Muṣuri, king of the city of Moab, Ṣil-Bēlu, king of the city of Gaza, Metinti, king of the city of Ashkelon, Ikausu, king of the city of Ekron, Milki-ašapa, king (of the city of) Gebal (Byblos), Matan-Baʾal, king of the city of Arvad, Abī-Baʾali, king of the city of Samsimurruna, Budu-ili, king of (the city of) Bīt-Ammana, Aḫī-Milki, king of the city of Ashdod, twelve kings of the coast of the sea; Ekištura, king of the city of Ediʾil, Palāgurâ, king of the city of Kitrusi, Kīsu, king of the city of Sillûʾa, Itu-andar, king of the city of Pappa, Eresu, king of the city of Silli, Damasu, king of the city of Kurî, Admēsu, king of the city of Tamesi, Damūsi, king of the city of Qarti-ḫadasti, Unasagusu, king of the city of Lidir, Buṣusu, king of the city of Nuria, ten kings of the land of Iadnana (Cyprus) in the middle of the sea; total of twenty-two kings of the land of Hatti, of the shore of the sea, and of the middle of the sea. I sent orders to all of them for large beams, tall pillars, very long crossbeams of cedar (and) cypress, grown on the Mount Sirāra and Mount Lebanon, which since ancient times had waxed very tall, and sprouted in height, *aladlamme* (bull colossi) of *pindû*-stone, *lammasu*-statues, *apsasātu*-statues, thresholds of baked brick, of alabaster, *pindû*-stone, breccia, small breccia, *alallu*-stone, *girimḫilibû*-stone, from the midst of the mountain region, the place where they were created, for the need of my palace, with difficulty and great effort, (vi.1) I had them drag to Nineveh, my lordly city.

(vi.2–8) In a favorable month, on a propitious day, on that foundation platform, I built on top of it great palaces for my lordly dwelling. A house of the king, which was ninety-five large cubits in length, and thirty-one large cubits in width, which among the kings, my fathers, no one had built, I built. (With) thresholds of alabaster, as its lower course, I surrounded it; and I extended over it beams of tall cedars.

(vi.9–14) A palace of white limestone, and palaces of ivory, ebony, boxwood, sissoo wood, cedar, cypress, for my royal dwelling, and my lordly leisure, I had artfully made; and I extended over it tall beams of cedar wood. Doors of cypress, whose fragrance is sweet, I tied up with bands of silver and copper, and I hung in their gates.

(vi.15–21) *Aladlammu* and *apsasatu* of *pindû*-stone that, like their appearance turn back the chests of evil, large *aladlammu*-s, and lions facing one another, *apsasatu* arranged in pairs, polished *lamassu*-s I formed of bright copper, and *aladlammu* of white limestone to the right and to the left I had hold their bolts.

(vi.22–26) Large columns of copper, tall columns of cedar wood, boards, crenellations of their gates I stood around that palace. A narrow band of ivory and lapis lazuli I had made, and I had it surround the archivolt and *kur/mat-ig-qu* (vault?) like a crown. Like a rainbow, I had it surround all of the gates.

(vi.27–29) Nails of silver and gold and bright copper I drove into them. The might of Aššur my lord, the acts which he had done in the enemy lands, I engraved inside it by work of engravers' chisels.

(vi.30–34) A great orchard, resembling (Mount) Amanus, where all aromatics and fruit are gathered together I planted alongside it. Its courtyard greatly I enlarged, and its walkways very much I widened. For watering the horses in its midst I directed to it a channel, and I made it gurgle like a canal.

(vi.35–43) After that palace, from its foundations until its crenellations I finished and completed to perfection, I filled it with luxury. Its wall plaster (*šallaru*) is stirred with beer, its plaster (*kalakku*) is mixed with wine; the carriers of shovel, pickax and brick basket, the doers of the work, the carriers of the (builder's) hod, in cheerful songs of joy, happiness of heart, radiant countenance spend their days. Its work in happiness and joy, hymns of blandishment I completed, and I called its name: Eš-gal-šid-dù-dù-a "The Palace of Counting Everything."

(vi.44–53) Aššur, Bēl, Nabû, Ištar of Nineveh, (and) Ištar of Arbela, all the gods of the land of Assyria, I invited into its midst, and I sacrificed before them abundant, pure sacrifices, and I presented my gifts. Those gods, in their steadfast hearts blessed my kingship. All the princes and people of my land, at tables of feasting, dining and celebration I seated in its midst; and I made their frames of mind joyous. I had their innards imbibe wine and beer. I poured on their heads oil and fine ointment.

(vi.54–57) At the command of Aššur, king of the gods and the gods of the land of Assyria, their creator, in good flesh, happy heart, and bright insides, satisfaction of long life, inside it forever may I dwell, and be satisfied with its luxury.

(vi.58–61) At the New Year, in the first month, all of the thoroughbreds, mules, camels, military equipment, implements of war, all the soldiers, plunder of the enemy, annually and without cease may I count within it.

(vi.62–64) Inside that palace, may a good protecting spirit and a good female protecting spirit, guardian of my royal path, who makes my innards happy forever may they be seen, may they not leave its side.

(vi.65–74) In future days, among the kings, my sons, whom Aššur and Ištar call his name to rule the land and the people – when that palace will become old and fall into ruins, may he renew its ruins. Just as I, placed the inscribed monuments inscribed with the names of the king, the father who created me, with the monuments inscribed with my name, so you, as I, see the monument inscribed with my name and anoint it with oil. Offer sacrifice, place it with the monument inscribed with your name. May Aššur and Ištar hear your prayer.

(Colophons)

REFERENCES

Texts: Thompson 1931; Borger 1956:36–66; Leichty 2011:9–26. Translations: Oppenheim, *ANET*, 289–292; Cogan 2008:131–137.

ESARHADDON'S HEIDEL PRISM (Nineveh B) (4.40)

Victor Avigdor Hurowitz

(i.1–13) Palace of Esarhaddon, great king, mighty king, king of totality, king of the land of Assyria, governor of Babylon, king of the land of Sumer and Akkad, son of Sennacherib, king of the land of Assyria, son of Sargon, king of the land of Assyria, the king who, by the encouragement of Aššur, Sîn, Šamaš, Nabû, Marduk, Ištar of Nineveh, (and) Ištar of Arbela, the great gods, his lords, went again and again from the rising of the sun (east) to the setting of the sun (west), and has no rival.

(i.14–37) Conqueror of the city of Sidon, which is in the middle of the sea; who flattens all its settled area; its walls and its dwelling I uprooted, and threw them into the middle of the sea; and I destroyed the place where it had been. Abdi-milkutti, its king, who had fled before my weapons into the middle of the sea, like a fish, from the middle of the sea, I hunted him down, and I cut off his head. His stored up possessions, silver, precious stones, elephant hides, ivory, ebony, boxwood, clothing of trimmings and linen, whatever it is called, treasure of his palace, in great quantities I plundered. His wide people, who have no number, cattle and sheep, donkeys, I led into the midst of the land of Assyria, and gathered together the kings of the land of

Hatti, and the entire coast of the sea. In another place, I had them build a city, and I called its name "the city of Kār-Esarhaddon (Port Esarhaddon)." People, captured by my bow, of mountain and the sea of the rising of the sun (east), I settled in it. I appointed my officer (eunuch) over them as a provincial governor.

(i.38–56) Moreover, Sanduʾarri, king of the city of Kundi (and) the city of Sisû, a fierce enemy who does not fear my lordship, who abandoned the gods, and put his trust in the difficult mountains, and Abdi-Milkutti, king of the city of Sidon made as his ally – I trusted in Aššur, my lord, and like a bird from the midst of the mountain I hunted him, and I cut off his head. In order to display the might of Aššur my god to the people, the head of Sanduʾarri and of Abdi-Milkutti I hung around the necks of his magnates, and with singers and lyres I passed again and again through the squares of Nineveh.

(i.57–63) The one who plunders the land of Arzâ, on the border of the Brook of Egypt, who, Asuḫili, its king, along with his advisors threw into chains, and I led to the city of Aššur. At the side of the city gate, inside the city of Nineveh, with a bear, a dog and a pig I seated him, tied up.

(ii.1–4) And Teʾušpa, the Cimmerian (*gimmirrāya*), the Umman-mānda, whose place is far away, in the land of the land of Ḫubušna, along with his entire (*gimir*) army, I beat with weapons.

(ii.5–15) Who tramples the necks of the people of the land of Cilicia, mountaineers who dwell in the mountain ranges, at the side of the city of Tabal, who trusted in their mountains, and from previous days did not submit to my yoke. Twenty-one of their cities, along with the little cities in their borders I surround, I captured, I plundered their plunder, I destroyed, I tore down, I burnt in fire. The rest of them who had no sin or crime I imposed upon them the yoke of my lordship.

(ii.16–19) The thresher of the land of Barnaki, a dangerous enemy, who dwells in the land of Til-Ašurri, which in the mouths of the people of the city of Meḫrānu, is called Pitānu.

(ii.20–23) Scatterer of the people of the land of the Manneans, the uncontrolled Gutians, who the troops of Išpakaya, the Ašguzayan, his ally who could not save him, killed by weapons.

(ii.24–33) The banisher of Nabû-zēr-kitti-līšir, son of Merodach-baladan, who relied on the king of (the land of Elam), and did not save his life. Naʾid-Marduk, his brother, in order to serve me, fled from the land of Elam, and came to me in Nineveh, my lordly city, and kissed my feet. The Sealand in its entirety, the dominion of his brother, I made see his face (serve him).

(ii.34–45) Plunderer of the land of Bīt-Dakkuri, which is in (the land of Chaldea), enemy of Babylon; capturer of Šamaš-ibni, its king, a rogue, a criminal, who does not fear the name of the Lord of Lords, who took away by violence the fields of the sons of Babylon and Borsippa; and because I know fear of Bēl and Nabû, I returned those fields, and I made them (the fields) see the sons of Babylon and Borsippa (= I entrusted the fields to the citizens of Babylon and Borsippa). Nabû-šalim, son of Balasu, I seated on his (Šamaš-ibni's) throne, and he drew my harness.

(ii.46–62) The city of Adumutu, the fortress city of the land of Arabia, which Sennacherib, king of the land of Assyria, the father who created me, had captured, and its property, its possessions, its gods (divine statues), along with Apkallati, queen of the land of Arabia, plundered, had taken to the land of Assyria, Hazael, king of the land of Arabia, with his heavy visitation gift, came to me in Nineveh, my lordly city, and kissed my feet. Because he begged me to give him his gods (divine statues), and I had mercy on him; and those gods (divine statues), I restored their ruins, and the mighty deeds of Aššur, my Lord, and an inscription of my own name I had written on them; and I gave them to him in return. (The lady) Tabuʾa, who had grown up in my palace, I placed as king over them; and with her gods I returned her to her land.

(iii.1–8) Sixty-five camels above the earlier tribute of my fathers I added and imposed upon him. Afterwards, the god brought Hazael to his destiny (killed him), and Iaʾulû, his son, I seated on his throne, and ten mina of silver, a thousand select stones, fifty camels, a thousand bags of aromatics, above the tribute of his father, I added to him; and imposed upon him.

(iii.9–36) The land of Bāzu, whose place is far away, an oblivion of dry land, ground of salt, a place of thirst, one hundred and forty double hour marches, ground of sand (*baṣṣu*), thorns, and gazelle-toothed stones, twenty double hour marches over ground of snakes and scorpions, which, like ants fill the field. Twenty double hour march over (Mount) Ḫazû, a mountain of *saggilmud*-stone, I sent behind me and I traversed, which from ancient times, no earlier king before me had gone, by command of Aššur, my lord,
In its midst I went dominantly. Eight kings, which I killed in that regions, their gods, their possessions, their property, their people, I plundered into the middle of the land of Assyria. Layalê, king of the city of Yadiʾ, who from before my weapons had fled, heard about the plundering of his gods, and to

Nineveh, my lordly city, he came before me, and he kissed my feet. I had mercy on him, and I said to him "Aḫulap" ("it is enough!"). His gods which I had plundered, the might of Aššur, my lord, I wrote upon them, and I gave to him in return. That region of Bāzu I made see his face (assigned to him to rule). My lordly tax and tribute I established upon him.

(iii.37–52) Bēl-iqīša, son of Bunani, the Gambulean, who at a distance of twelve double hour marches over land, like a fish, his dwelling place is situated in water and reeds. By command of Aššur, my lord, dread fell upon him, and following his own council, the tax and tribute, fat, unblemished bulls, double pairs of white mules, he took from the land of Elam, and brought before me to Nineveh, and kissed my feet. I had mercy on him, and I soothed his heart. The city of Ša-pî-Bēl, his fortress city, I strengthened its fortifications, and he, along with his bow troops, I brought inside it, and like a lock, in face of the land of Elam, I locked it.

(iii.53–61) (Mount) Patušarra, the region alongside the salt field, which is inside the (land of the) distant Medes, which among the kings, my fathers, no one had trampled the dust of its land, Šidirparna (and) E-parna, strong city chieftains who don't submit to my yoke, they, along with their people, horses of their riders, cattle, sheep, donkeys, (Bactrian) camels, their heavy plunder I plundered to the land of Assyria.

(iv.1–10) Uppiš, mayor of the city of Paritakka, Zanasana, mayor of the city of Partukka, Ramateia, mayor of the city of Urukazabarna, the Medians, whose place is far away, who in the period of the kings, my fathers, the territory of the land of Assyria, did not pass into, and did not step on her ground – the terrifying fear of Aššur, my lord, overwhelmed them; and they brought to me to Nineveh, my lordly city, large, warhorses, and lapis lazuli mined from their land, and kissed my feet.

(iv.11–20) Because of the mayors who had raised hands against them, they beseeched my lordship, and asked for my help. My eunuchs, provincial governors of the territory of their countries I sent with them, and the people who dwell in those cities they trampled, and made them submit to their feet. Tax and tribute of my lordship I fixed upon them annually.

(iv.21–31) After Aššur, Šamaš, Bēl, Nabû, Ištar of Nineveh, and Ištar of Arbela made me stand triumphantly over my enemies, and I filled my heart's desire with all of the widespread enemies, which by encouragement of the great gods, my lords, my hands had captured, the temples of the holy places of the land of Assyria and the land of Akkad I had them build, and I adorned them with silver and gold, and I made them bright like the day time.

(iv.32–53) At that time, the Palace of Muster, which is in the midst of Nineveh, which the kings who came before me, my fathers, had built – for the mustering of the camp, counting the warhorses, the mules, the chariots, equipment and implements of war, and plunder of my enemies, everything, whatever be its name, which Aššur, king of the gods, gave me as my royal portion, for the horses to run wild (and) the parading of the chariots, that place was too small. People of the lands, captured by my bow, I made them carry hoe and brick basket, and they molded bricks. That small palace I razed in its entirety, and much land as an addition, I cut out of the midst of the swamp, and I added to it. With strong limestone from the mountains I filled up the foundation platform.

(iv.54–v.12) I called up twenty-two kings of the land of Hatti, of the shore of the sea (and) of the middle of the sea. All of them I commanded, and large beams, tall pillars, (v.1) horizontal crossbeams of cedar and cypress from (Mount) Sirāra and (Mount) Lebanon, *lamassu*-statues, *aspassātu*-statues, thresholds of baked brick, of alabaster, *pindû*-stone, *turminû*-breccia, *turminubanda*-breccia, *Engišû*-stone, *alallu*-stone, *girimḫilibî*-stone, from the midst of the mountain region, the place where they are created, with difficulty and great effort, I had them dragged to Nineveh.

(v.13–23) In a favorable month, on a propitious day, on that foundation platform, I built on top of it great palaces for my lordly dwelling. A strong house, which is ninety-five large cubits long, thirty-one large cubits wide, which among the previous kings, my fathers, no one had built, I built. High beams of cedar wood I stretched out above it.

(v.24–32) Doors of cypress wood, whose fragrance is sweet, I tied up with bands of silver and copper, and I hung in its gates. *Aladlammu*-statues and *lamassu*-statues of stone,
Which, because of their appearance, turn back the breast of evil, guard the steps, protect
The walk of the king who created them, to the left and right I placed at their bolts.

(v.33–39) A palace of interlocking limestone and cedar wood, for my lordly leisure, I artfully constructed. *Lamassu*-statues of polished copper, both of which look forward and backward, in pairs, I erected within it.

(v.40–45) High beams of cedar wood, with crossbeams as a cornice, I stood in its gates. Around that palace, a narrow band of obsidian and lapis lazuli,

I had made, and I surrounded it like a wreath. With vaults and *matgiqu*-s, like a rainbow, I surrounded all the gates.

(v.47–53) Nails of pure silver and bright copper I drove into it. The mighty acts of Aššur, my lord, which in enemy lands, he did for me time and again, by the craft of sculptors, I depicted within it.

(v.54–58) An orchard, resembling the (Mount) Amanus, in which every type of aromatic plant and tree are collected, I placed alongside it. Its courtyards I made very large // Its walkways I made very wide.

(vi.1–9) In order to water my horses within it I made a canal flow, and I made it gurgle like a brook. That palace, from its foundations until it crenellations I constructed and completed, and I filled it with luxury. I called its name: Ešgalšiddudua, "The Palace of Administering Everything."

(vi.10–24) Aššur (and) Ištar of Nineveh, all the gods of the land of Assyrian into its midst I invited, and luxurious, pure sacrifices I offered before them; and I presented them my gifts. Those gods, in the steadfastness of their heart, blessed my kingship. The magnates and people of all my lands, in banquet and feast, on tables of celebration, I seated inside it; and I made their moods joyous. Wine and *kurunnu*-wine I made their innards imbibe. Oil and fine oil I poured over their heads.

(vi.25–37) By command of Aššur, king of the gods, and all the gods of the land of Assyria, in good health and happy heart, radiant insides, and ripe old age, may I always dwell within it, and may I be sated with its luxury. At the New Year festival, in the first month, all of the warhorses, mules, donkeys, camels, military gear, equipment of war, all the troops plundered from the enemies, annually, without cease, may I count within it.

(vi.38–40) In the midst of that palace, may good *šēdu*-spirits and good *lamassu*-spirits, who guard my royal steps, and make my insides joyful, endure forever, and never depart from its side.

(Colophon)

REFERENCES

Text: Heidel 1956; Borger 1956:37–64; 1996:381. Translations: Oppenheim, *ANET*, 290–292.

AŠŠURBANIPAL'S RASSAM PRISM (A) (4.41)

Victor Avigdor Hurowitz

Aššurbanipal is mentioned in the Bible only once, in an Aramaic letter where he is called Osnapar (Ezra 4:10), and is said to have deported several peoples from Babylonia and Elam and settled them in the city of Samaria and the rest of the province of "Beyond the River." In his many royal inscriptions, Judah is mentioned only once, in a list of twenty-two kings of the Mediterranean coast, which includes Manasseh, king of Judah (edition C). But there are numerous references to Aššurbanipal's activities in lands surrounding Judah including Egypt, Lebanon, Transjordan.

The Rassam Prism (Prism A)[1] is a ten-sided prism[2] bearing 1,302 lines of text, dating to the eponym of Šamaš-da''inanni (perhaps 644–643 BCE).[3] This prism is sometimes called Aššurbanipal's annals, but it is not an annalistic composition, and it is preferable to refer to it as his *res gestae*,[4] because, although the military ventures are described serially and labeled individually, they are numbered not by eponym (*līmu*) or regnal year (*palû*) but by "campaign" (*gerru*).[5] More significant to breaking with the strictly annalistic form, the campaigns are not ordered chronologically, year by year, but in geographical sequence counterclockwise, going from southwest (Egypt), to

[1] See Borger 1996:1–85. There are thirty-three exemplars of Prism A (Borger 1996:1–4). The classic, previous edition was Streck 1916 1:xvii–xxi; 2:2–91. For a discussion of the textual variants among Ashurbanipal's inscriptions see Cogan 2005. For a full translation see Luckenbill, *ARAB* 2:290–323, §§762–840. For translation of selected passages on the Egyptian, Syro-Palestinian and Arabian campaigns, see Melville 2006. For the apology, first Egyptian campaign, Gyges incident, and Šamaš-šumu-ukīn war, see Hecker *TUAT* 74–84; on the Egyptian and Tyrian campaigns, see Oppenheim *ANET*, 294–301; on the Egyptian and Tyrian campaigns, see Cogan 2008:149–157, 160–161.

[2] Some scholars such as Streck 1916; Luckenbill, *ARAB* 2:290; and Oppenheim, *ANET*, 294 refer to it as a "cylinder." I have adopted Borger's (1996) designation.

[3] For attestations of this eponym see Millard 1994:82–83. Although designated "post-canonical" by Millard, Reade (1998:257) has dated it to Ashurbanipal's 22nd year. For historical background, see Grayson 1991b:142–161; Radner 2011. For recent studies of historical and other aspects of the individual *gerru*s, see the references in the outline of the text.

[4] We could also call it his autobiography because even though not written by the king himself, it starts, "*anāku* ..." and is phrased throughout in the first person singular, the voice speaking being that of Ashurbanipal. For the various autobiographical modes in Mesopotamian historiography, and the "pseudo I" of the royal inscriptions in particular, see Machinist 2003.

[5] See Tadmor 1981:21.

west and northwest (Phoenicia, Lydia), east (Mannea), southeast (Elam) and further south (Arabia). The ninth *gerru* actually ends in the Mediterranean costal cities Usû and Akkû, captured on return from Arabia (ix.115–128). This return to the west brings his conquest of the world full circle.

This order follows the arrangement of the so-called "summary inscriptions" (also known as *Prunkinschriften*, or "display inscriptions")[6] and has two advantages. On the one hand, by not employing specific, identifiable dates expressed in the terms *palû* or *līmu*, Aššurbanipal exempts himself from having to explain inactive or unsuccessful years even while maintaining a verisimilitude of chronological continuity and a constant stream of victories. On the other hand, the geographic ordering brings to the fore the world-encompassing scope of Assyrian power and domination.[7]

The Rassam Prism is segmented by ruled lines on the tablet, dividing the inscription into thirteen sections. A brief outline of the text follows:

I. Introduction (Pedigree, selection, titles, education, prosperity) (i.1–51)
II. First *gerru* (South: Egypt; Tarqû [Terhaqa)[8] (i.52–ii.27)
III. Second *gerru* (Egypt, Cush; Tašdamanê – continuation) (ii.28–48)
IV. Third *gerru* (West: Phoenicia; Northwest: Lydia) (ii.49–125)
  A. Mediterranean Coast: Tyre, Arwad, Tabāl, Cilicia, Arwad[9] (ii.49–94)
  B. Lydia (Gyges)[10] (ii.95–125)
V. Fourth *gerru* (East: Manneans; Aḫšēri)[11] (ii.126–iii.26)
VI. Fifth *gerru* (Far East and South: Elam and Gambulu; Babylon and Šamaš-šumu-ukīn)[12] (iii.27–127)
  A. Teumman[13]; Umman-nikaš; Tammaritu[14]; Dunānu of Gambulu (iii.27–69)
  B. Babylon: Šamaš-šumu-ukīn[15] (iii.70–127)
VII. Sixth *gerru* (Babylon: Šamaš-šumu-ukīn, continuation) (iii.128–iv.109)
VIII. Seventh *gerru* (Far East: Elam; Umman-aldaš) (iv.110–v.62)
IX. Eighth *gerru* (Far East: Elam; Umman-aldaš; Susa; Pa'ê) (v.63–vii.81)
X. Ninth *gerru* (South: Arabia; Uʾateʾ, Abī-Yateʾ; West: Ušû, Akkû)[16] (vii.82–x.5)
XI. Finale – (In Assyria [Nineveh]) (x.6–39)
  A. Umman-aldaš taken to Assyria (x.6–16)
  B. Tammaritu, Pa'ê, Umman-aldaš, Uʾateʾ taken to Assyria (x.17–23)
  C. Victory celebration in Emašmaš temple (x.24–39)
XII. Urartu (Ištar-dūri) (x.40–50)
XIII. Building Report (*ina ūmēšu*): Building the *bīt ridûti* (x.51–120)
  A. Building the *bīt ridûti* (x.51–108)
  B. Request to rebuild: Blessing and Curses (x.109–120)

(i.1–7) I, Aššurbanipal, creation of Aššur and Mullissu, eldest prince of the Succession Palace (*bīt rīdûti*, lit. "adjoining palace"),[17] whom Aššur	a Jer 1:5	and Sîn, lord of the crown, in distant days, by pronouncing his name, called (him) for kingship, and in his mother's womb[a] created him for shepherd-

[6] See Gerardi 1987. This practice, which is essentially a hybrid of the annalistic and the summary inscription formats, is followed earlier in Esarhaddon's Thompson Prism (Nineveh A) (see Hurowitz 2009).

[7] Irene Winter has suggested that the battle scenes on the walls of the throneroom in Assurnasirpal II's Northwest palace at Kalhu are arranged geographically (southwest, west, north, east), and that this arrangement reflects a statement in one of this kings inscriptions that the he has "brought under one authority ferocious (and) merciless kings from east to west." See Winter 1983:24. For similar geographical ordering in the reliefs of Shalmaneser III, see Marcus 1987.

[8] For the Egyptian campaigns, see Spalinger 1974; Fales 1981; Onasch 1994.

[9] See Lamprichs 1995:166–181.

[10] For the encounter with Gyges, see Gelio 1981. For the literary history of this pericope and the unique characteristics of the tale in Prism A, see Cogan and Tadmor 1977:78–81. On the textual growth of this *gerru*, see Cogan 2009.

[11] See Ponchia 2002:257–262.

[12] For the Elamite campaigns, see Gerardi 1987; Potts 1999:276–288; Waters 2000:68–80, 117–118; 2002.

[13] See Waters 1999b.

[14] See Waters 1999a.

[15] For relations between Ashurbanipal and Šamaš-šumu-ukīn and the uprising, see Brinkman 1984:85–104; Frame 1992:102–190; Bartelmus 2007.

[16] For the Arabian campaigns and the variant textual versions describing them, see Weippert 1973; Ephʿal 1982:46–52, 142–169 and passim; and Gerardi 1992.

[17] Parpola 1970, 2:119–120.

ing the land of Assyria; Šamaš, Adad, and Ištar, by their firm (oracular) decision, declared my exercise of kingship.

(i.8–22) Esarhaddon, king of the land of Assyria, the father who created me, was attentive to the word of Aššur and Mullissu, the gods in whom he trusts, who had commanded him concerning my exercise of kingship. In the month of Ayyaru (Iyyar), the month of Ea, lord of humanity, on the twelfth day, a favorable, the SUM-NÍG (festival) of Gula, according to the princely utterance of the mouth, which Aššur, Mullissu, Sîn, Šamaš, Adad, Bēl, Nabû, Ištar of Nineveh, Šarrat-Kidmuri, Ištar of Arbela, Ninurta, Nergal, (and) Nusku, pronounced, (he, Esarhaddon) gathered the people of the land of Assyria, small and great, of the upper and lower seas. To guard my regency, and afterwards to perform kingship of the land of Assyria, a loyalty oath (sworn to) by the life of the great gods, he made them pronounce; he confirmed the treaty documents.

(i.23–40) In happiness and joy I entered the *bīt rīdûti*, an artful place, the bond of kingship, which Sennacherib, father of my father who bore me, had exercise within in it regency and kingship; where Esarhaddon, the father who created me, was born in its midst, grew up, exercised lordship of the land of Assyria, dominated all chieftains, and broadened his family, tied together relatives by marriage and family; and I, Aššurbanipal, learned within it the wisdom of Nabû, the entirety of the scribal art of all wise men, whatever there are, I sought out their learning. I learned to shoot a bow, ride horses, and hold the reins of a chariot. By command of the great gods whose names I have called, (and) have spoken their praise, they commanded me to perform kingship. They assigned me to sustain their holy places. In my stead, they answered my opponents and killed my enemies. Male, hero, beloved of Aššur and Ištar, descendant/great-grandson of kingship am I.

(i.41–51) After Aššur, Sîn, Šamaš, Adad, Bēl, Nabû, Ištar of Nineveh, Šarrat-Kidmuri, Ištar of Arbela, Ninurta, Nergal, (and) Nusku in goodness seated me on the throne of my father who created me, Adad, his rain he sent to me; Ea broke open for me his underground springs; five cubits high, grain grew in its furrows; the sheaves were 5/6th cubits long; success of the harvest, abundance of Nissaba; constantly caused blossoming in the cane brake; orchards, were luxuriant with fruit; cattle were abundant with offspring; in the term of my reign were plenty and abundance; in my years plenty was accumulated.

(i.52–61) In my first campaign I went to (the land of land of) Magan (Egypt) and the land of Meluḫḫa (Nubia). Tirhaka[b] (Tarqû), king of the land of Egypt and the land of Nubia/Ethiopia (Kusû), whom Esarhaddon, king of the land of Assyria, the father who created me, had inflicted his defeat (and) ruled his land; and he, Tirhaka, the might of Aššur and Ištar and the great gods, my lords, forgot, and trusted in his own strength. Against the kings, trusted representatives, whom, in the midst of the land of Egypt, the father who created me had appointed – to kill, rob and take away the land of Egypt he came against them. He entered and sat in the midst of Memphis, the city that the father who had created me had conquered, (and) had turned into territory of the land of Assyria.

(i.62–65) A swift courier came to me in the midst of Nineveh, and repeated (the news) to me. Concerning these deeds, my heart became furious; and my innards burned. I raised up my hands, I beseeched Aššur, and Ištar-Aššuritu.

(i.66–71) I called up my exalted forces which Aššur and Ištar, had placed in my hands. To the land of Egypt and the land of Nubia I went straight on the road. In the course of my campaign, twenty-two kings of the coast of the sea, the midst of the sea, and the dry land, servants who see my face, their heavy audience gifts carried before me, and they kissed my feet.

(i.72–74) Those kings, along with their forces, their ships, on sea and dry land, along with my soldiers on a way and a path I sent them off.

(i.75–77) To the aid and assistance of the kings, my trusted representatives, who are in the midst of the land of Egypt, the servants who my face, quickly I proceeded; and I went to the city of Kār-Banīti.

(i.78–89) Tirhaka, king of the land of Egypt, and the land of Kush, (while) within Memphis heard the progress of my campaign, and to wage war of weapons and battle, he called up against me his battle troops. With the encouragement of Aššur, Bēl and Nabû, the great gods, my lords, who go at my side, in a battle in a wide field I inflicted the defeat of his troops. Tirhaka, in the midst of Memphis, heard of the defeat of his troops. The awe-inspiring radiance of Aššur and Ištar overwhelmed him, and he went crazy. My majestic radiance covered him – that with which the gods of heaven and earth had adorned me – and he abandoned the city of Memphis, and in order to save his life he fled into Thebes (Nîʾ).[c] I seized that city. I brought my soldiers inside and settled (them) within.

(i.90–113) Necho,[d] king of the city of Memphis and the city of Sais; Šarru-lū-dāri, king of the city of *Pelusium*; Pišanḫuru, king of the city of Natḫû; Paqruru, king of the city of Pi-šaptu; Bukkunannīʾpi, king of the city of Ḫatḫiribi; Naḫkê, king of the city of Ḫininši; Puṭubišti, king of the city of

b 2 Kgs 19:9; Jer 37:9

c Nah 3:8; Ezek 30:14–16; Jer 46:25

d 2 Kgs 23:29, etc; Jer 46:2; 2 Chr 35:20, etc.

Tanis (Zoan); Unamunu, king of the city of Nathû; Ḫarsiaešu, king of the city of Ṣabnûti; Buʾama, king of the city of Mendes (Pindidi); Susinqu, king of the city of Buširu; Tapnaḫti king of the city of Punubu; Bukkunanniʾpi, king of the city of Aḫni; Iptiḫardēšu, king of the city of Piḫattiḫurunpiki; Naḫtiḫuruansini, king of the city of Pišadiʾâ; Bukurninib, king of the city of Paḫnuti; Ṣiḫâ, king of the city of Šiyautu; Lamintu, king of the city of Ḫimuni; Išpimātu, king of the city of Tayani; Mantimeʾanḫe, king of the city of Thebes – these kings, governors, trusted representatives, who in the midst of Egypt, the father who had created me had appointed, who in the face of the onslaught of Tirhaka had abandoned their posts of responsibility, (and) filled the desert, I returned; and where the posts of their responsibilities (had been previously), in their places I appointed them.

(i.114–117) The land of Egypt and the land of Kush, which the father who created me had conquered I took anew. The watches, I strengthened even more than in previous days, and I tied the ties. With much plunder and heavy booty, in wellbeing I returned to the city of Nineveh.

(i.118–122) Afterwards these kings, all those I had appointed, transgressed my loyalty oaths. They did not keep the oath of the great gods the good deeds I had done for them they forgot, and their heart planned evil. Lying words they spoke, and counsel which was unfortunate they counseled among themselves, saying: "Tirhaka, from the land of Egypt they will rip out, and you, what are we sitting for?"

(i.123-ii.3) To Tirhaka, king of the land of Kush, in order to make a treaty and peace they sent their mounted messengers, saying: "peace between us may there be, and let us be agreeable to each other; the land, among ourselves (lit. among each other), we will divide up, and may there be between us no other master." To the troops of the land of Assyria, the forces of my lordship, which as their reinforcements I had placed, they sought something evil. My eunuchs, these words they heard, (and) their mounted messengers along with their emissaries, they captured for me, and saw their lying acts. These kings they caught for me, and in chains of iron and shackles of iron they grasped (their) hands and feet. The oath of Aššur, king of the gods, overtook them; but those who had transgressed the loyalty oath of the great gods, the good in their hands I sought, and what I did to them (was) good; but people of the city of Sais, the city of Bindidi, the city of Ṣiʾnu and the rest of the cities, how many with them placed, plotted evil small and large, by weapons they felled, a single person did not escape from within; their corpses they hung on stakes, their skin they flayed, and clothed (with it) the walls of the city. These kings who sought evil to the troops of the land of Assyria, while they were still alive they brought to me to Nineveh.

(ii.8–19) On Necho, from among them, I had mercy, and I let his soul live. I imposed on him a loyalty oath more excessive than before. I clothed him in multicolored garments, and a golden *allu* (jewelry), as an insigne of his royal rank, I placed upon him. Bracelets of gold I tied on his hands. A dagger of iron for the belt, whose inlay is gold, I wrote upon it the calling of my name and gave it to him. Chariots, horses, mules for his lordly riding I presented him. My eunuchs, governors, I sent with him for his assistance. Wherever the father who had created me had appointed him for kingship in the city of Sais, I returned him to his position. Nabû-šēzibanni, his son, I assigned to Ḫatḫariba; sweetness and good I added more than of my father who created me and I did to him.

(ii.20–21) Tirhaka, in the place where he had fled, the terrifying appearance of the weapon of Aššur my lord overwhelmed him, and he died.

(ii.22–27) Afterwards, Tašdamanê (Tantamun), son of Šabakû, sat on his royal throne. The city of Thebes (and) the city of Heliopolis (Unu), he made as his fortresses; and he gathered his band, to fight with my troops, the sons of the land of Assyria, who were in Memphis; he stirred up his battle. Those people he captured and seized their escape route. A fast messenger came to me in Nineveh and told me.

(ii.28–48) In my second campaign, to the land of Egypt and the land of Nubia I took a straight road. Tašdamanê (Tantamun) heard the progress of my campaign and that I had trampled (set foot on) the border of the land of Egypt. He abandoned the city of Memphis, and in order to save his life he fled into the middle of Thebes. The kings, governors (and) trusted representatives whom in the middle of the land of Egypt I had placed, in front of me came to me, and kissed my feet. After Tašdamanê I took the road. I went to Thebes, his fortress city. The onslaught of my mighty war he saw, and he abandoned the city of Thebes. He fled to the city of Kipkipi. That city, in its entirety, by the encouragement of Aššur and Ištar, my hands captured. Silver, gold, choicest stones, the property of his palaces, whatever there was, clothes of colored fabric, linen, large horses, people, male and female, two tall pillars, fashioned out of pure silver alloy, whose weight is 2500 talents, standing in the gate of the temple, from their standing places I ripped them out, and I took to me to the land of Assyria. Heavy plunder without number I plundered from the midst of Thebes. Over the land of Egypt, and the land of Nubia I made my weapons shine bright, and

I established victory. With full hand, in wellbeing I returned to Nineveh, my lordly city.

(ii.49–62) In my third campaign, against Baal, king of the land of Tyre, who dwells in the middle of the sea, I surely went. He who did not observe my royal decree (and) did not heed the utterance of my lips. I constructed fortifications against him; I blocked his paths on sea and on dry land; their life I made narrow and cut short. I made him submit to my yoke. A daughter, issue of his body, and daughters of his brothers he sent to me to perform steward service. Yaḫimilki, his eldest son, who had never crossed the sea, as one he sent to me to do servitude to me. His daughter and his brother's daughters along with a large bridal gift I received from him. I had mercy on him, and the son, issue of his body, I returned and gave to him.

(ii.63–67) Jakinlû king of Arvad, who dwells in the midst of the sea, who was not submissive to the kings, my fathers, submitted to my yoke. His daughter with a large dowry (and) to perform stewardship to Nineveh I brought, and he kissed my feet.

(ii.68–74) Mugallu, king of the land of Tabal, who with the kings, my fathers, spoke treachery, his daughter, issue of his body, with large bridal gifts, to perform stewardship, to Nineveh he sent to me, and she kissed my feet. Upon Mugallu, large horses as an annual tribute I imposed upon him.

(ii.75–80) Sandašarme, the Ḫilakkaen, who to the kings, my fathers did not submit, did not tow their harness, a daughter, issue of his loins, with a great dowry to perform stewardship, to Nineveh he brought to me, and she kissed my feet.

(ii.81–94) After Iakinlû, king of the land of Arwad, died (lit. "stood on his mountain"), Aziba'al, Abiba'al, Adoniba'al, Sapaṭiba'al, Budiba'al, Ba'al-yašupu, Ba'alḫanû, Ba'al-maluku, Abīmilkī, (and) Aḫīmilki, the sons of Yakīn-ilu, who dwelt in the midst of the sea, came up to me from the midst of the sea, and with their heavy audience gift came to me and kissed my feet. I showed kindness to Aziba'al, and I assigned him to kingship of the land of Arvad. Abiba'al, Adoniba'al, Sapaṭiba'al, Budiba'al, Ba'al-yašupu, Ba'alḫanunu, Ba'al-maluku, Abīmilkī, Aḫīmilki, I dressed in clothing of multicolor cloth. I tied bracelets of gold to their hands. I caused them to stand before me.

(ii.95–106) Guggu (Gyges), king of the land of Lydia, a region which is across the sea, a distant place which the kings, my fathers, had not heard the mention of its name, Aššur, the god my creator, caused him to see my name in a dream, saying: "Grasp the feet of Aššurbanipal, king of the land of Assyria, and by (merely) mentioning his name, conquer your enemies." On the day he saw this dream, he sent his rider to ask of my wellbeing. (On account of) this dream, which he saw, he sent to me by the hand of his messenger, and (the messenger) repeated it to me. From the very day that he grasped my royal feet, the Cimmeraeans (*Gimirraya*), who exhaust his land, who did not constantly fear my father, and, as for me, did not grasp my royal feet, he (Gyges) conquered.

(ii.107–110) With the encouragement of Aššur, and Ištar, the gods, my lords, from among the chiefs of the Cimmereans (*Gimirraya*) whom he had captured, two chiefs in iron wooden bars of handcuffs, and iron fetters he held, and, along with his heavy visitation tribute he sent to me.

(ii.111–118) (Suddenly) his riders whom, to ask of my wellbeing, he constantly sent to me again and again, he caused to cease because he did not keep the word of Aššur, the god who created me, (but) in his own strength he trusted, and his heart swelled. His forces to the assistance of Tušamilki (Psammetichus), king of the land of Egypt, who had thrown off the yoke of my lordship, he sent, and I heard, and I beseeched Aššur and Ištar saying: "In front of his enemies, may his corpse be cast, and may they carry off his bones." As I requested Aššur, so it took place. Before his enemies his body was cast, and his bones were carried off.

(ii.119–125) The Cimmerians, whom he had trampled by the pronouncing of my name, invaded and devastated his entire land (*gimir mātīšu*). After him, his eldest son sat on his throne. The evil deeds, which because of the lifting up of my hands (my prayers) the gods, in whom I trust, had lain in front of the father who created him – in the hands of his messengers he reported to me, and he grasped my royal feet, saying: "You are the king whom the god knows. You cursed my father, and evil was placed on him. I am the slave who fears you; (please) bless, so that I may pull your harness."

(ii.126-iii.10) In my fourth campaign, I called up my armies. Against Aḫšēri, king of the Manneans, I had them take a straight road. By command of Aššur, Sîn, Šamaš, Adad, Bēl, Nabû, Ištar of Nineveh, Šarrat-Kidmuri, Ištar of Arbela, Ninurta, Nergal, (and) Nusku, I entered into the land of Mannea, and I walked about dominantly. His strong cities, all around, which have no number, until the midst of the city of Izirti, I captured, and destroyed, I tore down, I burnt with fire. People, horses, donkeys, cattle and sheep from the midst of those cities I removed; and counted as booty. Aḫšēri, heard the progress of my campaign, and he abandoned the city of Izirti, his royal city. (iii.1) To the city of Ištatti, the city of his reliance, he fled, and kept a distance. That region I captured. (To the distance of) a fifteen day walk I destroyed it, and I poured out deathly silence. Aḫšēri, who does not fear my lordship, because of the word of Ištar who dwells in the city of Arbela, who long ago had spoken saying: "I (will cause) the death of Aḫšēri, king of the land of Mannea; as I have spoken, I will do." She delivered him into the hands of his servants, and the people of his land fomented rebellion against him. His body they cast into the streets of his city; they dragged around his corpse. His brothers, his family, the seed of his father's house, they felled by weapons.

(iii.11–26) Afterwards Uallî, his son, sat on his throne. The mighty acts of Aššur, Sîn Šamaš, Adad, Bēl, Nabû, Ištar of Nineveh, Šarrat-Kidmuri, Ištar of Arbela, Ninurta, Nergal, (and) Nusku, the great gods, my lords, he saw, and he submitted to my yoke. In order to save his life, he opened his palms; he beseeched my lordship. Erisinni, the son, his successor, he sent to me to Nineveh, and he kissed my feet. I had mercy on him, and my messengers of wellbeing I sent to him. A daughter, issue of his body, he sent to me to do stewardship. His earlier tribute, which during the reigns of the kings my fathers they had caused to cease, they carried to me. Thirty horses more than his previous treaty I added and imposed upon him.

(iii.27–43) In my fifth campaign, I sent straight on the road to the land of Elam. By command of Aššur, Sîn, Šamaš, Adad, Bēl, Nabû Ištar of Nineveh, Šarrat-Kidmuri, Ištar of Arbela, Ninurta, Nergal, and Nusku, in the month of Elul, the work of goddesses, the month of the king of the gods, Aššur, (and) father of the gods, Nunnamnir, like the onslaught of a mighty storm I covered the land of Elam in its entirety. I cut off the head of Teʾuman their king, the arrogant one who had plotted evil against me. Without number I killed his warriors. With my hands, alive I captured his fighters. Their corpes, like camel thorn and acacia, I filled the environs of the city of Shushan. Their blood I made flow in the Ulai (River). Its water I dyed like red wool.

(iii.44–49) Ummanigaš, son of Urtaki, king of the land of Elam, who, before Teʾuman, to the (land of) Aššur had fled, grasped my feet. With me I brought him to the land of Elam. I seated him on the throne of Teumman. Tammaritu, his brother, his third brother, who had fled along with him, I placed in the city of Ḫidalu for kingship.

(iii.50–69) After I had caused the weapons of Aššur and Ištar to shine brightly over the (land of) Elam and had established my strength and victory, upon my return, against Dunanu, the Gambulean, who had trusted in the land of Elam, I set my face. The city of Šapî-Bēl, the city of trust of the land of Gambulu, I captured. Inside that city I entered. Its people I slaughtered like sheep. Dunanu (and) Samʾaguni, who disturbed my exercise of kingship, I bound their hands and feet in fetters, iron handcuffs (and) iron chains. The remaining sons of Bēl-iqīša, his family, the seed of his father's house, as many as there are, Nabû-naʾid, Bēl-ēṭir, sons of Nabû-šum-ēreš, the governor of Nippur (*šandabakku*) and bones/mortal remains of the father who had created them, with the auxiliary troops (*Urbi*), and enemies of the people of the land of Gambulu, cattle, sheep, donkeys, horses, mules, from the midst of the land of Gambulu I took as plunder to the land of Assyria. The city of Šapî-Bel, the city of his confidence, I destroyed, I tore down, and dissolved in water.

(iii.70–79) At that time, Šamaš-šumu-ukīn, the untrue brother, to whom I had done good, (whom I) had placed him for kingship of Babylon, and whatever is considered appropriate for kingship I did and gave him, soldiers, horses and chariots I gathered up and filled his hands. Cities, fields, orchards, people dwelling within them I increased, and more than my father who created me had commanded I gave to him. But he, this good which I did to him, he forgot, and he sought out evil.

(iii.80–86) Above, on his lips, he spoke good; below, in his heart, he plans murder.[e] The sons of Babylon who were fond of the Assyrians, servants, seers of my face, he *isolated*, and untrue words he spoke with them. In a shrewd act of asking about my wellbeing, he sent them to Nineveh, (to come) before me.

(iii.87–106) I, Aššur-bāni-apli, king of Assyria, for whom the great gods had determined a good destiny, (and) had created him in justice and truth, those sons of Babylon, at tables of hospitality I stood them. In clothes of multicolored linen I clothed them. Bracelets of gold I tied to their hands. While those sons of Babylon I was standing within Aššur, and they were seeing the face of my administrator, he, Šamaš-šumu-ukīn, the untrue brother, who did not keep my loyalty oath – the people of Akkad, Chaldeans (and) Aramaeans, the Sealand from (the city of Aqaba) unto the city of Bāb-salimēti, servants who see my face, he incited to rebel in my hands; and Ummanigaš, a refugee, who grasped my royal feet, whom in the midst of Elam I had placed him for kingship, and kings of (the land of the) Gutian, Amorite (and) Meluḫḫa, who by the word of Aššur and Mullissu had been placed in my hands, all of them he made hostile to me, and with him they placed their mouths (cooperated).

(iii.107–117) The city gates of Sippar, Babylon, (and) Borsippa, he locked, and he cut off brotherhood. On the walls of those cities he brought up his fighters, and with me they waged war again and again. He held me back from performing my sacrifices before Bēl, the son of Bēl, the lamp of the god, Šamaš, and the hero, Erra, and he caused me to cease offering my sacrifices. In order to take away the cult center, the dwelling place of the great gods,

e Jer 9:3

whose temples I restored and decorated with gold and silver, (and) in their midst I placed appropriate things, he planned evil.

(iii.118–127) At that time, one (of my) seers lay down at night and saw a dream, saying: on the base of (the statue of the god) Sîn is written: "he who plans evil against Aššurbanipal, king of the land of Assyria, and instigating hostility, I will bestow on him an evil death. By fast sword of iron, falling of fire, starvation, affliction of Erra, I will shorten his life." This I heard, and I took confidence in the word of Sîn, my lord.

(iii.128–135) In my sixth campaign, I called up my armies against Šamaš-šumu-ukīn, I sent them on a straight road. In the midst of Sippar, Babylon, Borsippa, (and) Kutha, he together with his fighters I imprisoned, and seized their exits. Within the city and in the steppe, without number, I rendered over and over again his defeat. The remainder, by affliction of Erra (plague), want and famine, rendered up their lives (died).

(iii.136-iv.2) Ummanigaš, king of Elam, appointee of my hands, who accepted his bribes, rose up to his assistance. Tammaritu rebelled against him, and slaughtered him with the sword, together with his family.

(iv.3–20) Afterwards, Tammaritu, who after Ummanigaš sat on the throne of the land of Elam, did not ask the wellbeing of my kingship, went to the assistance of Šamaš-šumu-ukīn, my enemy brother, and in order to battle with my soldiers he rushed his weapons (armed forces). Because of the prayer which I prayed to Aššur and Ištar, they accepted my supplications, and heard the utterance of my lips. Indabigaš, his servant rebelled against him, and in field battle he inflicted his defeat. Tammaritu, king of the land of Elam, who over the severed head of Teumman had spoken insolence, that a lowly soldier of my troops had cut it off, saying: "Did they cut off the head of the king of the land of Elam, in the midst of his land, in the company of his soldiers?" (and) a second time he said: "Ummanigaš, how does he kiss the ground in front of the messengers of Aššurbanipal, king of Assyria?"

(iv.21–27) Because of these words which he slanderously uttered, Aššur and Ištar rushed against him (i.e. treated him insolently), and Tammaritu, his brothers, his family, the seed of his father's house, along with eighty-five princes, who go at his side, fled from before Indabigaš; and in their nakedness, on their bellies (lit. "hearts"), they crawled before me, and came to me at Nineveh.

(iv.28–36) Tammaritu kissed my royal feet, and he swept the ground with his beard. The floor of my chariot he grasped, and appointed himself to doing servitude to me, and in order to do his judgment (i.e. receive his punishment) and perform his assistance by command of Aššur and Ištar, he beseeched my lordship. Before me they (Tammaritu and his family) stood, and they praised the hero, my mighty gods who go to my assistance.

(iv.37–45) I, Aššurbanipal, (one of) broad heart (i.e. wise), who is not short-tempered, who expunges sins, I had mercy on Tammaritu, and he, along with the seed of his father's house, inside my palace had them stand. At that time, the people of Akkad who had placed themselves with Šamaš-šumu-ukīn, (and) plotted evil, famine grasped them. In their hunger, the flesh of their sons and their daughters they ate[f]; they chewed leather straps.

(iv.46–63) (The gods) Aššur, Sîn, Šamaš, Adad, Bēl, Nabû, Ištar of Nineveh, Šarrat-Kidmuri, Ištar of Arbela, Ninurta, Nergal, (and) Nusku, who go before me and kill my enemies, Šamaš-šumu-ukīn, my enemy brother, who was hostile to me, they threw him into the raging fire, and (thus) ended (lit. "destroyed") his life. Moreover, the people who had plotted for Šamaš-šumu-ukīn, my enemy brother, (and) had done these evil deeds, (but) who feared death, (and) their life in their faces was dear, and with Šamaš-šumu-ukīn, their lord, did not fall into the fire; those who, in the face of the cutting of the iron sword, the famine, the hunger, and the burning fire remained (and) took a distance – the net of the great gods, my lords, which cannot be escaped, swept them up. Not even one escaped; not a single survivor got out of my hand; they (the great gods) counted into my hands.

(iv.64–69) Chariots, processional carriages, parasols, his harem women, the property of his palace they brought before me. Those troops, the lies of their mouths, which had spoken lies about Aššur my god, and (against) me, the prince who fears him, had plotted evil, their mouths I cut out, established their defeat.

(iv.70–76) The rest of the people, who were still alive – by the *šēdu* and *lamassu* (statues), with which they had crushed Sennacherib, the father of the father who created me,[g] now, I, crushed those people during his memorial rite (*kispu*). Their cut up flesh I fed to the dogs, the swine, the jackals (vultures?), the eagles, the birds of heaven and the fish of the deep.

(iv.77–85) After I did these deeds, (after) I assuaged the hearts of the great gods, my lords, the corpses of the people whom Erra (god of plague) had felled, and who by famine and hunger had given their lives, the left-overs from what was eaten by dogs and pigs, which was spread across the markets and filled the streets, their skeletons from the midst of

f Deut 28:53–57

g 2 Kgs 19:36–37; Isa 37:37–38

Babylon, Kutha and Sippar I removed, and I threw them outside.

(iv.86–91) By the work of purification specialists I purified their daises; I cleansed their dirty (processional?) streets. Their angry gods and furious goddesses I calmed down by means of *taqribtu*-rites and lamentations. Their daily offerings which had diminished (become scarce), as in ancient days, in wellbeing I restored and established (anew).

(iv.92–96) The rest of the sons of Babylon, Kutha and Sippar who from the plague, massacre and famine had escaped, I had mercy upon them. I commanded to keep alive their souls, within Babylon I settled them.

(iv.97–109) The people of Akkad, along with Chaldeans, Arameans of the Sealand, who had assisted Šamaš-šumu-ukīn, and returned a single mouth (cooperated with him) (and) to cut themselves off had been hostile to me – by command of Aššur and Mullissu and the great gods in whom I trust their entire border I trampled. The yoke of Aššur which they had thrown off, I imposed upon them. Governors, trusted representatives, appointees of my hands, I appointed over them. Daily offerings, regular offerings, first fruit offerings of Aššur and Mullissu and the gods of the land of Assyria I established over them. Tax, tribute of my lordship yearly, without ceasing, I imposed on them.

(iv.110–132) In my seventh campaign in the month of Sivan, the month of Sîn, lord of oracular decisions, the highest ranking son, who goes before (the armies) of Bēl, I called up my troops, (and) against Ummanaldasi, king of the land of Elam, I sent on a straight road. I brought with me Tammaritu, king of the land of Elam, who had fled from before Indabigaš, his servant, and had grasped my feet. The people of the city of Ḫilmu, the city of Pillatu, the city of Dummuqu, the city of Sulaya, the city of Laḫira, (and) the city of Dibirīna, heard the mighty onslaught of my war, that I marched to the land of Elam. The awesome radiance of Aššur and Ištar, my lords, (and) the dread of my kingship overwhelmed them. They, their people, their cattle, their sheep, to perform my servitude, to the land of Assyria, fell (deserted?) to me, and they grasped my royal feet. The city of Bīt-Imbî, an earlier royal city (and) fortress of the land of Elam relied, which like a great wall, which lies across the face of the land of Elam, which Sennacherib, king of Assyria, father of the father who created me, had previously captured; and he, the Elamite, a city opposite the earlier city of Bīt-Imbî built a second (city), and fortified its wall, and he elevated its external wall. They called its name Bīt-Imbî. In the course of my campaign, I captured (it).

(iv.133–137) The people dwelling in its midst, who did not come out to me, and did not ask the wellbeing of my kingship, I killed. I cut off their heads. I cut their lips. To the astonished viewing of the people of my land I took (the heads) to the land of Assyria.

(v.1–5) Imba-appi, the trusted representative of the city of Bīt-imbî, the son in law of Ummanaldasi, king (of the land of) Elam, while still alive, I removed from the midst of that city, and I threw him hand and foot in iron chains, and I led him to the land of Assyria.

(v.6–14) The woman of the palace and sons of Teumman, king of the land of Elam – who because of a message from Aššur in my previous campaign I had cut off his head – with the rest of the people, dwellers of Bīt-Imbî, I removed, and counted as plunder. Ummanaldasi, king of the land of Elam, heard of the entry of my armies, which had entered the land of Elam, and he abandoned the city of Madaktu, his royal city, and he fled and died (lit. "ascended his mountain").

(v.15–20) Umbaḫabuʾa, who, after the land of Elam revolted, escaped to the city of Bubilu, and opposite Ummanaldasi sat on the throne of the land of Elam. Just as him, he heard, and the city of Bubilu, the city of his lordly dwelling, abandoned, and, like a fish, he took to the depths of the distant waters.

(v.21–27) Tammaritu, who had fled (and) grabbed my feet, I caused to enter the city of Shushan (Susa). I appointed him for kingship. (But) the good I did to him, (namely) that I had sent him help, he forgot, and he sought to do me evil, and capture my troops. This he said with his heart (to himself), saying: "The people of the land of Elam, to whom(?) do they turn? In the face of the land of Assyria they are. Will they come into me, and will they continually take as booty the booty of the land of Elam?"

(v.28–35) Aššur and Ištar, who go at my side, (and) make me stand over my enemies, examined the heart of brazen, rebellious Tammaritu, and demanded from his hand; from the throne of his kingship they caused him to rise, and they returned it to him, and for a second time caused him to submit to my feet.

(v.36–40) Because of these words, in the anger of my heart, that the perfidious Tammaritu had committed a crime against me, in victory and might of the great gods, my lords, through the land of Elam in its entirety I constantly marched dominantly.

(v.41–62) Upon my return safely and with full hands, the face of my yoke I turned to the land of Assyria. The city of Gatudu, and again the city of Gatudu, the city of Daʾeba, the city of Nadiʾ, the city of Dūr-Amnani, and again the city of Dūr-Amnani, the city of Ḫamānu, the city of Taraqu, the city of Ḫajūsi, the city of Bīt-kunukku-bīssu, the city of Bīt-Arrabi, the city of Bīt-Imbî, the city of Madaktu, the city of Šušan (Susa), the city of Bubê, the city of Kapar-Mardukšarrāni, the city of Urdalika, the city of Algariga, the city of Tûbu, the city of Tīl-tûbu, the city of Dunšarri, the city of Dūr-undāsi, and again the city of Dūr-undasi, the city of Bubilu, the city of Samunu, the city of Bīt-Bunaku, the city of Qabrina, and again the city of Qabrinama, the city of Ḫara' – these cities I captured, I destroyed, I tore down, I burnt by fire. (The statues of) their gods, their people, their cattle, their sheep, their property, their possessions, wagons, horses, mules, equipment, (all their) gear of battle, I plundered to me to the city of Aššur.

(v.63–76) In my eighth campaign, by command of Aššur and Ištar I called up my armies; against Ummanaldasi, king of the land of Elam, I sent them on a straight road. The city of Bīt-Imbî, which in my previous campaign I had captured, now the land of Rāši, the city of Ḫamānu, along with its environs, I captured; and he, Ummanaldasi, king of the land of Elam, heard about the capture of the land of Raši and the city of Ḫamānu, and the fear of Aššur and Ištar who go at my side overwhelmed him; and Madaktu, his royal city, he abandoned and fled to the city of Dūr-Undasi. The River Idide he crossed, and that river he placed as his fortress. He tied it up (fortified it) for battle with me.

(v.77–92) The city of Naditu, the royal city, including its regions I captured. The city of Bīt-Bunaki, the royal city, including its regions I captured. The city of Ḫartabanu, the royal city, including its regions I captured. The city of Tûbu, the royal city, including its regions I captured. Between the river (the bend of the river) in its entirety, the city of Madaktu, the royal city, including its regions I captured. The city of Ḫaltemaš, his royal city, I captured. The city of Šušan, his royal city, I captured. The city of Dīn-šarri, the city of Šumuntunaš, his royal city, I captured. The city of Pidilmu his royal city, I captured. The city of Bubilu his royal city, I captured. The city of Albinak his royal city, I captured. By encouragement of Aššur and Ištar, I proceeded and went against Ummanaldasi, king of the land of Elam, who did not submit to my yoke.

(v.93–112) In the course of my campaign, the city of Dūr-Undasi, his royal city, I captured. The troops, saw (the river) Idide, and raging wave, they were afraid of the crossing. Ištar, who dwells in Arbela, in a night vision to my soldiers revealed a dream, and thus she said to them, saying: "I will go before Aššurbanipal, the king whom my hands created." My troops relied on that dream, the (river) Idide they crossed safely. Fourteen cities, his royal dwellings, along with small cities which have no number, and twelve regions in the midst of the land of Elam, all of it, I captured, I destroyed, I tore down, I burnt in fire, I turned it into tells and rubble heaps. Without number I killed his warriors; with weapons I struck down his exalted fighters. Ummanaldasi, king of the land of Elam, in his nakedness escaped, and seized a mountain (disappeared).

(v.113–118) The city of Banunu, until the region of the city of Tasarra, entirely I captured. Twenty cities in the region of the city of Ḫunnir above the territory of the city of Ḫidalu, I captured, the city of Bašima and the cities around it I destroyed and tore down, I made piles of the people dwelling in their midsts.

(v.119–125) I destroyed (the statues of) their gods, I calmed the innards of the Lord of Lords (Marduk), (the statues of) his gods and his goddesses, his property and his possessions, people, small and great, I plundered to the land of Assyria. (A distance of) sixty double hour march of land, by the command of Aššur and Ištar, which they sent me, in the midst of the land of Elam I entered and walked constantly, dominantly.

(v.126-vi.6) On my return, (during) which Aššur and Ištar, made me stand over my enemies, the city of Šušan (Susa), the great holy city, the dwelling place of their gods, their secret place, I captured. By command of Aššur and Ištar, in the midst of his palaces I entered and sat in happiness. I opened their treasure houses in which silver, gold, property, possessions are stored within their midst, (vi.1) which the previous kings of the land of Elam until the kings who until this very day had gathered and placed, which no other foreigner besides myself had put his hand inside I took out to me, and numbered it as booty.

(vi.7–26) Silver, gold, property, possessions of the land of Sumer and Akkad, and all of the land of Karduniaš, which the previous kings of the land of Elam, all seven of them, had plundered and brought to the midst of the land of Elam: fine, red gold, bright *ešmarû*-silver, choice stones, precious jewelry appropriate for royalty, which the previous kings of the land of Akkad, and Šamaš-šumu-ukīn, to their allies, had squandered on the land of Elam – clothing, jewelry, appropriate for royalty, weapons of battle, appurtenances, anything for making war, appropriate to his hands, furniture and implements of all his palaces upon which they sat and lie down and from which they eat, drink, bath, anoint; chariots, procession-chariots, wagons, whose inlays are fine gold and *zaḫalû*-silver; horses, large mules, whose trappings were of gold and silver, I plundered to the land of Assyria.

(vi.27–47) The *ziqqurrat* of the city of Šušan (Susa), which had been decorated with lapis-lazuli (enameled) baked bricks, I destroyed. I peeled off the horns fashioned from bright copper. The god Šušinak, their mysterious god, who dwells in seclusion, whom no one has seen the making of his divinity, the god Šumudu, the god Lagamaru, the god Partikira, the god Ammankasibar, the god Uduran, the god Sapak, which the kings of the land of Elam constantly worshiped their divinity, the god Ragiba, the god Sungursara, the god Karsa, the god Kirsamas, the god Sudānu, the god Ayapaksina, the god Bilala, the god Panintimri, the god Nabirtu, the god Kindakarbu, the god Silagarâ, the god Nabsâ, those gods and goddesses, along with their jewelry, their possessions, their furnishings, along with Šangê the *buḫlalû* (Elamite priest) I plundered to the land of Assyria.

(vi.48–57) Thirty two royal statues fashioned from gold, silver, copper, alabaster from the midst of the city of Šušan (Susa), the city of Madaktu, the city of Ḫuradi, including the statue of Ummanigaš, eldest son of Umbadarâ, the statue of Ištarnanḫundi, the statue of Ḫallusi, the statue of Tammaritu, the latter, which by command of Aššur and Ištar performed servitude to me, I took to me to the land of Assyria.

(vi.58–69) I lifted up the *šēdu* and *lamassû* (statues), the guardians of the temples, as many as there were, I uprooted; raging wild steers appropriate to gates of the temples of the land of Elam until they did not exist I desecrated. (The statues of) its gods and its goddesses I numbered as wind. Their secret groves, into which no stranger is permitted inside and had not tread on their border, my combat troops entered their midst; they saw their secrets; they burned in fire.

(vi.70–76) The tombs of their earlier and latter kings, (who) did not fear Aššur and Ištar, my lords, who made the kings, my fathers tremble, I destroyed, I tore up, I revealed to the sun. Their bones I took to the land of Assyria, their spirits I condemned to restlessness. I deprived them (made them thirst?) of memorial food offerings (*kispu*) and water libations.

(vi.77–95) To a distance of a month and twenty-five days (march) I devastated the regions of the land of Elam; salt (and) cress I strewed over them. Daughters of the kings, sisters of the kings, until the former and later family of the kings of the land of Elam, trusted representatives, mayors of those cities, as many as I captured, master bowmen, governors, holders of reins (chariot drivers), third men on the chariots, open-crotched (runners/cavalrymen), soldiers of bows, *ša-rēši*-officers, military craftsmen, all artisans, whatever there are, men, male and female, small and great, horses, mules, donkeys, cattle and sheep, which were more numerous than locusts, I plundered to the land of Assyria.

(vi.96–98) The dust of the city of Šušan (Susa), the city of Madaktu, the city of Ḫaltemaš, and the rest of their holy cities I gathered and took to the land of Assyria.

(vi.99–106) In a month of days (a full month), the land of Elam, in its entirety I destroyed. The cry of the people, the steps of the cattle and sheep, the calling of good ululation, I made scarce in its fields, wild asses, gazelles, beasts of the field, whatever there are, in the meadow, I made crouch down in their midst.

(vi.107–124) The goddess Nanaya, who for 1635 years was angry, and went and settled in the midst of the land of Elam, a place not appropriate for her – and in that day, she and the gods, her fathers, called my name for lordship of the lands, the return of her divinity, she let my face see, saying: “Aššurbanipal, from the midst of the wicked land of Elam, will take me out, and he will bring me into the midst of Eanna.” The word of the command of their divinity, which in far-away times they had spoken, now they revealed to later people. The hands of her great divinity I grasped, and a straight road of joy of the heart she took towards Eanna. In the month of Kislev, the first day, I brought her into the midst of Uruk; and in Eḫilanna, which she loves, I set her in an eternal dais.

(vi.125-vii.8) The people, and the booty of the land of Elam, which by command of Aššur, Sîn, Šamaš, Adad, Bēl, Nabû, Ištar of Nineveh, Šarrat-Kidmuri, Ištar of Arbela, Ninurta, Nergal and Nusku, I robbed, (vii.1) the first portion I gave to the gods. The soldiers, the bows, the (wooden) shields, the artisans, the craftsmen, which I plundered from the midst of the land of Elam, I added to my royal band (of soldiers). The rest, to the holy cities, dwellings of the great gods, my provincial governors, my magnates, my entire camp, as sheep I divided up.

(vii.9–15) Ummanaldasi, king of the land of Elam, who had seen the rage of the mighty weapons of Aššur and Ištar, returned from the mountains, the place of his hiding, and in the midst of the city of Madaktu, the city which, by command of Aššur and Ištar I had destroyed, tore down, and plundered its plunder, he entered, and sat down, beating his breast in mourning in a place of mourning rites.

(vii.16–27) As for Nabû-bēl-šumāte, the grandson of Merodach-baladan, who had transgressed my loyalty oath, (and) thrown off the yoke of my lordship, who placed the kings of the land of Elam as his strength, (and) trusted in Ummanigaš, Tammaritu, Indabigaš, Ummanaldaš, the kings who exercised lordship of the land of Elam – my messenger, for the purpose of extraditing Nabū-bēl-šumate, while filled with anger, I sent to Ummanaldaš.

(vii.28–37) Nabū-bēl-šumāte, grandson of Merodachbaladan, heard the going of my messenger, who in the midst of the land of Elam had entered, and his heart pounded, he started trembling, his life before him was not dear, he desired death.

To his own groom he said, saying: "Smite me by weapons." He (and) his groom, with the iron swords in their belts, stabbed each other.

(vii.38–44) Ummanaldaš was afraid, and the corpse of that Nabû-bēl-šumāte, he laid in salt, and along with the head of his groom, who had smitten him by a weapon, he gave (it) to my messenger, and had him bring it to me.

(vii.45–50) His corpse I would not give over for burial. More than before I added to his death (I made him deader than before), and I cut off his head. Around the neck of Nabû-qātā-ṣabat, the minister of Šamaš-šumu-ukīn, my alien brother, who along with him, had gone to incite the land of Elam to hostility, I hung (it).

(vii.51–57) Paʾe, who opposite Ummanaldaš, had exercised lordship of the land of Elam, the awe inspiring radiance of the fierce weapons of Aššur and Ištar, which once, twice and thrice they poured down upon the land of Elam, he remembered, and had a broken heart (i.e. was distressed). From the midst of the land of Elam he fled, and he grasped my royal feet.

(vii.51–81) People, survivors of the city of Bīt-Imbî, the city of Kuṣurteʾin, the city of Dūr-šarri, the city of Masutu, the city of Bubê, the city of Bīt-Unzaja, the city of Bīt-Arrabi, the city of Ibrat, the city of Dimtu-ša-Tapapa, the city of Akbarina, the city of Gurukirra, the city of Dunnu-Šamaš, the city of Ḫamanu, the city of Kaniṣu, Aranziaše, the city of Nakidāte, the city of Dimtu-ša-Simane, the city of Bīt-qatatti, the city of Ša-Kisaja, the city of Subaḫtê, the city of Tīl-Ḫumba, who in my previous campaign, who before the mighty weapons of Aššur and Ištar, had fled, and captured the city of Salatri, the difficult mountain – those people, who ⟨in⟩ Salatri, the mountain had placed as their fortress, the awe-inspiring-radiance of Aššur and Ištar, my lords, overwhelmed them. From the mountain, the place of their refuge, they fled to me, and they grasped my feet. To recruit them for bow (service), to my royal band (of soldiers), which they (the gods) placed in my hands, I added (them).

(vii.82–93) In my ninth campaign, I called up my troops. Against Uʾateʾ, king of the land of Arabia, I sent on a straight path – who had transgressed my loyalty oath – the good I had done him he did not observe, and he threw off the yoke of my lordship, which Aššur had imposed upon him (so that) he pulled my yoke. To ask of my wellbeing, he cut off his feet (i.e. ceased coming), and he withheld my audience gift, his heavy tribute. As (in the case of the land of) Elam, he heard the lying speech of the land of Akkad, and he did not keep my loyalty oath.

(vii.94–106) Me, Aššurbanipal, king, pure high priest, the pious slave, creation of the hand of Aššur, he abandoned; and to Abī-yateʾ, Ayamu, first born of Tēʾri, armed forces he gave to them. To the assistance of Šamaš-šumu-ukīn, my alienated brother, he sent, and put his mouth (i.e. cooperated). The people of the land of Arabia, along with him, he incited to hostility (to me), and they constantly robbed the robberies of the people whom Aššur, Ištar and the great gods had given me, (and) to shepherd them had placed in my hands.

(vii.107–124) By command of Aššur and Ištar, my troops, in *girā* (?) the city of Azar-ilu, the city of Ḫirataqaṣaya, in the city of Edom, in the pass of the city of Iabrudu in the city of Bīt-Ammani (Ammon), in the region of the city of Ḫaurīna, in the city of Moab, in the city of Seʾir, in the city of Ḫargê, in regions of the city of Ṣubiti (Zobah), in great numbers I slaughtered; without number I imposed his defeat. People of the land of Arabia, all that stood with him, I smote with weapons; and he, before the mighty weapons of Aššur flew, and escaped at a distance. The tents of their dwellings they (my troops) set on fire, they burnt with fire. Uʾateʾ, sickness came upon him, and alone he fled to the land of Nebaioth.

(viii.1–7) Uʾateʾ, son of Hazael, son to the brother of the father of Uʾateʾ, son of Bīr-Dāda, who placed himself for kingship of the land of Arabia, Aššur, king of the gods, the great mountain, changed his disposition, and he came before me.

(viii.8–14) In order to display the praise of Aššur and the great gods, my lords, I imposed upon him a great punishment, and I placed upon him a neck stock, and I tied him up with a bear and a dog, and I made him guard the city gate within Nineveh, (named) "The Entrance to the Place of Control of the World."

(viii.15–29) Moreover, he, Ammuladi, king of the land of Qedar, rose up to fight the kings of the Amurru, whom Aššur and Ištar, and the great gods had caused to see my face (caused to serve me). With the encouragement of Aššur, Sîn, Šamaš, Adad, Bēl, Nabû, Ištar of Nineveh, Šarrat-Kidmuri, Ištar of Arbela, Ninurta, Nergal, (and) Nusku, I inflicted his defeat. They (my troops) seized him alive, along with Adiya, wife of Uʾateʾ, king of the land of Arabia; and they bought (them) before me. By command of the great gods, my lords, a dog collar I placed upon him, and I made him guard the lock/bolt.

(viii.30–43) By command of Aššur, Ištar, and the great gods, my lords, concerning Abī-yateʾ (and) Ayamu, son of Tēʾri, who went to the assistance of Šamaš-šumu-ukīn, my hostile brother, to enter

Babylon, his helpers I killed; I inflicted his defeat. The remnants who entered into the city of Babylon, in want and starvation they eat each other's flesh.[18,h] In order to save their lives, from inside (the city of Babylon) they came out to me, and my armed forces, which were placed against Šamaš-šumu-ukīn, a second time they inflicted his defeat, and he, alone, fled, and in order to save his life, he grabbed my feet.

h Lev 26:29; Deut 28:53–57; Jer 19:9; Ezek 5:10; 2 Kgs 6:28–29; Lam 2:20; 4:10

(viii.44–51) I had mercy upon him, and a great loyalty oath, by the life of the god, I made him swear, and instead of U'ate', son of Hazael, to kingship of the land of Arabia, I placed him. And he, along with the land of Nebaioth, he placed his mouth (cooperated), and the oath (sworn) by the life of the great gods he did not fear, and he robbed the robbery of the territory of my land.

(viii.52–64) With the encouragement of Aššur, Sîn, Šamaš, Adad, Bēl, Nabû, Ištar of Nineveh, Šarrat-Kidmuri, Ištar of Arbela, Ninurta, Nergal, (and) Nusku, Natnu, king of the land of Nebaioth, whose place is far away, from whom U'ate', had fled, heard; and the might of Aššur who had encouraged me; (Natnu) who at any time to the kings, my fathers, had not sent his messengers, did not ask about the wellbeing of their kingship – in fear of the conquering weapons of Aššur he approached me, and asked me the wellbeing of my kingship.

(viii.65–72) And Abī-yate', first-born of Tē'ri, who does not remember the good, does not observe the oath of the great gods, words of lies with me he spoke, and he placed his mouth (cooperated), with Natnu king of the land of Nebaioth, and his armed forces he called up against me to rise up in evil against my territory.

(viii.73–78) By command of Aššur, Sîn, Šamaš, Adad, Bēl, Nabû, Ištar of Nineveh, Šarrat-Kidmuri, Ištar of Arbela, Ninurta, Nergal, (and) Nusku, I called up my troops, and against Abī-yate' I sent them off on a straight path.

(viii.79–103) The Tigris and the Euphrates in their swollen high-water, they safely crossed; they proceeded on a distant road; the ascended again and again high mountain ranges; they traversed again and again forests whose shadow was broad; between many trees, thorns, brambles, a road of sharp bushes, they safely crossed over and over again. A desert, a place of thirst and *kakkaltu* (for water drawing; or "of parching thirst"[19]), which the bird of heaven does not seek out, (where) wild asses, gazelles, do not graze in it, an hundred double hours march over ground from Nineveh, the city beloved of Ištar, first ranking wife of Enlil, after U'ate', king of the land of Arabia, and Abī-yate', who had gone with the forces of the land of Nebiaoth, they proceeded and went. In the month of Sivan, the month of the god Sîn, the first ranking first born son, who goes before the armies of Enlil, the 25th day, the Procession Day of Bēlet-Bābilī, the honored of the great gods, from the city of Ḫadattâ, I set out. In the city of Laribda, the fortress of the seal makers, by the cisterns of water I pitched my camp.

(viii.104–119) My troops, drew water for the drinking vessels, and they proceeded and went to a land of thirst, place of *kakkaltu*,[20] as far as the city of Ḫurarina, between the city of Iarki and the city of Azalla in the desert, a distant place, where there are no beasts of the field and a bird of heaven does not place its nest. I inflicted the defeat of Isamme', the *a'lu* (confederation?) of the god Atarsamayin and the land of Nabioth. People, donkeys, camels, and flock, their robbery without number I robbed. Eight double-miles march overland my troops went time and again dominantly, in wellbeing they returned to me, and in the city of Azallu they drank quenching water.

(viii.120-ix.8) From the heart of the city of Azallu as far as the city of Quraṣiti six double hour march over land, a place of thirst, and *kakkaltu*[21] they proceeded; they went. The *a'lu* (confederation) of Atarsamayin (ix.1) and the Qedarians of U'ate', oldest son of Bīr-Dāda, king of the land of Arabia, I surrounded. (The statues of) his gods, his mother, his sisters, his wife, his family, the people of the land of Qedar, in its entirety, donkeys, camels, and sheep, whatever by the encouragement of Aššur and Ištar, my lords, my hands had captured, the road to the land of Damascus, I directed their feet.

(ix.9–24) In the month of Ab, the month of the Bow-Star, the daughter of Sîn, the heroine, the third day, the evening of the festival of king of the gods, Marduk, from the city of Damascus I set out. Six double hours march over land, the entire night, I proceeded and went to the city of Ḫulḫulitu. At Mount Ḫukkurina, the difficult mountain, I caught the *a'lu* (confederation) of Abī-yate', first born of Tē'ri, the Qedarite; I inflicted his defeat; I plundered his plunder. Abī-yate', Ayamu, son of Tē'ri, by the command of Aššur and Ištar, my lords, in a battle of war, while they were still alive, I captured with my hands. Hands and feet, I threw on them

18 Like sheep.

19 KAL-KAL-*tu* can be read *kalkaltu/kakkaltu* "a device for drawing water" (*CAD* K 49b, s.v. *kakkaltu*); *galgaltu* "hunger" (*CAD* G 14b, s.v. *galgaltu* A); or *laplaptu* (*CAD* L 94b, s.v. *laplaptu*; *CAD* M/1 12a, s.v. *madbaru* b).

20 See n. 19.

21 See n. 19.

iron chains, with the plunder of their land I took them to the land of Assyria.

(ix.25–41) The fugitives who fled from before my weapons, were afraid and they held on to Mount Ḫukkuruna, the difficult mountain. In the city of Manḫabbi, the city of Apparu, the city of Tenuquri, the city of Zayauran, the city of Marqanâ, the city of Saraten, the city of Enzikerme, the city of Taʾnâ, the city of Saraqa, a place of cisterns, and springs of water, of every sort, I made guards stand watch over them, and water, for resuscitating their life I withheld. Watering I made dear to their mouths, in the thirst and *kakkaltu*[22] they gave up their lives, the rest of the camels, their mounts, they cut open, for their thirst they drank blood and water of excrement (urine), those who had ascended into the middle of the mountain came in and took a distance. Not even one escaped. A survivor did not get out of my hands. In the place of their refuge my hands caught them.

(ix.42–52) The people, male and female, donkeys, camels, cattle and sheep, without number I plundered to the land of Assyria. All of my land with Aššur had given me in its entirety, all around I filled it, up to its limit. I apportioned camels like sheep. I divided among the people of the land of Assyria. In the middle of my land, a camel for a shekel and a half of silver they bought in the market gate.[i] (To) a tavern keeper as a gift; (to) a brewer for a breaker, (to) a gardener for his cucumber patch of greens camels and slaves are sold over and over.

(ix.53–74) Uʾateʾ, along with his troops, who did not keep my loyalty oath, who before the weapon of Aššur, my lord, had run away, and fled before them, Girra the warrior felled them. Want occurred among them, and in their hunger they ate the flesh of their sons.[j] By all the curses which are written in their loyalty oath,[k] in accordance to what had been decreed for them by Aššur, Sîn, Šamaš, Adad, Bēl, Nabû, Ištar of Nineveh, Šarrat-Kidmuri, Ištar of Arbela, Ninurta, Nergal, and Nusku, young camels, young asses, calves and spring lambs on seven nursing animals will suck, but they will not satisfy their stomachs with milk.[l] The people of the land of Arabia, one to one will ask each other, saying: "For what reason did these evil events come upon the land of Arabia?" saying: "because we did not keep the great loyalty oaths of (the god) Aššur, we sinned against the good/covenant of Aššurbanipal, the king, beloved of the heart of Enlil."[m]

(ix.75–94) Mullissu, the beloved/wild cow of Enlilship, heroine of the goddesses, who with Anu and Ellil is triumphant in position, gored my enemy with her heroic horns. Ištar, who dwells in Arbela, clothed with fire and adorned with radiance, over the land of Arabia rains down flames. Girra, the hero, ties together battle, and smote my enemies. Ninurta, the arrow, great hero, son of Enlil, in his sharp arrow will slit the throat of my enemies. Nusku, revered advisor, who makes my lordship prominent, who by command of Aššur, Mullissu, the heroine, mistress of battle, goes at my side, and guards my kingship, has taken the front of my army, and has felled my enemies. The onslaught of the weapon of Aššur and Ištar, the great gods, my lords, who in waging war go to my assistance, the troops of Uʾateʾ, heard, and rebelled against him.

(ix.95–102) He was afraid, and from the house where he fled he came out to me, and with the encouragement of Aššur, Sîn, Šamaš, Adad, Bēl, Nabû, Ištar of Nineveh, Šarrat-Kidmuri, Ištar of Arbela, Ninurta, Nergal, and Nusku, my hands captured him, and I sent him to the land of Assyria.

(ix.103–114) Because of the raising of my hands (prayer) which to capture my enemies I constantly receive, by command of the gods Aššur and Mullissu, with the chariot beam, held in my hand, I pierced his jaw. I placed a lead rope in the cheek of his face, I put a dog collar upon him, and in the city gate to the rising of the sun, which was in the midst of Nineveh, which is called by the name "Entrance of Control of the World," I had him guard the lock. In order to praise the glory of Aššur and Ištar and the great gods, my lords, I had mercy on him and kept alive his life.

(ix.115–121) Upon my return, the city of Usû, whose dwelling place is situated on the coast of the sea, I captured. The people (of the city of) Usû, who did not approach their provincial governor, and did not pay tribute, their annual gift, I killed. Among the non-submissive people I did judgment, their gods, their people, I plundered to the land of Assyria.

(ix.122–128) The non-submissive people of Akko I killed. Their corpses impaled on stakes, around the city I surrounded it (with them). The rest of them I took to me to the land of Assyria. I organized them into a (military) unit, and to my numerous troops, which Aššur gave to me, I added (them).

(x.1–5) Ayamu, the first born of Tēʾri, with Abīyateʾ his brother, stood with my troops and did battle. In the battle of war, while they were alive, with my hands I caught them. In Nineveh, the city of my lordship, I flayed their skin.

(x.6–16) Ummanaldaš, king of the land of Elam, who long ago Aššur and Ištar, my lords, had called to perform my service, by command of their exalted divinity which is immutable, afterwards, his coun-

i 2 Kgs 7:1, 17, 18

j Deut 28:53–57

k Deut 29:19, 26

l Lev 26:26

m Deut 29:23–24; 1 Kgs 9:8–9

22 See n. 19.

try rebelled against him, and in face of the uprising of his servants, which they fomented against him, he fled alone, and grabbed the mountain (disappeared). From the mountain, his house of refuge, the place to whence he fled, as a hawk I hunted him down, and while he was alive I took him to the land of Assyria.

(x.17–23) Tammaritu, Paʾe, and Ummanaldaš, who after each other had exercised lordship of the land of Elam, who by the strength of Aššur and Ištar, my lords, I made him submit to my yoke, Uʾateʾ, king of the land of Arabia, who by command of Aššur and Ištar, I had inflicted his defeat, I took him from his land to the land of Assyria.

(x.24–39) After, in order to perform a libation, I went up into Emašmaš, their lordly dwelling, before Mullissu, the mother of the great gods, the first ranking wife, beloved of Aššur, performed the rites of the Akitu House, the yoke of procession I made them grasp, to the gate of the temple they marched beneath me (as I rode in it). I pressed my nose (a gesture of submission); I praised their divinity. I extolled their might in the assembly of my troops, which Aššur, Sîn, Šamaš, Adad, Bēl, Nabû, Ištar of Nineveh, Šarrat-Kidmuri, Ištar of Arbela, Ninurta, Nergal, and Nusku, those not submissive to me made submit to my yoke (and) in triumph and might caused me to stand over my enemies.

(x.40–50) Ištar-Dūri, king of the land of Ararat, who the kings, his fathers, to my father constantly sent (messages of) brotherhood; now, Ištar-Dūri, the might of the deeds which the great gods had determined for me, heard, and as a first-born to his father constantly sends lordship, and he, in this wise, constantly sent to me thusly: "May there be wellbeing to the king, my lord." In fear and submission, his heavy audience gift he sent before me.

(x.51–71) At that time, the *bīt-rīdûti* (house of succession), the substitute for the palace in the midst of Nineveh, the exalted city, beloved of Mullissu, which Sennacherib, king of the land of Assyria, father the father who created me, had built for his royal dwelling, that *bīt-rīdûti*, in joy and gladness had grown old, its walls had collapsed. I, Aššurbanipal, the great king, the mighty king, king of totality, king of the land of Assyria, king of the four quarters, because I had grown up within that *bīt-rīdûti*, (and) Aššur, Sîn, Šamaš, Adad, Bēl, Nabû, Ištar of Nineveh, Šarrat-Kidmuri, Ištar of Arbela, Bēlet-parṣī, Ninurta, Nergal, and Nusku, had guarded my regency, (and) their sweet shade, their protective canopy of wellbeing they extended over me, from when I sat on the throne of my father who had created me, the constantly performed lordship of the lands and the widespread people – constantly, tidings of happiness, of capturing my enemies, they bore to me within it. On my bed at night, my dreams were made good, at dawn my cledons were beautiful.

(x.72–108a) That dwelling keeps its occupants happy, and the great gods determines his destiny for good. Its ruins I removed. In order to broaden its walkways, I tore it down all around. Fifty brick courses, at the site of its old structure, its form I formed, its foundation platform I filled. Since I feared the temples of the great gods, my lords, that foundation platform its form I did not make very high. In a good month, on a favorable day, on top of that foundation platform I laid its foundations, I made its brickwork firm. With choice beer and wine, I mixed its mortar; I pounded its plaster. In wagons of the land of Elam, which by the command of the great gods, my lords, I had plundered to build that *bīt-rīdûti* the people of my land, inside them carried its bricks. Kings of the land of Arabia, which had sinned against my loyalty oath, who, in the battle of war, while alive had grasped my hands, to build that *bīt-rīdûti* I made them carry hoes and corvée baskets; I had them bear baskets for earth. Those who molded its bricks and its corvée baskets spent their days in joyous song. In happiness and joy, from its foundations to its crenellations I finished it. More than before I widened its dwelling, I made its works glorious. Tall beams of cedar, growth of Mount Sirara and Mount Lebanon, I extended over it. Doors of conifer wood whose fragrance is sweet I tied together with bands of copper, and I hung in its gates. Tall pillars I coated with bright copper, and architraves of the door openings I stood in its portico. That *bīt-rīdûti*, my royal dwelling, all around it I completed, I filled it with luxury. An arboretum containing all trees bearing all kinds of fruit, I planted all around it. The work which I had done I completed, and sumptuous sacrifices I sacrificed to the gods, my lords. In happiness and joy I inaugurated it. I entered into it in joyous song.

(x.108b–120) In distant days, among the kings, my sons, which Aššur and Ištar, will call his name to lordship of the lands and people, when that *bīt-rīdûti* becomes old and collapses, may he renew its ruins. The monuments bearing an inscription of my name, and of my father, and of my father's father, eternal seed of kingship, may he see, and may he anoint it with oil. May he offer sacrifices, may he place inscriptions of his own name with the monuments. May all the great gods that are inscribed on this monument, grant him might and triumph as they grant me. Whoever, will destroy the monument with the inscription of my name, of my father, my father's father, and will not place it with his monuments, may Aššur, Sîn, Šamaš, Adad, Bēl, Nabû, Ištar of Nineveh, Šarrat-Kidmuri, Ištar of Arbela, Ninurta, Nergal, and Nusku, judge him with my judgment with the calling of my name.

(Colophon)

A NEO-ASSYRIAN LETTER TO THE GOD

THE LETTER TO THE GOD AŠŠUR RECOUNTING SARGON'S EIGHTH CAMPAIGN (714 BCE) (4.42)

F. M. Fales

(1) (Col. I)[1] To Aššur, father of (all) the gods, the mighty lord who inhabits Eḫursagkurkurra, his great temple, the very best of health! To the gods of destinies and the goddesses who inhabit Eḫursagkurkurra, their great temple, the very best of health! To the gods of destinies and the goddesses who inhabit the city of Aššur, their great temple, the very best of health! Greetings to the city and its people, greetings to the palace which stands in its midst! To Sargon, the holy priest, the servant who reveres your great divinity, and to his army, the very best of health![2]

(6)[3] In the month of Du'uzu, which prompts the right decisions for mankind[4] – the month of Ninurta, the valiant firstborn of Enlil, the almighty among the gods – of which the lord of wisdom Ninšiku had written in an ancient tablet (that it was proper) to gather my army and to gather my encampment, I departed from Kalḫu, my royal capital, and forded furiously the Upper Zab in its full flood.[5] On the third day, so as to muzzle the mouth of the vainglorious (and) to bind the legs of the wicked, I reverently prostrated myself before the gods Enlil and Mullissu,[6] and I made the armies of the gods Šamaš and Marduk jump across the Lower Zab, whose crossing point is arduous, like a (mere) ditch. Into the passes of Mt. Kullar, a high mountain of the country Lullumû – which they call Zamua – I entered. In the district of Sumbi, I held a review of my army; I inspected the number of steeds and chariots. With the mighty support of Aššur, Šamaš, Nabû, and Marduk, I set course for the third time to the interior of the mountains. To the lands of Zikirtu and Andia I directed the yoke of Nergal and Adad, whose standards precede me.[7]

(15) I climbed between Mt. Nikippa and Mt. Upâ, high mountains which all types of trees cover, whose interior is a wilderness, and whose entry is terrifying, over whose environs a shadow extends as in a cedar forest, (so that) the traveller of their roads never sees the sunlight. I crossed the Pûya, a

---

[1] Line 1. This is the first of the four columns (2 on the Obverse, 2 on the Reverse) in which the 430-line tablet (37.5 × 24.5 cm) was subdivided, each column holding approx. 110 lines (but cf. at line 426 for the last column). The sole extant exemplar, Louvre AO 5372 (as well as the additional fragments held in Berlin: cf. at lines 96 ff.) originally came from Aššur, and was acquired from the antiquities dealer J. E. Géjou in 1910, after having been smuggled from the archaeological site while the German excavations under W. Andrae were still in progress (cf. Grayson 1983:16; Pedersén 1986:41–76, and esp. p. 71 no. 477, with Andrae's excavation number 17681 and photograph number 5280). For the hand-copy of the densely written text, see Thureau-Dangin 1912, pl. I–XXII; photographs are given *ibid.*, pls. XXIII–XXX. The initial section (lines 1–5) is unique for the presence of horizontal rulings drawn after each line across the column. Quite differently, the remainder of the text before the summary and the colophon (lines 6–414) is subdivided in 14 sections or episodes of varying length – mainly corresponding to changes in geographical setting – which are equally set apart by horizontal rulings (cf. Kravitz 2003:81). These markers of the episodes, which were typographically reproduced in the editions of Thureau-Dangin 1912 and Mayer 1983, will be pointed out in the critical apparatus below.

[2] Lines 1–5. For the formal beginning of the text relating Sargon's eighth campaign (henceforth = Sg. VIII) as the *salutatio* of a letter addressed to the god Assur, and its implications, cf. Oppenheim 1960:133; Levine 2003:112*–113*. For other contemporary exemplars of correspondence between kings and gods, cf. Leichty 1991 (Esarhaddon's letters to the gods) and SAA 3, nos. 41–47 (epistolary replies of the Assyrian gods to various kings).

[3] Lines 6 ff. The description of the overall literary style of the text is given by Hurowitz 2008:105, n. 8: "… it is written in a hybrid style. Many passages, such as those describing Sargon's rampage through long lists of vanquished cities, are in unembellished prose and similar passages are found in other Assyrian royal inscriptions. But many passages including lyric descriptions of strange lands are in an elevated style which can be called "poeticized prose" because of the integration into prose sentences of parallelistic structures in many forms. The extant editions and translations totally ignore these features and present the text as if it is prose." Hurowitz further recalls (*ibid.*) that Fales 1991 is the sole attempt hitherto to present parts of the Akkadian text "reflecting their literary texture." In the present translation, an attempt to set out internal differences in style and content will be made merely through paragraphs and section subdivisions. The extensive and elegant play by the author of Sg. VIII with words in pairs (e.g. verbs and nouns from identical roots, or similar-sounding items), singled out both by Foster (2005) and Van de Mieroop (2010:427) is of course impossible to recover here.

[4] Line 6. Episode 1 (departure, beginning of campaign in the mountains, approach to the land of Ullusunu, the Mannean) starts here. Cf. *CAD* 1/I, 129a, where an unexplained pious etymology of the month name Dumu.zi is suggested for the meaning of this line.

[5] Line 8. The geography of Sg. VIII (centered on the present-day areas of Iraqi Kurdistan and NW Iran) has formed the object of extensive discussions, focusing on the identification of the ancient toponyms *per se* (cf. the works by Levine 1977, Vera Chamaza 1984, Lanfranchi 1995, and Salvini 1995a quoted in the bibliography) and in their sequential position within the account for the reconstruction of the campaign itinerary. Specifically, the location of the Urartian fortresses in relation to lake Urmia has been a major dividing point: did Sargon reach the "rolling sea" from the south, keeping to its western shore (i.e. following the so-called "short route", cf. Muscarella 1986, Salvini 1995a) or did he encircle it, in an E→N→W→S itinerary along its shores (the "long route", advocated e.g. by Zimansky 1990, Liebig 1991, Reade 1995, and others: cf. Kroll 2012)? And could he even have reached Lake Van (as suggested by Thureau-Dangin in 1912, but with no more recent support)? The implications of this complex historical problem are plentiful and multi-faceted, since they not only touch upon physical geography in an overall landscape which is still nowadays difficult to survey in detail, but also upon the comparative testimonial of available Neo-Assyrian sources (from royal inscriptions of previous kings and of Sargon himself, to epistolary texts sent to Sargon or his Crown Prince Sennacherib in the years before/after 714 BCE), as well as upon Urartian sources retrieved in various – possibly relevant – archaeological settings (cf. Salvini 1995a), and finally upon the still incomplete record of excavated sites from Urartu or its neighboriung polities.

[6] Line 9. For the political-ideological implications of this passage, see Fales 1991:135–136; Hurowitz 2008:111.

[7] Line 14. For the "confusing" syntax of this passage, see Vera Chamaza 1992:111.

river between them, all of twenty-six times, and my army in its massed body was unafraid of its high waters. Mount Simirria (is) an imposing mountain peak, which rises up like the blade of a spear, its summit – the abode of the goddess Bēlet-ilī – high above the (other) mountains, whose peak touches the heavens above and whose foundation reaches inside the netherworld below. Moreover,[8] like the back of a fish, it has no passage from side to side[9] and its ascent is very difficult, both forward and backward, and on its sides ravines of mountain gullies are cut, a fearsome spectacle to behold,[10] inadequate for the ascent of chariots and high-spirited horses, and with a passage too laborious for heavy infantry[11] to negotiate.

(23) With the wide understanding and broad knowledge[12] which the gods Ea and Bēlet-ilī have bequeathed to me, and which make me widen my stride to overwhelm the land of the enemy, I provided my vanguard[13] with strong bronze pickaxes, and they smashed the tall mountain pinnacles as if they were of limestone, making a good road. I stood facing my army,[14] and I made the chariots, horsemen, and combat troops marching at my side fly over it like valiant eagles. The rank and file and the light infantry[15] I brought up after them. The camels and pack mules bounded in succession over its peak, like wild goats reared on the slopes. I brought up the abundant Assyrian troops in good order over its steep ascent and built an encampment on the summit of that mountain. The mountains Sinahulzi and Biruatti – far-off ranges, whose cover is of sweet-smelling wild leek and spicy plants – and Turtani, Sinabir, Ahšuru, and Suya: these seven mountains[16] I traversed with difficulty. I crossed the rivers Rappâ and Arattâ, their rapids in seasonal flooding, as if they were irrigation ditches. I descended towards the land of Surikaš, a district of Mannaea[17] on the border of Karallu and Allabria.

(32) Ullusunu[18] the Mannaean heard of my expedition's approach, (and) because I had never failed to back his cause, year by year, he, together with his magnates, the elders, the advisors, his royal family, the governors and the officers who administer his land, came forth quickly from his land in a pleasant state of mind and a joyful countenance, without hostages. He came to me from his royal capital Izirtu to Sinihini, a fortress at the boundary of his land. His tribute of horses in yoked teams, along with their trappings, along with cattle, and small livestock, he brought me, and kissed my feet. I arrived at the city Latašê, a fort which is on the river of the land Laruete, a district of Allabria;
I received from Bel-apal-iddina of Allabria his tribute of horses, cattle, and small livestock, and I went down to the land of Parsuaš. The chieftains of the lands Namri, Sangibutu, Bit-Abdadani, and of the land of the strong Medes heard of the approach of my expedition; the devastation of their territories in my previous regnal year was still in their minds, and thus terror spread over them. They brought me their heavy tribute from the heart of their lands and handed it over to me in Parsuaš.

(42) From Daltâ of the land Ellipi, Uk-satar,[19] Durisi, Satar-esu, chieftains of the river country; (from) Anzî of the city Halhubarra, Pâ-ukku of the city Kilambate, Uzî of the city Mâli, Wakirtu of the city Nappi, Makirtu of the city Bit-Sagbat, Kitakki of the city Wariangi, Mašdaya-ukku of the city Kingaraku, Uzi-tar of the city Qanta'u, Pâ-ukku of the city Bit-Kabsi, Humbê of the city Bit-Zualzaš,

8 Lines 18–20. The description of Mt. Simirria is, in point of fact, basically organized in the relative mode, as visible from the verbs in the subjunctive: thus the break between clauses has been inserted here simply for reasons of clarity, although it has a faint justification in the presence of an *ú* at the beginning of line 20. According to Van de Mieroop (2010:421–422) Mt. Simirria, being in Sargon's home territory, enjoys a description with feminine attributes, whereas Mt. Wauš, fully embedded within a hostile environment (lines 96–102) has masculine ones, despite the many literary parallels between the two presentations of the landscape.

9 Line 20. The expression *idu ana idi* is rendered "d' un côté à l' autre" by Thureau-Dangin (and see also *CAD* M 44a, "from side to side", which has been taken up here, on the basis of the comparison with the slippery back of the fish), but "side by side" by Luckenbill; cf. also *CAD* I/J 14b, for a further interpretation, "on either side", which has the benefit of parallels from cultic contexts.

10 Line 21. Thureau-Dangin's reading was *a-na i-tap-lu-us-sa ina ênê*[II], albeit with a basically accurate translation ("dont la vue inspire la crainte"); it should however be corrected to *a-na i-tap-lu-us ni-ṭil* IGI.2. (cf. *CAD* Š 3:132b).

11 Line 22. For the interpretation of the Assyrian military term *zūk šēpē* as "heavy infantry," cf. Fales 2009.

12 Line 23. Thureau-Dangin's *ša-ri kar-še* ("le souffle intérieur") must be read *šá-dal kar-še* (Mayer 1983:70).

13 Line 24. The word *sag/kbu* was correctly understood by Thureau-Dangin ("mes pionniers"); but not, it would seem, by Luckenbill ("I had (my men) carry mighty bronze pickaxes in my equipment").

14 Line 25. Thureau-Dangin (1912:6) read *miḫ-rit um-ma-ni-ia aṣ-bat*, "Je pris la tête de mes troupes", and this interpretation has been followed by most authors (Mayer 1983:71: "Ich setzte mich an die Spitze meiner Truppen"; Foster 2005:792: "I took the lead position before my army" – which takes into some account the basic meaning of *meḫretu*, "opposite side"); but already in 1972 Von Soden, *AHw* 640b had suggested to read the verb as *az-ziz*[!], thus understanding "I stood facing my troops," as pointed out by Vera Chamaza 1994:117a.

15 Line 26. On the term *kallāpu*, cf. Fales 2009.

16 Line 29. The overall count comprised the previously named Mt. Simirria, plus the six toponyms listed here. Cf. also Vera Chamaza 1992:112–113.

17 Line 31. Foster (2005:793) omits "of Mannaea."

18 Line 32. For the PN and its attestations, cf. *PNA*, 1374a–1375a.

19 Line 42. Elsewhere in NA texts attested as Uaksatar; a possible Median equivalence to the name given as Cyaxares in Classical sources has been suggested (*PNA*, 1353b).

Uzu-manda of the city Kisilaha,[20] Burburazu of the city Bit-Ištar, Bagbarna of the city Zukrute, Darî of the city Šaparda, Ušrâ of the city Kanzabakani, Šarruti of the city Karzinû, Mašdakku of the city Andirpatianu, Akkussu of the city Usi.., Birtatu of the city Ṣiburayyu, Zardu-ukku of the city Harzianu, Mašdakku of the city Arad-pati, Satar-panu of the city Barikanu, Karakku of the city Urikayyu – horses swift of knee, hot-tempered mules, camels (such as are) native to their land, cattle, and small livestock I received.

(51)[21] I set out from the land of Parsuaš, and I drew near to the land Missi, a district of the land of the Mannaeans. Ullusunu, together with the people of his land, in the loyalty of servitude, awaited my expedition in the city Sirdakka, his fortress. As if he had been one of my eunuchs or one of the governors of Assyria, he had piled up stocks of flour and wine to feed my troops. He delivered to me his eldest son, with presents and audience gifts, and entrusted to me his stela, so as to ensure his rulership.[22] I received his tribute of large-sized horses in yoked teams, of cattle, and of small livestock, and he prayed me to back his cause. Together with the magnates and the administrators of his land, he implored me, crawling on all fours as if they were dogs, that I block the access of the people of Kakmē[23] – a wicked enemy – from his land, and that I rout Rusa[24] in pitched battle, that I bring back home the dispersed Mannaeans, and that I stand victoriously over his enemy, (so as) to achieve all his wishes. I had pity on them, received their supplication,[25] listened to their weeping speeches, and spoke my mercy.[26]

(60) With the supreme power that Aššur and Marduk granted me, (having) made my weaponry superior to that of all the rulers in the world, I promised them to overthrow the land of Urartu, to restore their (legitimate) boundaries, and to allow the troubled Mannaeans to rest; (at this) they became confident. Before king Ullusunu, their lord, I spread a richly endowed table,[27] thus exalting his rule over that of Iranzu, the father his begetter.[28] I had them take place at a joyful repast with the Assyrians, and they blessed my kingship before the god Aššur and the deities of their land.

(64) Zizî, of the city Appatar, and Zalaya of the city of the Kitpataeans, city lords of the land Gizilbunda, a territory which is located in the far-off mountains, a remote place blocking the route of the lands of Mannaeans and Medes like a barricade – the people inhabiting these cities trusted in their own strength and recognized no overlordship. None, among the kings my forerunners, had seen their dwelling-places nor had heard their name nor had received their tribute. (But) thanks to the powerful bidding of the god Aššur, my lord, who granted to me as a gift the subjection of the mountain rulers and the receipt of their presents, they came to hear of the advance of my expedition, and fright of my fearsome aura overtook them, with terror striking them in their very land. Their tribute of countless horses in yoke teams, of cattle, and of small livestock, they brought forth to me from Appatar and Kitpat, and conveyed it in my presence in the city of Zirdiakka of Mannaea. They begged me to spare their lives, and they kissed my feet so that I should not destroy their fortified emplacements. Accordingly, I appointed a representative over them for the well-being of their land, and I assigned them to my eunuchs and to the governor of Parsuaš.

(74)[29] I set out from Zirdiakka, a fortress of the land of the Mannaeans. I covered speedily thirty

[20] Line 46. On the possible Iranian etymology of this PN ("Powerful"), see *PNA*, 1425b.

[21] Line 51. Episode 2 (tribute of Ullusunu and pledge of mutual alliance, approach to Gizilbunda and tribute therefrom) starts here.

[22] Line 54. As already implied in Luckenbill's slightly verbose translation, and suggested outright by Foster in a footnote (2005:794, n. 1), the expression *a-na kun-ni šar-ru-ti-šu* should refer to the son's future accession to the throne, written up in a royal inscription which Ullusunu entrusted to the Assyrian king.

[23] Line 56. As explained in Fuchs 1994:440–441, Kakmē was the name of Urartu in the Mannaean language, and the two toponyms are interchangeable in various passages of Sargon's royal inscriptions.

[24] Line 56. ^{I}*Ur-sa-a*. This is the first occurrence of the Urartian king's name in the text: cf. *PNA* 1054a–1057b s.v. Rusa, where the variant writings ^{I}*Ur-sa-a*, ^{I}*Ru-sa-a*, and ^{I}*Ru-sa-a-a*, attested at random in the Sg. VIII, are noted; the meaning of the name is obscure. Of the three Urartian kings bearing this dynastic name, the present one should be the best-known Rusa I, son of Sarduri III, and father of Argišti, possibly already on the throne under Tiglath-pileser III or Shalmaneser V; Sargon himself states in line 92 that Rusa was in power before his time. For a different opinion, cf. Roaf 2011.

[25] Line 59. The term *utnēnu/utnennu*, "prayer, supplication" recurs in line 161, referring to Sargon himself before his gods, and in line 400 for a worshipper statue: cf. *CAD* U/W 336a–b.

[26] Line 59. Lit. (with Thureau-Dangin), "I said to them: '*aḫulap*!'", i.e. employing the well-attested exclamation with which a superior (god or king) grants compassion and mercy, and which a subordinate/worshipper hopes to obtain from him (see *CAD* A 1:213b–215a). Mayer (1983:73, line 59) translates *aḫulap* as "Es ist genug!", while Foster renders it as "What a pity!"

[27] Line 62. For *takbittu*, which in itself means "honor, dignity, important position", but which can also be used in the *ARI* as a semantically exaltative qualifier of an adjacent noun, and thus be translated as "important, rich/copious, exaggerated *etc*.", cf. *CAD* T 70a–b; *AHw* 1306a. Cf. also line 261 below.

[28] Line 62. Foster takes the expression literally, "I placed his chair higher than that of Iranzu," in the wake of Thureau-Dangin, "plus que pour Iranzu le père qui l'a engendré, j'élevai son siege," of Mayer (1983:73, line 62), and of *CAD* (T 70a); however the image should be rather understood with an ideological connotation, since Iranzu was most likely long dead at the time of the repast.

[29] Line 74. Episode 3 (Panziš) starts here.

"double-hours"[30] of territory between the land of the Mannaeans, Bit-Kabsi, and the land of the mighty Medes. I approached Panziš, its strong fortress, which keeps guard over the lands of Zikirtu and Andia, constructed against both these districts to prevent the escape of fugitives and to block the invasion of enemies. I reinforced the structure of that stronghold, and brought within it grain, o[il,[31] wine], and war materiel.

(79)[32] From Panziš I set out, fording the river Ištar-aurâ, and approached the land of A'ukanê, a district of the land of Zikirtu. Metatti of Zikirtu – who had cast away the yoke ⟨of Aššur⟩[33] and had scorned Ullusunu the king, his lord, neglecting his vassalage to him, putting his trust (instead) in Rusa the Urartian who, like him, had no discernment, (and was) an ally who could not save his life – climbed up in fear Mt. Wašdirikka, a difficult mountain, and his body trembled when he saw the advance of my expedition from afar. He assembled all the people of his land and amidst difficulties made them ascend mountains (so) remote, (that) their (hiding-)place could not be detected. As for him, (not even) Parda, his royal capital, retained value in his eyes; he forsook the property of his palace, and headed outward.[34] He mobilized his horses and combat troops and brought them to assist Rusa his ally as reinforcements. I killed his fearsome combat forces who were stationed at guard on the pass of Mt. Wašdirikka. All in all, I conquered twelve of their strong and fortified cities – Ištaippa, Saktatuš, Nanzu, A'ukanê, Kabani, Gurrusupa, Raksi, Gimdakrikka, Barunakka, Ubabara, Sitera, Taštami, Tesammia[35] – together with eighty-four settlements around them. I destroyed their fortified enclosures, I set on fire the houses within them, I demolished them like a deluge, I piled them up like ruin mounds.

(91)[36] I set out from A'ukanê, and I drew nigh to Wišdiš, a territory of the land of the Mannaeans which Rusa had taken away from it. Before my time,[37] Rusa the Urartian (already was) one who failed to observe the bidding of Aššur and Marduk, who had no reverential fear of the curse of the lord of lords, a mountain-dweller, offspring of a murderous lineage, who had no discernment, whose lips uttered (only) words of hostility and foolishness, who did not keep the venerable command of Šamaš, the great justice of the gods, and who – year after year – never failed to violate his prescriptions.[38] After all his previous misdeeds, he committed the grave crime of destroying his land and causing the downfall of his people.[39]

(96)[40] In Mt. Wauš, an imposing mountain, the peak of which, with a layer of clouds, reaches to the innermost sky – a place through which, since time immemorial, no offspring of humankind had passed, and no traveller had ever viewed its innermost parts, and above which no winged bird of heaven had passed, [nor buil]t a nest to teach its fledglings to spread their wings, a high mountain, which stands up like a dagger tip, chasms and precipices of far-off mountains [cutting][41] its interior, (and where both) during severe heatwaves and the rigor of winters, (whether) the Bow-star and the Arrow-star [cast][42] their glow mornings or

30 Line 75. A *bēru*, "double-hour" is conventionally made to correspond to 10.8 kms. (Powell 1987–1990:467a); thus the distance indicated here should be equal to ±325 kms.

31 Line 78. Against Mayer 1983:74, Vera Chamaza 1994:117a, believes that only "wine" could have fit within the relatively small break.

32 Line 79. Episode 4 (against Metatti of Zikirtu) starts here.

33 Line 80. The integration of ⟨^{d}*Aš-šur*⟩ here, given by Mayer 1983 only in translation, is advocated by Vera Chamaza 1994:117a, on the basis of numerous parallels.

34 Line 84. On the syntax of this clause, cf. Vera Chamaza 1992:115.

35 Lines 87–89. In point of fact, the listed toponyms are thirteen; but only Mayer (1983:77) seems to have marked this discrepancy through punctuation in his translation. It is not clear if a scribal mistake crept in here, or else if perchance A'ukanê, as (also) referring to the entire territory, was not included in the count.

36 Line 91. Episode 5 (against Wišdiš, pitched battle of Mt. Wauš) starts here.

37 Line 92: Foster (2005:796) follows Mayer (1983:77)in interpreting "before my arrival", which is ambiguous in its possible reference to a mixed temporal and spatial dimension. In point of fact, *ellāmū'a* means "before me", so it must, in agreement with Fuchs (*PNA*, 1054b), represent a purely chronological indication, "before my time" (cf. *ad* line 56, above).

38 Lines 92–94. This heavily derogatory passage on Rusa is aptly and closely compared by contrast to the glowing praise of Sargon in lines 112–115 by Van de Mieroop 2010:419–420.

39 Line 95. With the translation "qui (méritait) la ruine de son pays et la défaite de son people," Thureau-Dangin clearly understands the "land" and "people" as Rusa's own, whereas Foster (2005:796), following Mayer (1983:77) inserts "(Ullusunu)" as referent of the pronominal suffix in both cases.

40 Lines 96–109, marked by a number of central lacunae in the original edition (Thureau-Dangin 1912:16–19 and Table V, XXIV), were largely restored on the basis of texts from the Berlin Museum: O. Schroeder's 1922 copy of the composite duplicate text KAH II, 141, Col. I, and the fragment VAT 8698a. The ensuing readings were presented by E. Weidner, AfO 12 (1937–1938), 144–145; see now Mayer 1983:76–79. For some reason, Luckenbill's 1927 edition quoted Schroeder's copies (p. 73) but did not take full advantage of them, thus leaving numerous lacunae in the relevant passages.

41 Line 99. The restitution in the break is based on the expression in l. 21, above: cf. Vera Chamaza 1994:117a.

42 Line 100. Vera Chamaza 1994:117b would restore [*na-pa-ḫu*] in the break, on the basis of multiple parallels.

evenings,[43] snow is continuously piled up over it day and night, and its entire appearance is [mantled in frost][44] and ice, (where) the body of anyone crossing its boundary is struck by stormy gales, and his flesh is stung by the depths of winter.

(There) he (= Rusa) had raised his great host, including his auxiliaries. To back the cause of Metatti of Zikirtu, he assembled his fighters, competent in battle, the mainstay of his host, and the [....... of t]heirs he readied.[45] The horses, their swift-running mounts, he [....., and made them] bear weapons. Metatti of Zikirtu, who from [......][46] had been given help [......],[47] who had won over [to his side][48] all the rulers of the mountains, his neighbors, and received their help for the massed body of his troops and auxiliaries [......], he held them in contempt.[49] Praise of his prowess in battle [he proclaimed (?), and he ......], equalling my strength. (Col. II) His (= Rusa's) heart yearned to fight with me in an open field battle, and he planned mercilessly to repulse the host of the god Enlil and Aššur. (Thus), he drew up a battle line at a spring of that mountain, and he sent me a messenger (challenging me) to battle and to man-to-man combat.[50]

(112) I (am) Sargon, king of the four edges of the earth, shepherd of Assyria, who observes the oath (to) the gods Enlil and Marduk, who is attentive to the decision of Šamaš,[51] scion of Baltil (= the city of Aššur) – the city of (ultimate) wisdom and broad understanding –,[52] who waits with reverence upon the words of the great gods and does not question their designs,[53] the legitimate king of gracious speech, to whom a deceptive word is a taboo, (and) from whose mouth (expressions of) evil and wrongdoing never come forth, the wisest of the kings of the world, who was generated in intelligence and reason, who upholds with his hands reverence for gods and goddesses.[54]

(116) To Aššur, king of all the gods, lord of all the lands, begetter of everything,[55] king of all the great gods, who encircles the edges (of the earth), all-poweful lord of Assyria who, in the great fury of his anger, crushes the rulers of the world and pulver-

[43] Line 100. As explained by Foster (1995:796, n. 1) the coupled reference to the "Arrow-star" (*Canis maior*) and the "Bow-Star" (*Sirius*) must be connected to the previous climate/seasonal indications and the following times of day: the morning rising of the two stars (which were closely connected in 1st millennium astrological tradition: see e.g. Rogers 1998) coincided with the summer, the evening rising with the winter. Thus the entire passage implies that Mt. Wauš was snowed over at all times. The missing verb is integrated *u[štabarr]û* in *CAD* Š 3:229a–b, which refers to other passages in the *ARI* concerning the rising of Sirius.

[44] Line 101. Vera Chamaza 1994:117b, after *AHw* 1284a, envisages [*ḫi-it-lup ḫal-pu-u*] in the break, which has been followed in the present translation. The partially similar integration "[is locked in frost]" is suggested by Foster (2005:796), whereas Luckenbill (1927:80) has "is covered (?) with sleet and ice."

[45] Line 104. Thus, with all previous translators, but perhaps *uzakki-ma* should be rather understood in a technical sense, "he mobilized."

[46] Line 106. Luckenbill (1922:80) suggests "days of old(?)" in the break.

[47] Line 106. Foster (2005:796) understands the signs [ ]-*ti-iš* before *šá-kín* to represent the end of an adverb expressing a comparison, "had been his ally like a[ ]"; while Weidner, Luckenbill, and Mayer do not attempt interpretation. Cf. on the other hand *AHw* 972b; *CAD* R 271a, for a reading *iš-šá-kín*, with a passive meaning.

[48] Line 107. The present interpretation implies that the verb read by Weidner and all others after him as [*i-tu*]-*ram-ma* could have been preceded in the break by *ana idi-šu*, "to his side"; however, in this case, the D-stem of *târu* seems to be required (*CAD* T 275b), so perhaps [*ú-tir*]-*am-ma* (or similar form) might be worth considering.

[49] Line 108. This passage, with only [ ]*il-qa-a še-tu-šun* remaining at the end of the line (Mayer has erroneously *še-šun*), is particularly difficult to reconstruct. In general, however, it would seem to imply that, for all of the troops that Metatti of Zikirtu had brought personally to the field, and despite all his efforts in engaging neighboring mountain rulers to the cause, the Urartian king felt no real respect for these minions of his. The following lines, in point of fact, indicate clearly that Rusa considered himself a full equal of the Assyrian ruler, and thus was ready to "match the strength" of the latter.

[50] Line 111. Cf. *CAD* E 88a; also, with different nuances, *CAD* T 202a. The present interpretation intends to underscore a possible further specification of *šutelup ananti* (lit. "to mingle in battle") on the previous *taqrubtu*, "battle" – the essential point of the narration here being, that Rusa was spoiling for an open field, and pitched, battle (*tušāru*) with the Assyrians (cf. *CAD* T 138b). Cf. also Vera Chamaza 1992:117, for previous and different interpretations.

[51] Line 112. The term *dīnu* is understood by all previous translators in the sense of "judgment," with general reference to Šamaš as god of justice (cf. *CAD* P 512b; Mayer 1983:79, "Rechtsspruch"), but the clause might more specifically be taken to cite the deity as patron of *bārūtu*, i.e. as ultimately responsible for the "yes/no" decisions resulting from queries requiring extispicy – a practice to which Neo-Assyrian kings freely resorted, as shown by the abundant texts assembled by I. Starr in SAA 4.

[52] Line 113. BAL.TIL^{ki}. For this reference on Sargon's part to the so-called "Baltil ideology" of Assyrian kingship, which reappears in the historically crucial text of the "Assur Charter," cf. most recently Fales 2013:222, and n. 105, with previous references. As for the following URU *né-me-qi*, it must be admitted that Thureau-Dangin's rendering (1912:21), "la ville de science," remains quite attractive. See also line 429 below.

[53] Line 113. Thus, in basic agreement with Luckenbill (1927:80) and Mayer (1983:79; cf. also *CAD* S 140b), and differently from Thureau-Dangin (1912:21: "qui ne s' approche pas de leurs bornes") and Foster (2005:797: "(who) does not trangress the bounds they have set").

[54] Line 115. Foster (2005:797) seems to accept the reading by Thureau-Dangin (1912:20), *pa-liḫ* DINGIR.MEŠ *ù* ^{d}*Iš-ta-ri* ("who sustains with his own hands anyone who reveres divinities"), but Mayer (1983:78) and *CAD* (R 383a) envisage the construct infinitive *pa-laḫ* here, with a more fluid translation.

[55] Line 116. The text has *a-lid* BI-*ri*, but as already noted by Thureau-Dangin (1912:21), it should represent no more than a scribal mistake for *a-lid gim-ri*, attested elsewhere in Sargon's royal inscriptions: see now the relevant quotes in *CAD* A 1:292b. Thus, the translation by Luckenbill (1927:80), "creator of (prophetic) vision" must be rejected, while the footnote by Foster (2005:797) is uncalled-for.

izes the impious,[56] the supreme hero, from whose trap the evildoer cannot escape and who uproots whoever does not fear his oath[57] – (to him,) who ragingly destroys in dire battle whoever fails to fear his name, (or) trusts in his own strength, (or) has forgotten the greatness of his divinity and speaks boastful words, (by) smashing his weapons and scattering to the wind his tightly packed corps – (and) who (instead) makes his terrible battle-axe proceed at the side of whoever observes the sentence of the gods and has faith in the favorable decision of Šamaš, by continuously revering Aššur – the Enlil of the gods – (thus) causing him to stand in triumph over enemy and foe.

(123) Since I had never yet trespassed the boundaries of Rusa the Urartian, the borders of his broad land, nor had I yet poured the blood of his warriors on the open field, I raised my hands (in prayer, that) I might effect his repulse, turn his insolent words against him, and make him carry the burden of his sins.[58] Aššur, my lord, heard my righteous words, and this was pleasing to him; he turned toward my just prayer and agreed to my plea. He sent at my side his furious arms which crush the insubmissive at their (very) appearance, from dawn to sunset.

The sleepless troops of Aššur, who had come a long way, were weary and fatigued from having crossed over countless distant mountains of difficult ascent and descent, (so that) their countenances were distraught. (But) I gave no relief to their exhaustion,[59] I gave no water to quench their thirst, I placed no bivouac nor did I construct a fortified encampment; I did not give orders to my elite troops, I did not assemble my corps, I did not bring those to the right and left back to my side,[60] I paid no attention to my rearguard. I was not afraid of his (= Rusa's) massive troops, I disregarded his cavalry, I did not (even) cast a glance at[61] the mass of his armored elite units.

With my single war-chariot and the horsemen who ride at my side, who never abandon me, whether in enemy or friendly territory – the formation of the training center of Sin-aḫu-uṣur[62] – I plunged into his midst like a raging arrow, I obtained his defeat and turned back his attack. I made a huge massacre of his (men), spreading the corpses of his warriors like (drying) malt so as to fill the mountain valleys. I made their blood flow, river-like, in ravines and gullies; I dyed the steppe, the countryside, and the plains red, as if with poppies.[63] At his feet, I slaughtered like sacrificial sheep his combat troops, the mainstay of his army, as well as the bowmen and lancers, and severed their heads. In the midst of the fray, I shattered the weapons of his chief officers, his counsellors, and his courtiers, and captured them along with their mounts. I took prisoner 260 (people, between) his royal family, his chief officials, his governors, and his horsemen, (after) having dispersed their battle formation.

(139) And as for him, I confined him in the gathering of his own encampment. I smote his horses in yoked teams from under him with spears and arrows. To save his life, he forsook his war-chariot, mounted a mare, and took flight before his men. I caused the downfall of Metatti of Zikirtu,[64] together with the coalition of his neighboring kings, and I scattered their forces; I drove back the army of Urartu, the

56 Line 117. A difficult clause: with Mayer 1983:78, account is taken of a possible integration, *uš-ta⟨-aḫ⟩-ši-la la-na-a-te*, from *ḫašālu*, accepted by Foster (2005:797), "(who) pulverizes their bodies", although a Št-stem of this verb is not attested elsewhere. Thureau-Dangin's translation (1912:21) was only partial, "les princes du monde, ...," while Luckenbill's rendering (1927:81) was radically different, "and made the ignoble their equal(?)." On the other hand, the translation in Luckenbill seems to imply an interesting solution for the last word in the line, which presents a difficult *la-na-a-te* ("form, stature," not attested in the plural, and moreover with no accompanying pronominal suffix), and which might rather (with Vera Chamaza 1994:117b) be understood as *la na-a-de*$_4$, thus yielding altogether "who pulverizes the impious."

57 Line 118. Lit., "and the root of him who is not afraid of his oath is pulled out": cf. Vera Chamaza 1992:118, for this inversion of subject and tense on the previous relative clause.

58 Line 124. Cf. also Fales 1991:137.

59 Lines 129 ff. This passage is interestingly ambiguous: by describing in some detail the fact that the troops were in such a condition of fatigue following their long and difficult march that no normal measure of repose, reorganization and organized array was possible, it would actually seem to underscore the lack of time involved, in view of the enemy's full readiness to do battle in a tactical location which had been long since, and aptly, chosen. This (initially negative) difference of military readiness between the Assyrians and their enemies is then made to work, from the literary and ideological point of view, as the indispensable cause of the king's heroic decision to go it alone on his personal war-chariot, with only a handful of choice fighters, so as to effect an exemplary slaughter of enemy forces. Cf. Fales 1991:140–141, for this motif of the "(heroic) one against the many", which, as for the latter, also extends to the multiplicity of allies which Rusa and Metatti had called to their side to stop the single Assyrian expeditionary force.

60 Line 130. With Mayer 1983:80, an integration *⟨ú⟩-te-ram* is called for here.

61 Line 131. The preposition *a-na* is erroneously repeated twice: cf. Mayer 1983:80.

62 Line 132. This man – the only Assyrian other than Sargon to be named in the account before the colophon (Van de Mieroop 2010:423) – was the brother of the king, who bore the title of *sukkalmaḫḫu*; cf. *PNA*, 1128b, and Niederreiter 2005, for other texts and figurative/archaeological evidence concerning this "Grand vizier."

63 Line 135. Mayer (1983:81) translates *illūriš* as "wie Anemomen"; and similarly Foster 2005:798, "like anemone-flowers." However, *AHw* 373a, to which this interpretation goes back, drew the identification of the plant *illūru* from Campbell-Thompson's DAB (p. 141), nowadays considered basically unreliable; thus e.g. *CAD* I/J 87a–b, and *CDA* 127a render *illūru* noncommittally as "a red flower." The translation "poppy" given here is thus merely meant to lend visual substance to the parallelism conveyed by the text, and it has been chosen because this flower is more frequently and widely known for its red-blood/scarlet color than the anemone, which has a variety of possible hues.

64 Line 141. Foster 2005:798, translates *ú-šam-qit* as "slew," but – apart from the meaning of *maqātu* Š as "to cause s.o.'s downfall, ruin," etc. – there is no supporting evidence of Metatti's death on the battlefield of Wauš: cf. *PNA*, 757b.

evil enemy, together with its allies, and within Mt. Wauš he (= the enemy) took to his heels.[65] Their horses clogged the ravines and the gullies, while they, like ants in panic, negotiated even the most difficult paths. I went up after them, with the rage of my mighty weapons. I filled the rises and downward inclines with the cadavers of fighters. For six "double-hours" of terrain, from the mountain of Wauš to Zimur, the mountain of jasper, I was on his (= Rusa's) trail at arrow's length.[66] Those men who were left, who had fled to get away with they lives, and who I had let go so as to glorify the strength of Aššur my lord – the mighty god Adad, valiant son of Anu, let loose his immense thunder against them, and with his storm-cloud and hail finished off the remainder.[a]

(148) Rusa, their ruler, who had trespassed the bounds of Šamaš and Marduk and who did not honor his oath to Aššur, king of the gods, became fearful at the din of my powerful weapons, and his heart palpitated like a rock-partridge fleeing before an eagle. Like one wanted for murder, he decamped from Ṭurušpâ, his royal capital, and like a restless vagrant[67] he hid in a recess of his mountains. Like a woman in travail, he lay on his bed, refusing all food and drink in his mouth,[b] and inflicting on himself illness without remedy.

I established the power of Aššur, my lord, for all time to come over the land of Urartu; forever after, I left behind me an unforgettable fear of him. In furious battle, I provided the land of Urartu with the bitter taste of the greatness of my overpowering strength and of the assault of my all-powerful weapons, which have no rival in the four edges of the earth and which never turn back in retreat. I covered the people of Zikirtu and Andia with the venom of death; I barred the access of the evil enemy from the land of the Mannaeans, thus causing the heart of Ullusunu, their lord, to rejoice and light to shine forth on his distressed people.

a Josh 10:11

b 1 Sam 28:20–23; 1 Kgs 21:4–7

(156) I am Sargon, guardian of righteousness, who never oversteps the bounds of Aššur and Šamaš, who reveres Nabû and Marduk with ceaseless humility; I achieved my heart's desire with their firm consent. In triumph I stood before my haughty foes. I spread devastation over all the mountains,[68] and I imposed silence and wailing upon the enemy populations, (while) I entered my fortified encampment in happiness and rejoicing, accompanied by players on lyres and flutes. To Nergal, Adad, and Ištar, lords of battle, to the gods dwelling in heaven and earth and the gods who dwell in Assyria, I made precious offerings of glorification. I stood before them in a pose of reverence and supplication, and I extolled their divinity.[69]

(162)[70] I interrupted my campaign to Andia and Zikirtu, where my countenance was directed, and I turned toward the land of Urartu. I conquered the entire land of Wišdiš, a territory of Mannaea which Rusa had taken away and turned over to himself, its settlements so abundant as to be numberless like the stars in the sky. I crushed like potsherds their powerful fortifications down to their fundaments, and made them into bare ground. I opened their countless grain-stores and had my men eat barley beyond measure.

(167)[71] From Wišdiš I set out, and approached Ušqaya, a great fortress at the outer boundary of Urartu, which, at the pass of the land of Zaranda, bars the territory like a door and (even) holds back the messenger, and which stands out, on Mallau, the mountain of juniper, like a boundary stake over

[65] Line 142. For the verbal clause in the 3rd p. sg., obviously referring back to the *nakru lemnu*, cf. *CAD* N 2:199a; see also Mayer 1983:83.

[66] Line 145. Lit. "at arrow point" (cf. Foster 2005:799). What is probably expressed here is Sargon's claim to have remained hard on the heels of Rusa – i.e. virtually at shooting distance with his bow – for all of six *bērus* (= approx. 66 km) in the latter's flight. Mayer's rendering (1983:83) "mit der Pfeilspitze" is less significant.

[67] Line 150. The comparison *kī munnabti ṣayyādi* is understood by Mayer (1983:83) as "wie ein ruheloser Fluchtling", whereas Thureau-Dangin (1912:27), and then Luckenbill (1927:83), and finally Foster (2005:799) view *ṣayyādu* as corresponding to "hunter"; in this case, however, the translation consistently implies underscoring an "animal," or collectively "game," as referent of *munnabtu*. Moreover, since the present clause immediately follows the one with *kī tābik dāmi*, a comparison equally portraying a wretched human condition seems more likely here.

[68] Line 158. Integration KUR.MEŠ-*e ka-la-šu*⟨*-nu*⟩ required, as suggested by Mayer 1983:84.

[69] Line 161. Cf. Fales 1991:135–138, for the view that the ideological-literary motif of a radical opposition in moral conduct between the "righteous king" (Sargon) vs. the "treacherous enemy" (Rusa), which begins at the very opening of the text, ends here in its first, and main, manifestation; an opposition along the same lines will be briefly taken up again regarding Urzana in lines 309–312, due to the king of Muṣaṣir's (forced) defection to an allegiance with Rusa.

[70] Lines 162–309. This middle part of Sg. VIII was analyzed by Fales (1991:142 ff.,) who noted the difference with the ideological perspective on the enemy previously offered in the text: "from the previous individual 'snapshots' of the fighters for whom Urartu was reputed, of the defenders placed in its most formidable strongholds, of the self-satisfied inhabitants of its cities, we are brought again to a topical and homogeneous picture – the homogeneity of a cowardly enemy crowd fleeing in slightly variant states of panic at the arrival of the Assyrian army" (p. 142). Further, "ideologically, the total devastation of the enemy's assets functions as a consequence of the abandonment of the city on the part of the latter; it is the substitute for a direct military confrontation, for the fight and the consequent carnage of the enemy, which cannot take place. Since the enemy is absent, the ideological 'toll' is taken by the things which he has abandoned; these things are desecrated, violated, brought to naught in the enemy's stead" (p. 143). A further point is that, in this part, Rusa is conspicuously absent as a physical antagonist (p. 147): he will return to the scene of the text only briefly, and "by proxy" from the literay point of view, upon hearing of Urzana's defeat and of the plunder of Muṣaṣir (lines 411–413).

[71] Line 167. Episode 6 (against Ušqaya) starts here.

the meadows of Subi, clothing it in radiance. The population of that territory has no equal in all the land of Urartu for their skill with cavalry. Every year, they take the very young, thoroughbred foals born in their vast country, which they raise for his (= Rusa's) royal army. Until they are taken to Subi – the territory that the people of Urartu call "Mannaea" – and their prowess is not checked, they do not attempt to ride them, nor do they teach them to advance, turn, and retreat, (as is) expected in battle, or harness them to a yoke.[72]

These men, (both) of the fortress and of the territory, observed the rout of their lord Rusa, and their legs went slack like roots on a riverbank; (and when) their battle-tested vanguard, in flight before (my) arms and (already) enveloped in the poison of death, (finally) came upon them,[73] reporting to them of the valor of Aššur, my lord, who left none to escape alive among all their fighters, they became still as death.[74] They turned into ruins the city of Ušqaya, the mainstay of their land, along with its surrounding settlements, left behind their possessions, and took a road of no return.

I ascended to that fortress with the attack of my mighty weaponry, I ransacked its vast goods and brought them to my encampment. Its massive wall, the foundation of which was laid on mountain bedrock and which measured eight cubits in its thickness, starting from its crenellations and reaching to its deepest fundament, I demolished altogether and razed down to the ground. I set fire to the buildings inside, and turned to ashes their tall beams. As if they were brushwood piles, I burned 115 settlements in its environs, and covered the face of the sky like a dust storm with their smoke. I made its open fields as if a deluge had devastated them; its inhabited settlements I heaped up like rubbish dumps.

I destroyed and leveled down to the ground the city of Aniaštania, his herding center, built on the border of the land of Sangibutu, between Ušqaya and Tarmakisa, along with 17 settlements around it. I set their tall roof beams on fire, I burned their crops and their chaff. I opened up their grain depots and storehouses and let my troops devour the barley supplies beyond measure. I let loose the livestock of my encampment on his flatlands like a swarm of locusts, and they pulled out the pasturage which was his support, and laid waste his meadows.

(188)[75] From Ušqaya I set out, and reached the steppeland,[76] source of his livestock, which they call Sangibutu. Tarwi and Tarmakisa are powerful fortresses which were built in Dalaean territory, cultivated environs (with) abundant grain stores of his. Their fortifications are very strong, their enceintes are well-packed, their moats are deeply dug and surround their perimeters. Inside them, the horses – the reserves of his royal army – are placed in stalls and supplied with fodder year after year. The people living in that territory saw the lordly actions that I had repeatedly performed in the settlements all around them, and they became terrified. They abandoned their settlements and fled for their lives to a dry expanse, a land of thirst, like a desert.[77] I covered that territory like a bird-snare; among its fortified cities I stirred up combat; their strong fortresses I destroyed, beginning at the crenellations and reaching to their foundations, and razed down to the ground. I laid on fire the buildings within them, I turned to ashes their tall beams. I burned their plentiful crops. I opened the grain stores and fed my troops on barley beyond measure. Thirty settlements in their environs [I burned as if they were brushwood piles, and like a dust storm] covered the face of the sky with their smoke.[78]

(199)[79] I set out from Tarmakisa and reached [...................]. Ulḫu, a stronghold at the foot of

[72] Lines 170–173. The description seems to imply that the horses of Ušqaya were by and large kept undisciplined until their selection for actual training within Rusa's armed forces, differently from elsewhere, where they should have been preliminarily broken in. However, unless one should understand that they were left to roam completely in the wild – and thus, one may ask, where would the local "skill" be rooted? – a suggestion that they were ridden bareback may be put forth (i.e. with *ṣe-ru-uš-šú-un ḫal-la la ip-tu-ma* meaning here that no formal riding apparel was used; cf. already Fales 1991:133). See also Dalley 1985:42 for a (largely unacknowledged) translation of the passage which has provided interesting suggestions.

[73] Line 175. The implication here should be that the "vanguard" (*ālik pānišunu*) was the last to arrive in its retreat, well after the general rout of the troops had been amply observed by the natives of Ušqaya.

[74] Line 176. The translation of *CDA* 213a, is followed here, although Foster's (2005:800) rendering, "they were as good as dead," is ingenious. All other authors follow closely Thureau-Dangin (1912:29), "ils devinrent comme morts."

[75] Line 188. Episode 7 (against Tarmakisa) starts here.

[76] Line 188. With *AHw* 572a, the alleged ^{KUR}*Ba-ri*, accepted by all authors following Thureau-Dangin (1912:30) must be understood as *mad*!*-ba-ri*, "steppe, open countryside." Quaintly enough, even Mayer (1983:84) missed the correction published by his teacher Von Soden in 1972. The same correction appeared in *CAD* M 1:12a (1977), but was overlooked by Foster (2005:801).

[77] Line 193. As noted by Van de Mieroop (2010:423), this comparison "is quite inappropriate for the lush Zagros Mountains, which elsewhere in the text are said to contain mighty waterfalls." However, a negative opinion on (the enemy's) natural environment is topical in the Assyrian royal inscriptions.

[78] Line 198. This clause is for some reason omitted by Foster (2005:801).

[79] Episode 8 (against Ulḫu) starts here. Lines 199–232 were philologically elaborated, on the basis of the Assur fragment KAH II, 141, by B. Meissner (1922). Their content and ideological significance were the object of detailed study by Zaccagnini 1981; see also Fales 1991:142–147.

[Mt. Kišpal,[80] ....], and its people, like a fish, to [....................], they [could not] drink and could never be sated. Following his heart's desire, Rusa, their king and lord, had [....................], and discovered sources of water. He dug a main ditch to carry the flowing water,[81] and [................waters] of abundance, like the Euphrates, he caused to flow. He had countless irrigation channels depart from its midst [, and ....][82] he provided irrigation for the meadowland. His arable land, which was uncultivated since days of yore [............he plan]ted,[83] and caused fruit and grapes to pour down like rain.[84] He caused plane-trees and *šurathu*-trees – the pride of [his] palace – to [extend their branches (?)] like a forest, (and) to bear a (shaded) covering over his cultivated areas. And (so), over his abandoned meadowland, the *araḫ*[*ḫu*-song he brought back, and], like a deity,[85] he made his people intone the sweet *alala*-work cry. (From) 300 measures of seed[86] he made a cornfield of grain sp[rou]t in its fur[rows], and in the sale he multiplied the yield.[87] The waste area of his agricultural land he made like a meadow [............] greatly in the spring,[88] (so that) grain and pasturage were unceasing, winter and summer. He turned it into a corral for horses and cattle, and he taught his entire inaccessible land the use of camels, (so that they could) heap up (further) weirs. He built a palace, a royal residence for his leisure on the bank of the canal, roofing it with cypress beams of pleasant scent. The city of Sarduriḫurda, a fortress to guard him, he [built] on Mt. Kišter, and brought therein [people from the land of .... ti]b/na[89] to protect his country.

(213)[90] When the people of that territory heard of the painful matter which I had set in action against Rusa, they cried "Woe!" and struck their thighs in grief. They abandoned Ulḫu, their stronghold, even up to Sarduriḫurda, the fortress of their support, and fled at night to a recess in the difficult mountains. In my heart's wrath, I [enveloped] the borders of that territory like a fog, and I compacted (its) breadth and length like ice.[91]

In Ulḫu, the city of Rusa's relaxation, I entered as a lord, and triumphantly I walked around [within] the palace, seat of his kingship. Its strong wall, made of stone from a massive mountain, I crushed minutely like a clay bowl with [iron] axes and iron [daggers], and leveled it to the ground. The long juniper beams that roofed his palace I [tore out], I hacked them

[80] Line 200. The restoration, based on the further reference to this mountain in Sargon's Annals, was already suggested by Thureau-Dangin (1912:32–33); see now Fuchs 1994:443, for the Khorsabad Annals, line 140 (text *ibid.*, p. 112). However, as noted by this author, account should be also taken of the reference to KUR*Kiš-te-er* in line 212 of our text.

[81] Line 203. The translation takes account of the detailed study of the Ulḫu water system in Laessøe 1951 (esp. p. 27).

[82] Line 204. Zaccagnini 1981:265, integrates "[with the waters which he rais]ed?" here, presumably on the basis of the [...]*lu-ú* which concludes the break. Foster (2005:802) takes after him, "[with the water he brought]."

[83] Line 205. Integration suggested by Zaccagnini 1981:265; a verbal form in the preterite here is justified by the closing enclitic *-ma*, while Foster's "[thereafter]" (2005:802) is unclear in its origin.

[84] Line 205. Foster (2005:802) suggests that the final verb *ušaznin* should depend on the initial *ugaršu* ("His fields ... would shower down"), but the subject of the clause is clearly the technically-minded and proficient king, as implied by Meissner, Zaccagnini and Mayer, whereas Luckenbill (1927:86) is noncommittal ("and made fruit and grapes as abundant as the rain"). Cf. also Vera Chamaza 1992:121, who believes "that the *tertium comparationis* of the 'fruits and grapevine' in the expression GURUN *ù* GEŠTIN *ki-ma zu-un-ni u-ša-az-nin* (line 205) is represented by the abundance of the 'rain.'"

[85] Line 207. The expression GIM DINGIR is omitted by Zaccagnini (1981:265) and Foster (2005:802), but had been clearly read by Meissner (1922:114).

[86] Line 208. One may wonder whether this could have been a standard measure of capacity for grain (Vera Chamaza 1992:121–122).

[87] Line 208. The integration *ina* AB.[SÍN.MEŠ (*-šú*)], "in its furrows," is accepted by all authors of recent date, while a decided uncertainty surrounds the reconstruction of the next verbal form, *ú-šaḫ*-[x]-*ib-ma*. Both Zaccagnini (1981:265) and Foster (2005:802) integrate -[*ri*]-, thus deriving it from **ḫarāpu*, "to be early", as does *CAD* K 550a ("early grain," etc.), while Mayer (1983:88) refers back to **ḫanāpu*, "to sprout, flourish" (*ú-šaḫ*-[*ni*]-*ib-ma*), which is followed here as more plausible. Meissner (1922:114) had instead integrated *ú-šaḫ*-[*bi*]-*ib-ma*, from **ḫabābu*, "ließ er durchfließen."

[88] Line 209. Luckenbill's (1927:87) integration here, although not critically marked out, is of a certain interest: "flooding them abundantly in springtime." Meissner (1922:115), on the other hand, had suggested "[indem sie grünten] gar sehr Frühjahr."

[89] Line 212. As noted by Vera Chamaza (1994:118a), this reconstruction is quite uncertain; certainly no professional nor ethnic group [-*ti*]-*b*/*na-a-a* is immediately apparent.

[90] Lines 213–214. Zaccagnini (1981:266) notes that these two lines on the population's apprehension of Sargon's violence and its immediately subsequent flight to far-off places act as a brief, but unequivocal, narrative "bridge" between the extended tale of the enemy king's commendable deeds and the following account of Sargon's systematic undoing of all of them (lines 215–232). From a different point of view, Vera Chamaza (1992:122), points out that "up to line 212 the Urartian king leads the action which is characterized by simple formulations. The change of subject in lines 213–214 does not cause any complication."

[91] Line 215. Luckenbill (1922:87) renders "On front and flank I harassed it frightfully", taking directly from Thureau-Dangin (1912:35, "de manière à causer l'effroi"); but the adverb derives precisely from *šurīpu*, "ice," cf. *CAD* Š 3:347a.

with pick[axes][c] and brought them to Assyria.[92] I opened up his grain depots and storehouses, and let my troops devour beyond measure his abundant barley supplies. I entered his hidden wine cellars, and the vast troops of Assyria drew fine wine in waterskins and leather buckets, as if it were river water. I blocked up the outlet of the canal, the watercourse of his sustenance, and turned the copious waters into a mire. I obstructed the murmuring offshoots which branched off from its midst, and I exposed to the sunlight [even the deepest(?)] of their pebbles.[93] I let my furious warriors enter into his pleasant gardens – the characteristic of his city, which were adorned with fruit and grapes, dripping like raindrops – (Col. III) and they made the noise of iron pickaxes roar like thunder.[d] They plucked its many fruits, countless in quantity, and they left no pleasure for many years to come for the perturbed heart.[94] His great trees, the feature of his palace, I spread out like (drying) malt;[95] his famous city I sullied, I put to shame his territory. Those tree-trunks, as many as I had cut down, I heaped up and set on fire. I uprooted their plentiful crops, countless like reeds in a canebrake; not a single ear of barley was left to identify the destruction (area).[96] His verdant meadowland, which was flecked like reddened pottery-glaze, and the cultivated plots, planted with spring growth and sprouting shoots, I overwhelmed like the Storm-god with chariotry, cavalry, and the tread of my infantry, and I turned the meadows – the sustenance of his horses – into wasteland. I utterly destroyed Sarduriḫurda, their great stronghold, together with 57 settlements all around it in the district of Sangibutu, and I reverted it to bare ground. The beams of their roofing I set on fire and reduced them to ashes.

c Ps 74:4–6

d Deut 20:19

(233)[97] I set out from Ulḫu and reached the hamlets of the land[98] above(?) the strong cities[99] of the district of Sangibutu; this was a populated territory, occupied by his (= Rusa's) State, which kings who came before him had taken over since earliest times to enlarge their territories. The cities of Ḫurnuku, Ḫardania, Gizuarzu, Šaš-zizza, Upper Ḫundurnu, [....................], Watzunza, Arazu, Ša-Sinia, Lower Ḫundurnu, El[....................]nak, Ṣittu-arzu, Zirma, Surzî, Elladinia, Dag[....................], Ṣurzialdiu, Armuna, and Kinaštania: in all, 21 strong cities [........, which like bus]hes – the offshoot of mountainsides – thrust up from the peaks of Mt. Arzabia, solid fortresses surronded by [massive(?) walls] – 120 brick courses was the height of their parapets – and [outfitted (?)] for the stationing of armed men [........], to be let out (?), they are clad in terror for the execution of battle. Very deep moats for the protect[ion ...., and the .... for] entrance into their city-gates are equipped with towers. Streams carrying floods of water in [plenty[100] ...; of ......] in their plains there was no interruption. Their population, in abundance and weal[th ...., (and of) .....], as much as available, spread out the hoard. Great palaces, equal to [............ (within which) .... (and)] wooden furnishings (?) were spread out, fitting for royalty. Rafters of cypress, sweet of fragrance [....................] and which wafted into the senses of anyone entering them (= the palaces) like *ḫašurru*-cedar.

(247) The people of Sangibutu district, both living in the territory and living in all those cities, [saw] the dust-cloud of my expedition from one "double-

92 Line 218. The practical sequence of actions in the Assyrians' pillage of Rusa's handsome beams is not entirely clear. Considering that they were "torn out" from the roofing (the verb *nasāḫu* is restored by all) and then they were shipped to Assyria (where they could be usefully employed in their intact state in public buildings, e.g. in the new capital Dur-Šarrukīn), what specific action was carried upon them in between? The verb *umaḫḫiṣ* does not leave much space for a non-destructive activity (e.g. *CAD* M 1:83a–b quotes this passage under "to smash, to destroy, to kill"), and the use of the *kalappu*-ax for hacking wood has a parallel in line 224, being also used by other Assyrian rulers for heavy work on rock surfaces (cf. *CAD* K 66b). On the other hand, this very problem seems to have been noted, and tackled, by previous translators; thus Zaccagnini (1981:267) has "I stroke (*sic*: for 'struck') them," while Foster reasonably (but with no real justification) renders "I smoothed them." Thus, the present translation, following Mayer's (1983:91: "(ich) behaute"), may be taken as explicitly ambiguous – also because the solution to the "puzzle" might be viewed in a hyperbolic scribal insertion of a further image of devastation, which at the end defeats the overall purpose of the clause itself.

93 Line 222. The integration is suggested by Zaccagnini (1981:287) and is taken up by Foster (2005:803), while Mayer (1983:90) leaves the textual gap as it stands.

94 Line 225. As noted by Foster (2005:813), this line was collated and studied by B. Landsberger 1942:165, with reference to a passage in Gilgamesh (9:VI 51), in which a garden is considered "a pleasure to behold."

95 Line 226. See already at line 134, and *CAD* Š 2:343b.

96 Line 228. Cf. *CAD* M 2:236. Differently Mayer (1983:91): "um die Lahmlegung der Arbeit zu erkennen."

97 Line 233. Episode 9 (against Sangibutu) starts here. On the difficulties of this section (esp. to line 245), marked by many gaps, cf. Vera Chamaza 1992:123.

98 Line 233. *a-na a-tu*[*r*] *un-na-te*, according to Mayer (1983:92); the suggestion of "hamlets of the land" stems from *AHw* 1421a; see also *CAD* U/W 161b. It may be recalled that M. Van Loon, *BiOr* 44 (1987), 259, had suggested A.AB.[.BA] *un-na-te*, but – as noted by Vera Chamaza 1994:118a – the "sea of the land" yields scarce sense in this context.

99 Line 233. Cf. *AHw* 1421a, *CAD* U/W 161b, for *unnātu*, "land," a term restricted to Sargon's inscriptions, which follows *a-tu*[*r*], "village(s)" (cf. *adurû* /*edurû*). Notice however *CAD* R 283a, where the following *re-eš* URU.MEŠ-*ni dan-nu-ti* is not understood as an adjective ("the foremost of the fortified cities," or similar; thus also Mayer 1983:93; Foster 2005:803), but as an adverb ("above"), and is considered to follow the restoration [*ana abun*]*nate*, although the latter is unconfirmed elsewhere (e.g. in *CAD* A 1:89b–90a).

100 Line 243. Vera Chamaza (1994:118a) suggests that [*ḫe-en-gal-li*], "plenty, plentifulness," might be integrated here.

hour" away,[101] (and) confusion spread over the entire border of Urartu. For their observation of the territory against the ene[my],[102] towers had been built on the peaks of mountains, and had been erected [....................].[103] They saw the kindling of brushwood (signalling) the approach of the [........] enemy, and the torches (lit) morning and evening,[104] and they informed [......]. They feared the wild onslaught of my combat, which is unrivalled, and a deathly hush was poured out over them, so that they be[came as dead men].[105] They did not even raise their face[106] at their numerous possessions, they forsook their mighty fortifications and they hid in a recess.[107] I covered that territory like a thick night cloud, and overwhelmed the entirety of his strong cities like a converging floodwater.

(254) I advanced for a stretch of terrain of 12 "double-hours" between Mts. Arzabia and Irtia, high mountains, and pitche[d ca]mp. In the remote recesses of their interior I moved along my fierce warriors like wild sheep, and [they spa]red not a single scout to hear their orders. I had the vast host of Aššur swarm over all their settlements like locusts, and I made my ag[gressive] plunderers penetrate their bedrooms. Goods, property and prized items [of their houses/palaces (?)] they brought back to me, and I laid hands on their piled-up treasuries. I made auxiliaries and footsoldiers be[aring bows and spears scale] their walls, and made wreckers take up position at (?) the battlements and the cornice.[108] I pulled out the beams of cypress-wood that roofed the palaces, and the people from Mannaea and the land of [N]a'ir[i ....][109]; I [crushed]their high enclosure walls, as firmly based as mountains,[110] down to their foundations, like sand. I ignited their elaborate residences, and caused the smoke thereof to rise up, covering the sky like fog. I let my entire host load on horses, mules, camels and donkeys their huge stores of grain, which they had piled up in silos over a long time for the sustenance of land and people, and piled them up anew inside my encampment, (as high) as ruin-mounds. I nourished my people on plentiful and satisfying food, and they joyfully prepared ample provisions[111] for their return march to Assyria. I cut down his exuberant orchards,[e] I chopped down the large number of his vineyards, and (thus) put his drinking to an end. I cut his vast forests, the trees of which are tangled like an inaccessible reed-bed, and I laid waste his cultivated land. I gathered all his cut-down tree-trunks like the debris collected by a dust storm,[112] and set them on fire. I set 146 settlements of its environs aflame like a brushwood pile, and their smoke shrouded the sky like a dust storm.

e Deut 20:19

(269)[113] I set out from the powerful cities of Sangibutu and reached the district of Armarili. The city Bubuzi, the fortress of Ḫundur – ringed by a double wall, the opening of (each) tower connected with a corresponding drawbridge of rope(?)[114] – the cities of Ayyalê, Ṣini-išpalâ, Ṣini-unak, Arna, Sarnî, (in all) seven strong cities, together with 30 settlements around them, which lie at the foot of Mt. Ubianda: I destroyed their region and I made it into bare ground. I set fire to the beams of their roofings and reduced them to ashes. I opened up their stores and granaries, and fed my troops their grain rations, abundant beyond any count. I ignited the harvest which supported his people and the hay,

[101] Line 248. Vera Chamaza (1992:122) suggests the possibility that in *ša a-na* 1 DANNA *ru-qi-iš iš-tu* UGU ^{KUR}*Ur-ar-ṭi*, an *iprus*-form from *šētû*, "to spread out, to extend" might be involved; but this meaning applies to *šeṭû* (*CAD* Š 2:343a–b), used in Sg. VIII in analogies, and not to *šētu*, "to remain, to be left over, to escape" (*ibid.*, 341b–343a), which is moreover rare in 1st millennium sources.

[102] Line 249. Mayer (1983:92) integrates *a-na na-a*[*k-re*(?)], whereas *CAD* D 145b understands an expression *ša na-gu-ú a-na na*[*-gi*], "from district to district" to be meant here.

[103] Lines 249–250. Foster (2005:804) integrates "provided with [stores of firewood for signals]", whereas *CAD* U/W 387b links *šu-zu-uz-za* to *dimāte*.

[104] Line 250. Cf. *CAD* Q 249b–250a.

[105] Line 251. The integration proposed by Thureau-Dangin (1912:40), *ik-*[*šu-du mi-tu-ti-iš*], accepted by Luckenbill (1927:89), was still repeated in *CAD* Š 1:108a, whereas Mayer (1983:94) read *ig-l*[*ud-du ta-ḫa-zi*] (see also *AHw* 274a), and this reading is taken up by Foster (2005:804), "they were too af[raid to fight]."

[106] Line 252, Quite efficaciously, Foster (2005:804) has "Without so much as a glance at *etc.*"

[107] Line 252. Thureau-Dangin (1912:40) integrates *e-mid-du šá-*[*ḫa-at* KUR*-šú*], in parallel with line 150 above, and this connection is supported by *CAD* E 139b, while Mayer (1983:94–95) reads simply *šá-*[*ḫa*]*-tu*, "drängten sich an die (Berg)flanken." On the other hand, Foster (2005:804) translates "(they) disappeared," presumably taking into account the further idiomatic expression *šadâ(šu) emēdu*, "to resort to the mountain," i.e. "to disappear" (*CAD* E 140a).

[108] Line 258. This passage is a *hapax legomenon* for the professional designation *nāqiru* "wrecker." cf. *CAD* N 1:335b.

[109] Line 259. Vera Chamaza (1994:118b) find this integration of Mayer's questionable on historical-geographical grounds.

[110] Line 260. *ša ki-ma* KUR.MEŠ*-e šur-šud*$^{!}$ (or more probably *-šu*$^{!}$)*-du*: thus Foster's (2005:804) "strongly built on the mountains" is inexact. Cf. Vera Chamaza 1994:188b.

[111] Line 264. For *ṣu-ud-de-e tak-bit-ti*, cf. line 60 above.

[112] Line 267. *kima ḫimmāt ašamšūti*: Foster (2005:805) omits the parallel by oversight.

[113] Line 269. Episode 10 (against Armariali) starts here.

[114] Line 270. The clause *pi-i di-im-ti tu-bal-e ma-ḫi-re ru-uk-ku-su* is considered obscure by *CAD* T 445a, but an alternative reading *tu-bal e-ma ḫi-ri* with *ḫīru* A, "ditch, moat" is suggested in *CAD* Ḫ 201a. As noted by Foster (2005:805), the reading *tu-bal-e ma-ḫi-re* goes back to Borger, *BiOr* 14 (1957), 121a, and is taken up in *AHw* 1364b; see also Mayer 1983:97, "Richtschnur." Vera Chamaza 1992:123 merely renders the passage as "at (their) entrances towers were built with corresponding *tubale*."

the sustenance of his livestock, as if it were brushwood, and his rural area I made into barren land. I cut down their orchards[f] and I felled his forests; I gathered in a heap and set ablaze the entirety of his tree-trunks.

f Deut 20:19

During my transit, I went to Arbu, the ancestral city of Rusa, and to Riar, the (prize) city of Sarduri. Seven settlements in their environs, in which his brothers and his royal family had settled and which were heavily guarded – these settlements I destroyed and made like bare ground. A temple of Ḫaldi, his god, I set on fire like brushwood, and I defiled its cella.

(280)[115] I set out from the land of Armariali, I traversed Mt. Wizuku, the cypress mountain, the bulk of which was in breccia-stone, and I approached the land of Ayadi. The cities of Anzalia, Kwayain, Qallania, Bitay, Alu-arza, Qiuna, Allî, Arzugu, Šikkanu, Ardiunak, Dayazuna, Gêta, Bâniu, Birḫiluza, Dêzizu, Dilizia, Abaindi, Duain, Ḫasrana, Parra, Ayasun, Aniaštania, Baldu-arza, Šaruardi, Šumattar, Šalzî, Albûri, Ṣiqarra, and Old Wayais – his thirty strong cities, were arranged in order along the shore of the rolling sea on the detritus of great mountains and set up in a straight line. The cities of Argištiuna and Qallania, his powerful fortresses, are constructed among them; they emerge like stars from atop Mts. Arṣidu and Maḫunnia, and their substructures are visible for a height of 240 cubits.[116] His fighters, crack troops[117] of his army, skilled in battle, armed with shields and spears, the support of his country, were installed inside them. They saw the conquest of Armariali, the territory alongside theirs, and their legs shook; they abandoned their cities and their possessions, and flew away like birds inside those fortresses. I sent up copious troops to their cities, and they looted their goods in large quantities, (making them) their own possessions. I demolished their strong walls, together with 87 settlements in their environs, making them reach ground level. I set fire to the buildings within, and turned to ashes their covering beams. I opened up their grain depots and storehouses and let my troops devour the barley supplies beyond measure. I cut down their orchards and chopped down their woods; I gathered all their tree-trunks and set them ablaze.

(297)[118] I set out from the land of Ayadi, and crossed the rivers Alluria, Qallania, and Innaya. I approached the city Wayais, his supply district on the lower side of the frontier with Urartu, on the borders of Nairi. Wayais was his stronghold and a great fortress, more reinforced than all his (other) fortresses and clever in its workmanship; his most ferocious combat troops (and) the scouts who brought in information on all the lands around were stationed inside it. He (= Rusa) had brought up his governors with their contingents in it, and had manned its mighty rampart with fighters.[119] I took that fortress from the back; I smote his warriors before its city gate like sacrificial sheep. I cut down their orchards and chopped down their woods; I gathered all their severed tree-trunks and set them on fire. I set ablaze the cities of Barzuriani, Walṭuquya, Qutta, Qippa, and Asapâ, five mighty fortress, as well as 40 settlements in their environs.

(306)[120] I set out from the city of Wayais, and I approached the territory of Yanzû, king of the land Nairi. Yanzû, king of the land Nairi, came to me from Ḫubuškia, his royal city, four "double-hours" of land away, and kissed my feet. Inside Ḫubuškia, his city, I received from him his tribute of horses in yoked teams, oxen, and small livestock.

(309) During my return march, Urzana of Muṣaṣir,[121] a worker of sin and sacrilege, violator of the oath of the gods, who did not submit to (my) lordship, an insolent mountain dweller who sinned against the loyalty oath to Aššur, Šamaš, Nabû, and Marduk, and (thus) rebelled against me, interrupted the return march of my expedition, by not (coming to) kiss my feet with a heavy audience-gift of his. He withheld tribute, obligation gift, and his personal audience-gift, and he did not (even) send a single envoy to inquire on my health.[122] In the

115 Line 280. Episode 11 (against Ayadi) starts here.

116 Line 288: cf. *CAD* K 44b–45a. Mayer (1983:97) overinterprets: "sind bis (zu einer Höhe von) 240 Ellen von ihren Unterbauten aus zu sehen," while Foster (2005:805) translates, less literally, "and (they) looked down 240 cubits below."

117 Line 289. Mayer (1983:96) reads *a-šá-re-tú*, but Vera Chamaza (1994:118b) corrects to *a-šá-re⟨-du⟩-ut*, on the basis of *AHw* 78b, s.v. *ašarēdu(m)* 3.

118 Line 297. Episode 12 (against Wayais) starts here.

119 Line 301: Luckenbill (1922:92) seems to have taken *ú-šal-mi* as a form of *šalāmu* ("(he) kept his fighters safe behind its mighty wall"), but already Thureau-Dangin (1912:47) had translated "il avait enfermé (ses) combattants," thus recognizing that the verb is *lam/wû* in the causative stem: cf. *CAD* L 76a.

120 Line 306. Episode 13 (against Yanzû, king of Nairi) starts here. It is the shortest episode of all, only 3 lines in length.

121 Line 309. Episode 14 (against Urzana of Muṣaṣir) starts here. For the name Urzana, its writings and attestations, cf. *PNA* 1420a–1421b. For the possible location of Muṣaṣir (Ardini in Urartian), cf. Salvini 1993–1997; and most recently Radner 2012:247–253, who points to the site of Sidekan at a height of ca. 1000 meters above sea level in the first ranges of the Zagros, nowadays in northeastern Iraq.

122 Lines 309–312. These derogatory epithets applied to Urzana by Sargon stemmed from the shift in political allegiance by the king of Muṣaṣir who, after a period of vassalage to Assyria, had been defeated by Rusa – as recorded in the Urartian-Assyrian bilingual stele of Topzawa and its more fragmentary duplicates at Movana and Mergeh Karvan (cf. CTU 1:497–508 for these texts) – and been forced to accept Urartian overlordship. See the convincing historical reconstruction by Dubovský 2006b.

rage of my heart, I had all my chariotry, my abundant cavalry, and my entire army take the road to Assyria.

With the great support of Aššur[123] – father of all the gods, lord of all the lands, ruler of the totality of heaven and earth, begetter of ⟨everything(?)⟩,[124] lord of lords, to whom, from time immemorial, Marduk, the Enlil of the gods, presented the deities of land and mountain[125] of the four regions of the earth, so that they might honor him again and again, none excepted, and that he (= Aššur) might let them enter the Eḫursaggalkurkurra with their stacked riches – and at the supreme command of Nabû and Marduk – who had taken a (favorable) course in the position of stars for the setting of my weapons in motion – and (at) a favorable sign for the seizing of power – (whereby) the (Moon)-god Magur, lord of the corona, remained eclipsed for more than one watch to predict the defeat of the land of Gutium[126] – and at the invaluable assent of the heroic god Šamaš – who caused reliable omens to be inscribed for me on the (findings of a sheep's) liver, (indicating) that he would go by my side[127] – with just my own single battle-chariot, and a thousand fierce horsemen, bearing bows, shields, and lances, my wild warriors, experts in combat, I mobilized an expedition against Muṣaṣir and I took the difficult road (thereunto).

(322) I brought my troops up to Mt. Arsi'u, a mighty mountain, whose climb, like steps in sequential ridges, had no (real) ascent.[128] I crossed the Upper Zab, which the people of the lands of Nairi and Ḫabḫi call Elamunia. (I proceeded) between the mountains called Šeyak, Ardikši, Ulāyū, and Alluri, high mountains, lofty elevations (with) steps of narrow ledges, which defy description[129] – among them there is no track for the passage of heavy infantry, and mighty waterfalls within them have carved their way, the roar of their discharge resounding like thunder for a "double-hour" around,[130] and every coveted evergreen, fruit tree or vine (grows) in a tangle like a reed-bed, and (all this) is greatly fearful for whoever approaches their entrances – and through which no king had ever passed, and whose innermost regions no prince prior to me had ever seen.[131] I cleared away their mighty tree-trunks and broke up their stepped ledges with bronze axes. I made good among them a narrow passage, a strait route which the heavy infantry could negotiate only sideways. I laid my war-chariot on the (troops') necks, while I, riding on horseback, stood facing my troops.[132] I narrowed my warriors who go by my side, with the(ir) horses, into a single file and made them go through their narrow places. I gave orders to my officers, to the governors with their contingents, that he (= Urzana) should not flee, and sent (them) in haste.

(334)[133] (Col. IV). [................. the arri]val(?) of my expedition he saw, and [....................], [....................] the people [....................]

[123] Lines 314–321. On the syntactical complexity of this long clause, cf. Chamaza 1992:125.

[124] Line 314: ⟨*gim-ri*⟩ was integrated after *a-lid* by Thureau-Dangin (1912:48), and this solution has been followed since. See the parallel expression in line 116, above.

[125] Line 315. Thureau-Dangin's (1912:49) "dieux du pays et des montagnes" for DINGIR.MEŠ KUR *ù* KUR-*i* has been generally followed; only Foster (2005:807) for some reason translates it as "the gods of heaven and netherworld." Cf. also *CAD* A 2:206b, with the more reductive nuance "gods of home and abroad."

[126] Line 318: ᵈMÁ.GUR₈ is one of the names of the Moon-god Sîn based on the lunar crescent which was conventionally depicted lying flat with the horns upwards, so as to give the impression of a cross-section lengthways of a boat with a high, curving prow and stern at either end: cf. *RlA* 7 (1987–1990), 192a; Potts 1997:122. The expression *ú-šá-ni-ḫa* EN.NUN literally means "prolonged one watch" and clearly refers to an eclipse extended in time, on the basis of parallels in astrological omens for the Moon (cf. *CAD* A 2:104b–105a). The lunar omen predicted the defeat of Gutium: this traditional geographical designation/concept was comprehensively equated with the mountainous lands of the Zagros (Urartu, Media, Elam) in Sargon's inscriptions and elsewhere at this time (cf. Fuchs 1994:435).

[127] Line 319: cf. *CAD* A 2:96a, 135a (with varying translations). The reference is to the well-known practice of *bārūtu*, extispicy performed on a sheep's liver for a count of favorable/unfavorable features in response to a query previously addressed to Šamaš; the Neo-Assyrian texts relating to this traditional Mesopotamian divinatory technique are published in SAA 4.

[128] Line 322. The clause *ša mūlūšu kî mēlê simmilti mūlâ la išû* is variously understood. Considering only the translations in which *sim-mil-ti* was read correctly, cf. *CAD* M 2:14b: "whose ascent is impossible (lit. has no ascent) like the rungs of a ladder"; whereas *CAD* S 274b, which quotes/translates lines 325 and 329 but not this passage, understands *simmiltu* as "referring to a vista of receding ranges of mountains and to mountain ledges." Foster (2005:107) gives an abridged rendering: "whose heights are unscalable ridges" – which however contradicts the *mūlâ la išû* of the text. More to the point is the attempt by Mayer (1983:101), "dessen Höhen wie eine Treppenrückwand keinen Aufstieg haben." The present rendering, somewhat in line with the latter, does not imply that Mt. Arsi'u was impassable in its ascent, but that to the contrary it was wearying in its unending sequence of scarcely sloping stepped passages.

[129] Line 325: *ša ni-ba id-ku-ma*: "which defy description" is already due to Thureau-Dangin (1912:51, "qui excluent toute description") and then to Luckenbill (1922:93); it is taken up by Foster (2005:807), albeit with reservation, while Mayer (1983:101) has "mit nicht zählbaren Stufen." An alternative possibility for reading was put forth in *CAD* N 2:205b: *ša ni-ba ed-ku* (read *-lu?*)*-ma*, but without translation (and see the same view in Foster 2005:813).

[130] Line 326: cf. *CAD* Š 3:123a.

[131] Line 328: *du-rug-šu-un* is neither "whose trails" (Luckenbill 1922:94) nor "the pathways thereof" (Foster 2005:807), but rather "whose innermost/most remote regions": cf. *CAD* D 191a, and Mayer (1983:101), "ihr Inneres." For "path, trail, track," cf. on the other hand *daraggu* in line 325 above.

[132] Line 331. Cf. line 25, above.

[133] Lines 334–342 describe cultic activities regarding the Urartian succession to the throne: see already Oppenheim 1960:140–141, Salvini 1995a:43–44, with previous references, and most recently Kravitz 2008:86–91.

strengthened [....................]; [................ Urar]-tu, and to Muṣaṣir, his royal seat, and the seat of Ḫaldi, [his god, the god the deity that is highest in] Urartu to its entire extent. They know no god above him in heaven and earth, [....................] his name, [............. without] the permission of whom neither scepter nor crown is taken up. The(se) insignia of shepherdship [and royalty of] the ruler and shepherd of Urartu, [after his death (?)],[134] they would bring to him (= Ḫaldi), and they would introduce whichever among his sons was to take his throne in Muṣaṣir to Ḫaldi with gold and silver and every precious item of the treasure of his palace, and they would provide him with gifts. Countless hefty oxen and fattened sheep they would offer before him, and they would prepare a meal for his entire city. [In the presence of] Ḫaldi, his god, they would put on him (= the successor) the crown of lordship, and have him lift up the scepter of kingship over Urartu, and his people would [accla]im his name.

Over this city, I caused my troops' fearsome war-cry to roar like thunder, and the inhabitants [within it[135] ....]; his (= Urzana's) people, (down to) the old men and women, climbed on the roofing of their houses and wept bitterly. To save their lives, they crawled on all fours, [wringing][136] their hands [........].

(346) Because king Urzana, their ruler, had not held in awe the name of Aššur, had cast away the yoke of my lordship, and forgotten his service, I designed to carry off the people of that city and I commanded the remotion of Ḫaldi, the object of trust of the land of Urartu. I imperiously made it sit before his own city-gate, (while) I deported his wife, his sons, his daughters, and his royal family. I included (them) together with 6,110 people,[137] 12 mules, 380 donkeys, 525 cattle, and 1,235 small livestock,[138] and brought them within the wall of my encampment. I imperiously entered [the city of M]uṣaṣir, residence of the god Ḫaldi, and I took residence as a lord in the palace, the dwelling of Urzana.

(351) I broke open the seals of the caches of their amassed [storerooms], which were overflowing with piled-up treasures, thus:[139] [34 talents and 18 mi]nas of gold,[140] 167 talents and 2½ minas of silver, white bronze,[141] tin; carnelian, lapis-lazuli, agate (?) – a selection of precious stones in abundance; [*n* (items, comprising) chairs] of ivory, ebony, and boxwood, together with wooden caskets, whose mountings were prepared with gold and silver; [*n* (items, comprising) tab]les of ivory, ebony, and boxwood, of large size, worthy of a king, whose mountings were prepared with gold and silver; 8 (items, comprising) strong wooden cutting platters (?)[142] and wooden basket-shaped vegetable bowls of ivory, ebony, and boxwood, whose mountings were prepared with gold and silver; 6 (items, comprising) wooden vessel stands, potstands, screens, stools, and potstands for cupbearers of ivory, ebony and boxwood, with mountings of gold and silver;

6 (items, comprising) gold knives with golden handles (shaped like) pine cones, a small gold knife, a gold fly whisk, and a bowl of alabaster inlaid with precious stones and gold; 11 (items, comprising) a silver bowl – the property of Rusa (himself) – with its lid,[143] bowls from the land of Tabal with gold handles, silver helmets, silver arrows with gold inlay; 34 (items, comprising) silver bowls with strong, small, and thin finger-decoration; *luṭṭu*-cups and *susanu*-ware in silver; 54 (items, comprising) bowls of massive silver, ⟨with⟩ their [lids (?), drink]ing-bowls decorated (with?) *ṣipratu*-ornaments and crescents, rings of silver; 5 (items, comprising) silver quivers, bowls,

134 Line 339: since the god provided religious sanction for the Urartian succession to the throne, it is reasonable to suggest that a fleeting mention of the previous king's death could have been made in a break in this line, or even in the previous one. Already Oppenheim (1960:141) had integrated "whichever of the sons of the (deceased) king holds the throne" in his translation. On the other hand, the Urartian-Assyrian bilingual inscription of Kelišin (CTU 1:141–144; and cf. Salvini 1995a:43) relates of a joint cultic visit to the temple of Ḫaldi in Muṣaṣir by king Išpuini and his son Menua, with copious offerings of animals to the god. Thus, Ḫaldi could have theoretically provided religious validation for the royal succession even before the assigned time for the event was due.

135 Line 343. The integration [*lìb-bi-ša*.....] is suggested by Vera Chamaza 1994:118b.

136 Line 345. The integration was suggested by Luckenbill (1922:94), but is not taken up by subsequent authors.

137 Line 349. The number is given as 6170 in Sargon's Annals, line 154 (Fuchs 1994:114).

138 Line 349. The sheep and goats are numbered 1,285 in line 424 below, although the other categories tally with the count given here. The numbers of livestock given in the Annals show greater differences: cf. Fuchs 1994:114, lines 154–155, for 692 mules and donkeys, 920 cattle, 1,225 sheep and goats.

139 Line 351. Cf. *CAD* K 466b, largely followed here. The subsequent section comprises itemizations subdivided by individual lines, comprising a number, plus the description of a specific lot of mixed precious objects. For the single (categories of) looted objects, cf. the detailed study by Mayer 1979.

140 Line 352. The quantity is restored after the Annals, line 155 (Fuchs 1994:114).

141 Following Mayer 1979:582, URUDU= *erû* is here rendered as "bronze," although ZABAR = *siparru* occurs three times in lines 369, 400, and 406. Foster (2005) renders consistently URUDU as "copper."

142 Line 355. The term *maḫraṣu* is uncertain, cf. *CAD* M 1:104a–b; *CDA* 191a; Mayer 1979:582: "um ein Mobelstück handeln muß, wird man wohl am ehesten an eine Platte oder an einen Tisch denken dürfen, auf dem beispielsweise Fleisch tranchiert oder vorgeschnitten wurde."

143 Line 358. The name of the Urartian king must have been inscribed on the object or on the lid.

vessels for liquids and [fi]re,[144] censers from the land of Tabal and thuribles of silver;

13 (items, comprising) bronze basins, bronze cauldrons, bronze wash-basins, bronze vessels, bronze tureens, bronze pans; 24 (items, comprising) bronze stands, bronze basins, bronze dishes, bronze vessels, bronze wall-rings, bronze hooks, bronze lamps; 120 (items, comprising) bronze utensils, heavy and light, the craftsmanship of their land, the names of which are not easy to write down;[145] [*n*] (items, comprising) an iron stove, iron fire-rakes, hooks of iron, tongs of iron, lamps of iron; 130 (items, comprising) garments of multicolored cloth of linen, purple wool and plain wool, garments of red wool from the lands of Urartu and Ḫabḫi – together with the (other) goods of his palace, (all this) I looted and I piled up his property.

(367) I sent my officers and my soldiers to the temple of Ḫaldi. (I took the statue of) Ḫaldi, his god, and of Bagbartu, his goddess, together with the copious possessions of his temple, as many as there were, thus:[146] [*n* +] 3 talents and 3 minas of gold, 162 talents and 20 minas, 6 shekels of silver, 3600 talents of bronze in pieces; 6 shields of gold[g] which were hung to the left and right in his cella and shone with brilliance, and heads of snarling lions protruded from their centers – their weight amounted to 5 talents and 12 minas of red shining (gold).[147] [1 ......], a horned [.....], the locking-bar of his gates, of poured refined gold weighing 2 talents; 1 latch of gold, in the shape of a human hand, that secured the double door, with a winged Deluge-monster placed recumbently above it, (and) 1 bolt of gold, holding the latch, (thus) strengthening the security of the temple and protecting the goods and riches accumulated (therein), and 2 gold keys in the shape of crowned female protective geniuses, holding rods and rings, the semblance of whose feet were made to trample snarling lions – these four items (formed) the closure of the door decorating the inner sanctuary, of a (combined) weight of 2 talents and 12 minas of gold, holding the door and making it fast;[h]

1 great golden sword, the weapon at his side, weighing 26 minas and 3 shekels of gold;[148] 96 (items, comprising)[149] silver spears, silver helmets, silver bows, silver arrows, with mountings and inlays of gold; 12 (items, comprising) strong silver shields, the outer bands of which were decorated with Deluge-monsters, lions, and wild bulls;[150] 67 (items, comprising) silver basins, silver stands, silver braziers, and fruit baskets of silver, with mountings and inlays of gold; 62 (items, comprising) silver libation vessels, silver pomegranates, silver implements with no equal, with mountings and inlays of gold; 33 (items, comprising) silver chariots, silver bows, silver quivers, silver rods, silver staffs, silver *manziaše*-containers, silver shields, silver spiked helmets (?), throw-spears (?) and emblems of silver; 393 (items, comprising) silver plates, heavy and light, the craftsmanship of Assyria, Urartu, and Ḫabḫi;

2 horns of great wild bulls, with mountings and inlays ⟨of gold⟩ and golden rivets surrounding on all sides their mountings;[151] 1 gold harp for the carrying out in full of the rites of the goddess Bagbartu, spouse of Ḫaldi, covered with a selection of gems; 9 (items, comprising) garments, his (= Ḫaldi's) divine clothing,[i] with golden bands and golden rosettes, their seams held together with golden filigree; 7 pairs of leather boots covered with gold stars, together with a silver whip, with decorative twine and inlay of gold; 1 ivory bed,[j] (with?) the resting surface of silver,[152] (his) divine resting place, inlaid with precious stones and gold; 139 (items, comprising) ivory staffs, ivory tables, fruit baskets of ivory, daggers of ivory, knives of ivory and ebony with golden mountings; 10 (items, comprising) boxwood tables, cutting platters of boxwood, supports of ebony and boxwood, with

g 2 Sam 8:7; 1 Kgs 10:17
h 1 Kgs 14:26; 2 Kgs 24:13; 2 Chr 12:9; 36:7
i Judg 8:27; 17:5; 18:14–20
j Amos 6:4

[144] Line 361. *mukarrise* [*nab*]*le* is very uncertain in its interpretation and even in its reading: cf. *CAD* N 1:27a, which considers *nablu* B a further type of vessel, with no relation to *nablu* A, "fire."

[145] Line 364. As noted by Mayer (1979:585), these "difficult" names must have been Urartian native terms.

[146] Line 368. For some reason, this line is omitted by Foster (2005:810).

[147] Line 371. Cf. *CAD* S 128a, where however the traditional reading *kal-bi*, "dogs," instead of *lab-bi*, "lions," is repeated. The heads of the snarling beasts are to be seen protruding in profile in the well-known scene of the sack of the temple on Sargon's relief from Khorsabad, which unfortunately has come down to us only in the drawing by Eugène Flandin (Botta and Flandin 1849: pl. 141; Albenda 1986: pl. 133). For the second relative clause, (5 GUN 12 MA.NA *sa-a-mu ru-uš-šu-ú ti-iṣ-bu-tu* KI.LÁ), the literal translation would be "… which contain 5 talents, 12 minas of red shining (gold) in weight" (cf. Chamaza 1992:126). As noted by Mayer (1979:586), a practical function for the six golden shields weighing approx. 25 kgs. each may be ruled out; they should have thus represented either votive gifts or Muṣaṣir's state reserve of gold preserved in the temple in the form of large shields.

[148] Line 377. This sword – the first item on the list of Ḫaldi's vast treasure – with its 12.5 kg in weight, was obviously beyond comparison with its counterparts for humans (approx. 1 kg), as noted by Mayer 1979:587.

[149] Line 378. From here on, the scribal layout and logic of the list follows that of Urzana's palace: one line, overall numbering of the items, and descriptive list of the latter.

[150] Line 379. Decorative bands such as the ones here described are well known from archaeological finds of Urartian metalwork: cf. Van Loon 1966:116–118, and fig. 13, for the fourteen shields discovered at Karmir-Blur dedicated by Urartian kings to Ḫaldi, with three concentric rings, alternately containing a procession of embossed lions and bulls.

[151] Line 384: Mayer (1979:588) suggests that the two richly decorated horns could have fulfilled the token role of drinking vessels for the god and his spouse.

[152] Line 388: thus, with Mayer (1983:109), whereas *CAD* M 1:117a, considers the sign ZÚ an erroneous scribal interpolation.

gold and silver mountings; 2 portable altars with assorted gems, proper divine ornaments and jewelry for Ḫaldi and his spouse Bagbartu;

25,212 (items, comprising) bronze shields,[k] heavy and light, bronze spiked helmets, bronze hauberks, bronze round helmets; 1,514 (items, comprising) bronze spears, heavy and light, and heavy bronze spear points, bronze throw-spears (?), bronze lances, with their bronze lance racks; 305,412 (items, comprising) bronze swords, heavy and light, bronze bows, bronze quivers, and bronze arrows;[153] 607 (items, comprising) bronze kettles, heavy and light, bronze wash basins, bronze ewers, bronze tureens, and bronze vases; 3 (items, comprising) heavy bronze vessels of 50 liquid measures capacity,[l] together with their heavy bronze stands;[154] 1 huge bronze cauldron of 80 liquid measures capacity,[m] together with its huge bronze stand, which the Urartian kings would fill with wine libations to make cultic offerings before Ḫaldi;

4 bronze statues of (divine) door attendants, watching over his (= Ḫaldi's) gates, their height four cubits, with their socles in cast bronze;[155] 1 worshipper statue, standing for the king, (gift) of Sarduri son of Išpuini, king of Urartu,[156] its base in cast bronze; 1 bull, a cow and her calf, made of bronze, belonging to the temple of Ḫaldi, of which Sarduri son of Išpuini made a votive offering,[n] and on which he wrote an inscription;[157] 1 statue of Argišti, king of Urartu[158] – who wore a star-studded crown of divine status, and whose right hand was raised in blessing – together with its housing, for a weight of 60 talents of bronze; 1 statue of Rusa, with his two riding horses and one charioteer, their bases cast in bronze, with a boast of himself, viz., "With my two horses and my single charioteer, my hands took over the kingship of Urartu," engraved on them.[159]

(405) (These things) I plundered, together with his (other) rich possessions, countless, not including the innumerable utensils of gold, silver, tin, bronze, iron, ivory, boxwood and all other types of wood, which the troops of Aššur and Marduk removed from the city, palace, and temple.[160] The property from the palaces of Urzana and the god Ḫaldi, together with his enormous riches, which I removed from Muṣaṣir, I loaded on my vast body of troops, and had it drawn to Assyria. I reckoned the people of the district of Muṣaṣir with the Assyrians, and imposed upon them service and corvée as (upon) Assyrians.

Rusa[161] heard (the news), and he fell to the ground, shredded his garments and bared his arms.[162] He tore off his royal headdress, plucked out his hair, pounded[163] his chest with both (hands), and he threw himself face down. His heart stood still, and his temper burned (inside), bitter laments were placed in his mouth. I caused wailings of lamenta-

k 1 Kgs 14:27; 2 Chr 12:10
l 1 Kgs 7:38
m 1 Kgs 7:23; 2 Kgs 16:7
n Exod 32:4–6; 1 Kgs 12:28

153 Lines 392–394. Mayer (1979:589) suggests that this detailed count of weapons indicates that within the temple the city arsenal with its depots of materiel was also included. According to his count, some 8,400 men could have been equipped with the listed shields, body armor, and helmets, whereas some 9,250 men could have been armed with the swords, bows and arrows (counting an average of 30 arrows for each quiver). Whether the idea of an arsenal within the temple is acceptable or not – against the alternative possibility that this was merely an immense hoard of bronze votive objects for the deity, as might be indicated by the subsequent bronze items of non-military use –, a preliminary question remains open: were the objects physically inventoried by the Assyrian soldiers, or was their count in Sg. VIII based on inventories retrieved within the sanctuary itself? The latter solution appears the most likely one; the possible existence of Urartian lists of goods, consulted by the Assyrians, might be inferred from line 364, above.

154 Line 397. Objects such as these, placed in the forecourt of the building, are depicted in Flandin's drawing of the bas-relief of the Assyrians' sack of the temple (Botta and Flandin 1849: pl. 141; Albenda 1986: pl. 133).

155 Line 399. Two of these statues facing one another in standing position, their hands raised in an attitude of reverence, are visible flanking the main entrance to the temple in Flandin's drawing (*loc. cit*).

156 Lines 400–401. Both here and in the following line, Sarduri (written, with "improper encoding" as *Issar-duri, ᵈ15-BÀD) is said to be the son of Išpuini, who was in fact his successor: it is thus possible that Sargon's scribes systematically misrepresented the Urartian royal genealogy, which the bilingual Urartian-Assyrian Kelišin stela gives instead correctly: cf. A. Fuchs' opinion in *PNA*, 568b.

157 Line 401. Cf. *CAD* E 252b, for *equ*, another *hapax legomenon* of this inscription. A cow and a calf in suckling pose are in point of fact vaguely visible beside the right-hand worshipper statue in Flandin's drawing (*loc. cit.*).

158 Line 402. This was Argišti I, son of Menua and father of Sarduri II, who reigned in the early 8th century BCE, also well known from Urartian texts: see *PNA*, 129a.

159 Line 404. Foster (2005:811) renders "(inscribed with) his self-glorification," but in fact the text states clearly that the inscription was *ba-rim* EDIN-*šú-un*, "engraved on them": cf. Luckenbill 1922:98, and *CAD* B 102b–103a. Van de Mieroop (2010:426) notes that here, and in the previous description of the Urartian coronation ceremony, "Sargon's account may be unique in stressing that Rusa was a legitimate king."

160 Line 407. Foster (2005:811) omits translation of *ša ul-tú* URU É.GAL-*lim* É.DINGIR.

161 Lines 411–413. This passage is aptly termed "Rusa's de-coronation" by Kravitz (2008:88), according to whom it was (belatedly) inserted into the narrative, along with other features linking Muṣaṣir with Urartian kingship, in order to recapitulate the overall Eighth Campaign account as portraying the confrontation between Sargon and Rusa (*ibid.*, 91), and the latter's disabling by the Assyrian king through the destruction of Ḫaldi's temple. In other words, it restored the ideological focus of the inscription on its initial premises (*ibid.*, 93). The novelty of the description is also underscored by Van de Mieroop (2010:427), although he notes that some of the gestures recur in later Assyrian official accounts (even Esarhaddon ripped his clothes in frustration upon hearing of his brothers' plot against him).

162 Line 411. "Bared his arms": cf. *CAD* I/J 12a, with Luckenbill 1922:98. Differently Mayer (1983:111), "seine Kraft verließ ihn," and Foster (2005:812), "threw up his hands (in despair)."

163 Line 412. "Pounded": Thureau-Dangin (1912:64) read *ú-dan-nin* with "lecture incertaine", due to the badly preserved signs; Mayer (1983:110) leaves the word blank. Cf. on the hand the reading *ú-rep-pi*[!]-*is* in *CAD* K 356a, and *CAD* R 151b–152a, and taken up by Foster (2005:813).

tion throughout the entire territory of Urartu and I established perpetual mourning in the Na'iri-lands.[o]

o Lam 1:1; Isa 3:26

(415)[164] With the exalted strength of my lord Aššur, with the power and the might of the gods Bēl and Nabû, my divine helpers, with the firm assent of Šamaš, the supreme judge of the gods, who opened the way and established (his) aegis over my troops, with the greatness of Nergal, the mightiest of the deities, who marched at my side and protected my encampment, I came out from the district of Sumbi through Mts. Nikippa and Upâ, difficult mountains, to Urartu. In Urartu, in Zikirtu, in the land of the Mannaeans, in Na'iri and in Muṣaṣir, I proceeded to and fro in a lordly fashion like an aggressive lion, spreading fear and finding no one to repulse me. I defeated the vast armies of Rusa the Urartian, Metatti the Zikirtean in pitched battle; I conquered a total of 430 settlements in 7 districts of Rusa the Urartian and I laid waste his land. Of Urzana the Muṣaṣirian, I took away his god Ḫaldi and his goddess Bagbartu, together with the copious possessions of his temple, together with 6,110 people, 12 mules, 380 donkeys, 525 cattle, 1,285 small livestock, his wife, his sons, and his daughters. I came out through the pass of Mt. Andarutu, a difficult mountain, opposite the city Ḫipparna, and returned in safety to my land.

(426)[165] One charioteer, 2 horsemen, and 3 infantry-men were killed.[166] Ṭab-šar-Aššur, chief treasurer, brought the main (enemy) informers to the god Aššur, my lord.[167]

Tablet of Nabû-šallimšunu, chief royal scribe, chief copyist, and scholar of Sargon, king of the land of Assyria, son of Ḫarmakku, royal scribe, from Baltil (= the city of Aššur).[168] (Report) delivered in the eponymate of Ištar-duri, governor of Arrapḫa.[169]

[164] Line 415. A horizontal line sets apart this summary of victories from the preceding text.

[165] Line 426. A horizontal line separates this part (colophon) from the preceding text. As may be seen from the hand-copy (Thureau-Dangin 1912: pl. XXII) and photograph (*ibid.*, pl. XXX), the availability of space at the end of Col. IV allowed these last five lines of Sg. VIII to be written out with a triple-sized line spacing on the preceding text, and even with wide horizontal intervals in the distribution of the signs within each line.

[166] Line 426. As long recognized, this total reflects only a token number of Assyrian causalties for memorial-ceremonial purposes, somewhat in line with the commemorative monuments/ceremonies to a single "Unknown Soldier" in our day and age. Rather, it may be asked if the 3-2-1 ratio for the deceased of different corps which were the object of the symbolic commemoration, could have reflected the relative status of such units within the Assyrian army of the late 8th century BCE.

[167] Line 427. For Ṭab-šar-Aššur, chief treasurer (*masennu rabiu*) of Sargon, eponym in the year 717 BCE, cf. *PNA*, 1344–1346, and esp. 1345a. The accompanying clause is trickier than it would seem at first sight: Foster (2005:813) translates "I send herewith to Assur my lord the best orator, Tab-shar-Assur, chief steward," taking *ul-te-bi-la* as a 1st p. sg., while previous interpretations varied to a great degree (cf. Levine 2003:118*). On the other hand, focusing on the plural ^{LÚ}EME.SAG^{MEŠ}, Levine (*ibid.*, 114*) suggested the interpretation "Ṭab-šar-^{d}Aššur, the chief steward, brought the major informants to Aššur, my lord," understanding that they were the eye-witnesses brought to testify to the deity on the veracity of the campaign account. The translation presented here accepts this perspective, also in the light of the contemporaneous letter SAA 5:55, which is a report to Sargon on the capture of an Urartian ^{LÚ}EME "informer" who was traveling over the mountains by Assyrian scouts.

[168] Lines 428–429. For Nabû-šallimšunu, royal scribe, cf. *PNA* 870b–871a. For his father, cf. *PNA*, 460b. The GN Aššur is written BAL.TIL^{ki} like in line 113, above. The fact that the text was discovered at Aššur (see at line 1, above) in an archive in a private house belonging to a family of exorcists might be somehow tied to the family origins of its author, since other scribes are also present/mentioned in the same archive (*contra*, Van de Mieroop 2010:431).

[169] Line 430. For Ištar-duri (or Issar-duri), governor of Arrapḫa, eponym of the year 714 BCE, cf. *PNA*, 569b.

REFERENCES

Botta and Flandin 1849; Dalley 1985; Dubovský 2006; Fales 1991; 2009; 2014; Foster 2005; Fuchs 1994; Hurowitz 2008; Kroll 2012; Kravitz 2003; Laessøe 1951; Lanfranchi 1995; Leichty 1991; Levine 1997; 2003; Liebig 1991; Luckenbill 1927; Mayer 1979; 1983; Meissner 1922; Muscarella 1986; 2012; Niederreiter 2005; Oppenheim 1960; Pedersén 1986; Potts 1997; Powell 1987–1990; Radner 2012; Reade 1995; Roaf 2012; Rogers 1998; Salvini 1993–1997; 1995a; 1995b; Schroeder 1922; Thureau-Dangin 1912; Van de Mieroop 2010; Van Loon 1996; Vera Chamaza 1992; 1994; 1995–1996; Weidner 1937–1938; Zaccagnini 1981; Zimansky 1990.

NEO-ASSYRIAN LETTERS

TWO LETTERS RELATED TO ASSYRIAN ACTS OF "PSYCHOLOGICAL WARFARE"

Eckart Frahm

The following two letters provide examples of how Assyrian kings and their officials put psychological pressure on their opponents to force them into submission. The letters bring to mind the famous episode in 2 Kgs 18–19 that describes how an emissary of Sennacherib, the *rab šāqê*, sought to convince the people of Jerusalem to submit to Assyria.

A LETTER FROM THE REIGN OF TIGLATH-PILESER III (4.43)

The reign of the Assyrian king Tiglath-pileser III (744–727 BCE) marked the beginning of the greatest expansion the Assyrian state had ever seen. Among the countries affected by the king's aggressive politics was Babylonia, Assyria's southern neighbor. Early in his reign, Tiglath-pileser had helped the Babylonian ruler Nabonassar (Nabû-naṣir) to quell a rebellion of various unruly Aramean and Chaldean tribes, whereupon Nabonassar had become his vassal. Babylonia remained loyal to Assyria for more than ten years, but in 732 BCE, after the short reign of Nabonassar's son and successor Nabû-nadin-zeri (733–732 BCE), a series of rebellions brought a certain Mukin-zeri on the Babylonian throne, a governor of the Chaldean state of Bit-Amukani who severed all ties with Assyria. Mukin-zeri served as king of Babylonia in a very volatile political climate until he was finally defeated by the Assyrian army and replaced by Tiglath-pileser himself in 729 BCE (see Brinkman 1984:42–43).

The letter translated here was probably written in 730 BCE (thus Luukko 2007), during the brief period of Mukin-zeri's tenure as Babylonian king (note that Dubovsky 2006a:163, prefers a dating "before Tiglath-pileser's invasion [731 BCE]"). It documents the efforts of two officials who served in an Assyrian garrison in Babylonia to convince the citizens of Babylon to give up their support of the new king and allow the Assyrians to enter their city. Mukin-zeri himself is apparently not present in Babylon during this episode.

The letter bears the excavation number ND 2632 and the museum number IM 64084 (Iraq Museum Baghdad). It belongs to an archive that was found in 1952 by British archaeologists in Calah near the ziggurat terrace, in a chamber designated ZT 4 (Saggs 2001:1). The letter poses significant difficulties. The present author is grateful to Mikko Luukko for providing him with a prepublication of his edition (2012, no. 98), which represents a substantial step forward over previous attempts to understand the text.

(Lines 1–4) To the king, my (sic!) lord, your servant(s) Šamaš-buna'i and Nabû-nammir. May all be well with the king, my lord, and may Nabû and Marduk bless the king, my lord.[1]

(Lines 5–19) On the 28th day (of the month), we went to Babylon, took our stand in front of the Marduk Gate[2], and spoke with the citizen(s) of Babylon. (Z)asin(n)u,[3] a servant of Mukin-zeri, (and?) some(?) Chaldean(s) (who) were with him, came out (too), standing with the citizens of Babylon in front of the gate.[4] We ourselves spoke to the citizens of Babylon as follows: "The king has sent us to you, saying: [Let me speak(?)] with the citizens [of Babylon] through your mouths. ... of Babylon ... I shall establish your *kidinnūtu*-privileges[5] and will come to Babylon.' "[6]

1 For other attestations of Šamaš-buna'i and Nabû-nammir, see Ambos 2011b and Baker 2001b, respectively. Because of the reference to the Babylonian gods Nabû and Marduk in the blessing formula, one wonders whether the two may have been ethnic Babylonians, but the letter is written in Neo-Assyrian language and script.

2 The Marduk Gate was one of two gates that provided access into Babylon through the eastern wall of the city. See the plan in George 1992:17.

3 Saggs reads [I]⌜*A*⌝-*si-nu*, whereas Baker 2001a and Luukko 2012:104 assume the name is actually Zasin(n)u, reading [I]⌜*Za*⌝- instead of [I]⌜*A*⌝ -at the beginning. Without collation, it is difficult to establish which reading, if any, is correct. Note that in *PNA* 3/2, the name Zasin(n)u is not included.

4 A different understanding of lines 6–11 was suggested by Barjamovic (2004:83), who translates: "We took our stand in front of the Marduk Gate, where we talked with 'the Man of Babylon.' Asinu – a servant of Mukin-zer the Chaldean – was (also) present at his side. They came out and stood with 'the citizens of Babylon' in front of the gate." Barjamovic assumed that the 'Man of Babylon' is a high official, perhaps the chairman of the city assembly (2004:84), and that the term 'citizens of Babylon' refers in the letter to a council of men representing the city (2004:65–67). Grammatically, Barjamovic's rendering of the text is well founded. ⌜DUMU⌝ TIN.TIR[ki] in line 7 (and line 36) is indeed a singular. Since, however, neither the expression 'Man of Babylon' nor 'citizens of Babylon' is otherwise used to designate specific officials or institutions, I prefer to follow Luukko's translation (2012:104) and to assume that the scribe simply forgot to write the plural determinative MEŠ. Note that the letter includes other grammatical inaccuracies, for instance, the repeated inconsistencies in the use of the 1st person singular and the 1st person plural.

5 Cities that received *kidinnūtu*-privileges were exempted from paying certain taxes and from doing corvée work for the crown. During the Neo-Assyrian period, a number of important Assyrian and Babylonian cult centers were granted *kidinnūtu*. The Assyrian emissaries promise *kidinnūtu* to the citizens of Babylon to lure them into agreeing to their requests.

6 My translation of lines 13–18 is based on the many new readings suggested by Luukko in his 2012 edition. I remain slightly skeptical, however, with regard to his restoration of line 16 ([*a*]-*na* [*du*]-*r*[*a-ri*? *š*]*a* ⌜TIN.TIR⌝[ki] ⌜*ù*⌝) and therefore have left it untranslated.

(Lines 19–30) We had long discussions with them, (but some) ten powerful men[7] did not agree to come out and speak with us, sending us messages (instead). We ourselves said to them: "Open the gate and let us enter Babylon," (but) they(?)[8] did not agree, saying: "(If?) we let you (masc. pl.) enter Babylon, what shall I say to the king when the king comes himself?" (They say(?)) when the king comes they will open the gate, (but) they do not believe that the king (really) will come.

(Lines 31–38) We spoke to them as follows: "Aḫu-...[9] and the servants of Mukin-zeri shall be entrusted to you (masc. pl.) until the king comes. We ourselves shall return(?) to Kar-Nergal."[10] Thus we spoke with the citizen(s) of Babylon. Whatever the news from them is, we will send a white donkey[11] to the king, my lord.[12]

(Lines 39–44) The people of the Litamu tribe[13] have written to us, saying: "We are servants of the king. On the 30th day (of the month), we will come and speak with you (masc. pl.), and our leaders will go to the king." When they come, we will bring them before the king, my lord.

(Lines 44–50) The report about Dilbat[14] is still the same. With regard to [what] the king, my lord, wrote to me, Mukin-zeri [......] we ourselves [......] to [...] ... We will send a detailed report[15] to the king [my lord].

7 In line 19, I follow Luukko's reading ERIM.ME[Š] ⸢KALAG⸣.MEŠ, which fits the traces better than Saggs's ERIM.ME[Š] ⸢*ḫa*⸣-*meš* "five men." The new reading, if correct, would invalidate Barjamovic's suggestion (2004:83–84) that the expressions "five men" and "ten men" in the letter do not designate random numbers of people, but rather specific groups of representatives, an idea based on the observation "that city-state officials consistently appear in groups of ten or fifteen in the instances where letters mention visits from Babylonia." Who the men were who stayed inside the city instead of joining the negotiations with the Assyrian envoys remains unclear.

8 Text: "he," unless one reads *i-ma-gúru* at the end of line 24.

9 Perhaps, the name is to be read, with Luukko, as Aḫu-ila'i.

10 A city in northern Babylonian that had remained under Assyrian control during the rebellion of Mukin-zeri and served as an Assyrian garrison.

11 In his 2007 article, Luukko assumed the animal in question was a horse and felt reminded by the passage of references to white horses in Rev. 6, 2 and Rev. 19, 11–16. His 2012 edition, however, recognizes that the logogram ANŠE denotes donkeys and not horses. Whether the white color of the animal really symbolizes peaceful intentions, as argued by Luukko, remains somewhat uncertain.

12 For a number of readings in lines 31–38 that deviate from Saggs's edition and are followed here, see Luukko 2007.

13 An Aramean tribe in southern Babylonia that is mentioned several times in Tiglath-pileser's inscriptions (see RINAP 1, 202, for references).

14 The letter ND 2717 (Saggs 2001:22–25) mentions that at some point Mukin-zeri urged the citizens of Babylon to join a Chaldean raid on orchards in Dilbat, but that they refused, with the exception of a few temple slaves of Marduk, to follow this order (lines 48′–53′).

15 *ni-ḫar-ra-ṣa*!, which is often used in hendiadys with *šapāru*, is written in smaller script on the left edge of the tablet, aligned with line 50. Saggs read the word as *ni-mur-ra-a* and took it as a note added by a royal secretary after the letter had been read to the king, meaning "We have seen (it)." However, for grammatical reasons, this interpretation cannot be correct.

REFERENCES

Copies: Saggs 1955:51, Pl. IV; Saggs 2001: pl. 2. *Editions*: Saggs 1955:23–26 (NL 1); Saggs 2001:19–21; Luukko 2013: no. 98. *Discussions*: von Soden 1972:47; Barjamovic 2004:60–61, 65–66, 76, 83–84; Fales 2005:176; Dubovsky 2006a:163–166; Luukko 2007 (lines 31–38).

A LETTER FROM THE REIGN OF ASSURBANIPAL (4.44)

In 652 BCE, Šamaš-šumu-ukin, king of Babylon (667–648 BCE), instigated a revolt against his brother, the Assyrian king Assurbanipal (668–631 BCE). For the following four years, the two brothers and their respective allies fought each other in a bloody war that ended, after the Assyrians had besieged Babylon for many months, with the defeat and death of Šamaš-šumu-ukin and the destruction of large parts of Babylon (see Frame 1992:131–190).

The letter translated in the following is from the beginning of the revolt; it was dispatched, according to a note in line 43, on the 23rd Iyyar (the second month) of the year 652 BCE. In the letter, Assurbanipal appeals to the citizens of Babylon not to join in rebellion with their king, Šamaš-šumu-ukin. He asks them to support the Assyrian cause instead. In case they comply, Assurbanipal promises to treat the Babylonians with respect and leave their various privileges in place.

The letter is a small rhetorical masterpiece and a testimony to the high esteem in which the art of persuasion was held in imperial Assyria. It flatters the citizens of Babylon and appeals to their pride. The letter is written in Assyrian script, but its language is, interestingly, almost consistently not Assyrian but Babylonian (exceptions include *abat šarri* in line 1 and the form *idabbūni* in line 5). Clearly, the Assyrian king thought it necessary to appeal to the citizens of Babylon in an idiom they would understand without any problems. This is reminiscent of the episode in 2 Kgs 18:19–37, in which the *rab šāqê*, dispatched by Sennacherib to convince the citizens of Jerusalem to give up their resistance, does so "in the language of Judah," that is, Hebrew. When the high officials sent to him by Hezekiah ask him to speak to them in Aramaic, the diplomatic language of the age, which they say they understand, the *rab šāqê* responds: "Has my master sent me to speak these words to your master and to you only, and not also to the people sitting on the wall ...?" (2 Kgs 18:26–27).

The last line of our tablet indicates that it served as an archival copy of a message to be delivered to the citizens of Babylon by a certain Šamaš-balassu-iqbi, whose mission was similar to that of the officials who had to deal with the Babylonians after the outbreak of the Mukin-zeri rebellion under Tiglath-pileser III (see the letter translated in the preceding section). We have no corroborative evidence that the message ever reached the Babylonians (see Frame 1992:139), but there is no particular reason to believe that it did not. In fact, our letter is not the only missive Assurbanipal sent to the citizens of Babylon during the Šamaš-šumu-ukin rebellion. A very similar but longer one, K 2931 (edited by Parpola 2004), was probably dispatched at about the same time, unless it is a discarded draft; it alludes to skirmishes between Assyrian and Babylonian troops and an even earlier message Assurbanipal sent to the Babylonians. ABL 517 (newly translated by Parpola 2004:229) is an archival copy of a letter Assurbanipal sent at some point during the siege of Babylon, which had started in 650 BCE. This last attempt by the Assyrian king to win the Babylonians over proved as futile as the preceding ones.

The letter translated in the following is inscribed on a perfectly preserved tablet that was found during Layard's early excavations in Nineveh, probably in the area of Rooms XL and XLI in the Southwest Palace on the citadel mound of Kuyunjik (see Reade 1986). It is part of the Kuyunjik Collection of the British Museum and bears the museum number K 84.

(Lines 1–3) Word of the king (Assurbanipal) to the citizens of Babylon: All is well with me. Your hearts can be glad.[1]

(Lines 3–24) I have been told of all the empty words[2] that this no-brother of mine (Šamaš-šumu-ukin)[3] has spoken to you and I have heard them. (They are indeed) empty – do not believe them. I swear by Aššur and Marduk, my gods,[4] that I have neither taken into consideration in my heart nor ordered with my mouth any of the evil things with which he has charged me. Instead, it is trickery in which he has engaged, (pondering): "I will besmirch the (good) name of the citizens of Babylon, who love him (Assurbanipal),[5] along with my own." (But) I, for my part, will not listen to this. Your brotherhood[6] with the Assyrians and the *kidinnūtu*-privileges[7] of yours that I established continue until now – you are in my heart.[8] You, for your part, shall likewise not listen to his empty utterances. Do not besmirch your name, which in my judgment and that of all the lands is (so) good, and do not make yourselves guilty before (the) god.

(Lines 25–40) I also know that there is another matter about which you are concerned in your hearts. (You say to yourself): "Now that we have become hostile to him (Assurbanipal), it will be to our reproach."[9] (But) there is no reproach. There is none at all because (your) name is so excellent. As for (the possibility of) your siding with my enemy (in the future), that would (indeed) be the same as bringing reproach upon yourselves and violating an oath before (the) god. Now, though, I am writing to you as if you have not (yet) sullied yourselves with him in this affair.[10] Let me see an answer to my letter immediately.

(Lines 40–42) That wretch rejected by Marduk (i.e., Šamaš-šumu-ukin) should not damage through my hands the commitment that I have made before Bel.[11]

(Lines 43–45) Month of Ayyaru (Iyyar), 23rd day, eponym: Aššur-duru-uṣur (652 BCE). Šamaš-balassu-iqbi[12] delivered (the letter).

---

1 The standard introduction of letters sent by Assyrian kings. Gallagher 1999:203 compares this line to the introduction of the *rab šāqê*'s "second speech" to the people of Jerusalem in 2 Kgs 18:28–35 ("Hear the word of the Great King …") and points to a number of additional parallels, both structural and lexical, between ABL 301 and that speech.

2 Literally: "words of wind (*šāru*)." *Ruaḥ*, the Hebrew counterpart of *šāru*, can be used in the sense of "something negligible" or "unreliable" as well.

3 Assurbanipal is so disappointed in Šamaš-šumu-ukin that he denies him his status as a brother and does not even mention his name.

4 Claiming both Assur and Marduk as his "personal" deities is a *captatio benevolentiae*: Assurbanipal seeks to convey to the citizens of Babylon that he was not only devoted to the Assyrian "national" god (Aššur), but also to that of Babylonia (Marduk).

5 That they shall "love" (*ra'āmu*) Assurbanipal is one of the things Esarhaddon's so called 'Vassal Treaties' require of the subjects and vassals of the Assyrian king; see SAA 2, no. 6:268. In Deuteronomy (e.g., Deut 11:1), love of god replaces love of the king.

6 While Assurbanipal renounces his brotherly tie to Šamaš-šumu-ukin, he reaffirms the metaphorical brotherhood that exists between himself and the citizens of Babylon.

7 See note 5 to the "Letter from the Reign of Tiglath-pileser III" above (4.43). As far as we know, Babylon and Sippar were the only Babylonian cities that enjoyed a *kidinnūtu*-status under Assurbanipal.

8 My translation of this sentence follows Barjamovic 2004:76, and Parpola 2004:227.

9 I prefer Moran's translation over Parpola's "will be a burden on us" (Parpola 2004:227, reading *biltu* instead of *piltu*).

10 Assurbanipal tries to convince the Babylonians that there is still time for a peaceful solution. The only thing they have to do is withdraw their support from Šamaš-šumu-ukin.

11 This translation seems preferable to the one given by Parpola (2004:228): "May this man whom Marduk hates not deprive from my hands the troop which I have put together for Bel." Some uncertainty, however, remains.

12 Nothing else about this man is known. See Ambos 2011a.

REFERENCES

Copies: IVR[2] 45; ABL 301. *Photo*: http://www.cdli.ucla.edu/dl/photo/P393748.jpg (CDLI). *Editions*: Waterman 1930:208–209; Pfeiffer 1935:70, no. 81. *Translations and discussion*: Oppenheim 1967:169–170; Moran 1991 (full translation of the letter and edition of the rev.); Frame 1992:131, 138–139; Gallagher 1999:202–205; Barjamovic 2004:61, 76; Parpola 2004; Radner 2006:150–151.

A PRINCELY LETTER

Eckart Frahm

A LETTER FROM ULULAYU (SHALMANESER V) TO HIS FATHER TIGLATH-PILESER III (4.45)

The Assyrian king Shalmaneser V (726–722 BCE), whose birth name was Ululayu, is credited in the Bible (2 Kgs 17:1–6; 2 Kgs 18:9–12) with the conquest of Samaria, which took place in the last year of his reign; he probably also conquered Sam'al and Que. Before he ascended the Assyrian throne, he served as Tiglath-pileser III's crown prince. In this capacity, it was his duty to deal with various state matters, both domestic and foreign, especially when his father travelled or went on campaigns. The prince, still called Ululayu at this time, kept his father informed on such occasions by writing him letters, five of which (apparently archival copies of the original missives) have been found in Calah. One of the letters is included here because it deals with the travels of emissaries from a number of Western countries, including Ashdod and Moab; it can be compared to SAA 1, 110, a letter from the reign of Sargon II that mentions emissaries from Egypt, Gaza, Judah, Moab, and Ammon (translated in *COS* 3.96). The letter translated in the following bears the excavation number ND 2762 and belongs to an archive that was found in 1952 by British archaeologists in Calah near the ziggurat terrace, in a chamber designated ZT 4 (Saggs 2001:1).

(Lines 1–8) To the king, my lord, your servant Ululayu. May all be very well with the king, my lord! [Assyria] is well, the temples are well, and all the forts of the king are well. The heart of the king, my lord, can be glad indeed.[1]

(Lines 9–17) Emissaries[2] from Kummuḫu (Commagene), Carchemish, Marqasi, Sam'al, Sidudu (Ashdod), and Moab have come,[3] passing the cities Turbisiba (Til-Barsip) and Guzana[4] without my permission.[5] I have written about this matter, and they have been held up in Kubanaši.[6]
(gap of two lines)

(Lines 20–33) I had written to the Chief-Marshall[7]: "The emissaries must not proceed," but they (nonetheless) left and proceeded. Now they are in Kubanaši, (as is) a second emissary from Marqasi. I have sent letters to Kubanaši. The orders I sent (are as follows): They shall write letters. When those have been brought to me, I will dispatch them [to the king], my lord. When the king, my lord, moves on, someone should write to me, and I will come and meet with the king, my lord. [May I (soon) hear] the king, my lord's answer.

---

1 The introductory address is typical for letters written to Assyrian kings by their crown princes. It is also attested in the letters Sennacherib sent to his father Sargon II while serving as his crown prince.

2 The Akkadian word for "emissary," *ṣīru*, is related to Biblical Hebrew *ṣīr* (e.g., Isa 18: 2; 57:9; Jer 49:14), which has the same meaning.

3 The passage about the emissaries can be compared to a long list of western rulers whose tribute is mentioned in Tiglath-pileser's "Summary Inscription 7" (Tadmor 1994:154–175 = RINAP 1, no. 47), a text written in 729 BCE or shortly after. Tiglath-pileser's list includes the names, among others, of Kuštašpi of Kummuḫu, [Pisiriš of Carchemish], Panammû of Sam'al, Tarḫulara of Gurgum (a Neo-Hittite state whose capital was Marqasi, modern Maraş), Salamanu of Moab, and Jehoahaz of Judah; a reference to Ashdod may have been lost in a gap. The emissaries are said to have brought gold, silver, tin, iron, lead, garments, and many other products to Assyria. As pointed out by Tadmor (1994:265–268), the states mentioned in the second part of the list, which includes the reference to Moab, had become Assyrian vassals in 734 BCE at the earliest. This year can therefore be considered a likely *terminus post quem* for our letter. It is almost certain that the emissaries mentioned in the letter brought tribute to the Assyrian king.

4 Til-Barsip, modern Tell Ahmar, is situated on the eastern bank of the Euphrates in Syria, while Guzana, modern Tell Halaf, is in the eastern Habur region. Both cities were on the main road between the Assyrian core area and the Levant. The Bible refers to Guzana as "Gozan" and identifies it as one of the places to which the Israelites were deported after the defeat of Samaria in 722 BCE (2 Kgs 17:3–6; see also 1 Chr 5:26).

5 Before Sargon II conquered Carchemish in 716 BCE, Til Barsip seems to have been the usual entry point for people coming to Assyria from the west (see Radner 2004:100). Guzana was another important urban center on the way. Perhaps the emissaries were not supposed to pass these cities because they had to register there and make arrangements with local officials that would ensure they would not miss the king.

6 Kubanaši, also known as Kubaniša, was a town in the province of Guzana, perhaps modern Tell Ḫanāfiz.

7 Assyrian: *turtānu*, a title rendered as *tartān* in the Hebrew Bible (Isa 20:1; 2 Kgs 18:17). The letter seems to indicate that Til-Barsip was still part of the "Province of the Chief-Marshall" during the reign of Tiglath-pileser III (see Radner 2004:99).

REFERENCES

Copies: Saggs 1959: pl. XLIII; Saggs 2001: pl. 34. *Editions*: Saggs 1959:159–160 (NL 50); Kessler 1980:203–206; Saggs 2001:182–184; Radner 2004:100–101; Vera Chamaza 2005:148–150; Radner 2006:122–123.

MARI INSCRIPTIONS

LETTER TO THE GOD NERGAL (*ARM* 1.3) (4.46)

Adam E. Miglio

ARM 1.3 (4.46) and *FM* 7.38 (4.47) provide a succinct history of kingship at Mari in the final decades before Hammu-rabi of Babylon destroyed the city. This letter was addressed by Yasmah-Addu, the king of Mari, to the god Nergal. Yasmah-Addu began his missive with a history of kingship at Mari. He presented this history as a generational feud between the dynasty of Ila-kabkabu, which included Shamshi-Adad and Yasmah-Addu, and the dynasty of Yagid-Lim, which included Yahdun-Lim and Sumu-Yamam. Yasmah-Addu's history in his letter provided a theological explanation of the past. Yasmah-Addu's brief historical account of kingship illustrated how the god had rewarded those who obeyed divine commands, whereas those who disobeyed the gods were subject to divine punishment. Yasmah-Addu's theological perspective of history, then, culminated in the conclusion to the letter, which seems to contain Yasmah-Addu's petition for an heir to succeed him. It should be noted, however, that Yasmah-Addu was followed by Zimri-Lim, who claimed to be the son of Yahdun-Lim.

(Lines 1–4) [Speak to] the venerated [Ner]gal,[1] who spoke to me: [thu]s says Yasmah-Addu, your servant and devotee.

(Lines 5–22) Since my birth, anyone who offended a god was ruined[2]; everyone should follow divine commands.[a] In the past Ila-kabkabu and Yagid-Lim swore a solemn oath by the god to one another. Ila-kabkabu had not committed an offense against [Yag]id-Lim, Yagid-Lim however committed an offense against Ila-kabkabu.[b] You called him to account[3] [and] marched [at] the side of Ila-kabkabu so that [Ila-ka]bkabu destroyed his fortress [and] captured his [son], Yahdun-Lim. [Then, when] Shamshi-Adad [ascended] to the [throne of his father, he did not commit an offense against Y]agid-Lim,[c] [despite] the offense [that] Yagid-L[im] had com[mitted against] Ila-kabkabu.[4]

(Lines 1′–5′) [Because of the offense] that he (Yahdun-Lim) [commit]ted against Shamshi-Adad and [because] he had confined [x x x x] of the god, [his] s[on Su]mu-Yamum, forced Yahdun-Lim from Mari.[d]

(Lines 6′–19′) Sumu-Yamum went on acting just like his father, Yahdun-Lim, and he himself [did] inappropriate things.[e] He destroyed your house, which former kings had b[uilt], and made a house for his wife.[f] You called him to account and his servants killed him. You proceeded to return all of the banks of the Euphrates [to] Shamshi-Adad. [*Because of*] the offense that Sumu-Yamam committed [against] Shamshi-Adad, [you re]turned [the city of Mari] and the banks of the Euphrates [to him]. (Then,) he took me and established me [with sovereign]ty at Mari. [When] he established me [with soverign]ty at Mari ....[5]

(Lines 23′–28′) *N*[*ow*], why [*did you take*] (my) son from me? Former (kings) requested expansive territory [from you]; (but) I requested [l]ife and offspring [from you].[g] Do not covet those who *are (still) living*! The land ....[6]

a Deut 28:15–68
b Ezek 17:12–29
c Jer 22:15
d 2 Sam 15:13–37
e 1 Kgs 15:1–3, 25–30; 2 Kgs 15:8–9; 21:18–32; 23:31–37; 24:8–9; 2 Chr 33:21–23
f 1 Kgs 7:8
g Gen 12:1–3; 25:21; 1 Sam 1; 2 Sam 7; 18:18, 33

1 There is some evidence to suggest that letters addressed to deities during this period were delivered to temples so that a religious functionary, like the *āpilum*-prophet (cf. *FM* 7:38 [see 4.47 below]), could reply to them (Ellis 1987:251–256; Charpin 2002:22–23).

2 The sense of lines 5–6 (5) *iš-tu ṣí-ti-ia ma-am-ma-an* 6) [*š*]*a a-na* DINGIR *ú-ga-al-li-lu ú-ul i-ba-aš-ši*) seems to be that those who committed offenses against the god(s) would be invariably punished; hence, it states a 'retribution principle' of sorts ([Durand 1998:74]; see also Bodi 2010:195–200).

3 The verbal hendiadys in line 14 (*te-el-qé-e-ma ta-ša-al-šu*) may be translated, "You went ahead and questioned him" (cf. line 10′) *ta-al-li-ik-ma ta-ša-al-*[*š*]*u*; line 12′–13′) *te-el-qé-ma ... tu-ut-t*[*e-e*]*r*). Nergal's action was in response to gods' roles in securing oaths and threatening retribution against those who violated sworn agreements.

4 There are approximately eight lines missing.

5 Three fragmentary lines are preserved: (20′) [.... *a*]*m da-re-e-em* 21′) [...]-*i-it a-wi-lu-tim* 22′) [...]-x-*kum*).

6 There are the traces of three additional lines.

REFERENCES

Text and Collations: Charpin and Durand 1985:339–342; Durand 2000:72 (= LAPO 18 931).

MESSAGE FROM ADDU FOR ZIMRI-LIM (*FM* 7.38) (4.47)

Adam E. Miglio

This letter was sent by Nur-Sin to Zimri-Lim, the king of Mari. It is not certain what office Nur-Sin held in Zimri-Lim's administration, but it is clear from his dossier that he was frequently privy to events in the western polity of Yamhad. In this letter, Nur-Sin recounted a message for the king from the *āpilum*-prophet of the god Addu.

The message of the *āpilum*-prophet was similar to the message in *ARM* 1.3 (4.46) in that it was embedded within a theological history of kingship at Mari. The message from the *āpilum*-prophet in *FM* 7.38 delineated the god's expectations for the king, Zimri-Lim. Literarily, the *āpilum*-prophet's message is significant because it invoked mythological imagery of the god Addu battling Tiamat, which is akin to a well known scene from the Babylonian Creation Epic, *Enuma Elish*, where the god Marduk is described defeating Tiamat.

(Lines 1–2) Speak to my lord, (Zimri-Lim): thus says Nur-Sin, your servant.
(Lines 3–10) Abiya the *āpilum*-prophet of Addu, the lord of Alep[po], came to me and said: "Thus says Addu, 'I gave all of the land to Yahdun-Lim and because of my weapons he had no rival. He abandoned me, however, so I gave to Shamshi-Adad the land that I had (previously) given to hi[m].[a] As for Shamshi-Adad ....[1]
(Lines 1′–10′) ... so I restored you. I returned you to the thro[ne of the house of your father]. I gave to you the weapon[s] that I (used to) combat the Sea.[b] I anointed you with the oil[c] of my resplendence;[2] (now) no one will sta[nd] before you! Hear my one [c]ommand:[d] When a litigant appeals to you and says, 'I have been wr[o]nged,'[3] be there to render a verdict! Res[pond to him ju]stly![e]
(Lines 11′–17′) [T]his is what I w[ant] from you.[f] When you g[o out] on a (military) campaign, do not le[ave] without (performing) an extispicy. When I am present[g] at my extispicy, you will go on (military) campaign. If (this is) [not] the case, you should not (even) go out of the gate.' "[h]
(Lines 17′–20′) This (is what) the *āpilum*-prophet spoke to me. I hear[by send to my lord the hair of the *āpilum*-prophet] and the fri[nge][4] (from his garment).

a 1 Sam 28:16–18; 2 Sam 3:9–11; 9:7; 1 Kgs 11:12–14
b Pss 7:11–13; 65:6–8; 74:12–15; 89:8–10; Isa 27:1
c 1 Sam 16:13
d Exod 20:1
e Exod 23:6; Ps 82:3–4; Isa 56:1
f Mic 6:8
g 1 Sam 3:10
h Judg 1:1–2; 20:1, 23, 28; 1 Sam 28:5–7; 30:8; 1 Kgs 22:5–7; 2 Kgs 3:11–12

1 There is a lacuna of several lines.
2 In the translation above, the form *nam-ri-ru-ti-ia* in line 4′ is understood to be related to the verbal root *nawārum*, "to be bright" (cf. the emphasis on purity [*šūpûm, elēlum*] found in A.3152+M.5665+ [4.51]; cf. also Ebeling 1953:98, which is a later ritual against lightning that describes Addu as "the one whose brilliance illuminates ...." [*ša ša-ru*]-*ru-šu ú-nam-ma-*[*ru*]). Alternately, this noun has been connected with the root *mrr*; see Durand 1993:53–54.
3 For the expression *ḫabtāku* accompanied by the verb *šasûm*, see *ARM*(*T*) 26/2: p. 299 (cf. *ARM* 26.5 [4.55, n. 7]).
4 The hair and the fringe of a prophet's garment could be sent to a diviner (*bārûm*), who would then use them to verify the prophet's message by means of a divinatory procedure.

REFERENCES

Text and Collations: Durand 1993:41–61; *FM* 7.38 (= Durand 2002:133–135).

REPORT ON *ḪAPĪRŪ*-ACTIVITIES IN THE BALIH REGION (*ARM* 2.131) (4.48)

Adam E. Miglio

The kingdom of Upper Mesopotamia, which Shamshi-Adad established with his sons Yasmah-Addu and Ishme-Dagan, was centered in the Habur at the city of Shubat-Enlil (Tell Leilan). This kingdom stretched from the banks of the Tigris to the Euphrates and included several adjacent regions as well. The three letters from Shamshi-Adad's reign that are included below (4.48–4.50) share a focus on regions to the west of the upper Habur – from the Balih to the Beqaʿ. In this letter, *ARM* 2.131 (4.48), the high-ranking official Mashum[1] wrote to Yasmah-Addu about a military event in Syria's Balih region, known in the sources from Mari as the land of Zalmaqum. Mashum and a military leader named Sin-tiri were in Zalmaqum, near the regional center of Shubat-Shamash. They reported how they had encamped at the city of Himush across from the opposing military leader, Yapha-Addu, who was holed up in the city of Zallul. According to Mashum, Yapha-Addu had rallied 2,000 *ḫapīrū*-troops[2] against Yasmah-Addu and his father Shamshi-Adad. Later sources indicate that Yapha-Addu would continue to be active in Zalmaqum even after the death of Shamshi-Adad, during the reign of Zimri-Lim (cf. *FM* 6.5 [4.57]).

1 Mashum was a secretary for the military (DUB.SAR MAR.TU) in *ARM* 2.60.
2 The term *ḫapīrum* was a socio-political designation most often used as a pejorative that referred to unruly elements in Bronze Age Near Eastern society.

(Lines 1–4) Speak to my lord, (Yasmah-Addu): thus says Mashum, your servant.
(Lines 5–23) Sin-tiri sent to me for reinforcements and I arrived before him at Shubat-Shamash[3] together with (my) troops. The next day (the following) report about the enemy came: "Yapha-Addu has secured the city of Zallul on the opposite side of the Euphrates' riverbank. Moreover, he is staying in the midst of that city along with 2,000 troops of the *ḫapīrū* from the land."[a] This information reached me[4] and I quickly left Shubat-Shamash along with the troops who were with me as well as with the troops who were with Sin-tiri. Then, I secured the city of Himush, which is across from Zallul.
(Lines 24–32) The cities are 1,800 meters apart. (As a result), he saw the reinforcements of the land when I secured the city of Himush, (which is) across from him, and he sent fire-signals.[b] Then, all of the cities on the other side of the riverbank from the land of Ursim received his (message).
(Lines 33–36) The enemy[5] troops who are assembled together in the citadel[6] are numerous. Because they will not disperse the troops, I will not draw near to (attack) the city.
(Lines 37–39) I have conducted this tablet to my lord from the banks of the Euphrates. The troops and the livestock are well.

a 2 Sam 20:6
b Jer 6:1

3 Shubat-Shamash was an important city in the region of the Balih River (cf. A.1610+ [4.63]) for which several locations have been suggested (see Durand 1997:131; Guichard 2014a:111; Charpin and Durand 1986:183; Ziegler 2009:206–207; cf. Charpin and Ziegler 2003:104, n. 246). Shubat-Shamash may have been another name for the city of Hanzat (see Arkhipov 2014:267–272; cf. A.1098 [4.56]).

4 Cf. the collocation in lines 9–10 (*maqātum* + *ṭēmam*) and in line 16 (*maqātum* + *awātam*) with the expression *maqātum* + *wūrtum* in *ARM* 10.5 (4.61, n. 6 below).

5 The translation above follows the collation in Durand 1998:76, n. 160: *na-[a]k-rum* (see further the remarks by Durand 1998:77, n. g).

6 The Akkadian phrase *zumur libittim* (SIG$_4$) may be translated "… the interior of the mudbrick (structure)." In context, it may have designated the hold of citadel-type construction akin to what is known from excavated sites in Syria such as at Tell Mardikh (cf. Durand 1998:77, n. h).

REFERENCES

Text and Collations: *ARM* 2.131; Durand 1998: 75–78 (= LAPO 17 491).

REQUEST FOR INFORMATION ABOUT THE CONFLICT WITH SUMU-EPUH (*ARM* 5.17) (4.49)

Adam E. Miglio

This letter was sent to Yasmah-Addu from Ishhi-Addu, the king of Qatna. Qatna was a polity located in western Syria near modern-day Homs (Tell el-Mishrife). Prior to the sending of this letter, these two kings had established amicable relations, which were realized by Ishhi-Addu giving his daughter in marriage to Yasmah-Addu. Yet in this missive Ishhi-Addu wrote to Yasmah-Addu regarding reports that Sumu-epuh, the king of Aleppo, had defeated Shamshi-Adad in battle. Ishhi-Addu indicated that he was inclined to believe these reports, since the envoys of Yasmah-Addu and Shamshi-Adad had stopped arriving at Qatna. Moreover, Ishhi-Addu invoked a similar experience in the recent past as further reason to believe the reports about Sumu-epuh's victory. He compared the present circumstances with a prior conflict involving the Turukkeans, a population east of the Tigris in the vicinity of the upper and lower Zab Rivers, who had interrupted envoys going back and forth from Qatna. Ishhi-Addu's missive, then, concluded with his assurance that he would remain loyal in the battle against Sumu-epuh regardless of whether Sumu-epuh's reports were true, and he also insisted that Yasmah-Addu give him an honest report about the conflict.

(Lines 1–2) Say to Yasmah-Adad: thus says Ishhi-Adad your brother.
(Lines 3–15) Sumu-epuh is repeatedly sending Nuzians[1] and messengers throughout the entire land, saying: "I assembled the Turukkeans and sent troops [am]ong the Turukkeans. I defeated Shamshi-Adad and plundered his land." This is (the message) he is repeatedly sending. When I heard, I was extremely concerned.[2] Moreover, now your envoys that typically arrive (here) have not (done so) for many days. At first I did not (want to) believe this report, but I have since believed (it), because your envoys no longer come to me.

1 It may be that the *nu-zé-e* (line 3) were inhabitants of ancient Nuzi, Yorghan Tepe, though this identification is not certain (Durand 1998:375).

2 In this letter Ishhi-Addu emphasized the need for sincerity and truthfulness. He did this, in part, by repeatedly using *libbum* ("heart"), which is the grammatical subject for the verbs "to fear, be concerned" (*adārum*) in line 11, "to trust" (*qiāpum*) in lines 13–14, and "let me know" in line 53 (literally, "let my heart know"). Additionally, it should be noted as a point of comparison that Ishhi-Addu insisted that he knew the "heart" (*libbum*) of Shamshi-Adad and of his son and that they were dishonest (lines 32–33, 38).

(Lines 16–26) Previously, when the Turukkeans revolted in the interior of the land,[3] you[4] would detain your envoys and my envoys there. You would not send the merchants who would typically come here. (At that time), there was no one who explained the matter to me! At present, he has similarly cut off the route of my envoys and your envoys. For this (reason) I have believed (his report)![a]

(Lines 27–41) What, then, is the (current) situation? Why am I uninformed about your success or [yo]ur misfortune? Now I myself have come to conclude that you consider me to be an outsider and an enemy.[b] (And) I know what you are thinking; it seems that you are contemplating: "If we write to Ishhi-Adad about this matter, then he will turn to Sumu-epuh for peace and they will conclude peace with one another." This (is what) you are considering. But even if Shamshi-Adad would conclude peace with Sumu-epuh, I, myself, will not make peace with Sumu-epuh as long as I live!

(Lines 42–49) Now if that which Sumu-epuh reported is correct and the Turukkeans are rebelling, (then) go and levy one man per street! Will not 2,000–3,000 troops be marshaled? Why has your father not given those troops for which I asked? I[f] you [truly] are my brother, I will (only) want (what) you [wa]nt!

(Lines 50–54) Quickly [s]end to me (regarding) that report which Sumu-epuh proclaimed – [i]f [th]is (report) is correct or not, (if) this is (or) is not (the case)! Let me know! Keep me informed!

a 1 Chr 19:1–4
b Prov 25:13

[3] The phrase "the interior of the land" (*i-na li-ib-bi ma-tim*) in this context connotes the region of the Habur 'Triangle' (Ziegler 2014:277–278; cf. A.1025 [4.65, n. 6]; M.6009 [4.71, n. 7]).

[4] Ishhi-Addu addressed both Yasmah-Addu and his father, Shamshi-Adad, in lines 16–41 by using second-person plural forms.

REPORT ON A SKIRMISH IN THE BEQAʿ VALLEY (A.3552) (4.50)

Adam E. Miglio

The military leader Muti-bisir wrote this letter to Yasmah-Addu, the king at Mari. Muti-bisir, much like Mashum and Sin-tiri (cf. *ARM* 2.131 [4.48]), had encamped across from a city in which there were enemy troops. In the case of Muti-bisir, however, he was installed at nearby Rahizum, which was far from Mari, being located in the upper Beqaʿ Valley.[1] In fact, Muti-bisir reported that the troops opposing him at Rahizum included Canaanites as well as *ḫabbātū*. The land of Canaan is the western-most geo-political horizon named in the letters found at Mari (the most notable Canaanite city mentioned in other letters from Mari being Hazor). As for the *ḫabbātū* mentioned in this missive, this term is akin to the term *ḫapīrum*[2] in that both designations could be applied to 'unruly' elements in Middle Bronze Age society.[3]

(Lines 1–4) Speak t[o] my lord, (Yasmah-Addu): thus says Muti-bisir, your servant.

(Lines 5–14) We are camped across from the city of Rahizum at the city of Dubba[4] – about which I have previously written several times t[o] my lord – and the desolate area (of) the city of Yarih is (only) 600 meters away from Rahizum. Now I looked beside [x x] and [I saw] 2,00[0 troops x x]. And Halu-samuh [x x x] to that city [x x x] among the *plu*[*nder* x x x]....[5]

(Lines 1′–12′) "[x x x] some [x x x] died, some [x x and] some the face of which/whom has been *dest*[*royed*.] In the opening of the tower [x x x]."[a] The refugees [spoke] this report [to me]; now his death is certain. I informed the district of Yatar-Hammu. Let his flocks be given in its/his place.[6] The *ḫabbātū* and the Canaanites are staying at Rahizum and we are able to see one another!

(Lines 13′–16′) The troops are well! My lord should not be concerned about his troops. I am sending this tablet to my lord on the 24th day of the month of Kinnum.[7]

a Judg 9:52–54

[1] The location of Rahizum in the Beqaʿ Valley is based upon its correlation with the toponym Ruhiṣu that is mentioned in the later el-Amarna letters 53 and 191 (Durand 1987:220).

[2] See the introduction to *ARM* 2.131 (4.48).

[3] Cf., for example, *ARM* 26.24 and *ARM* 28.40. For a discussion of the term *ḫabbātum* with special attention to the Tell Leilan letters, see Eidem 2011:1–22.

[4] The translation above follows the collation of Durand, who read *du-ub-ba-a* for the toponym (Durand 1987:219).

[5] There is a lacuna of several lines.

[6] Dossin read the end of line 8′ ⌜x⌝*iš-ša-ak-nu*. Given the space between the preceding word, *pu-*[*h*]*i-šu*, and the effaced sign, a likely restoration is ⌜*li*⌝*-iš-ša-ak-nu*. As for the interpretation of the line, Durand has suggested that this may be an instance in which the corpse of an individual (i.e. Halu-samuh) was reported dead (line 7′) and then exchanged for flocks (Durand 1998:30–31). At the same time, it may be that someone was being remunerated for a physical structure or something else that had been destroyed in line 7′. The fragmentary nature of the tablet and a lack of other sources concerning the precise event mentioned in these lines make it difficult to determine with certainty what transpired.

[7] The letter has been tentatively situated in the second month of the *limmum* of Nimer-Sin (Charpin and Ziegler 2003:124, n. 397).

REFERENCES

Text and Collations: Dossin 1973: 277–282; Durand 1998: 29 (= LAPO 17 456).

EPIC OF ZIMRI-LIM (A. 3152+M.5665+) (4.51)

Adam E. Miglio

The Epic of Zimri-Lim was inscribed on a single tablet that contained two columns on each side. The tablet was recovered in the palace at Mari and is one of the relatively few literary compositions found in the excavations at the site. The narrative poetry of this text instructs an audience to listen to the accomplishments of Zimri-Lim from early in his reign. It begins with an account of the divine selection of Zimri-Lim as king (i.12–17). Then, it recounts the gods' support for Zimri-Lim in his military conflicts and the king's military successes. Throughout the composition, Zimri-Lim's character and actions evince the divine favor that had been shown to him. In particular, the king is repeatedly likened to the god Addu. For example, Zimri-Lim is described as "resplendent" (i.16) just like the god (ii.27). And several of the king's actions on the battlefield evoke characteristics of the god Addu in battle (e.g. i.27–33; ii.17–19). At the same time, the king is also portrayed as an effective leader among his troops during the military campaign. Zimri-Lim inspires his warriors to victory as he endures the hardships of the battle alongside them. The text concludes with Zimri-Lim at Terqa, petitioning Dagan, the god who established kings along the central Euphrates River.

(Column i.1–37)
I will extol [Zimri-L]im,[1] wild bull of the battle,
I will forever repeat the renown of the [her]o,
[Zimri-Li]m, the heir of Yahdun-Lim, pre-eminent among the mobile pastoralists,
[The one who destroys the fortificatio]ns of the enemy!
I will exalt [the hero of *Itur-*]*Mer* (now) you must listen attentively,
[Pay attention to] my [w]ords about *the one who pursues* the adversary,
[*the one who subdues*] his enemy,[2]
[*the hero who read*]*ies* his lance [x x x],
[*the one who captures* land] after land!
[Zimri-L]im, the one who readies[3] his lance [x x x x x],
[*The one who captur*]*es* land after land!
In the [wo]mb, the gods gave (him) his name,
May the pronouncement[4] of Anum, the wild bull of his land,[5] be holy![6]
The gods gave him the name Zimri-Lim,
May the pronouncement of Anum, the wild bull of his land, be holy!
⸢*He*⸣[7] exulted the resplendent[8] king and,

---

[1] The translation above follows the restorations in Guichard 2014a, unless otherwise noted.

[2] The text clearly described the enemy of Zimri-Lim as grammatically singular, using mimation in some instances (e.g. *na-ak-ri-im* in ii.30). Yet other forms are equivocal, such as ii.19 (*na-ak-ri*) and iii.45 (*na-ak-ri-ku-nu*). It should be further noted that mimation is occasionally lacking on singular nouns in the composition (Guichard 2014a:85).

[3] The Akkadian collocation is *petûm šukurram*, which may be literally translated "to open the lance." The expression may allude to a ritual that consecrated the weapons for battle (cf. Guichard 1999:39–41).

[4] The word *zikrum*, translated "pronouncement" (*CAD* Z 112–116, s.v. *zikrum* A), refers to the act of naming Zimri-Lim in the previous poetic line. At the same time, the word *zikrum* can mean "image" and may also allude to the role of the king as the representative of the god (cf. *CAD* Z 116, s.v. *zikru* B, which is likely from the same etymon as *zikrum* A). Cf. Gen 1:26–28.

[5] The syntax of this line (i.13), which is repeated two lines later, may intentionally equivocate about whether Zimri-Lim (i.e. the "pronouncement of Anum") or whether the god Anum is the wild bull of the land (*zi-ik-ru* ^{d}*a-nim* ⸢*li*⸣*-te*$_9$*-li-il ri-im ma-ti-šu*). By so doing it may draw a connection between the god and Zimri-Lim (cf. i.1).

[6] The phrase here in i.13 (and repeated again in i.15) may be translated "Let the pronouncement of Anum be made pure" (*zi-ik-ru* ^{d}*a-nim* ⸢*li*⸣*-te*$_9$*-li-il*), understanding the form ⸢*li*⸣*-te*$_9$*-li-il* as a Dt-stem. Literarily, these lines should be compared with iii.31 and iii.33, where the king (LUGAL) receives the command (*zi-ik-ru-úš*) of Dagan, the pre-eminent one (*e-te*$_9$*-el*). The intratextual allusion between these lines emphasized the extensive divine support for Zimri-Lim's kingship.

[7] The verbal form in this line is a Š-stem from the root *rabûm*, but as Guichard notes the initial sign cannot be confidently deciphered: it is either a *lu* or an *ú*. It is unclear, therefore, if the form is in the 1st or 3rd person (⸢*lu/ú*⸣*-ša-*⸢*ar*⸣*-bi-ma*). If it is a 1st person form (⸢*lu*⸣*-ša-*⸢*ar*⸣*-bi-ma*), then one may translate: "Let me exult the resplendent king ...." In this case, line 16 is an interjection that celebrated the newly established king, Zimri-Lim. At the same time, it is noteworthy that the last use of a 1st person verbal form to express the voice of the narrator was in i.5, which may incline one to tentatively expect a 3rd person form. If it is a 3rd person form (⸢*ú*⸣*-ša-*⸢*ar*⸣*-bi-ma*), then line 16 would depict Anum as the one who established Zimri-Lim as king. Anum was ascribed the role of legitimating kings during the Old Babylonian period, for example, in the prologue to Hammu-rabi's law-stele (i.1–49, along with Enlil) and in the *Great Revolt against Naram-Sin* (line 5).

[8] The word *ša-pé-e-em* is probably best understood as a form derived from the verb (*w*)*apûm*, hence "resplendent" (Guichard 2014a:33). It is noteworthy that the forms *ša-pu-ú* (i.27), which may also be from the root (*w*)*apûm* (cf. n. 15 below), and the similar sounding form *šu-*⸢*pu*⸣ (ii.17) are used in the composition to describe the god Addu, thereby facilitating a comparison between the god and the king.

he has made Enlil's enemy his adversary![9,a]
Amidst the Habur and the Euphrates,
In the place where Addu rendered his judgment,
He[10] raised his voice (and) he scattered[b] his[11] lair,[12]
He frustrated his intentions to the four corners of the earth.
The land plundered the possessions of his hands,
The pure gold in the city of Bisan.[13]
He cut through the enemy like a knot of rope,[14]
(and) the earth drank the blood of soldiers.
Annunitum goes at his right (side),
Addu, the resplendent,[15] raised his voice.
He raised his voice, shattered the lance of the enemy,
He poured out his rage[16] on the land[s]!
Zimri-Lim, who breaks the lance of the enemy,
Poured out his rage on his enemy.
The fury of (his) combat cu[t through] the intense flame at the (battle)front,[17]
Who is greater than you [that] he could extinguish it?[18]
(It was) you (who) opened the mountain's narrow passage,
which is bolte[d sh]ut (with) a door of stone slabs.
Zimr[i-Lim is the one who o]pens the entrances of the fort,
which are (each) b[olted shu]t (with) a door of wood and stone ....[19]

(Column ii.1–48)
Zimri-L[im xxx],
Like an equid [xxx].
Before the troop[s xxx],
The one riding on a *šiḫāmum*-equid[20] [xxx].[c]
[There is n]o obstacle before him,
so the enemy was soaked through like [xxx],
A fugitive [did] not e[scape] from among the rear-guard.[d]
While opening two [x x x],
The young goatbuck[21] killed [his] ene[mies],
Whirlwinds turned against them.[22,e]
He did not fear the one going at his right,
The son of Enlil, La-gamal,[23] *the prince*,
And his support prevented *the warriors' fleeing*.[24]
He harvested his soldiers like reeds,[f]
Warriors fell like a tamarisk tree,

a Exod 23:22
b Lev 26:33; Deut 32:26–27; Ps 92:9; 144:6
c Jer 8:16; Ezek 38:14–16; Hab 1:7–9
d Josh 8:22; Judg 3:29; Jer 46:6
e Isa 28:2; 30:30; Jer 23:19; Ezek 13:13
f Jer 9:21; Mic 4:12

9 Line 17 is joined to line 16 by *-ma*, which conceptually connects Anum's associations with kingship and Enlil's conflict with his enemies. These concepts are also coupled in the *Great Revolt against Naram-Sin*, which is one of the few "canonical texts" recovered from Mari (see Charpin 1997b), where the king is given the title "anointed of Anum" (*pa-ši-iš* ᵈ*A-nim*) followed by the designation "military commander of Enlil" (GÌR.NITÁ ᵈEn-líl) Cf. also the characterization of Anum and Enlil in *Atra-hasis* in which Anum was "king" (*ša-ar-ru* i.7) and the "presider" (*be-el ṭe-mi*, iii.5) and Enlil is repeatedly called the "warrior" (*qú-ra-du*).

10 The description of Addu "raising his voice" (*id-di ri-ig-ma-aš-šu*) is a common means for expressing the storm god's powers associated with thunder (cf. Ps 29).

11 The antecedents for the masculine singular suffixes in lines 20 and 21 seem to be the singular nouns in i.17 (*na-ak-ri* and *za-ri-šu*; cf. note 2 above).

12 Cf. *ARM* 26.199 (4.66 below).

13 Bisan is a city located along the central Euphrates River Valley.

14 The word "knot," *kiṣrum*, which is used in the simile of i.24, is a term that in other contexts has the meaning "soldiers" (e.g. ii.3 and iii.38 below).

15 Alternately, the form used here (*ša-pu-ú*) may be derived from the verb *šapûm*, "to be dense, to billow," hence invoking Addu's associations with the storm (see note 8 above).

16 In this context the Akkadian word *imtu* refers to the destructive effects of the storm, which Addu pours out on Zimri-Lim's enemies. It is noteworthy that the cognate Hebrew form *ḥēmāʰ* is used with storm-god imagery in the Hebrew Bible (e.g. Isa 66:15; 42:25.23; Jer 23:19; 30).

17 I:32 is very difficult: *pu-tam ta-an-pí-ih-tam is-ri-*[*im*] ⌜*i*⌝*-ša-at qa-ab-lim*. The "fury of (his) combat" in line 32 (⌜*i*⌝*-ša-at qa-ab-lim*) describes Zimri-Lim's action; fire is a common image in descriptions of battle (e.g. ii.40, below). The image of "fire" (*išātum*, IZI) is also connected with Addu, who is "the one who makes lightning strike and who carries … fire" ([*mu-*]*šab-riq bir-qí na-áš* ... IZI; Ebeling 1953:96). In i.32 the complements to the verb are the noun *ta-an-pí-iḫ-tam*, which is derived from this verbal root *nuppuhum* "to kindle, to blow" (cf. the effects of Addu described as *nipih išāti inna*[*phu*] Ebeling 1953: 100), and *pu-tam*. As for the verb itself, it seems to be *š/sarāmum*, "to cut, split" (see Guichard 2014a:39). In the context, then, the resultant image from the verb *š/sarāmum* and its compliments (*ta-an-pí-iḫ-tam* and *pu-tam*) may be comparable to the imagery found in the Ugaritic tradition of the storm god, where Balu's lightning broke through the clouds (see Pardee 2005:168). If correct, the imagery in i.32 furthers the comparison between Zimri-Lim and the god Addu by portraying the king's fiery combat as piercing the flames at the battlefront in a manner similar to the storm god's use of lightning to cut through the clouds. It is tempting to understand the verb *š/sarāmum* to mean "to strike (to flame), kindle," but the difficulty with this interpretation is that the verb *š/sarāmum* is not attested with this connotation to my knowledge (cf. Ps 29:7, where *ḥṣb* meaning "to cleave, to split" may convey the idea of "striking a fire," though this interpretation of the Hebrew root *ḥṣb* is not certain either).

18 The verb *balûm/belûm* concludes the image from the previous line, being a verb that was most frequently used with the meaning to extinguish fires (*išātum*; cf. previous note), but also at times being used to describe the concluding of wars.

19 There are approximately fourteen lines missing.

20 For the term *šiḫāmi*, see Durand and Guichard 2012:14–15.

21 "Young goat buck" is a translation of the Akkadian word *lalium*. Elsewhere, related imagery of a goat buck (*ka*/*izzum*) is associated with ferocity in warfare, for example in the Old Babylonian literary text "The Song of Bazi" (see George 2009:7, l. 34–3). Cf. Dan 8:1–8.

22 The god Addu was connected with the meteorological phenomena of "whirlwinds" or "sandstorms" (*ašamšūtum*).

23 La-gamal, whose name means "merciless," was connected with the underworld. In Old Babylonian sources he was associated with the city of Terqa and appeared in tandem with the deity Yakshudum/Ikshudum (meaning "He [who] captured," a nominalized form of *kašādum*; cf. *ARM* 13.3, Rouault 2011).

24 For the epigraphic and syntactic difficulties of ii.12–13, see Guichard 2014a:16, 46.

The earth drank his (enemy's) blood.
Once Addu was irrevocably *manifest*,[25]
Zimri-Lim, the leopard of battle,[g]
The powerful one who captures (his) adversary, who utterly destroys (his) enemy,[h]
Opened his mouth and spoke,
He addresses his men:
"A womb created you,
Just like you, a mother bore me![i]
This same battle is against me (and) *my plan ⌜changed,⌝*
The four corners (of the land) are hostile against you![j]
Now the land [x x x x] ⌜put in order for me,⌝
The enemy is ass[em]bled [x x x],
To the battle [x x x]!"
[*The wild bull of king*]*s*, the resolved one, once [x x x x],
Zimri-Lim, the resolved one, once [he accomplished his] objective,
He commanded his *sukkal*,
Directed his *sugāgū*:[26]
"Let my warriors, the mobile pastoralists, draw near to me,
let my (chief) herdsmen[27,k] enter before me![l]
With the regular conscripts, the inhabitants of the banks the Euphrates,
I will certainly act according to your counsel!"
Having heard what he spoke,
Ashmad, the *merḫûm*[28] addressed him:
"What do you fear about the Shubarean (people)?
(I swear that)[29] the fury of your combat cannot be turned back!
Chilling fear is (in) the shadows of the forest's trees,
At least in the trunks of (those) that were not cut by the blade of the axe!
Shubartum is scattered like the sheep of the pasture,[m]
[*Here*] the provisions are readied for (each) soldier.
[Oh Zimri-L]im, let them see your heroism,

g Ezek 38:14–16; Hos 13:7
h Ps 68:2
i Job 31:15
j Ezek 7:2
k 2 Kgs 3:4
l Mic 5:5–6
m Num 27:26–17; 1 Kgs 22:17; Ezek 34:5–6; Nah 3:18
n Deut 7:16; Jer 21:7
o Jer 49:32
p Gen 21:14–15
q Jer 2:23–24
r 1 Sam 14:31–33
s Deut 31:6; Josh 1:6; 10:25; 1 Sam 4:9; 2 Chr 32:7–8

[x x x] Let him extol your name!"
[The king rejoiced at the wor]d of the *merḫûm*, your servant,
[x x x] the harvester of the field ....[30]

(Column iii.1–50)
[He] filled the field(s) with their allies.
Being clad with armor, pity was his (only) prescription,[n]
Everyone in his way is felled.
Donkeys are seen (being) plundered (and) overcome,
The warriors (of the enemy) strew (the ground),
The battlefield is smeared with their blood.[o]
Until the king accomplished his objective,
He, then, trampled Ida-maraṣ under his feet.
He only drank from water-skins,[p]
Counted among the soldiers, everything was arduous.[31]
Great are the soldiers who went (on campaign) with him:
Like the onager[q] (eating) the straw in the steppe,
His men devoured meat[32];
They took heart (and) gained strength.[r]
Zimri-Lim goes like a standard before them,
He turned back to (each of) the weary and encouraged (him):
"Be strong and press on;[s]
The enemy will see your fortitude!"
Fire burned (within) them,
Their appetites were kindled![33]
They arrayed with daggers, swords, (and) lances,
(With) weapons menacing[34] their [x x]⌜x⌝.
[x x x x x]⌜x⌝ that which remains of the steppe,
⌜x⌝[x x x x, m]ost competent Eshtar.
When [x x x x x x x x x x],
He placed [his] officials [along the banks] of the River.
[He queried] the god[s] who were not (yet) summoned [to] campaign;

25 Line ii.17 is epigraphically uncertain. Guichard tentatively read: *a-ki*$^{!?}$*-i*$^{?}$ ⌜^{d}IŠKUR$^{?}$⌝ *šu-*⌜*pu*⌝ *a-na* ⌜*ḫu-ur*⌝*-ri-im* (Guichard 2014a:16).

26 A *sugāgum* was a local authority. *Sugāgū* are known to have overseen various types of social groups, such as tribal and mobile pastoralist populations or settled, townspeople. The word is related to the West-Semitic root *śgg* or *śg'* "to be great" (Durand 1997:208).

27 Akkadian *mār nāqidum*.

28 For the *merḫûm*, see the introduction to M.6060 (4.52), below. For Ashmad, see the introduction to *FM* 8.43 (4.54).

29 The construction in ii.40 is an oath in which the protasis is stated and the apodosis is ellipted (*la ú*[*s-sà*]*-ḫi-ru i-ša-at* ⌜*qa-*⌝*-ba-li-ka*; cf. *ARM* 28.95 [4.75, n. 2]).

30 There are five lines missing.

31 The description in these lines emphasized the king's sacrifices on the campaign along side his soldiers. Animal skins were suited for use on military campaigns because they could be transported more easily than ceramic vessels. Yet animal skins were not able to keep liquids as cool as ceramic.

32 The word *šīrum*, translated "meat," might also be rendered "flesh" (cf. ii.20). The metaphor of devouring or "eating" (*akālum*) one's enemy is well attested in Akkadian literature (e.g., *FM* 6.5: 37 [4.57]).

33 Line iii.20 (*ka-ar-šu-šu-nu ši-wi-tam la-am-du*) expressed an idea similar to that found in the preceding line, namely that the troops were inspired. The noun *šiwītum* is understood, following Guichard 2014:58, who connects it with the verbal root *šawûm* "to roast."

34 The verb translated "menacing" may be related to the Ugaritic verbal root *š-r*, which seems to be transitive. Thus it may be that an object for the verb was contained in the break at the end of the line.

They quickly answered the king (with a) 'Y[es],'[35]
(and) the interior of the [lan]d was kindled to battle.
The hero does not march on campaign by himself.
The king, by the command of Dagan, the pre-eminent one,[36]
Inspected his *men (who were like) his family*.
Zimri-Lim, by the command of Dagan, the pre-eminent one,
(had) Itur-Mer, the warrior, (as) his aid!
(By) the *āpilum*-prophet,[37] he saw (Dagan's) sign,[t] the pre-eminent one of his land,
(and) the king was greatly encouraged.
Addu marches on his left side,
Erra, the ferocious, on his right side.
He posted his units along the banks of the Habur,
At night he went on to lead them.
He summoned the diviners and mobilized (the troops):[38]
"Shamash, the warrior, answered me,
Today I will capture the enemy!
Oh my heroes, strive [x x x x],
Consider your enemy as [x x x x x]."
His warriors heard the com[mand of *his lips*],
Like the most excellent bird trap, they overwhelmed [their enemies].
The one who fled was [x x x x x],
The one who passed by was turned back [x x x].
Zimri-Lim [x x x x x x x x][39]

(Column iv.1–11)
[x x x x x x x x x x x]
[x x x x] he caused to establish,
He filled the land [x x x x].
[As for those who] responded (with) hostility (toward) Zimri-Lim,
They did not live; they died.
Once the king accomplished his objective,
He entered before Nunamnir.[40]
He offered his sacrifice in Ekisiqqa,[41]
In Terqa, the beloved (city) of Dagan.
Life, prosperity, and strength,[42]
Zimri-Lim requested from Dagan.[u]

t 1 Sam 10:7
u 2 Chr 1:11

35 The imagery in iii.26–27 may be that of Zimri-Lim enlisting the gods via divination to march as his military support (26) *la na-bi-iú-tim it-ti* DINGIR.[MEŠ *i-ri-iš a-na*] ⸢*re*⸣*-di-im* 27) *ar-hi-iš* LUGAL *i-pu-lu a*[*na-na-am*]). Additionally, it may be noted that a few lines later, not only are the diviners explicitly mentioned as accompanying Zimri-Lim into battle (iii.41), but divination is again alluded to in the king's speech to the troops (iii.42–43) where he recounted the response of Shamash, the god to whom queries were frequently posed (see further Guichard 2014a:65). Cf. perhaps 2 Sam 24; 1 Chr 21.

36 Cf n. 6 above.

37 For the *āpilum*-prophet, see *ARM* 26.199 (4.66) and *FM* 7.38 (4.47).

38 The translation above understands the form *ú-za-ak-ki* as related to the verb *zakûm* "to mobilize," which may also be found in *FM* 2.116 (4.60 below). The advantage to this interpretation is that it implies an audience (i.e. the troops) for the direct speech that follows. At the same time, one may translate the form, "He ... made a purification sacrifice" (for *zakûm* as an offering, see Durand 2008:520–521).

39 There are four lines missing.

40 Nunamnir is a Sumerian name for Enlil.

41 Ekisiqqa is the temple of Dagan at Terqa.

42 Cf. *ARM* 1.3: 25–26 (4.46).

REFERENCES

Text: Guichard 2014a.

OATH FOR AN OFFICIAL DURING THE REIGN OF ZIMRI-LIM (M.6060) (4.52)

Adam E. Miglio

M.6060 is a fragmentary tablet that preserves portions of an oath that was sworn to Zimri-Lim. Zimri-Lim imposed similar oaths on many of the functionaries in his administration, especially those who had previously served under the former king of Mari, Yasmah-Addu (cf., for example, the introduction to *FM* 2.116 [4.60]). This oath, while incomplete, is notable because it encapsulated the duality of Zimri-Lim's authority over both mobile populations in the steppe as well as over more sedentary, settled populations (lines 22′–23′). Unfortunately, the fragmentary nature of the text makes it impossible to know for certain what type of functionary might have sworn this oath. It has been suggested that it may have been imposed upon a collective of mobile pastoralists.[1] Alternately, the first person verbal forms and the recurrent mention of the pasture (*rîtum* [lines 4′, 9′] and *nawûm* [line 22′]) and mobile pastoralists (*ḫanûm* [line 22′]) may suggest that this oath was for a *merḫûm*. The *merḫûm* primarily resided in the pasturelands and was responsible for mobile pastoralist populations (cf. *FM* 8.42 [4.54]; A.1098 [4.56]). At the same time, the *merḫûm* also came into frequent contact with settled populations in cities (cf. *FM* 6.5 [4.57]).[2]

1 Durand 1991:50–53.

2 Miglio 2014:73, n. 53.

(Lines 1′–5′) [If x x x x x] he strikes [...], [*I will not fle*]*e* and ⌜x x⌝[x] not light, not [...]. [Let] the hand of my enemy [*bring an e*]*nd* to the pasture and extinguish my tribe.

(Lines 6′–9′) [Now] my attention is (given) to my princes[3] [and] their [h]eirs.[a] If not, ⌜let⌝ [x x x t]heir [x x x. Z]imri-Lim [x x x x x x] the land and the pasture ....[4]

(Lines 15′–27′) (I swear that) I will not trample[5] [x x x] this [oa]th, [which] I swore by my gods to Zimri-Lim my lord, the son of Yahdun-Lim, the king of Mari and of the land of the mobile pastoralists.[6] (I swear that) I will [not] commit an offense against Zimri-Lim. [When] I hear a conspiratorial word either in the mouth of the mobile pastoralists of the steppe or in the mouth of the peoples of the cities, saying: "Zimri-Lim [and] his heir will not exercise authority over us," I will not get invol[ved] [wi]th evil (plots) against Zimri-Lim and his he[ir].

a 2 Sam 7; Isa 11:1

[3] The word translated "princes," *mādarum*, can designate royal family members, such as the son of a king (e.g. *ARM* 28.32 and A.818 [see Durand 2004:159 n. 256). Durand has suggested that it is related to the root *ʾdr*, meaning "to fear" (see Durand 2001–2002:755; see also Durand 1991:21).

[4] There are traces of five fragmentary lines.

[5] The verb *ú-še-pu-ma* (line 19′) is extremely rare. The only attestation listed in the *CAD* is from a lexical list *malku* = *šarru* (cf. *CAD* Š/2 307, s.v. *šêpu*). The lexical list *malku* = *šarru* glosses lesser known Akkadian words, and occasionally loan words from West Semitic languages, with well-known Akkadian words. The entry that contains the verb *šêpum* includes synonyms for the Akkadian verb *etēqum*, "to go pass, cross over:" *ba-ʾ-u, še-e-pu, na-pal-ṭu-ú* = *e-te-qu*. Noting this, Durand has observed that the Akkadian verb *etēqum* is used with *nīšum* to convey the idea of "transgressing an oath," and he has suggested that in the oath above the verb *šêpum* seems to be used similarly (Durand 1997:465–466). *Šêpum* may be able to be compared with the Hebrew *šʾp*, which is not without its challenges in the Classical Hebrew lexicon, but is found with the connotations "to trample upon" (e.g. Amos 2:7; 8:4).

[6] Cf. Yahdun-Lim's titulature, where his kingship was described in terms of "Mari and the land of the Simal" (e.g. RIME 4:E4.6.8.6; Cavigneaux and Colonna d'Istria 2009).

REFERENCES

Text and Commentary: Durand 1991: 50–53; Durand 1997: 464 (= LAPO 16 297).

UPDATE FROM THE COURT OF YARIM-LIM OF ALEPPO (A.2988+) (4.53)

Adam E. Miglio

The selection of letters below from Zimri-Lim's reign have been arranged in chronological order, with a few exceptions, so as to give a sense of the significant events from his roughly thirteen-and-a-half year period. One of the earliest letters from Zimri-Lim's reign may be A.2988+[1] (4.53), which was written by a Mariote representative in the court of Aleppo named Yatar-kabkab. If this is the case, this letter provides a glimpse into how Zimri-Lim established his position within the international landscape by negotiating diplomatic relationships with the western polity of Yamhad, centered at Aleppo, and the eastern polity of Eshnunna (Tell Asmar).[2]

(Lines 1–4) Speak to my lord: thus says Yatar-kabkab, y[our servant].

(Lines 5–20) [My lord spoke] the following [regard]ing Eshnunna: "When you [g]o up, you should s[tand] before Yarim-Lim (of Aleppo) [and re]port on Eshnunna, saying: 'Eshnunna is repeatedly sending to me about peace. The first time, he sent his messenger to me, I returned him to the border. A second time he sent to me, and (again) I returned his messenger to the border. Then, after that, a dignitary[3] came and I returned him to the border,' asking: 'Without Yarim-Lim how can there be peace with Eshnunna?' "

(Lines 20–36) Now when I recounted this (message) to him, he responded to me: "If his demands have changed (and he is no longer) claiming, 'This is my border,' then he should stop sending up his troops. [*Let him de*]*tain*[4] this (envoy)!" That man does not want (to accept) either the [en]voys that are repeatedly coming up or [peac]e with Eshnunna.[a] He is saying: "Am I not better for him (i.e. Zimri-Lim) than Eshnunna? Do I not have troops as

a 2 Sam 10:1–4; 1 Kgs 5:1; 2 Kgs 17:4; 2 Chr 32:31; Ezek 17:15; Prov 13:17; Isa 52:7

[1] For the possible date of this letter to Zimri-Lim year 0, see Charpin 1992: §101.

[2] This letter contains orthographic oddities, most notably the use of the *ú* sign as the conjunction alongside the conventional *ù* sign.

[3] Literally, "one who rides a donkey" (cf. Zech 9.9).

[4] The end of line 25 is fragmentary. Charpin has restored the verb *esērum*: *a-nu-*[*um li-s*]*i-ir* (Charpin 1991:161–162). If he is correct, the king of Aleppo not only wanted the Eshnunnean messenger to be turned back from Mari, but he wanted Zimri-Lim to imprison him when he arrived.

Eshnunna? As for the city that is his enemy (and about which) he spoke, saying, 'This city is our enemy,' I will indeed go along with my troops in order to return[5] that city to his authority."[b]

b 1 Kgs 22:4; 2 Kgs 3:7

[5] The verb *târum* is used several times throughout A.2988+ (cf. lines 13, 15, 17 and line 36) and may have rhetorical significance. The repetition of this verb may be intended to focus attention on the fact that Zimri-Lim's loyalty to Yarim-Lim, which he had demonstrated by repeatedly turning back the Eshnunnean envoy, had earned him the return of a contested city.

REFERENCES

Text and Translations: Charpin 1991:161–162; Durand 1997:441–443 (= LAPO 16 282); Ziegler 2006:53–54.

REQUEST FOR PERMISSION TO RAID THE FLOCKS OF ISHME-DAGAN (*FM* 8.43) (4.54)

Adam E. Miglio

Ashmad, a *merḫûm*,[1] sent this letter to Zimri-Lim. Ashmad is mentioned in A. 3152+M.5665+ (4.51), where he is said to have supported the king on his military campaigns into the land of Shubartum. In this letter, however, Ashmad described his plan for raiding the flocks of Ishme-Dagan, the son of Shamshi-Adad. Ashmad's leadership among the mobile pastoralists (*ḫanûm*) illustrates how the *merḫûm* as well as the mobile pastoralist populations related to and supported Zimri-Lim. Additionally, Ashmad's letter preserves a route that structured the recurrent movements of the mobile pastoralists across the steppe and along the rivers of Syro-Mesopotamia.[2]

(Lines 1–4) Speak to my lord: thus says Ashmad, your servant.
(Lines 5–16) All of the mobile pastoralists assembled and said: "Send to our lord so that our lord turns us loose and we may raid Ishme-Dagan's sheep at Rapiqum and Yabliya,[3] return to the banks of the Euphrates, and give many [she]ep to our lord.[a] Then, our [lo]rd will not be continually asking us for [many] sheep." This is what all the mobile pastoralists said to me with a single voice.
(Lines 17–35) Now if th[is] is what my lord desires, he should no[t st]and in the way of the pastoralists, his servants. Let my lord be attentive to this tablet and at o[nc]e – (even) on the very same da[y] – put a reply to my [t]ablet into the hand of the (very) messenger who brought this tablet of mine (to you). Then, let it arrive (back) to me before Ramum[4] so that after Ramum I may[5] embark on that journey and we may capture those sheep. [W]e should go down to fi[gh]t before the fe[as]t of Eshtar; *we should return* ⌜x x x⌝ *be*[*cause* x x x]. Regarding [these] sheep, I will g[ive] half (of them) to our lord and the (other) half is apportioned for [our] lord's servants.[b] [Only let me hear] the command of my lord and I will go and supply my lord with many sheep![c]

(Lines 35–46) When leaving, [the route] will be kept (secret).[6] I will set out f[or Mo]unt Murdi as (if I was) going to the camp[7]; but the remainder (of the route) will be different. I will covertly go [t]o Qattunan. Then, I will go along the [edge of the] steppe [in order to capture] those [shee]p (which

a 1 Sam 25:5–9; 2 Sam 13:23

b Isa 9:3; Prov 16:19; Num 31:27

c 1 Sam 30:21–26

[1] For the *merḫûm*, see the introduction to M.6060 (4.52).
[2] Durand dated this letter to Zimri-Lim year 1 (Durand 2005:152).
[3] Rapiqum and Yabliya were located south of Mari in the region of Suḫum. These cities are elsewhere paired in the letters from Mari, for example, in an account of a military expedition from Rapiqum to Yabliya (*ARM* 26.477) as well as in a report about Eshnunnean raids on the flocks from these cities (*ARM* 26.504).
[4] The celebration of *rāmum* was accompanied by the erection of commemorative stones; it also could be associated with the new moon (e.g. *FM* 8.41; Durand 2008:353–356).
[5] Lines 26–27 may also be translated "… so that after Ramum ⟨we⟩ may embark on that journey …" (26) *ak-ki-ma wa-ar-ki ra-me-e-im* 27) KASKAL *ša-a-ti* ⟨*nu*-⟩*uṣ-ṣú-ma*; Durand 2005:150), although this translation requires an emendation. At the same time, the form *uṣ-ṣú-ma*, which is what was written on the tablet, may be interpreted as a first-person singular form. A singular form is not inconsistent with Ashmad's recounting of the journey in lines 37–41, where he also used first-person singular forms. By comparison, Ashmad's description of raiding the sheep used plural verbs (lines 28–30). It may also be noted that the text is not characterized by numerous, if any, scribal mistakes; the only other possible error is at the end of the letter, where the tablet is fragmentary and hence difficult (cf. n. 10 below).
[6] Durand has suggested the reading [KASKAL] ⌜*in*⌝*-na-ṣí-*[*ir*] for line 35 and has translated, "ma route sera secrète" (Durand 2005:152; Durand 2004:139). Cf. line 29 (*a-pá-zi-ir-ma*) "I will covertly go …;" cf. A.1098:38 (4.56): "My lord's [secret plan] must be kept" ([*pi-ri-iš-ti*] *be-li-ia lu na-aṣ-ra-at*).
[7] For the term *maḫanum*, which designates an encampment of Simal mobile pastoralists, see Durand 2004:144–146.

are at Rapiqum and Yabliya).[8,d] My lord should not be lax [ab]out this mission of mine![9] My lord must quickly send a response to my tablet before Ramum.

(Lines 47–49) Additionally, [x x of][10] Ida-maraṣ (and) Shamshi-Adad, king of Nahur, have installed Asqur-Addu.

d Josh 8:3–7

[8] The route described in this letter begins in the environs of the Mount Sinjar, the western part of this range being known as Mount Murdi (Wäfler 2001:132 and the bibliography there). The proposed route, then, proceeded from the western side of Mount Sinjar to the west, toward the Habur River valley and the city of Qattunan, before turning south along a path that skirted the Jezirah ("along the [edge of the] steppe"). The route's terminus was at the cities of Rapiqum and Yabliya, which were located along the Euphrates River valley in the region of Suḫum, south of Mari (see Durand 2004:197).

[9] The translation "mission" is based upon the proposal by Durand, who compared the word *napsuḫtum* with the Hebrew root *pś'*, meaning "to march" (Durand 2005:153).

[10] In addition to the epigraphic challenges (see further Durand 2005:152–153), there are two interpretive difficulties in lines 47–49. First, the historical allusion found in lines 47–49 is obscure. Second, the syntax of these lines is challenging. As it regards the historical context, it has been suggested that the Shamshi-Adad mentioned in lines 48 may have been a ruler from Nahur during the opening months of Zimri-Lim's reign (Durand 2005:153, n. g). As for the syntax of these lines, the translation above tentatively understands Shamshi-Adad to be a part of a compound, asyndetic subject. Alternately, Durand has suggested an emendation: "Moreover, the sons of Ida-maraṣ have installed Asqur-Addu, ⟨a servant⟩ of Shamshi-Adad of Nahur" (47) *ša-ni-tam* [DUMU(?)].MEŠ *i-da-ma-ra-aṣ* 48) ⟨ÌR⟩ ^{m}*sa-am-s*[*i*]-^{d}IŠKUR LUGAL *ša na-hu-ur*^{KI} 49) ^{m}*às-qúr*-^{d}IŠKUR *iš-ku-ú-nu*; Durand 2005:152).

REFERENCES

Text: Durand 2005:150–153.

ADVICE FOR THE KING ON HOW TO DEAL WITH PERSONNEL (*ARM* 26.5) (4.55)

Adam E. Miglio

Bannum was a *merḫûm*[1] who supported Zimri-Lim during the first eight to twelve months of his reign. According to a sealing that is likely to be attributed to Bannum, he was "a servant of Yahdun-Lim, who returned the heir of Yahdun-Lim to his place."[2] Thus Bannum claimed to have had a role in helping Zimri-Lim secure the throne at Mari. *ARM* 26.5 (4.55), A.1098 (4.56), and an oath that was sworn to the king mentioning Bannum by name[3] confirm this *merḫûm*'s pronounced political influence during Zimri-Lim's reign. *ARM* 26.5 (4.55), in particular, is an important source because it provides a glimpse into Bannum's staunch commitment to the interests of the Simal tribe to which he and Zimri-Lim belonged.

(Lines 1–2) Speak to my lord: thus says Bannum, your servant.
(Lines 3–27) Is it appropriate that Asqudum constantly provides you with lib[elous][4] (information) and that you repeatedly listen (to) his words?[a] When you prepared for the campaign and stayed for seven days at the *unqatim*-(ritual)[5] in the temple of Dagan (at Terqa), you left me at Mari and instructed me, saying: "The (very) day I leave the *unqatim*-(ritual) come meet me at Terqa." This is what you said to me. But I was detained at Mari and (when) Asqudum spoke libelous words to you, you appointed him the *sugāgum*[6] of Hishamta. Then, again he deceived you with (his) words and you appointed Enlil-ipush as majordomo of Hishamta. When I arrived at Saggaratum, I heard about this matter and I said "I have been wronged."[7] I discussed the matter with you, saying: "How can you appoint an Ekallatean[8] as *sugāgum* of Hishamta? And you (also) have appointed Enlil-ipush to majordomo!" This is what I said to you. Then, I relieved that man (from his post) and I made

a 1 Sam 24:9

[1] For the *merḫûm*, see the introduction to M.6060 (4.52).

[2] TH 72.15:3–6, cited in Charpin and Durand 1985:324.

[3] Durand 1991:117–118.

[4] The phrase *lā šināti* ("libelous things"), which is partially restored here, was used four additional times in this letter (lines 13, 29, 34, 69) as well as in another letter from Bannum (*ARM* 26.6). The repetition of the phrase *lā šināti* alongside the other negative characterizations of Bannum's opponents (e.g. *daṣātum* [line 15], *lemuntum* [lines 32, 34, 68], ŠU-UḪ-ḪU [line 45, see below n. 12]) serve as points of comparison for Bannum's presentation of himself and others whom he trusted to be reliable (*taklūtum* [line 46]).

[5] For the term *un-qa-tim* (lines 7, 10), see the discussion *ARM*(*T*) 26/1:84.

[6] For the *sugāgum*, see A.3152+M.5665+ (4.51, n. 26).

[7] Cf. *FM* 7.38 (4.47, n. 3).

[8] "An Ekallatean" (DUMU *é-kál-la-tim*) was a designation used to for someone who was loyal to Ishme-Dagan, the son of Shamshi-Adad, after the latter's death (Guichard and Ziegler 2004:242–244).

Bel-shunu, your servant, take the position of majordomo – he is fat like a pig that you would slaughter[9] (and) no one will persuade you [about him].[10]
(Lines 28–52) Asqudum, (who is) my captive,[11] harbors malice in his heart. You should appoint servants to official positions who will not displease my lord, himself, or the Simal. Know that that man's motivation is evil and (that) he speaks libel to my lord with wicked intentions. He has appointed former servants of Ishme-Dagan to official positions. Ishme-Dagan will hear this news and be very pleased, (thinking): "My former servants [hold] offices and will a[ct] to return this land (to me) – I do not (need to) spend (even) one morsel of bread!" My lord should ⸢not⸣ co[nsent to] the word of that man because that man will not [*hesitate*] to obstruct the palace. My lord must not depend on that man; he is disloyal.[12,b] Trustworthy diviners are in the service of my lord. Those men are Simalites; they are devoted to my lord, alone. Let my lord have that man sent to me. If not, I will bring Asqudum's household and Hali-hadun's household into the palace.[13] Let that man arrive quickly!
(Lines 53–58) Additionally, when my lord left Saggaratum, (Asqudum) said to you: "I am ill. Without a trusted person, the possessions of my lord are delayed in Saggaratum."[14] What possessions were left on that day for a lack of porters?
(Lines 59–70) On another matter, is it appropriate that Sumu-hadum[15] wrote to my lord, saying: "I intercepted the tablets of Shamshi-Adad?" Who is this [mess]enger of his who intercepted [thos]e tablets and conducted (them) to me? And to whom, (then), did I not give [a reward]? The messengers of S[umu-hadu]m did [not ac]quire those [table]ts and so [I did not give] them a reward. If a defeat [...], if yes [...]. Know that this man [spoke e]vil [and] libelous [words] to my lord. My lord should [know]!
(Lines 71–76) Finally, they indeed hid the 200 sheep of Zu-Hadnim which they con[veyed] to you in the evening.[c] I, (however), seized those sheep. I will guard them until you arrive here. You will hear (more) about those sheep when you arrive.

b 2 Sam 3:6–27
c 1 Sam 15:9–15

[9] According to Bannum, it seems that Bel-shunu's being "fat like a pig" qualified him for the office of majordomo (*abūt bītim*). It may be that the characterization of Bel-shunu as *kabārum* ("to be fat") was meant to convey that he was a strong candidate for the position.

[10] The phrase in line 26, *ma-am-ma-an qa-at-ka la i-ṣa-ab-ba-tu-*[*šu-um*], may be literally translated "... no one will seize your hand [for him]." Bannum may be indicating that the king would not need to offer any political favors in return for securing Bel-shunu's appointment (see previous note).

[11] The phrase in line 28, *kišid qātīya*, literally means "the acquisition of my hand" and seems to evoke the image of taking captives in warfare (see *ARM*(*T*) 26/1:85, which compares the letter *ARM* 26.408). It should be noted in the context of *ARM* 26.5 (4.55), however, that it does not seem that Bannum was claiming that Asqudum was a prisoner under his immediate supervision, for later in the letter (lines 49–52) he requested that the king send Asqudum to him.

[12] Durand notes that the reading of the signs ŠU, UḪ, and ḪU in line 45 are epigraphically certain (*ARM*(*T*) 26/1:85). Morphologically, however, the form is unclear. The contextual meaning is plainly negative, hence Durand translated this word "fondamentalement hostile;" my translation "disloyal" is merely a guess based upon the context, in particular the word's juxtaposition with *taklum* ("trustworthy").

[13] For Hali-hadun, see *ARM* 10.157 (4.64). For the inventorying of officials' households at Mari, see van Koppen 2002.

[14] The quotation of Asqudum is understood to continue from lines 54 through line 56 (*ARM*(*T*) 26/1:84). Accordingly, I understand that Bannum was questioning Asqudum's claim to be a reliable (*taklum*) servant of the king (cf. Heimpel 2003:178).

[15] Sumu-Hadu was a former functionary of Yasmah-Addu (see the introduction to *FM* 2.116 [4.60]).

REFERENCES

Text and Translations: *ARM* 26.5; Heimpel 2003:177–178.

ADVICE FOR THE KING ON INTERNATIONAL POLITICS AND THE MOBILE PASTORALISTS (A.1098) (4.56)

Adam E. Miglio

This letter, along with *ARM* 26.5 (4.55), is an important source for understanding Bannum[1] and his role during the early reign of Zimri-Lim. In this missive,[2] Bannum advised Zimri-Lim about how to negotiate his relationship with the kings of Ida-maraṣ, citing the precedent of Yahdun-Lim, Zimri-Lim's father. He also counseled Zimri-Lim about his campaign to Kahat, a city located along the southern reaches of the Jaghjagh River in the upper Habur. Kahat was a strategic city to which Shamshi-Adad's harem had fled after he died. Lastly, Bannum instructed Zimri-Lim how to deal with the mobile pastoralists' concern regarding Bannum's absence from their encampments (*nawûm*) in the steppe.

[1] For Bannum, see the introduction to *ARM* 26.5 (4.55).

[2] This letter has not been fully edited; the first nineteen lines, several lines at the end of the obverse and beginning of the reverse as well as the concluding lines of the tablet have not been published.

(Lines 20–30) (Bannum wrote): Dwell in the land of Musilan[3] along with your main troops. Also, write to the fathers[4] of Ida-maraṣ and to [Aduna]-Addu[5] so that they come before you; conclude a treaty[6] and speak forthrightly with them! Put their men at your disposal and establish your (mobile pastoralist) encampments[7] in their districts. Let your messengers be continually before Aduna-Addu. Previously, when Yahdun-Lim went to that land, he offered gifts to the fathers of Ida-maraṣ. His (mobile pastoralist) encampments (dwelt) in safety; there was neither dishonesty nor offence. Now you should do just as your father!

(Lines 31–38) Moreover, if you go to the fortresses that are constantly writing to you [and] have drawn near to Kahat[8] without (your) main troops and not having sworn a solemn oath by the gods, then Yarim-Addu has many brethren, who are loyal to him – (including) Ashmad[9] (who is) among the mobile pastoralists. (So) I hope that my lord's secret plan was not disclosed to Yarim-Addu and that that man will not carry out some malicious plan in the midst of the city. My lord's [secret plan] must be kept![a]

a 2 Sam 17:1–16

(Lines 6′–15′) And i[f] the mobile pastoralists have pressured you to appoint another *merḫûm*,[10] saying: "[S]ince Bannum, our *merḫûm*, is dwelling along the banks of the Euphrates, we will appoint another [*me*]*rḫûm*." You should respond to them [sa]ying, "Previously he stayed in (your) encampments where he secured the foundations of the Simal, Numha, (and) Yamut-bal.[11] Then, he went to the banks of the Euphrates, (where) he liberated fortresses and established your status along the banks of the Euphrates. Now because I had to quickly leave, I have left that man to maintain control of the fortresses along the banks of the Euphrates. Then, when I arrive (back at Mari), I will send your *merḫûm* to you." You should respond to them (with) this (message) ....

3 Musilan was situated in the western reaches of the Habur Triangle.

4 This designation as "fathers" evokes the standing of the kings relative to others in the system of international politics (cf. the introduction to *FM* 2.117 [4.59]).

5 Aduna-Addu was a king at the city of Hanzat, which was located in the region of the Balih River (cf. *FM* 6.5 [4.57]; *ARM* 2.131 [4.48, n. 3]).

6 The collocation "to kill a donkey" (*qaṭālum ḫârum*), which is used here in the text above, expressed the notion of concluding a treaty. The phrase described the ritual practice of slaughtering a donkey that accompanied the conclusion of a treaty. *ARM* 2.37, for example, records such a ritual: "I went to Ashlakka to kill the donkey (6) *a-na ḫa-a-ri-im qa-ṭá-li-im*) between the (Simal) mobile pastoralists and Ida-maraṣ. They brought me a puppy and a female goat, but out of respect for my lord I did not allow (the use of) a puppy or a female goat. (Instead) I had a foal, the son of a she-ass, slaughtered (11) [*ḫa*]*-a-ra-am* DUMU *a-ta-ni-im* 12) [*a*]*-na-ku ú-ša-aq-ṭì-il*); I established peace between the (Simal) mobile pastoralists and Ida-maraṣ."

7 The term *nawûm*, used here in line 25, seems to designate "(mobile pastoralist) encampments," as it does on numerous other occasions in the letters from Mari. Cf. line 29: "His (mobile pastoralist) encampments (dwelt) in safety" (*na-wu-šu ša-al-ma-at*) and in line 9′ "Previously he stayed in (your) encampments" (*pa-na-nu-um i-na na-wi-im ú-ši-ib-ma*); cf. also *FM* 6.5 (4.57, n. 9).

8 Kahat may be identified with Tell Barri (Wäfler 2001), although Guichard has suggested it should be found at Tall al-Hamidiya (Guichard 1994:244; followed by Durand 1997:51).

9 For Ashmad, see the introduction to *FM* 8.43 (4.54); Ashmad is also mentioned in A.3152+M.5665+ (4.51).

10 For the *merḫûm*, see the introduction to M.6060 (4.52).

11 This statement suggests that Bannum's oversight of mobile pastoralists in the steppe included populations not only from the Simal, but also from the Yamut-bal and Numha.

REFERENCES

Text: Charpin 1998: 100, n. 34; Villard 1994: 297, n. 33; Guichard 2014a: 112, n. 72

REPORT ON ZALMAQUM AND THE *ŠEPÂTUM* IN THE UPPER HABUR (*FM* 6.5) (4.57)

Adam E. Miglio

Zakura-Abum, a *merḫûm*,[1] sent this letter to Zimri-Lim. In his letter, Zakura-Abum informed the king about the conflict in Zalmaqum, in particular Aduna-Addu's victory at Hanzat. Additionally, Zakura-Abum reported on the *šepâtum*, which was an exchange between the mobile pastoralists (*ḫanûm*) and the settled populations in the upper Habur. The *šepâtum* seems to have been a provision of grain that the sedentary peoples of the upper Habur gave to the mobile pastoralists,[2] while the sedentary populations, in return, received livestock from the mobile pastoralists.[3]

1 See the introduction to M.6060 (4.52).

2 See further Guichard 2002:161–163.

3 Zakura-Abum continued to be involved with the *šepâtum* later in Zimri-Lim's reign, while he was located at the small polity of Zalluhan (see *ARM* 28.79; see further Guichard 2014b).

(Lines 1–4) Speak to my lord, Zimri-Lim: thus says Zakura-Abum, your servant.
(Lines 5–19) The mobile pastoralists are entirely your forces[4] and all of the mobile pastoralists are expectantly waiting for your arrival. Also, all of fortresses are continually writing to me: "Let our lord, [k]ing Zimri-Lim, come so that we may open up (our gates for him)."[a] I sent a complete report (about this matter) to you (via) Hatna-Ilu. You wrote to me: "Let the mobile pastoralists assemble before me." I, of course, went (to the meeting). My lord, (however), was delayed, so I had a tablet taken to Adal-shenni. Adal-shenni gave an honest answer to me about the *šepâtim* of the mobile pastoralists and the pasture, saying: "I am still accou[nt]able for the shortfall as it concerns the donkey-loading[5] and the sating of the mobile pastoralists." This is how Adal-shenni responded to me.[b]
(Lines 20–30) Now Nusugganu, the king of [Shinami], has [established] an order for his district: "No one should give grain for the *šepâtim* to the mobile pastoralists." The 3,000 equids for the mobile pastoralists have returned to me empty, reporting (that) Nusugganu, the king of Shinami, (complained): "Why is your lord constantly writing to Adal-Shenni, yet he has not written to me?" For this reason, he will not give the *šepâtim* to the mobile pastoralists.
(Lines 30–50) Moreover, Yapah-Addu[6] and Supri-erah went to Yarim-Lim, the man of Yamhad, and (to) Aplahanda of Carchemish. They took the lead of Yarim-Lim and Apla[hand]a along with their troops and (then) we[nt] to devour Zalmaqum and Aduna-Addu. Yarim-Lim and Ap[lahanda wrote to] Adal-shenni and Shipti-[ilu, then all of the mobile pastoralists] as[sembled] themselves [together]. I objected: "I cannot allow you [to leave] without my lord!" Now [Adun]a-Addu and Zalmaqum [dealt a de]feat to Yarim-Lim [and A]lpahanda. [*They*] *brou*[*ght*] *grain* [*to me*].[7] [When] they heard this [message], the mobile pastoralists who are stationed [here ass]embled [to go] to Mount Yamisim ....[8]
(Lines 60–70) Additionally, do [not be discouraged] about the defeat that Aduna-Addu and Zalmaqum dealt to Yarim-Lim and Aplahanda. Let my lord quickly come [and] advise the mobile pastoralists and its encampments.[9] [If my lord] is delayed, [then] let me go before the kings of Zalmaqum and I will advise the mobile pastoralists.

a Judg 9:3; 2 Sam 2:4; 2 Kgs 10:5

b 1 Sam 25:1–11

[4] This letter has several orthographic peculiarities. As a result, it is not easy to determine if the form *e-mu-ka* in line 5 should be understood as being derived from *emum*, "family," or *emūqum* "troops." If the former, line 5 could be translated, "The mobile pastoralists are the whole of your family (by marriage)" (Guichard 2002:122, 156–157). If the latter, the form would be an orthographic variant for *emūqum* (Durand 2004:186–187).

[5] The infinitive *wakāpum* is most likely related to the noun *ukāpum*, "a packsaddle" (Guichard 2002:124–125).

[6] The Yapah-Addu mentioned in this letter is probably the same person named in *ARM* 2.131 (4.48) (Guichard 2002:125).

[7] The clause in line 47 is badly damaged: [*ù šu-nu*] *še-e ub-ba-l*[*u*(?)-*nim*.

[8] Traces of nine fragmentary lines are preserved. Based upon the identifiable words or phrases in these lines, it seems that the same general topic of the letter continues: "[x x] message, which [x x] to my lord .... A word .... Grain for the mobile pastoralists .... A sacrifice .... The mobile pastoralists ... Isqa .... The mountain ...."

[9] The Akkadian translated "its encampments" is *na-we-šu*; cf. A.1098 (4.56, n. 7).

REFERENCES

Text: *FM* 6.5 (= Guichard 2002:121–125).

REQUEST FOR ZIMRI-LIM TO RECIPROCATE SUPPORT (*ARM* 28.77) (4.58)

Adam E. Miglio

This letter was written by Ibal-Addu to Zimri-Lim some time before the former's accession to the throne of Ashlakka.[1] Ibal-Addu's missive provides an insight into the events that transpired in the aftermath of Shamshi-Adad's death, when the kingdom of Upper Mesopotamia collapsed. At that time numerous local dynasts reasserted their claims over their ancestral cities. Ibal-Addu's letter reveals how he had cooperated with Zimri-Lim in hopes that both would be able to reclaim their patrimonies in the wake of Shamshi-Adad's death. Yet Ibal-Addu complained that his support for Zimri-Lim had not been reciprocated.[2] In fact, other sources from Mari indicate that Ibal-Addu waited up to three years to claim the throne at Ashlakka.

[1] Kupper 2001.

[2] A situation similar to that of Ibal-Addu in this letter is recounted in *FM* 6.18, where a certain Sumu-Lanasi also recalled an agreement he had made to support Zimri-Lim's reconquest of Mari in return for assistance regaining his ancestral throne. Yet after Zimri-Lim had been enthroned, Sumu-Lanasi complained to the new king at Mari: "Certainly (it was the case that) when you, my lord, and I spoke in the garden with the man of Karkamiš at Muzu-L[im], our mat[ter] was decid[ed]. But n[ow], the god of your father made you ascend to your father's throne, but when I arrived to the house of [my] father, Yumraṣ-[El] was dwelli[ng] in my city" (*FM* 6.18:5–15).

(Lines 1–4) Speak to [my father,] Zimri-Lim: thus [says Iba]l-Addu, [*your son*].
(Lines 5–13) [I dispatched my companions while my father] stayed [at] Tuttul. [My father made] them [take up] weapons against Ishme-Dagan[3] and then had them go down to Mari. Now my father, himself, has capt[ured] the city of Mari! If it is acceptable to my fa[the]r, let my father rel[eas]e [those] men so that they may [bury] the bodies of those who have died.[a]
(Lines 14–25) As for those who are (still) alive, let my father [place] (them) under the authority of [PN] and Abi-sar, the commander. The men whom I se[nt] to my father are like me. But (if there is) (any) man that is under [my] auth[ority] who is otherwise – (who is) a hindrance[4] to my father – then let my father write [to me] so that I may discharge [him] (from duty). (Yet) have not these men (even) died for [your] renown and for all the land? Because of this, let my father repay to [me] this favor by releasing them (from their service). Do not detain them![5]
(Lines 26–32) Moreover, my father has defeated his enemy and ascended to the throne of his father. Yet as for me, I have still not ascended to the throne of my father. I am (merely) a commoner![6] Let my lord confer to me what he should confer to me! Now in my land the servants of my father are numerous ....[7]

a Gen 50:5; 1 Sam 31:11–13; 1 Kgs 11:15–16; Ps 79:3

3 Ishme-Dagan was the son of Shamsi-Adad and brother of Yasmah-Addu. After Shamshi-Adad's death, Ishme-Dagan ruled as king at Ekallatum (cf. *ARM* 1.3 [4.46]; *FM* 8.43 [4.54]; and *ARM* 26.5 [4.55]).
4 The word *ḫi-ki-it* in this context is understood as a construct form of a nominal that is derived from the verb *ḫakûm* "to wait, lie in wait" (cf. below *ARM* 28.95 [4.75, n. 7]).
5 It was customary for allied kings to entrust troops into one another's care (cf. *ARM* 28.95:43–64 [4.75]).
6 Many kings bore the designation "the man (LÚ/*awīlum*) of GN." By comparison, Ibal-Addu asserted that he was merely a commoner (*muškēnum*).
7 There are traces of six fragmentary lines.

REFERENCES

Text: *ARM* 28.77.

INFORMATION FOR ZIMRI-LIM REGARDING DIPLOMACY AND INTERNATIONAL POLITICS (*FM* 2.117) (4.59)

Adam E. Miglio

International politics were customarily framed using household language. For example, the relationship of 'father-son' expressed a political hierarchy between two kings, in which the 'father' was the king of higher standing. Alternately, if two kings shared the status of 'brothers,' they were acknowledging their equality as sovereigns.[1] In this letter Ishhi-madar, an official of Zimri-Lim, advised the king at Mari on international politics. For Ishhi-madar, it seems that the statuses of Zimri-Lim vis à vis two kings – Hammu-rabi of Babylon and Simah-ilane, the king of the Numha polity centered at Kurda – were intertwined. This letter affords a glimpse into the complex and dynamic international 'system' during Zimri-Lim's reign.

(Lines 1–4) Speak to my lord: thus says Ishhi-madar, your servant.
(Lines 5–26) When we arrived at Mari with our lord [x x x x], we discussed the matter of Simah-ilane with our lord, saying: "Let our lord attempt to have Simah-ilane go out (from) the place where he is staying, so that our lord may create an indivisible bond between the Simal and the Numha.[2] As soon as our lord makes Simah-ilane leave, (our lord) should write to Hammu-

1 See Lafont 2001.
2 The clause in lines 12–15 may be rendered, "Let our lord make the Simal and Numha into a single finger that cannot be separated" (12) DUMU *si-ma*(!)*-le-em ù* DUMU *nu-ma-ḫa-a* 13) *a-na ú-ba-nim iš-te-et* 14) *ša a-na ša-ta-qi-im la i-re-ed-du-ú* 15) *be-el-ni li-te-er*). The phrase "a single finger that cannot be separated" was used in the letters from Mari to express political solidarity (see Lafont 2001:259).

rabi (of Babylon) as (his) son." My lord heeded the advice of his servants: he wrote to Hammu-rabi (of Babylon) as (his) son and made Simah-ilane leave (the place where he was staying). And when my lord wrot[e to Hammu-rabi, he] did not [object to you] writing as a son.[3] My lord [should know] this!
(Lines 27–42) Now concerning the fact that [Simah-ilane] has not w[ritten] my lord as s[on] [but has addressed my lo]rd as a brother, the *sugāgū*[4] and [the elders] of the Numha[a] w[ent and] adv[ised] Simah-ilane, saying: "Why should you write to Zimri-Lim as son? Just as Ashtamar-Addu regularly wrote to Yahdun-Lim as brother, you also should typically write to Zimri-Lim as a brother."[5] Simah-ilane wrote to my lord as (his) brother in keeping with the counsel from the *sugāgū* and elders of the Numha. Our lord should not harbor any anger against us because of this.
(Lines 43–51) Additionally, concerning the delegation led by Asqur-Addu, those men were imprisoned upon [their] arrival because my lord discussed [the matter with Simah]-ilane. [Now that] they have been imprisoned, when will they be released? [O]n account of (the situation with) those men, we are not (even) able to speak to the *land*.[6] The situation is insulting!
(Lines 52–56) When my lord has an audience with Simah-ilane, let my lord inquire about these men. Simah-ilane must not detain them! Let my lord seriously consider this tablet of mine.

a 2 Sam 10:3–5; 16:20–23; 1 Kgs 2:13–25; 12:6; Esth 1:13–14

3 The translation above is based upon the following restoration of lines 22–25: 22) *ù i-nu-ma* [*a-na ḫa-mu-ra-bi*] 23) *be-lí iš-pu-r*[*a-am*] 24) *ma-ru-tam ša-pa-*[*ru-um*] 25) *mi-im-ma ú-*[*ul iq-bi-kum*]. If correct, it would seem to be that Ishhi-madar wanted the king of Mari to secure the loyalty of Simah-ilane so that he could write to Hammu-rabi of Babylon as a son. It is notable that concern for Zimri-Lim's status relative to Hammu-rabi of Babylon was a topic for consideration some years later in the letter A.2968:3–15, when Zimri-Lim's status before Hammu-rabi was again connected with his standing vis à vis the kings in the upper Jezirah. A.2968 was a report from Itur-Asdu, whom Zimri-Lim had sent on a diplomatic mission to Hammu-rabi of Babylon. Itur-Asdu wrote: "I led my lord's (diplomatic) mission and I safely delivered the audience-gift to Hammu-rabi (of Babylon with) which my lord commissioned me. On the first day, when I [enter]ed into Babylon, I did not have an audience with Hammu-rabi. On the second day, early in the morning, I le[d] the messengers of the man of Turukku and (other) allies who accompanied me (on) the expedition and I went to the palace-gate to give the content of my mission. When I arrived, the mi[nister] of foreign (affairs for Hammu-rabi of Babylon) came out of the palace before me. He as[k]ed me (the following based) upon a written message from his lord: '[Whom] do I greet first, you or the man of Turukku?' As for me, I was annoyed and I answered him, saying: 'Do you consider the man of Turukku to be equal to my lord? I, myself, led the Turukku and the allied messengers and conducted them here! They have come by the written order of [my lord]!' Then, he (i.e. the minister of foreign affairs for Hammu-rabi) asked me 'Why do the kings of [the land] of Shubartum continually write as 'brothers' to your lord and (why) are they not writing as sons?'" (Guichard 2004a:16–22). At the same time, a different solution to lines 21–25 of the letter above has been offered by Lafont, who translated: "Il a fait sortir Simah-ilane, mais (après cela), lorsque mon seigneur a écrit à Hammu-rabi, il ne s' est plus jamais adressé à lui en tant que fils" (*FM* 2.117 [4.59]: 21) [^{m}]*si-ma-aḫ-i-la-a-né-e* ⸢*ú-še-ṣi*⸣ 22) *ù i-nu-ma* [*a-na ḫa-mu-ra-bi*] 23) *be-lí iš-pu-r*[*a-am*] 24) *ma-ru-tam ša-pa-*[*ru-um-ma*] 25) *mi-im-ma ú-*[*ul iš-pu-ra-aš-šum*; Lafont 1994:211).

4 For the *sugāgum*, see A.3152+M.5665+ (4.51, n. 26).

5 Ashtamar-Addu was the king at Kurda prior to Simah-ilane. It is noteworthy that one extant letter from Simah-ilane to the king of Mari, Zimri-Lim, addressed him as 'brother' (*ARM* 28.162). As for other kings of Kurda that came after Simah-ilane, they wrote to Zimri-Lim as 'brother,' 'servant' (Bunu-Eshtar in *ARM* 28.164, 165) and 'son' (Hammu-rabi in *ARM* 28.166).

6 Lafont read *ma*?-*tim*^{KI} and indicated in the hand copy that the *ma*-sign was effaced (Lafont 1994:210, 212).

REFERENCES

Text: *FM* 2.117 (= Lafont 1994:210–213).

COUNSEL FOR ZIMRI-LIM ABOUT PREPARATIONS FOR CAMPAIGN (*FM* 2.116) (4.60)

Adam E. Miglio

Sumu-hadu was a governor (*šāpiṭum*) who had served during the reign of Yasmah-Addu. After Yasmah-Addu's reign was over, however, Sumu-hadu swore a loyalty oath to Zimri-Lim, the new king at Mari.[1] In this letter, Sumu-hadu wrote to Zimri-Lim about preparing for a campaign to Shubat-Enlil, the capital where Shamshi-Adad had resided. According to Sumu-hadu, Turum-natki, the king of Apum, supported Zimri-Lim's campaign (cf. *ARM* 10.5 [4.61]). Sumu-hadu planned to have the mobile pastoralists from the Yamina assemble with him, whereas the king was encouraged to have the mobile pastoralists from the Simal to rally to him. Moreover, Sumu-hadu advised that Zimri-Lim should garner support from Qarni-Lim, the Yamut-bal king at Andarig, and Simah-ilane, the Numha king at Kurda, before campaigning to Shubat-Enlil.

1 For an oath sworn by Sumu-hadu to Zimri-Lim, see Durand 1991:26–28; also, Lion 2001:176–177 (cf. the oath M.6060 [4.52]).

(Lines 1–2) Speak [to] my lord: thus (says) Sumu-hadu, your servant.

(Lines 3–27) I heard [the tablet of] my lord and the tablet of Turum-natki[2] [that my lord] sent to me. [When] I heard these [tab]lets, I dictated a tablet and then sent (it) [to] Iṣi-Epuk and Yashub-Dagan, whom my lord *commissioned*[3] among the mobile pastoralists of the Yamina[4] with returning sheep from the open country. I (said to them): "My lord's tablet reached me (while) on a journey (and) the message of my lord's tablet was this: 'Let the *sugāgū*[5] and the elders of Mutebal know (that) Turum-natki and the men dwelling at Shubat-Enlil are continually writing to me, your lord, to liberate the city of Shubat-Enlil, saying: "Come, seize this city and take its silver, its gold, and its plunder!" Now you certainly know that the treasures of Shamshi-Adad are inside that city! Go with your lord on this campaign, along with your brothers the Simal, so that the one who does not have a slave may acquire for himself a slave, the one who does not have a female slave may acquire for himself a female slave, and the one who does not have a donkey may acquire for himself a donkey.[a] Savor the plunder and establish the renown of your lord! They should heed th[is message].' You (i.e. Iṣi-Epuk and Yashub-Dagan) should bring the *sugāgū* and elders [to Dur Yahdu]n-Lim,[6] before my lord so that my lord can assure them and take action concerning the campaign (to Shubat-Enlil)." I [dutifu]lly dictated the letter and [sent it] to [them].

(Lines 27–37) Previously they (i.e. Iṣi-Epuk and Yasub-Dagan) said to me: "[…] of our lord […] of ourselves […] and [we kissed] the feet of our lord." Now let [my lord] delay the journey [to] Shubat-Enlil [until the en]d of this month. [x x x so that] the Yamina may [re]turn to my lord, kiss the feet of my lord and so that my lord may appease them. Let the canal work be supervised!

(Lines 37–47) Now regarding the plan of raiding the land about which my lord wrote to the Simal mobile pastoralists – let th(ose) mobile pastoralists arrive and let that plan [be considered]! The Simal mobile pastoralists will certainly gather there before my lord and the Yamina mobile pastoralists should gather here. Moreover, my lord will command any regular conscripts of the Yamina from the banks of the Euphrates that I prepare (for the campaign).[7] I am reviewing the matter of the troops so that my lord will go with a well-prepared army, will establish renown for himself, and will take for himself the valuables of that city, (especially) the treasures of Shamshi-Adad. Let my lord delay (just) this month!

(Lines 47–60) Additionally, if Qarni-Lim and Simah-ilane are not speaking honestly with my lord, my lord should send [a tablet] to both of [them] while my lord is preparing for the campaign he will go on and (from which) he will bring back the valuables of that city for [himself]. Then, they will join with my lord in [this] matter. Otherwise, they [will hear] about it after[wards] and they will [not fo]llow my lord with [their] troops. Moreover, they will trouble my lord, ally with [the man of Esh]nunna against us, or make [unreason]able demands of us. Therefore, wri[te] (about) their involvement now, and afterwards they will follow my lord with their troops. Then, my lord will approach Shubat-Enlil as a great leader.

a Num 31:9–11; Deut 2:35; Judg 5:30

2 Turum-natki is elsewhere attested as the king of Apum (e.g. *ARM* 10.5 [4.61]). In *FM* 2.116 (4.60), Turum-natki's name is misspelled ˹*tu*˺-*rum-na-ak-te*; this is just one of several scribal errors that may be found in this letter (e.g. line 3 [*ṭup-pí b*]*e-lí*⟨*-ia*⟩; line 11 *li-*⟨*iš-*⟩*mu-ú*; line 13 *k*]*a*⟨*-ia*⟩*-an-tam*; line 38 *iš-pu-*⟨*ra*⟩*-*˹*ru*˺; line 41 *an-*⟨*na-*⟩*nu-um*; line 48 *i-*⟨*ša*⟩*-ri-iš*).

3 The verbal form in line 8 is not certain. Epigraphically, Eidem commented that the AK and LA signs were fairly clear (Eidem 1994:208). Given that the text has other scribal mistakes (see the previous note), the translation above follows the emendation proposed by Eidem 1994:204, who suggested the reading ⟨*ú*⟩*-*˺*t*[*a(?)-a*]*k*⟨*-ki*⟩*-la-šu-nu-ti*.

4 Sumu-hadu was careful to distinguish the tribal identity of the mobile pastoralists (*ḫanûm*) that he wrote about. By comparison, often times the designation *ḫanûm* was used as shorthand to refer to the Simal mobile pastoralists in the letters from Mari, especially when it was used by a *merḫûm* who served among the Simal mobile pastoralists (cf. *ARM* 28.95 [4.75, n. 2]) or the king, Zimri-Lim, who also belong to the Simal tribe.

5 For the *sugāgum*, see A.3152+M.5665+ (4.51, n. 26).

6 Dur Yahdun-Lim was located upstream from Mari, perhaps at Deir ez-Zor. The importance of the city is evinced not only by Yahdun-Lim's building inscription (RIME 4 E4.6.8,1) but by the inscription of a governor (*šaknum*) at Terqa (RIME 4 E4.6.11.2001) who identified Yasmah-Addu as the "king (LUGAL) of Dur Yasmah-Addu," (i.e. Dur Yahdun-Lim).

7 Cf. A.3152+M.5665+ (4.51).

REFERENCES

Text: *FM* 2.116 (= Eidem 1994:204–208).

SHIMATUM INFORMED ZIMRI-LIM ABOUT HER HUSBAND'S POLITICAL ACTIVITIES (*ARM* 10.5) (4.61)

Adam E. Miglio

Shimatum was Zimri-Lim's daughter, whom he had married to Haya-Sumu, the king of Ilan-ṣura. In this letter, Shimatum wrote to her father about the activities of her husband, Haya-Sumu. According to Shimatum, Haya-Sumu planned to capture Shubat-Enlil, the former capital of Shamshi-Adad. Shimatum recounted events similar to those found in Sumu-hadu's letter above (*FM* 2.116 [4.60]), although she seems to indicate that Haya-Sumu and Turum-natki had joined together in a political alliance. In addition to the political information provided by Shimatum, her more personal tone toward her father at the end of her missive is noteworthy. In her concluding remarks, Shimatum stated Zimri-Lim's importance to her in patrimonial terms. For Shimatum, Zimri-Lim was her caretaker *par excellence*, as if he was both her father and brother. A similar sentiment may also be noted in other letters that Shimatum and her sisters sent to their father in which Zimri-Lim was addressed as 'my star,' a term of reverent endearment.[1]

(Lines 1–2) Sp[eak] to my lord: thus says Shimatum, your servant.

(Lines 3–23) Concerning the message that my lord w[ro]te to me about Simah-ilane,[2] the man of the Numha – Simah-ilane, went to enter Shubat-Enlil. Then, Turum-natki[3] and Haya-sumu combined their troops and they sent him along with their army's main contingent. Haya-Sumu and Turum-natki swore an oath by the gods with one another and they assembled their troops (together). Previously, Turum-natki had committed an offense and was [hosti]le toward Haya-Sumu. Now by my lord's command,[4] [Haya-S]umu has reached an [ag]reement with Turum-natki and th[ey] (act) in [solida]rity; they are going on a campaign to Shubat-Enlil! [N]ow Haya-Sumu t[ook] payment from Samiya[5] and he [se]nt a scouting expedition to Shubat-Enlil.

(Lines 24–31) Additionally, my lord's command has not been disregarded.[6] Concerning the me[ssa]ge of Maṣi-El about whom my lord se[n]t to me, sayi[ng] "Let the men have him draw near to Shubat-Enlil," trusted men had him approach Shubat-Enlil. Now the man is the subject of questions[7]; he has entered, though he has not yet come out (of the city).

(Lines 32–40) Furthermore, my [hear]t was anxious because (after I had written to you) once (or) twice I did not hear news from my lord. Now my heart is [exceeding]ly overjoyed to hear from my lord! For to [wh]om else could I [lo]ok apart from my lord? You are a father and brother to me.[a]

[a] 1 Sam 13

1 This letter contains several scribal errors (e.g. see n. 4 below) as well as several linguistic peculiarities, which have led to speculation that Shimatum may have written the letter herself (see Durand 2000:433).

2 In line 5 Simah-ilane's name is spelled *si-ma-i-la-ḫa-ni-e-em* (see Streck 2013, who has analyzed it as meaning "listen, Oh God, to the humble;" cf. Durand 2000:433, n. b).

3 For Turum-natki, see the introduction to *FM* 2.116 above.

4 Following Durand's suggestion, I have supplied the preposition *ina* in line 15: *i-na-an-na* ⟨*i-na*⟩ *qa-bé-e be-lí-ia-ma* (Durand 2000:433, n. f).

5 Samiya was a former functionary of Shamshi-Adad who continued to exercise authority at Shubat-Enlil after Shamshi-Adad had died.

6 The expression *wu-ú-ur-ti be-li-i[a]a-na qa-qa-ri-im ú-ul im-qú-ut* is unusual in Akkadian and may be literally translated, "My lord's command has not fallen to the ground." At the same time, it is reminiscent of the expression found, for example, in 1 Sam 3:19 or Isa 55:11 (cf. *ARM* 2.131 [4.48, n. 4).

7 The form *šu-úl* is understood as a D-stem from the verb *šâlum*, "to ask" (Durand 2000:133–134).

REFERENCES

Text and Collations: *ARM* 10.5; Durand 2000:431–434 (= LAPO 1222).

IMPORTANT INFORMATION ABOUT BUNU-ESHTAR RELAYED TO THE PALACE (A.1215) (4.62)

Adam E. Miglio

Yassi-Dagan, a military commander of Zimri-Lim (cf. A.1025 [4.65] and *ARM* 2.130 [4.67]), sent this message to Sammetar, a functionary that resided at Mari while the king was away from the city. Yassi-Dagan was primarily concerned with the conduct of Bunu-Eshtar, a member of the Numha, who had aspirations to be the king at Kurda (cf. *FM* 2.117 [4.59]; *FM* 2.116 [4.60]; and *ARM* 10.5 [4.61]). He recounted Bunu-Eshtar's self-described plight in exile during Shamshi-Adad's reign as well as Bunu-Eshtar's insistence that he receive support from the *merḫûm*[1] and other elites (*wēdûtum*) for his installation as king. Yassi-Dagan's letter provides remarkable insight into the practice of harboring elite refugees who aspired to kingship (*kaltū*).[2] These refugees made claims to kingship and, therefore, were supported as rivals to enthroned dynasts. In this letter it is striking that Bunu-Eshtar had written thinly veiled threats about someone named Yamṣi-malik, whom Bunu-Eshtar was harboring as a possible rival to Zimri-Lim. Historically, it should be noted that Bunu-Eshtar succeeded in securing the throne at Kurda for several years.

(Lines 1–2) Speak to [Sammetar]:[3] thus says [Yassi]-Dagan.

(Lines 3–10) I heard [the tablet that you sent] to me. As for (the possibility of) Yatar-[kabkab][4] or [Yamṣi]-Addu residing in the city of Nahur (about) which you wrot[e to me, the king] has not yet install[led] anyone for [that] city. The king's departure has been del[ayed]. Itur-Asdu[5] has been mentioned, but as of yet has not been installed. Now have Yatar-kabkab or Yam[ṣi-Ad]du come to that city just as you wrote [to me].

(Lines 11–32) Another thing, Bunu-[Eshtar de]vised and dictated a tablet for me and then sent (it) to me. On this tablet it was written: "Speak to Yassi-Dagan: thus says [Bunu-Eshtar]. Previously when I resided in Zalbar, Shamshi-Adad wrote to the ki[ng] of Zalbar about my return. The king of Zalbar,[6] (however), devised (a plan in which) instead of me he turned over some man (who was) ready and willing, (who) said 'here I am.'[a] Aminum (then,) returned that man as (if he was) me and Shamshi-[Adad kill]ed that man. So as for me, the kin[g of] Zal[bar saved my life]! Since I left Zalbar I have resided at Kurda. Now is this truly proper that Zimri-Lim ascended to the throne of my father without a share in an inheritance, while I am a vagabond? Call in the *merḫûm* and the servants of the elites so that they can make me ascend to the throne of my father." This is what Bunu-Eshtar devised and wrote to me.

(Lines 33–40) He devised thi[s message] and [sent] the tablet [to me] because his servants reported to him that when he writes something unacceptable to the king (of Mari) I refute (it) before the king. I have heard that [table]t and I have presented an answer to his [mes]sage before the king (of Mari). My lord heard that tablet and the king set the message (of Bunu-Eshtar) before the *sugāgū*.[7]

(Lines 40–52) Additionally, Bunu-Eshtar wrote to the king (of Mari): "Yamṣi-Malik, the son of Abi-Madar is staying with me." Then, the king replied to him: "Is this proper[8] that you are ra[ising up] Yamṣi-Malik, my servant, [to] support[9] (him) as my *kaltum*. Now as for me, I have not raised your *kaltum* against you, a son of Dairum, [your servant], who is staying with me even now. You should do [just as K]azallu(k) and block [*the sour*]*ce* of the spring!"[10] At length, the king wrote this and more [to him].

(Lines 52–55) In the gate of the pa[lace it is well]! May the wellbeing of the district, your complete [report], and your tablets continually be before the king!

a Gen 22:1, 11; 31:11; 46:2; Exod 3:4; 1 Sam 3:1–10; Isa 6:8

1 For the *merḫûm*, see the introduction to M.6060 (4.52).

2 This word is known, to date, only from the palace archive at Mari where it is most often spelled with an i-vowel (e.g. *ki-il-ti* in *ARM* 28.115 [4.69]). A plausible origin for this word is the West-Semitic root *qlṭ*, where the cognate verbal form in Aramaic connotes receiving or harboring a refugee and the Hebrew nominal form *miqlāṭ* designates a refuge or place of asylum (cf. Durand 2004:183, n. 388).

3 Charpin and Durand have discussed the firm basis for the restoration of Sammetar as the recipient of this letter (Charpin and Durand 2004:104).

4 For Yatar-kabkab, see A.2988+ (4.53).

5 Itur-Asdu (alternately Yatur-Asdu) was an important official, who was eventually installed by Zimri-Lim as a local authority at the city of Nahur (cf. *ARM* 28.51 [4.68] and *ARM* 28.115 [4.69]).

6 The GN in line 18 is spelled *za-ar-ba-al*⌜KI⌝; cf. *za-al-ba-ar*KI (lines 16, 17, 24).

7 For the *sugāgum*, see A.3152+M.5665+ (4.51, n. 26).

8 This phrase echoes the loaded question of Bunu-Eshtar, which Yassi-Dagan reported earlier in the letter: "Is this truly proper that Zimri-Lim ascended to the throne of my father without a share in an inheritance …?" (in lines 26–27).

9 See *ARM(T)* 28: 209.

10 The saying in lines 48–50, while fragmentary and somewhat abstruse, seems to be a proverbial expression that encouraged dealing with the problem at its source (49) [*me-eḫ-re/re-še-et-*]*-e-et i-ni-im mu-ul-li-*[*e-em-ma*]; 50) [*ki-ma k*]*a-sa-lu-uk*KI *te-te-ne-ep-p*[*é-eš*]). For the spelling of the city of Kazallu(k), cf. *ARM* 26.365.

REFERENCES

Text: Charpin and Durand 2004:99–115.

UPDATE FOR THE KING ABOUT EVENTS DURING THE WAR WITH ESHNUNNA (A.1610+) (4.63)

Adam E. Miglio

Ibal-pi-El, a *merḫûm*,[1] wrote this letter to Zimri-Lim during the war against Eshnunna. He informed Zimri-Lim that the forces of several kings from the upper Habur as well as the troops of the mobile pastoralists (*ḫanûm*) had joined together and that they were ready for Zimri-Lim to lead them. Ibal-pi-El also reported on hostilities at the city of Talhayum, in the western reaches of the upper Habur. Talhayum was closely connected with the Simal, as was indicated by a later king of Talhayum, Yawi-Ili. Yawi-Ili recalled the Simal's relationship with the city: "Previously during the reign of your father, Yahdun-Lim, we turned over the land of Yapturum, a (capital) city of Talhayum, and its villages, to the Simal."[2] In this text (A.1610+), however, the king of Talhayum as well as several mobile pastoralists of the Simal were reported to have been killed as a result of an uprising instigated by persons from the land of Zalmaqum (cf. M.6009 [4.71]).

(Lines 1–3) Spe[ak] to my lord: thus says Ibal-pi-E[l], your servant.
(Lines 4–20) The kings of Ida-maraṣ, Haya-Sumu, Sammetar, Shub-ram, Ibal-Addu, Tamarzi, Hammi-kuna, Yamut-lim, Lime-Ad[du], and Zakura-abum have assembled [toget]her with [their] tro[ops] and the [tr]oops of the land of Apum. They have joined up with Qarni-Lim and the mobile pastoralists. The (very) day I sent this tablet to my lord the troops started out for Harbu of the Yamut-bal. Qarni-Lim and all of the kings of the land are awaiting the coming of my lord. The Simal and the troops are well.
(Lines 21–42) Moreover, the king has written to me two or three times since last year, to dispatch troops to Hammi-epuh, the king of Talhayum. I consulted with the *sugāgū*,[3] the servants of my lord, about the dispatching of troops and have not sent troops. Thereafter, my lord com[posed a firmly] (worded) tablet and [my lord] wrote (that I should) [dispatch] 30 troops. [The tablet of my lord reached] me at Hamadanim. Because I was encamped before the enemy, I set apart 20 troops and sent (them) to Talhayum. (The land of) Zalmaqum heard about [th]ose tr[oops e]ntering (into Talhayum) and it assembled. It stationed (itself) at the gate of Talhayum and an uprising took place inside the city. They killed their king![4] Now Nuhmuna-Addu, a man of Ibal-ahu, was a witness and Hali-hadun[5] (was) [his] witness[a] as well as 30 mobile pastoralists (along with them).
(Lines 43–49) They have cut off the head of their [kin]g and the heads of (30 mobile pastoralists)[6] [and] sent (them) [t]o Shubat-Shamash.[7] They also killed the 20 mobile pastoralists whom I dispatched. My lord should know this!

a Deut 19:15

1 For the *merḫûm*, see the introduction to M.6060 (4.52).
2 *ARM* 13.144:26–29.
3 For the *sugāgum*, see A.3152+M.5665+ (4.51, n. 26).
4 Hammi-epuh was the king of Talhayum who had been killed.
5 Ibal-pi-El, a *merḫûm*, likely mentioned Hali-hadun because he would have been seen by Zimri-Lim as a reliable witness (see *ARM* 10.157 [4.64]).
6 There is a near duplicate of this letter that was recovered from Mari (A.1212) as well as another fragmentary tablet that describe this event (A.1188; see Durand 1988:109–110). These additional sources seem to indicate that there was a total of 50 mobile pastoralist troops that were killed at Talhayum in this event (see Durand 1988:110).
7 Shubat-Shamash was an important center in Zalmaqum (see *ARM* 2.131 [4.48, n. 3]). Sending the heads of those who had been decapitated to Shubat-Shamash was an attempt by the populations from Zalmaqum to intimidate the city (cf. 2 Kgs 10:7–8).

REFERENCES

Text and Commentary: Durand 1988:108–110; 1998:266–268 (= LAPO 17 604).

A BRIEF REPORT TO THE QUEEN (*ARM* 10.157) (4.64)

Adam E. Miglio

Hali-hadun was a leader among the mobile pastoralists, perhaps even serving as *merḫûm* during the reign of Zimri-Lim.[1] He wrote this brief letter to Addu-duri, the queen mother at Mari, and reported that the king was still residing in the upper Habur at the time of his writing. Hali-hadun further indicated that he had been involved in the negotiations for peace between the Numha king Bunu-Eshtar and the Yamut-bal king, Qarni-Lim (cf. *FM* 2.116 [4.60]; A.1215

1 See Guichard 2002:155; for the role of the *merḫûm*, see the introduction to M.6060 (4.52).

[4.62]; A.1610+ [4.63]; A.1025 [4.65]; and *ARM* 2.130 [4.67]). The peace that Hali-hadun negotiated between Qarni-Lim and Bunu-Eshtar, however, did not last long and tensions between the Numha and Yamut-bal persisted on-and-off throughout the rest of Zimri-Lim's reign (e.g. *ARM* 2.130 [4.67]).

(Lines1–4) [S]peak [to] my [q]ueen, [Ad]du-du[ri]:[2] thus says Hali-hadun, your servant.
(Lines 5–17) Since I left you, I have not been idle. My lord is staying at Ashlakka, but he sent me to the district of the Numha and Yamut-bal. I [established] peace and well-be[ing] between [Bunu-Eshtar] and Qarni-Li[m, the Numha] and the Yamut-bal.[a] Rejoice!
(Lines 18–23) When I arrive safe and sound before you and have an audience with you, you will realize all that I have done and that I have not been idle.
(Lines 24–25) The king and the troops are well!

a 1 Kings 12

[2] Durand's collation has confirmed the recipient of the letter: *[a-na be-]el-ti-ia* [^{d}IŠK]UR-*d[u-ri]* (Durand 1998:277, n. 17).

REFERENCES

Text and Collations: *ARM* 10.157; Durand 2000:277 (= LAPO 1092).

LONG REPORT ON THE CRISIS AMONG THE KINGS IN THE UPPER JEZIRAH (A.1025) (4.65)

Adam E. Miglio

Yassi-Dagan, a military commander for Zimri-Lim, wrote this long letter to the king of Mari during the war with Eshnunna. Zimri-Lim had left the upper Habur in order to deal with insurrections along the banks of the Euphrates (cf. A.1215 [4.62] and *ARM* 2.130 [4.67]). Yet Yassi-Dagan candidly informed the king that his withdrawal to the banks of the Euphrates had fueled speculations and suspicions among the kings in the upper Habur. In particular, Yassi-Dagan named Sasiya, the king of Turukkum (cf. *ARM* 5.17 [4.49]), as someone who was encouraging distrust of Zimri-Lim. Sasiya emphasized that the withdrawal of the king from the upper Habur was suspicious. Sasiya, furthermore, called attention to the fact that Zimri-Lim had restored his relationship with Qarni-Lim, even after Qarni-Lim had switched his allegiance to the man of Eshnunna. Thus, according to Yassi-Dagan, Sasiya argued that Zimri-Lim's behavior was a likely indication that he had concluded peace with Eshnunna and that he had abandoned the kings in the Sinjar and the upper Habur in their fight against Eshnunna. At times in his letter, Yassi-Dagan himself seemed perplexed by the king's actions and at one point even indicated that these problems could have been addressed if Zimri-Lim had merely arranged for the mobile pastoralists (*ḫanûm*) to be in the region. Thus Yassi-Dagan urged the king to remedy the situation by having the *merḫûm* send mobile pastoralists to the region.

(Lines 1–2) Speak [to my lord]: thus says [Yassi-Dagan],[1] your servant.
(Lines 3–13) [Since] my lord has left for the [banks] of the Euphrates, allied kings [and] all of the [lan]d had (their opinion) formed against my lord and their sentiment has [sh]ifted! Previously, I discussed this matter with these kings, saying: "Indeed, my lord will take the lead of the mobile pastoralists. He will quickly come and tear the talon of Eshnunna out of this land and he will save it!"[a] This is what I said to them and I assuaged their fear. But when these kings heard that my lord went to the banks of the Euphrates, they were [di]stressed and their sentiment changed. (They said): "Where is your lord, the one who will come and save us and drive out Eshnunna? He has gone to the banks of the Euphrates!" This is what those kings discussed.
(Lines 13–27) Moreover, Sasiya circles about Hadnu-rabi and his land in order to destroy it and he has turned opinions against my lord. Now he discussed the matter with the kings, saying: "Where is Zimri-Lim, whom you seek out as your father and whom you follow after when he rides in the palanquin?[2] Why does he not come and save you?" This is what Sasiya said to Bunu-Eshtar, Hadnu-rabi, Sharrum-kima-kali, Zimriya and (other) [ki]ngs. And [they] do not pay close attention to the (disingenuous nature) of that man's message. It seems that he speaks to them with f[ul]l sincerity, but he is spinning lies. So they began to denounce my lord before Sasiya, (but) they did n[ot know] that he sp[oke] (to them) with false pretenses and that (he) was, (in fact,) at pe[ace] with Eshnunna. [Now] that man, (Sasiya), has as a complaint against my lord that my lord left for the banks of the Euphrates. (He is saying): "Zimri-Lim swore an oath by the god with Qarni-Lim and [the man] of Eshnunna. For this reason [he] has not come to us, but (instead)

a 1 Sam 11

[1] The expeditor of this letter may be confidently reconstructed on the basis of line 84.
[2] See Arkhipov 2010.

left and wen[t] to his land." (For) [t]hese, among others reasons, that man is opposed to my lord.

(Lines 27–33) C[alumny] is constantly being spread about my [lord]. Tablets from Zimri-L[im] repeatedly go [to] Shallurum,[3] saying: "Dra[w near] to your lord, [otherwise] I will go to my lord and [c]onfer with my lord, (the king of Eshnunna); my lord is the lord of their lord!" And these tablets are (also) going from Shallurum to Nidat-Sin, (who is) the overseer (of the troops of) Babylonia.

(Lines 33–40) Additionally, it was reported to me that my lord previously sent a herdsman[4] to Qarni-Lim and that the tablet which he carried contained the following (message): "Speak to Qarni-Lim: thus says Zimri-Lim. Regarding the secret message which I have sent to you (with this) herdsman, quickly take care of this matter!" They (i.e. the kings) heard that tablet and they started to become angry (with) my lord. It is as if my lord has made peace with Eshnunna; all the land is afraid.

(Lines 40–56) Next these kings went to Sasiya as did each contingent-leader throughout the land. And likewise, Yaphur-Lim, the contingent-leader who was with him, and I went along. They arrived before Sasiya, and Sasiya, ignoring all other matters,[5] further laid into my lord, saying: "What is this that Zimri-Lim has done? Last year he came up to the land[6] and the kings (of the land) accepted him as their father and leader. He gave troops to Hadnu-rabi; he took my cities, he plundered sheep and he left my land in ruins. Afterwards, the man of Eshnunna came up, but Zimri-Lim left and went to his land. He did not save you! Now he has returned and sworn an oath by the god with Qarni-Lim and the man of Eshnunna and has (once again) gone back to his land." Sasiya said this, among other things, and they (i.e. the other kings) complained against my lord.

(Lines 57–66) Also, they spoke to him about going to Karana, but he did not agree (to it), saying: "He is joined with Hadnu-rabi (with whom he has a) mutual aggression (pact).[7] So I will fight, (but) will not go to Karana! I will perform an extispicy here and if the omen is auspicious, I will fight with the man of Eshnunna. Alternately, if the omen is inauspicious, I will not fight but (instead) will write to Hammu-rabi so that supplemental troops come up from Babylon. Then, Zimri-Lim will arrive and we will fight." This is what that man discussed, but these words of his that he spoke are false pretenses; (he) is at peace with Eshnunna.

(Lines 67–71) At this time the kings and all of the land are infuriated with my lord. Bunu-Eshtar got up and spoke to Sasiya: "Zimri-Lim held back his good troops, but he sent to us the poor(ly provisioned) troops so that we will die with them!" Moreover, he repeatedly called the mobile pastoralists "*scavengers*."[8]

(Lines 72–83) The kings and all of the land are looking for my lord. (Yet) if only b[efore] my lord had decided to leave he had arranged for the mobile pastoralists, (who are) with my lord, to have come (here), then some time ago Eshnunna would have broken camp and this land would have returned (to follow) after my lord! Now let my lord confer with his servants and commission extispicies regarding his deliberations. And should the results of the extispicies about the arrival of my lord be favorable, let him come! Otherwise, let my lord write to the *merḫûm* so that the *merḫûm* can take the lead of 1000 or 2000 mobile pastoralists and come to us! (Then), [whe]n the days are pleasant and hand(s) are warm, let us fight with Eshnunna![b]

b 2 Sam 11:1

(Lines 84–93) [Now] do not let my lord say (to himself): "Yassi-Dagan, my servant, is [th]ere, (but) he is [not] sending to me everything [that] he hears!" An urgent message of everything I am hearing I am promptly wri[ting] to my lord. Now regarding Hadnu-rabi – [about] this (matter) my lord should not be worried! (Rather), my lord should be con-

3 Shallurum was an Eshnunnean military leader.

4 Yassi-Dagan indicated that a herdsman (*nāqidum*) carried the alleged message negotiating peace with Qarni-Lim and with the king of Eshnunna. This detail was probably not unrelated to the complaint later in the letter that the (Simal) mobile pastoralists were conspicuously absent from the region of the Habur Triangle or to Yassi-Dagan's insistence that the king have the *merḫûm* send troops of the mobile pastoralist. That is, the perception among the kings in the Habur 'Triangle' that the (Simal) mobile pastoralists and their troops had withdrawn because they had concluded peace with Qarni-Lim and the king of Eshnunna was likely reinforced by the fact that a herdsman (*nāqidum*) had been sent to Qarni-Lim.

5 This phrase may be translated, "leaving aside his right and his left" (*i-mi-it-ta-šu ù šu-mi-il-šu i-zi-ib-ma*).

6 Cf. *ARM* 5.17 (4.49, n. 3); M.6009 (4.71, n. 7).

7 The phrase *ú-ba-nim na-ḫi-ip-tim* ("an aggressive finger") describes Hadnu-rabi. The translation above takes into account the fact that at Mari a single finger was a symbol of solidary created through an alliance (see *FM* 2.117 [4.59, n. 2]). In the context of A.1025 (4.65), I have guessed that the phrase *ú-ba-nim na-ḫi-ip-tim* conveyed the idea that Hadnu-rabi had a mutual defense and/or aggression pact; thus Sasiya's response suggested that he wanted to avoid triggering a pact that would draw Eshnunna further into conflict with the kings of the region (for an example of a mutual aggression pact between Zimri-Lim and Hammu-rabi of Babylon, see Durand 1986). Yassi-Dagan, however, claimed that the real reason Sasiya did not want to trigger this mutual aggression pact was because he had already negotiated peace with Eshnunna.

8 The mobile pastoralists were designated "shredders" (*ṭà-ri-pu*, line 71), perhaps evoking the activities of wild predatory animals (cf. Hebrew *ṭérep, ṭ^{e}rēpā^{h}*). The translation "scavengers" is merely a suggestion based upon a comparison with the usage of the root in Hebrew and based upon the context of the letter. In Yassi-Dagan's letter, Bunu-Eshtar may be understood to be charging Zimri-Lim with withholding the mobile pastoralists only to have them return like scavengers once the local kings and their troops had been defeated by Eshnunna. This interpretation is congruent with Yassi-Dagan's subsequent reflections upon how Zimri-Lim should have arranged for the mobile pastoralists to been in the upper Habur earlier (see also Durand 1998:154).

cerned [about] the banks of the Euphrates! [It is out of] duty [I wrote] (all this) to my lord. Let my lord consider (the matter) and act [according to] his great royal status!

REFERENCES

Text and Collations: Kupper 1990; Durand 1998:146–154 (= LAPO 545).

ACCOUNT OF PROPHETIC RESPONSES TO THE CONFLICT WITH ESHNUNNA (*ARM* 26.199) (4.66)

Adam E. Miglio

Sammetar sent this letter to Zimri-Lim near the conclusion of the war with Eshnunna (cf. A.1610+ [4.63], *ARM* 10.157 [4.64], and A.1025 [4.65]). He hoped to convince the king of Mari that the peace that Eshnunna proposed was a ruse. Sammetar most likely opposed *détente* with the man of Eshnunna because he had a great deal to gain by the ongoing fighting with Eshnunna; he was a direct beneficiary of the nearby enemy lands that were recurrently robbed in the course of the war.[1] Thus Sammetar relayed prophetic messages and conversations with Lupahum, an *āpilum*-prophet of Dagan, and one message from a *qammātum*-prophetess that supported his position against Eshnunna. Sammetar's argument is well developed. He contended that Lupahum had always supported the war with Eshnunna (lines 5–28), that Lupahum had proved himself to be a credible prophet in the course of the war (lines 29–40), and that Lupahum's message had been confirmed by a *qammātum*-prophetess of Dagan (lines 41–57). Yet Sammetar's efforts to persuade the king to continue the war with Eshnunna seem to have failed, as Zimri-Lim concluded peace with Eshnunna not long after Sammetar sent this missive.

(Lines 1–4) Speak to my lord: thus says Sammetar, your servant.

(Lines 5–16) Lupahum, the *āpilum*-prophet of Dagan, arrived here from Tuttul. He conveyed the message that my lord charged him with (while he was) at Saggaratum, (saying): "Entrust me to Dagan." And they answered[2] him: "Everywhere you go, well-being will gr[e]et you. Battering ram and (siege)-tower will be given to you. They[3] will go at your side and be your support."[a] This is the response they gave him at Tuttul.

(Lines 16–28) When he arrived from Tuttul, I conducted[4] (him) to Der and he brought my bolt[5] to the goddess Deritum. Previously he had brought the standard[6] and said: "The standard is not fastened; water is flowing.[7] Strengthen the standard!" Now he has brought my bolt (and) thus it was written (on the bolt): "I hope you[8] do not trust in the peace of Eshnunna and let your guard down; be even more vigilant than before!"

(Lines 29–40) Moreover, he spoke to me: "I hope he will not swear a solemn oath with the man of [Esh]nunna without asking the god. (Rather, the king should do) just as (he did) previously when the Yamina came down to Saggaratum and dwelt (there), at which time I said to the king: 'Do not conclude a treaty[9] with the Yamina! I, (Dagan),

[a] 1 Kgs 22:1–28

[1] See further Durand 2012a, n. 29.

[2] The plural subject of the verb *i-pu-lu-šu* seems to be unnamed religious functionaries at Tuttul to whom Lupahum conveyed the king's message (Durand 2012a:259).

[3] It is not certain who or what is the implied subject of the verb *i-il-la-ku*. It may be that the subject is the "Battering ram and (siege)-tower," which will accompany Zimri-Lim in battle. Alternately, it may be referring to the gods who supported Zimri-Lim in battle (cf. A.3152+M5665 iii:37–38 [4.51]; Durand 2012a:259).

[4] The subject of the verbs in lines 17–22 has been understood in one of two ways. I have followed most translators, interpreting the initial form as a first-person singular verb: "I conducted (him)" (*ú-še-er-di-ma*, line 17). The subsequent forms, then, are treated as third-person forms: "he brought" (*ú-bi-il*, lines 18, 19, 22; *ARM*(*T*) 26/1: 427; Heimpel 2003:252–254; Nissinen 2003:30–32). According to this interpretation, an overarching interest of the letter is to establish Lupahum's consistency and credibility as an advisor in the war against Eshnunna. In this case, the missive seems to introduce the *āpilum*-prophet's message from Tuttul (lines 5–16) only to show his consistency by recounting the messages he gave at Der (lines 16–28). Thereafter, Sammetar reminded the king of Lupahum's track record in dealing with the conflict with the Yamina (lines 29–40) and provided confirmation of Lupahum's message by appealing to an outside source, a *qammātum*-prophetess (lines 41–57). More recently, however, Durand has suggested that all of these verbs should be understood as first-person singular forms, in which Sammetar is the subject of the verbal forms (Durand 2012a:260–261).

[5] Or "bolts."

[6] For the term translated "standard" (*šernum*), see Durand 2012a: 263–264.

[7] The image of flowing water is repeatedly used in this missive to symbolize military defeat (cf. also A.3080 [4.73]).

[8] The subject of this verb is feminine, which in the context is most likely the goddess Deritum.

[9] Cf. A.1098 (4.56, n. 6).

will drive them from the burrows of their lairs[10] and the River will finish them off for you.' [N]ow he should not swear a sol[em]n oath with the man of [Esh]nunna without asking the god." This is the message that Lupahum spoke to me.
(Lines 41–57) Two [d]ays later a *qammātum*-prophetess of Dagan at Ter[qa] came and spoke [to me, say]ing: "Beneath chaff water flo[ws]![11] They are continually writi[ng to you] (and) they are sending their gods [to you], but they are planning an act of deception in their hearts.[b] The king should not swear a solemn oath without consulting the god!" She requested a *laharum*-garment and a nose-ring, so I g[a]ve (them) to her. She delivered her instructions in the temple of Belet-Ekallim before the h[igh priestess, Ini]b-shina. I have sent to my lord a repor[t on the matter] which she spoke to me. Let my lord consider (it) so that he can act as the great sovereign (that he is).
(Lines 58–63) Lastly, I immediately sent Abi-Epuh (to find) Yanṣib-Dagan, the regular conscript from Dashran, (about) whom my lord wrote (with instructions) to cut off his head. That man was not found, so he put his household and his people in[to] slavery. The next day a tablet from Yasim-Dagan reached [me], saying: "That man has arrived here with me!" Let my lord write [to me] whether or not I should release his family.

b Jer 6:14; 8:11; Ezek 13:10

10 It may be that the signs ḪU BU UR RE E are a *purussûm*-noun (such as *ukullûm*, *rugummûm*) from the Akkadian verb *ḫepērum* ('to dig'). *Purussûm*-nouns from verbal roots often function as *nomina actionis* for typical or planned activities (GAG § 56o). The morphology, therefore, would convey a meaning such as "tunneling, burrowing" (cf. Arabic *ḥufra*, "hole, burrow"), which is the basis for the translation given above. While the noun *ḫupurrûm* is otherwise unattested, to my knowledge, it should be noted that this root might be attested elsewhere at Mari, designating digging implements (*ka-pa-ar-ra-tim*; see Durand 2005:12; cf. Durand 1998:153 n. x, which remarks on the spelling with *k* at Mari). Alternately, one may understand the signs HU BU UR RE E as two words: *hubur rê* and a resultant translation would be, "I will drive the shepherds of their clans into the Hubur ...." In the latter case, the Hubur is understood as the river of the underworld (see Charpin 2002:25; followed by Nissinen 2003 and Durand 2012a). Cf. A.3152+M5665 (4.51, n. 23).

11 This same message attributed to the *qammātum*-prophetess is recounted in two additional letters (*ARM* 26.197 and *ARM* 26.202); see the bibliography in Nissinen 2003:30.

REFERENCES

Text and Collations: *ARM* 26.199; Durand 2012a.

REPORT ON THE UPPER JEZIRAH IN THE AFTERMATH OF THE WAR WITH ESHNUNNA (*ARM* 2.130) (4.67)

Adam E. Miglio

Yassi-Dagan (cf. A.1215 [4.62] and A.1025 [4.65]) sent this letter to the king of Mari after the war with Eshnunna (cf. A.1610+ [4.63]; *ARM* 10.157 [4.64]; and A.1025 [4.65]; *ARM* 26.199 [4.66]). In his letter, Yassi-Dagan revealed that Bunu-Eshtar was quite sick. At the same time, however, Yassi-Dagan wanted to impress upon Zimri-Lim that Bunu-Eshtar was still actively instigating conflicts between the Numha and Yamut-bal. The struggle between Qarni-Lim, the Yamut-bal king at Andarig, and Bunu-Eshtar, the Numha king at Kurda, seems to have centered upon control of the city of Shubat-Enlil (cf. *FM* 2.116 [4.60]).

(Lines 1–2) Speak to my lord: thus says Yassi-Dagan, your servant.
(Lines 3–8) My lord is not paying (close enough) attention to the matter of Bunu-Eshtar! That man is like a broken down cart. He does not leave his house, yet he arrogates to himself greatness. He has offered his patronage and has won over all of the kings of the land of Ida-maraṣ to his side; now they follow after him![a]
(Lines 9–32) Qarni-Lim revealed his plan to proceed to Shubat-Enlil. [Bu]nu-Eshtar responded by dispatching Silillam[1] along with the troops of the Numha to (the city of) Kasapa against Qarni-Lim. Then, he wrote to the kings of the land of Ida-maraṣ and they have detained (any) Yamut-bal dwelling in their houses according to Bunu-Eshtar's command. Bunu-Eshtar heard that Qarni-Lim was staying at Andar[ig] and that we were passing by (the city). Then, he dispatched Saggar-abum along with his main troops to Kasapa. Moreover, Silillum was pursuing us with 1000 troops. Yet the protective spirit of my lord accompanied me and my lord's campaign was safe. I have entered Shubat-Enlil and have sent this tablet from Shubat-Enlil. My lord must not be caught off guard by Bunu-Eshtar's plans.[2]

a 2 Sam 15:5–6

1 Silillum was a military commander (GAL MAR.TU) under Bunu-Eshtar. Saggar-abum, who is mentioned just a few lines later, bore this same title at a later date, though perhaps he already had this role at the time of the writing of this letter (see Durand 1997:525–526).

2 Alternately, "My lord must not be caught off guard by Bunu-Eshtar's shrewdness" (31) *a-na ṭe₄-mi-it ša bu-nu-iš₈-tár*; Durand 1997:526).

(Lines 33–40) I heard about the census along the banks of the Euphrates. My lord should give strict orders so that my lord has troops at his disposal and so he can return all of the land of Ida-maraṣ to his side when it is springtime.[b]

b 2 Sam 11:1

REFERENCES

Text and Collations: *ARM* 2.130; Durand 1997:524–526 (= LAPO 16 336).

RATIONALE FOR NOT GOING TO MARI (*ARM* 28.51) (4.68)

Adam E. Miglio

Not long after the conflict with Eshnunna there were several years of relative stability during which Zimri-Lim was not involved in a large-scale war. During this period, there were many letters sent to Mari from Zimri-Lim's vassals in the upper Habur. These letters provide insight into the local politics of the region. One of the best-documented vassals of Zimri-Lim from this region is Ibal-Addu, the king of Ashlakka. Ibal-Addu had supported Zimri-Lim's conquest of Mari (*ARM* 28.77 [4.58]) before becoming the king at Ashlakka, where he ruled throughout most of Zimri-Lim's reign.

(Lines 1–2) Speak to my lord: thus says Ibal-Addu, your servant.
(Lines 3–5) The city of Nahur is well (and) Ashlakka is well. The heart of my lord should not be worried.
(Lines 6–23) Also, I hope that my lord is not upset with me because I have not come and had an audience with my lord. The year was difficult. The commoners, the citizens of Ashlakka, have left to cross the mountain for survival. Additionally, the *ḫapīrū*[1] have become ho[st]ile. Yet [I am] protecting the city of [my lord]! Now Itur-Asdu,[2] the servant of my lord, knows (that) it is on account of these (things) I have not gone down t[o] my lord. My lord should not be irritated. Herewith I have conducted three slaves (as) the portion of my lord as well as one ox and one deer for the feast of Eshtar.[a]

a 2 Sam 19:31–37

1 See the introduction to *ARM* 2.131 (4.48).
2 For Itur-Asdu, see *ARM* 28.115 (4.69) and A.1215 (4.62, n. 5).

REFERENCES

Text: *ARM* 28.51.

COMPLAINT TO ZIMRI-LIM ABOUT IBAL-ADDU (*ARM* 28.115) (4.69)

Adam E. Miglio

The upper Habur was a crowded political landscape in which there was constant competition among the kings of the region. In *ARM* 28.115 (4.69), Yaphur-Lim, the king of Izallu, wrote to Zimri-Lim and complained about his neighboring king, Ibal-Addu (cf. *ARM* 28.77 [4.58] and *ARM* 28.51 [4.68]). Yaphur-Lim's primary frustration was that Ibal-Addu was harboring a rival claimant, a *kaltum*, to the throne of Izallu (cf. A.1215, [4.62]).[1] It is noteworthy that Yaphur-Lim was not alone in charging Ibal-Addu with harboring a rival claimant; Zakura-Abum, after becoming king at Zalluhan (cf. *FM* 6.5 [4.57]), leveled a similar accusation against the king of Ashlakka.[2]

(Lines 1–4) [Speak to my lord: thus says] Yaphur-Lim, your servant.
(Lines 5–32) Is what Ibal-Addu is doing right? When my lord was staying at Nahur, I spoke to my lord (there) at Nahur about my *kiltum*, who was dwelling with Ibal-Addu. My lord summoned Ibal-Addu and you questioned him, asking: "Where is (that) man?" Ibal-Addu replied to my lord: "He is staying in Talhayum." Then, my lord asked Ibal-Addu, "When will that man come?" And Ibal-Addu answered you: "He will arrive tomorrow." (But) this man is (really) in Ashlakka! He is repeatedly

1 For the *kaltum* see the introduction to A.1215 (4.62).
2 Cf. *ARM* 28.53.

telling my lord lies! He did not heed the word that my lord spoke at Nahur or at Shusha. Now Ibal-Addu has provided that man with a house, fields, grain, and everything he needs at Ashlakka (and) he is telling him: "Don't worry about anyone at all." Meanwhile, the bread in my mouth is bitter![a]

(Lines 33–47) Moreover, I spoke to Yatur-Asdu:[3] "Since you are the representative of my lord at Nahur, why is my *kiltum* at Ash[la]kka?" [Ya]tur-Asdu responded to me: "I sent troops and they will apprehend him." (Yet) Yatur-Asdu went to Ashlakka and [my] *kiltum* was with him and with Ibal-Ad[du]. He provides food and drink, and Yatur-Asdu does not (so much as) say a word. Let my lord see that which Ibal-Addu is doing! A[s] a great household, he is raising a *kilt*[*um*]!

....[4]

a Prov 20:17; Lam 3:15

3 For Yatur-Asdu (i.e. Itur-Asdu), see *ARM* 28.51 (4.68) and A.1215 (4.62, n. 5).

4 There seem to be traces of four or five additional lines on the tablet, judging from the photo and handcopy.

REFERENCES

Text: *ARM* 28.115.

REPORT ON RUSE INVOLVING THE KING OF GUTIUM (M.11495) (4.70)

Adam E. Miglio

Elam, located in western Iran, was a significant political power during Zimri-Lim's reign. It was a watershed event, therefore, when the Sukkal of Elam led a campaign into Syro-Mesopotamia. Just prior to this campaign, the Sukkal of Elam had been allied with Hammu-rabi of Babylon and Zimri-Lim against the city of Eshnunna. However, immediately after the defeat of Eshnunna, the Sukkal provoked a war with several of his former allies, including Hammu-rabi and Zimri-Lim (cf. M.6009 [4.71]; A.2730 [4.72]; A.3080 [4.73]; and M.13014 [4.74]). Hammu-rabi and Zimri-Lim eventually responded by swearing a mutual aggression pact against the Sukkal of Elam.[1] Yet the Elamites' advance into northern Mesopotamia led to the removal of many of Zimri-Lim's allies in the region, and numerous local powers seized upon these moments of unrest as an opportunity to expand their authority (cf. M.6009 [4.71]). In the case of this letter, a military commander for the Gutium plotted how to secure support from the Sukkal of Elam against his king.

(Lines 1′–12′) ...[N]ow this matter is unusual.[2] Hammu-rabi said: "A commander of the troops for the king of Gutium[3] whose estate[4] is in the open country of Eshnunna, emigrated to Eshnunna three years ago.[a] He has now devised the (following) message for the Sukkal of Elam: 'I should go and speak (to the Gutian king that) I remembered my lord and my land and am returning (to them)! Let me say (this) and do (it) at once.'"

(Lines 13′–19′) He devised this (message) and then that man went to his land. When he arrived at the city, the king w[as] not there. He realized (that) his lord was not there and because his lord was n[ot] there, he sent to the army of Elam at a *stronghold*[5] [that was nearby]. It has [pl]undered three of [our] citi[es] and the p[lunder] of Gu[tium xxx] before [....]

a 1 Sam 13:37–38

1 See Durand 1986.

2 There are an uncertain number of lines missing at the beginning and at the end of the tablet. From the photo, it appears that about half, or just a little more than half of the tablet has been preserved: the bottom half of the obverse, the lines that continue onto the lower edge, and the lines at the top half of the reverse.

3 The Gutians were located in the Zagros Mountains in the vicinities of the upper and lower Zab Rivers (Durand 1998:376).

4 Literally, "his land" (*ma-as-sú*).

5 Lines 16–17 read: 16) *a-na ṣa-bi-im* ELAM.MA *ša* [*ri*]-*iš$_{15}$-dú-u*[*m*] 17) [*qé-er-bu i*]*š-pu-ur-ma*. The translation above follows Durand, who has tentatively postulated that the form [*ri*]-*iš$_{15}$-dú-u*[*m*] is a nominal from the root *ršd*, meaning "(military) stronghold" (Durand 2012b:186, n. 3).

REFERENCES

Text: Durand 2012b:185–186.

ACCOUNT OF UNREST AT TALHAYUM (M.6009) (4.71)

Adam E. Miglio

Ibal-El, a *merḫûm*,[1] wrote this letter to the king regarding matters in the western reaches of the upper Habur, at the city of Talhayum. According to the report from Mesiran, a certain Samsi-erah along with troops of the *ḫapīrū*[2] had been smuggled into the city of Talhayum, perhaps by the elders of the city.[3] In the chaos that ensued within the city, Talhayum's king was killed, and the people of the city established a new king (cf. A.1610+ [4.63]). Ibal-El's source, Mesiran, indicated that while Zimri-Lim's *ḫaziānum*-official was still alive, the loyalties of the new king at Talhayum were not certain. Before concluding, then, Ibal-El also updated Zimri-Lim on a treaty with Ida-maraṣ and Ishme-Addu as well as his dealings with Asqur-Addu.

(Lines 1–2) [Speak] to [my] lord: thus says Ibal-El, [your servant].
(Lines 3–30) Mesiran, the man of Isq[a, went to Zabalum] and thus wrote to me: "[The citizens of Talhayum] rebelled against their lord, Yawi-Ili, [and killed him]. During the night Samsi-e[rah] along with the *ḫapīrū* [and the citizens of Luhaya] who regularly [fo]llow him, were let [into] Talhayum. Sam[si-e]rah gathe[red] silver and the g[oods of the *palace*] and immediately he *to[ok them away*]. Then, the [*ḫ*]*apīrū* and the citizens of Luhaya who had enter[ed] into Talhayum with him started plundering[4] the houses of the commoners. The people of Talhayum were alarmed and defeated the *ḫapīrū* and the men of Luhaya – one hundred and forty men (total). Then, they established another king from among their people[5]; but the *ḫaziānum*-official of my lord is well. In no way is (this) kingship [*legitimate*].[a] Now where will Talhayum look? (It may look) eit[her t]o my lord, to Ida-[maraṣ, or] to Zalmaqum. It is not y[et] clear where it will [lo]ok!" This is what Mesiran [wrote to me] from Zabalum. So I wrote (back) to him: "Discern the intentions of that city and send (them) [to me]!"

a Jer 41:1–3

(Lines 31–41) Moreover, concerning the land of Ida-maraṣ and Ishme-[Addu] who constantly write to me for peace, at this point the elders of the land have not arrived here so I have not yet concluded [the treat]y.[6] W[hen] the elders of the land [arrive, I will conclude] a treaty with t[hem …]. The expedition of the men of Id[a-maraṣ is near to] the land[7] [x x]. Then, I will indeed c[ome] to [my] lo[rd] for the feast of Eshtar.
(Lines 42–47) Additionally, the very day [that] I sent the tablet [to] my lord, the elder[s of the land] arrived [to conc]ude their [t]reaty. [I sent this tablet] to [my] lord from Ma[lahatum].
(Lines 48–55) Also, Asqur-Addu […]. Thus he wr[ote to me:] "Since […]. Now let us meet, you and I, at any village [that you nam]e, so that I may have a word with you." But I wrote to him: "Write your message on a tablet and send (it) to me!"

1 For the *merḫûm*, see M.6060 (4.52).
2 See the introduction to *ARM* 2.131 (4.48).
3 See Guichard 2011:44–46.
4 Durand 1997:88.
5 For additional details regarding this event, see Durand 1988.
6 See A.1098 (4.56, n. 6).
7 See *ARM* 5.17 (4.49, n. 3); cf. A.1025 (4.65, n. 9).

REFERENCES

Text: Guichard 2011:67–71.

ADVICE FOR ZIMRI-LIM ON HOW TO RESPOND TO ATAMRUM (A.2730) (4.72)

Adam E. Miglio

Ibal-El, a *merḫûm*,[1] wrote this letter to Zimri-Lim regarding the relatively new Yamut-bal king at Andarig, Atamrum. Ibal-El provided Zimri-Lim with two responses to Atamrum's demands. In the first half of the letter, Ibal-El seems to offer a rationale for rejecting Atamrum's request for troops. Ibal-El's explanation recalled several earlier events, including an instance involving the former king of Andarig, Qarni-Lim (cf. *FM* 2.116 [4.60]; A.1610+ [4.63]; A.1025 [4.65]; *ARM* 2.130 [4.67]; and A.2730 [4.72]). In the second half of the letter, Ibal-El responded to Atamrum's ultimatum that the Simal mobile pastoralists (*ḫanûm*) should withdraw from the land of Ida-maraṣ. Ibal-El insisted

1 For the *merḫûm*, see the introduction to M.6060 (4.52).

that the king should remind Atamrum that the land of Ida-maraṣ had been the long-standing customary pastoral route (*nigḫum*) used by the Simal mobile pastoralists.

(Lines 1–2) Speak t[o] my lord: thus says Ibal-El, your servant.
(Lines 2–19) Concerning the message of Atamrum, who wrote to my lord "Dispatch troops," my lord should reply (to him): "Ask Hammu-rabi (of Kurda), Hadnu-rabi, and Sharru-kima-kalima – the kings who are your allies – and (ask) Yanuh-samar, your servant! Between me and Sharrya, (however), blood-(bond) and a solemn (promise) have been established! 100 mobile pastoralists and 100 of my servants from the borders of the Euphrates – (a total of) 200 of my trusted servants, leaders of my land – were present with me at (the ceremony of) blood-(relations)[2] when I swore an oath by the god to him. Similarly, when my father, the Sukkal, sent to me for troops (and after) I dispatched (them to him), I wrote to Qarni-Lim: 'Are you not my blood-(relation)? Send your troops to me, so that they can camp in my camp!' (But) he did not furnish his troops and they called him to account.[3] Also, I wrote to Sharriya (of Razama): 'Are you not my [bloo]d-(relation)? Send troops! Let [your troops] camp in my troops' c[amp]!'"
...[4]
(Lines 27–29) ... "If [you] bes[iege] another city, (then) I will send troops." Write this to him!

a 2 Sam 14:28–33

(Lines 30–50) Now concerning the land of Ida-maraṣ about which he, (Atamrum), wrote to you "Withdraw from that land," you should answer him: "Just as the land of Yamhad, the land of Qaṭna and the land of Amurrum are the customary pastoral route[5] of the Yamina and in that land the Yamina are sated with grain and they graze their pastures, (so too) Ida-maraṣ has been from the distant past the customary pastoral route of the (Simal) mobile pastoralists. What offense has the (Simal) mobile pastoralists committed against Ida-maraṣ? What is good for the (Simal) mobile pastoralists is (also good for) Ida-maraṣ! Why, then, have the people of Ida-maraṣ committed an offense against the (Simal) mobile pastoralists? They have taken the lives of the people under my authority! They have led away young men and women, my daughters-in-law and my servants as plunder! They have attacked the sheep, cattle, donkeys, and livestock of my land! Have I wronged him in any way or set fire to his grain?[a] It has (always) been my customary pastoral route! Why has it committed an offense against me?" Let my lord respond (with) this (information) and other things that my lord has at his disposal.

2 The statement in line 8 *da-mu ... ša-ak-na* and in line 11 *i-na da-mi iz-zi-zu* refers to a ritual in which blood was used (cf. lines 14, 18). A similar expression is attested in a contemporary letter from Tell Leilan: "blood-(relations) were established between us" (89:34) *da-mu-ut-tum i-na* [*b*]*i-ri-ni iš-ša-ka-na*; cf. also the Mari letter A.4350 cited in Charpin and Ziegler 2003:51, n. 191). It is noteworthy that in the aforementioned letter from Tell Leilan, there may be a connection between this expression and the ritual slaughtering of a donkey, a practice associated with treaty-making (Eidem 2011:311–317; cf. A.1098 [4.56, n. 6]). Additionally, one may compare the expression *lapātum* + *dāmam*, which is attested at Mari and Tell Leilan, with the well-known Akkadian collocation *lipit napištim* (see further Eidem 2011:315–317).
3 Cf. *ARM* 1.3 (4.46).
4 There are seven lines missing.
5 For the term translated "customary pastoral route" (*nigḫum*), see Durand 2004:118–121; Miglio 2014:85–106.

REFERENCES

Text: *ARM*(*T*) 26/2: 33, n. 24; Durand 2004:120–121.

REPLY TO ZIMRI-LIM'S CONCERNS ABOUT THE WAR WITH ELAM (A.3080) (4.73)

Adam E. Miglio

Hammi-ishtamar, a military leader among the Yamina, wrote this letter to Zimri-Lim. Hammi-ishtamar was responding to the king of Mari, who seems to have been concerned about the arrival of the Elamite troops along the banks of the Euphrates. The king had insisted that the Elamites would not differentiate between the Yamina and Simal populations, implying that the Yamina had as much to be concerned about as the Simal king, Zimri-Lim. Hammi-ishtamar, however, reported the reason for his delayed arrival and encouraged Zimri-Lim to not grow frustrated about his absence. Historically, it may be noted, however, that the Yamina were not especially supportive of the war with Elam.[1]

1 See Charpin and Ziegler 2003:224, n. 499 and the bibliography cited there.

(Lines 1–4) Speak to my lord: thus says Hammi-ishtamar, your servant.
(Lines 4–26) I have listened to the tablet that you sent to me. My lord wrote concerning the troops – all of the troops are (now) readied! My lord drafted a long tablet and sent it to me, (saying): "May god not bring the adversary and enemy to the banks of the Euphrates! May your god and Dagan, lord of the land, break the weapon of the Elamites! If, (however), they indeed arrive at the banks of the Euphrates, (then) they will not make distinctions,[2] as (there are between) the termites of the riverbank[3] of which it can be said that one (is) white and the (other) one black! Will they say, 'this city is Simal and this city is Yamina?' They will not make comparisons, just as the floodwaters of the river (which move) from up(stream) to down(stream).' "[4,a] [Why] has my lord written this letter?

a Isa 8:7

(Lines 27–41) My lord should not be frustrated with me because I have not come before my lord. My lord knows that the *sugāgū*[5] and mobile pastoralists are dwelling with me at Samanum. Moreover, it has been the case that they were not able to meet up with their brothers who live in the city for some time. (As a result), they have stayed a very long time (at Samanum). My lord should not be frustrated; I will arrive before my lord on the day after this tablet.

[2] For the verbal form *uš-ta-pa-ra-sú* (line 17, "they will not make distinctions") and *uš-ta-ma-ḫa-ru* (line 24, "they will not make comparisons"), see Miglio 2014:180–189.
[3] The phrase *ri-im-ma-tim ša ki-ša-di-im*, translated above "termites of the riverbank" is equivocal and may be rendered "beads of a necklace."
[4] For the extent of Hammi-ishtamar's quotation of Zimri-Lim's letter, see Anbar 1993:158–160.
[5] For the *sugāgum*, see A.3152+M.5665+ (4.51, n. 26).

REFERENCES

Text: Durand 1990b:104–106; Durand 1998:488 (= LAPO 17 733).

REPORT TO ZIMRI-LIM ON REACTIONS TO THE WAR WITH ELAM (M.13014) (4.74)

Adam E. Miglio

Similar to the sentiment near the end of the war with Eshnunna (cf. *ARM* 26.199 [4.66]), there seems to have been a mixed response to the Elamite campaigns into Syro-Mesopotamia. In this letter, Su-nuhra-halu, a high-ranking official in Zimri-Lim's administration, reported on the differing reactions within the household of Igmil-Sin, a commoner (*muškēnum*), to the Elamite's advance.

(Lines 1–2) Speak to my lord: thus says Shu-nuhra-halu, your servant:
(Lines 3–34) Some man (who was) a servant of a commo[ne]r [that] was [bo]und (and) shackled *detained us*[1] when we administered an oath by the god in the countryside and we entered after the gods into the city [by] the gate of Annunitum. He said to us: "When the troops of the Elamites devoured [all] the land of Shubartum, [we] heard the [report that the k]ing was going up [against the El]amites on a campaign. Then, the mother of Igmil-Sin, my lord, spoke [to Igmi]l-Sin, my lord, (saying): 'He will go up [against the Ela]mites, (so) your [household] – whether it is ready or not – should [enter into] the fortress and wait for us.' [Thus] his mo[ther] spoke to him. [But] he responded to her: 'Go and dwell in [a fortress,] (but) will you find [your deliverance]?'[a] He said (this) [to] his mot[her because] of the bad [ne]ws about the fortress of Sumu-Epuh.[2] His [mother] was terrified, so she le[ft; but each] of the men is going with him, [saying]: '[I will indeed g]o against the enemy of the king. I will oppose the [Elam]ites [with weapons]! I will achieve [my objective]! And if the enemy approaches, I will exclaim (before them that) I [will bring] you low, preserve the well-being of my household and receive great [praise]!' [For th]is reason he has been estr[anged] from his mother. [Now] each man among his relatives [x x x x] who hears ...."[3]

a Esth 4:3

[1] For a discussion of the difficult form *is-ni-in₅-né-ti-[ma]* in line 6, see Charpin and Durand 2003:61.
[2] The fortress of Sumu-epuh was located along the Euphrates River, north of the city of Emar (Durand 1990a:66, cf. 39, n. 1). An Elamite victory at the fortress of Sumu-epuh would have been a significant event in the western reaches of Syria.
[3] Several lines are missing; the left edge of the tablet was not preserved.

REFERENCES

Text: Charpin and Durand 2003:64–69.

UPDATE ON A LAND-DISPUTE IN THE UPPER JEZIRAH (*ARM* 28.95) (4.75)

Adam E. Miglio

In this letter, Shub-ram (cf. A.1610+ [4.63]), wrote to Zimri-Lim to update him about a legal dispute over the city of Shunhum. The problem was that Ili-Eshtar of Shuna claimed the city, but Ili-Addu had seized control of it. This dispute was to be resolved by the River ordeal. Then, after the ordeal, Haya-Sumu would award the city to the rightful owner. Zimri-Lim had established Haya-Sumu as a close ally in the upper Habur; in fact, Zimri-Lim had married two daughters to Haya-Sumu (cf. *ARM* 10.5 [4.61]). Yet Shub-ram reported to Zimri-Lim that Ili-Eshtar, the king of Shuna did not accept Haya-Sumu's authority. Moreover, Shub-ram recounted that Ili-Eshtar had found support from Atamrum, the king of Andarig (cf. A.2730 [4.72]). Shub-ram even accused Ili-Eshtar of having his military commander, Kirru, commandeer troops from Kiduhhu and of having colluded with Ishme-Dagan.

(Lines 1–2) Speak to my lord: thus says Shub-ram, your servant.

(Lines 3–14) Previously, while my lord was staying at Tadum, Ili-Eshtar, the man of Shuna, sent to my lord regarding the city of Shunhum: "That city is my city! He has seized it with troops! Moreover, Ili-Addu, the man of Kiduhhu is continuously attacking me." When he wrote this and other (things) to my lord, my lord spoke and gave me the (following) instructions: "Let Ili-Eshtar and his elders, Ili-Addu and his elders, you, and the elders of the land of Apum, (its) elites, assemble so that Haya-Sumu can give a legal provision for you. You should accept the judgment that Haya-Sumu gives to you." This is what my lord instructed me.

(Lines 14–34) When Haya-Sumu returned [fr]om my lord, at the appointed time that Haya-Sumu had established, I – along with the elders of the land of Apum, (its) elites and Ili-Addu and his elders – we (all) went before Haya-Sumu [just as] my lord instructed. But he (Ili-Eshtar) did not come and he did not send his elders. (Instead) he sent Zakku, his servant, and some messenger along with him. Then, Haya-Sumu gave this legal provision for us: "If that city is (indeed) your city, let two men and two women from Shuna take [d]ust from that city and let them undergo the River ordeal.[1,a] They will state: 'That city is indeed my city. [L]ong ago it was given as the allotment of the Yabasu (clan of the Simal). (I swear that) the people of Apum in fact gave it as a gift.'[2] Let them state this (and) undergo the River ordeal in order to take that city. Otherwise, let [two] men (and) two women from Apum tak[e] dust from that city and undergo the [Ri]ver ordeal, saying: 'That city (is) Shub-Ra[m]'s (city). It was indeed allotted to the mobile pastoralists since long ago.'[3] Let them say [t]his (and) undergo the ordeal, in order to take that city." This is the legal provision that Haya-Sumu gave to us, but (Ili-Eshtar) did not accept it.

(Lines 35–42) He is a thief[4] – he is robbing the inhabitants of Apum! Rising early, he plunders, and (he continues) into the night. I constantly write (to him), but he will not answer. He will not [accept] the legal provision. (And) when I send my messengers to him, my lord Atamrum repeatedly re[vil]es (them) and makes many complaints.[5] Those who were reviled [be]fore him, I made testify before

a Num 5:11–31

[1] The River ordeal, which is also known from the laws of Hammu-rabi of Babylon (laws 2 and 132), was a means to adjudicate a legal dispute after 'traditional' legal options had been exhausted. In other words, if a verdict could not be reached through a typical trial, then a divine determination was sought. The sources from Mari indicate that the ordeal was practiced at the city of Hit, which was located on the Euphrates River about halfway between Mari and Babylon. It seems that a participant in the River ordeal submitted to a ritual in which water was poured on their hands, after which they swore an oath by the god. The next step in the ordeal, however, is not as clear, but it may have involved swimming in the Euphrates River while carrying a millstone (cf. Charpin 1986).

[2] Line 26 is tentatively understood as a negative oath in which the apodosis is omitted (LÚ *a-pa-a-yu*⸢KI⸣ *a-na qí-iš₇-tim la id-di-nu-šu*; cf. A.3152+M.5665+ [4.51, n. 29]; see Durand 2004:147, n. 189). According to this interpretation, the interests of the Simal's Yabasu clan aligned with those of the mobile pastoralists (*ḫanûm*) mentioned elsewhere in the letter. Alternately, one could translate this clause as a negative oath (and in line 30, as a positive assertory oath with *lū*; cf. n. 3 below). In this case, Shub-ram would be understood to represent the interests of a mobile pastoralist group (*ḫanûm*) that did not exactly align with those of the members of the Yabasa clan mentioned in the letter.

[3] Cf. Durand has restored and understood line 30 as an interrogative clause: "Was it given long ago as an allotment to the mobile pastoralists?" ([*ki i*]*š-tu aq-d*[*a*]*-m*[*i*] ⸢*a*⸣*-n*[*a*] ḪA.LA HA.NA^{KI} *lu-ú na-di-*[*in*]).

[4] I have followed the reading *ḫa-bi-it-ma*, suggested by Durand 2000:255, n. 86 (cf. *ARM*(*T*) 28:134–136).

[5] The word *mi-ig-re-tim* in line 39 is likely to be related to the lemma *magīrtum* (Durand 2000:157; cf. *ARM*(*T*) 28:136).

Haya-Sumu.[6] [My lord] should send to [Ha]ya-Sumu so that he may decide this [matter].
(Lines 43–63) Additionally, eighty troo[ps] from Kiduhhu [along with Kirru], their commander, are in his presence. They are constantly raiding throughout the land of A[p]um and they incessantly taunt the city of Kiduhhu. [When] Ishme-Dagan went up (for a campaign), he dispatched those troops along with Kirru, their commander, to Ishme-Dagan and they went with Ishme-Dagan. At Talbaum, Ishme-Dagan and Hammu-rabi (of Kurda) swore an oath by the gods and those troops as well as Kirru, their commander, swore an oath by the gods. We questioned him, asking: "Why did you dispatch [t]roops to Ishme-Dagan?" He answered: "(They are) reservists and they have left." (While he is) here he insists again and again "they are reservists," but before Ishme-Dagan (he) says: "(they are) the troops of the man of Shuna and Kirru, the commander of Shuna's (army)."[b] Now my lord must review (the matter) of these men. He may consider those men reservists, (but) [beca]use these men went without my lord to Ishme-Dagan and swore an oath by the gods, these men are enemies of my lord. Let my [lo]rd lie in wait for[7] them![c] These men belong to the mobile pastoralists; they do not belong to his land. He is with my lord (which is where) he should stay. Let my lord dispatch his trustworthy servants with Tehum-Adal so that he can lead these men to my lord.
(Lines 64–65) I have hereby sent Tehum-Adal before my lord. Let my lord be attentive to his words.

b 1 Sam 29
c Judg 9:26–44; Hos 6:9

[6] The translation above for line 40 follows the collations by Durand, who read, *š*[*a*] ˹*i-na*˺ [*ma-a*]*ḫ-ri-šu it-ta-az-za-ru* ˹*ù*˺ [*ḫa*]-*ià-su-ú-mu uz-zi-sú*-[*nu*]-*ti* (Durand 2000:155, n. 80). Another reading of the tablet is given by Kupper, who transcribed the tablet: *š*[*u-nu ma-a*]*ḫ-ri-šu it-ta-az-za-ru* ˹*ù*˺ [*ḫa*]-*ià-su-ú-mu uz-z*[*i-iz*] ("T[hey] are reviled [be]fore him and Haya-Sumu is furio[us]" [*ARM*(*T*) 28:136]).
[7] For the verb *ḫakûm*, cf. *ARM* 28.77 (4.58, n. 4); see further Durand 2000:94; *ARM*(*T*) 28:107, n. c.

REFERENCES

Text: *ARM* 28.95; Durand 2000:154–157 (= LAPO 18 1000).

REPORT ON POLITICS IN THE UPPER JEZIRAH (*ARM* 28.44) (4.76)

Adam E. Miglio

Terru, the king of Urgish, wrote to Zimri-Lim after Elam had withdrawn from the upper Habur. In this letter, Terru wanted Zimri-Lim to know that he had been eager to reciprocate a favor for his lord. Also, he reported to Zimri-Lim how the Hurrayu opposed Shadum-Labu'a, the king of Ashnakkum, and had collectively decided to support a man named Ili-Sumu as a *kaltum* against Shadum-Labu'a. Historically, Ili-Sumu does not seem to have been successful in replacing Shadum-Labu'a.

(Lines 1–4) Speak to my lord: thus says Terru, your servant.
(Lines 5–21) Previously, my lord, sent to me by Halu-rabi,[1] asking: "What about the generous things that I have repeatedly done for Terru? Why has that man not once returned a favor?" When Halu-rabi said this, I made arrangements (in response to) the message that my lord sent to me (and) I returned a favor to my lord. When I made that decision, my city was present in order to stone me,[2] but my lord's god rescued me from the talon of the Sukkal of E[lam]. My lord should know this!
(Lines 22–37) My lord must not object to the fact I have not come before my lord. The Hurrayu are ho[stile] toward Shadu-Labu'a because of Ishme-Addu. Furthermore, in their [ang]er they elevated [Ili-su]mu as a *kaltum*[3] against [Sha]du-Labu'a. As for [m]e, I am holding the fortress of Ashnakkum! My lord, (however), should send Shadu-Labu'a (away) with honor. Once Shadu-Labu'a returns, I will come before my lord.

[1] One of the best-known persons with the name Halu-rabi in the letters from Mari was a local authority in the region known as Suḫum, which was located to the south of Mari (see Charpin 1997a:355–360; cf. *ARM* 14.117). This Halu-rabi was active during the events recounted in the letter above (and is known to have been involved with events in the upper Habur [cf. esp. *FM* 7.4]).
[2] In the *edito princeps*, Kupper argued that the action described here in lines 18–19 (*a-li i-n*[*a*] NA$_4$ *ka-ta-mi-im iz-zi-za-am-ma*) was a ritual that signaled cooperation and loyalty between parties (see further *ARM*(*T*) 28: 58 and n. c; Guichard 2003:213). Elsewhere it has been argued that this phrase indicated that the people of Urgish wanted to kill Terru for his actions (Guichard 2004b; see also Durand 2005:107–107; Sasson 2013:125).
[3] For the *kaltum*, see the introduction to A.1215 (4.62).

REFERENCES

Text: *ARM* 28.44.

TEXTS FROM ANCIENT CANAAN

ADMINISTRATIVE DOCUMENT FROM HEBRON (4.77)

Richard S. Hess

This is the only cuneiform tablet discovered at Tell er-Rumeideh (Tell Hebron), the site of ancient Hebron. Found in 1986 in excavations that uncovered what has been identified as Middle Bronze Age levels, it has affinities in script and grammar with Old Babylonian.[1] The left side and the lower edge of this small tablet[2] are missing (Anbar and Na'aman 1986–1987:3). The tablet has several vertical lines drawn down the obverse and reverse, to assist in organizing the records on each line. Solid lines are also drawn horizontally across the tablet beneath text lines 1, 2, 4, 6, 8, 9, 11, (before 1′), 1′, and 4′. The text is an administrative document wherein most lines identify the king, numbers of sheep and cattle, and a personal name.[3] Parts of a total appear at the end.

(Lines 1–11)

01.	shorn[4] [g]oat,	1 sheep/goat[5] for Padida,[6]	1 sheep/goat,	1 sheep with lamb,[7]	Hili-El[8]
02.	shorn [sheep with l]amb,	3 sheep,	3 sheep/goats,	2 sheep with lambs,	Hili-El
03.	[goa]t,	23 sheep,	15 sheep/goats,	1 sheep with lamb,	Hili-El
04.	...] the king.				
05.	...] the king,	19 sheep,	15 sheep/goats,	1 sheep with lamb,	Hili-El
06.	...] goat.				
07.	...] the king,	9 sheep,	11 sheep/goats,	2 sheep with lambs,	Hili-El
08.	...] the king,	shepherded	for Inti,[9]	2 sheep,	Sukuhu[10]
09.	...] the king,	9 sheep,	1 sheep/goat.		
10.			...]3(?) sheep/goats,	2 sheep with lambs,	
11.			... Hi]l[i-E]l.		
01′.			... ha]-di,	1 sheep with lamb	
02′.			were missing	1 sheep	
03′.	...] 1 [...]				
04′.	female collectors (of taxes).				
05′.	...] mature shorn [goat]s, 77 sheep for offerings				
06′.	...] a total of 46 sheep/goats.				

[1] However, Horowitz, Oshima, and Sanders 2006:88 note that the lack of mimmation on the participle form in rev. 4′ indicates a period later than that of the Hazor Middle Bronze Age tablets.

[2] Ibid. indicate measurements of the clay tablet as 6.2 × 5.2 × 2.3 centimeters.

[3] Cf. Hebron and texts related to herding, Gen 13:5–18; 35:27; 36:7.

[4] Anbar and Na'aman 1986–1987:6 had read this as ḪALxGAM, without knowing how to interpret it. However, Horowitz, Oshima, and Sanders 2006:90 read here (also lines 2 and 5′) as GÍR = *gazza* for "shorn."

[5] Horowitz, Oshima, and Sanders 2006:90 understand UDU.MÁŠ as Heb. *ṣōʾn*, including sheep and goats.

[6] "Addu has redeemed." Cf. similar name in Hazor 10 line 3, *ad-du-ap-di*.

[7] Horowitz, Oshima, and Sanders 2006:91, where UDU.NÍTA can refer to either male or female sheep.

[8] It is possibly W. Semitic, to be interpreted as "El is (my) strength." Cf. Abihail (Anbar and Na'aman 1986–1987:7) in Num 3:34; 1 Chr 2:29; 5:14; 2 Chr 11:18; Est 2:15; 9:29; and in Heb. epigraphy, cf. Albertz and Schmitt 2012:556. However, this second millennium BCE name may also be Hurrian from *ḫil(l)*. Cf. Hess 2007:158, n. 36.

[9] Likely a Hurrian PN; Anbar and Na'aman 1986–1987:7; Hess 2007:159 n. 36; Richter 2012:89. On the presence of Hurrian and Anatolian names at Hebron, cf. Hess 1996:210–212; Num 15:12; Josh 14:9.

[10] Hess 2007:159, n. 36.

REFERENCES

Albertz and Schmitt 2012; Anbar and Na'aman 1986–1987; Hess 1996; 2007; Richter 2012.

CYLINDER LETTER FROM TAGI TO LABAYA (Beth Shean 2) (4.78)

Richard S. Hess

This is the only known example of a cuneiform letter written on a cylinder seal. The question as to why Tagi chose this form and who the writers are remains unclear. W. Horowitz (1994; 1996; 1997; Horowitz and Oshima 2006:48–49) proposed that it was so written as an attempt to hide the letter from the pharaoh's officials. A. F. Rainey (1998:239–

242) notes that, while contemporary parallels existed for school exercises (EA 355) and for a lexical reference text (Aphek prism), a letter in this form is unparalleled. He proposes a scribal reference text for writing common epistolary formulas. N. Naʾaman (Goren et al. 2004:259) argues, on the basis of petrographic analysis of the clay, that the letter could not have come from the Amarna figure named Tagi, who ruled Gath-Carmel. It must therefore be another Tagi. While the name Tagi, a hypocoristic personal name containing a Hurrian element referring to "pure," is well attested in the Late Bronze Age (Hess 1993:153–155; 2003:42), it is not so clear that the clay must come from the same source as the sender. In the end, the short text fuels more questions than it provides answers.

(Lines 1–6) Say to Labaya, my lord. The message of Tagi to the king my lord:

(Lines 7–9) "I have heard your letter to me …"

REFERENCES

Goren, Finkelstein and Naʾaman 2004; Hess 1993a; 2003; Horowitz 1994; 1996;1997; Horowitz, Oshima and Sanders 2006; Rainey 1998.

THE TAANACH TABLETS (4.79A–D)

Richard S. Hess

Some 17 cuneiform pieces have been discovered at Taanach. The first fourteen were cuneiform tablets and fragments found in the excavations by E. Sellin in 1903–1904. This work also yielded a fifteenth piece, a cylinder seal. The remaining two texts, an administrative text of personal names and an alphabetic cuneiform text, were uncovered in the 1960's. Only four complete letters were identified in the collection: Taanach 1, 2, 5, and 6. These are translated here. All the cuneiform texts date from the 15th century BCE. The texts were first published by F. Hrozný (1904; 1905) in the original excavation report. In 1966, E. Gordon made a number of new collations and readings that were used by A. Glock, along with his own work, in 1983. A. F. Rainey (1999) provided a new edition of the tablets that are studied here. Horowitz and Oshima (2006) did their own collations of Taanach 1 and 6 in 2004. To date these remain the major editions of the letters. For the personal names, see the works of Gustavs 1927; 1928; Zadok 1996; and Hess 2003:37–40. Taanach 1 and 2 are exchanges between local rulers who are not Egyptian officials. Thus Akkadian was an accepted medium of communication between Canaanite officials in the 15th century BCE.

TAANACH TABLET 1 (4.79A)

In this text. Ehli-Teshub, a local town leader with a Hurrian name, writes to another Hurrian name bearer, Talwashur. The document may have accompanied a payment of fifty silver shekels that was due. Items of special interest to Ehli-Teshub appear in the final lines: a type of wood, myrrh, and the welfare of a servant girl or young woman.

(Lines 1–7) Say to Talwashur. The message of Ehli-Teshub:[1] Live well![2] May the gods seek your well being, the well being of your house, and of your sons.[3]

(Lines 8–11) You have written me concerning fifty (shekels) of silver. So I am giving fifty (shekels) of silver. How could I not do this?

(Lines 12–18) Why don't you send me news of how you are doing? Whatever news you have heard from there, write [m]e.

(Lines 19–30) Also, if there is even an inch of *zarninu* wood and of myrrh, give it to me. Send news about the servant girl, Kan[…], who is in Rubbutu[4,a]; about her well being. When she grows up, let him sell her for redemption money or to a husband.

a Josh 19:20

1 Both personal names here are Hurrian.
2 See Rainey 2006:75 here and throughout.
3 Cf. Hazor 10 lines 4–6 for a similar blessing.
4 Cf. Rabbith in the allotment of Issachar. Rainey 2006:75.

TAANACH TABLET 2 (4.79B)

As in the first tablet, a writer addresses Talwashur with a request for assistance of various sorts. Of special interest are chariot wheels. The *maryannu* class (a Hurrian term) maintained battle chariots. Papyrus Leningrad 1116A records that *maryannu* were sent to Egypt from Taanach in the fifteenth century BCE (Rainey 1999:153*–154*).

(Lines 1–4) Say to Talwashur. The message of Ahiyama: May the lord God[5] protect your life. You are a brother and a close friend in that place.

(Lines 5–9) It is in your heart that I have entered into an empty house.[6] Then give me an inch: two chariot wheels, a bow, and two *uppasannu*.[7]

(Lines 10–14) If the bow is completed and made, send it by means of Purdaya.[8] Then, command your towns and let them do their work.[9]

b Josh 2:19; 2 Sam 1:16; 1 Chr 12:20

(Lines 15–18) I am responsible[10,b] for everything that has been happening to the towns. Look, I will do what is good for you.

(Lines 19–24) If there are copper arrows, let them be given.
Let Elu-rapi[11] enter into Rehov.[12]
I will certainly send my man to you, and I will arrange a marriage.

[5] EN.DINGIR.MEŠ, either Baal God or lord God. The plural form with a singular verb may be a plural of majesty (Rainey 1999:158*). Cf. Hazor 10.20–22 and the apparently plural form of "God" in the biblical *'elohim.*

[6] This expression, also found in EA 102.11–12; and 316.18–20, indicates desolation (Rainey 1999:158*).

[7] This Hurrian word, denoting an object of wool or leather used as a harness or yoke, occurs at Nuzi and Alalakh, as well. See Richter 2012:493.

[8] This name is difficult to analyze. It may be Indo-Aryan. See Hess 2003:39.

[9] A feminine verb appears with URU, the logogram that is normally masculine in Akkadian. The West Semitic word for "town, city," however, is feminine and may have influenced this text (Horowitz, Oshima, and Sanders 2006:134). Cf. Hazor 3.

[10] Literally, "on my head." Cf. EA 326.18–19 (Rainey 1999:158*).

[11] This West Semitic name also occurs in Taanach 12.3 and elsewhere (Hess 1993:89).

[12] See Rainey 1999:158*–159* for analysis of this spelling as an Amorite form.

TAANACH TABLET 5 (4.79C)

Both tablets 5 and 6 are messages from Amanhatpa to Talwashur. Tablet 6 line12 associates Amanhatpa with Gaza. Tablet 5 line 15 mentions Megiddo. EA 242, 243, 244, 246, and 365 from Biridiya of Megiddo share a similar ductus and the use of the enclitic *-mi* (Horowitz and Oshima 2006:140; Rainey 1996, 2:31). A different figure, Amanhatpe, is mentioned in the Amarna correspondence, in EA 185 and 186, from Mayarzana of Hasi. There he appears as ruler of Tushulti (Hess 2003:29; cf. EA 185 above).

(Lines 1–3) Say to Talwashur. The message of Amanhatpa: May the storm god[13] protect your life.

(Lines 4–12) Send me your brothers with their chariots. Send me the horse(s) as your tribute along with gifts, and all the captives[14] who are with you.

c Judg 5:19; 1 Kgs 9:15

(Lines 13–15) Send them tomorrow to Megiddo.[15,c]

[13] Most likely identified as Baʿal but possibly (H)addu. ^{d}IM can refer to either as seen in Amarna personal names. Cf. Hess 1993:233–234, 236.

[14] Reading here *a-si*$_{17}$*-ri* with Horowitz and Oshima 2006:140. Alternatively, with Rainey 2006:76 as *a-ši-ri*, a special class of men. Cf. Richter 2012:54 for "prisoner."

[15] On the archaeological association of chariotry and horses with Megiddo, see Cantrell 2011:87–113.

TAANACH TABLET 6 (4.79D)

This is the most broken of the four Taanach letters translated here. Thus its translation is less certain than the others. The emphasis is on Talwashur sending various groups to Amanhatpa in Gaza, and perhaps on Talwashur himself appearing there.

(Lines 1–3) [Say to Ta]lwashur. [The message of A]manhatpa. May [the storm god prot]ect your life.

(Lines 4–11) [For]merly, you would send Bazunu son of Narsi to me. Furthermore, your own soldiers[16,d] are not in the garrison unit.[17] You neither come to me yourself nor do you send your brothers.

(Lines 12–17) Furthermore, I was in Gaza but you did not come to me. Now I [am going forth] to war but you are [...].[18]

d Gen 14:14

e Ps 102:21; Isa 42:7; 61:1

(Lines 18–22) [Fu]rthermore, [as for your] brothers [and your y]oung men, do [no]t [s]end [them to] me. [As for ...],[19] s[end them to] me.

(Lines 23–30) [No]w, as for the PO[Ws] whom I have redeemed,[e] [se]nd them. As for your [brothers] and their [...]. Furthermore, [... send] to m[e tomor]row and [...].

[16] Cf. Gen 14:14. This term is an Egyptian loan referring to retainers: *hanaku*. Rainey 1999:159*.

[17] So Rainey 1999:159*. Horowitz and Oshima 2006:141 "your retainers are not on guard."

[18] Rainey 1999:159* proposes: but you and your brothers are not.

[19] Ibid., proposes: [As for the horses,] your [tribute],

REFERENCES

Albright 1944; Glock 1983; Gustavs 1927; 1928; Hess 1993; 2003; Horowitz 2006; Hrozný 1904; 1906; Cantrell 2011; Rainey 1977; 1999; 2006; Richter 2012; Zadok 1996.

THE EL-AMARNA LETTERS (4.80–86)

Richard S. Hess

The El Amarna tablets represent the largest collection of letters and other literature emerging from Palestine before the writing of the Hebrew Bible. However, the letters are not limited to the land of Israel or even to the southern Levant. Originating across the eastern Mediterranean and the Middle East of the fourteenth century BCE, this corpus of about 380 cuneiform texts was rediscovered in 1887. They appeared at the abandoned site that became known as Tell el-Amarna in Egypt. The town was originally built as his capital by pharaoh Amenophis IV/Akhenaten and abandoned not many years afterward. At that time the movers left behind the old files that were no longer relevant. The remains of those archives comprise the corpus of Amarna tablets. Although some ten different museums house the surviving tablets that can be traced from the original archive, the three major centers are: the Egyptian Museum of Cairo (51 tablets), the Vorderasiatisches Museum of Berlin (200 tablets), and the British Museum of London (96 tablets).[1] While a number of initial publications began to appear, the most complete and most accurately produced work was that of Knudtzon 1915. It remains an important resource a century later.

PHARAOH TO KADASHMAN-ENLIL (EA 1) (4.80)

EA 1 provides a good example of the international correspondence found in the collection. El Amarna tablets 1–44 contain international correspondence and other related texts among the major ancient Near Eastern kingdoms. Those receiving and sending these communications included: Alashiya (Cyprus), the Hittite empire, Mitanni, Assyria, and Kassite Babylonia. EA 1 provides an illustration of correspondence from pharaoh Amenophis III (Akhenaten's father) to Kadashman-Enlil II, king of Babylon. As such it represents the concerns of two of the most influential nations of the fourteenth century BCE, wherein these and other texts provide a brief window into international landscape of the Late Bronze Age. In this letter the pharaoh is dissatisfied with the Babylonian envoys and expresses concerns about the Babylonian king's sister as well as general diplomatic issues.[2]

(Lines 1–9) Say to Kadashman-Enlil,[3] the king of Karduniash,[4,a] my brother. The message of Nibmuareya, the Great King, the king of Egypt, your brother. All is well with me. May all go well for you. May it also go well:
for your household,
for your wives,
for your children,
for your officials,
for your horses,
for your chariots, and
for your lands.
All is very well with me. It is well:
with my household,
with my wives,
with my children,
with my officials,
with my horses,
with my chariots, and
with my many troops.
In my lands it is very well.

a Gen 2:13

(Lines 10–25) Just now I have heard what you wrote to me about her: "Now you have asked for my daughter to become your wife. My sister, whom my father gave to you, is present with you. No one has seen her. Is she alive or is she dead?" These are your words that you wrote me on your tablet. Did you send someone important who knows your sister, who could speak with her, and who could identify her? Let one (like this) speak with her! The men you sent are useless. One was the [...] of Zaqara. The other was an ass herder from [...]. There was not one among them who [knows he]r, who is close to your father, and wh[o could identify her]. Further, [...] was given into [his] hand [t]o fet[ch it] for her mother.[5]

(Lines 26–36a) You (Kassite king) wrote: "You (pharaoh) addressed my messengers while standing in the presence of your wives, 'Look, this is

---

1 Tropper and Vita 2010:13–14.
2 Greenwood 2006:186.
3 Kadashman-EN.LÍL, where EN.LÍL is likely the Kassite deity Ḫarbe. This Kassite king's name can be interpreted as "trust of Ḫarbe." Cf. Hess 1993:95.
4 Kassite Babylonia.
5 Cf. Moran 1993:3. The "mother" is the name at Mari given to the woman who accompanies a woman given in marriage.

your lady standing before you.' However, my messengers did not recognize her as my sister who was with you." You also wrote, "My messengers did not recognize here. Who will identify her?"[6] Why don't you (Kassite king) send an important person who will tell you the truth about the wellbeing of your sister here? Then you can trust the one who enters to inspect her quarters and her relationship with the king.

(Lines 36b–50) You also wrote, "Could it have been the daughter of a commoner, a Kaskean, a Hanigalbatean, or a citizen from Ugarit whom my messengers saw? Who will believe them? The one who was with you did not open her mouth. No one believes th[em]." These were your words. If your [sister were d]ead, why would one conceal [her death] and present a differe[nt person]? May the god Amun [know … your] si[ster is alive. I have appointed a]s mistress of the household […] more than all the wives […].[7]

(Broken text)

(Lines 52–62a) … in the land of Egypt. You also wrote, "I [hav]e daughters who are married to lo[cal] kings. If my messengers visit the kings, they speak with the women and they [se]nd me a gift of greeting. The one with [you …]." These were your words. Perhaps y[our neighb]oring kings are wealthy. Then your daughters may acquire something from them and send it to you. What does your sister who is with me have? She could acquire something and I could send it to you. It is good that you give your daughters to obtain something of value[8] from your neighbors.

(Lines 62b–77) You also wrote the words of my father. Set them aside. Do not speak his words. "Now establish a loyal brotherhood between us." You wrote these words. Now we are brothers, you and I, both of us. Even so, I quarreled against your messengers because they said to you, "They gave nothing to those of us who went to Egypt." Of those who come to me, did anyone of them come [and not] receive silver, gold, oil, special clothing, and all sorts [of good, more than] in any other country? He speaks dishonestly to the o[ne who sen]ds him. The first time the messengers went to yo[ur father,] their mouth spoke lies. The second time they went, they spoke lies to you. So I thought, whether [I gi]ve them something or whether I don't give them anything, they will continue telling lies. So I decided that I would not gi[ve anything] to them.

(Lines 78–88a) You also wrote me, "You said to my messengers, 'Your master has no troops, and the young girl they gave me has no beauty.'" These were your words, but they are not true. Your messenger spoke to you in this manner. It can be learned for me whether or not there are troops. Why should I ask him whether your have troops or horses with you? Do not listen to your two messengers whom you sent here and whose mouths lie. Surely they have not shown you respect. They tell lies in order to escape your hand.

(Lines 88b–98) You spoke to me, "He put my chariots with the chariots of the town leaders. You did not watch over them individually. You delivered them[9] to lands that did not belong to you. You did not watch over them individually." Here are chariots. The chariots needed the horses of my land, all my horses. When you sent me [a vess]el to anoint the h[ea]d of the girl, you sent me one gi[ft] of pure oil.[10]

6 Cf. Cochavi-Rainey 2012:216.
7 Cf. Moran 1992:4.
8 Ibid., pp. 2, 4–5, "a nugget of gold." Cf. Cochavi-Rainey 2012:127, "a garment."
9 Greenwood 2006:189.
10 Cochavi-Rainey 2012:159, 217. For an alternative, "we are distressed," in place of "pure," see Moran 1992:5.

REFERENCES

Text: Rainey 2015:58–65; Knudtzon 1915. Translations and Studies: Cochavi-Rainey 2011; Greenwood 2006; Hess 1993; Moran 1992; Tropper and Vita 2010.

RIB-ADDA TO THE PHARAOH OF EGYPT (Amenhotep III) (EA 74) (4.81)

This letter[1] represents one of the longer and better preserved missives that Rib-Adda wrote to the pharaoh of Egypt.[2] EA 68–95 and 101–138 are clearly or likely written by this ruler of Byblos (ancient Gubla). Together they comprise by far the largest collection of letters from the Amarna corpus. Rib-Adda ruler of Byblos claims to endure threats inside of his city and outside of it. While some of his enemies, such as Abdi-Ashirta leader of Amurru, perish during Rib-Adda's career; Abdi-Ashirta's son and successor, Aziru, continues to pose a threat. Further danger arises from landless disruptors of society known as the Apiru. Although farther north at Alalakh, Apiru serve at the highest

1 I thank William Schniedewind for graciously providing access to the late Anson Rainey's prepublished collations and translations for this and the other Amarna letters from Canaan that are translated here. See now Rainey 2015.

2 Important recent studies and translations of this letter are found in: Youngblood 1961:122–154; Moran 1992:142–145; von Dassow 2006:201–203; Tropper and Vita 2010:139–142.

levels of the society, elsewhere they resemble those without inheritance and prospects, not unlike the men who surrounded the fugitive David (1 Sam 22:1–2). When Rib-Adda seeks assistance in Beirut, his brother replaces him in Byblos. He never seems to persuade the pharaohs, either Amenhotep III or his successor, to rescue him with military aid. Rib-Adda disappears from the written record in exile.

(Lines 1–5a) Rib-Adda says to the [his] lord, the king of lands, the great king, the king of battle: May [the lady] of Byblos grant power to the king my lord. I fall at the feet of my lord, my Sun, 7 times and 7 times.[a]

(Lines 5b–10a) May the king, the lord, know that Byblos the loyal maidservant of the king, has been secure since the days of his fathers. Now the king has withdrawn his hand from his loyal city.

(Lines 10b–15a) May the king inspect the tablets of his father's house (to see if) he was ever not a loyal servant in the city of Byblos. Do not be negligent of your servant. Surely the hostility of the Apiru forces is very severe against me, as the gods of your land [liv]e.

(Lines 15b–19a) Gone are our sons, [our] daughters, and the wood of our houses. They have been given to the land of Yarimuta in exchange for provisions for our lives.[b] "My field is like a woman without a husband, with no one to plow it."[3]

(Lines 19b–29a) All my towns that are in the mountains[4] or along the sea have joined the Apiru forces. Byblos and two towns still belong to me. Now Abdi-Ashirta has taken Shigata for himself. He said to the men of Ammia, "Kill your prince and become secure, like us." They were won over in accordance with his words and became like Apiru.

(Lines 29b–41) Now Abdi-Ashirta has written to the troops, "Assemble at the temple of NIN.URTA.[5] Then we will fall upon Byblos. See, there is no one who can save it from our hand. Then let us drive out the town leaders from the lands so that all the lands will join the Apiru forces. Let an alliance be made for all the lands so that our sons and daughters will be at peace forever.[c] If the king then comes forth, and all the lands are hostile to him, what can he do to us?"

(Lines 42–48) So they have made an alliance between them and I am extremely afraid, because there is no one who will save me from their hand.[d] Like birds placed in a cage,[6] so am I in the city of Byblos.[e] Why do you remain silent regarding your land?

(Lines 49–57a) Now, I have written to the palace but you do not hear my words. Look, Amanappa is with you. Ask him! He knows and has seen the trouble that is against me.[7,f] May the king listen to the words of his servant. So may he give his servant provisions and sustain his servant. I will guard his loyal city, with our Lady and our gods, for you.

(Lines 57b–65) May [the king in]spect his [lan]d and [his servant. So may he ca]re for [his] land. P[acify yo]ur [land!] May it seem go[od] in the eyes of the k[ing], my [lo]rd. May he send a man of his that he may stand (in my place). Then I will arrive before the king my lord. It is good for me to be with you. What can I do by my[sel]f? This is what I want day and night.

a Gen 33:3
b Joel 4:3
c Pss 21:5; 23:6
d Ps 17:7; Isa 36:20
e Prov 7:23; Eccl 9:12; Lam 3:52; Amos 3:5
f Gen 31:42; Exod 4:51; Deut 4:35; 2 Kgs 14:26; Eccl 6:5; Isa 58:3; Lam 1:1

3 Cf. parallels to this proverb in other Rib-Adda letters: EA 75.15–17; 81.37–38; and 90.42–44.
4 Here glossed with West Semitic *ḫa-ar-ri*; cf. Hebrew singular *har*.
5 A logographic reading of a divine name whose West Semitic form has not been identified. Cf. 2 Kgs 10:20–21.
6 Here glossed with W. Semitic *ki-lu-bi*. Cf. Jer 5:27; Amos 8:1–2.
7 Youngblood 1961:150.

REFERENCES

Text: Rainey 2015:454–457. Translations and Studies: von Dassow 2006; Moran 1992; Tropper and Vita 2010; Youngblood 1961.

LETTER FROM THE GENERAL TO RIB-ADDA OF BYBLOS CONCERNING THE RECOVERY OF LOST ASSES (EA 96) (4.82)

The general identifies himself as Rib-Adda's father. In this letter the prolific author of many epistles to the pharaoh refuses to allow citizens of Sumur to come to Byblos. Rib-Adda gives as his reason a plague that has injured the asses of the town of Sumur. However, the general warns Rib-Adda that, if the asses belong to the king (i.e., the pharaoh), they must be recovered. He mentions that he is also writing to the pharaoh and suggests that Rib-Adda guard Sumur.

(Lines 1–6) Say to Rib-Adda, my son. The message of the leader of the troops, your father. May your god[1] seek your welfare and that of your household.[a]

(Lines 7–14a) As to your saying, "I will not allow people of Sumur to enter my city[b]; there is disease in the city of Sumur," is the disease against the people or against the asses?

(Lines 14b–27) What is the disease that affects asses so that they cannot walk? Do you or do you not guard the asses of the king? No property of the king is lost.[c] Their owner may still search for them.[2] If the king is the owner of the asses, then search for the king's asses.[d] Why do you act this way toward the king's servants?

(Lines 28–33) Send men to guard the city. Look, I have written to the king about you. May he reply to me by letter regarding everything.

a Jer 29:7
b Josh 10:19
c 1 Sam 8:16
d 1 Sam 9:3

1 The use of the plural DINGIR.MEŠ to refer to a singular deity is not uncommon in the Amarna correspondence and elsewhere. Cf. the Taanach letter 2 for a special occurrence. For this singular as a plural in Babylonian usage, see Lambert 1960:67. For other occurrences associated with Byblos, cf. EA 74.57; 84.35; Youngblood 1962:25; Moran 1992:156; Smith 2008: 55–56. See also Hazor 10.21–22.

2 Rainey 1996, 3:120.

REFERENCES

Text: Rainey 2015:540–541. *Translations and Studies*: Lambert 1960; Moran 1992; Rainey 1996; Smith 2008; Youngblood 1962.

THREATENING LETTER FROM THE PHARAOH TO AZIRU (EA 162) (4.83)

This is a letter from the pharaoh to Aziru, leader of the land of Amurru. There remain about a dozen cuneiform letters authored by the pharaoh during the New Kingdom.[1] Several letters are preserved that were sent to the kings of Babylon (EA 1, 5, and 14) and of Arzawa (EA 31). He sent letters to Canaanite leaders at Ashkelon (EA 370), Gezer (EA 369), Achshaph (EA 367), and Ammiya (EA 99). Two pharaonic letters have also been found at Kamid el-Loz, ancient Kumidi. EA 163 is fragmentary. However, it is from Egypt's king and preserves the same conclusion as EA 162. The writing uses the same ductus. The ductus also matches the Kumidi correspondence. EA 162 remains the longest preserved cuneiform letter from the pharaoh to any vassal. It is important because Amurru lay near the border of those lands under Hittite control and those under Egyptian control. Despite Aziru's protests of loyalty (EA 157–161, 164–168), he appears to have been taken to Egypt (EA 169), perhaps as a result of his vacillation in loyalty between the Hittites and the Egyptians. Caught between the Hittite and Egyptian powers of his day, Aziru would eventually ally with the former.[2]

Although the upper left corner of the verso is missing, EA 162 is otherwise well preserved. There are 81 lines of text divided into twelve parts by eleven horizontal lines drawn across the tablet beneath lines 6, 11, 14, 18, 21, 29, 32, 38, 41, 54, and 77. A double horizontal line beneath the 81st line of text signals the end of the letter. These divisions reflect major areas of content and thus provide the equivalent of paragraph markers. After the initial introduction, the first five sections describe problems that the pharaoh finds with Aziru. He has listened to Rib-Adda of Byblos, given him refuge, and reinstated him as leader without informing the pharaoh. Further, Aziru has made alliance with the leader of Qedesh (presumably Etagama). Lines 30–41 (sections 6–8) constitute a charge to Aziru to change his behavior. The pharaoh warns Aziru that those whom he follows want to destroy him. He should be loyal to the Egyptian ruler rather than face his anger. The third section leaves behind the allegations and threats. In a manner similar to other letters from the pharaoh to his vassals, it describes Aziru's responsibilities. This includes a section in which Aziru (or a son of his) is commanded to appear personally before the pharaoh (lines 42–54). A second part includes a list of enemies to be turned over to the king's representative. The letter concludes with a formulaic statement of the pharaoh's health and power, presumably intended to intimidate.

(Lines 1–6) Say [to Aziru,] the leader[3] of the city of Amurru. [The messag]e of the king, your lord: 'The ruler of the city of Byblos[4] [has spoken] to you. He is the one whose brother threw him from the gate, [and who says, "T]ake me and bring me to my city. I will give you [a lot of silve]r. There is a lot of this property [but there] is nothing with me." ' He spoke to you[5] in this way.

1 Hess 1990a.

2 On the politics of Aziru, see Liverani (2004). On his role in the history of the region, especially the northern Beqaʿ, see Rainey in Rainey and Notley 2006:80–82.

3 Literally, "the man of the city …" (LÚ URU), also with found in the following line for "the man of the city of Byblos." Cf. 2 Sam 10:6, 8 for the use of "the man of Tob" to designate the leader of Tob. Note also the implications for this usage in the title of "the man" in Gen 2; Hess 1990b.

4 The pharaoh never names Rib-Adda, his chief antagonist in this letter. It may be that it was not the preferred custom for New Kingdom pharaohs to dignify their enemies by naming them, when that was deemed unnecessary.

5 The expression, "he spoke to you" (*iq-ba-ak-ku*), frames the quote from Rib Adda.

(Lines 7–11) Have you [no]t written to the king your lord [say]ing: "I am your servant as all the good city leaders [who are each] in the midst of their city"? You have done wrong by taking in a leader whose brother threw him from the gate of his own city.

(Lines 12–14) He is residing in Sidon and you have given him to the city leaders, following your own judgment. Don't you know the evil of men?

(Lines 15–18) If you are really a loyal servant of the king, why don't you denounce[a] him before the king, your lord by saying, "This city leader has written me, saying, 'Take me to yourself and bring me to my city.'"

(Lines 19–21) If you really acted loyally, (why then) is everything you wrote about them untrue? In fact, the king thought, "Everything you said is unfriendly."

(Lines 22–29) Now the king heard the following, "You are at peace with the leader of Qedesh, and you take food and strong drink together in brotherhood. It is true. Why do you act this way? Why are you at peace with the man with whom the king has a quarrel? If you really acted loyally, (why then) do you consider your own judgment but not his judgment? You don't consider what has happened to you because of the things you did not do previously. Still you are not with the king, your lord."

(Line 30–32) Consider those who teach you for their own benefit. They come to you to throw you into the fire. They lit the fire, and, as for you, you like it so much more.

(Lines 33–38) If you perform service for the king your lord, what is there that the king will not do for you? If you want to do any of this, and if you continue to hold on to these wrong things in your heart, then you will die by the royal axe, together with your whole family.

(Lines 39–41) Perform your service for the king your lord and you will live. You know that the king does not want to go to the whole land of Canaan when he is angry.[6]

a Dan 3:8; 6:25

b Exod 22:21; 23:9; Deut 23:7; 24:14, 17

(Lines 42–54) When you wrote, you said, "Let the king, my lord, allow me (to remain where I am) this year, that I may come to the king, [my lo]rd, next year. Otherwise, let my son [go] to {the king}." Now the king, your lord, has allowed you to remain this year, just as you said. You come or send your son, and you will see the king by whose sight all the lands prosper.[7] Do not say, "Let him allow (me to remain where I am) this year, too," If it is not possible to come before the king, your lord, send your son in place of yourself, to the king, your lord. If it is impossible, let him come.

(Lines 55–77) Now the king, your lord, listened when you wrote to him, "May the king, my lord, send me Ḫanni, the messenger of the king, once more. Then I will deliver the king's enemies into his hand." See, he comes to you, just as you said. So hand them over, omitting none of them.[8] See, the king, your lord, has brought you the names of his enemies on a tablet by means of Ḫanni, the messenger of the king. So hand them over to the king, your lord, omitting none of them. Fix bronze shackles on their feet. Here are the men you must deliver to the king, your lord:
Sharru with all his sons;
Tuya;
Leya with all his sons;
Pishyari with all his sons;
the son-in-law of Manya with his sons and his wives;
the commissioner who knows impiety, who has mocked a foreign guest[b];
Dasharti;
Baaluma[9];
Nimmahe who is a brigand in Amurru.

(Lines 78–81)
You should know that the king is as healthy as the sun in the sky. His troops, his many chariots from the Upper Land to the Lower Land and from the rising of the sun to the going in of the sun, are very well.

6 This and the preceding two sections focus on three increasingly dramatic word pictures to make their point. Lines 30–32 emphasize the rebellion of city leaders as fire. Lines 33–38 identify the axe as an instrument of death that Aziru will face. Lines 39–41 identify the pharaoh's rage as the source of the punishment that threatens Aziru. See Hess 1990a:143–144.

7 The opportunity to behold the life-giving prosperity of the pharaoh, and thereby to receive it, lies at the center of this section and forms the primary motivation for Aziru.

8 Extradition of royal enemies from the vassal's land forms a standard stipulation of suzerain-vassal treaties. Contrast Deut 23:15–16.

9 This West Semitic name is the only one on the list that is cannot be Egyptian.

REFERENCES

Text: Rainey 2015:802–807. *Translations and Studies*: Hess 1990a; 1990b; Liverani 2004; Rainey and Notley 2006; van der Westhuizen 2012.

LETTER OF MAYARZANA OF HASI TO THE PHARAOH ABOUT AMANHATPE'S CONQUESTS OF TOWNS IN THE REGION (EA 185) (4.84)

This text represents one of two letters written by Mayarzana, leader of Hasi, a site in the Beqaʿ. The other letter, EA 186, is much more damaged. The author appeals for assistance to fight Amanhatpe, another city ruler. Apiru have attacked, plundered, and burned four other towns. The iterative style of the repeated town destructions resemble other ancient Near Eastern conquest accounts, including that of Joshua 10:28–42.[1] The text is divided into seven sections that are separated by six lines drawn across the tablet following lines 8, 15, 20, 26, 36, and 41. Following a standard introduction, lines 9–41 recount the destruction of the towns. Lines 42–76 focus on Mayarzana's successful defense of his town and his charge that Amanhatpe is an Apiru, a traitor to the pharaoh.

(Lines 1–8) Say to the king, my lord, my god, [m]y Sun god. The message of Mayarzana,[2] the leader of Hasi, your servant, the dust beneath the feet of the king, my lord, my god, my Sun god, and the ground on which he treads. I have fallen [seven times] and seven times at the feet of [the kin]g, m[y lor]d, my god, my Sun god.[a]

(Lines 9–15) [May] the king, my lord, m[y go]d, my Su[n god, kno]w the action that Amanhatpe, the leader of Tushulti, did against the towns of the king, my lord; when the Apiru made war against me and [sei]zed the towns of the king, my lord, my god, my Sun god.

(Lines 16–20) The Apiru seized Mahsibti, a town of the king, my lord. They completely plundered it and sent it up in flames.[3] Then the Apiru took refuge with Ama[nhatpe].[b]

(Lines 21–26) The Apiru seized Giluni, a town of the king, my lord. They plundered it and sent it up in flames so that hardly a single house survived from the town of Giluni. Then the Apiru took refuge with Amanhatpe.

(Lines 28–35) The Apiru seized Magdali, a town of the king, my lord, my god, m[y] Sun god. They completely plundered it and sent it up in flames so that hardly a single house survived from the town of Magdali. Then the Apiru took refuge with Amanhatpe.

(Lines 36–41) As for Ushte, a town of the king, my lord; the Apiru seized it. They plundered it and sent it up in flames. Then the Apiru took refuge with Amanhatpe.

(Lines 42–49) See! The Apiru attacked Hasi, a town of the king, my lord. We engaged the Apiru in battle and we defeated them. Forty Apiru soug[ht refuge] with [Amanha]tpe. He received [those who] escaped and they gathered in his town. Therefore, [Ama]nhatpe is one of the Ha[piru.]

(Lines 50–60) We hear[d tha]t the Apiru were with Amanhatpe. So my bro[thers,] my so[ns,] your servants, dispatched chariots to Amanhatpe. My brothers said to Amanhatpe, "Hand over the Apiru traitors to the king, our lord. [We] want to interrogate the Apiru who took refuge with you. They captured the towns of the king, my lord, and they have set them on fire."

(Lines 61–64) He agreed to hand over the (forty) Apiru. However, he took them by night and he fled to the Apiru. See! Amanhatpe is a traitor.

(Lines 65–76) May the king, my lord, interrogate him! He (Amanhatpe) has deserted from him. So may the king, my lord, not remain silent without investigating Amanhatpe.[4] As to any other man, may he not bring traitors to the loyal land of the king, my lord. The [kin]g, my lord, will interrogate Amanhatpe, the traitor, and banish (him) from his presence.[5] We will obey. See! I am a loyal servant of the king, my lord.

a line 8 "seven times" Gen 33:3

b lines 18–19 "sent it up in flames" Josh 11:11

1 See Hess 1998
2 This name has affinities with Sanskrit but remains unclear as to its etymology. See Hess 1993:111.
3 For the emphasis on both verbs see Rainey 1996, 2:159, 162; 3:240.
4 See Rainey 1996, 3:23.
5 Literally, "expel(?) from him."

REFERENCES

Text: Rainey 2015:866–871. Translations and Studies: Hess 1993; 1998; Rainey 1996.

LABAYA OF SHECHEM WRITES THE PHARAOH TO EXPLAIN HIS LOYALTY (EA 252) (4.85)

As the first of three letters from Labaya leader of Shechem to the pharaoh, this text provides some of the most vivid imagery and rhetorical forms.[1] Labaya attempts to persuade the pharaoh of his innocence and of the oppression of his enemies. The preface omits honorifics toward the pharaoh that occur in EA 253 and 254, Labaya's other letters. This may suggest a more defiant tone of the ruler of Shechem. Throughout the letter the most frequent verb is *ṣabātu* "to seize, capture." This occurs five times, and always precedes URU, the logogram for "town." Thus the chief concern of the author is that enemies have seized one of his towns and will seize another if things continue as they are. The first and final occurrences of this key verb appear in a similar phrase. Lines 6–7 contain the pharaoh's command, "Guard the men who seized the town." Near the end of the letter, lines 28–29 conclude, "I will indeed guard the men who seized the town …" The lines in between constitute Labaya's justification for not obeying the pharaoh earlier. Indeed, following the commands of lines 6–7, we would expect an obedient response, "I do/will guard the men." The absence of such an immediate response would have surprised the pharaoh and drawn his attention to the following lines that interrupt the obedient statement of lines 28–29. This consists of three parts: the wrong done to Labaya (lines 9–15), the manner in which that wrong renders passivity dangerous (lines 16–22), and the final assurance of loyalty despite the danger (lines 23–28a).

In the first part of this response, Labaya emphasizes his loyalty with a threefold repetition of the verb, *tamû* "to swear," in line 10. Likely this oath was sworn before a divine image. Yet at the same time that Labaya was performing this exemplary act of loyalty, his "own" divine image was stolen. The following parallel expression, "the plunderers of my father," invite the understanding that not only was the town that Labaya's father had passed on to him captured by the enemy. "My god," here understood in parallel with "my father," as an image of the ancestor, was also stolen. Yet Labaya was slandered before the pharaoh (lines 13–15) with the result that his loyalty is questioned and he is misunderstood.

The proverb regarding the ant forms the focus of the second part of Labaya's defense in lines 16–22. No proverb like this occurs in the Bible. It suggests an attitude of defiance and overt resistance against those who would destroy the leader of Shechem. However, Labaya is not so bold to write this explicitly. It would no doubt contradict the command of the pharaoh. Instead, he appeals to this proverbial analogy from the animal world. If an ant responds in this manner, how much more should Labaya!

Nevertheless, the final section, lines 23–31, consists of a willingness to "fall beneath" Labaya's enemies and to suffer death, should the pharaoh require this of him. Indeed, Labaya here is ready to affirm his loyalty in which he will "guard the men who captured the town and my god." The repetition of the verb, "guard," emphasizes the loyalty of Labaya, despite the implicit right Labaya claims to wreak vengeance like the ant. This proverb lies at the center of this rhetorically sophisticated missive designed to persuade the pharaoh of Labaya's loyalty and to lead him to agree with the leader of Shechem that it is necessary to fight back.

(Lines 1–4) Say to the king, my lord. The message of Labaya[2] your servant. At the feet of the king, my lord, I fall.

(Lines 5–13) Because you wrote, "Guard the men who captured the town," (I respond) How can I guard the men? The town was captured during a battle. When I swore peace and while I swore,[3] an officer was swearing with me. The town and my god[4] were captured.

(Lines 14–15) I have been slandered before the king, my lord.

a Prov 6:6; 30:25

(Lines 16–19) Furthermore, when an ant is swatted, does it fight back[5] and bite the hand of the man who swats it?[a]

(Lines 20–22) How can I show fear these days? Another town of mine will be seized.

(Lines 23–28a) Furthermore, if you also say, "Fall beneath them so that they might smite you," I would do it.

(Lines 28b–31) I will indeed guard the men who captured the town and my god, the plunderers of my father. And I will indeed guard them.

1 Cf. Hess 1993:96–103. For the tablet with transliteration, translation, and commentary, cf. Bezold and Budge 1892:no. 61; Knudtzon 1915:807; Albright 1943 (also *ANET*, 486); Halpern and Huehnergard 1982; Moran 1992:305–306.

2 The name is WS for "lion" plus the hypocoristic suffix, "*-ya*." The name is common among WS names of the late second millennium and the first millennium BCE. Cf. Hess 1994:103.

3 This phrase (line 10) translates two *kî* clauses that contain the same verb form, *it-mì*. Like the preceding phrase, with its *i-na nu-kur-te*, the clauses describe the circumstances during which the attack takes place.

4 The form, *i–li*, can be analyzed as a verb from the root, *le'û* (cf. Halpern and Huehnergard 1982), the customary indications of a guttural, a broken writing, or an additional vowel sign, are absent. However, the form "my god" may be found as part of personal names such as *i-li-mil-ki* and *i-li-ra-pí-'i* (Hess 1993a:204; 1993b:97).

5 *ti-qà-bi-lu* as a prefixed form of D stem *qubbulu* "to fight." Rainey (1996, 2:148) suggests a D stem of *kapālu* "to curl up."

REFERENCES

Text: Rainey 2015:1022–1025; Knudtzon 1915. *Translations and Studies*: Albright 1943; Bezold and Budge 1892; Halpern and Huehnergard 1982; Hess 1993a; 1993b; Moran 1992; Rainey 1996.

TELL EL-HESI LETTER (EA 333) (4.86)

The first cuneiform tablet found in the land of Israel was discovered at Tell el-Hesi in 1892 (Sayce 1893). When Knudtzon (1915:944–947) published his work on the Amarna tablets, he included this text and numbered it as EA 333. It is related to the events in and around Lachish as described in EA 329–332. The letter is written by Papu to the Leader. Papu is an Egyptian name occurring only here (lines 2 and 22) in texts from the region (Hess 1993:122–123). He may be an Egyptian administrator writing to the pharaoh with a report concerning the politics of the region. Hilprecht's photo (1896: plate 24 numbers 66–67) and copy (plate 64 number 147) were remarkably accurate. The transliteration and translation of Albright (1942), published fifty years after the discovery, continues to prove useful.

(Lines 1–3) [Say to the L]eader.[1] [The message of] Papu. At your [fe]et I fall.

(Lines 4–7) May you know that Shipti-Balu[2] and Zimrida[3] have conspired to be disloyal.[4,a]

(Lines 8–14) Shipti-Balu said to Zimrida: The troops of the town of Yaramu[5,b] wrote to me, "Give me [...] + 1 bows, 3 daggers, and 3 swords."

a Ezek 16:57; 28:24, 26

b Josh 10:3, 5, 23; 12:11, 35; 21:29; Neh 11:29

(Lines 15–18) "If I go out against the royal land, you join with me and alongside of me."

(Lines 19–23) He still answers me, "Act against the government! He who acts against the king is Papu. Therefore, send him before me!"

(Lines 24–26) Now I send Rabi-ilu. He will indeed answer him [in] this matter.

1 LÚ.GAL "great man," also used of the Egyptian administrator, Haya, in Aphek letter 7 line 1.

2 For this reading and Ugaritic parallels, cf. Hess 1993:143–144. Shipti-Balu is the leader of Lachish. He has a West Semitic name. Cf. biblical Jehoshaphat.

3 Ibid. 169–170. Like his conspirator, Zimrida has a West Semitic name (cf. biblical Zimri). For the dominance of West Semitic names among town leaders in the Shephelah and along the entire East Mediterranean coast (except around Akko), see Hess 2006.

4 This understands the verb in line 5 as a D-stem 3rd masculine plural imperfect West Semitic of *šwṭ*. See Albright 1942:33–34, n. 8; Moran 1992:356–357, n. 3; Rainey 1996, 2:175. Probably the infinitive appears in line 20 and the 3cs preterite in line 21.

5 Jarmuth (Khirbet el-Yarmuk)? So Albright 1942:36, n. 30.

REFERENCES

Text: Rainey 2015:1220–1221; Knudtzon 1915. *Translations and Studies*: Albright 1942; Hess 1993; 2006; Hilprecht 1896; Moran 1992; Rainey 1996; Sayce 1893.

CUNEIFORM TEXTS FROM HAZOR 8, 10, 12, 18 (4.87A–D)

Richard S. Hess

The excavation of the largest Bronze Age tell in modern Israel, Tel Hazor, has produced eighteen fragments and complete documents ranging in date from the Middle Bronze Age through the Late Bronze Age (Horowitz and Oshima 2010; Horowitz forthcoming). These cuneiform texts include a variety: inscribed vessels and jar handles, a court record, a school tablet, administrative documents, letters, a multiplication table, administrative documents, a clay liver model, and two fragments of a law collection. Only Taanach, with its fewer (fifteen) cuneiform texts, can compare to Hazor in terms of the quantity and diversity of writing in the region. Hazor is the only city in Southern Canaan to be mentioned in the Mari texts. In terms of its size and written remains, it dominated the region throughout the second millennium BCE Bronze Age (cf. Josh 11:10).

HAZOR 8 (4.87A)

This letter fragment dates from the Middle Bronze Age. It seems likely that Ibni-Addu, the king of Hazor known from Mari texts addressed to Hazor, is intended here.[1] Although none of the three personal names are completely preserved they are likely all West Semitic forms. Irpa-Addu may be a litigant in the lawsuit of Hazor 5, where this name also appears (Horowitz 1992:166; 2006:78).

1 Bonechi 1992.

(Lines 1–2) Say to Ibni-[Addu]. The message of Irp[a-Addu …]

(Lines 3–4) Regarding your bringing of the young woman[2] in the ch[arge of …]

(Lines 5–8) One woman, Aba[…] ob[jected …] She said as follows, "Until […]" She said[3] […]

2 Logogram MÍ.TUR for *ṣuḫārtim*, "young woman." See Na'aman 2004:92–99 for the occurrences of this noun in Canaan and its implication of a woman of subservient status.

3 *iq-bi-am* with the uncontracted ventive, an indication of an Old Babylonian form, similar to the forms at Mari. See Rainey 1996, 2:31; 1999:155*.

HAZOR 10 (4.87B)

This letter is entirely preserved. Along with a three-line administrative text, this Late Bronze Age letter was discovered in 1996 at Hazor's royal palace. It resembles the Amarna letters from Hazor (EA 227 and 228) and the Taanach correspondence from the Late Bronze Age.[4]

(Lines 1–3) Say to Puratpurta.[5] The message of Adduapdi(?).[6]

(Lines 4–6) May the gods and the Sun-god seek your wellbeing,[a] the well being of your house, the well being of your sons, and of your land.

(Lines 7–12) You have written me by means of Yarima:[7] "Send the women of the young men[8] and whatever is necessary for them."

(Lines 13–22) I said: "I am indeed sending." Now Yarima is here. Ask him. Here they are. They had departed / moved away[9,b] from work. The god(s)[10] have decided/judged[11,c] between me and them.

a 1 Sam 1:17

b Gen 12:8; 26:22; Job 9:5; 14:18; 18:4

c Pss 7:12; 50:6; 58:12; 75:8; 82:1, 8

4 Horowitz 2000:16.

5 This name is best analyzed as either Kassite or Hurrian. It represents the presence of "northern" names bearers in and around the Beqa and Jordan Valleys in the Late Bronze Age. For the name's analysis, see Horowitz 2000:23–24; Hess 2003:41; 2006:355. For the presence of northern personal names, see Hess 1997; 2006. Northern (especially Hurrian and, less so, Anatolian and Indo-Aryan) names may occur in the traditions preserved in the book of Joshua, in names such as Piram, Hoham, Sheshai, and Talmai. See Hess 1996.

6 The last two signs of this name are read *-um-mi* in Na'aman 2004:95, following E. Weissert. However, see the collation of Horowitz 2006:81. In either case, the name is West Semitic.

7 A West Semitic name.

8 Na'aman 2004:95, "the wives of the *ṣuḫārū*."

9 Analyze *ip-ta-nu* as a Gt stem of *panû*, "depart, move away from." This glosses the West Semitic suffix conjugation of *'tq* "to move on." Horowitz 2000:22.

10 On the use of the plural DINGIR.MEŠ with a singular verb see EA 96.4–6.

11 The Akkadian G perfect *parāsu* (here *parāšu*) with the West Semitic *šāpaṭ*, a synonymous vocable.

HAZOR 12 (4.87C)

This Middle Bronze Age letter provides a list of textiles[12] and luxury goods (including metal work). It is followed by a command to move these goods to the writer who is at Mari and who intends to go on to Ekallātum (Horowitz and Wasserman 2004). This text preserves important evidence of Hazor's connection with Mari, perhaps the Mari of Samsî-Addu.[13] Horowitz and Wasserman (2004) suggest that this texts describes items for a marriage between Samsî-Addu's son, Yasmah-Addu, and a princess of Qatna.

(Lines 2′–19′)[14]
02′ 60 [luxury g]arments
03′ 60 delicate cloths of best quality; 120 delicate cloths [of second class quality];
04′ 60 *sakkum* cloths of best quality; 120 *sakkum* cloths [of second class quality];
05′ 60 *zakûm* cloths of best quality; 120 *zakûm* cloths of second class quality;
06′ 10 linen garments of the finest quality; 30 *sak burêm* covers;
07′ 10 linen cloths; 10 linen cloths;
08′ 20 *lamaḫuššu* (wool) robes;
09′ 20 clean *sakkum* cloths; 20 *ḫalû* garments;
10′ 60 wool *ḫalû* garments; 120 scarves;
11′ 180 of the finest articles of clothing[d]; 120 *i'lu* bands.
12′ 300 articles of clothing of second class quality; 1,000 felt cloths;
13′ 300 long shirts of patchwork;
14′ 300 beaded shirts;
15′ 180 felt shirts;
16′ 1,000 headbands;
17′ 5,000 headdresses; 3,000 silver rivets;
18′ 1,000 gold rivets;
19′ 2,000 bows; 2,000 bronze …

d Josh 7:21; Judg 14:12–19

12 Hazor textiles are mentioned in the international Amarna correspondence, EA 22 ii 41, and EA 25 iv 40. Cf. Moran 1992:83 n. 36; Horowitz, Oshima, and Sanders 2006:83 n. 21.

13 Ziegler and Charpin 2004.

14 On the logographic readings and their interpretation, see Horowitz and Wasserman 2000:170–174; 2006:84–85. Line 1' is broken.

(Lines 20′–27′)
Let them send (these items) quickly to me at Mari. Something bad could happen.[15] After I have reached the city of Mari, I will go on to Ekallatum to make sacrifices and celebrations. You should not be negligent to make the arrangements. [. . .] Let them watch [. . .]

[15] Cf. EA 8 for a report of merchants who were captured and murdered near Hannathon and Acco.

HAZOR 18 (4.87D)[16]

Excavations at Hazor in the summer of 2010 yielded two Middle Bronze Age cuneiform fragments of a collection of laws in the style of Hammurabi and the other Old Babylonian legal collections. However, these laws do not match with any existing legal collection. Thus they suggest a distinctive legal tradition at Hazor contemporary with Hammurabi. This is the first evidence for a Bronze Age legal tradition among the archives and written materials of Canaan in the second millennium BCE. It demonstrates the presence of written laws in this region, and invites further study in light of the later biblical legal traditions. It can no longer be maintained that the biblical authors of their legal materials necessarily had to reach beyond the West Semitic world to find antecedents.

Fragment A (preserving portions of the beginnings of five lines)
[If . . .], 12 shekels of [silver . . .]
If the n[ose . . .], 10 (shekels) to the owner of the sl[ave . . .]
If the tooth[. . .], 3 shekels of silver to [the owner of the slave . . .]

Fragment B (preserving three lines of which only part of the second line is readable)
[. . .] to the ow[ner of the slave . . .]

[16] See Horowitz, Oshima, and Vukosavović 2012.

REFERENCES

Bonechi 1992; Hess 1996; 1997; 2003; 2006; Horowitz 2000; Horowitz and Oshima 2010; Horowitz, Oshima and Sanders 2006; Horowitz, Oshima and Vukosavović 2012; Horowitz and Shaffer 1992; Horowitz and Wasserman 2000; 2004; Na'aman 2004; Rainey 1996; 1999; Ziegler and Charpin 2004.

MEDICAL TEXTS

THE PRACTICE OF MEDICINE

JoAnn Scurlock

Ancient Mesopotamian medicine benefited from the expertise of two specialists, one of whom (*asû* = the "pharmacist") collected the information recorded in the pharmacological texts (4.88A), assisted in devising treatments, and dispensed medicines to patients whose medical problem was already known. The other (*āšipu* = the "doctor") diagnosed and treated patients using a growing corpus of diagnostic and therapeutic handbooks (and/or a friendly "pharmacist") to help him in his work.[1] The diagnostic system was a flexible one, allowing for both what we would consider to be "natural" and "supernatural" causes. In addition to malfunctioning body parts (4.88B) and specially named syndromes (4.88C–E), the "natural" causes, ancient Mesopotamians attributed diseases to the baleful influence of gods (4.88F–G), ghosts and demons (4.88H–J) and witchcraft (4.88K–M). These "supernatural" causes were not part of a separate system of diagnosis but, on the contrary, behaved in exactly the same way as the "natural" causes with one exception. Certain classes of disease as, for example, fevers and skin conditions lent themselves to a system of assigning a group of similar diseases to a group of related spirits and/or allowed for variations within a single syndrome to be attributed to the interference of specific gods.[2] Last but not least, medical text commentaries (4.88N) allow us a peek into the minds of ancient Mesopotamians.

1 See Scurlock 1999.
2 For a full discussion, see Scurlock and Andersen 2005:429–528.

REFERENCES

Scurlock 1999; Scurlock and Andersen 2005:429–528.

BEGINNINGS OF PHARMACOLOGY (KADP 1)[1] (4.88A)

JoAnn Scurlock

List of plants are an old tradition in Mesopotamia; they found their way westwards as part of the scholastic tradition by means of which Sumerian and Akkadian were taught to non-native speakers. A curious late echo of this tradition appears in Bar Hebraeus, who includes a list of plants in his account of the third day of creation. Apparently beginning in the Late Bronze Age and in Assyria, scholars also began to compile plant lists, a tradition with a bright future in the Mediterranean World culminating in the work of the mid-1st century CE Cilician, Dioscorides. These lists were intended to aid in the recognition and use of medicinal plants. They also aimed to sort out the tangled mess created by empire of similar or identical plants with different names in different languages or with fanciful and curious popular names, as well as the difficulties of identical names for more than one plant. Ultimately, the goal was to combine this with other information about plants of interest such as their appearance, habitat and medical uses into one grand compendium. KADP 1 is the earliest exemplar of this compendium known to us by its ancient name of URU.AN.NA. Of medical texts, this compendium was the last to receive canonical form, which it did under the aegis of the Assyrian king Aššurbanipal.

KADP 1 col. i–iv together form a one-tablet version of the later multi-tablet series. Column v is formatted as what we call a vademecum, that is a text specifically designed to collect plant uses. Unlike the normal vademeca, however, KADP 1 col. v organizes by plant (all the uses of a particular plant) rather than by plant use (all the plants useful for a particular medical problem). A number of the entries duplicate information gathered together into a separate pharmacological treatise known as the "Nature of Plants" (*Šammu šikinšu*).[2]

(Col. i.1–4) *Urânu*, *tullal* (and) *sikillu* are equivalent to *maštakal*. It (*maštakal*) is a plant for purification.
(i.5–7) ŠAKIR is *šakirû*. It (*šakirû*) is equivalent to ⌜"sunflower"⌝ and *arzatu*.
(i.8–9) *Kazallu* is equivalent to *ararianu*. *Išbabtu* is equivalent to *mullaḫtu*.
(i.10–11) *Atartu* and *erišti eqli* are equivalent to *ḫasarratu*.
(i.12–13) *Erišti ereši* and *erišti kasî* are equivalent to *šambaliltu*-fenugreek.

1 For the restorations of numerous broken entries and the odd collation, see the *CAD* under the plant names in the lexical sections. Parts of column v are translated in Böck 2011b.
2 An edition of this series appears in Stadhouders 2011 with the translation in Stadhouders 2012.

(i.14–16) URU.TI.LA is *ḫarūbu*-carob. "White plant" (Ú BABBAR) is *ṣarbātu*-poplar resin.
(i.17–18) "Black plant" is *aktam*.[3] "Red plant" is *ḫaṭṭi re'i* ("shepherd's staff").
(i.19–21) "Green plant" is *irrû*-coloquinth. It (*irrû*-coloquinth) is equivalent to "life plant" and wild *imḫur-lim*.
(i.22–23) "Daughter of the field" is equivalent to *ararû*.[4] *Erišti eqli* is eqivalent to *iptu*.
(i.24–25) *Anunutu* is ^{Ú}ÁB.DAR. *Adumatu* is what *kana(š)u* is called in this country.
(i.26–27) *Ḫurmu* is equivalent to *karān šēlibi* ("fox grape"). It (*karān šēlibi*) is a plant for the liver.[5]
(i.28–30) *Ananiḫu* is equivalent to *urnû*. *Šibibiānu* and *šimru* are equivalent to *zibû*.
(i.31–32) *Arzallum* is "Fine Hair" (SÍG SAL.LA). It (*Arzallum*) is equivalent to *ḫašḫur api* ("swamp apple").
(i.33–35) *Daddaru* is equivalent to ˹*kurdinnu*˺. *Tarupadi* is equivalent to [*laptu*-turnip]. KI.LUḪ.ḪA is equivalent to [...].
(ii.1–3) [...], ˹*piqû*˺ and ˹*na(m)ṣabu*˺ are equivalent to the [seed of the *pillû*-mandragora].
(ii.4–5) [*Baltu*-thorn] is a plant for ˹*maškadu*˺.[6]
(ii.6–8) [...] is a plant for [...], [...] and [...].
(ii.9–10) [*Azallû*] is a plant for depression.[7] It ([*Azallû*]) is equivalent to *ḫurṣatu*.
(ii.11–12) [*Gurgurru*] is "[ox] lung" plant. It ([*gurgurru*]) is equivalent to ˹*ḫurmu*˺.
(ii.13–14) [*Ata'išu*] is a plant [that grows wild]. ^{Ú}KUR.KUR is [*ata'išu*].
(ii.15–16) ˹*Zariqu*˺ and ˹*kamullu*˺ are equivalent to [*kassibu*].
(ii.17–21) (too fragmentary for translation)
(iii.2′–3′) [^{Ú}ḪAB] is "plant for *bu'šānu*." It is equivalent to [...].
(iii.4′–6′) A plant for ˹wolf˺ [attack] is a plant for "wandering about."[8] Garden [...] and [...] are plants for "wandering about."[9]
(iii.7′–8′) "Silver [blossom]" is *nuṣābu*. Yellow "Gold [face]" is similar to *nuṣābu*.
(iii.9′–10′) ˹*Sapalginu*˺ and ˹*namulḫu*˺ are equivalent to *kurkanû*.
(iii.11′–13′) ˹*Ḫazallunu*˺ is equivalent to *buṭnānu*. ˹*Puḫpuḫḫu*˺ is an exceptionally large plant.
(iii.14′–17′) *Imḫur-ašna* is "long [plant]," "fish [intestines]," "˹milk-giving˺ [plant]" and "dog ˹intestines˺."
(iii.18′–19′) ˹*Aruššu*˺ and *labišu* are equivalent to *amuššu*-onion.
(iii.20′–21′) ˹*Kuniphu*˺ is equivalent to *ezizzu*-onion. ˹*Ezizzu*-onion˺ is a ˹plant˺ for the lungs.[10]
(iii.22′–23′) (too fragmentary for translation)
(iii.24′–25′) ˹TU$_9$˺.NIM is *saggilatu*. *Uḫḫulu qarnānu* is a plant for "wandering about."
(iii.26′–27′) *Kudimārānu* is equivalent to *saḫlānu*. ^{Ú}NIM.È is *kuṣimānu*.
(iii.28′–30′) ÚR.TÁL.TÁL is *memētu*. *Alluzu* is equivalent to *šimaḫu*-boxthorn. It (*šimaḫu*-boxthorn) is a ˹plant˺ for intestinal prolapse.
(iii.31′–34′) ˹*Bukānu*˺ (GIŠ.GAN) is equivalent to *siḫpu* (= inner *kiškānu* bark). [...] is equivalent to *kana'(š)u*. [*Urṭu*] and [*edenâ*] are plants for *šaššaṭu*.
(iii.35′–36′) ˹*Puglānu*˺ is a [plant of the canebrake]. [...] is equivalent to [...]
(iii.37′–38′) [KI.^{d}ŠEŠ.KI] is ˹*aṣuṣimtu*˺. [Plant for ...] is ˹*aṣuṣimtu*˺ for cattle.[11]
(iii.39′–41′) (too fragmentary for translation)
(iii.42′–44′) [*Akak nāri*] is equivalent to *alapû*. [...] is equivalent to [...] [...] is equivalent to [...]
(iii.45′–47′) (too fragmentary for translation)
(iv.1–8) (too fragmentary for translation)
(iv.9–11) ˹*Ḫazallunu*˺ is equivalent to *ṣibūru*. *Ḫabi*(?)-*bānu* is a plant for the lungs and a late (blooming) plant.
(iv.12–13) ˹"Sweet plant"˺ is ˹*arariānu*˺. [...] is equivalent to [...]
(iv.14–16) ˹*Tubāqu*˺ is equivalent to ˹*kamkādu*˺. [...] is equivalent to [...]. [...] is its fruit.
(iv.17–21′) (too fragmentary for translation)
(iv.22′–23′) "Its mother" is a plant [to be used to make glazes]. "Its son" is equivalent to [*labubītu*].[12]
(iv.24′–26′) *Ēlilu* is equivalent to [wild *maštakal*]. *Urbatu*-rush is equivalent to [*niaru*-papyrus]; its seed is equivalent to ˹*kungu*˺.
(iv.27′–28′) *Šizbānu* is equivalent to ˹*ḫilabānu*˺. *Namḫarû*[13] is equivalent to "˹Ištar's bed˺."
(iv.29′–30′) *Šigguštu*[14] is equivalent to *elligu*-stone (plant). *Qulqullânu*[15] is equivalent to ˹*dukdumu*˺.
(iv.31′–32′) *Baru*-cereal and *kiššenu*-peas are ˹*šuḫu*˺-peas (= large peas).

3 For more information in pharmacological texts on this plant, see BAM 1 i.19–20; ii.25, 28; BAM 421 i.34′; BAM 426 ii.20′; KADP 1 v.42; BAM 380:14–15//BAM 381 iii.4–5//STT 92 iii.30′–31′.
4 For more information in pharmacological texts on this plant, see BAM 1 i.55.
5 For more information in pharmacological texts on this plant, see BAM 1 ii.11, 49.
6 See Scurlock and Andersen 2005:257–258.
7 See Scurlock and Andersen 2005:382–383.
8 The reference is to rabies. See Scurlock and Andersen 2005:21–23, but see 4.88J for a correction to the discussion.
9 See *CAD* R 147. To note is that listeriosis is a completely inappropriate interpretation, since human beings do not suffer from "staggers."
10 See Scurlock and Andersen 2005:42–48, 177–184.
11 Restoration is based on a similar entry for donkeys.
12 For more information on this plant, see KADP 33:4–5 (Stadhouders 2011:25).
13 The plant appears in KADP 33:12–13 (Stadhouders 2011:25–26).
14 The plant appears in BAM 379 i 34//SpTU 3.106 obv. 12′ (Stadhouders 2011:19).
15 The plant is mentioned in a medical commentary SpTU 1.51 r. 9.

(iv.33′–34′) GÚ and *abšu* are *kakkû*-peas (= small peas).
(iv.35′–37′) GÚ.GAL is *ḫallūru*-chickpea. GÚ.TUR and *abšu lagu* are (other names for) *lallangu*.
(iv.38′–39′) GÚ.[ḪAB] ("stinky bean") is *kiššenu*-pea. ⟨GA⟩ BA.[RA] ("beaten" milk) is ⌜*eqidu*-cheese⌝.
(iv.40′–41′) *Pinnaru*-cheese[16] (smells/looks like) ⌜*kabû*-dung⌝. *Pinirtu* is the equivalent of *qarratḫu*.
(iv.42′–43′) GA ḪAB (sour milk) is called ⌜*nagāḫu*⌝ and *kisimmu*.
(iv.44′–45′) *Ašūḫu*-pine is the equivalent of ⌜*miḫru*⌝-fir. *Lammu*-almond is equivalent to ⌜*dulbu*⌝-plane tree.
(iv.46′–47′) *Šunû*-chaste tree and *kanirḫu*-tree are equivalent to ⌜*ṣilurtu*⌝-tree.
(iv.48′–49′) *Šallūru*-plum is equivalent to ⌜*ḫaḫḫu*⌝-pear. Wild *šallūru*-plum is equivalent to [wild] *ḫaḫḫu*-pear.
(iv.50′–51′) *Urzīnu*-tree is equivalent to ⌜*mušku*⌝-tree. "Fruit of the trees" (*mutḫummu*) means from the trees [of the garden].
(iv.52′–53′) *Qatrānu*-resin is the sap of [*erēnu*-cedar]. "Assorted aromatics" are similar to [...]
(v.1) Green [*girimmu*-berry] is a plant for dog bite. It is to be ground (and) [daubed] on the [bite].
(v.2) White [*girimmu*-berry] is a plant for impotence.[17] It is to be ground (and) [given to drink] in first quality beer.
(v.3) Red [*girimmu*-berry] is a plant for Lamaštu.[18] It is to be ground (and) [rubbed gently on] (mixed) with oil.[19]

(v.4) Fresh [*maštakal*] is a plant for dog bite.[20] It is to be ground (and) [daubed] on the ⌜bite⌝.[21]
(v.5) ⌜*Maštakal*⌝ is a plant for "hand" of god. It's leaf is to be wrapped in a tuft of wool (and) [put] ⌜on⌝ [the person's neck].

(v.6) ⌜*Šakirû*⌝ [seed] is a plant for "hand" of god.[22] Its leaf is to be ground, [poured] into water (and) [used in a bath].
(v.7) ⌜*Šakirû*⌝ [root][23] is a plant for toothache.[24] It is to be ground (and) [put] ⌜on⌝ the [tooth].
(v.8) ⌜*Šakirû*⌝ is a plant for a ⟨woman⟩ having difficulty giving birth.[25] It is to be ground (and) [rubbed gently on, (mixed)] with oil.

(v.9) [...] is a plant for dog bite. It is to be ground (and) [daubed] on the [bite].
(v.10) [...] is a plant for snake bite. It is to be ground (and) [...].

(v.11) [...] is a plant for impotence. It is to be ground (and) [gently rubbed on], (mixed) with oil.
(v.12) [...] is a plant for a ⟨woman⟩ having difficulty giving birth. It is to be ground (and) [...]

(v.13) [...] is a plant for scorpion sting and (the resulting) ⌜numbness⌝.[26]
(v.14) It is to be poured into water (and) used to ⌜bathe⌝ the person.

(v.15) ⌜*Ṣaṣuntu*⌝ is a plant for [*samānu*-cellulitis].[27] It is to be ground (and) ⌜rubbed gently on⌝ (mixed) with oil.
(v.16) [*Ṣaṣuntu*] is a plant for there not to be wild animals in a person's house. It is to be ground, [poured] into [water]
(v.17) (and) sprinkled in the house.

(v.18) ⌜*Maštakal*⌝ is a plant for the holy water vessel[28] (and) to be eaten on the day of the disappearance of the moon.
(v.19) Male *maštakal* is a plant for sorcerous rituals not to approach a person. It is to be eaten on the day of the disappearance of the moon.

(v.20) *Maštakal* seed is a plant to stop nosebleed. It is to be wrapped in a tuft of wool (and) put into the (nasal) opening.[29]
(v.21) You saturate the wool (with it). It is to be put into his nose.[30]

(v.22) *Maštakal* seed is a plant to obtain an erection. You spin its leaf in red-dyed wool
(v.23) (and) it is to be put under his bed.

---

16 This is presumably the same word as Turkish *peynir*.
17 See Scurlock and Andersen 2005:111–113.
18 See below, 4.88H–J and Scurlock and Andersen 2005:483–485.
19 See also CTN 4.194:2.
20 See Scurlock and Andersen 2005:21.
21 Restorations are from context.
22 CTN 4.194:5 has "seed."
23 Restoration is based on CTN 4.194:6.
24 See Scurlock and Andersen 2005:418–423.
25 See Scurlock and Andersen 2005:270–271.
26 See Scurlock and Andersen 2005:289–290.
27 Restored from BAM 1 ii.19. See Scurlock and Andersen 2005:62–66.
28 Pace Böck 2011b, this is not a disease. *Maštakal* is one of the standard plants to end up in the holy water vessel as part of purificatory rites.
29 The translation assumes a *parras* form of *batāqu*: "to cut through" meaning, essentially, a permanent breach (in the skull). In BAM 524 ii.11′, *maštakal* seed is similarly wrapped in wool and inserted in "the mouth of the lungs."
30 This is reading: SÍG!.ÀKA NIGIN *ina bat-tàq* GAR SÍG!.BA *ta-ṣa-bu ana* KIR_4.BI GAR-*nu*. Böck 2011b apparently reads SÍG!.ÀKA NIGIN *ina* MÚD K[A!.GI.NA] DIB.BA *ta-ṣa-bu ana* KIR_4.BI GAR-*nu* and translates: "in ein Wollbüschel wickeln, im 'Blut' des Hämatit-Steines durchfeuchtest du es, (danach) auf seine Nase legen." Both readings require emendations. My reading requires a new word to be added to the lexicon, albeit based on a known root with appropriate meaning. Böck's reading requires, literally, getting blood out of a stone.

(v.24) *Tarmuš* is a plant for sorcerous rituals[31] not to approach a person. It is to be ⸢eaten⸣ on the day of the disappearance of the moon.
(v.25) *Tarmuš* is a plant for snakebite. It is to be ground (and) ⸢rubbed gently on⸣ (mixed) with oil.

(v.26) *Imḫur-lim* is a plant for snakebite. It is to be ground (and) ⸢rubbed gently on⸣ (mixed) with oil.
(v.27) *Imḫur-lim* is a plant for sorcerous rituals not to approach a person. It is to be ⸢eaten⸣ on the day of the disappearance of the moon.
(v.28) *Imḫur-ašna* is a plant for ⸢sorcerous rituals⸣ not to approach a person. It is to be ⸢eaten⸣ on the day of the disappearance of the moon.

(v.29) *Sikillu* is a plant for purification. It is to be used to ⸢purify⸣ the person on the day of the disappearance of the moon.
(v.30) *Sikillu* seed is a plant to dispel *kišpu*-witchcraft. Its leaf is to be used to [wash] the patient's ⸢hands⸣ on the day of the disappearance of the moon.
(v.31) *Sikillu* seed is a plant for snakebite. It is to be ground, (mixed) with oil (and) [rubbed gently on].

(v.32) *Ardadillu* is a plant to dispel *kišpu*-witchcraft. Its leaf is to be used to [wash] the patient's [hands] on the day of the disappearance of the moon.
(v.33) *Ardadillu* seed is a plant for "hand" of god. Its leaf is to be wrapped in a tuft of wool (and) put on the person's neck.

(v.34) *Ankinūtu* is a plant for departing ditto ("hand" of god). It is to be wrapped in a tuft of wool (and) put on the person's neck.

(v.35) *Urânu* is a plant for removing *umṣātu*-lesions[32] is to be ground, poured into well water,
(v.36) baked in an oven (and) used to irrigate the person.

(v.37) *Urânu* leaf is a plant for *guraštu*.[33] It is to be dried, crushed,
(v.38) mixed with cedar resin (and) rubbed gently on the ⸢shaved⸣ head.

(v.39) *Urânu* root is a plant for *guraštu*. It is to be dried, crushed,
(v.40) mixed with cedar resin and ghee (and) rubbed gently on the shaved head.

(v.41) *Urânu* root is a plant for *bennu*.[34] It is to be wrapped in a tuft of wool (and) put on the person's neck.

(v.42) *Aktam* is a plant for sore hips. It is to be ground, poured into well water,
(v.43) baked in an oven (and) used to massage the hips.
(v.44) It is to be crushed (and) used to bandage the hips.

(v.45) [*Aktam*] is a plant for sore eyes.[35] It is to be ground, mixed with milk (and) used to bandage the eyes.

(v.46) [*Aktam*] is a [plant] for sore eyes. It is to be pressed-out while still fresh (and) its liquid
(v.47) is to be dropped into the [eyes].

(v.48–55′) (too fragmentary for translation)

(v.56′) [...] is a [plant for ...]. It is to be ground, (mixed) with oil (and) rubbed on gently.
(v.57′) [...] is a [plant for ...]. It is to be ground, (mixed) with oil (and) rubbed on gently.

(v.58′) [...] is a [plant] for sore [...]. You ⸢spin⸣ (it) in red-dyed wool
(v.59′) (and) it is to be put under his bed.

(v.60′) [...] is a [plant] for sore [...]. You spin it in red-dyed wool
(v.61′) (and) it is to be put under his bed.

(v.62′) [...] is a plant for snakebite. [...] in the gate [...].
(v.63′) [...] is a plant for snakebite. [...] in the gate [...].

(v.64′) [*azallû*] is a plant for ⸢forgetting⸣ depression (*nissatu*).
(v.65′) [It is to be eaten or drunk] on an empty stomach.

(v.66′) [*azallû*] is a plant for crushing sensation in the chest (*ḫuṣ ḫēpi libbi*).[36] It is to be ground, [(mixed) with oil and rubbed gently on].

(Col. vi) (too fragmentary for translation)

31 For more on witchcraft and sorcery, see below 4.88K–M.
32 See Scurlock and Andersen 2005:230–231.
33 See Scurlock and Andersen 2005:234.
34 The category seems to refer to seizures of infectious etiology. See Scurlock and Andersen 2005:83–84.
35 See Scurlock and Andersen 2005:185–202.
36 See Scurlock and Andersen 2005:710, n. 14.

REFERENCES

Böck 2011b; Scurlock and Andersen 2005:21–23, 42–48, 62–66, 83–84, 111–113, 177–202, 230–231, 234, 257–258, 270–271, 289–290, 382–383, 418–423, 483–485, 710, n. 14; Stadhouders 2011 and 2012.

"NATURAL" CAUSES: SICK LIVER (BAM 92) (4.88B)

JoAnn Scurlock

BAM 92 is classic in clearly demonstrating the close relationship between pharmacological texts on the one hand and therapeutic texts on the other. On the one hand, the text is generally formulated as a collection of physician's treatments, which describe the observed symptoms and give the patient's diagnosis followed by instructions for the treatment. To save space, all treatments other than the first were generally indicated simply by "If ditto" which we have generally rendered as "Alternatively." From the preserved symptoms, we may conclude that this text was designed to deal with lung problems (i.35′–ii.9′) and liver problems (i.1′–4′, ii.22′–34′, iii.10–17, iii.38′ff) treated, as these conditions generally were, with some combination of bandages and potions.

Hinted at indirectly (ii.23′–34′) is the ancient Mesopotamian physician's golden rule of medical ethics. Amebiasis causes hepatic abscesses that can rupture into the peritoneum[1] causing peritonitis and, without modern surgery, death. The ancient Mesopotamian physician did not cheat his patients by pretending to cure the incurable. If the abscess had ruptured, it was time to let the patient know that he was going to die. If, however, the abscess had not ruptured into the peritoneum, and the ancient physician knew this by testing to make sure that the umbilical area "continued to be supple," then there was hope, and treatment could be instituted.

Lines i.5′–7′ have a duplicate[2] that formats the text in a manner suggestive of a pharmacist's treatment, that is, it lists the plants first and appends a label of the type: "so many plants for such and such a condition." One might expect from this to find other connections with pharmacological texts. Indeed, according to preserved vademeca, *aktam* seed was to be ground, mixed with oil and used in a potion for "sick lungs" drunk on an empty stomach while the tongue was held.[3] In addition, *aktam* seed was used for the liver.[4]

Even clearer is the fact that a number of plants, including some of those recommended in lines i.8′–22′ are cited in BAM 92 for potential use by themselves: *imḫur-lim* (ii.28′–29′); *imḫur-ešra* (ii.30′); *tarmuš* (ii.31′–32′); "late blooming wildflowers" (ii 33′); *šagabegalzu* (ii.34′–35′); *ḫazallūnu* (ii.36′–37′), *šimāḫu* (ii.38′), *ḫaltappānu* (iii.1–2), *lulumtu* (iii.3–4), *kurkānû* (iii.5–6), *nuṣābu* (iii.7–8) and *šammi buʾšāni* (iii.9). These treatments, and the manner in which they are presented (even in one case noting that a plant grows in the canebrake) suggest that these lines might actually been copied by the *āšipu* from an *asû*'s compendium with modifications to fit the new context.

Indeed, there is significant overlap between lines ii.28′–iii.9 and the preserved vademeca. BAM 1 ii.47–52 and BAM 421 i.32′–37′,[5] the "plants for the liver" sections, consist entirely of plants listed in BAM 92, and/or its duplicate BAM 161, to the point where it is actually possible to restore BAM 92 from the vademeca. For example, lines ii.28′–30′ are essentially identical with BAM 1 ii.50–52//CT 14.37 [Rm 357]:3–5,[6] as may be seen from the following citations.

> *Imḫur-lim* is a plant for the liver. It is to be ground (and) given to drink (mixed) with beer. (BAM 1 ii.50//CT 14.37 [Rm 357]:3)
>
> *Imḫur-ešra* is a plant for the liver. Ditto (It is to be ground and given to drink mixed with beer). (BAM 1 ii.51//CT 14.37 [Rm 357]:4)
>
> *Tarmuš* is a plant for the liver. Ditto (It is to be ground and given to drink mixed with beer). (BAM 1 ii.52//CT 14.37 [Rm 357]:5)

Similarly, the two plants: *karān šēlibi* ("fox grape") and *ḫašḫur api* ("swamp apple") that appear as part of the potion only in one of the duplicates to BAM 92[7] feature in the vademeca. BAM 1 ii.49 envisages the use of *karān šēlibi* ("fox grape") for the liver, ground, boiled in ghee and used as a salve. *Ḫašḫur api* ("swamp apple") is similarly to be used for the liver,[8] ground, mixed with beer or wine and used as a potion.[9] One of these plants actually appears in the pharmacological series Uruanna, which lists *karān šēlibi* ("fox grape") as a plant both for the liver[10] and for the cold season.[11]

1 Harrison 1987:773, 775.
2 BAM 161 vii.17–19.
3 BAM 1 ii.25; STT 92 ii.8.
4 BAM 421 i.34′.
5 So also BAM 426 and STT 92, but the texts are too fragmentary to be sure of this.
6 Two of the enumerated plants also appear in BAM 421 i.35′, 37′ and BAM 426 ii.10′, 11′ as plants for the liver.
7 BAM 161 vii.20–21.
8 BAM 426 ii.12.
9 BAM 1 ii.48; cf. STT 92 ii.25′.
10 KADP 1 i.27; CT 37.29–32 i.57′.
11 KADP 2 ii.3; CT 37.29–32 i.58′.

Armed with the knowledge of the properties of individual plants, then, it was possible for the ancient pharmacist or physician to devise more complex treatments as in BAM 92 i.8′–22′, which uses many of the same plants listed individually elsewhere in the text for one great potion. Similarly, CT 51.197, col. ii of which also seems to deal with liver problems, lists plants to be used singly in the style of a vademecum (ii.1′–5′) followed by a complex treatment (ii.6′–8′) which contains many of the same plants as BAM 92 but differently combined.

(i.1′–4′) [If ...] from his anus [...] ⸢his⸣ face [...] yellow, that person (has) winter "[sick] ⸢liver⸣."[12] Its bandage is [...].
(i.5′–7′) [If] ⸢ditto⸣ (a person has winter "sick liver"): you roast *aktam* seed. You grind (it) ⸢with⸣ myrrh.[13] You have him drink (it) in wine. If he ⸢vomits⸣, he should recover.[14]
(i.8′–22′) [Alternatively], you mill-grind and sift *qutru*-thorn seed, flax seed, *nikiptu*, *ḫaṭṭi re'i* ("shepherd's staff"), *mirišmara* leaves, *ḫaluppu*-tree leaves, [...], *supālu*, *ṣadānu* and *ninû*-mint. You mix in *barirātu*. You make a dough [with] *kasû* [juice]. You rub him gently with oil. If you bandage (him with it), he should recover. You grind together ⟨(*karān šēlibi*)⟩, *imḫur-lim*, *imḫur-ešra*, *tarmuš*, *paṭrānu*, ⟨(*ḫašḫur api* ["swamp apple"])⟩, *šagabegalzu*, *ḫaltappānu*, "late blooming wildflowers," *ṣibūru*-aloe, *allumzu*, ⟨*qutru*⟩ (and) *šammi bu'šāni*. You have him drink (it mixed) with sweet [wine] on an empty stomach. He should recover.[15]
(i.23′–34′) [If a person]'s ⸢umbilical area⸣ continues to be supple, etc.,[16] you grind together *biṣṣūr-atāne*-shell, *sikillu*-plant, *šakirû*, *burāšu*-juniper (and) *ata'īšu*. [You mix it with ...] (and) drip (it) onto his umbilical area. You make these plants into a dough with beer (and) you decoct (it).[17] You massage (it) into waterproof leather. You grind *tarmuš* and station (it) on top of the massaged stuff. You bandage him (with it). He should recover.[18]
(i.35′–ii.9) [If a person] continually produces [white *su'ālu* phlegm ...][19] ⸢continually vomits⸣ and [...], you mill grind and sift [...], *barirātu* and *kukru*. You make (it) into a dough with soured wine and vinegar (and) massage (it) into waterproof leather. You bandage his upper back and thorax (with it) until his lips are clear (of phlegm) and then [you take it off. As soon as] his lips have cleared, [you ... and have him drink (it mixed) with] ⸢first quality⸣ [beer] on an empty stomach while holding [his tongue]. If [he vomits], ⸢he should recover⸣.

(ii.22′–27′) If a person's liver [...], you crush together (and) sift ⸢these⸣ eight plants: [... shekels of ...] fat, [... shekels of] *burāšu*-juniper, [... shekels of] *ṭūru*-aromatic, [... shekels of] *baluḫḫu*-aromatic resin, 2 shekels of [...] (and) 3 shekels of [...]. You massage it into tawed(?) leather [and bandage him with it].
(ii.28′–29′) Alternatively, you grind *imḫur-lim*. If you have him drink it (mixed) with beer, ⸢on an empty stomach⸣, [he should recover].
(ii.30′) Alternatively, you grind *imḫur-ešra* [and have him drink it] (mixed) with first quality beer.
(ii.31′–32′) Alternatively, ⸢you grind⸣ *tarmuš*, a plant of the canebrake, (and) [have him drink it] (mixed) either with water or with first quality beer.
(ii.33′) Alternatively, you grind "late (blooming) wildflowers" [and have him drink it (mixed)] with [...].
(ii.34′–35′) [Alternatively], you grind ⸢*šagabegalzu*⸣ [and have him drink it mixed with] ⸢wine⸣.[20]
(ii.36′–37′) Alternatively, you grind *ḫazalluna* [and have him drink it] (mixed) with wine.
(ii.38′) Alternatively, you grind *šimāḫu* [and have him drink it] (mixed) with wine.
(iii.1–2) Alternatively, you grind *ḫaltappānu* [and have him drink it] (mixed) with first quality beer.
(iii.3–4) Alternatively, you grind *lullumtu* seed (and have him drink it) (mixed) with first quality beer.
(iii.5–6) Alternatively, you grind *kurkānu* (and have him drink it) (mixed) with first quality beer.
(iii.7–8) Alternatively, you grind *nuṣābu* (and have him drink it) (mixed) with first quality beer.[21]
(iii.9) Alternatively, you grind *šammi bu'šāni* (and have him drink it) (mixed) with first quality beer.
(iii.10–17) If a person has "sick liver" (and) his liver "turns over" so that his eyes are full of *aḫḫāzu*-jaundice, (and) blood incessantly comes to his mouth, to cure him, [you ...] *kasû* (and) have him drink (it) (mixed) with cold water. [...][22]
(iii.28′–32′) (too fragmentary for translation)
(iii.33′–37′) (For the liver), you grind together ⸢*tarmuš*⸣, *imḫur-lim*, [*imḫur*]-⸢*ešra*⸣, *ḫašû*-thyme (and)

[12] See Scurlock and Andersen 2005: 6.134.
[13] The duplicate BAM 161 vii.17–19 omits the if-clause and notes that the *aktam*-seed and myrrh are "two plants for winter liver." The difference in format suggests that a pharmacist's treatment has been adapted for use by the physician.
[14] Restored from BAM 161 vii.17–19.
[15] Restored from AMT 22/5:3–8//BAM 161 vii.20–25.
[16] The dangling *-ma* indicates something left out, in this case that the patient has "winter sick liver."
[17] See below, 4.88E ad obv. 14–15.
[18] Restorations are based on BAM 574 iv.43–46.
[19] Restored from AMT 50/3 r. 6, which describes patients with pneumonia attributed to witchcraft.
[20] Restored from BAM 1 ii.47. This also appears in BAM 421 i.36′ and STT 92 ii.24′.
[21] This appears also in CT 51.197 ii.4′.
[22] See Scurlock and Andersen 2005: 6.116.

˹*atā*ʾ*išu*˺. If [you have him drink it mixed with] first quality ˹beer˺ on an empty stomach, he should recover.

(iii.38′ff) [If] a ˹person˺ has ˹sick liver˺ (and) his knees, his liver and his upper back hurt him ...[23] (Col. iv) (too fragmentary for translation)

[23] See Scurlock and Andersen 2005: 6.128.

REFERENCES

Scurlock and Andersen 2005:116, 128, 134.

"NATURAL" CAUSES: JAUNDICE (BAM 578 iv.26–46)[1] (4.88C)

JoAnn Scurlock

BAM 578 is classic in demonstrating the close relationship between diagnostic and therapeutic texts. Sometime in the Neo-Assyrian period, the accumulation of therapeutic material made it necessary to serialize the data. We are fortunate in having fragments of a catalogue that explains the divisions of the resulting Therapeutic Series into subseries, gives the order of the tablets in each sub-series, and provides a summary of the contents.[2] From this, we know that BAM 578 represents Tablet 3 of the seventh sub-series of the Nineveh recension, which is longer than the Assur recension by at least two tablets. BAM 578 iv.26–46 represents a common pattern of organization that allowed the ancient physician to find treatments in the Therapeutic Series for diseases diagnosed by means of his diagnostic texts.[3] First, the problem to be treated (in this case a form of jaundice) is described using material drawn from these diagnostic texts (iv.26–27), followed by treatments for the problem (iv 28–42) and capped off by symptoms that indicate untreatable forms of the disease (iv.43–46). Also to be noted is a very nice bit of "magic" (iv.33–34) buried right in the middle of the medicine. The ancient physician was smart enough to supplement the plant and other natural medicines at his disposal with carefully designed rituals that allowed the patient to participate in his own cure.

(iv.26–27) If a person's flesh is yellow, his face his yellow and black (and) the base of his tongue is black, it is called ˹*aḫḫāzu*˺ (jaundice without wasting).[4] You grind a large steppe dwelling *pizzalurtu*-lizard (and) you have him drink (it mixed) with beer. The *aḫḫāzu* inside him should be excreted.

(iv.28–29) If a person is full of *aḫḫāzu*, you grind *burāšu*-juniper (and) have him drink (it mixed) with beer. You grind *kikkirānu*-juniper berries (and) alum. If you have him drink (it mixed) with oil and beer, he should recover. You grind *kukru* (and) have him drink (it mixed) with beer. You grind *ḫašû*-thyme (and) have him drink (it mixed) with beer. You grind *buṣinnu* root[5] (and) have him drink (it mixed) with water. You grind myrrh (and) have him drink (it mixed) with milk.

(iv.30) If a person is full of *aḫḫāzu*, you grind *šūšu*-licorice root (and) decoct (it) in beer. You let (it) sit out overnight under the stars (and) have him drink (it).

(iv.31–32) If a person is full of *aḫḫāzu*, you fumigate ˹him˺ with *aṣuṣimtu* (and) *anunūtu* (mixed) with incense and, if you rub him gently with the blood of a steppe dwelling *anduḫallatu*-lizard, ˹he should recover˺.

(iv.33–34) You take used grease from both door posts of the main gate. You pour (it) into oil (and) repeatedly ˹rub him gently˺ (with it). He should go straight home on a reddish road. ˹He should cross˺ an abandoned bridge.

(iv.35–36) If *aḫḫāzu* afflicts a person, you take male *pillû* root which grows on the north side (and) have him drink (it mixed) with beer. You grind ˹*ḫašû*-thyme˺, [...] and *kurkānû*-turmeric (and have him drink it mixed) with beer. You grind *kikkirānu*-juniper berries (and) have him drink (it mixed) with beer. (You have him drink) *imḫur-lim* (and) *imḫur-ešra* (mixed) with beer. [(You have him drink) ...] root [(mixed) with beer].

[1] For the rest of this fascinating text, see Scurlock 2014: 2.5.7. For a German translation, see Böck 2011a: 78

[2] For details, see Scurlock 2014: 1.3.1.

[3] For a full publication of the Diagnostic and Prognostic Series (= DPS), see Scurlock 2014: 1.1.

[4] This is a variant of the entry in DPS 9:13 (see Scurlock 2014: 1.1.9). For more on jaundice in ancient Mesopotamian texts, see Scurlock and Andersen 2005:138–142, 191–192; Haussperger 2001 and Haussperger 2012:257–261.

[5] Correcting Böck 2011a:78.

(iv.37) If ditto (*aḫḫāzu* afflicts a person) or *amurriqānu*, ⌜you grind⌝ *burāšu*-juniper (and) ⌜myrrh⌝ (and) ⌜have him drink (it)⌝ (mixed) with beer.

(iv.38) Alternatively, you soak(?) alum (and) black alum together in beer (and) clarify (it). [...]

(iv.39) Alternatively, you grind 15 grains[6] of *anzaḫḫu*-frit. You soak(?) (it) in beer (and) clarify (it). You pour pressed-out oil into it (and) [have him drink it] ⌜on an empty stomach⌝.

(iv.40–41) Alternatively, you grind *kalû*-paste (and) have him drink (it mixed) with oil and beer. You have him drink *bīnu*-tamarisk seed (mixed) with beer. [You have him drink] *bīnu*-tamarisk seed (mixed) [with oil]. You grind *bīnu*-tamarisk seed (and) have him drink (it mixed) with oil and beer. You have him drink *šūšu*-licorice root (mixed) with oil and beer. You grind *imḫur-ešra* (and) [have him drink it mixed with ...].

(iv.42) Alternatively, you pour *šūšu*-licorice root (and) *nurmû*-pomegranate root into water. You bake (it) in an oven. You take (it) out, filter (it and) let (it) cool. You have him drink (it) repeatedly (mixed) with [...].

(iv.43–44) If *aḫḫāzu* rises to a person's eyes so that his eyes are ⌜covered⌝ with a network of yellow threads, his insides are puffed up (and) return bread and beer (to his mouth), if that person lingers, he will die.[7]

(iv.45–46) If a person is sick with *aḫḫāzu* and his head, his face, his whole body and the base of his ⌜tongue⌝ [are affected], the *asû* (pharmacist) is not to lay his hands on that patient (to treat him); that person will die; he will not [live].[8]

6 This will have been delivered in three separate doses of 5 grains each. As is explained in BAM 578 iv.16, "If you give him too much (of it), he will die."
7 See Scurlock and Andersen 2005: 6.39, 6.118, 9.39.
8 See Scurlock and Andersen 2005: 6.139.

REFERENCES

Böck 2011a:78; Haussperger 2001; Haussperger 2012:257–261; Scurlock and Andersen 2005:138–140; 6.39, 118, 139; 9.39; Scurlock 2014: 1.1; 1.3.1; 2.5.7.

"NATURAL" CAUSES: COUGH (BAM 552 with BAM 549) (4.88D)

JoAnn Scurlock

BAM 552 is a classic for the mix of no-nonsense and sometimes quite sophisticated therapies with charming bits of "magic." This text forms a fragment of the reverse of the fifth tablet of the sixth subseries of the Therapeutic Series, and contains treatments for conditions of the lungs. Our current knowledge of the existing fragments of this reverse allows us to place BAM 549 col. iv in the missing lines at the end of BAM 552 col. iii and before the beginning of col. iv. The treatments consist mostly of potions for productive and dry coughs (BAM 552 iii.1′–7′ff; BAM 449 iv.0–5′, 12′–20′; BAM 552 iv.1′–7′, 15′–16′) with one glorious distillate daub as a backup (BAM 552 iv.8′–14′).[1] This is combined with direct address to the cough, inviting it to pick up its chair and go elsewhere (BAM 549 iv.6′–11′).

BAM 552[2]
(iii.1′–2′) [If ...] you ⌜gently rub⌝ [his chest] and his shoulders with [...], *erēnu*-cedar (and) [...].
(iii.3′–7′ff) If a person is sick with *su'ālu*-cough[3] and [has phlegm], [you put] *kasû*, *ḫašû*-thyme (and) [...] on [his] tongue. [You have him drink] *aktam*, ⌜*ḫašû*⌝, [...], 1 shekel of *kasû*, 4 [shekels of ...] (and) ½ shekel of [...] (mixed) with beer.
BAM 549[4]
(iv.0–3′) If a person has a dry *su'ālu*-cough [...] pressed out oil. You grind together [these] three plants: *antaḫšum*-vegetable, *nuḫurtu* and sweet *kalû*-clay; [you mix it] with honey and ghee. ⌜If⌝ you have him drink (it) repeatedly on an empty stomach, [he should recover].
(iv.4′–5′) If a person has a dry *su'ālu*-cough, he cannot produce (phlegm) (and) [cannot shout out] Halleluyah, to cure him, you grind together *urnû*-mint (and) gazelle droppings (and) [have him drink it] (mixed) with beer on an empty stomach.

1 For more details, see Scurlock 2014: 2.4.2.
2 The text is restored from AMT 81/1 iii.8′–16′.
3 See Scurlock and Andersen 2005:178–179.
4 Col. iv.0–5′ are restored from AMT 81/1 iii.17′–29′ and BAM 551 iii.1′–7′; iv.6′–11′ are restored from ABRT 2.11 ii.21–26 and BAM 553:1′–4′; iv.12′–20′ are restored from BAM 550 iv.1–8 ff.

(v.6′–11′) *Su᾽ālu*-cough, *Su᾽ālu*-cough, *Su᾽ālu*-cough, strong is [its] ⸢grip⸣; it has set up its throne between the lungs. Go out, *su᾽ālu*-cough. It is not [your] dwelling place. May Gula, mistress of life, raise the root of thick sputum, *guḫḫu*-cough and *su᾽ālu*-cough. Spell and Recitation. Recitation for [*su᾽ālu*-cough]. Its ritual: You recite the recitation over his chest and you have him drink (it).

(iv.12′–15′) If a person [has] *su᾽ālu*-cough and phlegm, you boil 10 shekels of *maštakal* in 1 *qû*-measure of first quality beer. When it has boiled, [you have him drink it]. Afterwards, you have him drink 1 *qû*-measure of sweet beer. At the same time [...].

(iv.16′–18′) Alternatively, you ⸢grind⸣ *ninû*-mint [and have him drink it mixed with ...]. Alternatively, you [grind] *burāšu*-juniper and [...]; you leave it out overnight under the stars (and) [have him drink it mixed with ...].

(iv.19′–20′) If a person [is sick] with *su᾽ālu*-cough and *ḫaḫḫu* (bloody sputum), you [...] in water [...]

BAM 552[5]

(iv.1′–3′) [...] 5 shekels of *kasû* [...]. You have him drink (it mixed) [with] ⸢beer⸣.

(iv.4′–5′) If a person ⸢is sick with⸣ *su᾽alu*-cough, you grind "white plant." If you have him drink (it mixed) with pressed-out oil on an [empty] stomach, he should recover.

(iv.6′–7′) Alternatively, ⸢you grind⸣ *nuḫurtu*. If you have him ⸢drink⸣ (it mixed) with wine on an empty stomach, he should recover.

(iv.8′–14′) If he does not experience improvement with the previous treatments, [you put out] a bronze soup bowl. You crush *nīnû*-mint. You mill grind (and) sift *šūšu*-licorice root, [...], *antaḫšum*-vegetable (and) *kukru*. You ⸢pour⸣ [...] oil, beer and ghee over it. [You bore a hole in] a *burzigallu* bowl (and invert it over the other bowl). [You cover] its sides with a dough made of emmer (flour). You boil it over a fire. You stick in a reed straw. He should suck (it) up hot [into his mouth] and, if ⸢you slap⸣ it onto his lungs with the reed straw, he should recover.

(iv.15′–16′) If a person [is sick with] *su᾽ālu*-cough, *ḫaḫḫu* and thick sputum in the ⸢lungs⸣, you have him drink powdered *saḫlû*-cress in first quality beer ⸢on an empty stomach⸣.

5 Col. iv.4′–16′ are restored from AMT 81/1 iv.1′–5′ and BAM 548 iv.2′–15′.

REFERENCES

Scurlock and Andersen 2005:178–179; Scurlock 2014: 1.3.1, 2.4.2.

"NATURAL" CAUSES: FEVER; HEADACHE; SKIN LESIONS; EARS; EYES (4.88E*)

JoAnn Scurlock

Labat (*RA* 53.1ff. [AO 11447])[1] is one of many known extracts from the Therapeutic Series. It was, according to its colophon, produced by a scribe in the proud tradition of Aššur scribes, who traced their lineage back to one Adad-uballiṭ.[2] Unlike many extracts that jump about all over the place, this seems to more or less follow the series order, beginning with fever and headache (obv. 2–21, drawn from Tablets 1–3 of the first sub-series), proceeding on to skin problems on the head and body (obv. 22–r. 17, drawn from Tablets 4–5 of the first sub-series). It finishes with treatments for the ears (r. 18–32, drawn from Tablets 1–2 of the second sub-series). This tablet was originally followed by a further extract tablet beginning with the eyes (drawn from the third sub-series). Of particular interest are r. 8–17, which demonstrate the close relationship between the Therapeutic Series and the Diagnostic and Prognostic Series from which many of the descriptions of skin lesions are cited.[3]

(obv. 2) [If (you want)] to remove ⸢fever⸣ of the head, you crush *saḫlû*-cress. You make (it) into a dough [with] *kasû* juice. You shave (his head and) bandage (him with it).[4]

(obv. 3) [Alternatively], you ⸢make *saḫlû*-cress⸣ (and) roasted grain flour ⸢into a dough⸣ with *kasû* juice. You shave (his head and) bandage (him with it).[5]

(obv. 4–6) (Fragmentary)

(obv. 7–9) *Erēnu*-cedar, *šurmēnu*-cypress, *suādu*, myrrh, *burāšu*-juniper, *kukru*, *kasû*, *ḫallūru*-chick pea, *kakku*-lentil, date rind, *saḫlû*-cress, winnowed beerwort, *ininnu*-barley, *imbû tamtim* (and) malt (are plants for) a bandage for the head.

1 The text is edited in its original publication in Labat 1959; a new edition with a new copy appears in Geller 2007.

2 For more on this subject, see Geller 2007:4.

3 See below for specific references.

4 Restored on the basis of Heeßel and al-Rawi 2003: i.1–2. The parallel was suggested in Geller 2007:8.

5 Restored on the basis of Heeßel and al-Rawi 2003: i.3–4. The parallel was suggested in Geller 2007:8.

(obv. 10–13) *Kukru* flour, *burāšu*-juniper flour, flour of roasted *kasû*, wheat flour, roasted grain flour, *ḫallūru*-chick pea flour, *kakku*-lentil flour, flour of old sesame residue, emmer flour, flour of roasted *saḫlû*-cress, malt flour (and) "dove dung" (*ḫarūbu*-carob) flour are twelve flours for a bandage for the head. If it is winter, you heat (it) in beer dregs (and) if it is summer in *kasû* juice (and) bandage (him with it).[6]
(obv. 14–15) To calm pulsating temples,[7] you mix *kukru*, *asu*-myrtle, *kasû*, old sesame residue (and) *balukku*-aromatic with *isqūqu* flour. You decoct (it)[8] in beerwort and beer (and) bandage him (with it).[9]
(obv. 16–17) Alternatively, ⌜you mix⌝ *kukru*, *burāšu*-juniper, myrrh, *atāʾišu*, *imbû tâmti*, *kibrītu*-sulphur (and) ⌜Dilmun(?)⌝ dates with *baluḫḫu*-aromatic resin, *ṭūru*-aromatic, fat (and) wax (and) bandage (him with it). (This is) a ⌜tested⌝ treatment.
(obv. 18–19) Alternatively, ⟨you crush (and) sift⟩ *kukru*, *burāšu*-juniper, *ruʾtītu*-sulphur, *atāʾišu*, *kalgukku*-clay, *imbû tâmti* ⟨(and) *nikiptu*⟩. You mix (it) with fat from the kidney ⟨of a wether⟩ and wax. You recite the recitation UR.SAG ᵈASAL.LÚ.ḪI[10] over it. You make (it) into a dough (and) bandage (him with it).[11]
(obv. 20–21) (You mix) *kukru*, *burāšu*-juniper, *atāʾišu*, myrrh, *ṭūru*-aromatic, *baluḫḫu*-aromatic resin (and) date rind with wax, fat from the left kidney of a wether (and) *erēnu*-cedar resin. This is for a conventionally proportioned[12] bandage (for the head).[13]
(obv. 22–24) If a person's head is full of sores, you make roasted ox dung ⌜into a dough⌝ with hot water. For one day, you cool his head (with it) until it is moistened. You shave him (and) wash him with urine until the blood comes out. Afterwards, you crush *saḫlû*-cress (and) make (it) into a dough with *kasû* juice. You bandage his head (with it and) keep doing this to him until he recovers. This is an experiment that is part of oral tradition (i.e. the teacher treated a patient while the student watched).[14]
(obv. 25–26) If a person's head has *kiṣṣatu*,[15] you wash his head with *aktam* (and) *uḫḫulu qarnānu* (mixed) with hot water. You grind *ašqulālu* (and) *urânu* [and mix it with oil]. If you ⌜rub (it) gently on⌝, he should recover.[16]
(obv. 27) Alternatively, ⌜you grind⌝ "white plant" (and mix it) with sheep fat. You grind *aktam* (and mix it) with oil. You grind *imḫur-lim* (and mix it) with *kibrītu*-sulphur oil (variant: with naphtha).[17]
(obv. 28) Alternatively, you dry (and) crush the excrement of a *ḫurri*-bird (shelduck?) If you repeatedly wash[18] his head (with it, mixed) with water, he should recover.[19]
(obv. 29) Alternatively, you dry, crush (and) sift green foliage of *mussukānu*-tree. You wash his head with water (and) repeatedly [rub him gently] (with it).[20]
(obv. 30–33) If a person's head is full of *kibšu*,[21] *kiṣṣatu* (and) *gureštu*, you dry together in the shade, crush (and) sift these five plants: *kibrītu*-sulphur, *uḫḫūlu qarnānu*, *rikibti arkabi*, *tiṭṭu*-fig cuttings (and) *bīnu*-tamarisk bark. You (mix it) with urine (and) wash his head (with it). The *kibšu*, *kiṣṣatu* (and) *gurartu* should be extinguished.[22]
(obv. 34) To remove *kiṣṣatu*, you wash his head with natron (mixed) with honey. [...]
(obv. 35–36) If a person's head is full of "sweet" lice bites, (you mix) the plant that resembles *kamunu*-

6 This entry appears also in Heeßel and al-Rawi 2003: i.24–29.
7 See Scurlock and Andersen 2005:311–314.
8 See *AHw* 933b and *CAD* R s.v. *rabāku*. Heeßel 2011:46, n. 112 follows Goltz in disputing Landsberger's identification in favor of "making a paste." The argument is that boiling and filtering (as one would do in preparing a decoction) are separately mentioned and that, therefore, *rabāku* must be something else. However, grinding plants and mixing them with oil or fat, a.k.a. making a paste, is also separately mentioned and cannot, by the same logic, be what is meant. A *ribku* can be solid, since in this and a number of other passages (for references, see *CAD* R 321), you make a *ribku* into a dough using a hot liquid. Alternatively, it can be a liquid as in BAM 106 obv. 1–10 (Scurlock 2014 2.2.4) where a *ribku* is baked and then filtered, hardly possible with a solid. A survey of currently available references suggests that what was contemplated was indeed a decoction, made by crushing plants and cooking them in boiling liquid. The resulting decoction could be left as a liquid or, by the simple expedient of adding flour and continuing to cook the mixture, a virtually solid substance could be obtained.
9 This entry appears also in Heeßel and al-Rawi 2003: i.12–15.
10 The recitation appears also in AMT 19/1 iv!.13′//BAM 482 iv.32′; BAM 520 ii.12′–18′; BAM 508 i.15′–21//K 6239 ii.9′–17′//K 8211 ii.9′–18′//LKA 145 obv. 10–15, r.1//BM 123362 r.16′–19′; BAM 216:15′. It found a home in *Utukkū lemnūtu* 10 (see Geller 2007:8, n. 27).
11 This entry appears also in Heeßel and al-Rawi 2003: i.16–19/BAM 8:1–4 from which come the additions and restorations.
12 The term is conventionally taken to be an ethnic slur against Apišaleans; more probably we are dealing with *apšītu* which would represent a Sumerian loanword for "agreed proportion" (*CAD* A/2 197).
13 This entry appears also in Heeßel and al-Rawi 2003: i.20–23 from which come the restorations. Note also the similar BAM 124 iii.38–39.
14 Heeßel and al-Rawi 2003: i.5–11 had what is either an identical or a very similar entry, depending on whether Heeßel's reading of GAZI^SAR is correct or not. In any case, the procedure appears to be identical and has been used to restore the text.
15 See Scurlock and Andersen 2005:213–214.
16 A similar entry appears in BM 41282+41294 ii.14′, from which come the restorations.
17 A similar entry appears in BM 41282+41294 ii.15′ from which come the restorations.
18 *Ḫapāpu* is an Aramaic loanword; see *CAD* Ḫ 84a.
19 The entry appears also in BM 41282+41294 ii.19′ from which come the restorations.
20 The entry appears also in BM 41282+41294 ii.20′–21′ from which come the restorations.
21 See Scurlock and Andersen 2005:234–235.
22 Restored from the similar BAM 33:1–8//AMT 6/1:9–11//BM 41282+41294 ii.8′–11′.

cumin (and) [whose] ⸢name⸣ is *murru*[23] with oil (and) [if] you [repeatedly] rub [him] gently (with it) in an upwards direction(?),[24] [he should recover].[25]
(obv. 37–38) You wash him with one shekel of *kalgukku*-clay, ½ shekel of *labanātu*-incense (and) ¼ shekel of *kibrītu*-sulphur. It is good for getting rid of lice. This is an experiment (gloss: the curse)[26] of Šamaš, the divine lord who keeps me alive.
(obv. 39–40) If there is *luḫigātu*[27] in a person's body, to remove the *luḫigātu*, you firmly rub his skull. You daub *qutru* from the top of an oven on it. If you bandage him (with it), the hair should sprout.[28]
(obv. 41) Alternatively, you grind *anzaḫḫu*, white *anzaḫḫu* (and) black *anzaḫḫu*. You mix (it) with ghee (and) gently rub (it) on his skull. If you bandage (him) with sheep's *sar'u*,[29] he should recover.[30]
(obv. 42) If a person is sick with *kurāru*,[31] you rub him gently with ghee. You grind "white plant" and [daub] it on [the sore].[32]
(obv. 43) Alternatively, you plaster him with undiluted vinegar. [You grind . . .]-clay [and daub it on].
(obv. 44) Alternatively, you plaster him daily with a *samānu*-insect. Honey, ghee [. . .]
(obv. 45–r. 7) (Either lost or fragmentary)
(r. 8–9) If a sore comes out on a person's body and, as a consequence, his face and his eyes are swollen (and) his sight is difficult and (his eyes) drift downstream,[33] it is ⸢called⸣ *ašû*. You grind *kasû*, *saḫlû*, *kakku*-lentils (and) *šaššugu*-tree leaves over a fire (and) [drip it] into the fire (gloss: drop by drop).[34]
(r. 10–11) If (a sore comes out on a person's body and) it is hot like a burn and does not contain liquid or if it is full of tiny *bubu'tu*-blisters, it is ⸢called⸣ *išītu*.[35] You dry and grind (*kasû*, *saḫlû*, *kakku*-lentils and *šaššugu*-tree leaves). You make (it) into a dough with *kasû* juice. If you bandage (him with it), he should recover. You [make] riverbank mud [into a dough] with *kasû* juice [and bandage him with it].
(r. 12–13) If (a sore comes out on a person's body and) it is red (and) small and hurts him, it is called *ziqtu*.[36] You mix myrrh (and) wax with fat from the kidney of a wether. You massage (it) into leather (and) bandage (him with it). You mix myrrh, *baluḫḫu*-aromatic resin (and) wax with sheep fat (and) bandage (him with it).[37]
(r. 14) You make malt [flour], "dove dung," *kukru*, *burāšu*-juniper, (and) *kakku*-lentil flour into a dough with beer dregs [and bandage him with it].
(r. 15–17) If (a sore comes out on a person's body), it is red and hurts him and it holds all of them,[38] that sore is called *pindû*.[39] To remove it, you grind together these five plants: *kukru*, ⸢*burāšu*-juniper⸣, [. . .], *nikiptu* (and) [. . .] seed. You decoct (it) with *isqūqu*-flour made from ⸢*barirātu*⸣ in beer in a *tamgussu*-vessel until decocted.[40] You massage (it) into waterproof leather (and) bandage (him with it).[41]
(r. 18–21) If it (continually) hurts a person and continually jabs him in his ears like (a case of) "hand" of ghost, you separately press out oil of *kanaktu*-aromatic, oil of "sweet reed" (and) oil of *burāšu*-juniper. You mix (them) together and pour (them) into his ears. You wrap a lump of ⟨emesalim⟩[42]-salt in a tuft of wool and insert (it) into his ears. You mix winnowed beerwort, *ḫallūru*-chick pea flour, *kakku*-lentil flour, emmer flour (and) *kasû* flour in

23 This is a direct citation of *Šammu šikinšu* (CTN 4 196+195 ii.12′ – Stadhouders 2011:16) but with a different recommended use.
24 Reading AN-*šú*.
25 The entry appears in BM 41282+41294 ii.22′–23′ from which come the restorations.
26 Attributing recitations to divinities is fairly commonplace, but the end of the line sounds more like a personal name. The bit about curses is either a misunderstanding of the text by the glossator, or they had really fierce copyright protection in those days.
27 Geller 2007:10, 16 prefers an alternative reading which would mean literally: "affliction of vinegar-spots" if you take *ṭābātu* as "vinegar." Geller 2007:16 takes these as "sweet" (*ṭabu*), although that is usually rendered instead by *matqu*. A third possibility would connect this with "salt" (*ṭabtu*). Sometimes, it is obvious why ancient scribes used Sumerograms.
28 The entry appears also in BAM 497 ii.7′–8′//AMT 1/3:3′–4′, whence come the restorations.
29 Geller 2007:10, n. 43 suggests that this is an Assyrianism for *sarbu*: "tallow, fat."
30 The entry appears also in BAM 497 ii.9′//AMT 1/3:5′, whence come the restorations.
31 See Scurlock and Andersen 2005:233–234.
32 The entry appears also in BAM 3 i.48, which has provided the restorations.
33 This is cited from DPS 33:4 (see Heeßel 2000:353–374; Scurlock 2014: 1.1.33). See Scurlock and Andersen 2005: 9.31, 10.96 but with one possible modification, followed here. Instead of the eyes being "red," the eyes would be "drifting downstream." The reference is either to conjunctivitis ("red") or to encephalomyelitis ("drift downstream" = horizontal nystagmus), both of which occur with measles. Measles is one of the conditions included under the ancient diagnosis of *ašû*. For details, see Scurlock and Andersen 2005:224–226.
34 The entry also appears in AMT 84/6 ii.5′–7′, which has provided some of the restorations.
35 This is cited from DPS 33:15 (see Heeßel 2000:353–374; Scurlock 2014: 1.1.33). See also Scurlock and Andersen 2005: 10.173.
36 This entry, also cited in AMT 30/2:11′, is drawn from DPS 33:42 (see Heeßel 2000:353–374; Scurlock 2014: 1.1.33). See also Scurlock and Andersen 2005: 10.108.
37 The treatment appears also in AMT 30/2:13′–14′, whence the restorations.
38 After a suggestion by Geller 2007:11–12. This is apparently cited from DPS 33:27 (see Heeßel 2000:353–374; Scurlock 2014: 1.1.33), whence come the restorations.
39 See Scurlock and Andersen 2005:231–232. If Geller's suggestion is correct, NA references to a lesion called "fire" are to be instead read as references to *pindû*.
40 See above ad obv. 14–15.
41 This entry appears also in BAM 264 ii.23′–24′.
42 This appears only in BAM 503 ii.64′.

equal quantities with *erēnu*-cedar oil. You decoct (it) in beer (and) bandage him (with it). He should recover.[43]

(r. 22–24) If inside a person's ears, it hurts him like (a case of) "hand" of ghost, (these) fifteen plants: *burāšu*-juniper, *kukru*, *ṣumlalû*, *nikiptu*, *asu*-myrtle, *šimeššalû*-boxwood, *ballukku*-aromatic, "sweet reed," *atāʾišu*, *maštu* (= *šammi ašî* seed), *kalgukku*-clay, *kasû*, *kurkanû*, *baluḫḫu*-aromatic (and) *erēnu*-cedar are a tampon for "hand" of ghost. You sprinkle (it) with *erēnu*-cedar resin (and) insert (it) into his ears.[44]

(r. 25–26) If a person's ears contain pus, to cure him, you mill-grind (and) sift ʿtheseʾ seven plants: myrrh, *šupuḫru*-cedar, *kasû*, *annuḫāru*-alum, *gaṣṣu*-gypsum, *ḫašû*-thyme (and) "white plant." You wind (it) into a burl (and) insert (it) into his ears.

This is a tested tampon.[45]

(r. 27) Alum, "white plant" (and) kiln slag are three plants for a tested tampon for the ears.[46]

(r. 28) Alum, *gaṣṣu*-gypsum and ʿkiln slagʾ are plants for a tampon for the ears.

(r. 29–30) *Kukru*, *burāšu*-juniper, myrrh, *ballukku*-aromatic, *erēnu*-cedar, "sweet reed," *suādu*, *kasû* (and) *kalgukku*-clay are nine plants for a fumigant for the ears.[47]

(r. 31–32) If a person's ears continually roar, ⟨you crush and sift⟩[48] *burāšu*-juniper, *kukru*, *ballukku*-aromatic, *aktam* (and) winnowed beerwort. You boil it in beer. You bandage him with it while it is still hot. This is a [tested] treatment.[49]

(r. 33) If a person's eyes are full of blood[50] and become dimmed, ʿsaḫlû, lišān kalbiʾ seedʾ … (catch-line)

---

[43] This entry appears also in BAM 503 ii.63′–66′//Heeßel and al-Rawi 2003: i.30–36. The wash and tampon are the same as those of BAM 3 iv.12–13. The wash and bandage are the same as those of BM 59593:3–9. For these texts, see Scurlock 2006a: nos. 161, 162 and 160.

[44] This entry appears also in BAM 3 iv.17–19//Heeßel and al-Rawi 2003: i.37–42. For these texts, see Scurlock 2006a: nos. 163a–b.

[45] This entry also appears in BAM 3 iv.20–22//BAM 410:5′–7′//CTN 4.113 ii.16–20// Heeßel and al-Rawi 2003: i.48–50, which has been used to restore the text.

[46] Heeßel and al-Rawi 2003: i.46–47 has this entry, but substitutes *gaṣṣu*-gypsum (IM BABBAR) for the "white plant" (Ú BABBAR).

[47] This entry appears also in BAM 3 iv.33–34//BAM 503 i.31′–32′//Heeßel and al-Rawi 2003: i.43–45, which have been used for the restorations. The same treatment, with a recitation added, appears in BAM 506:6′–7′//BAM 508 iv.3–10//CT 51.199:5–13. For these texts, see Scurlock 2006a: nos. 139a–b.

[48] These instructions are provided by the duplicate.

[49] This entry appears also in BAM 3 iv.25–27, which adds: "You pour sheep fat and *burāšu*-juniper (oil) over his head. If you repeat this procedure for five days, he should recover." For these texts, see Scurlock 2006a: no. 157.

[50] For a discussion of this problem, see Fincke 2000:126–128.

REFERENCES

Fincke 2000:126–128; Geller 2007; Heeßel 2000:353–374; Heeßel and al-Rawi 2003; Heeßel 2011:46, n. 112; Labat 1959; Scurlock and Andersen 2005:213–214, 224–226, 231–235, 311–314; 9.31, 10.96, 10.108, 10.173; Scurlock 2006a nos. 139a–b, 157, 160–162, 163a–b; Scurlock 2014: 1.1.33, 2.2.4.

"SUPERNATURAL" CAUSES: THE MOON GOD SÎN: HERPES (KAR 211) (4.88F)

JoAnn Scurlock

KAR 211[1] is a very interesting example of an early diagnostic text from Aššur from the Middle Assyrian period. The material contained in this and similar texts was redacted by the Babylonian Esagil-kin-apli (ca. 1050 BCE) into what we know as the Diagnostic and Prognostic series. In the process, entries formerly grouped, as here, around diagnostic categories were partially rearranged so that the symptoms affecting the head were listed first, and so on, down the body to the toes. In the process, lines i.4′–9′ and i.19′–20 ended up more or less together in Tablet 3, whereas i.21′–22′ were bumped to Tablet 4 and so on. Since the Diagnostic and Prognostic Series is only partially preserved, it is not entirely clear whether all the material available in Aššur (e.g. i.13′–18′) made it to Babylonia and was included somewhere in the sections now lost to us. There does seem to have been an outlying diagnostic series in Assyria, of which we will be seeing an example later (4.88K), but this may simply have been due to a preference for organization of diagnostic material by diagnostic category and not to any major deficiencies in the main series.

Assyrian and Babylonian diagnostic texts typically do not list all the symptoms of a single disease entity in a single entry and then move on to other subjects. Instead, multiple entries in sequence allow for the varying signs and symptoms that appear at separate stages of a disease to be separately examined. Contrasting references allow for differential diagnosis. So, in the first section of KAR 211 (i.4′–13′), it is explained how Sîn's fever differed from

---

[1] A new copy and recent edition of this text appear in Heeßel, 2010:171–177.

that caused by two demons of disease, *aḫḫāzu* (biphasic fever with jaundice)[2] and Lamaštu (typhus/typhoid).[3] More details on Sîn's fever appear in the fuller context of the Diagnostic and Prognostic Series Tablet 17 as follows:[4]

DPS 17

(90) If in the morning he is hot (and) in the evening he is cold and trembles, "hand" of Sîn.[5] = KAR 211 i.12′

(91–92) If in the morning he is hot, in the evening he is cold (and) in middle of the night he says, "Ua," his dying brother is bound with him.[6]

(93) If in the morning he is hot (and) in the evening he is cold, "hand" of Sîn.[7]

(94) If in the morning he is hot and his hands and his feet tremble, "hand" of Sîn.[8]

In the second section of KAR 211 (i.14′–22) symptoms appearing in different phases of the disease are listed as separate entries. Confusing the issue somewhat for the modern reader is another interesting feature of the ancient Mesopotamian diagnostic system. The sequellae of wounds were assigned to the "hand" of various gods on the basis of symptoms produced by that divinity in non-trauma contexts.[9] So, the trauma references to *aḫḫāzu* and Sîn give information about symptoms to be found in those spirits' fevers and have correspondingly been listed together with the direct references in KAR 211 to complete the diagnostic picture.

The key to decoding the system is to find the organizing principle behind it. In this case, what has pulled down the diagnosis of "hand" of Sîn are the skin lesions mentioned in i.19′–20′. Besides causing the lesions of tuberculoid leprosy,[10] the Babylonian moon god Sîn (and his two children, Šamaš and Ištar), also produced varying colors of *bubuʾtu*-blisters. The full context is given in the Diagnostic Series Tablets 3 and 9 as follows:[11]

DPS 3

(100) [If from] his ⸢head⸣ to his feet, he is full of red *bubuʾtu* and his skin/body is white, he was "gotten" in bed with a woman; "hand" of Sîn.[12] = KAR 211 i.19′–20′

(101) [If from] his ⸢head⸣ to his feet, he is full of red *bubuʾtu* and his skin/body is dark, (he was "gotten" in bed with a woman); ("hand" of Sîn).[13]

(102) [If] ⸢from⸣ his head to his feet, he is full of *bubuʾtu* and his skin/body is yellow, (he was "gotten" in bed with a woman), "hand" of Ištar.[14]

(103) [If] ⸢from⸣ his head to [his feet], he is full of white *bubuʾtu* and his skin/body is dark, (he was "gotten" in bed with a woman), "hand" of Šamaš.[15]

(104) [If from his] head to [his] ⸢feet⸣, he is full of dark[16] *bubuʾtu* and his skin/body is red, (he was "gotten" in bed with a woman), "hand" of [Šamaš].[17]

DPS 9

(47) If his face is full of red *bubuʾtu*, "hand" of Sîn; he will get well.[18]

(48) If his face is full of white *bubuʾtu*, "hand" of Šamaš; he will get well.[19]

[2] See Scurlock and Andersen 2005:33–34.
[3] See Scurlock and Andersen 2005:483–485.
[4] See Heeßel 2000:194–217; Scurlock 2014: 1.1.17.
[5] See Scurlock and Andersen 2005: 19.261.
[6] See Scurlock and Andersen 2005: 2.12, 19.261.
[7] See Scurlock and Andersen 2005: 19.261.
[8] See Scurlock and Andersen 2005: 3.23, 19.261.
[9] For details of this system, see Scurlock and Andersen 2005:465–482.
[10] See below, 4.88G.
[11] For a full transliteration and translation of these tablets, see Scurlock 2014: 1.1.3, 1.1.9.
[12] See Scurlock and Andersen 2005: 3.233, 4.18, 10.85.
[13] See Scurlock and Andersen 2005: 10.85.
[14] See Scurlock and Andersen 2005: 10.86.
[15] See Scurlock and Andersen 2005: 10.87, 19.106.
[16] GI_6 can be either *ṣalmu*: "black" or *tarku*: "dark."
[17] See Scurlock and Andersen 2005: 10.87, 19.106.
[18] See Scurlock and Andersen 2005: 3.232, 4.16, 10.82.
[19] See Scurlock and Andersen 2005: 10.83.

(49) If his face is full of black *bubu'tu*, "hand" of Ištar; he will die.[20]

These blisters are common lesions of pox diseases for which the ancient physician had a "natural" causes category, namely *ašû*.[21] In addition, they are characteristic of herpes, a sexually transmitted disease almost certainly referred to in i.19′–20′.[22] Of interest is that there is a herpes encephalitis whose specific signs match closely those of the fever described as being caused by "hand" of Sîn. To the symptoms given in KAR 211 (and possibly originally given in the broken sections at the end) may be added the following from the Diagnostic and Prognostic Series.[23]

(DPS 4.24) If his "left" temple hurts him and ⟨his eyes⟩ drift downstream for five days, "hand" of Sîn [...].

(DPS 5.39′) [If his "left" eye droops and] his ⸢jaws⸣ shake, "hand" of Sîn.

Even more information appears in one of the tablets of the outlying Neo-Assyrian diagnostic series, STT 89, as follows:[24]

STT 89

(205) If the patient's body is hot (and then) cold (and) his affliction keeps changing (for the worse), "hand" of Sîn = DPS 18.1[25]

(206) [If] his eyes are "soaked," "hand" of Sîn ≅ KAR 211 i 13′

(207) [If] his eyes drift downstream, "hand" of Sîn

(208) [If] his "left" eye droops and his jaws shake, "hand" of Sîn = DPS 5.39′[26]

(209) If his "left" temple hurts him and (his eyes) drift downstream, "hand" of Sîn = DPS 4.24.[27]

KAR 211

(i.4′–6′) [(If in)] his head he burns with fever (and) over the course of a ⸢day⸣ [(it leaves him and then)] (later) it overpowers him (and) flows over him [(for two days as in affliction by) a ghost] and the plantar surfaces[28] [(of his feet feel cold, and when the fever releases him)], his hands and his feet are hot as in affliction by a ⸢ghost⸣, [(*aḫḫāzu*). If (the course of the fever is regular), he will get well][29] = DPS 3.79–80.[30]

(i.7′–9′) If he was injured on the head and, consequently, chills [(keep falling on him, his face flushes and turns pale)] (and) when his affliction falls upon him, his mentation is altered and [(he twists)], affliction by ⸢*aḫḫāzu*⸣. [(His days may be long but he will die of it.)][31] = DPS 3 91–92[32]

(i.10′–11′) If he is hot and then cold (and) [(he continually asks for)] a ⸢lot⸣ of water ⸢to⸣ bathe in, [(⸢"hand"⸣ of Lamaštu)] (var. "hand" of Sîn), [...]. = DPS 19–20.9′.[33]

(i.12′) If in the morning he is hot (and) in the evening he is cold and ⸢trembles⸣, [("hand" of Sîn)].[34] = DPS 17.90.[35]

(i.13′) [If] his eyes are continually "soaked" and his hands and his feet shake, ["hand" of Sîn].

(i.14′) [If] he was injured ⸢on⸣ one side of his face and his mouth is turned (to one side), "hand" of Sîn or [...].[36]

20 See Scurlock and Andersen 2005: 10.84.
21 See Scurlock and Andersen 2005:224–226 and above, 4.88E, r.8–9.
22 See Scurlock and Andersen 2005:91–93.
23 For a full transliteration and translation of these tablets, see Scurlock 2014: 1.1.4, 1.1.5.
24 For STT 89 lines 103–214, see Stol 1993:91–98.
25 See Heeßel 2000:218–225; Scurlock 2014: 1.1.18.
26 For this entry in context, see Scurlock 2014: 1.1.5.
27 For this entry in context, see Scurlock 2014: 1.1.4.
28 For the interpretation of KI.TA as "plantar surface," see Adamson 1981:128.
29 See Scurlock and Andersen 2005: 3.30.
30 For this entry in context, see Scurlock 2014: 1.1.3
31 See Scurlock and Andersen 2005: 13.127, 19.187.
32 For this entry in context, see Scurlock 2014: 1.1.3
33 See Heeßel 2000:226–245 and Scurlock 2014: 1.1.19–20
34 See Scurlock and Andersen 2005: 19.261.
35 See Heeßel 2000:194–217; Scurlock 2014: 1.1.17.
36 Correcting Scurlock and Andersen 2005: 13.129. Pace Heeßel 2011:175, 176–177, the eye is not involved, and the reference is not to "epilepsy" but to cranial trauma. In i.14, the blade of an enemy sword has sliced through the patient's face severing the cranial nerves but doing no other damage. In i.15, the sword has penetrated to the brain, producing seizures. This is indeed a patient not likely to survive.

(i.15′–16′) [If] he was injured ⌜on⌝ one side of his face and his mouth is turned (to one side) (and) when it comes over [him], he collapses and spittle flows from his mouth, "hand" of Sîn; he will ⌜die⌝.[37]

(i.17′–18′) [If] a ⌜falling⌝ spell falls on him so that he ⌜trembles⌝ (and) shakes and his eyes [shed tears] or are "soaked," ⌜"hand"⌝ of Sîn.

(i.19′–20′) [If from] his head to his feet, he is full of red *bubuʾtu* and [(his skin/body is white/dark)], he was "gotten" in bed with a woman; "hand" of ⌜Sîn⌝[38] = DPS 3.100–101.[39]

(i.21′) [(If)] he was injured [(on his)] "right" [(temple)] and ⌜his⌝ eyes ⌜shed tears⌝, "hand" of [Sîn][40] = DPS 4.40.[41]

(i.22′) [(If)] he was injured [(on his)] ⌜"left"⌝ temple and his eyes are "soaked" (suffused), "hand" of ⌜Sîn⌝.[42] = DPS 4.41.[43]

---

37 See Scurlock and Andersen 2005: 13.130.
38 See Scurlock and Andersen 2005: 3.233, 4.18, 10.85.
39 For this entry in context, see Scurlock 2014: 1.1.3
40 See Scurlock and Andersen 2005: 19.200.
41 For this entry in context, see Scurlock 2014: 1.1.4.
42 See Scurlock and Andersen 2005: 19.200.
43 For this entry in context, see Scurlock 2014: 1.1.4.

REFERENCES

Adamson 1981: 128; Heeßel 2000: 197–245; Heeßel, 2010: 171–177; Scurlock and Andersen 2005: 33–34, 91–93, 224–226 465–485; 2.12, 3.23, 3.30, 3.232–233, 4.16, 4.18, 10.82–87, 13.127, 13.129–130, 19.106, 19.187, 19.200, 19.261; Scurlock 2014: 1.1.3, 1.1.4, 1.1.5, 1.1.9, 1.1.17, 1.1.18, 1.1.19–20; Stol 1993: 91–98.

"SUPERNATURAL" CAUSES: THE MOON GOD SÎN: LEPROSY[1] (4.88G)

JoAnn Scurlock

The disease at the center of the ancient disease category known as SAḪAR.ŠUB.BA (*saḫaršubbû*), which included other diseases with similar looking lesions in animals, is most likely to have been that form of leprosy most common in the Near East today. This is not the infamous *Lepromatous* leprosy, but the much milder tuberculoid form.[2] Unlike its dreaded cousin, tuberculoid leprosy has anesthetic skin lesions and, when treated, the lesions change color and become scaly or "put down dust," which is what SAḪAR.ŠUB.BA literally means. Patients with tuberculoid leprosy eventually "cure themselves," even without treatment.

This is not necessarily to be equated with the biblical priestly category of skin lesions producing cultic impurity (*ṣaraʿat*), although the lesions of tuberculoid leprosy were probably included in the category. Where our Emar text and the Biblical texts unquestionably meet is in one of the methods used to remove remaining impurities after the physician has finished his work. It is standard in Mesopotamia for things which are ill-omened to be neutralized via a ritual known as a NAM.BÚR.BI, lit. "its releasing." This usually takes the form of a transfer rite in which evil influences end up rubbed off and dumped in the river with the assistance of the Sungod Šamaš, whose participation is rewarded by sacrifice. In our Emar text, the lapis-colored wool indicates the Netherworld as the ultimate recipient of the evil. Unusual in standard Mesopotamian texts is the Emariot sacrifice of one bird and the releasing of another, reminiscent of Lev 14:1–9 which also employs wool, if of a different color.

(37–40) Where has it flown? It has escaped to the earth! Where is it standing? It should not be standing on the earth! Heaven seven times, earth seven times, from (my) sight seven times. May the evil *utukku*-demon, the evil *alû*-demon, the evil ghost, the evil *gallû*-demon, the evil god, the evil *rabiṣu* (bailiff)-demon (and) the evil tongue stand aside. By heaven may (it) swear; by earth may (it) swear.
(41–42) Before approaching (someone with) *saḫaršubbû*, you should recite the recitation ME.ŠÈ BA.DA.RI (a recitation for numbness) three times over him.[3]
(43–45) If there is *saḫaršubbû* on a person, you take *kukkušu* flour of barley. You bind (it) on him boiled

---

1 Tsukimoto 1999:199–200. This text, probably from Middle Babylonian Emar, was first published and edited in Tsukimoto 1999. Corrections to the recitations appear in Finkel 1999. For a discussion, see Böck 2007:64–65. The text is translated in Schwemer 2011:41–45 and transliterated and translated in Scurlock 2014: 2.3.3.
2 See Scurlock and Andersen 2005:70–73.
3 See Scurlock and Andersen 2005: 3.222

like a decoction[4] with an afterbirth and, after it has cooled, you take (it) off. The sore should [shed?] "dust." You gently rub honey (and) oil on the sore.
(46–49) If it is visible(?) *saḫaršubbû*, you grind noded(?) *pillû* root which the sun did not see when you pulled (it) out. You mix (it) together (and) repeatedly bind (it) on here (and) there (wherever there is a sore). You boil a placenta (and) pour *tubru*-fruit(?) on it. You wash the sore (and) rub (it) gently on after the sore has dried.
(50–52) If a person (has) *saḫaršubbû*, you grind *kamūnu* (and) *imḫur-ašnan*[5] (and) mix (it) together. You daub (it) on the sore (and) put a linen cloth on top. You repeatedly bind these plants on. In the morning, you daub on *pillû* root (and) *pillû* leaves (and) repeatedly bind (it) on. He should recover.
(53–54) If there is white *saḫaršubbû* on a person's body,[6] you dry (and) crush *ašāgu*, salt, barley flour, *ḫilēpu*-willow (and) male and female palm fronds.[7] If you rub (it) gently on him, he should recover.
(55) Ditto (If there is) yellow (*saḫaršubbû*) on his body, you repeatedly gently rub (him) with wild animal fat for seven days.
(56–57) Ditto (If there is) red and black (*saḫaršubbû*) on his body,[8] for seven days you repeatedly bind on snake oil, fish oil, hot[9] "human (fat)" from a grave (and) fat of a large snake (hunting) gecko.
(58–59) Ditto (If there is) red and white (*saḫaršubbû*) on his body,[10] you boil *ašāgu*-thorn root, salt, barley flour, *ḫilēpu*-willow (and) male and female palm fronds.[11] If you rub (it) gently on him, he should recover.
(60) Ditto (If there is) yellow (and) red *saḫaršubbû* (on his body), "hand" of Sîn.[12] To remove it, [if] ⸢you gently rub⸣ "human semen" [on him] for seven days, [he should recover].
(61–62) Ditto (If there is) red, white (and) black *saḫaršubbû* (on his body), "hand" of the person's god. To remove it, if you gently rub him with "lion fat" (and) fat of a large steppe-dwelling snake for seven days, he should recover.
(63–69) Ditto (If his body) is full of *saḫaršubbû*, you grind *nurmû*-pomegranate peel. You mix (it) with ghee while he waits for you. You have the person who is full of *epqēnu* sit on the threshold of his outer gate and you daub that *nurmû*-pomegranate peel around his sore. You also take dust from the threshold. If you rub (him) firmly (with it) seven and seven times (mixed) with saliva, on that same day, the ⸢*epqēnu*⸣ should be extinguished. He should recover. If he still has its complaint, you heat oil over a fire (and) burn (it with it). You do this repeatedly again and again and do not let anything come near (it). That [person] should recover.
(70–71) Ditto (If there is) red, white and black *saḫaršubbû* (on his body), "hand" of the person's god.[13] To remove it, if you repeatedly rub him gently (with) snake fat, giant[14] *ašāgu*-thorn, "lion fat" (and) fat of a large steppe-dwelling snake for seven days, he should recover.
(72–84) Plants for a person with *epqēnu*: he strikes (the sores) with a fig branch and then crushes (together) figs and raisins and then binds them (with it). On the second day at night, he releases them (from the bandage). If they are still white, he binds them (again) and releases them (from the bandage) on the third day. Whether the whiteness has disappeared or whether their whiteness is not yet finished, he crushes them with an obsidian knife and then you grind together alum, *kalgukku*-clay, *lurpānu*-mineral (and) *uḫḫūlu* in vinegar. You repeatedly bind (it on him) for seven days. He releases (them from the bandage) for two nights and on the second day, he binds (them). He releases (them from the bandage) for two days. On the second day, he binds (them). If the surface of his sores is uniform and red, he crushes together cracked[15] *šigūšu*-grain (and) *šarmidu* and if he daubs (it) on, he should recover. If he does not recover, you mix *paḫḫānu*-lizard blood or (blood of) a *ḫurri*-bird (shelduck) (and) blood of a frog with alum, *kalakuttu*-clay, *lurpānu*-mineral and with *uḫḫūlu*

[4] A survey of currently available references suggests that what was contemplated was indeed a decoction, made by crushing plants and cooking them in boiling liquid. The resulting decoction could be left as a liquid or, by the simple expedient of adding flour and continuing to cook the mixture, a virtually solid substance could be obtained. See above, 4.88E, ad obv. 14–15.
[5] This is the same as *imḫur-ešra*.
[6] See Scurlock and Andersen 2005: 10.133.
[7] Schwemer 2011:43 interprets this as male and female *buṣinnu* (^{GIŠ}*bu-ṣí-na*). However, sexual differentiation is otherwise unattested for *buṣinnu*, and is highly unusual for plants other than mandrake and date palms.
[8] See Scurlock and Andersen, 2005: 10.133.
[9] For this expression, see Scurlock and Andersen 2005:27. The fat is hot because it is allegedly being taken from a fresh corpse. Schwemer 2011:44 interprets this expression as *ḫarḫaru*: "scoundrel," which seems less likely. In either case, we are dealing with a plant and it is being used fresh rather than dried.
[10] See Scurlock and Andersen, 2005: 10.133.
[11] See above, lines 53–54.
[12] See Scurlock and Andersen 2005: 3.219.
[13] See Scurlock and Andersen 2005: 3.220.
[14] *Talmu* is Hurrian for "large."
[15] For the suggestion that this is GUD$_4$ for KUD: *šebru*, see Tsukimoto 1999:198. *Šebru* means literally "broken," a close equivalent to English "cracked" as in "cracked wheat." This quite ancient method of preparing grain for eating requires boiling, and then sun drying, the kernels.

and then repeatedly bind him (with it). He should recover.
(85–93) When he has recovered, he burns with fire whatever bandages he repeatedly bound on. He sets up a table before Šamaš. You put out a ⌜censer⌝ burning *burāšu*-juniper. You set out *mersu*-confection (made with) honey and ghee. That patient stands before Šamaš. You burn a *ḫurri*-bird (shelduck) and a crab before Šamaš. [And] you wipe him off with (another) *ḫurri*-bird (shelduck) and then he releases it. And when you have the patient stand ⌜before⌝ Šamaš, ⌜you⌝ bind his head and his hip region with lapis-colored wool (dyed with dye) from the garden. When he comes out from before Šamaš, you throw the lapis-colored wool from his head and his hip region [and] all of the ritual paraphernalia which was placed before Šamaš into the river. The river will carry off its evil. And the patient should unburden his heart before Šamaš.
(94–97) ⌜If⌝ a person is unable to pour out his urine, you crush together honey, figs, raisins, dates, strich shell, *elkulla*, *šuliliānu*, "silver blossom" (and) "gold blossom" into little pieces. If he drinks (it mixed) with beer or wine, he should recover. You recite the recitation: "(I will cast for you a spell) that drives away every illness"[16] three times over the patient.

[16] For the full text of this recitation, see Böck 2007:45–46, 150–158.

REFERENCES

Böck 2007:45–46, 64–65, 150–158; Finkel 1999; Schwemer 2011:41–45; Scurlock and Andersen 2005: 3.219–220, 3.222, 10.133; Scurlock 2014: 2.3.3; Tsukimoto 1999.

"SUPERNATURAL" CAUSES: THE DEMONESS LAMAŠTU: DIAGNOSTIC AND PHARMACOLOGICAL TEXT EXCERPTS (4.88H)

JoAnn Scurlock

Lamaštu was a baby-snatching demoness who seems, in Jewish folklore, to have been crossed with another creature, the *lilītu*-demoness, producing the Lilith. According to her ancient Mesopotamian back story, Lamaštu was a daughter of Anu who got herself thrown out of heaven when she proved to have a taste for human flesh: "The daughter of Anu comes before Enlil, her father, crying: 'Bring me what I ask of you, my father Enlil: the flesh of mankind which is not good (to eat), the coagulated(?)[1] blood of men'" (4R^2 58 ii.33–36).[2]

Her problem was that she was a frustrated mother who caused abortions in pregnant women and deaths in young children due to her over-eagerness to nurture and suckle babies: "The daughter of Anu daily counts the pregnant women; she goes around after those (about to) give birth. She counts up their [months]; she marks the days (of their confinement) onto the wall. For the lying-in women giving birth (this) is (her) incantation: 'Bring me your sons so that I can give them suck; let me put the breast into the mouth of your daughters.'" (LKU 33:18–22).

It was hardly surprising that she had no husband or lover to provide her with children of her own, since she was lion-headed monster with donkey teeth (4R^2 58 i.36; Farber 1987:257:11) and clawed feet (SpTU 3.84:63) only slightly redeemed by wings like a *lilītu*-demon (LKU 33:15). She also ran about half naked (SpTU 3.84: 64), lived in the swamp, and wore an Elamite topnot (4R^2 28 ii.31–32), when she bothered to comb her hair at all. She was so awful looking that she literally withered trees just by leaning on them: "She leans on a *bīnu*-tamarisk, it loses its foliage. She leans on a date-palm, she strips off its dates. She leans on an *allānu*-oak or a wild *buṭnu*-terebinth, she makes it shrivel up" (KAR 239 ii.11′–13′).

In the Diagnostic and Prognostic Series, there appear a number of references to Lamaštu of which the most revealing are the following:

> (DPS 3.45–46) If his head continually afflicts him and fever (has) its seat[3] equally all over (and) when his illness leaves him, he has dizziness and trembles (and) ⌜if⌝, [when] his confusional state comes over him, his mentation is altered so that he wanders about without knowing (where he is) as in affliction by a ghost, Lamaštu afflicts [him]. He will come through.[4]

[1] For the translation, see Civil 1982:2, n. 4.
[2] This and the other rituals of the canonical series have been fully edited in Farber 2014.
[3] UNU = *šubtu*; see *CAD* Š/3 172b s.v. *šubtu* A lex. section.
[4] See Scurlock and Andersen 2005: 3.25, 19.227; Scurlock 2014: 1.1.3.

(DPS 9.11) If his face is yellow, Lamaštu afflicts him.[5]

(DPS 13.69) If his abdomen gets hot and gets cold (and) he asks for a lot of water and then drinks it, "hand" of Lamaštu.[6]

(DPS 13.70) If his abdomen gets hot and gets cold (and) he continually asks for a lot of water to bathe in, "hand" of Lamaštu.[7]

(DPS 16.14–15) If it afflicts him for one day (and) for one day it releases him (and) when his confusional states come over him, his limbs continually hurt him, he is feverish and trembles, sweat falls upon him and then he finds relief and continually asks for a great deal of water to drink, "hand" of Lamaštu; he will get well.[8]

(DPS 40.51) If fever and *li'bu* grips an infant and he is continually cold, affliction by Lamaštu (var. "hand" of the daughter of Anu).[9]

(DPS 40.52) If an infant is hot and then cold and he asks for a lot of water to drink, affliction by Lamaštu (var. "hand" of the daughter of Anu).

(DPS 40.53) If an infant's abdomen gets hot (and) gets cold and he asks for a lot of water to drink and drinks it, "hand" of Lamaštu.[10]

(DPS 40.54) If the air of an infant's "right" nostril gets cold and that of the "left" gets hot, "hand" of Lamaštu.

From this description, it is possible to identify a real disease or group of diseases with which the patients described in these references will have been ill. Most promising is the typhus/typhoid group. This acccounts for Lamaštu being said to "live in the swamp" as well as her characterization as a frustrated "mother" (*ummu* – a pun on "fever") and the "daughter" of Anu (*martu* – a pun on "jaundice"). As for her predilection for pregnant women and young children, this may have been an attempt to distinguish typhus from typhoid since the two diseases have significantly different mortality rates in children and in the likelihood of a pregnant woman losing her fetus.[11]

Conventional wisdom has it that the expert we are calling the "pharmacist" treated only diseases with "natural" causes. As so often in this field, however, conventional wisdom is quite wrong. For a patient afflicted by Lamaštu, there were a number of pharmacists' treatments of which a sample is the following:

(BAM 423 i.18′–19′) Shoots of *baltu*-thorn are a plant for Lamaštu. (It is to be ground and rubbed gently on mixed with oil). Shoots of *ašāgu*-thorn are a plant (for Lamaštu). (It is to be ground and rubbed gently on mixed with oil).

(BAM 379 iii.36′) (*Kazallu*) is a plant for affliction by Lamaštu. It is to be ground and rubbed gently on (mixed) with oil.

(BAM 379 ii.7′–8′//CTN 4.195 iii.4–5) The plant which resembles the *murrānu*-tree and whose seed is as white as a *ḫallūru*-chick pea is called "lone plant." It is a plant for removing Lamaštu.[12]

(KADP 1 v.3//CTN 4 194:2) Red ⸢*girimmu*-berry⸣ is a plant for Lamaštu. It is to be ground [and rubbed on gently] mixed with oil.

The pharmacist and the physician also had at their disposal more complex combinations of medicines as in the following example.

(BAM 183:16–19) Snake skin, *šamaškillu*-onion peel, flax seed, *kibrītu*-sulphur, *saḫlû*-cress, hair combings, *kukru*, *kasû* and unsifted flour are a total of nine drugs (lit. "plants"): a fumigant for ⸢Lamaštu⸣

What is essentially this same treatment appears in the canonical series of mostly magical rituals against Lamaštu.

5 See Scurlock and Andersen 2005: 3.26, 19.223; Scurlock 2014: 1.1.9.
6 See Scurlock and Andersen 2005: 19.230; Scurlock 2014: 1.1.13.
7 See Scurlock and Andersen 2005: 19.231; Scurlock 2014: 1.1.13.
8 See Scurlock and Andersen 2005: 3.20, 13.84, 19.225. For the text in context, see Heeßel 2000:171–193; Scurlock 2014: 1.1.16.
9 See Scurlock and Andersen 2005: 3.16, 19.224; Scurlock 2014: 1.1.40.
10 See Scurlock and Andersen 2005: 19.229.
11 For more details, see Scurlock and Andersen 2005:483–485.
12 See Stadhouders 2011:22.

(4R[2] 55 no. 1 obv. 36–37) These plants: *kukru*, *kasû*, unsifted flour, snake skin, *šamaškillu*-onion peel, flax seed, *kibrītu*-sulphur, *saḫlû* and hair combings are a fumigant (for Lamaštu).[13]

---

[13] This and the other rituals of the canonical series have been fully edited in Farber 2014.

REFERENCES

Civil 1982:2, n. 4; Farber 1987:257; Farber 2014; Heeßel 2000:171–193; Scurlock and Andersen 2005:483–485; 3.16, 3.20, 3.25–26, 13.84, 19.223–225, 19.227, 19.229–231; Scurlock 2014: 1.1.3, 1.1.9, 1.1.13, 1.1.16, 1.1.40; Stadhouders 2011:22.

"SUPERNATURAL" CAUSES: THE DEMONESS LAMAŠTU: FEVER (BM 35512)[1] (4.88I)

JoAnn Scurlock

BM 35512 is one of a number of texts collecting together treatments for fever. Some of these appear to be symptomatic treatments for elevated temperature, but several specifically mention Lamaštu (obv. 5–8, rev. 15–17) or her partner in crime "Anything Evil" (rev. 11–14), a demon apparently responsible for febrile delirium and convulsions. These treatments reflect that jumbled mix of what we would consider "magic" and what we would accept as "medicine" that characterizes pre-Christian traditions of medicine.

We might wish to supplement our medicines with prayer, but there is more to these rituals than simply the expansion of causality from one God to the complex of gods, ghosts, demons, malfunctioning body parts and witchcraft of ancient diagnoses. For us, combating disease is a matter of black and white, good vs. evil, with doctors as crusaders and the patient a somewhat fragile battlefield. Ancient physicians had a more humane and balanced view of the universe in which bad things were, witchcraft excepted, the result of a conflict of interests between human needs and desires and those of other beings. So an unhappy ghost might make demands on you that were, in their own way, as legitimate as those made by your own liver or stomach. As we have seen (4.88H), Lamaštu's need for children to suckle was perfectly natural, even legitimate or rather, it would have been if humans had not had to suffer as a result.

Demons in general were not the recipients of regular offerings in the cult, and the medicines given the patients in whom they caused diseases were the only food they got to eat. In dealing with them, therefore, the key was to administer whatever medicines seemed to be acceptable to them (as judged by whether the patient got well) combined with rituals that made it clear that they were to take their offerings and go away. Sympathy only goes so far when humans begin to suffer and die. So, for example, "Anything Evil" (rev. 11–14) was given back his fever by making his figurine from clay used to wipe off the body of the patient and then dispatched to the Netherworld by being left in the steppe at sunset tied to a thornbush and surrounded with a magic circle to prevent escape. He was not, however, sent off empty handed, being supplied with clothing and travel provisions for his journey with the god of justice, Šamaš, to witness. Even so, the patient was not, like Orpheus, to make the mistake of looking back, and just for good measure he went a different way home to confuse his tracks.

What is important about this text in particular is that it confirms the connection between the Diagnostic and Prognostic series of which it cites Tablet 33 line 4,[2] and the Therapeutic Series of which it is an extract text (rev. 18–20). What is more, Na᾿id-Marduk, who appears as the son of the author of the tablet, is a known *āšipu* who worked in the Ezida, temple of the Mesopotamian god of wisdom, Nabû, in Borsippa.[3]

(obv. 1–3) If fever afflicts a person, you grind together *kamūnu*-cumin, *kamantu*, *kamkādu*, *lišān kalbi* ("dog tongue"), male and female *nikiptu*, *kukru* (= "white aromatic"), *burāšu*-juniper, *azupīru*, fresh *karān šēlibi* ("fox grape") (and) *kamūn šadê*-fungus. You mix (it) with oil (and) pour (it) into a *tamgussu*-vessel. You drop a live *ṣurāru*-lizard into it (and) boil (it) over a fire [until] it has cooked. What you dropped in (i.e. the lizard), you take out and throw away. You let (the mixture) cool. You recite the recitation "The hatred(?) of his god has been loosened" three times over it and, if you rub him gently with it, he should recover.

(obv. 4) Alternatively, you grind together *ankinutu*, *burāšu*-juniper, *kukru* (and) *ṣumlalû*. You mix (it) with oil (and) rub him gently (with it). If it is ⸢winter⸣, you use (it) hot.

(obv. 5–8) Alternatively, you collect together dust from a crossroads, dust from a tavern, dust from the gate of the palace, dust from the gate of a temple,

---

[1] A transliteration and translation of partial duplicates to this text appear in Scurlock 2014: 2.2.1–2.2.2 and 3.2.3. I would like to thank the trustees of the British Museum for permission to translate this tablet.

[2] For a full edition, see Heeßel 2000:353–374. See also Scurlock 2014: 1.1.33.

[3] Hunger 1968:53–54, no. 136, 132 no. 467, 153.

dust from the gate of the house of a brewer, dust from the house of a cook, dust from the house of a rug weaver, dust from a boat going downstream (and) dust from quays and crossings. You mix (it) with oil. [You ...] a *šalālu*-reed. You take its pith and resin. You wrap (it) in a tuft of wool. Before Šamaš, you set up an offering arrangement. [You ...] the oil and this amulet on a wooden [...]. You recite [the recitation ...] times. You recite the recitation "Lamaštu, daughter of Anu" seven times before Šamaš over the oil. You put the amulet on his neck and if you rub him gently with this oil, he should recover.

(obv. 9–10) Alternatively, you dry (and) grind *ṣaṣuntu*, *aprušu* (and) *karān šēlibi* ("fox grape") (and) mix (it) with oil. You heat (it) in a *pūru*-vessel made from *algamešu*-stone and then rub him gently (with it). You twine together red-dyed wool, lion hair (and) hair of a virgin she-goat into a cord. You work *lišān kalbi*, *imḫur-lim*, *amilānu*, *ašqulalu*, and "ox dung" with them into the cord. If [you put it] on his neck, he should recover.

(obv. 11–13) If fever afflicts a person, you rub him gently with *ḫalulaya*-insect (mixed) with oil. You fumigate him with flax seed over coals. You hitch a stallion to a chariot on the left side and you cool down the ⸢horse⸣ on the left with old sheep fat. You drive (it) so that the ⸢horse⸣ sweats and then you rub the garment(?) of the patient gently with the old [sheep fat]. The day it afflicts him, you fumigate him (with) the fat one, two or three times. If a stranger fumigates him, he should recover.

(obv. 14–18) Alternatively, at noon, you take dust from shade and sunlight. You grind (it and) plaster from both doorposts, dust from the front threshold, dust from below a post-menopausal woman, dust from a tomb (and) *samīdu* (and) mix (it) with *pūru* oil. You boil it over a fire ⟨(in)⟩ a *pūru*-vessel made from *algamešu*-stone. You drop a live *ṣurāru*-lizard into it. You take (it) out and throw (it) away. You have him recite over it as follows. "The shade brings (shade) in proportion to the heat of the sunlight (The hotter the sun, the cooler the shade). Just as one door post does not approach the other, so may the sickness never approach the patient, so-and so, son of so-and-so. Just as should anyone step on the threshold, (he will never obtain anybody as a wife), so may (the illness) not obtain anybody (as a wife). Just as a drainpipe can never abandon its runnel and its riser, so may the sick person not be given up on. Just as a dead person does not change his kidney (i.e. toss and turn), so may the sick person not change his kidney: spell and recitation." You recite the recitation over it seven times and then rub him gently (with it).

(obv. 19) ⸢Alternatively⸣, you wrap *šurdunû* in a black cloth and, if you put (it) on his neck, he should recover.

(obv. 20) ⸢Alternatively⸣, if you fumigate him with fat from the kidney of a black ox, gazelle droppings, stag horn, "lone plant" (= "human bone"), *uḫḫūlu* ⸢*qarnānu*⸣ (and) *kibrītu*-sulphur over coals, he should recover.

(obv. 21) ⸢Alternatively⸣, you (rub him gently) with *imḫur-ešra*, dust from beneath a post-menopausal woman, *baltu*-thorn oil (and) *bīnu*-tamarisk oil (mixed) with oil (and you wrap it) in a tuft of wool (and put it on his neck).

(obv. 22) If ditto (fever afflicts a person), (and) on the second (day) he feels well, you (rub him gently) with a *ḫalulaya*-cricket, a fly from a dog (and) "dog's tongue" (mixed) with oil (and you put it on his neck) in a leather bag.

(obv. 23) Alternatively, you fumigate him with snake skin, scorpion stinger, *saḫlû*-cress, *sikillu* (= "soiled rag") (and) bristles over coals.

(obv. 24) Alternatively, (you wrap) ape hair (and) "lone plant" (= "human bone") in a tuft of wool (and put it on his neck).

(obv. 25) Alternatively, you sew up (a tuft of) black (hair) from the thigh of a donkey, (a tuft of) black (hair) from the thigh of a horse(!) (and) tanner's depilatory paste in a leather bag and (you also rub him gently with) *aprušu* (mixed) with oil.

(obv. 26) Alternatively, (you put) snake skin, scorpion stinger, "lone plant" (= "human bone"), *sikillu* (= "soiled rag"), *kutpû*-mineral, *mūṣu*-stone (and) *ṣaṣuntu* in a leather bag.

(rev. 1) [If ...] you fumigate him [with ...] over coals.

(rev. 2–3) [Alternatively, you ...] flax [seed and ...]. If you repeatedly rub him gently (with it), he should recover.

(rev. 4–6) [If ...] the flesh ⸢above⸣ is cold (but) [the bones below feel burning hot, fever with] ⸢*liʾbu*⸣-rash afflicts him. If you repeatedly rub him gently [with ...] (mixed with) oil, he should get well.

(rev. 7) [...] To remove fever, you moisten (it) with water and, if you cool him with it, he should get well.

(rev. 8–10) [If ...] it is continually grasped with the hands (and) [...], he is ⸢sick⸣ with [...]. In order for his illness not to be prolonged, you grind *ankinūtu* (and) powdered "lone plant." [...] If you keep doing this for [...] ⸢days⸣, he should recover.

(rev. 11–14) If fever continually afflicts a person, you take clay from a canal. You mix (it) with canal water. You wipe off the body of the sick person (with it and) make a figurine. On its left shoulder, you write "Figurine of 'Anything Evil.'" You take hair from the forehead of oxen and sheep. You weave (it) into a makeshift garment, a makeshift cloak (and) a makeshift turban. You arrange groats, beer bread, malt (and) [...] flour on *sēpu*-bread. In the late afternoon, you present your case (against "Anything Evil") before Šamaš. You take (him) out into the steppe region. You make (him) face the setting sun. and you tie (him) to a *baltu*-thorn or *ašāgu*-thorn and you surround (him) with a magic circle. You do not look behind you. [You take] another street (home from the one on which you came).

(rev. 15–17) (Garbled Sumerian recitation against the demoness Lamaštu) Recitation for cases where a fever afflicts a person. You write it on a cylinder seal. You put (it) on his neck and, [if you do not take it off for ... days], he should recover.

(rev. 18–20) "If a sore comes out on a man's body and his face and eyes are swollen, his sight is difficult and (his eyes) drift downstream (horizontal nystagmus), it is called *ašû*" (is the next line of the following tablet).[4] Thirty-four extracts from the series: "If a person's skull holds fever," copy of an original in the "house of Mister Work [work work]"[5] which [Luḫdu-Nabû], son of Nappaḫu [wrote] for his life and the life of [his] son Naʾid-Marduk.

[4] See Scurlock and Andersen 2005:224–226.

[5] This seems to be a variant of the "house of words." For other texts from this establishment, see below, 4.88N.

REFERENCES

Heeßel 2000:353–374; Hunger 1968:53–54, no. 136, 132 no. 467, 153; Scurlock and Andersen 2005:224–226; Scurlock 2014: 1.1.33, 2.2.1–2.2.2 and 3.2.3.

"SUPERNATURAL" CAUSES: LAMAŠTU AND WITCHCRAFT: RITUALS OF THE END OF THE MONTH ABU[1] (4.88J)

JoAnn Scurlock

Ebeling 1931 no. 30A is composite made up of Texts A (KAR 227), B (LKA 89) C (K 9860+), D (LKA 90), E (K 6793+), F (BM 98638)[2] and G (Si 747). It is a multi-column text of a complex ritual designed to combat the demoness Lamaštu here again, as in BM 33512, accompanied by "Anything Evil." The text has a fascinating relationship with a group of texts published as Abusch and Schwemer 2011: 8.7.1–2. In this group, which consists of a long and very complicated ritual with an accompanying memorandum tablet, it is imagined that an alcoholic patient who has contracted a fever[3] has been the victim of one or more particularly nasty pieces of witchcraft (Abusch and Schwemer 2011: 8.7.1:1–67′; 8.7.2:12).

In these alleged rites, the patient was made febrile through the rituals of a sorcerer or sorceress, who made figurines of him, clothed them with combed-out hair, covered their faces with sheep bile, and pierced them with a date palm thorn so as to produce the hair-fall, vomiting and aches and pains of the fever. To ensure that this would result in fatality, the evil enemy allegedly also manufactured figurines of the patient at the beginning of Abu in anticipation of one of four annual visits by ghosts at the end of the month (Abusch and Schwemer 2011: 8.7.1:17). With the arrival of the ancient Mesopotamian equivalent of Halloween, these figurines were handed over to Gilgamesh, one or more of the visiting ghosts of Abu and/or the ghost of the patient's relatives and made to cross the Hubur river to the Netherworld with the returning ghosts (Abusch and Schwemer 2011: 8.7.1: 17, 60′–61′). Having once done this, the patient could never return to the land of the living except as a ghost. Gilgamesh (Foster 1997) was a semi-legendary heroic early king of Uruk who, after death, lived on as the constellation Orion and as one of the judges of the Netherworld. He presided over a court consisting of the gods of the lower world, the Anunnaki. Since the 26th of Abu was the day the Annunaki made their decisions,[4] the victim of such a rite was pretty much doomed to die.

The ancient author of Abusch and Schwemer 2011: 8.7.1–2 reacts to this situation in standard fashion by protecting the patient with a specially manufactured amulet (Abusch and Schwemer 2011: 8.7.2:31–33; 8.7.1:106‴–117′), repeating the fever-infliction process on figurines made to represent a sorcerer and sorceress (Abusch and Schwemer 2011: 8.7.2:17–19; 8.7.1 A_3 ii.2′–7′) and then baking, burning, roasting, and otherwise disposing of them (Abusch and Schwemer 2011: 8.7.2:3–16; 8.7.1: 88″–98″, A_3 iii.4′–6′, 102‴–105‴).

[1] The text was first edited in Ebeling 1931:122, 124–133 (no. 30a). In his review, von Soden 1936:265–267 made numerous corrections. Since then, Abusch and Schwemer 2011:14 have found new duplicates and new joins to an already known duplicate, Haupt, *Nimrodepos* no. 53. The later text (without the new joins) is transliterated, translated and discussed in context in Lambert 1960:40. The prayers to the family ghost and the address to the skull were edited in Scurlock 1988:351–354, 357–361. The text as a whole is discussed in Schwemer 2007:200–201, 220 and Abusch 2002:76–78 and will be edited by them in the forthcoming AMD 8/2.

[2] A transliteration of this tiny fragment was kindly provided to me by D. Schwemer.

[3] With Abusch and Schwemer 2011:349 and pace Scurlock and Andersen 2005:22–23, this is not a reference to rabies.

[4] See Abusch and Schwemer 2011: 8.3 obv. 56.

In addition, a ritual was to be performed in imitation of the alleged dedication to Gilgamesh and the infernal powers in order, literally, to reverse the spell and to counter-inflict Lamaštu on the sorcerer or sorceress in a classic tit for tat. First, a skull was washed and anointed with oil (Abusch and Schwemer 2011: 8.7.2:20–21). Lamaštu was seated (as witness) to the ritual and given various presents as were the ghosts (Abusch and Schwemer 2011: 8.7.2:22, 23–27; 8.7.1:70″–72″). Clay figurines (of the sorcerer and sorceress) were tied into the skull's hem using bits of colored wool (Abusch and Schwemer 2011: 8.7.2:22–23; 8.7.1:73″–80″, 83″–87″), then gathered into it and sealed up with *šigūšu*-barley flour (Abusch and Schwemer 2011: 8.7.1:118‴–119‴) for dispatch together with Lamaštu to the Netherworld (Abusch and Schwemer 2011: 8.7.1: A_3 iii.7′–9′). A final appeal to the skull (Abusch and Schwemer 2011: 8.7.1:127⁗–139⁗) completed the preserved parts of the rite.

This last ritual is a close analogue to Ebeling 1931 no. 30A and, in the unfortunately fragmentary state of current preservation of the latter text, the presence of the memorandum version (Abusch and Schwemer 2011: 8.7.2) is something of a godsend. Ebeling 1931 no. 30A has an apparently somewhat more complex version of this ritual, and opens with the preparation of figurines not only of the sorcerer and sorceress but also of Gilgamesh, Namtar and "Anything Evil." Gilgamesh's figurine is the first to be manufactured (A 227 i.6–13).[5] As divine judge of the Netherworld allegedly previously suborned by sorcery, his cooperation was essential for the ritual. In addition to dressing him in a manner appropriate to his rank, the patient was to give him "ransom money" (A i.10) in order to free himself from the sorcerer's alleged dedication of the patient's figurine to Gilgamesh. This is a "gold ransom," to join a later "silver ransom" paid directly to "Anything Evil." The specification of a shekel (GÍN) weight for one of the presents (A i.11) is probably a reference to the Sumerographic writing of Gilgamesh's name (GIŠ.GÍN.MAŠ). The seven grains of gold and seven grains of silver (A i.13) and the fact that the description takes up the first 14 lines of text are probably an invocation of the Netherworld, whose number is 14. The miniature cedar boat, which is of the large cargo-boat variety (A i.12), is for use later in the ritual when it comes time to "make (the sorcerer and sorceress) cross the Hubur."

The Hubur was the river of the Netherworld, the ancient Mesopotamian equivalent of the Greek Styx. In our ritual, an ordinary river was being used as a stand-in. To make sure that it understood what was expected of it, a recitation was delivered to it (A i.15–23) with Gilgamesh as witness, his figurine being turned to face it(?)[6] for this purpose (A i.6). The idea was for the river to carry off "Anything Evil" in the form of a figurine made from clay taken from a potter's pit on the river banks. Since magic will not work unless it is paid for, the grains of silver given to Gilgamesh in Text A and poured into the potter's pit in Text B were to reimburse the river banks for clay taken from them for this purpose (A i.17–18). The remainder of the recitation is a pretty description of objects thrown into the river being turned this way and that and eventually being carried away by the current never to return (A i.20–22).

The next order of business was to make a figurine of Namtar (A i.23–26) to whom the sorcerer and sorceress was to be entrusted (D ii.5′, iii.3, iii.24; KAR 227 iii.17). He was represented as a tall, lion-headed human figure with a red face and body and yellow cat's eyes. Lurking in the background is the demoness Lamaštu, who as we saw in BM 35512 (4.88J), was often associated with "Anything Evil." The latter got a figurine (A i.27–28) dressed in everyday clothes plus shoes, a bag for the "travel flour" with which he was to provision her (A i.28) and a waterskin (A i.32), a good indication that the two of them were destined for a long journey together. "Anything Evil" received the patient's "silver ransom" money (A i.28–31), actually bits of all sorts of metals and stones plus the three colors of wool that, as explained in Abusch and Schwemer 2011: 8.7.2 rev. 21–23, formed a sort of hem into which the money and the two figurines of sorcerer and sorceress, also made of clay (A i.33), will have been tied. The reference is to the part of a marriage ceremony in which the bride had the brideprice returned to her by her father as a sort of indirect dowry.

As mentioned later in the recitation to the Anunnaki (D iii.15), this set of actions resulted in the "marriage" of the demon to the persons represented by the figurines. Since the figurines were a dowry of sorts, the insinuation was that "Anything Evil" was being married to Lamaštu, a standard in Lamaštu rituals, although not usually with Lamaštu playing the role of husband. In the ancient Near East, when the normal marriage payments were reversed, it meant that the couple would be moving in with the bride. In this case, this was literally true since Lamaštu's home was in the Elamite swamp, which was where the figurines would eventually end up after they were dumped in the river.

In the alleged original rite, the patient's figurine, marked by his spittle, hair, fingernails, bits of his garments or even dirt from his tracks was married to "Anything Evil." In the counter-rite, the patient is careful to be as unspecific as possible, making both male and female figurines and labeling them simply as those sorcerers who have afflicted the patient (A i.34–35). It is standard for prayers in witchcraft rituals to insist that the patient does not know his

[5] The reading of the name in the duplicate to Text A i.6 is conjectural. However, since the Gilgamesh prayer specifically mentions the giving of presents to him, one of which is a cedar boat, and since the first figurine is given presents among which there is unquestionably an oar of cypress, it is hard to imagine that the first figurine represented anyone other than Gilgamesh.

[6] The figurine is being turned in some direction. That it is being turned to face the river is conjectural.

enemy or even the house or city in which the alleged perpetrator lives.[7] The reason for this is that the magic he was employing is what the Azande called "smart" magic. It might more properly be referred to as justice magic, since it could be trusted to find and punish the guilty party whoever and wherever he or she was. The reason for the care taken in setting up the magic is that, in ancient Mesopotamia, false accusation bore the same penalty as the offense. In practical terms, the magic, would, in case of misuse, turn about-face and do to the patient whatever he was attempting to do to his enemy.

Now that all the figurines had been made, it was time to begin the ritual, properly speaking. The patient needed to be isolated and on top of the roof, which was where the ceremony was to take place (A i.36). The preparations and sacrifice are quite standard except for the libation of beer made from roasted grain flour (A i.38), not something usually offered to Šamaš or other gods of healing called in as guarantors of magic rituals. The reason for this oddity soon becomes apparent. Everybody involved as assistant in this ritual expulsion of "Anything Evil" gets something by way of offering – Namtar (A i.40), the skull (D i.5′), both family (D i.6′) and strange ghosts (D i.7′) and the Anunnaki (D i.8′), even Lamaštu who is called as witness indicating her interest in the proceedings (D i.4′). Everybody, that is, except for Gilgamesh. As the prayer delivered to him makes clear, most if not all of what are ostensibly offerings to Šamaš (A i.37–39) actually were to go to Gilgamesh, presumably, on condition that he did what was required of him. Since the Sungod visited the Netherworld during the night, he could easily have delivered Gilgameš's share to him in person.

A prayer was recited at this point to Šamaš (D i.11′–27′; A ii.1–5) of which very little is preserved. His role as god of justice was to see to it that justice was done in this case. This Šamaš prayer was followed by a prayer to Gilgamesh (E obv. 1–42; D ii.1′[8]–iii.9) which is much better preserved. Interesting in view of later tradition is to see Gilgamesh referred to as a Watcher (E obv. 3), originally a reference to judicial investigations performed as Orion in the night sky, which, for ancient Mesopotamians, was an extension of the Netherworld. Since Gilgamesh was a judge (E obv. 1, 4), we hear much about the ancient Mesopotamian legal process. The good judge was expected to question witnesses, to make an investigation, to judge the case and finally, to check once more to make sure that justice had been done (E obv. 7). It was in this way that he could ensure that his decisions were not overturned and his words not forgotten (E obv. 6).

Deciding whether the accused was innocent or guilty was not, however, the end of the judge's duties; he had also to apply the appropriate sentence, if any, which required the giving of a legal opinion. Later Islamic law gave the duty of providing the legal opinion (*fetwa*) to a separate expert (*mufti*) from the judge (*qadi*). Developed Roman law similarly separated legal experts (*juriconsults*) from judges. In ancient Mesopotamian sources, the process of judging the case (*dīnu dânu* – E obv. 12, 14 or *šipṭu šapāṭu* – E obv. 8) is separately mentioned from giving the legal opinion (*purussû parāsu* – E obv. 8, 13, 14), but both processes seem to have been performed by a single individual. If they had been separated into two functions as in later law, however, the judge would have been a *šāpiṭu* (*shopheth*) and the *juriconsult* a *pārisu* (*pharisee*). Given the "Babylonian captivity" and the fact that the Rabbinic descendants of the Pharisees are essentially the Jewish equivalent of a *juriconsult* or a *mufti*, it is hard not to think that this Akkadian expression is the actual origin of the term.

As is not uncommon, the prayers or recitations in magical texts make reference to the ritual *dromena* that accompany the spoken *legomena* of the ritual (E obv. 18–25), a fact which allows us to some extent to restore the broken parts of A i.7–13. Like Šamaš, Gilgamesh's role was as guarantor of the rite, with direct action on his part taking the form of pacifying the unhappy family ghosts (E obv. 40–41) and rendering the judgment (E obv. 42) that allowed the illness to be removed and the sorcerer and sorceress to be punished. "Anything Evil" (D ii.1′–3′) and the sorcerer and sorceress (D ii.3′–12′) could then be dispatched in picturesque fashion to the Netherworld.

This was not, however, before mention was made of their figurines (D ii.13′–17′, D ii.18′–19′) intertwined with mention of the figurine of "Anything Evil," and his silver ransom payment (D ii.17′–18′, D ii.19′–23′), thus verbally binding both the money and the witch figurines to the figurine of "Anything Evil." This payment is said to have been given not only in the presence of Gilgamesh (*ina* IGI-*ka*) but also of Lamaštu (*ina* TUŠ-*k*[*i*]) with a very nice distinction of legal terminology that, in ordinary contracts and legal cases, marks the difference between male and female witnesses (D ii.23′). In an ancient Mesopotamian court, men "stood" and women "sat" to witness. We saw Lamaštu "sitting" (as witness) in D i.4′ when offerings were made to the ghosts of family and strangers (D i.5′–7′). Nothing was said at that point (at least not in the preserved parts of the text) about any offerings to the sorcerer and sorceress as asserted in D ii.17′–19′. We may perhaps infer that, in order to claim their provisions, funerary (*kispu*)-offerings and water, the sorcerer and sorceress needed themselves to become ghosts.

7 Abusch and Schwemer 2011: 8.2:106–107.

8 This is the numbering given to D in Ebeling 1931:128. On the photograph of the tablet, there are actually several more lines more or less visible.

It is presumably Lamaštu who was to be impressed with the witchcraft figurines and their provisions (D ii.13′–19′) and with the ransom payment given to "Anything Evil" (D ii.19′–23′) of both of which she was to be the ultimate beneficiary. In this case, it will have been Lamaštu's word (D iii.1) that was to banish the sickness from the patient's body and she who was to entrust the sorcerer and sorceress to Netherworld figures (D iii.1–7). Otherwise, it is hard to imagine why there should be apparent duplication of instructions already once given (D ii.5′ = D iii.3; ii.9′ = iii.7). It would also be odd to find Gilgamesh being scolded about the prospect of letting the witches escape (D iii.2). Finally, it is noteworthy that the text repeats the "in your presence" with its masculine referent when it comes time to administer the oath (D iii.8), a function more obviously relevant to Gilgamesh.

So Gilgamesh reappears to administer the oath and to reap the benefits of the patient's gratitude for his cure (D iii.8–9). He also receives a libation and reverence (D iii.10–11). In Abusch and Schwemer 2011: 8.7.1–2's version of this ritual, the prayer to Gilgamesh was apparently omitted, and the libation directly associated with the prayer to Šamaš of D i.11′–27′; A ii.1–5, cited by incipit (Abusch and Schwemer 2011: 8.7.2:28–30).

The Anunnaki gods were the ordinary divine denizens of the Netherworld who formed the court over which Gilgamesh and the other judges presided. Since they had also been suborned, they, too, needed a prayer (D iii.12–31). Their role, as the text makes clear, was to issue a judgment, leaving the heavy lifting to the family ghosts. These were the next to be addressed, reminded of presents given them and of the presence at the ritual of Šamaš and Gilgamesh, and asked to take "Anything Evil" (A iii.16–17, A iii.20) and the sorcerer and sorceress (A iii.18–19) with them to the Netherworld. To note, as indicated only in the pronoun suffixes, "Anything Evil" is verbally placed on either side of the sorcerer and sorceress, thus preventing their escape. As a reward for their services, the ghosts were promised pure water in their water pipes (A iii.21–24). These are the victim's family ghosts that have been allegedly suborned by the sorcerer and sorceress, so the patient will have known where their graves were located and could easily refresh their water supply.

Next, there was the matter of the skull, to whom a recitation needed to be addressed. One of the interesting features of the month of Abu ghost festival was that it was a time when, not only did the family ghosts visit the living, but also the beggarly "ghosts of a nobody" could come into the community of the living and be fed. These were not friends of man, but they were hardly evil either, and they had once been human. So they were in some sense entitled to offerings, but not trusted to behave after they had gotten them.

Consequently, the skull is subjected to a long series of oaths (A iii.44–50) which nobody thus far appealed to in this ritual has had to swear, not even the family ghosts. The mention of a *nudunnû*-dowry (A iii.32) tells us that the skull is to be married (to Lamaštu) and is to be filled with the figurines and sealed up with dough as also in Abusch and Schwemer 2011: 8.7.1:118′′′–119′′′ which shares with Ebeling 1931 no. 30A a virtually identical recitation to the skull (Abusch and Schwemer 2011: 8.7.1:127′′′′–139′′′′).

Last, but by no means least, the little lion-headed figurine of Namtar needed to be given his instructions. This necessitated yet another recitation (D iv.5–15) similar in many ways to that of the skull since, like beggarly ghosts, demons were not the best at tamely doing what was asked of them. In this case, Namtar's job was as ferryman to take the figurines across to the "land of no return" (D iv.5–6), and to make sure that the returning ghosts took the sorcerer and sorceress down with them to the Netherworld (D iv.9). For good measure, Namtar was also subjected to a series of oaths to prevent escape (D iv.10–15).

At this point, Ebeling 1931 no. 30A more or less dies, leaving the final ritual instructions for us to restore. If we may do this using Abusch and Schwemer 2011: 8.71–72, then Lamaštu will have been seated once again, this time to receive two clay donkeys with travel provisions, her typical presents of housewifely items, a seal, a headdress of green *ḫašmanu*-wool, clothing, a silver ring and a grain of silver plus *kispu*-offerings (Abusch and Schwemer 2011: 8.7.2:22–27). This will also have been the point for the "marriage" of the sorcerer and sorceress figurines to "Anything Evil" and for the little figurines to be stuffed into the skull as "dowry."

The medium for the final dispatch of skull and contents will have been the tiny cedar boat model (A i.12; E obv. 23) that will have floated down the river, with Gilgamesh as ship's captain and Namtar as steersmen (D iv.5) manning the cypress oar, in order to send the lot of them off with the departing ghosts. We can know this pretty securely since there is another ritual, edited in Farber 1977:210–217,[9] that has a final recitation (BAM 323:87–88) that is identical to B iv.1′–3′. On the 29th of Abu, when it was customary for the ghosts to receive their food offerings (BAM 323:84), the little boat will have been loaded up and released, facing downstream, while the recitation was recited (BAM 323:84–86).

The colophon of Text B indicates that there was another ritual after this in the original from which our ritual was copied. This lost ritual dealt with a person whose figurines had been entrusted to a dead person. The colophon also

[9] See also Scurlock 2006a: no. 228.

identifies this text as belonging to the library of the famous Assyrian *āšipu*, Kiṣir-Aššur. One of the duplicates (Text E) bears the personal imprint of the scholar-king Aššurbanipal. It consists exclusively of the Gilgamesh prayer and, again according to its colophon, it was copied, checked and collated by the king himself "who trusts in Aššur and Mulissu and whom Nabû and Tašmetu endowed with broad understanding" to be kept in the palace for his own reading and to have it read to him. The colophon ends with a short prayer: "He who trusts in you will not come to shame, O king of the gods, Aššur."[10]

Ebeling 1931 no. 10A

(A i.1–14)[11] [If a ghost afflicts a person or Lamaštu] afflicts him [or Gilgameš or] the ⸢Anunnaki⸣ has seized him [or "Anything Evil"] afflicts him, [to] pacify the ⸢evil⸣ [sorcerous rituals and] to rescue [that person from] the ⸢Anunnaki⸣, you turn [a (stone) figurine] of ⸢Gilgameš⸣ which you have carved[12] [to face the river]. You station (him) at the river[13] and give him [a golden *mammu*-crown, a red *ḫuššu*-garment][14] (and) a ⟨silver⟩ ⸢*nibittu*-girdle⸣ as a gift. You bind [the golden *mammu*-crown][15] for the head(?) to the ⸢middle(?)⸣[16] of his head. You bind the silver ⸢*nibittu*-girdle⸣ to his waist. You put his (the patient's) golden ⸢ransom-money⸣ on his neck. You fasten a golden [ringlet] weighing 1 ⸢shekel⸣ to his hands and feet. You make a present to him of a cedar ⸢*makurru*-boat⸣ (with) an oar of cypress. You give him[17] seven grains of silver (and) 7 grains of gold. You recite the [recitation]: "⸢Clay pit⸣,[18] creatress of god and man."

(A i.15–22) You, clay pit, are creatress of god and man; you (Gilgameš),[19] the ⸢precious⸣ heavenly [stone],[20] the ⸢governor⸣ that gives orders. You, clay pit, have been ⸢purified⸣.[21] You have received your silver; you have taken in your [gift]. Your garment is spread out (to receive them). Your banks have no rival; your heart is wide; your banks take him away. May your banks take him; may your banks drive (him) away. Turn him round to before you; return him to before you. Take him so that he may be extracted (and) ⸢driven away⸣.[22] May he not return; may he not come near; may he not approach; [may he not] come close.

(A i.23–26) You recite this three times and then you pinch off clay from the clay pit. You make a figurine of ⸢Namtar⸣ one cubit tall. His head should be that of a lion (but) his hands [and] its [feet] that of a human being. You gently rub his face with red *šaršerru*-clay. On his right eye, you daub *kalû*-clay, (and) [on] his left eye, *kammu*-sumac. You gently rub his body with red *šaršerru*-clay.

(A i.27–32) You make a figurine of "Anything Evil." You dress him in a makeshift garment (and) a makeshift cloak. He should provide ⸢her⸣ (i.e., Lamaštu) with malt/travel provision-flour. You weigh out his (the patient's) silver ransom money (consisting of) silver, gold, copper, tin, lead, antimony, carnelian, lapis lazuli, *ḫulalu*-chalcedony, *muššaru*-serpentine, goat hair, ⸢wool⸣,[23] white wool, red wool, (and) blue wool and give (it) to him as a gift. You give him a *nibittu*-girdle, shoes, a *naruqqu*-sack (and) a waterskin.

(A i.33–35) You make a [figurine] of sorcerer and sorceress out of clay from the clay pit.[24] You write [their names on] their left shoulders: "[Whoever performed] ⸢sorcerous rituals⸣ against [so and so, son of so and so]."[25]

(A i.36–39) You isolate ⸢that⸣ [person] on top of the roof. [You sweep the ground]. You sprinkle pure water. Before Šamaš, [you set up] an offering arrangement. [You scatter a handful of flour].[26] You set out [a censer] (burning) *burāšu*-juniper. [You pour out a libation] of beer made from roasted (wheat)[27] flour. [You make a sacrifice]. [You bring near] the ⸢shoulder⸣, caul fat and (some of) the [roasted meat].

(A i.40–42; D i.4′–8′) [In the presence] of Šamaš, [you make a funerary offering] to [Namtar]. You

10 This is Hunger 1968: no. 319 (= Asb. Typ c-e).

11 Text A col. i is duplicated by Text B col. i of which there exists only a virtually illegible photograph. I have benefited in reading this text from collations of the original kindly provided me by Daniel Schwemer. For my restorations and my readings of his copied traces, he does not bear any responsibility.

12 The reading is based on Schwemer's collated traces.

13 This is added from Text B per Schwemer's collations,

14 Restored from Text E obv. 22.

15 Restored from Text E obv. 24.

16 Schwemer's collations allow for these readings, but only with exclamation points.

17 According to Schwemers collations, Text B has the grains being poured into the potter's pit.

18 The beginning of this and the following line follows Schwemer's collations, correcting Ebeling 1931: no. 40A.

19 The governor and giver of orders are clearly marked as masculine, whereas the clay pit is feminine.

20 After Schwemer's collations.

21 According to Schwemer's traces, the text originally had *qud-dušša* (ANŠE.LIBIR)-*ki*.

22 Text C obv. 1′ = Text A i.21.

23 Text B dies more or less at Text A i.30.

24 Text C ends at obv. 11′ = Text A i.33.

25 For the format of figurine names, see Scurlock 2006a: 49–50.

26 Restored from Text E obv. 20.

27 See Text E obv. 20.

⌜prostrate yourself⌝ [seven and seven times before] the ⌜Anunnaki⌝.[28] You prostrate yourself [seven and seven times before] Gilgameš. You seat [the Daughter of Anu] (as a witness).[29] [You wash a human skull with water]. You anoint (it) with oil.[30] You set out [hot broth[31] for] the ⌜ghost(s)⌝ of relatives. You pour out [beer] (made from) roasted grain[32] [for the ghost of a nobody].[33] [You offer *kispu*-offerings to] the Annunaki.

(D i.9′–12′) [The patient] lifts up [the figurine of sorcerer and sorceress in] his [hand] and you have him say as ⌜follows⌝ [before Šamaš: (Recitation): Great lord who makes] the ⌜things above⌝ and the things below [go aright],[34] you are the one to judge [the case of the wronged man and woman.][35]

(The rest of col. i of Text A is lost and the fragments of Text D i.13′–27′ despite some help from Text B[36] allow us only to understand that reference was made to "Anything Evil," witchcraft and family ghosts, including specifically the ghost of the patient's mother. Fortunately, the last bit of the Šamaš prayer is preserved on Text A col. ii.)

Ebeling 1931 no. 30A

(A ii.1–5)[37] May my sorcerer and sorceress, [my evil doer and facilitatress of evil] be distant from my body. [...] Head them towards the land of no return. You ("Anything Evil") are made to swear [not to come back]; you are made to swear not to return. [May] ⌜Gilgameš⌝ and Šamaš, the judge, [guide you] to [your] resting place.

(A ii.6) [You recite] this before Šamaš [and you say as follows:]

(E obv. 1–10) Gilgameš, perfect king, judge of the ⌜Anunnaki⌝, circumspect prince, neck stock of the people, restless watcher of the (four) quarters, director of the earth, together with the things below. You are a judge and check (your decisions) like a god. You stand in the earth; you complete the ⌜case.⌝ Your judgment cannot be altered; [your] ⌜word⌝ cannot be forgotten. You question, you investigate, you give judgment. You check (your decisions) and you make (them) ⌜go aright⌝. Šamaš has entrusted verdict and legal opinion to you. Kings, governors and princes kneel before you.[38] You inspect their exta; you give them a ruling.[39]

(E obv. Ii.11–17) I am so-and-so, son of so-and-so whose god is so-and-so (and) whose goddess is so-and-so. Illness has confronted me and, as a consequence, I kneel before you to judge the case and to give a legal opinion. Judge my case! [Give] my legal opinion. Remove the evil from my body. Drive out "Anything Evil" that stands ready to cut my ⌜throat⌝, "Anything Evil" that exists in my body, my flesh, and my muscles/blood vessels.

(E obv. 18–25) On this day, [I stand] before you. I have honored you; I have made you proud; I have shown you respect. [I have scattered for you][40] a pure handful of flour; I have poured out for you [beer] made from (roasted) ⌜wheat⌝ [flour]. [I have made a pure] sacrifice (and) offered you [some of the roasted meat. I have dressed you] in a red *ḫuššu*-garment; [I have given you] a *makurru*-boat of *erēnu*-cedar [with an oar of cypress]. [I have bound] a golden *mammu*-crown [to your head, a *nibittu*-girdle to your waist]. [I have placed (the patient's)] ⌜golden⌝ [ransom-money on your neck, a golden ringlet on your hands and feet].[41]

(Text E obv. 26–42 is fragmentary and allows us only to understand that a long list of problems was ennumerated including Lamaštu, Labaṣu and [*aḫḫāzu*], AN.TA.ŠUB.BA-epilepsy, *bennu*-seizures, *di'u*-fever, sleeplessness, Asakku-demon, all the various forms of witchcraft, anger of personal god and [goddess] due to offenses committed against them, and bad relations with family ghosts. We can pick up the thread again in Text E obv. 43 when Text D column ii begins to be more or less legible.[42])

Ebeling 1931 no. 30A

(D ii.1′–12′) [Through your] judgment, through ⌜your⌝ legal opinion, may he ("Anything Evil") ⌜rain down⌝ like the dew[43]; may he not return again and again. May he rise like the mist; may he not blow in with the wind. May their (the sorcerer's and sorceress') anger be ⌜dispelled⌝; may (their) witchcraft be distant from [my] body.[44] Entrust

28 Text D i.2′ = Text A i.41.
29 This is restored from Abusch and Schwemer 2011: 8.7.2: 22.
30 Restored from Abusch and Schwemer 2011: 8.7.2: 20–21.
31 Restored from Abusch and Schwemer 2011: 8.7.1:70″.
32 Reading from collation courtesy D. Schwemer.
33 This is a ghost whose relatives have died out. Text D i.7′ = Text A i.47.
34 This is the recitation mentioned by incipit in AMD 8/1 8.7.2:28–29.
35 Text D i.12′ = Text A i.52.
36 Text D i.21′ = Text B ii.1.
37 Text A ii.1 = Text D i.28′
38 Text C obv. 9 = Text A ii.14.
39 Text C obv. 10 = Text B ii.22.
40 See von Soden 1936:266.
41 This section is restored from Text A i.7–13
42 This is the numbering given to Text D in Ebeling 1931:128. On the photograph of the tablet, there are actually several more lines more or less visible.
43 Read from the traces as drawn by Schwemer with the help of LKA 70 ii.25, which also deals with "Anything Evil."
44 Text D ii.4′ = Text F ii.1′.

them to Namtar, the vizier of the Netherworld.[45] May they enter the great gate with the Anunnaki never [to return]; may they cross the Hubur river never to come back. May they enter the outer gate[46] (of the Netherworld); may they not meet [with the living].[47] [May] they be counted with the dead; may they not [be counted] with the living. May they be distant (and) far away from [my] ⸢body⸣.[48] [...]. May, the south wind, the north wind, the east wind (and) the west wind blow, but may their wind not blow – not even one wind of one of them.[49]

(D ii.13′–23′) The sorcerer and sorceress, [evil-doer and evil-doess, facilitater and facilitatress of sorcery][50] who performed, had performed, surrounded (or) had [me] surrounded with witchcraft, impregnatory witchcraft, sorcerous spittle (or) ⸢evil⸣ rituals[51] – now [I have made] a figurine of [that] sorcerer and sorceress.[52] I have given them their provisions. I have made an "Anything Evil" of [clay from the potter's pit] and then I [have made them] *kispu*-offerings (and) poured out water for them. I have given (them to) ["Anything Evil"] as a gift. [His silver] ⸢ransom payment⸣[53] [consisting of silver], ⸢gold⸣, copper, tin, [lead, antimony], carnelian, lapis lazuli, *ḫulalu*-chalcedony, [*muššaru*-serpentine, goat hair, wool], red wool, white wool (and) [blue] ⸢wool⸣,[54] the ⸢entire⸣ amount of silver [have I given him] in your (m.) presence (i.e. Gilgameš), in your (f.) presence (i.e. Lamaštu).

(D iii.1–7) At your word, let him be divided from my body. Seize the ⸢sorcerer⸣ and sorceress who pursue me for evil ends and do not let them go. Entrust ⸢them⸣ into the care of Namtar, the vizier of the Netherworld. [May] Ningišzida, chair bearer of the "broad earth" [strengthen] the watch over them. [May] Nedu, great gatekeeper of the Netherworld lock (the gate in) their faces. May they be ⸢removed⸣ from the living; may they be counted with the dead. From the road they travel may they never [return].

(D iii.8–9) Make them swear by my life (in) your (m.) presence (i.e., Gilgameš) that they will never come back. Bring me back to life so that I may [sing] your praises.

(D iii.10–11) You have him recite like this before Gilgameš. You make a libation and he prostrates himself. You present him to the Anunnaki and he [says]:

(D iii.12–31) You are the Anunnaki, great gods,[55] givers of legal opinions for the people below, judger of cases of all mankind. I am so-and-so, son of so-and-so, your servant with whom "Anything Evil" has gotten married so that he ⸢paralyzes⸣ me,[56] causes me to have convulsions and terrifies me. Great [gods] stand forth for me and judge my case, [give] me my legal opinion. Drive out from [my] body [the one who] ⸢afflicts⸣ me, etc.[57] Let the ⸢family⸣ [ghost(s)] seize them (the sorcerer and sorceress); may they not let ⸢them⸣ go. May they not become angry with [me]. May the sorcerer and sorceress receive [the illness from me]. Take ["anything"] evil which was laid on me (and) the sorcerer and sorceress to the land [of no return]. Entrust them [into the care of] Namtar, the vizier of the Netherworld. May Ningišzida, chair-bearer of the "broad earth" [strengthen] the watch over them. May Nedu, great gatekeeper of the "broad earth" [lock] their gate. ⸢May they not⸣ approach me, not come near me, not come close to me, not reach me.[58] [By] your august command that cannot be altered and your firm "yes" that cannot be changed, may [I], your [servant] ⸢recover⸣ (and) stay well so that I can make your greatness apparent (and) sing your praises.

(A iii.6–7) When this has been recited before the Anunnaki, before the ⸢ghost⸣ [of his family],[59] you have him say as follows:[60]

(A iii.8–24) (Recitation): You are the ghosts of my relatives, creators of everything, my father, my father's father, my mother, my mother's mother, my brother, my sister, my king, my kin and my relations, as many as sleep in the earth. I have made for you a funerary offering; I have poured you (a libation) of water.[61] I have honored you; I

45 Text D ii.5′ = Text A ii.43′.

46 A pun is intended here since *kamû*: "outer" also means "captive," so the "gate of those imprisoned." The ancient Mesopotamian Netherworld was imagined as a sort of prison for ghosts and demons.

47 Text D ii.8′ = Text E obv. 48.

48 Text D ii.10′ = Text A ii. "48" = Text F ii.8′.

49 Reading the illegible photograph as IM-*šú-nu a-a i-zi-qa šá* 1-*en šú-nu* IM 1-*en-ma*.

50 Schwemer's traces do not really fit this restoration, but it would certainly be appropriate to the context.

51 The translation follows Schwemer's reading of the traces.

52 Text D ii.16′ = Text E rev. 1.

53 The translation follows Schwemer's reading of the traces.

54 This is restored from KAR 227 i.29–31.

55 Text D iii.12 = Text E rev. 24′ which is its catchline (the first line of the next tablet in a series).

56 For the restoration, see von Soden 1936:266.

57 A dangling-*ma* indicates the omission of the "paralyzes, causes me to have convulsions and terrifies me." The translation follows Schwemer's reading of the traces.

58 Text D iii.27 = Text A iii.1.

59 Text A iii.6 = Text D iii.32.

60 Text A iii.7 = Text B iii.1.

61 Text A iii.12 = Text G:1′.

have made you proud; I have shown you respect. On this day, before Šamaš (and) Gilgameš stand forth and judge my case; give me a legal opinion. "Anything Evil" that exists in my body, my flesh (and) my muscles/blood vessels, entrust him into the care of Namtar, the vizier of the Netherworld. ⌜May⌝ Ningišzida, chair bearer of the "broad earth," strengthen the watch over them (the sorcerer and sorceress). [May] Nedu, great gatekeeper of the Netherworld [lock] (the gate) in their faces. Seize him ("Anything Evil") and take him down to the land of no return. May I, your servant, recover; may I stay well and, on account of sorcerous rituals may I invoke[62] your name. Let me pour cold water into your water pipe.[63] Keep me alive so that I may sing your praises.

(A iii.25–26) When this has been recited three times before the family ghosts, you have him say as follows before the skull.

(A iii.27–50) (Recitation): You are the ghost of nobody, you who have no one to bury (you) or to invoke (your name), (whose) name nobody knows, (but whose) name Šamaš, who takes care of (you) knows. Whether you be a man who is like a (living) man or whether you be a woman who is like a (living) ⌜woman⌝,[64] before Šamaš, Gilgameš, the Anunnaki, and the family ghosts, you have received a gift, you have been honored with a dowry. Listen to ⌜me⌝, to whatever I say. Whether he be an [evil] *utukku*-demon, or an evil *alû*-demon or an evil ghost, or Lamaštu or Labāṣu or ⌜*Aḫḫāzu*⌝, or *lilû*-demon or *lilītu*-demon or *ardat* ⌜*lilî*⌝-demon or nameless "Anything Evil" which continually afflicts me and ⌜pursues⌝ me, [which] is bound to my body, my flesh (and) my muscles/blood vessels and cannot be loosed – I have made a figurine of the sorcerer and sorceress who [have tied knots][65] against me before Šamaš (and) I have made a figurine of "Anything Evil" that afflicts me. I have entrusted [them] (to you) in the presence of Šamaš, Gilgameš and the Anunakki. Seize them and do not let them go; take them (with you) so that they may never return. [You] are made to swear by Šamaš who takes care of you.[66] ⌜You⌝ are made to swear by the great gods of heaven and earth. You are made to swear by the Igigi, the gods above. You are made to swear by the Anunnaki, the gods below.[67] You are made to swear by Lugalgirra, Ninazu (and) Ningišzida. You are made to swear by Ereškigal, queen of the Netherworld. If you let them go, then (you will be punished)![68]

(D iv.5–15) [You say to Namtar as follows]: O Namtar,[69] the one who ferries across the widespread peoples, [... to] the Land of No Return,[70] [....] them (the sorcerer and sorceress), [...] them. [...] May they (the ghosts) make them (the sorcerer and sorceress) go down (to the Netherworld). You are made to swear[71] [by the great gods of] heaven and earth. You are made to swear [by the Igigi, the gods above]. You are made to swear [by the Anunnaki, the gods below]. You are made to swear [by Lugalgirra, Ninazu and Ningišzida]. You are made to swear [by Ereškigal, queen of the Netherworld. If you let them go], then (you will be punished)! [...]

(B iv.1′–3′) Be distant, be distant 3,600 double-hours [from the body of so-and-so son of so-and-so]. ⌜Be far away⌝, be far away; be distant, be distant. You are made to swear by the great gods.

(B iv.4′ff) (Colophon)

62 The translation is based on Schwemer's collations.

63 Text A iii.23 = Text G:12′.

64 The translation is based on Schwemer's collations.

65 Restored from Abusch and Schwemer 2011: 8.7.1: 74″, 83″. The reference is to tying the patient's figurines into the hem of "Anything Evil," thus simultaneously "marrying" him to the demon and "binding" the demon upon him.

66 Text A iii.44 = Text B iii.36.

67 Text A iii.47 = Text D iv.1.

68 Text A iii.50 = Text D iv.4.

69 The name is written NAM.TAL as frequently with the plant known as $^{GI\check{S}}$NAM.TAR = *pillû*-mandragora.

70 The text gives this first in Sumerian and then translates it into Akkadian.

71 The oath is indicated by a "ditto" that refers to Text D iv.1–3.

REFERENCES

Abusch 2002:76–78; Abusch and Schwemer 2011:14, 349; 8.2:106–107, 8.3 obv. 56, 8.7.1–2; Ebeling 1931:122, 124–133; Farber 1977:210–217; Foster 1997; Hunger 1968, no. 319; Lambert 1960:40; Schwemer 2007:200–201, 220; Scurlock 1988:351–354, 357–361; Scurlock 2006a:49–50; no. 228; von Soden 1936:265–267.

"SUPERNATURAL" CAUSES: WITCHCRAFT: HYPOTHYROIDISM (STT 89)[1] (4.88K)

JoAnn Scurlock

STT 89, according to its own rubrics, represents tablets 33–34 of an outlying diagnostic series. Of interest here is the section dealing with "cutting of the breath,"[2] a form of witchcraft. We are predisposed to think of witchcraft as something imaginary; the ancient physician simply used witchcraft as another possible diagnostic category.[3] Among the real conditions included is what, from the description given in this text, we can recognize as hypothyroidism.[4] Lines 8–12 and 13–17 are classic for the technique of contrasting references and for the use of the enclitic *-ma* in medical texts to render "if." Two virtually identical cases appear before us; the first is fatal but the second only potentially so. The difference is whether or not the patient is able to keep down his food. Severe vomiting is a sign of abdominal ileus, and not good news for the patient. Lines 18–22 and 23–33 form another contrastive set of references. To note is that the parallel to lines 18–22 replaces the phrase about "cutting of the breath" with "If it is prolonged, he will die," and provides a treatment.

Lines 29–30 are a very nice description of the cerebellar ataxia with which some patients present. Modern doctors describe this as "The legs are lifted higher than necessary at the hips and are flung forward and outward in abrupt motions."[5] The god allegedly subborned to produce this particular set of symptoms, Šulpaea, was also responsible for similar movements that were involuntary.[6] The following symptom in Line 30 is broken, but must refer to the difficulty which patients have in balancing themselves when standing up, forcing them to stand with feet wide apart.[7]

Lines 43–56 are very interesting examples of a new set of magical practices with a long future ahead of them. The older sorcerous spells (23–37) simply dedicated a victim to a particular star[8]; the new style (43–56) combined a particular day of a particular month with a particular constellation to produce what would later be called a conjunction. For more on the development of this system of astrological sorcery, see Scurlock 2005–2006.

(1–7) [If a person . . .], that person has been given "cutting of the breath" to eat or drink or been rubbed with it (in oil) or his "cutting of the breath" figurines [have been manufactured] ⸢and⸣ made to lie with a dead person; he should recover.
(8–12) [If a person's eyes] seem continually to spin, his feet are continually sluggish, [his arms] feel numb, his flesh continually "binds" him, [he eats] and drinks ⸢and⸣ it does not stay down, (his) [flesh continually afflicts] him so that, [as if] he had been ⸢struck⸣ [with a weapon], his whole body gives him a stinging pain, messages of "cutting of the breath" have been performed against him before the ⸢Pleiades⸣; he will die.
(13–17) [If a person's eyes] seem continually to spin, his feet are continually ⸢sluggish⸣, [his arms] feel numb, his flesh continually ⸢"binds" him⸣, [he eats and] drinks and it stays down, (his) flesh continually afflicts him so that, [as if] he had been struck [with a weapon], his whole body gives him a stinging pain, if messages have been performed against him before the stars, he will die.[9]
(18–22) [If a person] is continually troubled and cramped, his eyes flutter,[10] his flesh feels numb, all of his teeth continually hurt him, (and) if he eats [bread] and drinks beer, he makes a loud growling noise, ⸢if⸣ "cutting of the breath" ⟨with soured milk⟩ has been practiced against that person, he will die.[11]
(23–27) If the muscles of a person's "right" thigh continually hurt him intensely, he continually has wasting of the flesh, his limbs are stiff, his mentation is altered so that he forgets whatever he has been doing (and) his phlegm is white, rituals have been performed against that person before Gula. On the twenty-seventh or twenty-eighth day (of his illness), that person will come to an end[12]; "hand" of "cutting of the breath"; he will die.[13]
(28–33) [If] the ⸢tip⸣ of a ⸢person's⸣ "right" foot stings him, the middle of his ⸢"left"⸣ upper back continually hurts him intensely, the muscle(s) of his

1 An edition of this section of STT 89 appears in Abusch and Schwemer 2011: 12.1.
2 The term is consistently translated in Abusch and Schwemer 2011 as "cutting of the throat." Either translation is correct, since ZI: *napištu* is both "throat" and "breath." I prefer the latter translation since we are talking about a magical process which does not literally cut your throat but which is designed to prevent you from breathing, thus bringing about your death.
3 For a listing of symptoms of all the various sorts of witchcraft together, see Schwemer 2007:170–177.
4 For a full discussion, see Scurlock 2014: 2.10.5–7.
5 Harrison, et al. 1987:95, 1741.
6 For details, see Scurlock and Andersen 2005:296.
7 Harrison, et al. 1987:95.
8 For an enumeration of possibilities, see Schwemer 2007:102.
9 Restored from BAM 453:7′–10′, which once provided a treatment. See Scurlock 2014: 2.10.5.
10 The reference is to frequent blinking, by contrast with the victim of Grave's Disease whose eyes "stand still," that is blink infrequently.
11 Restored from BAM 449 (4.88L) iii.13′–19′. See Scurlock 2014: 2.10.6.
12 For a discussion of this expression, see Abusch and Schwemer 2011:442.
13 Restored from BAM 449 (4.88L) iii.24′–27′. See Scurlock 2014: 2.10.6.

⸢leg⸣[14] are continually lifted up and they continually "jump" (when he walks but the leg is) ⸢firmly planted⸣(?)[15] (when he is) standing (and) his body feels numb, a binding has been bound against that person before Šulpaea [on] the 21st or 22nd day (of his illness). On the 27th or 28th day, his ⸢affair⸣ will be over; "hand" of "cutting of the breath"; he will die.

(34–37) [If] a ⸢person's⸣ muscles to "right" and "left" are made to dry out,[16] he continually [and incessantly?] produces blood from his mouth, and (what looks like) frothy beer [flows] (for) three [days], a ritual has been performed against that person before the Wagon Star (Ursa Major). If it lasts for ten days, he will die; "hand" of "⸢cutting⸣ of the [breath]," he will die.

(38–42) ⸢If a person's⸣ limbs are continually tense,[17] his [...] hurts him, his skull [...] afflicts him, his [stomach] continually heaves, he continually vomits, his "right" or "left" leg "jumps" (and) his "right" heel stings him, rituals have been performed against that ⸢person⸣; he should recover.

(43–47) If a crisis[18] begins on the 22nd day (of illness) [and] on the 27th, he ⸢brings up⸣ blood to ⸢his mouth(?)⸣, rituals have been performed on the 28th of Tašrītu and before the [...] star. On the 5th or 10th day, his ⸢affair⸣ will be over; "hand" of "cutting of the breath"; he will die.

(48–51) If his "right" buttock is hot (and) his "left" buttock is cold, his eyes become dimmed,[19] (and) blood flows from his nose/mouth,[20] rituals ⸢have been performed⸣ against that person [on] the fifth of Šabaṭu before Centaurus; ⟨"hand"⟩ of "cutting of the breath"; he will die.

(52–56) [If] a person's insides [are continually] colicky, his mouth or tongue is continually seized, he continually lies down (to sleep) in the cold of the morning (and) at night he jerks,[21] rituals have been performed against that person on the 10th(+) of Addaru [before] ⸢Scorpio⸣; ["hand"] of "cutting of the breath"; he will die.

(57–61) [If] the ⸢area between⸣ [a person's] shoulders continually hurts him and his teeth [ooze blood][22] (and) his ⸢hands⸣ (and) his [feet] sting him, [his figurines have been fed either] to a dog or a fish or a pig before [...] star. [...] his affair [will be over; "hand" of "cutting of the breath"; he will die].

14 For the restoration of "leg" see below, lines 38–42.

15 Reading [*kun*]-*ni*.

16 Pace Abusch and Schwemer 2011:400–401, these are muscles not veins and the skin does indeed dry out in this condition.

17 Literally, "they have been piled up in a heap" or, as we would say, "they feel all bunched up." For the interpretation, see Scurlock and Andersen 2005:292–293.

18 Pace *CAD* S 264, there is no reason to see this expression as a purely literary variant of the normal word for illness (*murṣu*). Instead, it would be good to follow the brilliant suggestion of *CAD* S 96–97 that the verb from which this is derived means: "to enter a critical stage of an illness." By this interpretation, the verb and the noun, when used by physicians, refer not to just any illness but a particularly serious illness or a dramatic change in an existing illness.

19 See Scurlock and Andersen 2005:186.

20 BAM 361:39–43 is a stone charm designed to ward off this eventuality before it occurred. See Scurlock 2014: 2.10.7.

21 BAM 361:44–48 is a stone charm designed to ward off this eventuality before it occurred. See Scurlock 2014: 2.10.7.

22 BAM 361:35–38 is a stone charm designed to ward off this eventuality before it occurred. See Scurlock 2014: 2.10.7.

REFERENCES

Abusch and Schwemer 2011:400–401, 442; 12.1; Schwemer 2007:102, 170–177; Scurlock and Andersen 2005:186, 292–293, 296; Scurlock 2005/2006; Scurlock 2014: 2.10.5, 2.10.6, 2.10.7.

"SUPERNATURAL" CAUSES: "CUTTING OF THE BREATH": RITUAL MESSAGES; SOUR MILK (BAM 449)[1] (4.88L)

JoAnn Scurlock

BAM 449 is a classic example of the mix of magic and medicine typical of anti-witchcraft texts. It is designed to treat what ancient Mesopotamians called "cutting of the breath" a complex of magical practices whose aim was, quite simply, to kill the victim. I omit the alleged since, as this text makes clear, some of these sorcerous practices were anything but imaginary. On the contrary, the animal whose throat had been cut while naming the patient's name and which was subsequently discovered on his doorstep, was directly involved in the apotropaic ritual, and great awkwardness was created if the evidence of the crime had been gotten rid of by an overzealous servant.

1 An edition of this text appears in Abusch and Schwemer 2011: 10.3.

In the first ritual (BAM 449 i.1–10), the animal remains are gathered into a pig skin for burial. The cutting of the throat of the pig that was to be used for the ritual – not the usual method of slaughter for pigs[2] – served to reverse the spell, as the recitation makes clear. The second preserved treatment (BAM 458 i.1′–7′) is unusual in requiring direct participation by the patient who is to rub himself with a prescribed salve at night when the doctor is not there to help.

The second preserved ritual (BAM 458 i.8′–13′; BAM 449 ii.1′–10′) was to counter a hexed doorbolt. This does not sound terribly serious, but the door was the main line of defense against demonic attack. As for why this particular bit of sorcery had the effect of hexing the door, the most probable explanation is that the rodent's name, *arrabu*, is similar in sound to *erēbu*, which means "to enter." In this ritual, the rodent is the intended agent of deliverance, receiving a deluxe burial including little bits of gold, etc. which are readily recognizable as the "ransom payment" given to "Anything Evil" in Ebeling 1931, no. 30A (see 4.88J). The unguented and tied up bundle was essentially an animal mummy of the sort made frequently in Egypt and with a similar purpose – to do the bidding of the manufacturer, in this case to fend off any and all attacks of "cutting of the breath" for the patient's lifetime. Unfortunately, the presence of the sorcerous remains was essential for this transformation, but as far as the current attack was concerned, the patient still had a prayer.[3]

The reverse of BAM 449 (iii.1′–12) concerns itself with a medical problem of which the only recoverable bit is a possible headache and the diagnosis of figurines entrusted to a ghost plus "hand" of curse. We are on firmer ground with BAM 449 iii.13′–27′ where it is specified that the "cutting of the breath" was accomplished by putting something poisonous in soured milk. The consequences of this nefarious practice for the victim are spelled out in some detail in STT 89 (4.88K), and we may identify iii.13′–27′ as the complex of hyper-and hypothyroidism.[4]

BAM 449
(i.1–10) If "cutting of the breath" has been performed against a person and is discovered, you take those (remains of) sorcerous rituals that were discovered (and) ⌜place⌝ them before Šamaš. You ⌜express⌝ your heart-sickness to Šamaš. Before Šamaš, you cut the throat of a pig over those sorcerous remains. You gather those sorcerous remains into the pig's skin. Before Šamaš, you have the person against whom "cutting of the breath" was performed say as follows. "Šamaš, may he who performed the 'cutting of the breath' not find me (but) may I find ⌜him⌝."[5] You have him say (this) seven times before Šamaš. Daily, [he should express] his heart-sickness to ⌜Šamaš⌝. [If you bury][6] those sorcerous remains which are inside the ⌜pig⌝ skin, that "cutting of the breath" [will] ⌜not⌝ [approach] that person.

(The rest of the column in BAM 449 is fragmentary or lost but the end of the column may be restored from BAM 458)

BAM 458
(i.1′–7′) [If you want] "cutting of the [breath]" [not to approach] ⌜that⌝ person, [during the day,[7] you rub him gently with] *qutru*-thorn, *šarmadu*, [. . .], *kibrītu*-sulphur, *sikillu*, *baltu*-thorn, *nikiptu*, [. . .], *šakirû*, *lišān kalbi* ("dog's tongue"), *kūṣi*[8] (and) *gaṣṣu*-gypsum [mixed with oil]. He should eat *azupīru*-safflower. During the night, he should repeatedly rub himself gently with *kibrītu*-sulphur, *imbû tamtim*, [. . .], *turminû*-breccia, *turminabandû*-breccia, "ox dung" plant, [. . .] and goose fat (mixed) with oil. The "cutting of the breath" [will not approach] the person.
(i.8′–13′) If "cutting of the breath" [has been performed against] a person using an *arrabu*-rodent [and] the *arrabu*-rodent with its throat cut is discovered in the person's house, in [that] house, the [door jamb], the door (and) the bolt is(!) hexed. You ⌜take⌝ that *arrabu*-rodent (and) place it [before Sîn]. You clothe it in a pure garment; you cover it with a linen cloth; [you anoint it with] ⌜fine⌝ oil. You have the person against whom "cutting of the breath" was performed kneel before Sîn and [you have him say] as follows. "My lord, lest I die before my time, [dispel] the sorcerous rites performed against me;

BAM 449// BAM 454
(ii.1–10) untie these knots that have surrounded me." You have him say this seven times before Sîn and you have him bend his nose (in prostration). That night, he should put out his portion for Sîn; on the fifteenth of the month, he should tell Sîn as much as is in his heart. He should pray daily. You take that *arrabu*-rodent and gather it into a mouse skin. You gather into it bits of silver, gold, iron, lapis lazuli, *dūšû*-stone (and) *ḫulālu-pappardillû*-stone. You pour oil, first quality oil, fine oil, *erēnu*-cedar oil, honey, ghee, milk, wine (and) vinegar into it.

2 For details, see Scurlock 2006b:29–30.
3 For more, see Schwemer 2007:222–225.
4 For a discussion, see Scurlock 2014: 2.10.5–7.
5 Correcting Abusch and Schwemer 2011: 408: 7.
6 Burial seems to be the standard method of disposal here.
7 Since the second salve specifies that it is to be rubbed on "at night," this seems a reasonable restoration for which there is room at the beginning of the line. This means, however, that there is probably not enough room also for NUMUN: "seed" before the *qutru*.
8 This appears in pharmacological texts as a type of rush. See *CAD* K 594.

You tie up the face, cover it with a linen cloth (and) gather it into a tomb. You make funerary offerings (for it). You make (it) proud, you show (it) respect. If you perform its rites for an inclusive seven days, any "cutting of the breath" which is performed against the person will not approach his body for as long as he lives.
(ii.11–15) If they have, without the person knowing about it, thrown that *arrabu*-rodent out of the house either into the river or into the street, that person against whom "cutting of the breath" was performed should put out his portion for Sîn on the fifteenth of the month. He should bend his nose; he should throw himself to the ground. He should express his heart-sickness. He should pour dust on his head. He should say seven times: "Give me assistance in this matter." The "cutting of the breath" will not approach that person.

(The remainder of column ii is fragmentary, but involves a regimen in which certain foods such as *laptu*-turnip are eaten at specific times and a salve is administered at nightfall)

BAM 449//Sm 1304//BAM 455//BAM 467
(iii.1′–4′) [If …] that ˹person˺'s [figurines] ˹have been entrusted˺ to a ghost; "hand" of curse. You ˹sew up˺ root of a lone-growing *baltu*-thorn (and) root of a lone-growing *ašāgu*-thorn [in the skin] of a virgin ˹she-goat˺ with a sinew from a dead cow. If you put it on his neck, it should be dispelled.
(iii.5′–7′) [Alternatively], you grind ˹together˺ *anzaḫḫu*-frit, *ḫuluḫḫu*-frit, *mūṣu*-stone, iron (and) magnetic hematite. You mix (it) with *šurmēnu*-cypress oil and leave it out overnight under the stars. In the morning, you gently rub his entire body (with it) before Šamaš. If he looks at red gold and steps on bitumen, it should be dispelled.
(iii.8′–12′) ˹Alternatively˺, you roast together two shekels each of seed from a lone-growing *bīnu*-tamarisk, *kikkirānu*-juniper berries, *atā᾽išu*, *urnû*-mint, swallow's nest, *karān šēlibi* ("fox grape") (and) *maštakal* and you grind (it) [in …] ˹shekels˺ of ghee (and) five shekels of pressed-out oil and you put it out (mixed) with cow's milk and ˹*bīnu*-tamarisk˺ [oil?] ˹and˺ you let (it) sit out overnight under the stars. In the morning, he should stand on dried ˹bitumen˺ before Šamaš [and] be given (it) to eat and, if he looks at gold and silver, it should be dispelled.
(iii.13′–19′) If a person is continually troubled and cramped, his eyes flutter, his flesh goes numb, all of his teeth continually hurt him, and if he eats bread and drinks beer, he makes a loud growling noise, "cutting of the breath" with soured milk has been practiced against that person. If it is prolonged, he will die.[9] Before it approaches him so that he dies, you crush together *urnû*-mint, *imḫur-lim*, flax seed (and) "lone plant" seed. You mix (it) with pressed out oil. You let (it) sit out overnight under the stars. In the morning, he should stand on dried bitumen before Šamaš and then you have him drink (it) and, if he looks at gold (and) silver, it (the "cutting of the breath") should be dispelled.
(iii.20′–23′) Alternatively, you mix 3 grains each of *atā᾽išu*, *azallû* seed, *urnû*-mint, *kazallu* seed, *karān šēlibi* ("fox grape") seed (and) *maštakal* seed with wild honey, oil, and first quality beer. You leave (it) out overnight under the stars. In the morning, you have (him) drink (it) before Šamaš. He should stand on dried bitumen and, if he looks at lapis, carnelian, gold (and) silver, it should be dispelled.
(iii.24′–27′) If the muscles of a person's "right" thigh continually hurt him intensely, he continually has wasting of the flesh, his limbs are stiff, his mentation is altered (and) he forgets whatever he has been doing (and) his phlegm is white, rituals have been performed against him before Gula. On the twenty-seventh or twenty-eighth day, his affair will be over; "hand" of "cutting of the breath"; he will die.[10]

9 See STT 89:18–22 (4.88K). This entry and its friends originally languished in the Unsolved Puzzles Appendix of Scurlock and Andersen 2005. This was Ap. 70.
10 See STT 89:23–27 (4.88K). This was Scurlock and Andersen 2005: Ap. 69.

REFERENCES

Abusch and Schwemer 2011:408; 10.3; Schwemer 2007:222–225; Scurlock and Andersen 2005: Ap. 69–70; Scurlock 2006b:29–30; Scurlock 2014: 2.10.5–7.

"SUPERNATURAL" CAUSES: "CUTTING OF THE BREATH": STAR-BORNE POISONS (AMT 44/4 + KMI 76A)[1] (4.88M)

JoAnn Scurlock

[1]AMT 44/4+ provides ritual help to patients with treatable hypothyroidism.[2] We know this because the symptoms are cited from STT 89:34–37 and 38–42 (4.88K). The alleged cause of these particular symptoms was sorcery performed with a bowl of water. Examples of such sorcerous practices exist from the Hellenistic period in Egypt.

AMT 44/4 lines 1–14 uses the classic technique of reversal, performing the sorcerous rite in reverse in order to send the witchcraft back to him or her who sent it. The red and [white] wool and the red beverage (wine) and the white one (water) signal the desired separation of the realms of the living (the red) and the realm of death as represented by the denizens of the night sky (the white).[3] The addition of blue, as in Ebeling 1931 no. 40A (4.88J) and the more generalized Abusch and Schwemer, 2011: 10.2 version of this ritual, adds to the mix the idea that the dead (white) should be separated from the living (red) and relegated to the Netherworld (blue).

Lines 15–27 contain a version of the reflection prayer of Maqlu, as noted in Abusch and Schwemer, 2011:399. To be corrected, however, is their New Wave mystical idea that the "pure and fleeting" reflection is being identified with in order to make the patient "immune and elusive" to witchcraft. It is, on the contrary, the reflection that is being protected from being literally stolen by the sorcerer and sorceress and used to inflict illness on its rightful owner. In the broader world of magic, this practice is referred to as "stealing someone's shadow," and "shadow" is what the word we are translating "reflection" literally means.

(1–14) [If] a ˹person's˺ muscles to "right" and "left" are made to dry out,[4] [he continually and incessantly(?) produces] blood from his mouth, and (what looks like) frothy beer flows (for) three days, [a ritual has been performed] against that person before the Wagon Star (Ursa Major). If it lasts for ten days, [he will die]; "hand" of "cutting of the breath," he will die. In order to save him from "hand" of "cutting of the breath," in the night, on bended knee,[5] [you install] a reed hut on the roof in the presence of the [Wagon Star]. Within the reed hut, you plant *urigallû*-standards to the four wind directions. [You set out] a ˹holy water vessel˺. You draw a magic circle around it. Inside the reed hut, you festoon the horn(s) of the *urigallû*-standards with red-dyed wool (and) [white wool].[6] He [should dress himself] in a ritually purified garment. The *āšipu* takes his right (hand) and makes ˹him˺ enter the reed hut. You cover a provisional reed altar[7] [with a … cloth]. You [scatter] dates (and) *sasqû*-flour. […] You set out a 1 *qû* vessel of beer (and) a 1 *qû* vessel of water. He should say as follows to the [Wagon] ˹star˺. "You be the judge – judge my case; [give me] a ˹legal opinion˺. [Do not accept] the evil sorcerous rituals. At your command, […]." He says this and [pours out] a libation [from the two vessels. "Hand" of "cutting of the breath"] will not approach that person […]

(15–27) If a person's limbs ˹are continually tense˺,[8] [his … hurts him, his skull … afflicts him], his stomach continually heaves, he [continually vomits, his "right" or "left" leg "jumps"] (and) his "right" heel [stings him, rituals have been performed against that person; he should recover]. In order for an evil ritual [not to approach] that person, [you fill a *kallu*-bowl with water]. [He should say as follows] to his reflection which is in the *kallu*-bowl. "[You are my reflection]; you are my pride; you are [my] (protective) ˹*lamassu*-spirit˺. You are my great reflection; you are [my] (protective) ˹*šēdu*-spirit˺.[9] [Do not accept witchcraft; do not accept sorcerous rituals]; do not accept murder; do not accept "˹cutting˺ [of the breath]"; do not accept sorcerous rituals and evil binding spells. [You are mine and I am yours. May nobody get to know you and] may "Anything Evil" not approach you at the

1 An edition of this text appears in Abusch and Schwemer 2011: 10.1.

2 See Scurlock 2014: 2.10.5–7.

3 For more on this sort of signaling, see Scurlock 2006a: no. 21:9, 12–13.

4 Pace Abusch and Schwemer 2011:400–401, these are muscles not veins, and the skin does indeed dry out in this condition.

5 The Akkadian has "squatted-upon leg," but the expression renders the same sentiment.

6 Correcting Abusch and Schwemer 2011:400: 6. If there are three types of wool, they will be red, white and blue, but if there are only two, they will have been red and white, as with the colors of the liquids poured out in libation. The similar PBS 1/2.121 (Abusch and Schwemer 2011: 10.2) can only help so far since it was, as its recitation makes clear, designed to combat any of the various sorcerous rites that might have been set using the Wagon star, and not just this one in particular.

7 This is from the same root as, but is not the same as, the normal word for reed altar.

8 Literally, "they have been piled up in a heap" or, as we would say, "they feel all bunched up." For the interpretation, see Scurlock and Andersen 2005:292–293.

9 Pace Abusch and Schwemer 2011:401, these spirits have nothing to do with "vital force." Your shadow/reflection might protect you, or others on whom it falls, but, for ancient Mesopotamians, your "vital force" was your breath.

⌜command⌝ of [Ea, Šamaš, Asalluḫi and princess Belet-ili."[10] When] you have said this (mistake for	"have had him say this"), [...] *gaṣṣu*-gypsum for him to crush [...]

[10] With Abusch and Schwemer 2011:399 and Schwemer 2007:228–230, this recitation is to be restored from the similar, if more multi-purpose, prayer in Maqlû.

REFERENCES

Abusch and Schwemer 2011:399–401; 10.1–2; Schwemer 2007:228–230; Scurlock and Andersen 2005:292–293; Scurlock 2006a: no. 21: 9, 12–13; Scurlock 2014: 2.10.5–7.

MEDICAL TEXT COMMENTARIES (Civil 1974:336–338)[1] (4.88N)

JoAnn Scurlock

In order to tease more meaning out of their texts, advanced ancient Mesopotamian students were taught to write commentaries as part of the lecturing and examination process. Any number of these commentaries are specifically labeled as involving oral explanations (*šūt pî*) and/or questioning (*maš᾽altu*) by experts[2] or as intended for the "reading" of physicians in training (LÚ.MAŠ.MAŠ BÀN.DA).[3] Some even indicate a locus for this activity, variously referred to as the "house of words" (*bīt dabībī*), or the "house of mister work, work, work" (É ᵐDÙ.DÙ.DÙ).[4] Given the lateness of these texts, we are presumably talking about something on the order of what the ancient Greeks called an academy. The result of all this activity was the production of commentaries such as the one edited in Biggs 1968 that makes what appears to me to be a reference to Nebuchadnezzar's destruction of the Temple in Jerusalem, and is as close as ancient Mesopotamia came to a philosophical treatise.[5]

The commentary from the "house of words" translated below was to a text of which we still have a fragment in BAM 77. The beginning of BAM 77 is broken, but the text apparently began with treatments for hurting hips and progressed to *mungu*-stiff knees before settling on problems with the spleen on the way to treatments for blood pouring out of the penis. This coverage may be inferred from the commentary's citation of the incipit of the commented text in lines 1 and 30 and of its catchline in line 31. *Tullal*, if that is the correct interpretation of the plant, is used in a treatment for sexually-transmitted urethritis involving *mungu* in BAM 205:12′//BAM 320:22′//Biggs 1969:68f. obv. 14′. One of the supernatural causers of urethtritis was the god Marduk, which may have provided the segue to the preserved parts of BAM 77. In any case, we have lost a three-day bandage and what appears to be instructions for the preparation of a solid decoction,[6] using a hot liquid and flour. We are on firmer ground with line 6, which picks up BAM 77:20′–21′: "If a person's spleen hurts him, he is unable to sleep day or night, his body ⌜holds⌝ fever and [the amount of beer he drinks and bread] ⌜he eats⌝ diminishes,[7] if he continually seeks out the shrine of Marduk, he should recover."

Of these lines, our commentator gives a brief summary, focusing on the part that interested him, namely the involvement of Marduk. From his perspective, Marduk was the cause of the problem via his planet Jupiter which had a lexical connection with spleens, and the treatment was effective because this problem-causing god was placated by the prayers at his sanctuary and by medicines which included ingredients that could in one way or another be connected with him. The reason for this interest is not far to seek. The (Persian period?) author was a lamentation priest of Enlil of Nippur, the Sumerian equivalent of Marduk. Among his jobs was the performance of lamentations on the occasion of an eclipse, something which, in later periods, he was expected to be able to predict. He also was very busy during festivals marking the changes of the seasons, particularly the Winter Solstice. As such, his interest in astronomy and the developing science of astrology was quite natural. The classical science of planetary melothesia owes much to speculations of this sort.[8]

[1] The text is transliterated with commentary but not translated in Civil 1974. For a discussion, see Frahm 2011:231–232.
[2] For references, see *CAD* M/2 354–355.
[3] See, for example, SpTU 1.33 (commentary on the 7th tablet of the Diagnostic and Prognostic series), 1.49–51, 3.100 (therapeutic text commentaries), 1.72 (malformed birth omens commentary).
[4] See, for example, SpTU 1.48, 1.51
[5] For more on this text, see Böck 2000 and Scurlock and al-Rawi 2006:369–374.
[6] For more details, see above, 4.88E, ad obv. 14–15.
[7] See Scurlock and Andersen 2005: 6.104.
[8] For more on this subject, see Reiner 1995:59–60.

Not every medicine used to treat spleen problems could be made to fit our lamentation priest's schema, most notably BAM 77:28′–29′ which he simply ignored. We may, from this fact, surmise, that the treatment came first and the analysis afterwards or, to put it differently, the object of the exercise was not to predict potential medicines but to explain why the medicines that worked were, in fact, working. Since our author was not himself either a physician or a pharmacist, he was in the position of a natural scientist explaining the bigger picture to his colleagues.

We do not concur with his conclusions, but we can still admire the ingenuity with which he found evidence to support his theories. The sucked medicine of the commentator's version of BAM 77:20′–27′ apparently contained[9] *arsuppu*-groats whose Sumerogram literally means "ox grain," and the alternative potion of BAM 77:24′ contained the lobe of an ox liver. The bull was the characteristic animal of warrior gods like Marduk.

The rawhide that was to be chewed in BAM 77:20′–27′ and in 37′–38′, 43′–45′ and 46′–50′ as well, was appropriate, as the commentary explains, due to its resemblance to the face of a falcon. The "real" connection is more likely to be the fact that the root for chewing, *kss*, is a pun on a word for falcon. The bird is, in any case, to be associated with Marduk.

BAM 77:30′–32′, 33′–36′ and 39′–42′ use dog spleen to treat splenomegaly. We know that this treatment will have worked, since it is essentially hormone replacement therapy. Our commentator made the same observation, but provided his own explanation. The text being commented on used goat rather than dog spleen and this was effective, as our commentator, explains, due to the goat's association with the goat-fish constellation (our Capricorn). This was the symbol of Marduk's divine father, the god of healing, Ea of Eridu.

BAM 77:33′–36′, 37′–38′ and 39′–42′ and 46′–50 use *anduḫallatu*-lizard, also for splenomegaly. This is connected to Marduk via a Sumerogram for the lizard which makes it out to be a fearsome dragon. In view of the imaging of Satan as a serpent, it is of interest to us that Marduk, whose color was red, boasts of being, essentially, a dragon. In its original context this was, of course, a compliment rather than a criticism.

Unfortunately, at this point BAM 77 breaks off, but the commentary allows us to understand that the commented text originally continued with treatments for urinary tract conditions,[10] for which the plant *nuṣabu* is commonly used. This appears in line 17 with a description drawn from a lost pharmacological text. The plant medicine was apparently to be sucked up accompanied by a charming punning recitation to be delivered by the patient. Just as spleen problems were blamed on Marduk via his planet Jupiter, Nergal got dunned for kidney problems via his planet of Mars. There are, of course, two kidneys and there was an associated constellation (the Gemini) connected to two by-forms of the god Nergal associated with two planets (Mercury and Mars) connected to two gods (Nabû and Nergal), of which only one was being singled out here. The most ingenious section of the commentary (lines 22–23) manages to dig this tidbit out of a simple direction involving a half day.

The remaining remarks give supplemental information about plants for which substitutes were available (quoted from pharmacological texts) or give explanations for unusual technical terms (and misspellings). So, for example, the verb *emēru* appears quite commonly in reference to stomachs but only rarely with reference to other parts of the body, as here.

(1) "If a person's hips continually hurt him." *Mungu*[11] is an illness.
(2a) *Tullal*(!)[12] is [...] (the tablet the scribe was copying from had been "recently broken").
(2b–3a) *ina* U_4.4.KÁM DU_8 means "it is to be taken off on the fourth day" [...] (the tablet the scribe was copying from had been "recently broken").
(3b) You filter (it while it is still) hot.
(4) È means "to filter"; BI means [...] (the tablet the scribe was copying from had been "recently broken"); ZÌ means "to break up into small pieces, (said) of flour."
(5) *dīšūtu* is the same as *dīšu*-grass.
(6) "If a person's spleen hurts him ... if he continually seeks out the shrine of Marduk, he should recover" is what it says.
(7) That is because (the same Sumerogram) ŠÀ.GIG stands (both) for Jupiter (Marduk's planet) and for the spleen.
(8–9a) You dry (and) grind *arsuppu*-groats (ŠE[!].GU_4: "ox grain"); alternatively, you dry (and) grind ox liver – that is, the lobe (of the liver).
(9b) Rawhide (looks) like the face of a falcon.
(10) Goat spleen; "goat spleen" is what it says.
(11) Capricorn is (the star of) Subartu and Eridu (Ea's cult center).
(12) "*Anduḫallatu*-lizard" is what it says. NIR.UŠUMGAL is the Sumerogram for *anduḫallatu*-lizard.
(13) "I, Marduk, am the *ušumgallu*-dragon of the Anunnaki and the *labbu*-monster of the Igigi."

[9] The first medicament is lost in a lacuna.
[10] See Böck 2008:299–300.
[11] For *mungu*, see Scurlock and Andersen 2005:249–250.
[12] See Civil 1974:337.

(14) PAP.ŠEŠ and SIM-*tum* are a masculine and feminine sieve.
(15) PAP (read PAPPUR).ŠEŠ means masculine sieve; SIM means "to sieve."
(16–17a) "May my lion (*labbu*) be calmed by (water from) the waterpipe (*naṣṣābu*); may my heart/insides (*libbi*) be calmed by sucking (*naṣābu*) (the medicine)."
(17b–18) *Nuṣābu* is a ^{Ú}*kukkānitu*-type plant with five branches.
(19) *ḫallapāna* is the same as *ḫaltappāna* and the equivalent of *tušru*.[13]
(20) "If a person's kidney hurts him, it is Nergal" is what it says.
(21a) The kidney planet is *Ṣalbatānu* (Mars).
(21b) $^{\text{GIŠ.Ú}}$GÍR.LAGAB is equivalent to *puquttu*-thorn.
(22a) *Mūṣu* is the same as stricture.[14]
(22b) MAŠ U_4(*tam*)-*mu* means "half (MAŠ) of (a pair of) twins (*tammu*)."[15]
(23) That is because half of it (*māšu*: "twin") is the syllable *ma*-. Secondly, MAŠ U_4-*mu* means "half a day."
(24) "His urethra." The urethra is a channel through the penis.
(25a) *šú-ḫi-šú* is (a mispelling) for *šu-uḫ-ḫa-šú*: "his buttocks."
(25b–26a) They (his buttocks) are distended (and) sting him. "To be distended" means "to swell."
(26b) "He cuts off" means "he cuts through."
(27a) MI ŠEŠ UT TIM is read *mi-šiš tam-tim*.
(27b) *ḫaḫḫinu*-thorn is equivalent to *puquttu*-thorn.[16]
(28) 24th extract tablet; treatments from the *Bīt dabībi* ("house of words").[17] The tablet is unfinished.
(29) No oral tradition (material derived from lectures) or questions from the mouth of an expert (exam questions) are to be found in it. (Everything here was looked up from written sources).
(30) (From) "If a person's hips continually hurt him"
(31) (to) "If blood pours from a person's penis(!)"
(32) Long tablet of Enlil-kāṣir, the *kalû*-priest of Enlil whose personal god is Nusku.[18]

13 This equation is also found, inter alia, in Uruanna texts KADP 2 ii.37; KADP 2 vi.31; KADP 6 v.7′; CT 37.29–32 ii.54′.
14 See Scurlock and Andersen 2005:102–103, with n. 28.
15 See Civil 1974:338.
16 This appears also in Uruanna texts KADP 2 iii.26; KADP 4:20.
17 This institution is also mentioned on BAM 401 and BAM 403 (see Civil 1974:336) as well as BM 59607 (see Geller 1990:122).
18 For more on this gentleman, see Frahm 2011:302–303.

REFERENCES

Biggs 1967:69; 1968; Böck 2000; 2008:299–300; Civil 1974:336–338; Frahm 2011:231–232, 302–303; Geller 1990:122; Reiner 1995:59–60; Scurlock and Andersen 2005:102–103, with n. 28, 249–250; 6.104; Scurlock and al-Rawi 2006:369–374.

BABYLONIAN LETTER

A NINTH-CENTURY LETTER FROM THE MIDDLE EUPHRATES TO CENTRAL SYRIA (4.89)

F. M. Fales

(Obverse)
(1)[1] Say to Rudamu[2]:
(2) thus (speaks) Marduk-apla-uṣur, your brother.[3]
(3) Good health to you!
(4) Also (say) to my brother thus:
(5) I have received the tablet which
(6) you sent to me with
(7) Bel-išdiya-kīni.[4] Even before your tablet
(8) was (available) for me to see, I wrote and
(9) dispatched to you the (following) tablet:
(10) "Yo[u ....]
(11) with m[e ....]"
(Lines 12–16) lost[5]

(Reverse)
(1′[6]) [...]Adad-nadin-[zeri].[7]
(2′) a man who ... s his god,[8] has been pocketing[9]

---

1 The present letter (Hama 6 A 334) was published in copy, photograph, transliteration and translation by Parpola 1990; the version given here follows this reliable *editio princeps* closely, save for minor details. The relevant tablet (4.9 × 7.8 cms) was retrieved in 1936 during the Danish excavations at the present-day site of Ḫamā on the Orontes river in central Syria, the ancient city of Ḫamat; it is presently kept in the Danish National Museum at Copenhagen. It comes from Building III of the ancient acropolis (nowadays a citadel for mainly military purposes), which also yielded other cuneiform texts of magical, divinatory, and medical content; since all these texts were found near the main entrance of the building, it is believed that an attempt to save them was effected in 720 BCE, when Ḫamat was about to fall to Sargon II of Assyria (Parpola 1990:257). The tablet was written by an "experienced scribe" in a writing close to 8th-century Neo-Babylonian cursive, and exhibits both Middle Babylonian (MB) and Neo-Babylonian (NB) language features (*ibid.*, and p. 263).

2 Obv. Line 1. The opening formula of the *salutatio*, urging the tablet to "speak" to the addressee, is typical of Babylonian epistolography. The name of the addressee, *Rudamu*, is a variant writing of the Luvian name Uratami(š), attested in five nearly duplicate inscriptions in hieroglyphic Luvian script on basalt blocks discovered in the acropolis of Ḫamat. The texts (HAMA 1–3, 6–7) indicate that Uratami(š), king of the city, was the son of Urḫilina, who is to be identified with Irḫulena/i, king of Ḫamat, leader of a vast alliance of North Syrian, Phoenician, and Transjordanian states, also including Ahab of Israel and an Arab contingent of camel troops, in the pitched battle at Qarqar on the Orontes against the invading Assyrian king Shalmaneser III (853 BCE; cf. Yamada 2000:169 ff.). Urḫilina kept on waging war against the Assyrians for several years (ca. 849–845 BC: cf. PNA, 564a–b); accordingly, Uratami(š) may be dated a generation later, ca. 840–820 BC (Hawkins 2000:402–403). The fact that the present tablet was also retrieved at Ḫamā makes the identification of the Luvian king Uratami(š) with our addressee Rudamu unequivocal; the implications of Reverse, lines 7′ and 12′ further indicate his royal status, while the parity of rank between the correspondents is implied by the appellative "brother" bestowed by the sender in a socio-political sense (Parpola 1990:260).

3 Line 2. *Marduk-apla-uṣur*. Cf. PNA, 711a for a man of this name, mentioned as ruler of the Middle-Euphrates state of Suḫu in the Black Obelisk of Shalmaneser III. Simply named by the Assyrians the "man from Suḫu" (cf. Rev. line 1′ below), he is said to have paid the Assyrians a tribute of silver, gold, gold buckets, ivory, spears(?), byssos, bright-colored garments, and linen (*RIMA* 3:150 A.0.102.90). Were this Marduk-apla-uṣur to be identified with the sender of the present letter – as is quite probable –, his chronological position would by and large tally with that of Rudamu, i.e after 840 BCE (see above, and cf. Parpola 1990:261). The polity of Suḫu – stretching in this period along the Euphrates from Rapiqu to the borders of Ḫindanu (i.e for a length of approx. 250 km) – had the city of Anat (in the present-day river island of Qal'at 'Āna in SW Iraq) as one of its main towns and sometimes as its capital (cf. Brinkman 1968:183 ff.): here, a British expedition carried out salvage excavations in 1981–1982 retrieving Neo-Assyrian antiquities as well as from other periods (Northedge *et al.* 1988).

4 Line7. A Babylonian name ("Bel, establish my foundation!"). Cf. PNA, 318a, for a man from Babylon with this same name in the time of Sargon II. In our case, it should refer to a messenger of Marduk-apla-uṣur who had borne back to Anat a previous letter from Rudamu: Parpola 1990:261 reconstructs in some detail a theoretical chain of letters on the basis of the mention of other epistolary texts in Obv. 5 and Obv. 8, reaching the conclusion that "the two rulers maintained a lively (almost hectic) correspondence at the time concerned."

5 The sole legible traces here are [... *n*]*a-a-a* at the end of line 14 which according to Parpola might be restored as [URU*Ḫi-in-da-n*]*a-a-a*, "Ḫindanaean," with reference to the polity lying just to the northwest of Suḫu on the Middle Euphrates.

6 A further line on the bottom edge of the tablet and the first one on the Reverse are also lost.

7 Rev. line 1′. *Adad-nadin-*[*zeri*]. This individual is attested as "governor of Suḫu and Mari," and as direct ancestor of Šamaš-reša-uṣur and his son Ninurta-kudurri-uṣur, who have left us numerous official inscriptions as independent governors of Suḫu in the early 8th century (see Ismail *et al.* 1983:19 f.; RIMB 2:282–285, texts S.0.1001.2–3, and *ibid.*, 295, 315, texts S.0.1002.1, 90 and *COS* 2:279, for their genealogy, and cf. PNA, 711a). The rivalry of Marduk-apla-uṣur with Adad-nadin-zeri indicated here and in the next line might be somehow reflected in the somewhat vaguer titulary attributed to the former by the Assyrians (see *ad* Obv. l. 2, above). Probably a subdivision of the territory of Suḫu between two competing rulers was underway at the time of this letter (with Adad-nadin-zeri possibly controlling the N/NW areas of Suḫu through which caravan traffic between Ḫamat and Anat necessarily flowed); however, their differences could also have concerned alternative political stances held vis-à-vis the advance of Assyrian arms in the Euphrates river basin. On the other hand, it may be noticed from Rev. line 4′, below that the two rulers were still entertaining correspondence, i.e. they continued to be somehow "on speaking terms."

8 Line 2′. The text has LÚ *ka*-ME DINGIR-*šú*, for which Parpola (1990:262) finds no single satisfactory reading/interpretation. In any case, the expression had a clearly derogatory meaning, implying some sort of impious action/behavior on Adad-nadin-zeri's part (with political connotations).

9 Line 2′: the text has *i-ta-kal*, lit. "eating up," with a possible meaning in the sphere of economy ("taking for himself/pocketing," *etc.*), although also "consuming" should not be ruled out. The exact context of the action is difficult to make out, although it is sufficiently clear that Marduk-apla-uṣur and Rudamu had common interest in some "goods" (*udē*, see next footnote), perhaps issuing from a regular caravan trade across the Syrian desert. Adad-nadin-zeri may have requisitioned some caravans of both parties as they were going through his particular territory (se note on Rev. line 1′, above, and cf, Parpola 1990:263).

(3′) [our] goods;[10] and I have	(9′) about my goods and get (them) back.
(4′) written to him. (Now) you,	(10′) Now,[13] may your messenger
(5′) protest[11] about your goods	(11′) come quickly!
(6′) and get (them) back![12]	(12′) May Anat and
(7′) He cannot withhold (them) from you.	(13′) and [*sic*][14] Ḫamat
(8′) I will (then) also protest	(14′) be strong,[15] strong![16]

10 Line 3′. Here, and in lines 5′ and 9′, the term *udē*, relatively frequent in MB and NB as a comprehensive term for miscellaneous (and usually precious) goods is used: cf. *CAD* U/W 24b. As already noted by Parpola (1990:263, n. 26), the Suḫeans were not above intercepting passing foreign caravans themselves: cf. now RIMB 2:300, text no. S.0.1002.3, for the proud and detailed report by the later "governor" Ninurta-kudurri-uṣur of having intercepted a caravan train from Tema and Saba' (i.e. resp. from the productive and trading centers of northern and southern Arabia, headed for Mesopotamia), whose leaders "had never come to me, and had never travelled to meet me" – i.e. possibly had not paid the required taxes for passage –, and of having captured the 100-man personnel, together with 200 camels and a vast booty of blue-purple wool, iron, and precious stones (*COS* 2:281–282).

11 Line 5′. Here, and in line 8′, are particular MB-NB forms (with *e*-vowel coloring) of the verb *tamû*, lit., "to swear, to take an oath," in legal contexts, often with the meaning of making a claim on stolen property: cf. *CAD* T 160a–165a. Parpola's translation is followed (see also *CAD* T 24b).

12 Line 6′. Here, as in line 9′, below, the scribe employed the verb *našû*, in the particular meaning of "taking back" something.

13 Line 10′. *enna* is a typically NB lexical item for "now"; cf. Parpola 1990:263.

14 Line 13′. The sign *ù* ("and"), already present in the previous line, is erroneously repeated here.

15 Line 14′. The text of this line has *lu* KALAG(erasure). MEŠ *dan-nu*. In both cases, the adjective *dannu*, "strong" is meant, but the slightly erased logograms (as visible from the photograph and Parpola's hand-copy on p. 259) refer to a plural form (consistent with the previous mention of both Anat and Ḫamat), whereas the syllabic *dan-nu* is in the singular – unless it should be taken as a form of scribal "gloss" to make the logograms understandable to the addressee.

16 Summing up, the historical interest of this isolated letter is that it sheds light on the long-range political and commercial relations between the state of Suḫu on the Middle Euphrates, of Babylonian heritage and culture, with the Luvian-ruled state of Ḫamat on the middle course of the Orontes (see the map in Parpola 1990:260). Whether this alliance was solely based on commercial interests, or it also had as its backdrop a geopolitical affinity concerning the need to counter Assyrian military and territorial expansion under the repeated thrusts of Shalmaneser III, is difficult to say with certainty. What is relatively clear, on the other hand, is that the two correspondents, Marduk-apla-uṣur and Rudamu/Uratamis, seem to have envisaged no difficulty in maintaining regular (and perhaps even intense) relations, despite the 400 km. distance between their homelands and the extreme harshness of the rocky Syrian desert in between – while, to the contrary, this arid and forbidding environment (probably also patrolled by camel-riding Arabs) seems to have been by and large "off limits" for the Assyrian armies, forced to cross westward from Mesopotamia to Syria along much more northernly itineraries in the grassy steppelands. Finally, this letter might go some way in clarifying the background of the dynastic change which occurred in Ḫamat some decades later (ca. 800 BCE), where an Aramaean named Zakkur rose to the throne. In the opening of his monumental Aramaic inscription (*KAI* 202, line 2), this king states clearly *'š 'nh 'nh*, a clause which was traditionally understood as "a humble/devout man am I," but which more recently has been re-interpreted as "a man of *'Anah* am I" (Millard 1990). While we are still in the dark concerning the concrete circumstances which brought (the ultimately pro-Assyrian) Zakkur to seize the throne of Ḫamat from the previous Luvian dynasty, starting out from his birthplace Anat/'Anah, the present letter clearly demonstrates that these two locations on opposite edges of the *Shamīya* desert had already been in close and intense contact for some decades.

REFERENCES

Brinkman 1968; Hawkins 2000; Ismail, Roaf, and Black 1983:191–194; Millard 1990:47–52; Northedge *et al.* 1988; Parpola 1990:257–265; Yamada 2000.

AKKADIAN BIBLIOGRAPHY

Abrahami, P.

2014 “Wool in the Nuzi Texts.” Pp. 283–309 in *Wool Economy in the Ancient Near East*. Ed. by C. Breniquet and C. Michel. Oxford: Oxbow Books.

Abusch, T.

2002 *Mesopotamian Witchcraft: Toward a History and Understanding of Babylonian Witchcraft Beliefs and Literature*. Ancient Magic and Divination V. Leiden: Brill/Styx.

Abusch, T. and D. Schwemer

2011 *Corpus of Mesopotamian Anti-Witchcraft Rituals*. Vol. 1. Ancient Magic and Divination 8/1. Leiden: Brill.

Adamson, P. B.

1981 “Anatomical and Pathological Terms in Akkadian: Part III.” *JRAS* 113:125–132.

Albenda, P.

1986 *The Palace of Sargon, King of Assyria*. Paris: ERC.

Albertz, R., and R. Schmitt

2012 *Family and Household Religion in Ancient Israel and the Levant*. Winona Lake: Eisenbrauns.

Albright, W. F.

1942 “A Case of Lèse-Majesté in Pre-Israelite Lachish, with Some Remarks on the Israelite Conquest.” *BASOR* 87:32–38.

1943 “An Archaic Hebrew Proverb in an Amarna Letter from Central Palestine.” *BASOR* 89:29–32.

1944 “A Prince of Taanach in the Fifteenth Century B.C.” *BASOR* 94:12–27.

Altman, A.

2012 *Tracing the Earliest Recorded Concepts of International Law: The Ancient Near East (2500–330 BCE)*. Leiden/Boston: Martinus Nijhoff.

Ambos, C.

2011a “Šamaš-balāssu-iqbi.” *PNA* 3/2:1192.

2011b “Šamaš-buna’i.” *PNA* 3/2:1195.

Anbar, M.

1993 “ועלה על כל אפיקיו והלך על כל גדותיו' יש' ח' 7” *ErIs* 24:158–160.

Anbar, M., and N. Na’aman

1986–1987 “An Account of Sheep from Ancient Hebron.” *Tel Aviv* 13–14:3–12.

Arkhipov, I.

2010 “Les véhicules terrestres dans les textes de Mari I.” Pp. 405–420 in *Language in the Ancient Near East: Proceedings of the 53e Rencontre Assyriologique Internationale, Vol. 1*. Ed. by L. Kogan, et al. Winona Lake: Eisenbrauns.

2014 “Toponymie et idéologie à l’époque amorrite: Les cas de Šubat-Šamaš et Ṣubat-Eštar.” Pp. 267–272 in *D’Aššur à Mari et au-delà: Entre les fleuves – II*. BBVO 24. Ed. by N. Ziegler and E. Cancik-Kirschbaum. Gladbeck: Pewe-Verlag.

Bagg, A.

2007 *Die Orts- und Gewassernamen der neuassyrischen Zeit, Teil I: Die Levante*. RGTC 7/1. Wiesbaden: Dr. Ludwig Reichert.

Baker, H. D.

2001a “Mukīn-zēri.” *PNA* 2/2:764–765.

2001b “Nabû-nammir.” *PNA* 2/2:854–855.

Baker, H. D. and Gentili, P.

2011 “Šamaš-mētu-uballiṭ.” *PNA* 3/2:1205.

Barjamovic, G.

2004 “Civic Institutions and Self-Government in Southern Mesopotamia in the Mid-First Millennium BC.” Pp. 47–98 in *Assyria and Beyond: Studies Presented to Mogens Trolle Larsen*. Ed. by J. G. Dercksen. PIHANS 100. Leiden: Nederlands Instituut voor het Nabije Oosten.

Bartelmus, A.

2007 “*Talīmu* and the Relationship between Assurbanipal and Šamaš-šum-ukīn.” *SAAB* 16:287–302.

Beckman, G.

1999 *Hittite Diplomatic Texts*. 2nd ed. SBLWAW 7. Atlanta: Scholars Press.

Berlejung, A.

1996 “Der Handwerker als Theologe: zur Mentalitäts-und Traditionsgeschichte eines altorientalischen und alttestamentlichen Berufstands.” *VT* 56:145–168.

1997 “Washing the Mouth: The Consecration of Divine Images in Mesopotamia.” Pp. 45–72 in *The Image and the Book*. Ed. by K. van der Toorn. Leuven: Peeters.

1998 *Die Theologie der Bilder: Herstellung und Einweihung von Kultbildern in Mesopotamien und die Alttestamentliche Bilderpolemik*. OBO 162. Fribourg: Universitätsverlag.

Bezold, C., and E. A. W. Budge

1892 *The Tell el-Amarna Tablets in the British Museum*. London: British Museum.

Biggs, R. D.

1967 *ŠÀ.ZI.GA: Ancient Mesopotamian Potency Incantations*. TCS 2. Locust Valley: J. J. Augustin.

1968 “An Esoteric Babylonian Commentary.” *RA* 62:51–58.

Blackman, A. M.

1924 “The Rite of the Opening of the Mouth in Ancient Egypt and Babylonia.” *JEA* 10:47–59.

Böck, B.

2000 “‘An Esoteric Babylonian Commentary’ Revisited.” *JAOS* 120/4:615–620.

2007 *Das Handbuch Muššu’u “Einreibung”: Eine Serie Sumerischer und Akkadischer Beschwörungen aus dem 1 Jt. vor Chr.* Biblioteca del Proximo Oriente Antiguo 3. Madrid: Consejo Superior de Investigaciones Cientificás.

2008 “Babylonisch-assyrische Medizin in Texten und Untersuchungen: Erkrankungen des uro-genitalen Traktes, des Endarmes und des Anus.” *WZKM* 98:295–346.

2011a Akkadische Texte des 2. und 1. Jt. v. Chr. 2: Therapeutische Texte 2.7.3. Pp. 75–78 in *TUAT* 5.

2011b Akkadische Texte des 2. und 1. Jt. v. Chr. 2: Pharmakologische Texte 4.6. P. 168 in *TUAT* 5.

Boden, P. J.

1998 "The Mesopotamian Washing of the Mouth (Mîs Pî) Ritual: An Examination of Some of the Social and Communication Strategies Which Guided the Development and Performance of the Ritual Which Transferred the Essence of the Deity Into Its Temple Statue." Ph.D. Dissertation. The Johns Hopkins University.

Bodi, D.

2010 *The Demise of the Warlord: A New Look at the David Story*. Hebrew Bible Monographs 26. Sheffield: Sheffield Phoenix.

Bonechi, M.

1992 "Relations amicales syro-palestiniennes: Mari et Hazor XIIIe siècle au." Pp. 9–22 in *Florilegium marianum, Memoires de N.A.B.U.* 1. Paris.

Borger, R.

1956 *Die Inschriften Asarhaddons Königs von Assyrien*. AfO Beiheft 9. Graz.

1961 "Zu den Asarhaddon-Verträgen aus Nimrud." *ZA* 54: 173–196.

1965 "Marduk-zākir-šumi I. und der Kodex Ḫammurapi." *Or* 34:168–169.

1982–1985 "Assyrische Staatsverträge." Pp. 155–177 in *TUAT* 1.

1996 *Beiträge zum Inschriftenwerk Assurbanipals – Die Prismenklassen A, B, C = K, D, E, F, G, H, J und T sowie andere Inschriften*. Wiesbaden: Harrassowitz Verlag.

2005 "Textkritisches zu "Mundwaschung" zu Walker and Dick Induction." *BiOr* 62:395–410.

Botta, P. É. and E. Flandin

1849 *Monument de Ninive*. Volume 1. Paris: Imprimerie Nationale.

Brinkman, J. A.

1968 *A Political History of Post-Kassite Babylonia, 1158–722 B.C.* AnOr 43. Rome: Pontificium Institutum Biblicum.

1984 *Prelude to Empire: Babylonian Society and Politics, 747–626 B.C.* Occasional Publications of the Babylonian Fund 7. Philadelphia: University Museum.

1990 "Political Covenants, Treaties, and Loyalty Oaths in Babylonia and between Assyria and Babylonia." Pp. 81–112 in *I Trattati nel Monda Antico: Forma, Ideologia, Funzione*. Ed. by L. Canfora, M. Liverani, and C. Zaccagnini. Rome: "L'Erma" di Bretschneider.

Cantrell, D. O.

2011 *The Horsemen of Israel: Horses and Chariotry in Monarchic Israel (Ninth-Eighth Centuries B.C.E.)*. History, Archaeology, and Culture of the Levant 1. Winona Lake: Eisenbrauns.

Cassin, E.

1982 "Heur et malheur du *ḫazannu* (Nuzi)." Pp. 98–117 in *Les pouvoirs locaux en Mésopotamie et dans les régions adjacentes*. Ed. by A. Finet. Brussels: Institut des Hautes Études de Belgique.

1986 "Forme et Identité des Hommes et des Dieux Chez les Babyloniens." Pp. 63–76 in *Corps des dieux*. Volume 7: *Le Temps de la Réflexion*. Ed. by C. Malamoud and J.-P. Vernant. Gallimard.

Cavigneaux, A. and L. Colonna D'Istria

2009 "Les découvertes épigraphiques des fouilles récentes de Mari. État des recherches en janvier 2009." *Studia Orontica* 6:51–68.

Charpin, D.

1991 "Le traité entre Ibâl-pî-El II d' Ešnunna et Zimri-Lim de Mari." Pp. 139–166 in *Marchands, diplomates et empereurs: études sur la civilisation Mésopotamienne offertes à Paul Garelli*. Ed. by D. Charpin and F. Joannès. Paris: Éditions Recherche sur les Civilisations.

1992 "La visite des messagers d' Ešnunna à Mari." *NABU* no. 101.

1986 "Les champions, la meule et le fleuve." Pp. 29–38 in *Recueil d'études en l'honneur de Michel Fleury*. Florilegium Marianum 1. Ed. by J.-M. Durand. Paris: SEPOA.

1997a "Sapîratum, ville du Suhûm." *MARI* 8:341–366.

1997b "La version mariote de L'«insurrection générale contre Narâm-Sîn»." Pp. 9–18 in *Recueil d'études à la mémoire de Marie-Thérèse Barrelet*. Florilegium Marianum 3. Ed. by D. Charpin and J.-M. Durand. Paris: SEPOA.

1998 "L' évocation du passé dans les lettres de Mari." Pp. 91–110 in *Intellectual Life of the Ancient Near East*. Ed. by J. Prosecký. Prague: Oriental Institute.

2002 "Prophètes et rois dans le Proche-Orient amorrite nouvelles données, nouvelles perspectives." Pp. 7–38 in *Recueil d'études à la mémoire d'Andre Parrot*. Florilegium Marianum 6. Ed. by D. Charpin and J.-M. Durand. Paris: SEPOA.

Charpin, D. and J.-M. Durand

1985 "La prise du pouvoir par Zimri-Lim." *MARI* 4:293–344.

1986 "«Fils de Sim'al»: Les origines tribales de rois de Mari." *RA* 80/2:141–183.

2003 "Des volontaires contre l' Élam." Pp. 63–76 in *Literatur, Politik und Recht in Mesopotamien, Festschrift für Claus Wilcke*. Ed. by W. Sallaberger, et al. Wiesbaden: Harrassowitz Verlag.

2004 "Prétendants au trône dans le Proche-Orient amorrite." Pp. 99–113 in *Assyria and Beyond: Studies Presented to Mogens Trolle Larsen*. Ed. by J. G. Dercksen. Leiden: Hederlands Instituut Voor Het Nabije Oosten.

Charpin, D. and N. Ziegler

2003 *Mari et le Proche-Orient à l'époque amorrite: essai d'histoire politique*. Florilegium Marianum 5. Paris: SEPOA.

Civil, M.

1974 "Medical Commentaries from Nippur." *JNES* 33:329–338.

1982 "Studies on Early Dynastic Lexicography I." *OA* 21:1–26.

Clifford, R. J.

1980 "The Function of Idol Passages in Second Isaiah." *CBQ* 42:450–464.

Cochavi-Rainey, Z.

2011 *The Akkadian Dialect of Egyptian Scribes in the 14th and 13th Centuries* BCE. AOAT 374. Münster: Ugarit-Verlag.

Cogan, M.

1977 "Ashurbanipal Prism F: Notes on Scribal Techniques and Editorial Procedures." *JCS* 29: 97–107.

2005 "Some Text-Critical Issues in the Hebrew Bible from an Assyriological Perspective." *Textus* 22:1–20.

2008 *The Raging Torrent: Historical Inscriptions from Assyria and Babylonia Relating to Ancient Israel*. Jerusalem: Carta.

2009 "Literary-Critical Issues in the Hebrew Bible from an Assyriological Perspective: Additions and Omissions." Pp. 401–413 in *Mishneh Todah: Studies in Deuteronomy and Its Cultural Environment in Honor of Jeffrey H. Tigay*. Edited by N. S. Fox, D. A. Glatt-Gilad, and M. J. Williams. Winona Lake, IN: Eisenbrauns.

COGAN, M. and H. TADMOR
1977 "Gyges and Ashurbanipal – A Study in Literary Transmission." *Or* 46:65–85.

CURTIS, E. M.
1990 "Images in Mesopotamia and the Bible: A Comparative Study." Pp. 31–56 in *SIC* 3.

DALLEY, S.
1985 "Foreign Chariotry and Cavalry in the Armies of Tiglathpileser II and Sargon II." *Iraq* 47:31–48.

DELLER, K.
1983 "Gab es ein König von Arrapḫe namens Muš-teya?" *Assur* 3/4:154–163.
1991 "Neuassyrisch *qanû*, *qinītu* und *tidintu*." Pp. 345–355 in *Mélanges Garelli*. Ed. by D. Charpin and F. Joannès. Paris: Éditions Recherche sur les Civilisations.

DIETRICH, M.
1992 "Der Werkstoff Wird Gott. Zum Mesopotamischen Ritual der Umwandlung Eines Leblosen Bildwerks in Einen Lebendigen Gott." *MARG* 7:105–126.

DOSCH, G., and K. DELLER.
1981 "Die Familie Kizzuk: Sieben Kassitengenerationen in Temtena und Šuriniwe." Pp. 91–113 in *Studies on the Civilization and Culture of Nuzi and the Hurrians in Honor of Ernest R. Lacheman*. Ed. by M. A. Morrison and D. I. Owen. Winona Lake, IN: Eisenbrauns.

DOSSIN, G.
1973 "Une mention de Cananéens dans une lettre de Mari." *Syria* 50:277–282.

DUBOVSKY, P.
2006a *Hezekiah and the Assyrian Spies: Reconstruction of the Assyrian Intelligence Services and its Significance for 2 Kings 18–19*. Rome: Pontifical Biblical Institute.
2006b "Conquest and Reconquest of Muṣaṣir in the 8th c. B.C.E." *SAAB* 15:141–145.

DURAND, J.-M.
1986 "Fragments rejoints pour une histoire élamite." Pp. 111–128 in *Fragmenta Historiae Elamicae: Mélanges offerets a M.-J. Steve*. Ed. by L. de Meyer, et. al. Paris: Éditions Recherche sur les Civilisations.
1987 "Villes fantômes de Syrie et autres lieux." *MARI* 5:199–234.
1988 "Les anciens de Talhayûm." *RA* 82/2:97–113.
1990a "La cité-État d' Imar à l' époque des rois de Mari." *MARI* 6:39–92.
1990b "Fourmis blanches et fourmis noires." Pp. 100–108 in *Contribution à l' histoire de l' Iran: Mélanges offerts à Jean Perrot*. Ed by F. Vallat. Paris: Éditions Recherche sur les Civilisations.
1991 "Précurseurs syriens aux protocoles néo-assyriens: considérations sur la vie politique aux Bords-de-l' Euphrate." Pp. 13–72 in *Marchands, diplomates et empereurs: études sur la civilisation Mésopotamienne offertes à Paul Garelli*. Ed. by D. Charpin and F. Joannès. Paris: Éditions Recherche sur les Civilisations.
1997 *Les documents épistolaires du palais de Mari*. LAPO 16. Paris: Les Éditions du Cerf.
1998 *Les documents épistolaires du palais de Mari*. LAPO 17. Paris: Les Éditions du Cerf.
2000 *Les documents épistolaires du palais de Mari*. LAPO 18. Paris: Les Éditions du Cerf.
2002 *Le culte d' Addu d' Alep et l' affaire d' Alahtum*. Florilegium Marianum 7. Paris: SEPOA.
2004 "Peuplement et sociétés à l' époque amorrite (I) les clans Bensim'alites." Pp. 111–197 in *Amurru III: Nomades et sédentaires dans le Proche-Orient ancien: Compte rendu de la XLVIe Rencontre Assyriologique International*. Ed by C. Nicolle. Paris: Éditions Recherche sur le Civilisations.
2005 *Le culte pierres et les monuments commémoratifs en Syrie amorrite*. Florilegium Marianum 8. Paris: SEPOA.
2008 "La religion amorrite en Syrie à l' époque des archives de Mari." Pp. 163–716 in *Mythologie et religion des Sémites Occidentaux*, vol. 1. OLA 162. Ed. by G. Del Olmo Lete. Leuven, Paris and Dudley, MA: Peeters.
2012a "La guerre ou la paix? Réflexions sur les implications politiques d' une prophétie." Pp. 251–272 in *Leggo! Studies Presented to Frederick Mario Fales on the Occasion of His 65th Birthday*. Ed. by G. B. Lanfranchi, et al. Wiesbaden: Harrassowitz Verlag.
2012b "Vengeance d' un exilé." Pp. 185–190 in *The Ancient Near East, A Life! Festschrift Karel van Lerberghe*. OLA 220. Ed. by T. Boiy, et al. Leuven: Peeters.

DURAND, J.-M. and GUICHARD, M.
2012 "Noms d' équidés dans les textes de Mari." *Semitica* 54:9–17.

EBELING, E.
1931 *Tod und Leben nach den Vorstellungen der Babylonier*. Berlin: Walter de Gruyter.
1953 *Die akkadische Gebetsserie "Handerhebung" von neuem gesammelt und herausgegeben*. Berlin: Akademie-Verlag.

EIDEM, J.
1994 "Raiders of the Lost City of Samsī-Addu." Pp. 235–274 in *Recueil d' études à la mémoire de Maurice Birot*. Florilegium Marianum 2. Ed. by D. Charpin and J.-M. Durand. Paris: Éditions Recherche sur les Civilisations.
2011 *The Royal Archives from Tell Leilan: Old Babylonia Letters and Treaties from the Lower Town Palace East*. Leiden: Nederlands Instituut voor het Nabije Oosten.

ELLIS, M. DEJONG.
1987 "The Goddess Kititum Speaks to King Ibalpiel: Oracle Texts from Ishchali." *MARI* 5:235–266.

EPHʿAL, I.
1982 *The Ancient Arabs*: *Nomads on the Borders of the Fertile Crescent 9th to 5th Centuries B.C.* Jerusalem: Magnes.
2005 "Esarhaddon, Egypt, and Shubria: Politics and Propaganda." *JCS* 57:99–111.

EPHʿAL, I., and H. TADMOR
2006 "Observations on Two Inscriptions of Esarhaddon: Prism Nineveh A and the Letter to the God." Pp. 155–170 in *Essays on Ancient Israel in Its Near Eastern Context: A Tribute to Nadav Naʾaman*. Edited by Y. Amit, E. Ben Zvi, I. Finkelstein, and O. Lipschits. Winona Lake, IN: Eisenbrauns.

FADHIL, A.
1972 Rechtsurkunden und administrative Texte aus Kurruḫanni. Unpublished Master's Thesis, University of Heidelberg.
1983 *Studien zur Topographie und Prosopographie der Provinzstädte des Königreichs Arrapḫe*. Baghdader Forschungen 6. Mainz am Rhein: Philipp von Zabern.

FALES, F. M.
1981 "A Literary Code in Assyrian Royal Inscriptions: The Case of Ashurbanipal's Egyptian Campaigns." Pp. 169–202 in *ARINH*.
1991 "Narrative and Ideological Variations in the Account of Sargon's Eighth Campaign." Pp. 129–147 in *Studies Tadmor*.
2005 "Tiglat-Pileser III tra annalistica reale ed epistolografia quotidiana." Pp. 163–191 in *Narrare gli eventi*. Edited by F. Pecchioli-Daddi and M. C. Guidotti. Studia Asiana 3. Rome: Herder.
2009 "The Assyrian words for '(Foot)soldier.'" Pp. 71–94 in *Homeland and Exile. Biblical and Ancient Near Eastern Studies in Honour of Bustenay Oded*. Ed. by G. Galil, M. Geller and A. R. Millard. VTSup 130. Leiden: Brill.
2014 "The Two Dynasties of Assyria." Pp. 201–238 in *From Source to History. Studies on Ancient Near Eastern Worlds and Beyond Dedicated to Giovanni Battista Lanfranchi on the Occasion of His 65th Birthday on June 23, 2014*. Ed. by G. Gaspa, A. Greco, D. Morandi Bonacossi, S. Ponchia and R. Rollinger. AOAT 412. Münster: Ugarit-Verlag.

FARBER, W.
1977 *Beschwörungsrituale an Ištar und Dumuzi*. Wiesbaden: Franz Steiner.
1987 "Rituale und Beschwörungen in akkadischer Sprache." In *TUAT* 2.
1990 "Review of Watanabe 1987." *ZA* 80:160–164.
2014 *Lamaštu. An Edition of the Canonical Series of Lamaštu Incantations and Rituals and Related Texts from the Second and First Millennia B.C.* Mesopotamian Civilization 17. Winona Lake: Eisenbrauns.

FINCKE, J.
2000 *Augenleiden nach keilschriftlichen Quellen*. Würzburger medizinhistorische Forschungen 70. Würzburg: Königshausen & Neumann.

FINKEL, I.
1999 "Magic and Medicine at Meskene." *NABU* 1999 no. 30.

FINKELSTEIN, J. J.
1981 "The Ox That Gored." *Transactions of the American Philosophical Society* 71/2:1–89.

FOSTER, B. R.
1997 "Gilgamesh (1.132)." Pp. 458–460 in *COS* 1.
2005 "The Eighth Campaign." Pp. 790–814 in *BM*.

FRAHM, E.
2009 *Historische und historisch-literarische Texte*. KAL 3. WVDOG 121. Wiesbaden: Harrasowitz.
2011 *Babylonian and Assyrian Text Commentaries: Origins of Interpretation*. Guides to the Mesopotamian Textual Record 5. Münster: Ugarit-Verlag.

FRAME, G.
1992 *Babylonia 689–627 B.C.: A Political History*. Leiden, Nederlands Historisch-Archaeologisch Instituut te Istanbul.

FRANKENA, R.
1965 "The Vassal-Treaties of Esarhaddon and the Dating of Deuteronomy." *OtSt* 14:122–154.

FRIEDMANN, A. H.
1987 "Toward a Relative Chronology at Nuzi." Pp. 109–129 in *General Studies and Excavations at Nuzi* 9/1. Ed. by D. I. Owen and M. A. Morrison. SCCNH 2. Winona Lake, IN: Eisenbrauns.

FUCHS, A.
1994 *Die Inschriften Sargons II. aus Khorsabad*. Göttingen: Cuvillier Verlag.

GALLAGHER, W. R.
1999 *Sennacherib's Campaign to Judah: New Studies*. SHCANE 18. Leiden: Brill.

GELB, I. J.
1962 Review of D. J. Wiseman, *The Vassal-Treaties of Esarhaddon* (London: The British School of Archaeology, 1958). *BiOr* 19:159–162.

GELIO, R.
1981 "La délégation envoyée par Gygés, Roi Lydie – Un cas de propaganda idéologique." Pp. 203–224 in *ARINH*.

GELLER, M.
1990 "Review of Erle Leichty, *Catalogue of the Babylonian Tablets in the British Museum*." *BSOAS* 53: 121–123.
2007 "Textes médicaux du Louvre, nouvelle édition: AO 11447, AO 7760 et AO 66774, Première partie." *Le Journal des Médecines Cunéiformes* 10:4–18.

GEORGE, A. R.
1986 "Sennacherib and the Tablet of Destinies." *Iraq* 48:133–146.
1992 *Babylonian Topographical Texts*. OLA 40. Leuven: Peeters.
2009 *Babylonian Literary Texts in the Schøyen Collection*. CUSAS 10. Bethesda: CDL Press.

GERARDI, P.
1992 "The Arab Campaigns of Aššurbanipal: Scribal Reconstruction of the Past." *SAAB* 6:67–104.
1987 "Aššurbanipal's Elamite Campaign: A Literary and Political Study." Ph.D. Dissertation, University of Pennsylvania.

GIORGIERI, M., and I. RÖSELER
1996 "Notes on the Mittani Letter." Pp. 281–284 in *Richard F. S. Starr Memorial Volume*. Ed. by D. I. Owen and G. Wilhelm. SCCNH 8. Bethesda, MD: CDL Press.

GLOCK, A. E.
1983 "Texts and Archaeology at Tell Taʿannek." *Berytus* 31:57–66.

GOREN, Y., I. FINKELSTEIN, and N. NAʾAMAN
2004 *Inscribed in Clay. Provenance Study of the Amarna Letters and Other Ancient Near Eastern Texts*. Tel Aviv University Sonia and Marco Nadler Institute of Archaeology Monograph Series 23. Tel Aviv: Emery and Claire Yass Publications in Archaeology.

Grayson, A. K.
1975 *ABC*. Reprint Eisenbrauns, 2000.
1991a "Assyria: Sennacherib and Esarhaddon (704–669 B.C.)." Pp. 103–141 in *The Assyrian and Babylonian Empires and other States of the Near East from the Eighth to the Sixth Centuries B.C.*, edited by John Boardman, et al. Vol. 3/2 of Cambridge Ancient History. 2nd edition. Cambridge: Cambridge University Press.
1991b "Assyria 668–635 B.C.: The Reign of Ashurbanipal." Pp. 142–161 in *Assyrian and Babylonian Empires and Other States of the Near East from the Eighth through the Sixth Centuries B.C.*, edited by John Boardman, et al. Vol. 3/2 of Cambridge Ancient History. 2nd edition. Cambridge: Cambridge University Press.

Green, A. R.
2004 "Esarhaddon, Sandaurri, and the Adon Papyrus." Pp. 88–97 in *Inspired Speech: Prophecy in the Ancient Near East, Essays in Honor of Herbert B. Huffmon*. Edited by J. Kaltner and L. Stulman. JSOTSup 378. London and New York: T&T Clark International.

Greenwood, K.
2006 "EA 1: Amenhotep III Rebuts Kadashman-Enlil II." Pp. 186–191 in *The Ancient Near East: Historical Sources in Translation*. Ed. by Mark W. Chavalas. Malden, Oxford, and Carlton: Blackwell.

Guichard, M.
1994 "Au pays de la Dame de Nagar." Pp. 235–274 in *Recueil d'études à la mémoire de Maurice Birot*. Florilegium Marianum 2. Ed. by D. Charpin and J.-M. Durand. Paris: Éditions Recherche sur les Civilisations.
1999 "Les aspects religieux de la guerre à Mari." *RA* 93:27–49.
2002 "Le Šubartum occidental à l'avènement de Zimrî-Lîm." Pp. 119–168 in *Recueil d'études à la mémoire d'Andre Parrot*. Florilegium Marianum 6. Ed. by D. Charpin and J.-M. Durand. Paris: SEOPA.
2003 "Lecture des *Archives royales de Mari*, Tome XXVIII: lettres royales du temps de Zimrî-Lîm." *Syria* 80:199–216.
2004a "'La malediction de cette tablette est très dure!' Sur l'ambassade d'Itûr-Asdû à Babylone en l'an 4 de Zimrî-Lîm." *RA* 98:13–32.
2004b "La lapidation à Urgiš." *NABU* no. 29.
2011 "Un David raté ou une histoire de *habiru* à l'époque amorrite: Vie et mort de Samsī-Ērah, chef de guerre et homme du peuple." Pp. 29–93 in *Le jeune héros: Recherches sur la formation et la diffusion d'un thème littéraire au Proche-Orient ancien*. OBO 250. Ed. by J.-M. Durand, et al. Göttingen: Vandenhoeck & Ruprecht.
2014a *L'Épopée de Zimrī-Lîm*. Florilegium Marianium 14. Paris: SEPOA.
2014b "Nouvelles données sur Zalluhān, un petit royaume des bords du Habur d'après les archive de Mari." Pp. 77–108 in *D'Aššur à Mari et au-delà: Entre les fleuves II*. BBVO 24. Ed. by N. Ziegler and E. Cancik-Kirschbaum. Gladbeck: Pewe-Verlag.

Guichard, M. and N. Ziegler
2004 "Yanûh-Samar et les Ekallâtéens en détresse." Pp. 229–248 in *Assyria and Beyond: Studies Presented to Mogens Trolle Larsen*. Ed. by J. G. Dercksen. Leiden: Nederlands Instituut voor het Nabije Oosten.

Gustavs, A.
1927 "Die Personennamen in den Tontafeln von Tell Taʿannek." *ZDPV* 50:1–18.
1928 "Die Personennamen in den Tontafeln von Tell Taʿannek." *ZDPV* 51:169–218.

Hallo, W. W.
1983 "Cult Statue and Divine Image: A Preliminary Study." Pp. 1–17 in *SIC* 1.
1988 "Texts, Statues, and the Cult of the Divine King." *VTSup* 40:54–66.

Halpern, B., and J. Huehnergard
1982 "El-Amarna Letter 252." *Or* 51:227–230.

Hämeen-Anttila, J.
2000 *A Sketch of Neo-Assyrian Grammar*. SAAS 13. Helsinki: The Neo-Assyrian Text Corpus Project.

Harper, R. F.
1913 No. 1239 in *Assyrian and Babylonian Letters Belonging to the Koyunjik Collection of the British Museum*, Part 12. Chicago: University of Chicago.

Harrison, T. and J. Osborne
2012 "Building XVI and the Neo-Assyrian Sacred Precinct at Tell Tayinat." *JCS* 64:125–143.

Harrison, T., et al.
1987 *Harrison's Principles of Internal Medicine*. 11th Edition. New York: McGraw-Hill.

Haussperger, M.
2001 "Krankheiten von Galle und Leber in der altmesopotamischen Medizin anhand des Textes BAM 578." *Würzburger medizinhistorische Mitteilungen* 20:108–122.
2012 *Die mesopotamische Medizin aus ärztlicher Sicht*. Baden-baden: Deutscher-Wissenschafts Verlag.

Hawkins, J. D.
1979 "Some Historical Problems of the Hieroglyphic Luwian Inscriptions." *AnSt* 29:153–167.
2000 *CHLI*.

Hecker, K.
2004 "Der Loyalitätsvertrag der Zakūtu." Pp. 91–93 in *TUAT* 2.

Heeßel, N. P.
2000 *Babylonisch-assyrische Dignostik*. AOAT 43. Münster: Ugarit Verlag.
2010 "Neues von Esagil-kīn-apli. Die ältere Version der physiognomischen Omenserie *alamdimmû*." Pp. 139–187 in *Assur-Forschungen*. Ed. by S.M. Maul and N.P. Heeßel. Wiesbaden: Harrassowitz.
2011 "Akkadische Texte des 2. und 1. Jt. v. Chr. 2: Therapeutische Texte 2.0, 2.3.1–3, 2.4.1–6, 2.17.1–3." Pp. 31–35, 45–61, 153–156 in *TUAT* 5.

Heeßel, N. P. and F. al-Rawi
2003 "Tablets from the Sippar Library XII. A Medical Therapeutic Text." *Iraq* 65:221–239.

Heidel, A.
1956 "A New Hexagonal Prism of Esarhaddon." *Sumer* 12:9–37, pls. 1–12.

Heimpel, W.
2003 *Letters to the King of Mari: A New Translation with Historical Introduction, Notes, and Commentary*. Mesopotamian Civilizations 12. Winona Lake: Eisenbrauns.

Hess, R. S.
1990a "Rhetorical Forms in EA 162." *UF* 22:137–148.
1990b "Splitting the Adam: The Usage of *ʾādām* in Genesis i–v." Pp. 1–15 in *Studies in the Pentateuch*. Ed. by J. A. Emerton. VTSup 41. Leiden: Brill.
1993a *Amarna Personal Names*. ASORDS 9. Winona Lake: Eisenbrauns.
1993b "Smitten Ant Bites Back: Rhetorical Forms in the Amarna Correspondence from Shechem." Pp. 95–111 in *Verse in Ancient Near Eastern Prose*. Ed. by J. C. de Moor and W. G. E. Watson. AOAT 42. Kevelaer: Butzon & Bercker; Neukirchen-Vluyn: Neukirchener.
1996 "Non-Israelite Personal Names in the Book of Joshua." *CBQ* 58:205–214.
1997 "Hurrian and Other Inhabitants of Late Bronze Age Palestine." *Levant* 29:153–156.
1998 "The Mayarzana Correspondence: Rhetoric and Conquest Accounts." *UF* 30:335–351.
2003 "Preliminary Perspectives on Late Bronze Age Culture from the Personal Names in Palestinian Cuneiform Texts." *Dutch Studies of the Near Eastern Languages and Literatures Foundation* 5:35–57.
2006 "Cultural Aspects of Onomastic Distribution throughout Southern Canaan in Light of New Evidence." *UF* 38:353–362.
2007 "Personal Names in Cuneiform Texts from Middle Bronze Age Palestine." Pp. 153–161 in *"He Unfurrowed His Brow and Laughed:" Essays in Honour of Nicolas Wyatt*. Ed. by W. G. E. Watson. AOAT 299. Münster: Ugarit-Verlag.

Hilprecht, H. V.
1896 *Old Babylonian Inscriptions, Chiefly from Nippur, Part II (= BE I/2)*. Philadelphia: University of Pennsylvania.

Holloway, S.
2007 "Review of E. Otto, *Das Deuteronomium: Politische Theologie und Rechtsreform in Juda und Assyrien*, BZAW 284 (Berlin/New York: Walter de Gruyter, 1999)." *JNES* 66: 204–208.

Holter, K.
1995 *Second Isaiah's Idol-Fabrication Passages*. BBET 28. Frankfurt am Main: Peter Lang.

Horowitz, W.
1994 "Trouble in Canaan – A Letter of the el-Amarna Period on a Clay Cylinder from Beth-Shean." *Qad* 27:84–86 (Hebrew).
1996 "An Inscribed Clay Cylinder from Amarna Age Beth Shean." *IEJ* 46:208–218.
1997 "The Amarna Age Inscribed Clay Cylinder from Beth-Shean." *BA* 60:97–100.
2000 "Two Late Bronze Age Tablets from Hazor." *IEJ* 50:16–28.

Horowitz, W., and T. Oshima
2010 "Ḥaṣor: A Cuneiform City in Canaan, A Retrospective and Look Forward." Pp. 483–490 in *Proceedings of the 6th International Congress on the Archaeology of the Ancient Near East, 5 May–10 May 2009, "Spienza," Università di Roma, Volume 3, Islamic Session, Poster Session, The Ceremonial Precinct of Canaanite Hazor*. Ed. by P. Matthiae, F. Pinnock, et al. Wiesbaden: Harrassowitz.

Horowitz, W., T. Oshima, and S. Sanders
2006 *Cuneiform in Canaan: Cuneiform Sources from the Land of Israel in Ancient Times*. Jerusalem: Israel Exploration Society and the Hebrew University of Jerusalem.

Horowitz, W., T. Oshima, and F. Vukosavović
2012 "Hazor 18: Fragments of a Cuneiform Law Collection from Hazor." *IEJ* 62:158–176.

Horowitz, W. and A. Shaffer
1992 "A Fragment of a Letter from Hazor." *IEJ* 42:165–166.

Horowitz, W. and N. Wasserman
2000 "An Old Babylonian Letter from Hazor with Mention of Mari and Ekallātum." *IEJ* 50:169–174.
2004 "From Hazor to Mari and Ekallātum: A Recently Discovered Old-Babylonian Letter from Hazor." *Amurru* 3:335–344.

Hrozný, F.
1904 "Anhang. Keilschrifttexte aus Taʿannek." Pp. 113–122, Tafeln x–xi in Ernst Sellin, *Tell Taʿannek*. Denkschriften der Kaiserlichen Akademie der Wissenschaften in Wien Philosophisch-Historische Klasse Band 50. Vienna: Carl Gerold's Sohn.
1906 "Anhang. Die neugefundenen Keilschrifttexte von Taʿannek." Pp. 36–41, Tafeln i–iii in Ernst Sellin, *III. Eine Nachlese auf dem Tell Taʿannek in Palästina*. Denkschriften der Kaiserlichen Akademie der Wissenschaften in Wien Philosophisch-Historische Klasse Band 52. Vienna: Alfred Hölder.

Hunger, H.
1968 *Babylonische und assyrische Kolophone*. AOAT 2. Kevelaer: Butzon & Bercker.

Hurowitz, V. A.
1989 "Isaiah's Impure Lips and Their Purification in Light of Akkadian Sources." *HUCA* 60:39–89.
2003 "The Mesopotamian God-Image: From Womb to Tomb – Review Article of Christopher Walker and Michael Dick, *The Induction of the Cult Image in Ancient Mesopotamia*." *JAOS* 123:147–157.
2006 "What Goes in is What Comes Out – Materials for Creating Cult Statues." Pp. 3–23 in *Text, Artifact and Image: Revealing Ancient Israelite Religion*. Ed. by G. Beckman and T. J. Lewis. BJS 346. Providence, RI: Brown University Press.
2008 "'Shutting Up' the Enemy – Literary Gleanings from Sargon's Eighth Campaign." Pp. 104–120 in *Treasures on Camels' Humps: Historical and Literary Studies from the Ancient Near East Presented to Israel Ephʿal*. Ed. by M. Cogan and D. Kahn. Jerusalem: Hebrew University Magnes Press.
2009 "A Monument to Imperial Control – Literary Observations on the Thompson Prism of Esarhaddon (Nineveh A)." Pp. 121–165 in *Homeland and Exile: Biblical and Ancient Near Eastern Studies in Honour of Bustenay Oded*. Edited by G. Galil, M. J. Geller, and A. R. Millard. VTSup 130. Leiden: Brill.

Ismail, B. Kh., M. Roaf, and J. Black
1983 "ʿAna in the Cuneiform Sources." *Sumer* 39:191–194.

Jacobsen, T.
1987 "The Graven Image." Pp. 15–32 in *Ancient Israelite Religion: Essays in Honor of Frank Moore Cross*, Ed. by Patrick Miller, Paul D. Hanson, and S. Dean McBride. Philadelphia: Fortress Press.

Jankowska, N. B.
1969 "Communal Self-Government and the King of the State of Arrapḫa." *JESHO* 12:233–282.
Kessler, K.
1980 *Unteruchungen zur historischen Topographie Nordmesopotamiens*. Wiesbaden: Harrassowitz.
Kitchen, K. A. and P. Lawrence
2012 *Treaty, Law, and Covenant in the Ancient Near East*. 3 Parts. Wiesbaden: Harrasowitz.
Knudtzon, J. A.
1915 *Die el-Amarna-Tafeln mit Einleitung und Erläuterungen*. 2 vols. Vorderasiatische Bibliothek 2. Leipzig: Hinrichs. Reprinted, Aalen: Zeller.
Koliński, R.
2001 *Mesopotamian* dimātu *of the Second Millennium* BC. BAR International Series 1004. Oxford: Archaeopress.
2002 "Tell al-Fakhar: A *dimtu*-Settlement or the City of Kurruḫanni?" Pp. 3–39 in *General Studies and Excavations at Nuzi* 10/3. Ed. by D. I. Owen and G. Wilhelm. SCCNH 12. Bethesda, MD: CDL Press.
Koppen, van F.
2002 "Seized by Royal Order: The Households of Sammêtar and other Magnates at Mari." Pp. 289–372 in *Recueil d'études à la mémoire d'Andre Parrot*. Florilegium Marianum 6. Ed. by D. Charpin and J.-M. Durand. Paris: SEPOA.
Kravitz, K. F.
2003 "A Last-Minute Revision to Sargon's Letter to the God." *JNES* 62:81–95.
Kroll, S.
2012 "Sargon II's 8th Campaign: A New View on Old Constructs." Pp. 10–17 in *The Eighth Campaign of Sargon II: Historical Geographical, Literary, and Ideological Aspects*. Ed. by S. Kroll, et al. n.p.: The Hasanlu Translation Project.
Kuntz, T.
1998 "At Harvard, a Political Sex Scandal That's Not News, but Ancient History." *The New York Times*, Sunday, October 18, 1998.
Kupper, J.-R.
1990 "Une lettre du général Yassi-Dagan." *MARI* 6:337–348.
2001 "Les débuts du règne d' Ibâl-Addu." *RA* 95:33–38.
Labat, R.
1959 "Le premier chapitre d' un précis médical assyrien." *RA* 53:1–18.
Laessøe, J.
1951 "The Irrigation System at Ulḫu, 8th Century B.C." *JCS* 5:21–32.
Lafont, B.
1994 "L' admonestation des Anciens de Kurdâ à leur roi (textes nº 117 et nº 118)." Pp. 209–220 in *Recueil d'études à la mémoire de Maurice Birot*. Florilegium Marianum 2. Ed. by Charpin and J.-M. Durand. Paris: Éditions Recherche sur les Civilisations.
2001 "Relations internationales, alliances et diplomatie au temps de royaumes amorrites." Pp. 213–328 in *Amurru II: Mari, Ébla et les Hourrites dix ans de travaux*. Ed. by J.-M. Durand and D. Charpin. Paris: Éditions Recherche sur les Civilisations.
Lambert, W. G.
1960a *Babylonian Wisdom Literature*. Oxford: Oxford University.
1960b "Gilgameš in Religious, Historical and Omen Texts and the Historicity of Gilgameš." Pp. 39–56 in *Gilgameš et sa Legende*. Edited by P. Garelli. RAI 7. Paris: Imprimerie Nationale.
Lamprichs, R.
1995 *Die Westexpansion des neuassyrischen Reiches. Eine Strukturanalyse*. AOAT 239. Neukirchen-Vluyn: Verlag Butzon & Bercker Kevelaer.
Landsberger, B.
1942 "Lexikalisches Archiv." *ZA* 34:152–169.
Lanfranchi, G. B.
1995 "Assyrian Geography and Neo-Assyrian Letters. The Location of Ḫubuškia Again." Pp. 127–137 in *NAG*.
Lauinger, J.
2011 "Some Preliminary Thoughts on the Tablet Collection in Building XVI from Tell Tayinat." *JCSMS* 6:5–14.
2012 "Esarhaddon's Succession Treaty at Tell Tayinat: Text and Commentary." *JCS* 64:87–123.
Leichty, E.
1991 "Esarhaddon's 'Letter to the Gods.'" Pp. 52–57 in *Studies Tadmor*.
1995 "Esarhaddon, king of Assyria." Pp. 949–958 in *CANE*.
2008 "Esarhaddon's Eastern Campaign." Pp. 183–187 in *Treasures on Camel's Humps: Historical and Literary Studies from the Ancient Near East Presented to Israel Eph'al*. Edited by M. Cogan and D. Kahn. Jerusalem: The Hebrew University Magnes Press.
2011 RINAP 4.
Levine, L. D.
1977 "Sargon's Eighth Campaign." Pp. 135–151 in *Mountains and Lowlands: Essays in the Archaeology of Greater Mesopotamia*. Ed. by L. D. Levine and T. C. Young, Jr. Bibliotheca Mesopotamica 7. Malibu: Undena Publications.
2003 "Observations on 'Sargon's Letter to the Gods.'" *Eretz-Israel* 27:111*–119*.
Levinson, B.
2010 "Esarhaddon's Succession Treaty as the Source for the Canon Formula in Deuteronomy 13:1." *JAOS* 130:337–347.
Levtow, N. B.
2008 *Images of Others: Iconic Politics in Ancient Israel*. Ed. by William H. C. Propp. Vol. 11, Biblical and Judaic Studies. Winona Lake, IN: Eisenbrauns.
Lewy, H.
1942 "The Nuzian Feudal System." *Or* 11:1–40; 209–250; 297–349.
1952 "Nitokris-Naqî'a." *JNES* 11:264–286.
Liebig, M.
1991 "Zur Lage einiger im Bericht über den 8. Felzug Sargons II. von Assyrien genannter Gebiete." *ZA* 81:31–36.

LION, B.
1999a "Les archives privées d'Arrapha et de Nuzi." Pp. 35–62 in *Nuzi at Seventy-Five*. Ed. by D. I. Owen and G. Wilhelm. SCCNH 10. Bethesda, MD: CDL Press.
1999b "L'*andurāru* à l'époque médio-babylonienne, d'après les documents de Terqa, Nuzi et Arrapḫa." Pp. 313–327 in *Nuzi at Seventy-Five*. Ed. by D. I. Owen and G. Wilhelm. SCCNH 10. Bethesda, MD: CDL Press.
2001 "Les gouverneurs provinciaux du royaume de Mari à l'époque de Zimrî-Lîm." Pp. 141–209 in *Amurru II: Mari, Ébla et les Hourrites dix ans de travaux*. Ed. by J.-M. Durand and D. Charpin. Paris: Éditions Recherche sur les Civilisations.
2010 "Les fortifications de Nuzi d'après une tablette du Louvre." Pp. 203–216 in *Festschrift für Gernot Wilhelm anläßlich seines 65. Geburtstages am 28 Januar 2010*. Ed. by J. C. Fincke. Dresden: ISLET.

LION, B., and D. STEIN
In press *The Tablets from the Temple Precinct at Nuzi*. Ed. by E. von Dassow. HSS LXV. Bethesda, MD: CDL Press.

LIPIŃKSI, E.
1999 "Ba'alu." *PNA* 1/2:242–243.
2000 *The Aramaeans: Their Ancient History, Culture, Religion*. OLA 100. Leuven/Paris/Sterling, VA: Peeters.

LIVERANI, M.
2004 "Aziru, the Servant of Two Masters." Pp. 125–144 in *Myth and Politics in Ancient Near Eastern Historiography*. Ed. by Z. Bahrani and M. Van De Mieroop. Ithaca: Cornell University Press.

LUCKENBILL, D. D.
1927 *ARAB* 2:73–100.

LUUKKO, M.
2004 *Grammatical Variation in Neo-Assyrian*. SAAS 16. Helsinki: Neo-Assyrian Text Corpus Project of the University of Helsinki.
2007 "How Could the Assyrian King Enter Babylon Conciliatorily?" NABU no. 71.
2012 *The Correspondence of Tiglath-Pileser III and Sargon II from Calah*. SAA 19. Helsinki: Helsinki University Press.

MACHINIST, P.
2003 "The Voice of the Historian in the Ancient Near Eastern and Mediterranean World." *Interpretation* 57:117–136.

MAIDMAN, M. P.
1994 *Two Hundred Nuzi Texts from the Oriental Institute of the University of Chicago*. SCCNH 6. Ed. by D. I. Owen. Bethesda, MD: CDL Press.
2010 *Nuzi Texts and Their Uses as Historical Evidence*. SBLWAW 18. Atlanta: Society of Biblical Literature.
2011 "Nuzi, the Club of Great Powers, and the Chronology of the Fourteenth Century." *Kaskal* 8:77–139.

MARCUS, M. I.
1987 "Geography as an Organizing Principle in the Imperial Art of Shalmaneser III." *Iraq* 49:77–90.

MAYER, W.
1979 "Die Finanzierung einer Kampagne (TCL 3, 346–410)." *UF* 11:571–595.
1983 "Sargons Feldzug gegen Urartu – 714 v. Chr.: Text und Übersetzung." *MDOG* 115:65–132.

MAYRHOFER, M.
2006 "Eine Nachlese zu den indo-arischen Sprachresten des Mittanni-Bereichs." *Anzeiger der philosophisch-historishen Klasse* (Österreichische Akademie der Wissenschaften, Wien) 141/2:83–101.

MCCARTHY, D.
1981 *Treaty and Covenant*. AnBib 21. Rome: Biblical Institute.

MEDVEDSKAYA, I.
1997 "The Localization of Hubuškia." Pp. 197–206 in *Assyria 1995. Proceedings of the 10th Anniversary Symposium of the Neo-Assyrian Text Corpus Project Helsinki, September 7–11, 1995*. Edited by S. Parpola and R. M. Whiting. Helsinki: The Neo-Assyrian Text Corpus Project.

MEIER, G.
1937–1939 "Die Ritualtafel der Serie 'Mundwaschung.'" *AfO* 12:40–45.

MEISSNER, B.
1914–1915 "Review of Harper 1913." *ZA* 29:216–222.
1922 "Die Eroberung der Stadt Ulḫu auf Sargons 8. Feldzug." *ZA* 34:113–122.

MELVILLE, S. C.
1999 *The Role of Naqia/Zakutu in Sargonid Politics*. *SAAS* 9. Helsinki: Neo-Assyrian Text Corpus Project.
2006 "Ashurbanipal." Pp. 360–368 in *The Ancient Near East: Historical Sources in Translation*. Edited by M. W. Chavalas. Oxford: Blackwell.

METTINGER, T. N. D.
1995 *No Graven Image? Israelite Aniconism in Its Ancient Near Eastern Context*. Coniectanea Biblica, OT Series 42. Stockholm: Almqvist & Wiksell International.

MIGLIO, A. E.
2014 *Tribe and State: The Dynamics of International Politics and the Reign of Zimri-Lim*. Gorgias Studies in the Ancient Near East 8. Piscataway: Gorgias.

MILLARD, A. R.
1970 "Fragments of Historical Texts from Nineveh: Middle Assyrian and Later Kings." *Iraq* 32:167–176.
1990 "The Homeland of Zakkur." *Semitica* 39:47–52.
1994 *The Eponyms of the Assyrian Empire 910–612 BC*. SAAS 2. Helsinki: Neo-Assyrian Text Corpus Project.

MORAN, W.
1991 "Assurbanipal's Message to the Babylonians (*ABL* 301), with an Excursus on Figurative *Biltu*." Pp. 320–331 in *Ah, Assyria ... Studies in Assyrian History and Ancient Near Eastern Historiography Presented to Hayim Tadmor*. Ed. by M. Cogan and I. Eph'al. Jerusalem: Magnes Press.
1992 *The Amarna Letters*. Baltimore: Johns Hopkins University.

MÜLLER, M.
1968 Die Erlässe und Instruktionen aus dem Lande Arrapḫa: Ein Beitrag zur Rechtsgeschichte des Alten Vorderen Orients. Unpublished Dissertation, University of Leipzig.

Muscarella, O. W.
1986 "The Location of Ulhu and Uiše in Sargon II's Eighth Campaign." *JFA* 13:465–475.
2012 "Sargon II's 8th Campaign: An Introduction and Overview." Pp. 5–9 in *The Eighth Campaign of Sargon II: Historical Geographical, Literary, and Ideological Aspects*. Ed. by S. Kroll, et al. n.p.: The Hasanlu Translation Project.
Na'aman, N.
2004 "The *ṣuḫāru* in Second-Millennium BCE Letters from Canaan." *IEJ* 54:92–99.
Northedge, A. *et al.*
1988 *Excavations at 'Āna*. Warminster: Aris & Phillips.
Niederreiter, Z.
2005 "L' insigne du pouvoir et le sceau du Grand Vizir Sîn-aḫ-uṣur (les symboles personnels d' un haut- dignitaire de Sargon II)." *RA* 99:57–76.
Nissinen, M.
1998 *References to Prophecy in Neo-Assyrian Sources*. SAAS 7. Helsinki: The Neo-Assyrian Text Corpus Project.
2003 *Prophets and Prophecy in the Ancient Near East*. SBLWAW 12. Atlanta: Society of Biblical Literature.
Noth, M.
1961 "Der historische Hintergrund der Inschriften von Sefire." *ZDPV* 77:118–172.
Novák, M.
1999 "The Architecture of Nuzi and Its Significance in the Architectural History of Mesopotamia." Pp. 123–240 in *Nuzi at Seventy-Five*. Ed. by D. I. Owen and G. Wilhelm. SCCNH 10. Bethesda, MD: CDL Press.
O'Connor, M.
1989 "Semitic **mgn* and Its Supposed Sanskrit Origin." *JAOS* 109:25–32.
Onasch, H.
1994 *Die assyrischen Eroberungen Ägyptens*. ÄAT 27. Wiesbaden: Harrasowitz.
Oppenheim, A. L.
1967 *Letters from Mesopotamia*. Chicago: The University of Chicago Press.
1960 "The City of Assur in 714 B.C." *JNES* 19:133–147.
Pardee, D.
2005 "On Psalm 29: Structure and Meaning." Pp. 152–182 in *Psalm 29: Composition and Reception*. Ed. by P. W. Flint and P. D. Miller. Leiden: Brill.
Parpola, S.
1970 *Letters from Assyrian Scholars to the Kings Esarhaddon and Ashurbanipal*. 2 Volumes. AOAT 5. Kevelaer and Neukirchen-Vluyn: Butzon & Bercker and Neukirchener.
1983 *Letters from Assyrian Scholars to Kings Esarhaddon and Assurbanipal*, Part 2: *Commentary and Appendices*. AOAT 5/2. Kevelaer/Neukirchen-Vluyn: Butzon & Bercker/Neukirchener.
1987 "Neo-Assyrian Treaties from the Royal Archives of Nineveh." *JCS* 39:161–189.
1990 "A Letter from Marduk-apla-uṣur of Anah to Rudamu/Urtamis, King of Hamath." Pp. 257–265 in *Hama II/2. Les objets de la période dite Syro-Hittite*. Edited by P. J. Riis and M.-L. Buhl. Hama 2/2. Copenhagen: Fondation Carlsberg.
2004 "Desperately Trying to Talk Sense: A Letter of Assurbanipal Concerning his Brother Šamaš-šumu-ukin." Pp. 227–234 in *From the Upper Sea to the Lower Sea: Studies on the History of Assyria and Babylonia in Honour of A. K. Grayson*. Edited by G. Frame. PIHANS 101. Leiden: Nederlands Instituut voor het Nabije Oosten.
Parpola, S. and K. Watanabe
1988 *Neo-Assyrian Treaties and Loyalty Oaths*. SAA 2. Helsinki: Helsinki University Press.
Pedersén, O.
1986 *Archives and Libraries in the City of Assur*, part II. Uppsala: University of Uppsala.
Peiser, F.
1898 "Studien zur orientalischen Altertumskunde." *MVAG* 3:227–271.
Pfeiffer, R. H.
1935 *State Letters of Assyria*. AOS 6. New Haven: American Oriental Society.
Podany, A.
2010 *Brotherhood of Kings: How International Relations Shaped the Ancient Near East*. Oxford: Oxford University Press.
Pomponio, F.
1990 *Formule di maledizione della Mesopotamia preclassica*. Brescia: Paideia.
Ponchia, S.
2002 "Mountain Routes in Assyrian Royal Inscriptions, Part II." *SAAB* 15:193–271.
Pongratz-Leisten, B.
1994 *Ina šulmi īrub: Eine kulttopographische und ideologiosche Programmatik der Akītu-Prozession in Babylonien und Assyrien im I. Jahrtausend v. Chr*. Mainz am Rhein: Phillip von Zabern.
Porada, E.
1947 *Seal Impressions of Nuzi*. Ed. by M. Burrows and E. A. Speiser. AASOR 24. New Haven: American Schools of Oriental Research.
Porter, B. N.
1993 *Images, Power, and Politics – Figurative Aspects of Esarhaddon's Babylonian Policy*. Memoirs of the American Philosophical Society Held at Philadelphia for Promoting Useful Knowledge 208. Philadelphia: American Philosophical Society.
Potts, D. T.
1997 *Mesopotamian Civilization. The Material Foundations*. London: The Athlone Press.
1999 *The Archaeology of Elam: Formation and Transformation of an Ancient Iranian State*. Cambridge World Archaeology. New York: Cambridge University Press.
Powell, M. A.
1987–1990 "Maße und Gewichte." *RlA* 7:457–517.
1991 "Epistemology and Sumerian Agriculture: The Strange Case of Sesame and Linseed." Pp. 155–164 in *Velles Paraules: Ancient Near Eastern Studies in Honor of Miguel Civil*. Ed. by P. Michalowski, et al. AuOrSup 9. Sabadell: Ausa.

Radner, K.
1997 *Die Neuassyrischen Privatrechtsurkunden*. SAAS 6. Helsinki: Neo-Assyrian Text Corpus Project of the University of Helsinki.
2004 "Salmanassar V. in den *Nimrud Letters*." *AfO* 50:95–104.
2006 Assyrische *ṭuppi adê* als Vorbild für Deuteronomium 28, 20–44? Pp. 351–378 in *Die deuteronomistischen Geschichtswerke: Redaktions- und religionsgeschichtliche Perspektiven zur "Deuteronomismus" – Diskussion in Tora und Vorderen Propheten*. Ed. by M. Witte, K. Schmid, D. Prechel, and J. C. Gertz. BZAW 365. Berlin/New York: Walter de Gruyter.
2006 "Briefe aus der Korrespondenz der neuassyrischen Könige." Pp. 116–157 in *TUAT*.
2007 "Esarhaddon, king of Assyria (681–669)." *Knowledge and Power*, Higher Education Academy Subject Centre for Philosophical and Religious Studies, knp.prs.heacademy.ac.uk/essentials/esarhaddon/.
2011 "Assurbanipal, King of Assyria (669–c. 630)." Higher Education Academy Subject Centre for Philosophical and Religious Studies, (n.p. [cited 29 January 2011]). Online: http://knp.prs.heacademy.ac.uk/essentials/assurbanipal/.
2012 "Between a Rock and a Hard Place: Muṣaṣir, Kumme, Ukku and Šubria – The Buffer States Between Assyria and Urarṭu." Pp. 243–262 in *Biainili-Urartu: The Proceedings of the Symposium Held in Munich 12–14 October 2007 (Tagungsbericht des Münchner Symposiums 12.–14. Oktober 2007)*. Ed. by S. Kroll, C. Gruber, U. Hellwag, M. Roaf, and P. E. Zimansky. Acta Iranica 51. Leuven: Peeters.

Rainey, A. F.
1977 "Verbal Usages in the Taanach Texts." *IOS* 7:33–64.
1993 "Manasseh, King of Judah, in the Whirlpool of the Seventh Century B.C.E." Pp. 147–164 in *Studies Kutscher*.
1996 *Canaanite in the Amarna Tablets: A Linguistic Analysis of the Mixed Dialect Used by the Scribes from Canaan*. 4 volumes. HdO 25. Leiden: Brill.
1998 "Syntax, Hermeneutics and History." *IEJ* 48: 239–251.
1999 "Taanach Letters." *ErIs* 26:153*–162*.
2015 *The El-Amarna Correspondence. A New Edition of the Cuneiform Letters from the Site of El-Amarna based on Collations of all Extant Tablets*. Edited by W. Schniedewind and Z. Cochavi-Rainey. HdO 110. Leiden and Boston: Brill.

Rainey, A. F., and S. Notley
2006 *The Sacred Bridge: Carta's Atlas of the Biblical World*. Jerusalem: Carta.

Reade, J.
1986 "Archaeology and the Kuyunjik Archives." Pp. 213–222 in *Cuneiform Archives and Libraries*. Ed. by K. Veenhof. PIHANS 57. Leiden: Nederlands Instituut voor het Nabije Oosten.
1995 "Iran in the Neo-Assyrian Period." Pp. 31–42 in *NAG*.
1998 "Assyrian Eponyms, Kings and Pretenders, 648–605 BC." *Or* 67:255–265.

Reiner, E.
1969 ANET.
1995 *Astral Magic in Babylonia*. Philadelphia: American Philosophical Society.

Renger, J.
1981 "Kultbild. A. Philologisch (in Mesopotamien)." *RlA* 6:307–314.

Richter, T.
2012 *Bibliographisches Glossar des Hurritischen*. Wiesbaden: Harrassowitz.

Roaf, M.
2012 "Could Rusa Son of Erimena Have Been King of Urartu During Sargon's Eighth Campaign?" Pp. 217–252 in *Biainili-Urartu: The Proceedings of the Symposium Held in Munich 12–14 October 2007 (Tagungsbericht des Münchner Symposiums 12.–14. Oktober 2007)*. Edited by S. Kroll, C. Gruber, U. Hellwag, M. Roaf, and P. E. Zimansky. Acta Iranica 51. Leuven: Peeters.

Rogers, J. H.
1998 "Origins of the Ancient Constellations. I: The Mesopotamian Traditions." *Journal of the British Astronomical Association* 108/1:9–28.

Roth, M.
1997 *Law Collections from Mesopotamia and Asia Minor*. 2nd Edition. SBLWAW 6. Atlanta: Scholars.

Saggs, H. W. F
1955 "The Nimrud Letters, 1952 – Part I." *Iraq* 17:21–56.
2001 *The Nimrud Letters, 1952*. CTN 5. London: British School of Archaeology in Iraq.

Sallaberger, W., B. Einwag, and A. Otto.
2006 "Schenkungen von Mittani-Königen an die Einwohner von Baṣīru. Die zwei Urkunden aus Tall Bazi am Mittleren Euphrat." *ZA* 96:69–104.

Salvini, M.
1993–1997 "Muṣaṣir. A. Historisch." *RlA* 8:444–446.
1995a *Geschichte und Kultur der Urartäer*. Darmstadt: Wissenschaftliche Buchgesellschaft.
1995b "Some Historic-Geographical Problems Concerning Assyria and Urartu." Pp. 43–53 in *NAG*.

Sasson, J. M.
2013 "'It is for this Reason that I have not Come Down to my Lord …' Visit Obligations and Vassal Pretexts in the Mari Archives." *RA* 107:119–129.

Sayce, A. H.
1893 "The Cuneiform and Other Inscriptions Found at Lachish and Elsewhere in the South of Palestine." *PEQ* 25:25–32.

Schroeder, O.
1922 *Keilschrifttexte aus Assur historischen Inhalts*, II. Berlin (= WVDOG 27).

Schützinger, H.
1984 "Bild und Wesen der Gottheit im alten Mesopotamien." Pp. 61–80 in *Götterbild in Kunst und Schrift*. Ed. by H.-J. Klimkeit. Bonn: Bouvier Verlag Herbert Grundmann.

Schwemer, D.
2007 *Abwehrzauber und Behexung: Studien zum Schadenzauber-glauben im alten Mesopotamien*. Wiesbaden: Harrassowitz.
2011 "Akkadische Texte des 2. und 1. Jt. v. Chr. 2: Therapeutische Texte 2.1.1–2, 2.2.1–2, 2.13–14." Pp. 35–45, 115–135 in *TUAT* 5.

Scurlock, J. A.
1988 "Magical Means of Dealing with Ghosts in Ancient Mesopotamia." PhD Dissertation: University of Chicago.
1999 "Physician, Conjurer, Magician: A Tale of Two Healing Professionals." Pp. 69–79 in *Mesopotamian Magic: Textual, Historical and Interpretive Perspectives*. Ed. by T. Abusch and K. van der Toorn. Ancient Magic and Divination 1. Groningen: Styx.
2005–2006 "Sorcery in the Stars: STT 300, BRM 4.19–20 and the Mandaic Book of the Zodiac." *AfO* 51:125–146.
2006a *Magico-Medical Means of Treating Ghost-Induced Illnesses in Ancient Mesopotamia*. Ancient Magic and Divination 3. Leiden: Brill.
2006b "The Techniques of the Sacrifice of Animals in Ancient Israel and Ancient Mesopotamia: New Insights Through Comparison, Part I." *AUSS* 44:13–49.
2014 *Sourcebook for Ancient Mesopotamian Medicine*. SBLWAW 36. Atlanta: Society for Biblical Literature.

Scurlock, J. A. and F. al-Rawi
2006 "A Weakness for Hellenism." Pp. 357–382 in *If a Man Builds a Joyful House* (Festschrift Leichty). Ed. by A. Guinan, et al. Leiden: Styx/Brill.

Scurlock, J. A., and B. R. Andersen
2005 *Diagnoses in Assyrian and Babylonian Medicine: Ancient Sources, Translations, and Modern Medical Analyses*. Urbana and Chicago: University of Illinois.

Smith, M. S.
2008 *God in Translation: Deities in Cross-Cultural Discourse in the Biblical World*. Tübingen: Mohr Siebeck.

Smith, S.
1925 "The Babylonian Ritual for the Consecration and Induction of a Divine Statue." *JRAS* 57:37–60.

Spalinger, A.
1974 "Assurbanipal and Egypt: A Source Study." *JAOS* 94:316–328.

Speiser, E. A.
1929 "A Letter of Saushshatar and the Date of the Kirkuk Tablets." *JAOS* 49:269–275.
1951 "Ancient Mesopotamia: A Light That Did Not Fail." The *National Geographic Magazine*, 99/1 (January–June 1951): 41–104.

Stadhouders, H.
2011 "The Pharmacopoeial Handbook *Šammu šikinšu*–An Edition." *Le Journal des Médecines Cunéiformes* 18:3–51.
2012 "The Pharmacopoeial Handbook *Šammu šikinšu*–A Translation." *Le Journal des Médecines Cunéiformes* 19:1–22.

Starr, R. F. S.
1937–1939 *Nuzi. Report on the Excavations at Yorgan Tepa near Kirkuk, Iraq*. 2 Vols. Cambridge, MA: Harvard University Press.

Stein, D.
1989 "A Reappraisal of the 'Sauštatar Letter' from Nuzi." *ZA* 79:36–60.
1993 *Das Archiv des Šilwa-teššup*. Vols. 8–9: *The Seal Impressions*. Wiesbaden: Harrassowitz.
1997 "Nuzi." Pp. 4:171–175 in *OEANE*.
2010 "The Nuzi Elite: Iconography of Power and Prestige." Pp. 355–367 in *Festschrift für Gernot Wilhelm anläßlich seines 65. Geburtstages am 28 Januar 2010*. Ed. by J. C. Fincke. Dresden: ISLET.

Stol, M.
1993 *Epilepsy in Babylonia*. Cuneiform Monographs 2. Groningen: Styx.

Streck, M. P.
2013 "Śimaʕ-ʔila-ʕanê(m), 'Listen, o god, to the humble.'" *Babel und Bibel* 7:291–298.

Streck, M.
1916 *Assurbanipal und die letzten assyrischen Könige bis zum Untergange Nineveh's*. 3 Volumes. VAB 7. Leipzig: J. C. Hinrichs'sche.

Tadmor, H.
1981 "History and Ideology in the Assyrian Royal Inscriptions." Pp. 13–33 in *ARINH*.
1982 "Treaty and Oath in the Ancient Near East." Pp. 127–152 in *Humanizing America's Iconic Book: Society of Biblical Literature Centennial Addresses*. Ed. by D. Knight and G. Tucker. Chico, CA: Scholars.
1983 "Autobiographical Apology in the Royal Assyrian Literature." Pp. 36–57 in *HHI*.
1994 *The inscriptions of Tiglath-pileser III, King of Assyria*. Jerusalem: The Israel Academy of Sciences and Humanities.
1999 "World Dominion: The Expanding Horizon of the Assyrian Empire." Pp. 55–62 in *Landscapes – Territories, Frontiers and Horizons in the Ancient Near East. Papers Presented to the XLIV Rencontre Assyriolgique Internationale, Venezia 7–11 July 1997*. Edited by L. Milano, S. de Martino, F. M. Fales, and G. B. Lanfranchi. HANE Monographs 3/1. Padova: Sargon.
2004 "An Assyrian Victory Chant and Related Matters." Pp. 269–276 in *From the Upper Sea to the Lower Sea: Studies on the History of Assyria and Babylonia in Honour of A. K. Grayson*. Edited by G. Frame and L. Wilding. Leiden: Nederlands Instituut voor het Nabije Oosten.
2006 *Assyria, Babylonia and Judah: Studies in the History of the Ancient Near East*. Edited by M. Cogan. Jerusalem: The Bialik Institute; The Israel Exploration Society. (in Hebrew).

Thompson, R.
1931 *The Prisms of Esarhaddon and Assurbanipal found at Nineveh 1927–1928*. London: The British Museum.

Thureau-Dangin, F.
1912 *Une relation de la huitième campagne de Sargon (714 av. J.-C.)*. Paris: Paul Geuthner.
1921 *Rituels accadiens*. Reprinted 1975. Osnabrück: Otto Zellar.

Tropper, J. and J.-P. Vita
2010 *Das Kanaano-Akkadische der Amarnazeit*. Lehrbücher orientalischer Sprachen Section I: Cuneiform Languages Volume 1. Münster: Ugarit-Verlag.

Tsukimoto, A.
1999 "By the Hand of Madi-Dagan, the Scribe and Apkallu-priest – A Medical Text from the Middle Euphrates Region." Pp. 187–200 in *Priests and Officials in the Ancient Near East*. Ed. by K. Watanabe. Heidelberg: C. Winter.

Van De Mieroop, M.
2010 "A Study in Contrast: Sargon of Assyria and Rusa of Urartu." Pp. 417–434 in *Opening the Tablet Box: Near Easter Studies in Honor of Benjamin Foster*. Ed. by S. C. Melville and A. L. Slotsky. CHANE 42. Leiden and Boston: Brill.

Van der Westhuizen, J. P.
2012 "An Egypt Amarna Letter (EA 162) and Word Order Variations of the Verbal Sentence." Journal of Semitics 21.2:374–415.
Van Loon, M. N.
1966 *Urartian Art. Its Distinctive Traits in the Light of New Excavations*, Leiden: Nederlands Instituut voor het Nabije Oosten.
Vera Chamaza, G. W.
1992 "Syntactical and Stylistical Observations on the Text of the VIIIth Campaign of Sargon II (TCL 3)." *SAAB* 6:109–128.
1994 "Der VIII. Feldzug Sargons II. Eine Untersuchung zu Politik und historischer Geographie des späten 8. Jhs. v. Chr. (Teil I)." *AMI* 26:91–118.
1995–1996 "Der VIII. Feldzug Sargons II. Eine Untersuchung zu Politik und historischer Geographie des späten 8. Jhs. v. Chr. (Teil II)." *AMI* 28:235–267.
2005 *Die Rolle Moabs in der neuassyrischen Expansionspolitik*. AOAT 321. Münster: Ugarit Verlag.
Villard, P.
1994 "Nomination d' un Scheich." Pp. 291–298 in *Recueil d' études à la mémoire de Maurice Birot*. Florilegium Marianum 2. Ed. by D. Charpin and J.-M. Durand. Paris: Éditions Recherche sur les Civilisations.
von Dassow, E.
2006 "EA 74: Rib-Hadda, Mayor of Gubla, to Amenhotep III, King of Egypt." Pp. 203–205 in *The Ancient Near East: Historical Sources in Translation*. Ed. by M. W. Chavalas. Oxford: Blackwell.
2014 "Levantine Polities under Mittanian Hegemony." Pp. 11–32 in *Constituent, Confederate, and Conquered Space: The Emergence of the Mittani State*. Ed. by N. Brisch, E. Cancik-Kirschbaum, and J. Eidem. Topoi: Berlin Studies of the Ancient World 17. Berlin: de Gruyter.
In press. "Alalaḫ and Nuzi in the Late Second Millennium." Ch. 4.5 in *A Handbook of Ancient Mesopotamia*. Ed. by G. Rubio. Berlin: de Gruyter.
von Soden, W.
1936 "Bemerkungen zu den von Ebeling in 'Tod und Leben' Band I bearbeiteten Texten." *ZA* 43:251–276.
1972 "Sanherib vor Jerusalem 701 v. Chr." Pp. 43–51 in *Antike und Universalgeschichte: Festschrift für Hans Erich Stier zum 70. Geburtstag am 25. Mai 1972*. Ed. by R. Stiehl and G. A. Lehmann. Münster: Aschendorff.
1991 Review of Parpola and Watanabe 1988. *WO* 22:188–195.
Wäfler, M.
2001 *Tall al-Hamidiya 3: Zur historischen Geographie von Idamaras zur Zeit der Archive von Mari und Šubat-enlil/Šehnā*. OBO 21. Göttingen: Vandenhoeck & Ruprecht.
Walker, C. B. F.
1966 "Material for a Reconstruction of the *Mīs Pî* Ritual." Ph.B. Dissertation. Oxford University.
Watanabe, K.
1983 "Rekonstruktion von VTE 438 auf Grund von Erra III A 17." *Assur* 3:164–166.
1987 *Die* adê-*Vereidigung anlässlich der Thronfolgeregelung Asarhaddons*. BaM Beiheft 3. Berlin: Mann.
1988 "Die Anordnung der Kolumnen der VTE-Tafeln." *ActSum* 10:265–266.
Waterman, L.
1930–1936 *Royal Correspondence of the Assyrian Empire*. Ann Arbor: University of Michigan Press.
Waters, M. W.
1999a "ABL 268 and Tammaritu." *ArOr* 67:72–74.
1999b "Teʾumman in the Neo-Assyrian Correspondence." *JAOS* 119:473–477.
2000 *A Survey of Neo-Elamite History*. SAAS 12. Helsinki: Neo-Assyrian Text Corpus Project.
2002 "A Letter from Ashurbanipal to the Elders of Elam (BM 132980)." *JCS* 54:79–86.
Weidner, E.
1932–1933a "Der Staatsvertrag Aššurnirâris VI. von Assyrien mit Matiʾilu von Bît-Agusi." *AfO* 8:17–27.
1932–1933b "Der Vertrag Šamši-Adads V. mit Marduk-zâkir-šumi I." *AfO* 8:27–29.
1932–1933c "Der Vertrag Asarhaddons mit mit Baʿal von Tyrus." *AfO* 8:29–34.
1937–1938 "Neue Bruchstücke des Berichtes über Sargons achte Feldzug." *AfO* 12:144–148.
1939–1941 "Assurbânipal in Assur." *AfO* 13:204–218.
Weinfeld, M.
1972 *Deuteronomy and the Deuteronomic School*. Oxford: Clarendon.
Weippert, M.
1973 "Die Kämpfe des assyrischen Königs Aššurbanipal gegen die Araber." *WO* 7:39–85.
Wilhelm, G.
1992 *Das Archiv des Šilwa-teššup*. Heft 4. *Darlehensurkunden und verwandte Texte*. Wiesbaden: Harrassowitz.
1993–1997 "Mušteja." *RlA* 8:498.
2004 "Hurrian." Pp. 95–118 in *Cambridge Encyclopedia of the World's Ancient Languages*. Ed. by R. D. Woodard. Cambridge: Cambridge University Press.
2006 "Briefe aus Nuzi." Pp. 101–105 in *TUAT* 3.
2012 "Šuppiluliuma I und die Chronologie der Amarna-Zeit." Ch. IV in *Kāmid el-Lōz* 20. *Die Keilschriftbriefe und der Horizont von El-Amarna*. Ed. by R. Hachman. Saarbrücker Beiträge zur Altertumskunde 87. Bonn: Rudolf Habelt.
Winter, I. J.
1983 "The Program of the Throneroom of Assurnasirpal II." Pp. 15–31 in *Essays of Near Eastern Art and Archaeology in Honor of Charles Kyrle Wilkinson*. Edited by P. O. Harper and H. Pittman. New York: The Metropolitan Museum of Art.
1992 "'Idols of the King': Royal Images as Recepients of Ritual Action in Ancient Mesopotamia." *Journal of Ritual Studies* 6:13–42.
Wiseman, D. J.
1958 "The Vassal-Treaties of Esarhaddon." *Iraq* 20:1–99, plates.
Yamada, S.
2000 *The Construction of the Assyrian Empire. A Historical Study of the Inscriptions of Shalmaneser III (859–824 BC) Relating to His Campaigns to the West*. SCHANE 3. Leiden and Koln: Brill.

Youngblood, R. F.
1961 *The Amarna Correspondence of Rib-Haddi, Prince of Byblos (EA 68–96)*. Ph.D. dissertation, The Dropsie College for Hebrew and Cognate Learning; Ann Arbor: UMI.
1962 "Amorite Influence in a Canaanite Amarna Letter." *BASOR* 168:24–27.
Zaccagnini, C.
1979 *The Rural Landscape of the Land of Arrapḫe*. Quaderni di Geografia Storica 1. Rome: Istituto di Studi del Vicino Oriente.
1981 "An Urartean Royal Inscription in the Report of Sargon's Eighth Campaign." Pp. 259–295 in *ARINH*.
Zadok, R.
1996 "A Prosopography and Ethno-Linguistic Characterization of Southern Canaan in the Second Millennium BCE." *Michmanim* 9:97–159.
Ziegler, N., and D. Charpin
2004 "Une lettre de Samsî-Addu découverte à Hazor?" *NABU* no. 4 (pp. 85–86).
Ziegler, N.
2006 "Zimrī-Lîm hat die Wahl einer Allianz mit Aleppo oder Ešnunna." Pp. 53–54 in *Texte aus der Umwelt des Alten Testaments*. Neue Folge, Band 3: Briefe. Gütersloh: Gütersloher Verlagshaus.
2009 "Die Westgrenze des Reichs Samsī-Addus." Pp. 181–209 in *Entre les fleuves – I*. BBVO 20. Ed. by E. Cancik-Kirschbaum and N. Ziegler. Gladbeck: Pewe-Verlag.
2014 "Le «coeur du pays» *libbi mâtim*." Pp. 273–289 in *D'Aššur à Mari et au-delà*: *Entre les fleuves II*. BBVO 24. Ed. by N. Ziegler and E. Cancik-Kirschbaum. Gladbeck: Pewe-Verlag.
Zimansky, P.
1990 "Urartian Geography and Sargon's Eighth Campaign." *JNES* 49:1–21.

SUMERIAN INSCRIPTIONS

KAR 4: THE CREATION OF HUMANITY (4.90)

Richard E. Averbeck

This myth focuses its attention on the creation of humanity. Four copies are known, three of them bilingual (Sumerian and Akkadian). The earliest copy is from the Old Babylonian period, and written only in Sumerian, suggesting that perhaps the composition itself was composed originally as early as the third millennium. Unfortunately, only the bottom right hand corner of the tablet is preserved, and what we have varies significantly from the other (bilingual) exemplars (see the remarks in Lambert 2013:350–351, and the first publication of Wilcke's copy of this Old Babylonian tablet on Lambert 2013: pl. 67).

The main bilingual tablet is mostly well-preserved, and dates to the Middle Assyrian period (ca. 1200–1000 BC; see Ebeling 1919 KAR 4 for a handcopy, and Landersdorfer 1917 pls. I–II for photographs). This is the main source for the following translation. Even this tablet is broken in some places and, in fact, was copied from an old tablet that was broken (see the colophon, lines 72–73, and the note on "break" written in Akkadian in lines 44–46). There appears to be a good deal of textual corruption even in the well-preserved lines (see, e.g., the remarks in Lambert 2013:351–352 and the notes below).

Lambert (2013:352–359 and 510–511) and Foster (2005:491–493) derive their translations from a combination of the Sumerian and Akkadian versions. Like Lisman (2013:60–62 and 330–336), the translation presented here is based almost exclusively on the Sumerian of KAR 4 and that of the other two bilingual exemplars (see Lisman 2013:330 and Lambert 2013:352 for the list of textual sources and Lambert pls. 65–66 for hand copies of the Neo-Assyrian tablets). Some consideration is given to the Akkadian when it is deemed helpful in the reading and translation of the Sumerian text. See Lambert (2013:352–359, 510–511) and Lisman (2013:60–64, 330–336) for transliterations of both the Sumerian and the Akkadian of KAR 4, and Lambert (2013:360) for a transliteration of the Old Babylonian exemplar. Lambert includes a brief commentary (2013:510–511) and Lisman a more extensive one (2013:62–64, 336–346).

The other two less complete copies date from the Neo-Assyrian period. In the case of the Neo-Assyrian copy from Ashurbanipal's library, the colophon tells us that this composition is the second tablet in a series of three. Before it came another tablet containing the double-column tablet of the so-called "Silbenalphabet" (i.e., syllable alphabet; see more on this below). After it came the first tablet of the composition known as Atraḫasis, since the incipit is given: *e-nu-ma i-lu$_4$ a-*[*me-lum*] "When the gods like m[an]" (Lambert 2013:352, 358; cf. also Lambert and Millard 1969:42–43).

Although there are no vertical lines indicating columns on the main tablet (KAR 4), nevertheless, it has three columns across the tablet, lined up and separated by visible spacing in most lines of the hand copy. On the actual cuneiform tablet itself, however, the column breaks are indicated not by visible spacing, but by enlarged vertical wedges at the end of the last sign in each column wherever the last sign ends with a vertical wedge. This makes the breaks between columns 1 and 2 and between columns 2 and 3 readily visible as these enlarged vertical wedges are lined up down the vertical axis of the tablet. This affords the tablet quite a striking appearance (see the photographs in Landersdorfer 1917, pls. I and II).

The second column contains the Sumerian edition of the mythic composition, and the third is its Akkadian translation. The first column contains the "Silbenalphabet" unit for each line. There is no discernible relationship between this first column and the composition contained in the following two, so it has not been included in the treatment here. The first column has its origin in third millennium scribal training (probably from Nippur) as an exercise in writing out (groups of) syllables. The first three lines of the Silbenalphabet read: (1) [m]e-me kúr-kúr (2) a-a-a-a-a (3) ku-ku lu-lu. By the Old Babylonian period, however, it seems to have lost its original function and was expounded as an esoteric text down into the Neo-Assyrian period (Lambert 2013:350–351 for discussion and p. 353 for bibliography; cf. Lisman 2013:337 and esp. Sollberger 1965:21–22).

The text has horizontal lines across the tablet between every one or two lines of cuneiform, and in one instance three lines (reverse lines 67–69), thus indicating "cases" of text. Scholars have managed this in different ways. The approach taken here is to number each line of cuneiform consecutively through the whole text (both obverse and reverse), but to combine the lines together in the translation when they are in the same case (e.g., lines 7–8 are treated as one unit). This way the reader can tell where these lines are drawn across the tablet. The cases actually correspond quite well to the clause and sentence sense units and flow of the composition.

The text falls into five main units followed by a colophon: (1) Introduction: the cosmic design, 1–6; (2) Enlil's deliberation among the gods, 7–20; (3) Creation of two model humans, 21–53; (4) Multiplication of animals and humanity, 54–66; (5) Lordship of Nisaba over humanity, 67–71; (6) Colophon, 72–73.

Obverse		
(1) After heaven was separated from earth,[1,a] its firm companion,[2] (2) so the mother goddesses could live there[3];	a Gen 1:1, 6–10	(3) after building up the earth to make the ground firm[4]; (4) when the designs[5] were made firm in heaven and earth

[1] For the separation of heaven from earth as a common motif in Sum. creation accounts, see Horowitz 1998:134–141 and compare, e.g., The Song of the Hoe *COS* 1.511 lines 4–5, "(Enlil) did hasten to separate heaven from earth, hastened to separate earth from heaven." The divine name Enlil means "Lord (*en*) Wind (*lil*)" (or "Breathe"). The fact that Enlil is the deity who separated heaven from earth corresponds well to heaven and earth with the space in between them being a place of wind, air, etc. This corresponds well to the waters above and below on the second day (Gen 1:6–8) and the dry ground/earth in the first part of the third day (Gen 1:9–10), yielding a three level cosmos: heaven (and waters) above, earth (and waters) below, with the surface of the earth (and sky) of animals and humanity in between.

Wolde (2009a and 2009b:184–200) proposes that *bārāʾ* "created" in Gen 1:1 means "to separate" or "differentiate," and that v. 1 should be translated "In the beginning God separated (or 'differentiated') the heaven and the earth" and, therefore, compares to the separation of heaven from earth in Sum. texts. One problem, among many others, with this reading of Gen 1:1 is that the Sum. texts consistently use the preposition "from" meaning "separated heaven from earth" and/or "earth from heaven." In Hebrew this would require the preposition *min* "from" between "heaven" and "earth" or, more likely, the use of *bēn* "between" before both "heaven" and "earth" similar to Genesis 1:4b (see, e.g., Becking and Korpel 2010:7–8 for a more complete discussion; cf. also Lisman 2013:206–207, n. 928 and the lit. cited there).

[2] The cuneiform sign for "companion" is *tab*, which consists of two parallel horizontal wedges. It could suggest the image of the male *an* "heaven" lying with the female *ki* "earth" in sexual union (Lisman 2013:62). This may add support to the concept of a previous cosmic marriage of the two, for which see Lisman 2013:77–81, 158–163, 181–182, 195–197. There is disagreement among scholars about how to understand all this. Speculation abounds but, basically, it appears the ancient Sumerians reasoned that, initially, *an* "heaven" and *ki* "earth" were an inanimate pair. There is no explanation given for the origin of this pair. They appear to be the starting point for creation in the Enlil/Nippur tradition, in contrast to the watery abyss starting point in the Enki/Eridu tradition (see Lambert 1980–1983:219–220 and 2008:28–30; cf. Gen 1:2). According to the former, the rain from heaven corresponds to the fertilizing semen deposited by the male *an* "heaven" on the female *ki* "earth" to create fertility. Perhaps they conceived of this fertility as that which brought them both to life as the animate deities, *An* and *Ki*, while still joined in cosmic union (the latter in the form of the great original Mother Goddess, sometimes known as Ninḫursaĝa "Lady of the Mountain Range").

Moreover, they may have thought of this cosmic union as eventually somehow producing not only a fertile earth but also a fertile heaven, the latter in the form of senior deities known as the Anunna gods (see lines 7–9 below; cf. Lisman 2013:27–30). From the third to the first millennia BCE, we have lists of En/Nin divine pairs (numbering from 2 to 21 pairs), always beginning with Enki/Ninki and ending with Enlil/Ninlil. This yields an ancestry for Enlil that goes back to Enki "Lord Earth" and Ninki "Lady Earth" (Note: this Enki is not to be confused with the well-known Enki[g] of Eridu referred to in lines 7–8 below). None of the pairs except Enlil/Ninlil are major deities with associated active religious cults. Lambert (1980–1983:219) argues that the intervening pairs, therefore, "serve only to ascribe remoteness to that first pair" (i.e., Enki/Ninki). Enlil, therefore, is the first major deity, the first of the Anunna gods and, along with the first great Mother Goddess, the progenitor or ancestor of all the rest. This would make sense in that "The Song of the Hoe" and other Sum. texts present Enlil, the greatest of the Anunna gods, as the one who originally separated heaven from earth and earth from heaven (see, e.g., Lisman 2013:26, 57–58; *COS* 1.511 and n. 1 above, and also Enki and the World Order, n. 4 in this volume).

In any case, KAR 4 begins with the long past separation of heaven from earth, assuming all that went before it according to the Enlil/Nippur tradition, as described above. Lines 1–3 recount this separation of the heaven from the earth, and the basic preparation of the landed world (*u*$_4$ ... *-ta* "from the day ..." = "after ..." clearly written in line 3, and probably to be restored in line 1 [see Lambert 2013:352]). Lines 4–6 introduce the time of the narrative that follows with "when ...," (*u*$_4$ ... *ba* in lines 4 and 6, lit. "in its (or 'that') day ...," meaning "when ..."; the *u*$_4$ at the beginning of line 4 applies to the *-ba* at the end of both lines 4 and 6). Thus, "after" those early days which were already long past (lines 1–3), later, "when" these designs for the Sum. world order had been put in place (lines 4–6), at that time the gods consulted about what to do next (lines 7 ff.).

[3] The separation of heaven from earth (line 1) led to the "mother goddesses" (= *ᵈama-ᵈinanna-ke*$_4$*-e-ne*, lit. 'mothers of Inanna'; see *COS* 1.516, n. 5) dwelling or living there (line 2). According to Enki and Ninmaḫ, at some point in primeval times the mother goddesses "were distributed in heaven and earth" (*COS* 1.516 line 6; Lisman 2013:48, 294; Lambert 2013:334–335). The previous two lines of Enki and Ninmaḫ (lines 4–5) refer to the birth of the Anunna gods, and then these mother goddesses being taken in marriage (*COS* 1.516 n. 4 and Lambert 2013:334–335). After their distribution in heaven and earth (line 6) the mother goddesses became pregnant and gave birth to the various minor gods, who were tasked with providing food for all the gods under the direction of the senior gods among them (lines 7–11). This led to the creation of humanity so that they could relieve the minor deities of their hard labor (see also The Song of the Hoe, *COS* 1.511–512).

KAR 4 also develops the theme of the creation of humanity to do the work of feeding the gods but, contrary to Enki and Ninmaḫ, this does not seem to be portrayed in terms of relieving the lesser gods of their hard labor (see the note on line 27 below). Instead, the creation of humanity is set forth as a plan worked out in the counsel of the Anunna gods (lines 7 ff.) after, and as a result of the fact that, they had established the basic designs of heaven and earth (lines 4–6).

[4] Instead of "to make the ground firm" (*ki ĝá-ĝá-e-dè*), Lisman (2013:330, 339) translates "in order to be able to establish cult places there" based on a line in the Abū Ṣalābīḫ temple hymn lines 11–12, which reads "Enlil has assigned plots of land to the Anunna" (*ᵈen-líl a-nun ki mu-ĝar-ĝar*). That understanding of *ki ĝar/ĝá* makes sense in that temple hymn context, but here the focus is on preparation of the earth for irrigation agriculture (see lines 4–6 and 13–15 below and also later lines, virtually the whole text). Temple building is also mentioned (lines 32–33, 49–51), but the focus throughout is on agricultural work and production. Here the text is telling us that the earth and ground were established so that they were well-prepared for the kinds of irrigation agriculture that would follow according to the designs of the gods (see line 5 and n. 5 below).

[5] The term rendered "designs" (*ĝiš-ḫur* written *ĝiš-ḫur-ḫur* to indicate plurality) regularly refers to the architectural plans for constructing buildings (see Gudea Cyl. A v 5, vi 5, vii 6, xvii 17, xix 20; see *COS* 1.421 n. 15), but can also denote, for example, battle plans (Gudea Cyl. B vii 15; for a full treatment of the term and its usage see Farber-Flügge 1973:181–191). Here it refers to the designs that the gods established for the layout and operation of the previously separated heaven and earth (cf. line 1). Lines 5–6 give some of the essential details of the plan for the land of Sumer, focusing on the water supply and its management for agricultural production. Everything, of course, begins with and depends on the Tigris and Euphrates (line 6; see also the same idea in Enki in the World Order lines 250–273 in this volume and Averbeck 2003:27–33).

(5) to establish levee and irrigation ditch in good order,[6]
(6) the banks of the Tigris and Euphrates being firmly fixed[7,b];
(7–8) An, Enlil, Utu (and/or Ninmaḫ),[8] and Enki, the great gods,
(9) the Anunna, the great gods,[9]
(10–11) sat down in a lofty dais grown high in awesomeness,[10,c] (and) Enlil himself deliberated (before them):[11,d]
(12) "Since the designs are firm in heaven and earth
(13) to establish dike and irrigation ditch in good order,
(14–15) the banks of the Tigris and Euphrates having been firmly fixed,[12]

b Gen 2:14
c Exod 26:33; 40:3; Lev 16:2
d Ps 89:5, 7; Job 5:1; 15:15; 38:7

6 The expression *e* (= *ég*) pa_5-*re* (= *pa*[*r*]) rendered "levee and irrigation ditch" is a standard combination that regularly designates "the whole hydraulic system, and stands for the whole lexical set of terms for artificial watercourses" (Civil 1994:109–110). The first term *ég* refers to manmade embankments. The original pictographic sign consists of a rectangular box open at the top (i.e., the open top of the ditch), two sides each drawn as double parallel lines to indicate the embankments on both sides of the ditch, and similarly the bottom of the ditch, . The pa_5 sign is similar, but with diagonal lines through the middle, perhaps to highlight the digging of the dirt out of the ditch, or the water flow area of the ditch. The common verb with pa_5 is "to dig" while with *e* it is "to pile up." Of course, it would be natural for the dirt that was dug out of the irrigation ditch to make the trench for the flow of water to be piled up along the sides of the ditch to make higher embankments (i.e., the two sides of the levee along the water channel). These are among the many rigorous agricultural occupations that humans will be tasked with later in this composition.

The width and depth of the channels and the height of the embankments would vary, depending on whether they were carrying the water to the fields (larger), or distributing the water through the fields (smaller). It is to be noted that the purpose of these channels was not only to distribute the water for irrigation, but perhaps even more for controlling the floods that could destroy ripening crops, houses, settlements, etc. Thus, for example, the same term *e* "embankment" could also be used for the embankments of the levees that formed overflow ponds to draw off the excess water when there was threat of destructive flooding. For a more complete discussion of the terminology, principles, and practices see esp. Civil 1994:67–72, 109–135 and also the still useful work of Kang 1973:421–440.

7 See n. 2 above for the relationship between lines 1–3 and 4–6. The *-a-ba* at the end of line 6 reaches back to the u_4 at the beginning of line 4, yielding the literal rendering of line 6, "in the day the Tigris and Euphrates were firmly fixed." As explained above (n. 6), levees and irrigation ditches not only depend on the water from the Tigris and Euphrates for the agricultural water supply they carry, but they also regulate that supply in order to minimize destructive flooding at the wrong time(s) of the year.

The design of the world as seen here begins with the basic set up, which is the work of the gods (lines 4–6), and then moves to that which would become the work of humanity, once they were created (lines 27–51). A similar pattern appears in Enki and the World Order, also treated in this volume (see the discussion of the latter text in Averbeck 2003:28–30).

8 Lines 67–69 of KAR 4 (see below) list the four deities as "An, Enlil, Enki, and Ninmaḫ," replacing Utu with Ninmaḫ and placing Enki just after Enlil. The Old Babylonian fragment seems to have both, yielding five deities in all, with the reading "An, Enlil, Utu, Ea (= Enki), and ^{d}*diĝir-maḫ* (= Ninmaḫ?)" (Lambert 2013:360 and 601, pl. 67 rev. lines 6–10). The term "Anunna" (line 9 here) does not recur in the context of lines 67–69. Some scholars emend line 7 to read Ninmaḫ, the female mother god, in place of Utu, the male sun god (see, e.g., Foster 2005:492 and Bottéro and Kramer 1989:503). In the rendering here, the main text of line 7 is left as it stands in the KAR 4 exemplar with Ninmaḫ put in parenthesis. Ninmaḫ may well be a better reading, however, since it would make sense to have a mother goddess among the four, especially with the close relationship between Enki and Ninmaḫ known from other compositions devoted to the creation of humanity (see, e.g., Enki and Ninmaḫ in *COS* 1.516–518; cf. also the remarks in Lambert 2008:27 and n. 9 below).

9 Some scholars translate lines 7–9 as "Anu, Enlil, Utu (or 'Ninmaḫ'), and Enki, the great gods, and the Anunna, the great gods," thus taking the four named deities as one group and the Anunna as a different group (see, e.g., Lambert 2013:354–355; Foster 2005:492; and Bottéro and Kramer 1989:503). Another approach is to take the repetition of the expression "the great deities" in lines 8 and 9 as an indicator that we have here only one group of deities – the four named deities are, in fact, the Anunna in this context (cf. Lisman 2013:330–331, 340, and the discussion in his n. 1441). The latter view is adopted here, but not considered certain. The lack of the "Anunna" in the parallel context of lines 67–69 may support this analysis (see n. 8 above and the text below). For more on Enlil and the Anunna, see n. 2 above.

10 As Miguel Civil has noted, the term *bára(g)* "dais" refers to a "'curtain of separation' (around the area reserved for the king and royal family or for a deity in a temple)." Accordingly, it is an early Semitic loanword from Akk. *parakku* "cult dais, sanctuary," and is related to both *parāqu* "to divide off" and *parāku* "to lie across, obstruct" (Civil 2007:21, 051.). Civil also proposes that we not translate "to sit ON the *bára(g)*" but "to reside in(side of) the *bára(g)*" (personal communication). In spite of the lexical confusion (see, e.g., *HALOT* 968–969), therefore, *bára(g)* does indeed seem to be related to the biblical *pārōket* that separated the holy place from the most holy place in the tabernacle, where the Ark of the Covenant was located (Civil 2007:21, n. 18; see, e.g., Exod 26:33; 40:3; Lev 16:2). There is some debate whether the biblical *pārōket* was simply a vertical hanging curtain, or whether it was also draped back on a wooden frame to form a canopy over the top of the Ark of the Covenant, underneath the roof of the tabernacle tent (see the discussions in *NIDOTTE* 3.687–689 and *TDOT* 12:95–97 and the lit. cited in those places).

The text of line 10 is corrupt. As it stands, the cuneiform reads: *bára-maḫ ní-te mu-un-KI-tuš mú-a* lit. "a lofty dais in awesomeness he sat (*ki* ?) grown high." Lisman (2013:331 and 340) suggests that we read *KI-tuš* as $durun_x$ meaning "to sit down," regularly written KU-KU in the plural. This seems likely, since *tuš* "to sit down" is written with the KU sign and KU-KU = *durun* for the plural of the same verb. This coordinates well with the plural Anunna as the subject from the previous line. The KI sign closely resembles KU, so it could easily be a mistake in the writing of the sign. Lisman also rearranges the line to place the *mú-a* "grown high" before, rather than after, the verb. This would be more normal Sum. grammar, but one wonders if the *mú-a* might be placed at the end of the line because of the pattern of *-a* at the end of a number of the previous lines.

11 Lambert (2013:355 and 510) rendered line 11 "And deliberated among themselves," based on his restoration of the Akk. version and the assumption that we should read *ad* gi_4-gi_4 "to take counsel, confer," rather than *šu* gi_4-gi_4 "to repeat (words)," which is what the cuneiform text actually reads (cf. Foster 2005:492; also see Bottéro and Kramer 1989:503 "et conférèrent" = "and they conferred"). Lisman (2013:331 and 340), however, points out that it must be only Enlil who does the speaking here, since the verb is singular as well as the pronoun *-ani* in the expression *ní-te-a-ni* "his self." So Enlil is not conferring or consulting with the other Anunna gods, but is deliberating before them about what they might do next. In lines 16–20, Enlil repeats his address to the Anunna gods. Then lines 21–23 introduce their response to Enlil in the following lines. There are similarities here to the "divine council" in the Hebrew Bible (e.g., Ps 89:5, 7). See Mullen 1980 and Heiser 2015.

12 For lines 12–14 see lines 4–6 above and the notes there.

(16–17) what is it that you would change? What is it that you would fashion?[13]
(18) Anunna, great gods,
(19–20) what is it that you would change? What is it that you would fashion?"
(21–22) The great gods, who were standing there, the Anunna, the gods who decree destiny,[14]
(23) two of them responded to Enlil:[15]
(24) "In Uzumua, the bond of heaven and earth,[16]
(25) we shall slaughter (the gods) Alla and Illa[17]
(26) to grow humanity (with) their blood.[18,e]
(27) Let the labor of the gods become its (humanity's) work assignment:[19,f]

e Gen 2:7; 9:6

f Gen 2:5–7

13 The Sum. version has Enlil addressing the Anunna gods as "you" directly in lines 16–20, with a few variants in the first person "we" in other copies. The Akk. version reads "we" consistently through lines 16–20 (see, e.g., Lisman 2013:331 and 341, line 16, "what can we change?"). Lambert (2013:354–355) translates them as alternatives, "What shall we/you make?" (reading the Akk. version verb *epēšu* "to do, make," rather than Sum. *bal* "to change").

14 Scholars debate the precise meaning of the very important Mesopotamian concept of Sum. *nam – tar* = Akk. *šīmta* (*šīmāti*) *šâmu*, rendered here conventionally as "decree destiny." See *CAD* Š 1.364 and the literature cited there, where it is proposed that, in the end, "it probably denotes the solemn pronunciation of binding words." See also the remarks and other literature cited in *COS* 2.418, n. 1; and also n. 3 in the treatment of Enki and the World Order in this present volume (4.90). Here in KAR 4 it is clear that it was the Anunna gods who were known to do this and from whom Enlil was expecting further solemn pronunciations that would set the agenda for the earth as it was designed.

15 Lambert (2013:355) translates here "Both groups answered Enlil," based on his view that the Anunna and "the great gods" are two different groups of deities (see lines 8–9 above and the remarks in n. 9; see also Foster 2005:492 and Bottéro and Kramer 1989:504). Lisman (2013:332 and 341), however, insists that there is only one group of deities: the four Anunna mentioned in line 8 are the same as "the great gods." So he renders the line "two of them answered Enlil." He suggests that perhaps it was Utu and Enki who responded, since An is relatively far removed and seldom engages in such a way in Sum. mythology. One could perhaps compare the approach to Enlil by the Anunna gods in The Song of the Hoe (*COS* 1:511–512). See also the last part of n. 20 below.

16 The term "Uzumua" is a place name, written *uzu-mú-a*^{ki} (i.e., with the post-position *-a* "in" and the post-determinative for a location *ki*). It means "In the place where flesh grows," and refers to a sacred site in Nippur, the city of Enlil. Similarly, "the bond of heaven and earth" is written *dur-an-ki-ke*$_4$ and, although it does not have the *ki* post-determinative, it refers to the place called the Duranki in the middle of Enlil's temple complex in Nippur (see *COS* 1:511, n. 5 and Foster 2005:492, n. 2).

17 Sum. ^{d}*NAĞAR* ^{d}*NAĞAR* is rendered "Alla and Illa" here as a reference to a pair of deities (see Krebernik 2002, followed by Lisman 2013:332, 342; cf. similarly Foster 2005:492 and Bottéro and Kramer 1989:504), perhaps "one for male and one for female" (Foster 2005:492, n. 3; cf. Lisman 2012:63). The lexical text An = *Anum* glosses ^{d}*NAĞAR* with *il-la*, *al-la*, *ḫa-a-a-u*, and *na-ĝar*, so perhaps the reduplication indicates such a pair. Lambert (2013:223–224, 355, 510) translates "the Alla deities," taking the reduplication to indicate plural deities, not a pair. See n. 31 below for a possible relationship between these two deities and the two humans created with their blood.

18 Lisman (2013:332) reads the verb *mú-mú-dé*, but Lambert (2013:354) has *mú-mú-e-dé*. Lambert's reading is correct according to both the KAR 4 hand copy and the photograph of the tablet (Landersdorfer 1917, pl. I). In any case, both would indicate the *-ed-e* non-finite verb, indicating purpose, "to grow" (Thomsen 1984:266–267; Edzard 2003:134–136). Exemplar A has Sum. *sağ ḫé-mú-mú* indicating the third person precative "let him grow" (Lambert 2013:354 and 510 for the relevant data on *sağ-mú-mú*), and the Akk. version has the first person plural precative, *i ni-ib-na-a* "let us grow," which would fit with the flow of the Akk. version from lines 24–25 into line 26 (i.e., all in the first person plural precative). The translation offered here follows the KAR 4 Sum. version. Lambert follows the Akk.

Mesopotamian textual traditions about the creation of humanity contain a mixture of motifs, some well-attested, and some not. One well-attested motif is that of "theomachy," the killing of a god or gods to obtain divine flesh and/or blood for the making of humanity, as the gods have proposed here in lines 24–26. Sometimes it includes mixing the blood and/or flesh with clay in order to infuse the clay with the divine essence. See, e.g., Atra-Ḫasīs lines 204–230 where the god Aw-ilu is slaughtered so that his flesh and blood could be mixed with clay to make humans (*COS* 1:451). Some see a parallel here with Gen 2:7, where the Lord God shaped the body of the man out of the dust of the ground and then breathed his own breathe into the man to give him life. Similarly, in Enuma Elish vi. 1–44, Marduk had Qingu killed because he had supported Tiamat in her battle against him, so that he could use his blood to fabricate humanity (*COS* 1:400–401). But in this latter case, as here in KAR 4, there is no mention of mixing the blood with clay. Generally, theomachy is limited to Akk. texts, not Sum.. KAR 4 is the only exception, where it is found in the both the Akk. and the Sum. versions.

The shaping of humanity out of clay, without theomachy, is a well-known motif in Sum. compositions. In one instance, it appears to involve the mother goddess shaping pieces of clay into properly formed humans, having them gestate within goddesses, and then assisting those goddesses in giving them birth (Enki and Ninmaḫ lines 24–37; see *COS* 1:517, nn. 18–22 and Lisman 2013:296–297, 306–307). Another text has humans made from clay by shaping the proto-type in a brick-mold followed by the institution of human reproduction (The Song of the Hoe lines lines 19–20, 27; see *COS* 1:511, nn. 8–9 but, in my opinion, Lisman 2013:324–325, 328 proposes a better reading of the text). For the tradition in which humans spring forth from the ground like plants, see lines 60–71 below.

19 This is the common rationale for the creation of humanity in Mesopotamian creation accounts. Sometimes it is clear that the minor gods have rebelled against their labor in providing for the gods, whether in Sum. texts (e.g., Enki and Ninmaḫ lines 9–23, 29–37; see *COS* 1:516–517 and Lisman 2013:294–297, 300–307; cf. also The Song of the Hoe in *COS* 1:512 and n. 3 above), or in Akk. (e.g., Atra-Ḫasīs in *COS* 1:450; cf. also very briefly Enuma Elish tablet vi lines 34–36 in *COS* 1:401). In other instances, as here in KAR 4, such rebellion is not indicated, at least not clearly. Here it appears that creating humanity to do the work of providing for the gods followed immediately upon establishing the basic design of the earth for irrigation agriculture (see lines 4–6 above). They had designed the Sum. world to work in a certain way, and they needed somehow to see that it actually functioned accordingly. This required humanity.

Gen 2:5 also refers to a time before the Lord God had created humanity: "as of yet there was no shrub on the earth and no plant had sprung up, for the LORD God had not sent rain on the earth and there was no one to work the ground." Here again the focus is on the need for both water and people to make the system work.

(28–29) to establish the boundary levees forever[20];
(30–31) to put hoe and work basket in its (humanity's) hand[21];
(32–33) for the temples of the great gods, (each one) worthy of a lofty dais,[22]
(34) marking out the irrigation districts,[23]
(35–36) to establish the boundary levees forever;
(37–38) to put the (irrigation) levees in proper order[24]; to establish (them) firmly[25];

(39–40) to make all different kinds of plants (i.e., crops)[26] plentiful for the temple estates in all four remote (corners of the land);
(41) [to] … the rains …;

Reverse

(42–43) to establish boundaries firmly (for) the dwelling grounds,[27] it (humanity) will surely pile up heaps of grain.

20 The verbal expression intended in line 29 is clearly *gi-⟨na-e-⟩dè* ("to establish") as in lines 36, 38, and 42 below. The term rendered "boundary levee(s)" in lines 28–29 and 35–36 is a compound of *e* (= *ég*) discussed in n. 6 above plus *sur* "to delimit, divide, mark off." In this context it refers to levees that would not only serve to control water flow, but also mark boundaries between the agricultural lands of the various temple estates of the deities. Lisman (2013:342) follows this understanding for lines 35–36, but suggests that here in lines 28–29 it may be used in a more general way, "perhaps referring to the boundary of Sumer (?)" This seems unlikely, since the levees (and canals) functioned internal to Sumer, not marking it off from outside regions. And, in any case, the context is organizing Sumer internally and making it fertile, not demarcating its boundaries.

Similar terminology is used for demarcating the boundary between Lagash and Umma in the Pre-sargonic inscriptions that recount the border disputes between these two major city-states. It is conceived of as a dispute between (the temple estates of) Ningirsu and Shara, their respective patron deities. For example, the Enmetena cone begins, "Enlil, …, demarcated the border (*ki e-ne-sur*) between Ningirsu and Shara" (Steible 1982:230 i 1–7; Cooper 1986:54). A few lines later the same text tells us that "Eanatum, ruler of Lagash, uncle of Enmetena ruler of Lagash, demarcated the border (*ki e-da-sur*) with Enakale, ruler of Umma. He extended the (boundary-) channel (*e-bi … íb-ta-ni-è*) from the Nun-canal to the Gu'edena …" (Steible 1982:232 i 32-ii 3; Cooper 1986:55). Here too the verb *sur* "to demarcate" is used in the same general context with *e* (= *ég*) "(boundary-) channel," where the issue is marking off and violating boundaries between the temple estate lands of Ningirsu/Lagash and Shara/Umma. The point of KAR 4 lines 28–35 is that the first work assignment to which humanity would need to devote themselves would be planning and establishing the boundaries between the field districts belonging to the various temple estates of the deities. This was to be done by establishing permanent boundary levees between them. The eleventh cycle of Enki and the World Order (EWO, lines 368–380) underlines the importance of establishing and maintaining the boundaries between the various temple estates and their lands. Enki placed Utu, the sun god and god of justice, in charge of making sure that this regular order was maintained (Averbeck 2003:54–56; see also these lines in the selections from EWO in this volume). This may support the notion that perhaps the two deities of line 23 are indeed Enki and Utu, as Lisman (2013:341) has suggested (see note 15 above).

21 For the importance of the hoe and the work basket as the primary working tools in Sumer, see The Song of the Hoe (e.g., line 10; *COS* 1:511, n. 6). Specifically, regarding the work basket, see the representation of it on the Urnanshe wall plaque (Roaf 1990:88; Suter 2000:253, fig. 37; see Cooper 1986:22–23 for a translation of the inscription), and the many foundation figurines of pious rulers carrying such baskets (see, e.g., the Roaf 1990:81, 112 with the discussion and lit. cited in Averbeck 2010:9–10). For the hoe, see the discussion in Averbeck 2003:44–47 and the lit. cited there.

22 For the actual meaning of "lofty dais," see note 10 above. For the importance of temples and temple building in creation texts in the ANE and the Bible see Van Leeuwen 2007 and Johnson 2014 and the lit. cited by them.

23 Lambert (2013:357) translates line 34 "To mark out field by field" and Foster (2005:492) "To add field to field" (cf. also Bottéro and Kramer 1989:504). Lisman (2013:333, 342) notes that *g̃iš – ḫur*, the verb in line 34, normally means "to design," and renders lines 32–34, "planning the houses of the great gods, befitting an exalted shrine, (and) meadows," but compare the translation and notes on lines 65–66 below. The Sum. reads literally, "(32) (for) the houses of the gods, (33) worthy of an exalted dais, (34) marking out the fields (*a-gàr-a-gàr-re g̃iš ḫur-ḫur-re*)." The compound verb *g̃iš – ḫur*, lit., "to scratch/sketch/dig the wood," refers to marking the actual boundaries of these field districts "upon" these fields (see the locative-terminative postposition *-e* at the end of *a-gàr-a-gàr-re*). The hoe and the work basket of lines 30–31 would be the basic tools for all such work (see, e.g., The Disputation between the Hoe and the Plow, *COS* 1:579, lines 65–78, and the discussion in Averbeck 2003:41–42).

In this context, as in other places, the term *a-gàr* (= Akk. *ugāru*; see the citations in *CAD* U/W 27–30) probably refers to "irrigation districts" in contrast to *a-šà* "fields" (see line 47 below; = Akk. *eqlu* "field," *CAD* E 249–252), which refers to the actual irrigated agricultural fields within the irrigation districts. See, for example, the combination "a field (*a-šà*) in the irrigation district (*a-gàr*)" (*CAD* E 250 meaning b and *CAD* U/W 29 meaning 3′).

24 Line 37 reads *e si sá-e-dè-zé-en*, but Lisman (2013:333, 342) is probably correct in seeing *-zé-en* as a scribal error, so that we have here another prospective infinitive, as in the lines before and after this line.

25 The "boundary levees" (*e-sur*, lines 28–36) brought the water to irrigation "levees" (*e*, lines 37–38; see note 6 above) for distribution of the water to the various agricultural fields of each temple estate (lines 39–51). Both levels of waterways required extensive construction and maintenance and, therefore, demanded an immense supply of human labor and the organizational infrastructure to manage it. The fields themselves were long and narrow so that the levees (i.e., ditches) on each side could readily supply water to all the rows of the field that lay between them (see Averbeck 2003:30–33, 39–43 and the lit. cited there; cf. also the modern day picture in Roaf 1990:127).

26 For the various kinds of crops, see Averbeck 2003:43–44 and the literature cited there.

27 Line 42 reads *ki-ùr-sur gi-na-e-dè*. Pettinato (1971:76, 81 n. 42) suggests *ki-ùr* belongs to the first column (the "Silbenalphabet" column, see the introduction above) even though it is written in the second (i.e., the Sum.) column. He reads the line ⟨*e*⟩*-sur gi-na-e-dè* "to make firm the boundary⟨ditch⟩." The tablet, however, definitely has *ki-ùr* in the second column (see Landersdorfer 1917: pl. II), as does the hand copy in KAR 4. Lisman (2013:333, 343) suggests that *ki-ùr-sur* "is probably a contamination of *ki-ùr* and *ki sur* ('to mark a boundary')" and translates lines 42–43, "to establish the boundaries of the dwelling grounds: then it (= *mankind*) will pile up heaps of grain."

Civil, in Lambert and Millard 1969:167–168, points out that *ki-ùr* primarily means "the land assigned to someone to live there, but still as an 'undeveloped plot.'" The tablet has the *sur* placed close to the *gi-na-* and removed from the preceding *ki-ùr*. If we reflect that in a literal translation, it would perhaps yield, "the dwelling ground, to establish the boundary firmly," suggesting the translation offered here above. The whole focus of the preceding lines (28–41) has been to establish firmly the boundaries between dwelling grounds of the various deities, and the prosperity of them all, which, in turn, lends itself to peaceful relations between them and less temptation to encroach one upon the other.

[lines 44, 45, 46: *break*][28]

(47) to make the fields[29] of the Anunna fertile;
(48) to make abundance plentiful in the land."[30]
(49) The feast of the gods being perfected,
(50) with the pouring out of cold water,
(51) in the great banquet hall of the gods worthy of a lofty dais

g Gen 1:5, 8, 10; 2:20

h Gen 1:26–28

(52–53) they were named[g] Ulleĝara and Anneĝara.[31,h]
(54–55) To make the abundance of the land plentiful in every kind of cattle, sheep, goats, fish, and birds,[32]
(56–57) Enul and Ninul,[33] whose pure mouths speak prayers,[34]

28 Akk. *ḫi-e-pi* = *ḫepû* "break" is written in both columns (Sum. and Akk.) of all three lines. This tells us that the ancient scribe was copying from a tablet that was broken in these three lines. The Silbenalphabet in the first column continues with no break in these lines. See also the colophon for the fact that the present tablet was copied and collated from an old one (lines 72–73 below).

29 See n. 23 on line 34 above. The term "field" here in line 47 is *a-šà* = Akk. *eqlu* and refers to the actual cultivated fields of the temple estates.

30 The continuous sequence of prospective infinitives that begins in line 26 concludes here in line 48 with the end result: because of humanity's labors there would be plentiful agricultural abundance throughout the land of Sumer, from one temple estate to the next (note esp. lines 39–40). It is most likely, therefore, that the pronouncement of the (two) Anunna gods that begins in line 24 ends here at line 48. Heidel (1963:70), Foster (2005:493), and Lisman (2013:334) end the quote at line 53, Bottéro and Kramer (1989:505) at line 69, and Lambert (2013:357–359) and Pettinato (1971:78–79) appear to have the quote running all the way through the end of the composition (i.e., they do not indicate a close quote anywhere).

Lambert (2013:351) maintains that the text makes good sense only up through line 27; that is, in lines 25–27 "the gods declare their plan to create man, but nowhere is the fulfillment of this plan described." He adds, "Indeed, the story is quite lost toward the end." However, if the quote ends at line 48, then the following four lines (49–53) function as a unit to tell us that everything was indeed successful. This is how they are understood here. Thus, line 54 begins a new unit, where the focus shifts away from humans and their work to produce abundant agricultural crops (lines 24–53) to the fertility and abundance of animals through successful human animal husbandry (lines 54–66). In fact, three new deities are introduced by name in lines 54–56. As in both Genesis 1 and 2, the creation humanity is closely associated with the creation of the animals. They belong together. Lines 67–71 form quite a good conclusion to the composition as a whole, and lines 72–73 constitute a colophon.

31 As remarked in the previous note, lines 49–53 as a unit report the successful conclusion to the creation of humanity and their function in producing agricultural abundance throughout the land (lines 24–48). There is some dispute over whether the names in line 52 are divine or human names, since the first begins with the divine determinative (i.e., ^{d}*ul-*). "An" the divine element of the second name does not have the divine determinative, but this is normal with the god An. See the discussion in Pettinato 1971:81; Lambert 2013:511; and Lisman 2013:343–344. The context, and the fact that two deities were slain to create them (see line 25 above), suggests that these are to be understood as the names of the first two prototype human beings. They were the models. One might compare this to Gen 1:27, where the two are created, male and female. Of course, in the biblical account the humans were created in the image of God as his likeness to maintain good order in the world, not to feed the gods.

The Sum. expression *mu pà(d)* means "to call/invoke the name," and here lit., "their names were called," which is a way of saying that these two model humans had come into being (i.e., they were now created). The corresponding Akk. expression is *šuma zakāru* "to call/invoke the name." It appears, for example, at the beginning of the creation myth Enuma Elish (see Lambert 2013:50–51, 469), where the text says that "earth beneath had not come into being" (lit. '(its) name had not been called') and "(not one of the gods) had come into being" (i.8). Then in line 10 we read, "Laḫmu and Laḫamu were formed and came into being." Similarly, at the end of his creative acts on days 1–2 and the first part of day 3 in Genesis 1, God "named" (the idiom is lit., "called the name to") day and night, the sky, and the earth and seas, respectively (Gen 1:5, 8, 10; cf. also the man's naming of the animals in Gen 2:20).

The names mean "The One Established (or 'Placed') by Ul" and "The One Established (or 'Placed') by An/heaven." The term "An," of course, means "heaven" and refers to the most-high god who is generally aloof from the contingencies of history. "Ul" is more debatable. Lambert (2013:415) suggests that it could mean "luxuriance," or perhaps "bud" (following Jacobsen). Either would make sense in a context of agricultural abundance. It could also be an adjective meaning "ancient" (= Akk. *ullû CAD* U/W 82–84 and cf. Lambert 2013:511, "Whom eternity established"), as in the expression *en-ul-e ĝar-ra* "established/placed by the primeval En/lord" in the Temple Hymns (Lisman 2013:344 citing Sjöberg and Bergmann 1969:20 line 65). In this case, the combined names could refer to the fact that the two humans originated in ancient primeval times and were placed on earth by heaven (i.e., the great gods).

32 The expression "in every kind of" is one possible rendering of Sum. *ne-ta-a* at the end of line 54 (Lisman 2013:334 has it at the beginning of line 55, but the tablet has it otherwise, Landersdorfer 1917: pl. II). It could represent a combination of *ní-te* "self" plus the post-position *-a* "in," or perhaps the demonstrative *ne* "this" plus the post-postpositions *-ta* "from" and *-a* "in." In either case, it seems to be an idiom meaning something like "in all kinds" or "variously," used in a distributive sense.

The prospective infinitive here begins a new series that has to do with animals and the human management of them, as opposed to agriculture (see lines 24–53 above for the latter). See also n. 30 above.

33 For Enul and Ninul, and En "lord" and Nin "lady" as multiple divine pairs in god lists, see now Lisman 2013:356, 358–359, 362 and remarks in Lambert 2013:415 and 2008:27–32. Lisman takes *-ul* in the lists to mean "bud, fruit," but it can also mean "ancient" (see the remarks on *ul* in n. 31 above). So perhaps we have here names that mean "Ancient Lord" and "Ancient Lady," referring to deities known for their antiquity. This would make sense in the context.

34 A look at the photograph of the tablet (Landersdorfer 1917: pl. II) suggests that we should read the verb as *siskur*$_2$ (= *siskur siskur* = Akk. *karābu* "to pray"), not *zur-zur* (= Akk. *kutennû* "to treat with honor"; compare Labat's sign list # 437 with # 438). See also the remarks in Lisman 2013:344, although he retains the reading *zur-zur*. The framing sign *zur* does indeed appear to display the *še* sign written within it, in which case it should be read *siskur*$_2$. Lambert (2013:358) has now come to accept this reading as well (contra his earlier reading of *zur-zur* according to *CAD* K 542 meaning 2).

(58) (and) Aruru,[35] being suited for lordship,[36]
(59) (they) drew up their own great designs.[37]
(60) Skilled worker after skilled, unskilled after unskilled,[38]
(61) like grain, this itself (humanity) is that which produces from the ground the verdure of the earth,[39]
(62) an unchangeable thing like unto an enduring star,
(63–64) for day and night[40] the feast of the gods being perfected,
(65–66) they themselves (humanity) drew up great plans.[41]
(67–69) An, Enlil, Enki, and Ninmaḫ, the great gods,[42]
(70–71) where they have created humanity, Nisaba stands there in her lordship.[43]

---

35 Aruru is the "creatress of mankind," whose main cult center is in Sippar (Lambert 2013:511). As the mother- and earth-goddess she is also known as Bēlet-ilī "lady of the gods" (= ^{d}*nin-ì-li*; Lisman 2013:360), Nintu(d) "lady who gives birth," and Mami/a, all three as alternate names in Atra-ḫasīs (i.189, 193, 198 etc. in *COS* 1:451 and n. 4; see also Lambert and Millard 1969:54–57), as well as Ninmaḫ "exalted lady," Ninmenna "lady of the crown," and Ninḫursag̃ "lady of the foothills." According to Sum. theology she is both the sister and wife of Enlil (*RlA* 1:160).

36 The text has *nam-nin*, which is strictly "ladyship," suitable to Aruru as a female deity, but contrast line 71 below, which has *nam-en* "lordship" for the goddess Nisaba. In the latter case it appears that *-en* refers to Nisaba's role as the great goddess who rules over humanity. See also n. 43 below.

37 The text actually reads *g̃iš-ḫur-gal-gal mu-un-IM-ZU-ḫur-ḫur-re*, but Pettinato (1971:76) reads *mu-un-*$^{\text{ní-ba}}$*-ḫur-ḫur-re*. Thus, *ní-ba* "their own" (= Akk. *ina ramānišunu* in the Akk. version) is mistakenly written imbedded in the verb rather than standing before it, as Lisman (2013:334, 344–345) has placed it. Lisman also restores ⟨*ne*⟩ at the end of the verb, but with the *-un-* in the verb prefix chain it is clearly a *ḫamṭu* transitive plural, so the verb ends *-re(š)*, which is often written without the *-š*.

38 Lines 60–66 return again to subject of humanity, but here we have not just two original human models (see lines 52–53 above), but now a multitude of them in two categories, skilled and unskilled. For Sum. *lú*$^{!}$*-IM* = the Akk. version *nû'u* "unskilled, uneducated, brute" see *CAD* N 2:356 where this text is cited (cf. Lisman 2013:334–335).

39 The meaning of this line is debated. Pettinato (1971:79), Bottéro and Kramer (1989:505), Foster (2005:493), and Lambert (2013:359, 511) all translate to the effect that humans grew up out of the ground like grain. Lambert, for example, has (the humans of line 60) "grew (?) out of the ground of their own accord, like barley." The question mark, however, indicates that he is uncertain about this rendering. He suggests that perhaps the line should be emended to mean that humans reproduce on their own like grain does, and refers to this pattern in Gen 1:11–12, 27–28. Lisman (2013:335, 345) ends up with something similar via a different analysis: "(61) – like grain, that of itself becomes green from the earth and that adorns the earth, (62) …" Thus, he interprets the line to mean that "Men's activities have to be like grain, that becomes green of itself, grows up and embellishes the earth … The task of men is self-evident, as is the growing etc. of grain" (Lisman 2013:344).

The Sum. text reads *še-gim ní-bi ne ki-ta sig*$_7$*(si*$_{12}$*)-sig*$_7$*(si*$_{12}$*) ki dím* (or *-gim*). A literal rendering might be given as follows: "like grain, itself, this one, from the ground, green things (or 'grows, sprouts'), the earth/ground, creates (or, 'fashions, adorns')." Lambert has the last sign as *-gim* "like," but both Pettinato and Lisman read *dím* "create, fashion, adorn," and the latter is the reading accepted here (these are two possible readings of the same cuneiform sign). Lisman (2013:345) suggests that *dím* = Akk. *bunnû* from *banû* B (*CAD* B 90–94) and means "to grow, beautify," but he seems to confuse *sig*$_7$, which has the lexical equivalent *bunnû* from *banû* B (see the remarks in Lambert 2013:469, 511) with *dím*, which has the equivalent *banû* A (*CAD* B 83–90) "to build, fashion, produce, create" (see also the explanation of the distinctions between these two verbs in *CAD* B 93). This creates problems for Lisman's translation and interpretation.

Perhaps there is a better way to render this line: "like grain, this one itself (humanity) is that which produces from the ground the verdure of the earth." *ní-bi* "itself" could refer to either the grain before it or collective humanity mentioned in the previous line, to which the following *ne* "this one" refers. In either case, *dím* is an active participle referring to "one who produces/creates," and what humanity of all kinds (line 60) produces or creates *ki-ta* "from the ground" is *sig*$_7$*(si*$_{12}$*)-sig*$_7$*(si*$_{12}$*)-ki* "the verdure (vegetation) of the earth" (*sig*$_7$ = *CAD* A2 300–301 *arqu* "green" plants, grass, etc.). If this is correct, then the initial phrase "like grain" does not refer to the humans themselves growing like grain from the ground, but to the humans growing all kinds of vegetation like grain from the ground. The meaning would be similar to the bilingual text that reads: Sum. *ú-šim edin-na ba-dù*: Akk. *urqīt ṣēri ibtani* "he created the vegetation of the steppe" (cited in *CAD* U/W 238).

40 The expression *u*$_4$*-gi*$_6$*-na-ta* is literally "from the day in his night." It could mean "from the break of day," referring to the fact that the work day began at day break, but it may also be an idiom for "day and night" or "by day and by night." In any case, the point is that the fulltime occupation and preoccupation of humanity was providing for the feasts of the gods.

41 Lines 65–66 read, *ní-te-a-ni g̃iš-ḫur-gal-gal-la mu-un-ḫur-ḫur-re*. For the verb form here, see n. 37 above. *ní-te-a-ni* is literally "himself" or "herself" singular, but here refers to humanity collectively (see the previous lines), and the verb is plural. The translation given here, therefore, renders the whole line in the plural.

42 For remarks on this list of gods see the discussion in nn. 8 and 9 above. Pettinato (1971:79), Bottéro and Kramer (1986:505), and Lambert (2013:359) attach the gods of lines 67–69 grammatically back to the previous sentence, but standard Sum. grammar would suggest that they belong to the following lines and serve as the subject of the verb in line 70 (see Lisman 2013:335–336 and similarly Foster 2005:493).

43 For *nam-en* "lordship" as it applies to the goddess Nisaba see n. 36 above. Nisaba (= Nidaba) is well-known as the goddess of grain, scribal lore, and record keeping. In The Song of the Hoe, for example, she is responsible for keeping the records of decisions, and for measuring out the dimensions of Eanna temple of the goddess Inanna in Uruk (see lines 30–34, 56–58 in *COS* 1:512). According to line 24 above, the original creation of humanity took place in the *uzu-mú-a*, which means "in the place where flesh grows," and refers to a sacred site in Nippur, the city of Enlil. The present line says that Nisaba is lord there. Lambert (2013:511) is concerned that Inanna is known to have been mistress there, but the close association between Inanna and Nisaba noted above should relieve any such concerns.

(72–73) Secret (knowledge): *Let the one who knows (this secret knowledge) reserve it (only for) the one who knows.*[44,i]	*i* Deut 29:29 (28); Dan 2:8, 19, 27–29, 30, 47	It is complete (and) collated; copy of an old (tablet). The hand of Kidin-Sîn, junior scribe, son of Sutû, scribe of the king.[45]

44 Lines 72–73 are the earliest known occurrence of the so-called "secrecy formula" that appears in texts from this time forward (i.e., from the Middle Assyrian period ca. 1500–1200 BCE) until the end of the cuneiform tradition (ca. 225 CE; Beaulieu 1992:98; Lenzi 2008:175). Most of them come from the Neo-Assyrian period or later (Veldhuis 2010:80; cf. also Beaulieu 1992). For substantial treatments of the secrecy formula in the cuneiform scribal tradition, see Rochberg (2004:210–219), van der Toorn (2007:24–29), Veldhuis (2010), and especially the full discussion in Lenzi (2008). The latter concluded that this formula was to be taken seriously as a strategy to protect a body of secret knowledge that was maintained among the ranks of certain specialized scribal scholars (*ummânū*): astrologers, diviners, physicians, exorcists, and lamentation priests. This knowledge purportedly originated with Ea (Sum. Enki), the god of secrets and wisdom, and was communicated through the ancient *apkallū* (antediluvian sages). Those who had this knowledge were considered competent and had the authority in the royal court to serve as intermediaries between the kings and the gods (Lenzi 2008:1–219 with summary pp. 377–380, 384–387).

Lenzi (2008:307–377 with summary pp. 380–386) argues that a similar kind of secrecy is mentioned in Deut 29:29(28) and Dan 2:8–47, and is reflected in the polemics of wisdom in Prov 8:22–31. He also suggests that it also manifests itself in the characterization of Moses as an *apkallu* figure in Deut 34:10–12. In the Bible, however, he points out that the secret knowledge from the divine council that came through the prophets was not delivered as knowledge to be kept secret, but as open revelation to all God's people.

45 For the cuneiform text of the later Neo-Assyrian colophon see Lambert 2013: pl. 66 (text K 4175 with other fragments), and also his transliteration on p. 358. In addition to the secrecy formula, which appears in another form but with the same basic meaning, the Neo-Assyrian colophon includes, among other things: (1) an introductory call to praise the goddess Nisaba (see lines 70–71 above and n. 43), (2) the incipit of Atra-ḫasīs (see Lambert and Millard 1969:42–43, Foster 2005:227–280, and COS 1:450–352; see also the remarks in the introduction above and in Lambert 2013:352), which means that Atra-ḫasīs would have been attached as the next (third) composition in the series of compositions to which KAR 4 belongs, and (3) finally, the incipit of the double columned Silbenalphabet that came before KAR 4 in the three composition series.

REFERENCES

Text: Ebeling 1919 (= KAR 4 handcopy); Lambert 2013: pls. 65–67; Landersdorfer 1917:62–76, pls. I–II (photographs of KAR 4); and ETSCL. Transliterations, Translations, and Studies: Bottero and Kramer 1989:502–508; Clifford 1994:49–51; Foster 2005:491–493; Hecker 1994:606–608; Heidel 1963:68–71; Lambert 2013:350–359, 510–511; Lisman 2013:60–64, 330–346; Pettinato 1971:74–85 and pl. I.

ENKI AND THE WORLD ORDER (4.91)

Richard E. Averbeck

"Enki and the World Order" (= EWO) is a long and relatively well-preserved Sumerian mythological composition (ca. 472 lines). There are a few lines missing here and there, and then especially near the end. A full critical edition is not yet available, but is currently under preparation by Jerrold Cooper (for now see Benito 1969, which is still useful, Kramer and Maier 1989, Römer 1993, and Vanstiphout 1997 with the literature cited there). Limitations of space do not allow a full presentation and treatment of the whole text here. Nevertheless, the substantial selections provided follow the basic outline of the composition, and include something from all four major units of the composition. The translation is newly made from the Sumerian text, largely based on the composite transliteration made available in ETSCL 1.1.3, which is grounded on the work of Miguel Civil, Joachim Krecher, Hermann Behrens, and Bram Jagersma. In some places other resources and readings are consulted and occasionally cited in the notes. I am especially grateful to the late lamented Åke Sjöberg for his kindness in making available to me M. W. Green's manuscript of EWO readings, which she prepared for the Pennsylvania Sumerian Dictionary project in the Tablet Room at the Museum of the University of Pennsylvania. The explanatory notes provided below are drawn largely from Averbeck 2003a and 2003b and the literature cited there, but other primary sources and more recent secondary sources are also consulted.

EWO divides naturally into four major sections. The first section opens with the author's third person praise to Enki (lines 1–60). In the second section, Enki praises himself twice in the first person (lines 61–139): (a) in his first self-praise Enki recounts how Enlil commissioned him and gave him the gift of the *me*'s and *nam-tar*, which refer to the various cultural components that made up the core of Sumerian life and culture, and the power to determine destinies, respectively (lines 61–85), and (b) in the second self-praise Enki proposes to take a journey through Sumer on his barge in order to fulfill his commission to establish proper order and prosperity in Sumer (lines 86–139). The third section, the long central part of the composition, recounts Enki's journey through the land, decreeing the destiny of the Sumerian world (lines 140–386). It comprises two parts. In the first part, Enki begins with Sumer as whole, and especially Ur, and moves from there to the surrounding regions of Magan, Meluḫḫa, and Dilmun (lines 140–249). In the second part, he comes back again to the Sumerian homeland itself where, in a twelve cycle series, he assigns specific deities to take charge of the functions of various regions and components of the Sumerian world order (lines 250–386). This third section is presented in full here. In the fourth section, Inanna complains to Enki that he had not assigned her any special functional powers in his decreeing of destinies, and Enki responds to her complaint (lines 387–471). In this last section, the lacunae in the text are the most extensive and tantalizing.

Scholars disagree about the basic nature of EWO as to whether it is an account of the creation of the cosmos (i.e., cosmogony; Horowitz 1998:142–143), a description of how the Sumerian world functioned with no real attention to the creation of the material world in the first place (i.e., cosmology, not cosmogony; Vanstiphout 1997:120–122), some kind of combination of the two, or something else (e.g., a foil for the exaltation of Inanna, where everything depends on the last section of the composition, which is unfortunately badly damaged and fragmentary; Kramer and Maier 1989:38). There are instances where Enki's decrees on his journey (esp. section 3 part 2, lines 250–386) seem to refer to the actual creation of key elements of the Sumerian material world (e.g., the Tigris and Euphrates rivers, lines 250–273), but in other places it appears that the material elements are in place already, only needing to be put in proper functioning order (as Vanstiphout has noted; e.g., Enki's calling upon the rain in lines 309–317). Moreover, the wording of the first part of Enki's journey (esp. lines 162–249; largely untreated here, but see the outline and notes 9–10 below) suggests that Sumer, Ur, Magan, etc. are already in existence.

Of course, cosmogony and cosmology are not mutually exclusive in ancient Near Eastern texts since, in such texts, how something is made has effects on how it functions, and it makes no sense to make something that has no function. Everything has to work together. In one sense, Enki's filling of the Tigris and Euphrates rivers (lines 250–273) creates Sumer, since without them there is no Sumerian world to arrange. The following two cycles (marshes and the sea, lines 274–308) naturally flow out of the flow of these two rivers from northwest to southeast, all the way through the Sumerian homeland. And the effectiveness of everything else in the following decrees depends completely on this river system, or is somehow attached and adjunct to it.

Whatever one concludes about the issue of cosmogony and/or cosmology in EWO, there are two lines near the end of the composition that suggest a different but related angle of view. Lines 451–452 use the verb gi_4 "return, restore" in saying, "... let the land (of Sumer) *restore* its (fertile) soil ... let the land (of Sumer) *restore* its (fertile) soil" (see the full rendering below and the note there). This suggests that perhaps it is not a matter of one or the other – material creation versus world order – but the maintenance or perhaps on occasion the restoration of world order and prosperity in Sumer based on the divine order that Enki initiated, the key components of which he placed under the control of the various deities listed. In this case, the focus would be on the ecosystem of Sumer rather than cosmogony and/or cosmology (see Averbeck 2003a:27, n. 10; 2003b:768–771).

At a certain point in the composition, the ritual side of all this makes an appearance too. At the turn from the second to the third section of the composition – at the very beginning of the Enki's journey (see lines 140–154) – there is a rather surprising shift in the text. As Enki makes himself ready to embark on his journey to determine destinies in Sumer and the surrounding regions, the text shifts from a *divine* point of view to that of *human priestly ritual activity*. This passage suggests a kind of conflation of the primarily mythological nature of the text with human ritual activities performed by the leaders and priests of Eridu. Sometimes myth is also articulated somehow in the ritual world. These lines appear to be an example of that. It seems that by bringing the human ritual world into the divine mythic world of the text, EWO lines 140–154 reflect some sort of ritual system or perhaps occasion with which EWO was associated. The ritual goal would have been to enact the concerns for restoration and/or maintenance of the Sumerian world order reflected in the mythology of EWO. These ritual procedures enabled the leaders and priests, on behalf of the whole population of Sumer, to actively participate in the restoration and/or maintenance of the Sumerian world order by engaging with the gods (especially Enki) and calling on them for their active participation in this essential matter (see further remarks Averbeck 2003b:769–771 and the literature cited there).

Basically, EWO programmatically sets forth the fundamental environmental, ecological, technological, economic, agricultural, architectural, pastoral, and industrial occupations and conditions that were the foundations of life in ancient Sumer. It begins with the lifeline of ancient Sumer, the watercourses of the Tigris and Euphrates rivers, the swamps and lakes that arose in connection with them, all the way down to the sea in the south (i.e., the Persian Gulf), and even the importance of rainfall (cycles 1–4). In turn, these rivers provided for the possibility of irrigation agriculture, which involved the work of digging canals and ditches, working the soil and planting crops with plows and teams of oxen, and the growth and harvesting of barley, lentils, and other crops (cycles 5–6). The making of bricks and use of them in the construction of buildings, domestic and otherwise, fills out the basic foundations of city life in ancient Sumer (cycles 7–8). Enki's work then turns to the highland and lowland plains, the places of wild game and pastoral activity – the place of the shepherd as opposed to the farmer (cycles 9–10).

Finally, the prosperity that came with the combination of all these resources brought with it the need to demarcate the boundaries between the various city-states in the alluvium (cycle 11) and establish the textile industry that was foundational to the development of trade (cycle 12). The latter was actually based on the pastoral resources of the plains that extended beyond the agricultural alluvium (cycles 9–10 above).

We know that these cycles were not viewed as presenting a complete picture in every important detail because in Inanna's complaint that follows five goddesses are mentioned along with the element(s) of culture over which Enki had placed them (lines 395–423, not treated here). Only one of them is mentioned in the previous 12 cycles (i.e., Nanshe, cycle 3). The other four include goddesses over giving birth to children, jewelry, metal working, and scribal practice. Nevertheless, the twelve cycles provide a general picture of the ancient Sumerian homeland and its ecosystem.

Section 1: Praise of Enki (lines 1–60)

(1) Exalted lord of heaven and earth, noble one, self-reliant one;
father Enki,[1] propagated by a wild ox, begotten by a mighty wild bull;
tenderly cared for by the great mountain, Enlil, beloved of holy An;
the king, celtis tree planted in the Abzu, who rises up above all the lands;
(5) the great dragon who stands in Eridu,
whose shadow reaches over heaven and earth;
a grove of grape vines that extends through the (whole) land;
Enki, lord of abundance of the Anunna gods …

[Further praise of Enki (lines 10–16)]

(17) Counting days and making months enter into their houses in order to complete years;
to present completed years to the assembly (for a) decision;
making a decision to put days in good order;
(20) father Enki, you are king among its assembled people[2];
you opening (your) mouth things multiply, (and) abundance emerges …[a]

a Gen 1:3, 6, 9, 11, 14, 20, 24, 26

[There follows a list of produce and Enki's powers of fertility (lines 22–60; partially broken)]

Section 2: Enki's Self-Praises (lines 61–139)

The First Self-Praise (lines 61–85)
(61) Enki, king of the Abzu, did indeed admire himself greatly, did rightly expound (his) all sufficiency:
"My father, the king of heaven and earth,
made (me) shine radiantly in heaven and earth,
my elder brother, king of all the lands,
(65) collected (all) the *me*'s (and) put (all) the *me*'s in my hand(s).[3]
From the Ekur, the house of Enlil,
to my Abzu in Eridu I brought all the skilled arts and crafts …

[*Enki praises his own powers of fertility, wisdom, and justice* (lines 68–74)]

(75) With Enlil looking out over the land, I am decreeing good destinies.
He has placed in my hand the decreeing of destinies at the place of the rising of the sun.
I am cherished by Nintu.
I am the one whom Ninḫursaĝ gives a good name.
I am the leader of the Anunna gods.

1 For a review of the early development of Mesopotamian religion, the central importance of Enki, Inanna, and Enlil, and the relationships between them in the Sum. pantheon from the fifth down into the third millennia BC, respectively, see now Averbeck 2014:45–51, 60–67 and the extensive literature cited there, with Lisman 2013:127–209, esp. 151–155 for further data and variations. The focus of EWO is, of course, Enki (line 2), the patron deity of Eridu in the far south of Sumer, who ruled as lord of the underground waters known as the Abzu from his main temple, the (*é*)*-abzu* ("[House of] the Abzu") in Eridu (George 1993:65). Enki was well-known for his many skills and great wisdom as well as his control of the *me*'s (see the note on line 65 below).

Enlil ("lord wind"; line 3) was known as the God of weather and the atmosphere. His temple was the *é-kur* ("House Mountain") in Nippur in northern of Sumer (George 1993:116). He became the chief and unifying deity of Sumer early in the third millennium probably also in association with the rise of Kish as the dominating political force even further to the north (see the title "king of Kish"). EWO was likely composed in the late third millennium BC and, therefore, has Enki blessed by Enlil, and arranging the Sum. world on his behalf so that abundance could flow to Enlil in the Ekur (see lines 62–67, 75–76, 130, etc.).

The third major deity who arises to prominence late in the story line of EWO is the goddess Inanna, whose main temple was the *é-an-na* ("House of Heaven"), the temple of both Anu and Inanna in Uruk (George 1993:67–68), located in central Sumer along the Euphrates. She was known to be aggressive in both love and war. Near the end of the myth she raises a complaint to Enki about his overlooking her in the distribution of divine responsibilities for the world order (lines 387–471). For the Anunna gods, see n. 4 below.

2 Enki is the god of wisdom, abundance, and prosperity, and often the creator and friend of humanity (see, e.g., Enki and Ninmaḫ *COS* 1:516–518 and as Enki/Ea in Atra-ḫasis *COS* 1:450–452). Thus, he is the king of the assembly of the people.

3 In this first self-praise (lines 61–139), Enki begins by proclaiming that his sovereign brother, Enlil, granted him possession of all the *me*'s, which were the basic elements of Sum. material culture, various cultural institutions (religious, social, and political), and the rules, principles, attributes, capacities, and functions that made the whole cultural system work properly (lines 61–67; see further explanation in Averbeck 1997:82, n. 98; *COS* 2:418, n. 2, 429–430, n. 61, and 431 n. 69).

Similarly, Enlil granted him control of the decreeing of destinies/fates (*nam-tar*, lines 75–76; = Akk. *šīmtu*, pl. *šīmātu*, which derives from the verb *šâmu* "to fix, decree"). He made Enki the one who determined how things work in heaven and earth. For a helpful discussion of the concept based largely on Akk. texts but also with reference to Sum., see Rochberg-Halton 1982. It refers primarily to the act of determining by decree (see also *CAD* Š 1:364 and the lit. cited there, where it is proposed that, in the end, "*nam-tar* probably denotes the solemn pronunciation of binding words"). Destinies that are decreed are "preordained or determined norms" that do not necessarily "remain unchanging or static." There is "a schematic order of all phenomena" that was "decreed by the gods." It could be maintained through regular ritual procedures, but could also be interfered with. It was also "susceptible to the forces of magic," which was the rationale of omens and divination (ibid., 365–368). It is often associated with creation, as in Enuma Elish line 8, which refers to the pre-creation time as that time *ši-ma-tu la ši-i-mu* "when no destinies had been decreed" (Lambert 2013:50–51).

(80) I am the one born as the foremost son of holy An."

After the lord had proclaimed his own magnificence,
after the great prince had pronounced praises (about) himself,
the Anunna gods took their stand there in prayer and supplication:
"O Lord who stands over skilled arts and crafts,
(85) who makes decisions; the praised one; Enki, praise!"[4]

The Second Self-Praise (lines 86–139)
(86) For a second time, to rejoice in (his own) greatness,[5]
Enki, king of the Abzu, did indeed did admire himself greatly, did rightly expound (his) all sufficiency:
"I am the Lord. I am the one whose word is upright.
I am the one in charge of everything ..."

[*Continued self-praise* (lines 89–105)]

(106) "In my Abzu, sacred song and incantation resonate everywhere for me.
My travel barge 'Crown,' the 'Ibex of the Abzu,' carries me there rejoicing in its heart.
Through the vast marshes to whatever place my heart chooses
(110) it sails. It submits to me."

[*Enki praises the operators of the barge and the joys of the journey* (lines 111–123)]

"The lands of Meluḫḫa, Magan and Dilmun,[6]
(125) me being Enki, let them look upon me.
Let the boat of Dilmun load up(?) with lumber.
Let the boat of Magan bind (its load up) sky-high.
Let the cargo boat of Meluḫḫa
transport gold and silver;
(130) let it deliver (them) to Nippur for Enlil, king of all the lands."

(131) To the one who has no city, to the one who has no house;
(to) the Martu nomads he granted livestock as a gift.[7]

[*The Anunna gods affirm Enki's self-praise* (lines 133–139; cf. lines 81–85 above)]

Section 3: Enki's Journey (lines 140–386)

Ritual Preparations for Enki's Journey (lines 140–161)
(140) For the great prince who travels in his land,
all the lords and rulers,
all the incantation priests of Eridu,
(and) all the linen clothed priests of Sumer

4 At the end of both Enki's first and second self-praise (lines 81–85 and 133–139, respectively) the Anunna gods affirm him with praise. Essentially, the Anunna were all the great gods of the Sum. pantheon. They have been thought to be the offspring of An and the mother goddess, Ningal/Ninḫursaĝa (see this tentative conclusion in Lisman 2013:166–170 and the primary and secondary lit. cited there; cf. also Lambert 2008:22–37 for analysis of the early god lists). There is considerable confusion in the scholarly discussion of the number, origin, identity, and function of the Annuna (= Akk. "Anunnaki"). According to lines 371–373 (in cycle 11) below, "For the Anunna gods, Enki did establish dwellings in the cities; he did establish plots in the fields." This suggests that, at least in EWO, the Anunna could be identified as the deities who had temple estates in the various city-states of Sumer during the third millennium BCE, since cycle 11 is primarily about Utu's control of the boundaries and relationships between these city-states and their temple estates. Here (lines 81–85 and 133–139) these Anunna gods praise Enki for bringing order to the whole realm and between them in their various regional temple estates under the authority of Enlil, the supreme deity in Sumer in the third millennium (see n. 1 above). For remarks on the temple estates in ancient Sumer, see n. 43 on lines 371–373 below.

5 Enki's second self-praise focuses first on his decree of good destiny for his home city (Eridu), and his temple there (the Abzu). It then turns to his determination to travel from there on his barge through the land of Sumer and even to Meluḫḫa, Magan, and Dilmun, ancient foreign places of trade for Sumer, to have them bring boatloads of their goods to Enlil in Nippur (lines 84–132). Although this part of the text is somewhat broken, Enki clearly states his intent to take such a trip (lines 107–108 and 115–118). The core of the composition clarifies his reason for the trip (lines 188–386), which was to decree the destinies throughout Sumer and the surrounding regions, since Enlil had granted Enki control of this power according to the first self-praise.

6 On the locations of these regional trade partners see n. 9 below.

7 Lines 131–132 interrupt the self-praise of this unit just before the final affirmation by the Anunna gods (see n. 5 above). See the note on lines 248–249 below for further discussion. There are two possible understandings of the term "Martu" in EWO, and they are not mutually exclusive (see Averbeck 2003b:764). On the one hand, Martu here may simply refer to "westerners" (Sum. *mar-tu* means "westerner"), who lived northwest of the Sum. heartland between the Tigris and Euphrates, and especially on both sides of the upper Euphrates (northern Syria). It could also include those Martu who appear to have lived on the desert fringes around the Euphrates even in the south, and possibly also north and east of the Tigris. In other words, the geographical nature of the context here in EWO may suggest that the term Martu refers to them in their western homeland, or at least outside of Sumer proper on the fringes around the Sum. homeland in several different directions.

On the other hand, in EWO the Sum. homeland is referred to by the Sum. term *kalam* (= "land, country"; lines 188–191, cf. also line 117 and elsewhere) while the foreign lands known as Magan, Meluḫḫa, and Dilmun are referred to by the term *kur* (= "land, foreign land, mountain"; lines 219, 238, cf. also line 124). There is no such geographical "land" term used to refer to the Martu in EWO (lines 131–132 and 248–249). They are described only by their lifestyle (non-urban tent dwellers) and their being granted the "animals (of the steppe)" (Sum. *máš-anše*). This may suggest that no particular geographical region is intended. We know that their Martu names, distinctive tribal identity, and even their pastoral nomadic lifestyle persisted even within the boundaries of Sumer (Bucellati 1966: 336–339, 346, 351–362; cf. Greengus 2003:64–65). So the mention of them in EWO may simply serve the purpose of distinguishing the Martu lifestyle from that of the Sumerians themselves, whether they lived inside or outside of the Sum. heartland. In this case, the two sets of Martu lines in the composition (lines 131–132 and 248–249) complete the description of their surrounding world not only on a literary level, but also in terms of ethnicity, lifestyle, and occupation.

performed the purification (rites) of the Abzu.[8]
(145) They stepped up (for) father Enki, in the holy place, the most excellent place.
(they) … in his rest chamber,
called (Enki's) name in its assigned place,
purified the exalted shrine, the Abzu,
brought the tall juniper, the pure plant into its midst,
(150) put in order the holy … on the exalted waterway of Enki,
ascended the main stairway of Eridu on the good quay,
loaded up the 'Ibex of the Abzu' at the good quay, the exalted quay,
set up the holy *uzga*-shrine,
(and) pronounced prayer after prayer there.

[*Seven lines badly broken or missing* (lines 155–161)]

Enki's Journey, Part 1 (lines 162–249)
[*Enki boards his boat and travels through the whole region decreeing destinies for Sumer* (lines 192–209), *Ur* (lines 210–218), *Meluḫḫa* (lines 219–237), *Dilmun* (lines 238–241), *and the enemy lands, Elam and Marḫaši* (lines 242–247).[9]

(248) To the one who has no city, to the one who has no house;
(to) the Martu nomads Enki granted livestock as a gift.[10]

Enki's Journey, Part 2 (lines 250–386)[11]
Cycle 1: Enki fills the Tigris and Euphrates rivers and puts Enbilulu in charge of the waterways (lines 250–273)
(250) After he had turned his eyes from there,[12]
after father Enki had indeed lifted (his eyes) onto the Euphrates river,[13,b]
like a raging bull he stood up triumphantly,
lifting up his penis, he ejaculated
and filled the Tigris river with flowing water.
(255) Being like a mother cow in its pasture, mooing for its calf in its scorpion infested pen,

b Gen 2:14

[8] As Enki readies himself to embark on his journey to determine destinies in Sumer and the surrounding regions, the text shifts from the divine perspective to human priestly ritual activity (lines 140–154; lines 155–161 are badly broken). Here there is a kind of conflation of Enki mythology with the human ritual activities performed by the leaders and priests of Eridu. They send Enki off on his journey with a flurry of purification rituals and prayers as he boards his procession boat. The ritual goal was to participate actively on a human level in the restoration and/or maintenance of the Sum. world that was the major concern of EWO as a myth (see further discussion in the introduction above, Averbeck 2003b:769–771, and the general remarks in Johnson 2014:43–44 as it relates to myth, ritual, cosmogony, and cosmology).

[9] Although it is not included in the translation here due to limitations of space, the first part of Enki's journey (lines 162–247) has him proclaiming decrees that would make Sumer a prosperous central region within its larger surrounding world. Meluḫḫa and Dilmun (lines 124–130, 219–241), and Magan (lines 124–130), were regular trading partners, while Elam and Marḫaši (lines 242–247) were frequent enemies in battle from the east (modern day Iran). Moorey (1999:xxi) and Potts (1995:1453–1459) place Dilmun, Magan, and Meluḫḫa to the south and east of Sumer. Dilmun is the coastal region of northeastern Saudi Arabia along the coast of the Persian Gulf. Magan is further to the southeast along the same coastline, but beyond the straits between the Persian Gulf and the Gulf of Oman, leading into the Arabian Sea. Meluḫḫa is still further east along the coast of Pakistan and western India, part of the so-called pre-Aryan Harappan Civilization of the Indus valley (see also further remarks in Averbeck 2003b:763).

Michaux-Colombot (2001) has collected all the data from ancient Mesopotamian and classical literary sources as well as the Uruk and Early Dynastic archaeological evidence for very early trade between Mesopotamia and Egypt. The conclusion reached is that "the Magan and Meluḫḫa problem must be left an open question." There are two possibilities. On the one hand, it could be limited to the southeastern Persian Gulf and beyond, the regions listed in the previous paragraph. On the other hand, Magan could have referred to the "North Arabian corridor linking Mesopotamia to Canaan and Egypt" which could have "shared the whole Arabian peninsula … with the Dilmun entity" further to the south and east along the Persian Gulf. Similarly, Meluḫḫa "may have meant the general offshore 'Indian' thalassocracy" of the northwestern Indian Ocean that reached all the way from India to the Red Sea and beyond (i.e., the Erythrean world), something like that established in the Mediterranean world by the Phoenicians from the coast of the Levant to Spain.

[10] Except for the explicit mention of Enki here in line 249, the same two lines about the Martu also occur at lines 131–132 above, where they fit the context neither in terms of content nor grammar (see Averbeck 2003b:762–763 and n. 7 above). Here in lines 248–249, however, they fit the flow of the narrative and separate the first part of Enki's journey (lines 162–247) from the second part, which follows immediately (lines 250–386). This suggests these two lines may have been inserted secondarily from here (lines 248–249) to there (lines 131–132), since some of the foreign regions mentioned in the previous lines here (lines 162–247) are also referred to there, just before lines 131–132. As remarked in n. 7 above, Martu lived on the fringes of Sumer both geographically and culturally.

[11] Part 2 of Enki's journey (lines 250–386) is the focus of concern in the composition: the proper development and maintenance of world order in the Sum. homeland. Here Enki initiates the various forces of nature and cultural phenomena necessary to make Sumer a prosperous place, and places the appropriate Sum. deity in charge of properly managing each one of them. For a summary of the twelve cycles see the introduction above. For the details of each cycle see the notes below and the more extensive treatment in Averbeck 2003a:27–59.

[12] The phrase "from there" refers either to all those regions surrounding Sumer reviewed in the previous lines (i.e., the first part of his journey, lines 162–249), or perhaps only the territory controlled by the Martu (lines 248–249; cf. n. 7 above on lines 131–132).

[13] The Euphrates and the Tigris rivers appear in alternating sequence in the translation given here (Euphrates lines 251 and 256; Tigris lines 254 and 258). There are two extant manuscripts of lines 250–257, both of which read Euphrates in line 251 and Tigris in lines 254. The main text reads Euphrates at line 256, but the smaller fragment has Tigris. See the renderings and remarks in Cooper 1989:87, n. 2 and Vanstiphout 1997:120, nn. 16–17. Again, I thank Åke Sjöberg for kindly making available to me M. W. Green's manuscript of EWO readings.

Jerrold Cooper has examined this element of the story in some detail and relates it to the sexuality of the Inanna-Dumuzi love poetry. He concludes that the rationale for it is to be found "in Enki's role as the ultimate source of fresh water irrigation, the fecundation that is the very basis of Babylonia's agricultural economy" (Cooper 1989:89).

Steinkeller (2001a with the additions in 2001b), following Heimpel's groundbreaking work on this problem (Heimpel 1987 and 1990), corrects the longstanding misconception that the watering of the Sum. heartland was accomplished largely by the Euphrates, with the Tigris not much involved. He points out that literary and other texts have long been known to connect the Umma/Lagash region with the irrigating and fertilizing waters of the Tigris. See esp. the very helpful maps in Steinkeller (2001a) 40 and 50, and his summaries of conclusions on pp. 40–41, 48–49, 55–56, and 64–65. The importance of both rivers is reflected here in EWO.

like a raging bull he ... the Euphrates river in his vigor.
He lifted up his penis and did indeed bring a wedding gift.
The Tigris river rejoiced in its heart like a great wild cow, it ... in its offspring.
It did indeed bring water, truly flowing water. Its wine will indeed be good.
It did indeed bring grain, truly fine grain. The people will indeed eat it.
It filled the Ekur, the house of Enlil (with) all kinds of things.
Enlil was happy with Enki. Nippur was glad.
The lord fastened on the diadem for lordship;
put on the proper crown for kingship.
He did indeed touch the ground with his left arm,
(so that) abundance did spring up from the ground for him.
The one who holds the scepter in his right hand;
who measures out the devouring (force of) the Tigris and Euphrates rivers
with his splendid mouth(?)[14];
there being plenty pouring forth from the palace like oil,
the lord of the destinies, Enki, king of the Abzu,
Enbilulu, the overseer of the waterways,[15]
Enki put (him) fully in charge.[16]

Cycle 2: Enki fills the marshes and reedbeds with fish and fowl (lines 274–277)[17]
He cal[led upon the marshes] and granted them many kinds of carp.
He cal[led upon the reed-beds] and granted them old dry reeds and fresh reed-sprouts.
[*Two missing lines and one badly broken*]
The one whose stretched out net fish cannot escape;
whose trap no animal that is born can escape;
whose snare no bird can escape;
... the exalted strong man(?), the son of ...
... the man who loves fish,[c]
Enki put (him) fully in charge.

c Gen 1:20–23

Cycle 3: Enki establishes a shrine in the south and puts Nanshe in charge (lines 285–308)
The lord founded a shrine, a holy shrine, its interior being skillfully woven together.
He founded a shrine in the sea, a holy shrine, its interior being skillfully woven together.[18]
The shrine whose interior is a tangled cord, a thing no man can know;
the shrine whose location is by the constellation "Field";

14 Lines 268–269 are especially difficult, but the idea seems to be that Enbilulu (see line 272 below) is being described here as the one who keeps the flow of the Tigris and Euphrates rivers under control so that it is productive for agriculture rather than destructive through flooding (see n. 15 below).

15 The rivers were both the lifeline of ancient Sumer and, at the same time, a major threat to the civilization that they spawned: "First, the alluvial plain south of Baghdad has a negligible slope (Baghdad, at 410 km from Basrah, is only about 33 m above sea level). This results in extremely unstable watercourses very sensitive to the pressures of the yearly flood and to sedimentation. Secondly, the flood comes practically at the same time as the cereal harvest, in April–May. Not only does the flood come at an inopportune time for the plants growth, but also menaces the crops themselves. Flood control has always been the central concern of farmer and king alike in the history of southern Mesopotamia" (Civil 1994:68, cf. also 110).

Since the flood as well as the harvest were in the spring of year (April/May), the goal was to control the flood and drain off excess waters so that it did not destroy the harvest, while at the same time capturing the flood waters and channeling them so as to flood fields where and when this was appropriate for the irrigation for the next year's agricultural cycle. This "was one of the major activities in Mesopotamian life" (Civil 1994:29 lines 2–4, and commentary pp. 68–69; cf. Jacobsen 1982:57–58), employing immense amounts of labor to keep the large-scale irrigation system intact, especially through communal efforts during the seasons when the actual fieldwork was minimal (see also the helpful summary in Eyre 1995:180–182, 185). It involved two main types of work: (1) earth moving, which included digging and/or dredging out canals and ditches as well as piling it up to make levees and dikes, and (2) the gathering, binding up, and mixing of reeds from the marshes with sand/earth to reinforce dikes and levees, and especially for preventing destruction during the annual time of the flood (Civil 1994:115, 121–122; see also n. 6 in the edition of KAR 4 in this volume, and the still useful discussion and illustrations in Kang 1973:421–440).

16 This rendering seeks to keep the Sum. poetic lines in order. A more English friendly translation of lines 271–273 would be: "the lord of the destinies, Enki, king of the Abzu – he did indeed put Enbilulu, the overseer of the waterways, in charge." See also, similarly, the concluding lines of each of the cycles that follow below.

17 The text of cycle 2 is relatively broken, although the general subject is clear: lagoons, marshes, and reed beds that teemed with fish and waterfowl. These arose naturally in the environment created by the two rivers, especially in the far south delta region near the Gulf, but also at various places along the meandering courses of the Tigris and Euphrates. The line that mentions the deity whom Enki placed in charge of this part of the Sum. world order is not readable, but he is said to be adept at netting fish and snaring birds, and known as one who loves fish (see further Averbeck 2003a:33–35 and the primary and secondary literature cited there).

18 The surging waters of the deep and the waters from the Tigris and Euphrates meet in the delta region. It is this confluence of the world of the rivers of Sumer with that of the sea that accounts for the description of this shrine in terms of the awesomeness of the sea and its waves. The sea is on the fringe of Sumer, so it is associated with the "deep" (Sum. *engur* = Akk. *apsû*; see line 294 below), which may refer to, among other things, the swamp regions in the far southeastern corner of Sumer (with the waterways "being skillfully woven together" like a "tangled cord," lines 285–287), below Sirara (see line 306), and the open sea beyond, as well as the "deep cosmic waters" below the surface of the earth and the sea, and even the underworld itself; see Horowitz 1998:334–347, esp. the citation of EWO lines 302–307 on p. 341 and the summary on p. 344.

the holy upper shrine whose location faces toward the constellation "Chariot."[19,d]
Its frightening sea being a rising wave whose splendor is terrifying,
the Anunna-gods, the great gods, do not dare to confront it.
It refreshes their hearts. The palace being in celebration over it,
the Anunna-gods were standing there in prayer and supplication.
For Enki they set up a lofty dais in the Eengura.[20,e]
For the lord, the flowing … (?)
The great prince … offspring … (?)
The pelican of the sea,[21] the boundary of … (?)
The shrine (of) good things, the shrine (of) everything that is born … (?)
The Ekur, the house of Enlil, he did indeed fill with all good things.
Enlil rejoiced over Enki. Nippur was glad.
She who sets sail … in the holy shrine,
who stimulates … copulation …,
who … over the great high flood of the subterranean waters,
the frightening waves, the inundation of the sea …,
who goes out from the … (?),
the lady of Sirara,[22] … fish …, Nanshe,
over the sea in all its wide extent,

d Job 9:9, 38:31–32; Isa 13:10; Amos 5:8; 2 Kings 23:5

e Exod 26:33; 40:3; Lev 16:2

f Pss 18:9; 29:7; 68:4, 33; 104:3–4; Deut 33:26; 2 Sam 22:10

Enki put (her) fully in charge.

Cycle 4: Enki institutes rain and storm and puts Ishkur in charge (lines 309–317)
He called upon the rain of heaven.
He positioned(?) it (there) as floating clouds.
He drives it(?) (along) … rising at the horizon.
He makes … mounds into fields.
The one who rides the great storm; who strikes with lightning flashes[f];
who blocks the midst of heaven with a holy door bolt;
the son of An, the canal inspector of heaven and earth[23];
Ishkur, the man of abundance, the son of An,
Enki put (him) fully in charge.

Cycle 5: Enki institutes agricultural field work and puts Enkimdu in charge (lines 318–325)
He prepared plow, yoke, and team.
The great prince, Enki, provided the leading long horned ox(?).
He opened the mouth of the holy furrow.
He made the grain grow in the cultivated field.
The lord who wears the diadem, the ornament of the high plain;
who (handles) the implements, the farmer of Enlil;
Enkimdu, the man of dikes and irrigation ditches,[24]

19 This is the only cycle in which constellations are mentioned (lines 288–289), specifically, the "Field" (Sum. ^{mul}*iku* consisting of four stars that make a square in the northern sky, like a field; later known as Pegasus after the winged horse in Greek mythology) and the "Chariot" (Sum. $^{mul\,giš}$*gigir* consisting of a combination of stars visible in the northern hemisphere during the winter, often illustrated by a chariot and charioteer; later known as Auriga, Latin for "Chariot"). The mention of constellations is somewhat puzzling (see Kramer and Maier 1989:49 and 220 n. 85), but it could perhaps refer to directional guides for those who traveled the sea. According to lines 301 and 307, Nanshe is "the one who sets sail (*u*$_5$-*a*) … in the holy shrine" and Enki puts here in charge of "the broad width of the sea."

20 Eengura = "the house/temple of the subterranean waters." For the meaning of *barag* "dais" see the more extensive note on KAR 4 line 10 in this volume. It refers to a niche for the deity and relates to the biblical *pārōket* that separated the holy place from the most holy place in the tabernacle, where the Ark of the Covenant was located (see, e.g., Exod 26:33; 40:3; Lev 16:2).

21 With regard to "the pelican of the sea" (*u*$_5^{mušen}$-*a-ab-ba*), in the composition known as *Nanshe and the Birds* Nanshe is closely associated with the pelican, perhaps because it is so large and majestic, and can be either a fresh water or a salt water bird (lines 1–22; ETCSL 5.9.1 and Civil 1961). From her "shrine in the sea" (line 286 above), Nanshe is in charge of the sea and its inundations as well as inducing sexual intercourse (line 302). The latter may be due to the close association between sexual intercourse and water/semen.

22 The compositions known as *The Home of the Fish* (ETCSL 5.9.1 and Civil 1961) and *Nanshe and the Birds* (ETCSL 4.14.3) are devoted to Nanshe, the goddess of the Sirara temple at NINA in the southern part of the Lagash district, near the Gulf (i.e., the sea). Her close association with Enki in the management of fish and birds is evident from references to her as "the child born in Eridu" and "the child of Enki" in *The Nanshe Hymn* (ETCSL 4.14.1 and *COS* 1:526–527 lines 8 and 61). *The Home of the Fish* and *Nanshe and the Birds* give us further information about the various kinds of birds and fish in the marshes, amid the reed beds, as well as those from the sea.

23 The god Ishkur is referred to here as "the canal inspector of heaven and earth" (*kù-gál-an-ki-a*, line 315), in contrast to Enbilulu, "the inspector of rivers/canals" (*kù-gál íd-da-ke*$_4$, line 272), who was in charge of maintaining the river system that was the basis of irrigation (see cycle 1 above). The distinction is important. Ishkur is in charge of the rains that come from the sky (lines 309–314), so he is said to do in both heaven and earth that which the latter does by means of the waterways on the ground. As Adams (1981:12–13) has observed, today, as in ancient Sumer: "… the amount of rainfall is, with rare exceptions, quite inadequate to produce a winter crop and is better regarded as only an occasional supplement to irrigation.… Heavy showers can be expected at any time from November through much of May, but they may not occur before December or even January and may be almost completely suspended for as much as two or three months during the growing cycle." Therefore, "it seems incontestable that agriculture was introduced into lower Mesopotamia only on the basis of irrigation."

24 For the terms "dikes (*e* = *ég*) and irrigation ditches (*pa*$_5$ = *pa[r]*)" see n. 6 on KAR 4 in this same volume, and the literature cited there. After sowing the crop in September/October, there came the removal of the remaining clods and then four irrigations over the winter months (November to February/March) as the crops grew and matured for the harvest in March/April/May (cf. also cycle 6 below; Civil 1994:31 lines 67–73, and commentary pp. 88–89, with Jacobsen 1982:59–61). See also Roaf (1990:127) for a picture of canal lines that remain on the Mesopotamian landscape even today, and Averbeck (2003a:40–44) for a summary of the whole complex of irrigation, cultivation, and agricultural work.

The amount of human labor needed to carry on large-scale irrigation of this kind was immense, thus accounting for much of the daily quotidian life of many of the common people in ancient Sumer (see Civil 1994:109–135 for a full discussion of the kinds of work involved in irrigation). Because irrigation resulted in "relatively high agricultural productivity, … large surpluses thus could be mobilized above the needs of the primary producers," so that a "… relatively high population density was attainable even at a fairly simple, only slowly improving level of technique. At least equally important, considerable proportions of the population could be maintained in specialized pursuits rather than agriculture itself" (Adams 1981:243; for further explanation see Adams 1981:242–252).

(325) Enki put (him) fully in charge.

Cycle 6: Enki supplies crops and fertility and puts Ezina in charge (lines 326–334)
The lord called upon the cultivated field and provided (it with) mottled barley.
Enki brought forth wheat, chickpea, and ...-meal; carp grain, mottled barley, and *innuḫa*-barley he heaped up in piles.
Enki redoubled the grain piles at the granary.
(330) With (the help of) Enlil he expanded the abundance among the people.
The one whose head and body are dappled, whose face is covered with date-syrup;
the lady who causes copulation, the vigor of the land, the life of the black-headed,[25]
Ezina,[26] the good bread, the (essential) thing of the whole world,
Enki put (her) fully in charge.

Cycle 7: Enki prepares hoes, brick molds, and bricks and puts Kulla in charge (lines 335–340)[27]
(335) The great prince bound the cord on the hoe[28] and prepared the brick mold.[29]
He made (the hoe) penetrate mother earth like precious oil.
The one who grasps the spiked tooth hoe, the corpse devouring snake;
who arranges the well-prepared brick mold (like) a shock of barley before the ewe;
Kulla, the man who ... sun-dried brick in the land,
(340) Enki put (him) fully in charge.

Cycle 8: Enki institutes the construction of buildings and puts Mušdama in charge (lines 341–348)
He tied the strings (in place); made the foundation (lines) straight.[30]
In the power of the assembly he established (the plan of) the house; properly performed the purification rituals.[31]
The great prince laid the foundations; set the bricks firmly on the ground.
He whose laid foundations do not sag;

[25] The "blacked-headed" are the Sumerians themselves.

[26] The name of the grain goddess is *ᵈezina₂* (= *ᵈašnan* written ŠE.TIR; ŠE = Akk. *še'u* "grain"). As the primary cereal crop they planted more barley than anything else because it is most resistant to salt. This was especially so, as the salinity in the soil increased over time. Wheat, various emmers (including emmer wheat), onions, and pulses (peas and chick-peas) were also grown, but in lesser amounts partly because they are less resistant to salt. We also have records of other lesser crops: garlic, flax, beans, lentils, and sesame. All of these are known from Sum. times, whether early or late, or both, but barley was always predominant (Jacobsen 1982:15).

[27] Irrigation agriculture brought with it not only high levels of production so that more people could be fed, but also required a large labor force. Therefore, irrigation and urbanization naturally developed side by side in ancient Sumer (cycles 7–8). Moreover, concentration of population and political organization in cities provided protection from natural disasters through diversification of resources and, at the same time, empowered them to compete with other urban centers for the limited natural resources available, including water (Adams 1981:242–243, 248–252).

[28] The expression "bound the cord on the hoe" seems to refer to binding the head of the hoe to the handle with a string/sinew (line 335; lit. *ᵍⁱˢal-e sa bí-sig₁₀* "[he] fixed a string upon the hoe"). The handle was apparently made of wood, and it would have one or more "teeth" (zú) made of wood or some other material. "The Disputation between the Hoe and the Plow" lines 2–4 describes it this way: "Hoe, made from poplar, with a tooth of ash; Hoe, made from Tamarisk, with a tooth of sea-thorn; Hoe, double-toothed, four-toothed" (*COS* 1:578). The regular hoe would have the blade(s) (i.e., its tooth or teeth) set at 90° to the handle, but there were many different kinds of hoes, some of which set the blade on the same plane as the handle, more like a pickax (see Civil 1994:71–72 comment on lines 10 and 12, and pp. 149–151). Kramer and Maier (1989:51) translate here "pickax."

[29] The "brick mold" was a rectangular wooden frame with no top or bottom that would be placed on the ground and filled with clay. The frames would usually be singular, but they could also be made in sets of two or three. Some kind of binding material would also be added to the clay mix to prevent the cracking of the brick. This could be straw, dung, pulverized sherds, or some other matter. The hoe would have been used to mix the clay for making the bricks. Brickfields were located near cultivated fields and their watercourses, since large amounts of water were needed for mixing the clay.

Once the clay had been properly pressed into shape in the brick mold and the excess clay cleaned off the top, the brick mold itself would be lifted up and off the brick so that it could be left to dry, perhaps only a day or two if the sun was hot, but sometimes for much longer periods of time (see Moorey 1999:305 and the pictures and explanation in Roaf 1990:31). The bricks were made in various shapes and types through the millennia. The flat rectangular shaped brick became standardized virtually everywhere during the last quarter of the third millennium BCE, but in first 600 years of the third millennium (Early Dynastic I–III) the plano-convex brick was popular in Sumer; flat on the bottom but convex shaped on the top, perhaps because the excess clay was not cleaned off the top of the mold (Moorey 1999:304, 306–309). See Roaf (1990:106–107) for a good view of the standard rectangular brick of Ur-Nammu's ziggurat at Ur and the manner of its laying in courses (ca. 2100 BCE; see also Averbeck 2003a:46–47 and the literature cited there for further explanation).

[30] For the use of strings and/or chalk lines to mark foundations and walls, and to line up bricks so walls are straight, etc., see now Averbeck 2010:22, 24–26 and the literature cited there.

[31] Cycle 8 is concerned with using the bricks of cycle 7 in the construction of buildings. According to the text, in addition to proper performance of purification rituals (*šu-luḫ*; see below), this involved the stretching of strings to guide the laying of foundation bricks straight according to the plan of the house, and then actually laying the foundations and the rest of the bricks. Enki put all this under the supervision of "Mušdama, Enlil's master builder (*šitim-gal*)," who was known for laying foundations so they do not sag (*nu-silig-ge*), building houses well and their vaults high (lines 343–346). From these lines we learn of the major concerns of builders, and even some of the dangers that come with inadequate building procedures.

For a careful discussion of building procedures see Moorey (1999:302–362), which includes the making of various kinds of bricks (see above, cycle 7), procedures for laying them in mundane and decorative ways, wall painting, plasters and mortars, the use of bitumen, various kinds of stone and wood (for roofing, walls, columns, doors, and interior decorations), and reeds (see in the remarks on cycle 2 above). For the building of the houses of the gods (i.e., temples) in the third millennium BCE, see now the extensive review in Averbeck 2010 (cf. more briefly Averbeck 2003a:48–49), where the Gudea Cylinders (Averbeck 2000) are the main text treated but other texts and pictures are also taken into consideration.

whose well-built houses do not collapse(?);
whose vault reaches to mid-heaven like a rainbow;
Mušdama, the master builder of Enlil,
Enki put (him) fully in charge.

Cycle 9: Enki supplies the high plains and puts Šakkan in charge (lines 349–357)[32]

He imbued the high plain[33] (with) a holy crown.
He attached a beard of lapis-lazuli on the highland plain; he wrapped (on it) a headdress of lapis-lazuli.
He perfectly lavished splendid greenery on the good place.[34]
He multiplied the animals of the highland plain; made them suitable (in number).
He multiplied the wild sheep and wild goats of the pastures; made them copulate.
The hero of the highland plain (who is) its crown, the king of the plain;
the great lion of the highland plain, the strong one, the great one, the exalted arm of Enlil;
Šakkan, the king of the foothills,[35]
Enki put (him) fully in charge.

Cycle 10: Enki supplies the lowland plains and puts Dumuzi-ušumgal-anna in charge (lines 358–367)

He built the sheepfold and made provision for (its) proper cleaning.
He established the cattle-pen and stocked (it) with the best fat and cream;
He made the dining hall of the gods overflow with prosperity.[36]
He made the plain that was fashioned for greenery attain abundance.[37]
The king, the faithful provider of the Eanna, the friend of An,
The beloved son-in-law of the young Suen, the holy spouse of Inanna,
the mistress, the lady of the great *me*'s,

---

32 As noted above, there were nomadic pastoralists who were not considered to be part of that homeland and Sum. culture proper, namely, the Martu (see lines 131–132, 248–249, and nn. 7 and 10 above). But that does not mean that no pastoral activities were engaged in within Sumer itself. On the contrary, it is a well-known fact that there was a symbiosis of sorts between the practices of animal husbandry and farming, and between pastoralists, farmers, and cities. Sometimes this even included Martu tribal groups and their herdsmen (Adams 1981:11, 250). EWO distinguishes between the "high, lofty, mighty, upland" (*uru*$_{16}$) "plain, steppe" (*edin*; line 349), also referred to as the "highland plain" (*an-edin-na*; line 350) where ibex and wild goats pastured (cycle 9), as opposed to the "(lowland) plain" (*edin*) of sheepfolds and cow-pens (cycle 10).

33 The highland plains were a place largely roamed by wild animals that multiplied and fed on the grasses and herbs of the foothill meadows (contrast the cow-pens and sheepfolds of cycle 10 below). Enki placed the god "Šakkan, king of the hill country" (or 'foothills' *ḫur-sag* line 356) in charge because, as the text puts it, he was muscular, like a lion, hefty and burly. Those who inhabited these regions would need to be vigorous and have the skills to hunt wild animals for their own subsistence and as part of their service to state and temple. It is known that the temples of the city-state centers were supplied, for example, with deer and other wild game probably brought in largely from these highland regions, along with birds and fish from the rivers and marshes (for the latter see cycle 2 above; Robertson 1995:446). The temple administrative texts actually retain records of fish and fowl.

34 The "holy crown" of the high plain, "beard of lapis lazuli," and "headdress of lapis-lazuli" appear to be "poetic images for the verdant vegetation of the steppe" (Kramer and Maier 1989:220, n. 99).

35 The term for "foothills" (*ḫur-sag* line 356) in particular, often refers to the slopes of the eastern mountains (beyond the Tigris to the north and east, visible from the Sum. plains), where there was "luxuriant vegetation, … wondrously fresh green pastures …, contrasting so markedly with the barren Mesopotamian plain" (Jacobsen 1970:118). This is the so-called pastoral corridor approaching the piedmont of the Taurus-Zagros mountain ranges (Adams 1981:135). It supplied some of the pasture for the herdsmen of certain nomadic pastoral tribal groups that were so significant in the economy of the Ur III state (ca. 2112–2104 BCE, see n. 37 below).

36 Sheep and cattle were certainly a source of meat, but the emphasis here is on "fat and cream" (dairy) production (line 359), which was an important part of the Sum. diet. Such foods brought balance to the regular fare of staple grains produced by irrigation agriculture, even luxury to the dining places of the gods (line 360). Shepherds and the farmers sometimes competed for resources, but they also relied on each other. And even the farmers had livestock to manage, partly as work animals, and perhaps also as a supplement to their agricultural produce (especially milk, butter, cheese, and other dairy products). The Farmer's Instructions mention that, "at the time the field emerges from the water" after the spring flood, the farmer should "not let the cattle herds trample it (anymore)" (Civil 1994:29 line 7 with comment pp. 70, 145). Thus, at certain other times cattle were allowed to wander and feed on the cultivated fields. Pasturing them in this way would not only feed the cattle, but also help keep the weeds down, assist with the preparation of the soil, provide natural fertilization by means of animal dung, and even thin out the young barley crop to prevent "lodging" when it came to maturity (Civil 1994:145, Eyre 1995:181, and Schwartz 1995:250). If grain crops are planted and grow too densely populated, when they ripen the heavy heads of grain can cause the plants to bend over and flatten out into the mud like waves under the effects of heavy rains and/or strong winds. This is called "lodging."

37 There were extensive networks of pastoralists in ancient Sumer. They functioned largely on the lowland plains, which were on the eastern periphery of Sumer and in the hinterlands of the core river basin region. At least in certain times and places, the lowland plains constituted "dimorphic zones" where sedentary agricultural life and nomadic grazing of herds could co-exist and, in fact, be mutually beneficial. The alluvial zone of irrigation agriculture was relatively narrow, so there was room for pastoral activity not only in the open ranges of the hinterland but also in the fallow fields and along the banks of the rivers of the alluvium itself. Because their livestock was moveable, the pastoralists tended toward a nomadic lifestyle, sometimes rather far ranging, even if they were closely linked with certain rural villages or large urban centers by family (tribal based) or through trade or production agreements (Adams 1981:135, 250, and Hesse 1995:209–211). Sometimes hostilities broke out between pastoralists and agriculturists and their urban centers over needed goods and resources, especially during times of climatic or environmental stress (see Adams 1981:135–136 and the literature cited there, and also Schwartz 1995).

The Third Dynasty of Ur (ca. 2112–2004 BCE) developed a massive system of administration at Drehem (Puzrish-Dagan, near Nippur) to manage the large numbers of animals, especially cattle, sheep, and goats, collected from the pastoralists in all regions controlled by the state. These were used to supply various state institutions and especially the temples. The animals were a major resource not only for sacrifices to the gods and for meat to be consumed, but also dairy products of various kinds as well as leather and wool for processing into textiles (for the latter see cycle 12 below; see also Adams 1981:147–148, Hesse 1995:210, and Robertson 1995:446–447).

who calls for copulation in the wide open streets of Kulaba,
Dumuzi-ušumgal-anna,[38,g] being the friend of An,
Enki put (him) fully in charge.

Cycle 11: Enki establishes cities, dwellings, and fields, and puts Utu in charge (lines 368–380)[39]

The Ekur, the house of Enlil, he did indeed fill with all good things.
Enlil rejoiced over Enki. Nippur was glad.[40]
He marked out the borders, fixed the boundaries.
For the Anunna gods,[41] Enki
did establish dwellings in the cities[42];
he did establish plots in the fields.[43]
The hero, the bull who charges out from the *ḫašur*-forest, who bellows fiercely;
the youth Utu, the bull who stands firm, pugnacious and powerful;
the father of the great city, the one who goes out from the horizon, the great herald of holy An;
the judge who renders the decision of the gods;
who wears the lapis-lazuli beard, who goes out from the horizon into holy heaven;
Utu, the son born by Ningal,
Enki put (him) fully in charge of heaven and earth as a whole.[44]

g Ezek 9:14

Cycle 12; Enki institutes the textile industry and puts Uttu in charge (lines 381–386)

He sorted out the tow from the fibers. He put the loom(?) in good order.
Enki greatly perfected the job of women.
For Enki the menial worker did … the wool … garment.
The dignity of the palace, the adornment of the king,
Uttu,[45] the faithful woman, the silent one,[46]
Enki put (her) fully in charge.

---

38 Enki charged Dumuzi(-ušumgal-anna "the dragon of heaven"), the spouse of Inanna (goddess of sexual fertility), with the care of the lowland plains. The reference to Inanna, Dumuzi's spouse, recalls the many myths and love poems about the marriage and sexual relationship between the two of them in the Sum. repertoire of literary compositions (see *COS* 1:540–543 for selections and Jacobsen 1987:1–98). This is the same Inanna who confronts Enki at the end of EWO for not giving her a special function in the Sum. world order.

39 The last two cycles focus specifically on urban organization and industry in the Sum. homeland. Cycle 11 is especially concerned with the problem of demarcating and maintaining the proper boundaries between the city-states, a problem that would be adjudicated by Utu, the sun god and judge among the gods. Cycle 12 is concerned with the making of textiles, a largely female industry with a female deity in charge. The fact that textiles were important as a trade commodity for ancient Sumer renders the special mention of king and palace understandable.

40 For remarks on Enlil and Enki and the relationship between them see n. 1 above.

41 See n. 4 above for remarks on the Anunna gods.

42 In Sumer the cities were located within the alluvium and the watercourses commonly flowed through them. In terms of city planning, the temples were located on the edge of the city, not at the center, and always at the point of highest elevation, whether by virtue of the terrain or through the construction of raised temple platforms or ziggurats, or both. Where palaces have been found, they were not on raised platforms, and they were separated from the temple complex either by distance or by a wall or canal. Canals, streets, and walls divided the city into sectors. Canals and streets also provided means of transport between different parts of the city. Fortified walls surrounded the major cities, enclosing the settlement mound as well as some non-settled areas (perhaps for growing fruits and vegetables). Aside from temple and palace sectors, there were also residential zones where both elites and commoners lived, and where one would also find various kinds of workshops. Much of the manufacturing was carried on in the residential areas (Stone 1995:236–243).

43 For recent discussions of the temple estate in ancient Sumer see Averbeck (2003a:56, 2010:6–8, 2014:41–48, and the lit. cited in those places). The temple in Babylonia was essentially a house, Sum. *é* and Akk. *bītu*. The terminology used was the same down through the millennia, and the basic functions of the temple as a household, or "temple estate," so to speak, remained the same as well. Sociologically, the temple as a household in ancient Sumer was able to organize life and society in a way that would have made sense to people on all levels of the society. Everyone fit into some kind of household, whether urban or not, whether elite or common, or anything in between. The temple, therefore, was able to unify the local society functionally.

Households, whether human or divine, worked for the common good under some kind of head of the household. The temple households of the Anunna gods (line 371; cf. n. 4 above) sometimes competed with each other, so there was need for adjudication, a job for which the sun god Utu was well-suited according to Sum. mythology (see line 370 with 377). The major historical sources for such boundary disputes are the Lagash inscriptions that recount the multi-generational battles between Pre-Sargonic Lagash and Umma over the agricultural land that stood between them (see the discussion and lit. cited in Averbeck 1994:93–98 and esp. Cooper 1983).

This concept of "temple estate" should be distinguished from "temple state" (Averbeck 2003a:55). The palace also certainly controlled land, and there is good reason to believe that private households not under the control of the state and temple institutions could also exercise their capacities for enterprise (see Robertson 1995:443–444 and esp. now Garfinkle 2012:18–27 and the lit. cited there). In any case, major temples had their own supporting estate as well as the administrative structure and labor supply to sustain it by means of land tenure labor (i.e., agricultural workers) and control of other regional resources (e.g., pastoralism, fowling, fishing, and hunting).

44 The last line of this cycle is different from all the others in that Enki puts Utu, the sun god and god of justice, fully in charge of "heaven and earth as a whole" (*an ki niĝin*$_2$*-na-ba*). Since Utu was the divine judge (line 377) among and between the Anunna gods (line 371–373), and Enki had demarcated boundaries between the temple estates of the various cities (lines 370–371), Utu would be the one who, in the end, adjudicated conflicts between temple estates and cities over their boundaries and fields. In this way, he was in charge of keeping Enki's whole system stable and workable.

45 Uttu (cf. Akk. *ettūtu* "spider") is naturally the goddess of weaving.

46 This description of Uttu corresponds to the fact that female dependents of various kinds were especially important in the fabrication of textiles in both the temple workshops and the palace industrial offices in ancient Sumer; see Robertson 1995:447, Adams 1981:148, and the overall explanation of procedures in textile fabrication in Bier 1995. Textiles were one of the most important trade commodities of ancient Sumer. Hundreds of thousands of sheep were sheared for their wool each year in the Lagash city-state alone during the last century or two of the third millennium BCE.

Section 4: Inanna's Complaint (lines 387–471)[47]

At that time, the only one who was left without a divine role;
the great woman of heaven, Inanna, left with no divine role;
before her father, Enki, Inanna
(390) did enter into (his) temple weeping and speaking a legal complaint:
"The determining of the destinies of the great gods, the Anunna gods,
Enlil did place in your hands.
Me being the woman, why did you treat me alone differently?
I am holy Inanna. Where is my divine role?"

[*Inanna complains that Nintud is the midwife, Nininsina is An's mistress, Ninmug makes fine jewelry, Nisaba is the scribe, and Nanše is in charge of fish and fowl for Enlil's table, but Enki had not given her any special function* (lines 395–423)]

Enki responds to his daughter, holy Inanna:
(425) "What was kept from you?
O mistress, what was kept from you? What can I entrust to you?
O maiden, what was kept from you? What can I entrust to you?
O woman, may you speak (with) a beautiful voice."

[*Enki's continued response to Inanna is partially broken, but he seems to highlight her beauty and pampered existence along with her warlike qualities and powers* (lines 429–450)]

(451) Now, surely the heart has overflowed its banks;
let the land (of Sumer) restore its (fertile) soil.
The heart of Enlil has surely overflowed its banks;
let the land (of Sumer) restore its (fertile) soil.
In (Enlil's) overflowing heart for(?) humanity[48]
he (Enlil?) will surely establish things … (?)

[lines 454–471 are badly broken]

(472) [Father Enki] praise!

---

[47] The last turning point in the composition is when the goddess Inanna comes to Enki and complains that he has not put her in charge of anything. The point of departure for her complaint is Uttu, the goddess of the textile industry, the final one in the previous twelve-fold cycle of divine appointments (lines 381–386). Inanna notes that other goddesses have also been included (lines 395–423). Why not her?

Inanna does not mention Uttu in her complaint, and four of the five goddesses mentioned in her complaint are not mentioned in the twelve cycles above (the exception is Nanshe, the third cycle, line 306). Vanstiphout (1997:125) suggests that "The gods mentioned in this subsidiary part derive their office from one or other of the general branches already allotted." Apparently, the previous list of twelve is meant to outline the larger framework of Sumer's world order without developing all the subsidiary elements of it.

There may be some connection between Inanna's complaint here in EWO and the composition known as "Inanna and Enki" (see *COS* 1:522–526), in which Inanna essentially steals the *me*'s from Enki in Eridu and takes them back to her temple in Uruk (see n. 3 above, and the lit. cited there, for remarks on the *me*'s). Gertrud Farber (1995:291) concludes that, in the composition Inanna and Enki: "Inanna visits Eridu and her father Enki, seeking revenge for having been neglected when all the other gods had their share of functions bestowed on them" in EWO. In fact, Inanna and Enki may be a secondary literary development composed as a sequel to EWO since there are so few extant copies and fragments of Inanna and Enki, especially as compared to EWO. One problem with this analysis, however, is that already here in EWO Inanna is referred to as "the lady of the great *me*'s" (line 364).

Vanstiphout (1997:131), following Bottéro, suggests that "Enki's refusal to incorporate Inana's warlike properties into the great and generative organization he is creating betrays an interest in *peace*." He adds, "*this* is the reason for the Inana episode: war and strife have no place in the correct, or good, or ideal life.... Of course, war and strife exist. The point is that they *should not*, in the ideal state of affairs as envisaged by Enki" (emphases his). This is a reasonable and possible interpretation, but the following lines (summarized, but not treated here; see the transliteration and translation in ETSCL 1.1.3) may suggest another conclusion.

Although the lines are partially broken, Enki appears to be listing and affirming her various qualities and powers, including her beauty as a woman as well as her associations with both love and war. Her warlike tendencies are not the problem. Instead, the real issue is that she is never satisfied with what she has. She always wants more. This is simply another part of the existing Sum. world order on the divine level, but a disruptive part that Enki is trying to keep under control. Her complaint here at the end EWO betrays this fact and is supported also, for example, by her attempt to obtain even the *me*'s of the underworld (*me-kur-ra*) in Inanna's Descent (see the transliteration and translation in ETSCL 1.4.1). This, in fact, did get her into very serious trouble, from which Enki himself extracted her, but only by means of his famous trickery, since not even Enki has control of the *me*'s of the underworld (see the further discussion in Averbeck 2003b:764–767, from which the analysis and interpretation proposed here vary to some degree).

[48] Lines 451–453 are the last three clearly legible lines on the extant tablets of EWO. Line 453 suggests that at least some of the following lines have to do with humans benefiting from the good fertilizing waters referred to in lines 451–452.

There is a good deal of correspondence between these lines near the end of EWO and the opening lines of Gudea Cylinder A i 5–9: (5) *šà gú-bé nam-gi*$_4$ (6) *šà-*^{d}*en-líl-lá gú-bé nam-gi*$_4$ (7) *šà gú-bé nam-gi*$_4$ (8) *a-g̃i*$_6$*-uru*$_{16}$ *nam-mul ní íl-íl* (9) *šà-*^{d}*en-líl-lá-ke*$_4$ ^{íd}*idigna-àm a-du*$_{10}$*-ga nam-tum* "The heart did surely overflow its banks; the heart of Enlil did surely overflow its banks; the heart did surely overflow its banks; the high tide, shining brightly, rising high; the heart of Enlil, being the Tigris river, it brings sweet water" (see the discussion of these lines in *COS* 2:419, n. 4). Compare these lines in EWO (451) *ì-ne-èš šà gú-bé nam-gi*$_4$ *kalam ki-bi ḫé-em-gi*$_4$ (452) *šà* ^{d}*en-líl-lá gú-bé nam-gi*$_4$ *kalam ki-bi ḫé-em-gi*$_4$ (see the translation above). The Gudea Cylinders begin with the same motif for the grant of prosperity from Enlil as part of the necessary background for Gudea's rebuilding of the Eninnu temple for Ningirsu in Lagash. In EWO it comes near the end of the composition because all that Enki has decreed for the world order brought the kind of prosperity to Sumer and especially to Enlil that would cause his heart to likewise overflow with blessings for the land and its people (i.e., "humanity," see line 453, *šà gú-bé gi*$_4$*-a nam-lú-u*$_{18}$*-lu-ka* and the rendering above). Note also the emphasis on *nam-tar* "decreeing of destiny" and the *me*'s in Gudea Cylinder A i 1–2 (see the rendering and remarks in *COS* 2:418, nn. 1–3), where the good decree of destiny leads to the abundance as it does here in EWO.

The multiple correspondences between these two compositions suggest that the primary concern of EWO was the *restoration* of world order in Sumer, or perhaps the reflex of that, the need to *maintain* that world order against erosion, whether physical alluvial erosion or other kinds of socio-cultural erosion of their civilization and its resources. The first halves of EWO lines 451–452 (cited above) refer explicitly to Enlil's heart overflowing to bring abundance to Sumer, and the second halves say: "let the land (of Sumer) restore (*gi*$_4$) its (fertile) soil" (see the earlier discussion of this passage in Averbeck 2003b:768–769, with some variation).

REFERENCES

Text, Transliterations, Translations, and Studies: Averbeck 2003a, 2003b; Benito 1969:77–160; Kramer and Maier 1989:38–56, 215–222; ETSCL 1.1.3; Römer 1993; Vanstiphout 1997.

SUMERIAN BIBLIOGRAPHY

Adams, R. McC.
1981 *Heartland of Cities: Surveys of Ancient Settlement and Land Use on the Central Floodplain of the Euphrates*. Chicago: University of Chicago Press.

Averbeck, R. E.
1994 "The Sumerian Historiographic Tradition and Its Implications for Genesis 1–11." Pp. 79–102 in *Faith, Tradition, and History: Old Testament Historiography in its Near Eastern Context*. Ed. by A. R. Millard, J. K. Hoffmeier, and D. W. Baker. Winona Lake, IN: Eisenbrauns.
1997 "Ritual Formula, Textual Frame, and Thematic Echo in the Cylinders of Gudea." Pp. 39–95 in *Crossing Boundaries and Linking Horizons: Studies in Honor of Michael C. Astour on His 80th Birthday*. Ed. G. D. Young, M. W. Chavalas, and R. E. Averbeck. Bethesda, MD: CDL Press.
2000 "The Cylinders of Gudea (2.155)." *COS* 2:417–433.
2003a "Daily Life and Culture in 'Enki and the World Order' and Other Sumerian Literary Compositions." Pp. 23–61 in *Life and Culture in the Ancient Near East*. Ed. by R. E. Averbeck, M. W. Chavalas, and D. B. Weisberg. Bethesda, MD: CDL Press.
2003b "Myth, Ritual, and Order in 'Enki and the World Order.'" *JAOS* 123:757–771.
2010 "Temple Building among the Sumerians and Akkadians (Third Millennium)." Pp. 3–34, 448–450 in *From the Foundations to the Crenellations: Essays on Temple Building in the Ancient Near East and Hebrew Bible*. Ed. by Mark J. Boda and Jamie R. Novotny. AOAT 366. Münster: Ugarit-Verlag.
2014 "The Third Millennium Temple: War and Peace in History and Religion." Pp. 41–67 in *Krieg und Frieden im Alten Vorderasien*. Ed by H. Neumann. RAI 52. Münster: Ugarit Verlag.

Beaulieu, P.-A.
1992 "New Light on Secret Knowledge in Late Babylonian Culture." *ZA* 82:98–111.

Becking, B. and M. C. A. Korpel
2010 "To Create, To Separate or to Construct: An Alternative for a Recent Proposal as to the Interpretation of ברא in Gen 1:1–2:4a." *JHS* 10:1–21.

Benito, C. A.
1969 "'Enki and Ninma?' and 'Enki and the World Order.'" Ph.D. Dissertation, University of Pennsylvania. Ann Arbor, Michigan: University Microfilms.

Bier, C.
1995 "Textile Arts in Ancient Western Asia." Pp. 3:1567–1588 in CANE.

Bottéro, J. and S. N. Kramer
1989 *Lorsque les deiux faisaient l'homme, mythologies mésopotamienne*. Paris: Gallimard.

Buccellati, G.
1966 *The Amorites of the Ur III Period*. Naples: Istituto Orientale di Napoli.

Civil, M.
1961 "The Home of the Fish: A New Sumerian Literary Composition." *Iraq* 23:154–175, plate 66.
1994 *The Farmer's Instructions: A Sumerian Agricultural Manual*. AuOrSup 5. Sabadell-Barcelona: AUSA.
2007 "Early Semitic Loanwords in Sumerian." Pp. 1–34 in *Studies Presented to Robert D. Biggs*. AS 27. Ed. by Martha T. Roth, et al. Chicago: Oriental Institute of the University of Chicago.

Clifford, R. J.
1994 *Creation Accounts in the Ancient Near East and in the Bible*. CBQMS 26. Washington, DC: The Catholic Biblical Association of America.

Cooper, J. S.
1983 *Rewriting History from Ancient Inscriptions: The Lagash-Umma Border Conflict*. SANE 2/1. Malibu: Undena.
1986 *Sumerian and Akkadian Royal Inscriptions*. Volume 1: *Presargonic Inscriptions*. New Haven: The American Oriental Society.
1989 "Enki's Member: Eros and Irrigation in Sumerian Literature." Pp. 87–89 in *DUMU-E$_2$-DUB-BA-A: Studies in Honor of Åke W. Sjöberg*. Ed. by H. Behrens, et al. Occasional Publications of the Samuel Noah Kramer Fund, 11. Philadelphia: The University Museum.

Ebeling, E.
1919 *Keilschrifttexte aus Assur religiösen Inhalts. Erster Band*. Heft 2. (= KAR 4). Leipzig: J. C. Hinrichs'sche.

Eyre, C. J.
1995 "The Agricultural Cycle, Farming, and Water Management in the Ancient Near East." Pp. 1:175–189 in *CANE*.

Farber, G.
1995 "'Inanna and Enki' in Geneva: A Sumerian Myth Revisited." *JNES* 54:287–292.

Farber-Flügge, G.
1973 *Der Mythos "Inanna und Enki" unter besonderer Berücksichtigung der Liste der me*. Studia Pohl 10. Rome: Biblical Institute Press.

Foster, B. R.
2005 *Before the Muses: An Anthology of Akkadian Literature*. Third edition. Bethesda, MD: CDL Press.

Garfinkle, S. J.
2012 *Entrepreneurs and Enterprise in Early Mesopotamia: A Study of Three Archives from the Third Dynasty of Ur (2112–2004 BCE)*. CUSAS 22. Bethesda, MD: CDL Press.

George, A. R.
1993 *House Most High: The Temples of Ancient Mesopotamia*. Mesopotamian Civilizations 5. Winona Lake, IN: Eisenbrauns.

Greengus, S.
2003 "Biblical and Mesopotamian Law: An Amorite Connection?" Pp. 63–81 in *Life and Culture in the Ancient Near East*. Ed. by R. E. Averbeck, M. W. Chavalas, and D. B. Weisberg. Bethesda, MD: CDL Press.

Hecker, K.
1994 "Ein zweisprachiger Schöpfungsmythos." Pp. 606–608 in *TUAT*, 3: *Mythen und Epen II*. Gütersloh: Gütersloher Verlagshaus.

HEIDEL, A.
1963 *The Babylonian Genesis*. Second edition. Chicago: University of Chicago Press.
HEIMPEL, W.
1987 "The Natural History of the Tigris according to the Sumerian Literary Composition Lugal." *JNES* 46:309–317.
1990 "Ein zweiter Schritt zur Rehabilitierung der Rolle des Tigris in Sumer." *ZA* 91:204–213.
HEISER, M. S.
2015 *The Unseen Realm*. Bellingham, WA: Lexham Press.
HESSE, B.
1995 "Animal Husbandry and Human Diet in the Ancient Near East." Pp. 1:203–222 in *CANE*.
HOROWITZ, W.
1998 *Mesopotamian Cosmic Geography*. Winona Lake, IN: Eisenbrauns.
JACOBSEN, T.
1970 *Toward the Image of Tammuz and Other Essays on Mesopotamian History and Culture*. Ed. by W. L. Moran. Cambridge, MA: Harvard University Press.
1982 *Salinity and Irrigation Agriculture in Antiquity*. BiMes 14. Malibu, CA: Undena Publications.
1987 *The Harps That Once ... Sumerian Poetry in Translation*. New Haven and London: Yale University Press.
JOHNSON, J. C.
2014 "The Cost of Cosmogony: Ethical Reflections on Resource Extraction, Monumental Architecture and Urbanism in the Sumerian Literary Tradition." Pp. 43–75 in *The Fabric of Cities: Aspects of Urbanism, Urban Topography and Society in Mesopotamia, Greece and Rome*. Ed. by N. N. May and U. Steinert. Leiden: Brill.
KANG, S. T.
1973 *Sumerian Economic Texts from the Umma Archive*. Sumerian and Akkadian Cuneiform Texts in the Collection of the World Heritage Museum of the University of Illinois. Volume 2. Urbana: University of Illinois Press.
KRAMER, S. N. and J. MAIER
1989 *Myths of Enki, The Crafty God*. Oxford: Oxford University Press.
KREBERNIK, M.
2002 "Geschlachtete Gottheiten und ihre Namen." Pp. 289–298 in *Ex Mesopotamia et Syria Lux*. Ed. by O. Loretz, et al. AOAT 281. Münster: Ugarit-Verlag.
LAMBERT, W. G.
1980–1983 "Kosmogonie." *RlA* 6:218–222.
2008 "Mesopotamian Creation Stories." Pp. 15–59 in *Imagining Creation*. Ed. by M. J. Geller and M. Schipper. Leiden: Brill.
2013 *Babylonian Creation Myths*. Winona Lake, IN: Eisenbrauns.
LAMBERT, W. G. and A. R. MILLARD
1969 *Atra-ḫasīs: The Babylonian Story of the Flood*. Oxford: Oxford University Press.
LANDERSDORFER, S.
1917 *Die sumerischen Parallelen zur biblischen Urgeschichte*. Münster: Verlag der Aschendorffschen Buchhandlung.
LENZI, A.
2008 *Secrecy and the Gods: Secret Knowledge in Ancient Mesopotamia and Biblical Israel*. SAAS 19. Helsinki: The Neo-Assyrian Text Corpus Project.
LISMAN, J. J. W.
2013 *Cosmogony, Theogony, and Anthropogeny in Sumerian Texts*. AOAT 409. Münster: Ugarit-Verlag.
MICHAUX-COLOMBOT, D.
2001 "Magan and Meluḫḫa: A Reappraisal through the Historiography of Thalassocratic Powers." Pp. 1:329–355 in *Historiography in the Cuneiform World*. Ed. by T. Abusch, P. Beaulieu, J. Huehnergard, P. Machinist, and P. Steinkeller. RAI 45. Bethesda, MD: CDL Press.
MOOREY, P. R. S.
1999 *Ancient Mesopotamian Materials and Industries: The Archaeological Evidence*. Winona Lake, IN: Eisenbrauns.
MULLEN, E. T., JR.
1980 *The Divine Council in Canaanite and Early Hebrew Literature*. HSM 24. Chico, CA: Scholars Press.
PETTINATO, G.
1971 *Das altorientalische Menschenbild und die sumerischen und akkadischen Schöpfungsmythen*. Heidelberg: Carl Winter, Universitätsverlag.
POTTS, D. T.
1995 "Distant Shores: Ancient Near Eastern Trade with South Asia and Northeast Africa." Pp. 3:151–1463 in *CANE*.
ROAF, M.
1990 *Cultural Atlas of Mesopotamia and the Ancient Near East*. Oxford: Andromeda Oxford Limited.
ROBERTSON, J. F.
1995 "The Social and Economic Organization of Ancient Mesopotamian Temples." Pp. 1:443–454 in *CANE*.
ROCHBERG, F.
2004 *The Heavenly Writing: Divination, Horoscopy, and Astronomy in Mesopotamian Culture*. Cambridge: Cambridge University Press.
ROCHBERG-HALTON, F.
1982 "Fate and Divination in Mesopotamia." Pp. 363–371 in *AfO* Beiheft 19 (= *RAI* 28).
RÖMER, W. H. Ph.
1993 "Aus »Enki und die Weltordnung«." Pp. 402–420 in *TUAT* 3: *Mythen und Epen II*.
SCHWARTZ, G. M.
1995 "Pastoral Nomadism in Ancient Western Asia." Pp. 1:249–258 in *CANE*.
SJÖBERG, Å. and E. BERGMANN
1969 *The Collection of the Sumerian Temple Hymns*. TCS 3. Locust Valley, NY: J. J. Augustin.
SOLLBERGER, E.
1965 "A Three-Column *Silbenvokabular A*." Pp. 21–28 in *Studies Landsberger*.

STEIBLE, H.
1982 *Die Altsumerischen Bau- und Weihinschriften*. Teil I. FAOS 5. Wiesbaden: Franz Steiner Verlag.

STEINKELLER, P.
2001a "New Light on the Hydrology and Topography of Southern Babylonia in the Third Millennium." *ZA* 91:22–84.
2001b "Addenda to 'New Light on the Hydrology and Topography of Southern Babylonia in the Third Millennium.' *ZA* 91:22–84." *NABU* number 3: 62.

STONE, E.
1995 "The Development of Cities in Ancient Mesopotamia." Pp. 1:235–248 in *CANE*.

SUTER, C. E.
2000 *Gudea's Temple Building: The Representation of an Early Mesopotamian Ruler in Text and Image*. CM 17. Groningen: STYX Publications.

TOORN, K. VAN DER
2007 "Why Wisdom Became a Secret: On Wisdom as a Written Genre." Pp. 21–29 in *Wisdom Literature in Mesopotamia and Israel*. Ed. by R. J. Clifford. Atlanta: Society of Biblical Literature.

VAN LEEUWEN, R. C.
2007 "Cosmos, Temple, House: Building and Wisdom in Mesopotamia and Israel." Pp. 67–90 in *Wisdom Literature in Mesopotamia and Israel*. Ed. by R. J. Clifford. Atlanta: Society of Biblical Literature.

VANSTIPHOUT, H. L. J.
1997 "Why did Enki Organize the World?" Pp. 117–134 in *Sumerian Gods and their Representations*. Ed. by I. L. Finkel and M. J. Geller. CM 7. Groningen: STYX.

VELDHUIS, N.
2010 "The Theory of Knowledge and the Practice of Celestial Divination." Pp. 77–91 in *Divination and Interpretation of Signs in the Ancient World*. Ed. by A. Annus. OIS 6. Chicago: University of Chicago.

WOLDE, E. J. VAN
2009a "Why the Verb *br*ʾ Does Not Mean 'to Create' in Genesis 1:1–2:4a." *JSOT* 34:8–13.
2009b *Reframing Biblical Studies: When Language and Text Meet Culture, Cognition, and Context*. Winona Lake, IN: Eisenbrauns.

INDICES

SCRIPTURE INDEX

All references to the Hebrew Bible follow its versification. When these vary from common modern translations the difference is marked with brackets: e.g., 1 Chr 6:54 [E 6:69]. Entire chapters are also marked: e.g., Dan 5 (Ch.). All references are for this *Supplements* volume alone. See *COS* 3:339–357 for the Scripture Index covering the first three volumes of *The Context of Scripture*.

GENERAL INDEX

All entrees reflect only the *Supplements* volume. The General Index for the first three volumes of *The Context of Scripture* is located in *COS* 3:359–403. When possible, all transliterations and spellings reflect the conventions of their respective contributors. Where forms differ among contributors, only one convention is followed in the index (e.g., both "Hatti" and "Ḫatti" appear in the *Supplements*, and the index adopts the latter). Page spans do not appear for items and/or topics that cross multiple consecutive pages, as the discerning reader will continue without such prompting. Where entries appear in footnotes, semicolons separate page numbers (indicated by commas everywhere else).